Account of the Revolutionary Movement in Bengal

Account of the Revolutionary Movement in Bengal

by

Hem Chandra Kanungo

with annotations by the Intelligence Branch, Bengal.

Edited

with a note on Hemchandra as a revolutionary

by

Amiya K. Samanta

Setu Prakashani

Kolkata Delhi

Account of the Revolutionary Movement in Bengal
by **Hem Chandra Kanungo**

First Edition : January, 2015
Cover Design : Dilip Ghosh

ISBN: 978-93-80677-66-8

Published by:
Archana Das & Subrata Das
on behalf of **Setu Prakashani**
12/A Sankar Ghosh Lane, Kolkata-700006
Phone : +91 33 2219 0704, +91 94330 74548

Outlet :
2, Shyama Charan Dey Street,
Kolkata - 700 073

Delhi Branch Office :
A-43, Mahendru Enclave, Galli No. 3,
G.T. Karnal Road, P.O. : Azadpur, Delhi - 110 033

e-mail : setuprakashani@gmail.com
Website : www.setuprakashani.com

Price : Six hundred and Fifty

Setting by :
Cynosure, 3/37A, Bejoygarh, Kolkata - 700 032
Printed by :
Imprinta, 243/2B, A.P.C. Road, Kolkata - 700 006

TO,

MY FRIEND

SUMIT SARKAR

Acknowledgement

When in 1995 a plethora of classified documents on the revolutionary terrorist movement available in the archives of the Intelligence Branch, West Bengal, were published in six volumes, Hem Chandra Kanungo's "Account of the Revolutionary Movement in Bengal" (Copy No. 4) was ignored as it was merely a translation of Hem Chandra's widely read book in Bengali, and not an Intelligence Branch document by itself. Now, the translation of Hem Chandra's book is published and I acknowledge with gratitude the help of the IB in this regard.

Besides I have obtained unpublished letters, rare photographs and documents from institutions like the Nehru Memorial Museum, the National Archives, both in New Delhi, the Record Room and the Museum of District Judge's court, Alipur, Kolkata, the State Archives, Kolkata, Sri Aurobindo Institute of Culture, Tollygunj, Kolkata. I am grateful to the officials of these institutions for their kind co-operation. The Assistant Commissioner, Kolkata Police Museum allowed me to take photographs of two revolvers used in the assassination of Naren Gossain, and of the parcel bomb made by Hem Chandra for Douglas Kingsford. He also provided me with the photos of Charles Tegart as Commissioner, Calcutta Police and Leonard Birley as Chief Secretary, Bengal. I am thankful to him and his staff.

Amiya K. Samanta

CONTENTS

Preface

Hem Chandra Kanungo's memoirs were serialised with the title of *Banglaya Biplab Kahini* (An Account of the Revolutionary Movement in Bengal) in monthly *Basumati* from April 1922 to April 1928, skipping, however, several issues in between. When it was published as a book in June 1928, it had a new title of *Banglay Biplab Prachesta,* (An Attempt at Revolution in Bengal) because, according to the author, "there cannot be any story of the revolution as no revolution has taken place in Bengal." In the book some of his observations and critical comments were further sharpened, but hardly any new fact was added.

Intelligence agencies all over the world review published materials with political contents and security implications as an essential part of the intelligence evaluation process. Accordingly, the books and articles written by the former revolutionaries came under their scanner during the British days. In point of time Aurobindo's *Kara Kahini*, published in a Bengali periodical named *Suprabhat* in 1909, was the first such publication. Its English version entitled "The Tales from Prison Life" was published later. Then in 1921 were published almost simultaneously Barindra Kumar Ghose's *Dwipantarer Katha* and Upendra Nath Bandopadhyaya's *Nirbasiter Atmakatha*. In 1922 Barindra's book was translated into English with the help of Nalini Kanta Gupta as "The Tale of My Exile" and was published from Pondicherry. Nalini Kishore Guha's *Banglaya Biplabbad* was published in May 1922 closely followed by Sachindra Nath Sanyal's *Bandi Jiban* in September 1922.

All these publications mentioned above were very much in the notice of the Intelligence Branch, Bengal. About *Bandi Jiban* an officer of the Intelligence Bureau of the Government of India wrote, "It gave an account of the terrorist movement in such a way as to arouse the immature minds to similar actions." It was translated into Hindi, Gurumukhi and Gujarati and had great influence on the patriotic students and youth in north India. In consequence the book was proscribed by the Government of The United Province in 1931. It would, however, be a gross exaggeration to say, as the reviewer has done, that "the author has sent more young men to the gallows or to prison for terrorism than any man who has lived in India".

In Bengal *Nirbasiter Atmakatha* had earned similar popularity more for its literary merit than as an inspiring and accurate account of the revolutionary movement. About Barindra's *Dwipantarer Katha* (The Tale of My Exile), Sachindra Nath Sanyal has written that only that part of the book is readable which has been copied word for word from *Nirbashiter Atmakatha*, and in the remaining part, Barindra has tried to hide more than what he has revealed. Nalini Kishore Guha, himself a revolutionary, has greatly eulogised the patriotism, courage and self-sacrifice of the young participants in glowing language in his *Banglaya Biplabbad* beside giving a list of revolutionary 'actions' from the Report of the Sedition Committee (1918) and contemporary news papers. It does not appear that the Intelligence Branch had taken any special notice of these three books.

The serialised version of Hem Chandra's *Banglaya Biplab Kahini* (Account of the Revolutionary Movement in Bengal) was translated by the I.B into English. Why did the IB attach such special importance to it as to translate the complete book, while other memoirs were merely reviewed by officers with knowledge in Bengali? Evidently Hem Chandra's views and observations, unencumbered by nationalist emotion and analysed in the light of his knowledge in Socialism and Marxism acquired in Europe, made his work different from other works of this genre. He has tried to trace the seeds of failure of the movement in the organisational laxity, in the enervating atmosphere of religiosity that enveloped the Manicktala group, in the social background of the members and above all, in the weakness of the leadership. The novelty of approach and the sharpness of all-pervasive criticism had attracted the attention of the intelligence analysts and policy planners. Hem Chandra was known to the authorities to be a man of unyielding nature as he declined to confess or disclose any secret about the organisation defying all threats and inducements. Even after he had undergone extreme hardship and humiliation in the Cellular Jail for four years, Charles Tegart, the redoubtable intelligence officer from Bengal, had found him as firmly non-communicative as he was before. His book, therefore, was not expected to disclose any secret; yet given his character, the account was likely to be much less biased and more truthful and dependable.

With the re-emergence of revolutionary terrorism in late 1920s and early 1930s throughout north India with increasing popular support and a distinct trend towards insurrectionary armed uprising, the Government felt somewhat bewildered. With no war situation existing and the demand for self-government and civil rights becoming stronger and stronger, the repressive measures started becoming counter-productive. In the context of growing terrorist violence, the author's ideological mind-set and his strong criticism of the movement from Marxist-Socialist standpoint became a valuable input for devising an anti-terrorist strategy.

The Government just about this time had started relaxing the stringent regulations prohibiting political literature into the jails and detention camps, where a large number of terrorist prisoners were incarcerated. Gradually, with visible and invisible indulgence of the Government the flow of Marxist and Socialist literature along with other political literature into all prisons including the Cellular Jail went on increasing. Marxist study circles grew up inside the jails and detention camps, issues of Socialism and Marxism and their applicability in the freedom struggle were discussed and even hand written papers containing writings on Marxism and Socialism were openly brought out by the prisoners. The Government, despite its strong distrust for Marxism as a subversive force, took the risk of using the ideology as a weapon against individual terrorism and religiosity in political movements in India. The consequences are all too well known. We may, however, hasten to add that the over-all political scenario with increasing participation of workers and peasants in freedom movement, growing disenchantment with individual terrorism of the revolutionary groups and introduction of a federal system with wider powers to the Indians were conducive to the acceptance of a new revolutionary ideology; and the Government acted as a great and conscious facilitator in this regard. In 1934 the Intelligence Bureau observed with ill-concealed satisfaction that the prisoners "in recent years have been intensively studying Communism and Socialism and have been impressed by the value of an armed mass revolution as a means of obtaining independence." (Terrorism in India, 1917-1936, P.65) In 1935 the Governor of Bengal admitted that the main on-rush of the wave of terrorism had been broken. By 1937 revolutionary terrorism became a glorious chapter in the history of India's freedom struggle.

It will, therefore, be seen that having appreciated the potentiality of the author's ideological inclinations which permeated the contents of the book, the IB made an exception and translated the serialised text into English, and printed only twenty copies in September,1928, so that the policy planners at all levels could study it and make their own evaluation. We have decided to free the book from the bondage of colonial confidentiality and to reprint this critique of the first phase of the revolutionary terrorist movement by one of the distinguished participants with a view to making it available to a much larger readership.

The serialised text was chapterised up to twelve chapters and the remaining text was not so divided. The English translation by the IB followed that. While publishing the book in Bengali the author divided the text after 12th chapter into seven more chapters making the total number of chapters 19. Accordingly we have also made 19 chapters in the English version with the same chapter headings as in the first Bengali edition. The IB's publication contained exhaustive notes on persons and events. We have retained those notes and have added, wherever necessary, new editorial notes on the basis of information now available. Besides we have added a fairly long account of Hem Chandra's revolutionary career both in India and abroad and of his life after release from jail. We have examined at length the validity or otherwise of Hem Chandra's criticism of Aurobindo, Barindra, the Swadeshi movement and other relevant issues of contemporary history. Some letters written from Paris mostly to his wife, Sarat, have been incorporated in the Appendix. The book first published more than 85 years ago still stands out as an honest and forthright memoir of the revolutionary movement.

Kolkata
10th November, 2014

Amiya K. Samanta

Hem Chandra Kanungo: A Rebel Extraordinary

Sachindra Nath Sanyal (1893-1943) spent nearly five years in the Cellular Jail where he had met Hem Chandra Kanungo for the first time. In his *Bandi Jiban*[1] he has recorded his impression of Hem Chandra. "When I went to Andaman Jail I, for the first time, saw him from a distance sitting on a stool and reading with deep concentration. His complexion was brown and his beard, a mixture of black and white, came down to his chest. He was wearing a pair of glasses. Hem Chandra had a very dignified and respectable look. He had a thoughtful face. His figure radiated a strong personality. Looking at him I was wondering this man must have been incarcerated for many years when his hairs had gone grey."[2] Sachindra had seen many veteran revolutionaries such as Barindra Kumar Ghose, Upendra Nath Banerji and Savarkar brothers who were co-prisoners; but none impressed him as much as Hem Chandra did. Although Hem Chandra was in the company of Barin and Upendra he stood apart for his unyielding character as a revolutionary. His stubborn resistance to threat and inducement for making confession became a legend among the revolutionaries. Sachindra after release on amnesty was returning to Calcutta on board the *S.S.Maharaja* in February 1920 along with the Alipur group and other similarly released prisoners. All of them were visibly very happy to return home after so much of suffering for so many years; but Sachindra was troubled by a dilemma. While his earnest desire was to dedicate himself to the service of the country, his family wanted him to marry and settle in family life. Sachindra writes, "The same elderly man, who attracted the admiring attention of the young man, when he first arrived at the island prison, came and stood by his side as a friend. Like a friend he frankly discussed his desires and aspirations and the old man counselled him on his future plans." Sachindra was much impressed. He writes," Hem Chandra was taking with him the books that he had collected during his long twelve years in prison for his son". In fact, the books would be Hem Chandra's companion for the rest of his life.

Sachindra was, however, critical of the two other members of Alipur group[3], namely Barindra and Upendra and of the Savarkar brothers too, for their conduct and attitude towards the protest movement launched by other political prisoners in jail. He was one of the leaders who organised cease work and hunger strike on several occasions in protest against oppression and torture, and in return he along with others had to suffer brutal punishment. Explaining the role of the veteran political prisoners on such occasions, Sachindra has written: "Having suffered terrible torture during long years of imprisonment in the Andaman jail, they had become mentally weak. When I was in jail on many occasions the political prisoners had clashed with the prison authority; we resorted to hunger strike or cease work in protest against torture. Not a single one of the old revolutionaries either participated in the strike or helped us in any way. On the contrary, I gained the impression from their conduct that they had become supporters of the Jail authority."[4] Troilokya Chakraborty (1889-1970), who was in the Cellular jail at the same time with Sanyal and played a leading role in the protest actions, has noted, "We were split into 'soft' and 'hard' groups. Savarkar brothers and Barin Babu and other Alipur case convicts came to the jail long time ago and they had to suffer much torture in the hands of the prison officials. At that time they were enjoying some privileges which they were not prepared to forsake by joining with us. Pulin Babu used to avoid troubles."[5] During their return journey Barindra on board the *S.S.Maharaja* in a somewhat repentant mood, had virtually confessed that he had been mentally weak and that is why he could not join the hunger strike in protest against the oppression and torture on the prisoners by the jail authorities. Those who had participated in protest actions had great courage and mental strength.

Hem Chandra read *Anandamath* at an early age and it "evoked a sense of patriotism" in him; but his patriotism was not solely inspired by the 'mother-in-bondage' image of the country or by the accounts of her past glory. He loved his country not because what she was in the past, but because it was only natural for him to love his own country and the people as he found them, and it was his duty to work for their emancipation. How to emancipate the country? According to Hem Chandra centuries of domination by foreign powers created a slave mentality as a result of which "we feel diffidence or disinclination to do something without precedence. The Italians, who were a slave nation like ours, have recently secured their freedom through the medium of secret society. By similar methods Russia has been enlarging her rights and privileges and entertaining the hope of securing her absolute freedom." The last example was that of the Boers who won the war against Britain and "secret societies alone made it possible". Since in the Boer war the secret society played a crucial role, the "Boer method[6] "was quite suited to our condition, and we decided to form secret societies."[7]

In tracing the inspiration for the secret society movement in India, Hem Chandra has stated that the anti-Ilbert Bill agitation had demystified the minds of the majority of the educated Indians of the spell that British rule in India had a higher moral and ethical purpose. In the closing years of the Nineteenth Century the Indians thought of 'freedom' from foreign rule and the idea of freedom at that time was merely "a desire to rid ourselves of the hatred, calumny, and disgrace to which we were subjected by the foreigners," and 'patriotism' primarily meant 'strong hatred for the oppressors and taking revenge for their misdeeds'. These ideas were germane to the formation of physical culture societies and secret societies for revolutionary action. His narration of the beginning of the secret society movement, the growth of the secret societies in Midnapur and Calcutta and the existential problems they faced in the pre-Swadeshi days are remarkably accurate and dependable. His approach is analytical, and is marked by witticism and sarcasm. While writing about events and persons he has occasionally used strong language and biting sarcasm, not caring for the persons who are at the receiving end.

Hem Chandra felt that mere political freedom achieved through the termination of British rule in India would not bring freedom to the people. India would have to be socially and economically liberated. As a matter of fact, social and economic liberation should have preceded political freedom. Hem Chandra has not, however, clarified whether secret society and terrorism were adequate means for achieving the objectives, and if they are not, what should be the alternative techniques of struggle and how the country would achieve social and economic liberation. Nevertheless, having accepted the secret society as the instrument for revolutionary movement, he remained faithful to it till the last. He had taken the oath of secrecy and allegiance to the leader and the society under all circumstances, and he steadfastly adhered to it spurning all inducements, threats and promise. He was, however, unsparingly critical of the lapses and failings of the leaders and the leading members of the society. At one stage he was so disenchanted that he even thought of breaking away from Aurobindo and Barindra's party and launching a new party of his own, if only adequate finance could be available. Since that was not forthcoming he returned to his old party and served it faithfully.

As the days passed, he noticed with great disappointment an increasing hold of religion on the secret society, and thought that the society and the struggle it waged became more and more sectarian. He disapproved of such a tendency and ridiculed the religious prayers and practices in the Manicktala Garden, which, according to him, would blur the vision, dilute the principal objective and make rational thinking difficult. He had differences with his leaders on various other issues; yet so long he was a member of the party he remained loyal to the leadership and did his job faithfully hiding his strong reservation about the style of running the secret society. He remained closely associated with Barindra, Upendra and others, both in Alipur and in the Cellular Jails, yet he was least influenced by their thoughts and conduct. Like Barin he never used to think that with the arrest his mission of struggle for freedom was over or he was no longer bound by the oath of secrecy of the revolutionary party. While almost all the members of the former Manicktala group after their release gravitated to Pondichery seeking peace and solace in spiritualism and religion, Hem Chandra devoted himself to photography and painting in his hometown, retaining, however, his faith in secularism and revolution. A few years after the publication of the memoirs[8] of Barindra and Upendra, he published an account of the revolutionary activities of the Manicktala group, entitled *Banglaya Biplab Prachesta,* which describes the growth of the early revolutionary movement in Bengal, with a critical appraisal of the thoughts and ideas of the pioneers. Unlike the works of his contemporaries, his book is not suffused with patriotic and nationalist sentiments, nor is it an excessive glorification of their activities or an apologia for their failures. His account is factually more accurate and therefore more dependable than many other books of the same genre. His criticism of the leadership and the movement, though at times harsh, are valid in essential points. He has not for a moment lost faith in revolutionary movement and has appealed to the younger generation to adopt new ideas and chart out the correct course through continuous criticism and self-criticism. Among the rebels, he was truly an extraordinary one.

1. Hem Chandra In Midnapur Secret Society

Born on 4 October, 1871 in a land-owning family of Radhanagar, a village on Midnapur-Orissa border, Hem Chandra left his studies while in BA class in Midnapur College to work as "a drawing master" in Midnapur Collegiate School, though he was never formally trained as an artist. He had, however, acquired certain mastery over brush and colour. Hem Chandra also did a stint as a demonstrator in the Chemistry department of Midnapur College--a job which later on helped him get admission in bomb-manufacturing class in Paris. But he gave up this job in Midnapur College to become 'Pound and Ferry Inspector' under the District Board. He was removed from this job only when he left for France in August 1906. He also tried his hand in business when he and his friend J.K. Naug, "started an aerated water business under the name *Dono and Co.*, a name made up from the initials of Dass and Naug and it also means a company of two". Eventually Naug bought his share." On his return from Paris in early 1908, he started a small business of fake jewellery, having learnt the business from S.R. Rana,[9] a jeweller in Paris.

He has not claimed in his memoirs that while in Paris for one and a half years he was ever enrolled in any Art school, but one of his friends said in the Session's Court that he was in an Art school and also learnt photography[10] in Paris. In Midnapur while working as a drawing teacher Hem Chandra came in touch with a gentleman, who for all practical purposes became his political *Guru*. He has called him "A Babu"[11] in his book to keep his identity under cover; but when he revised his book after independence in 1950, he identified 'A' Babu as Jnanendra Nath Bose, elder brother of Satyendra Nath Bose , both nephews of Raj Narain Bose. According to Hem Chandra, Jnanendra had been sub-editor of two English journals, and "therefore well-versed in politics," and "far more advanced in political thinking than the country's political leaders of the time". He used to read the news of Boer War everyday to Hem Chandra and would explain the trends of national and international politics of the time. "Of all the wonders of the Boer War, the one which struck me most was that a handful of uncivilised (I thought them to be so at that time.) Boers could have routed the enormously powerful British Army. Jnanendra Babu made it clear by citing examples from history that Secret Societies alone made this possible."[12]

The idea of 'freedom' was not very clear to many Indians, and according to Hem Chandra, all sections of the people never very strongly wanted 'freedom from British subjugation.' They, however, very strongly felt "a desire to get rid of the hatred, calumny and disgrace to which we were subjected by the foreigners;"[13] The predominant urge behind the formation of secret societies was to take revenge against individual perpetrators in the context of widespread racial hatred, insult and assault by the British on the Indians. The Boer war provided some inspiration to the Bengali youth because it was a war in which the poor Africans defeated the mighty British, proclaiming to the world that the British power was not invincible. Besides, Hem Chandra writes, "In October, 1899 when the news of Boer war reached Bengal, it was received not with the usual feeling of fear and disgust that the thought of war generally evokes in our mind but with a suppressed feeling of expectation and a feeble hope."[14]

In spite of being a staunch critic of *Anandamath* later in his life for its religious bias, Hem Chandra admits that the novel "evoked a sense of patriotism in him, besides giving the pleasure of reading a fiction". In his sub-conscious mind "it left a living and earnest impression." Jnanendra had taught him that religion had done much harm to the country and he sustained his statement by citing examples from history. Hem Chandra did never forget this lesson and from his experience in revolutionary politics, he had realised how true the statement was.

"In the middle of 1902", Hem Chandra wrote, "I heard from Jnanendra Nath that Aurobindo Babu had been trying to set up secret societies in Bengal, and that many important persons of Calcutta had joined it."[15] By that time, however, Jnanendra, Satyendra and Hem Chandra had already organised a secret society in Midnapur. Membership was not large, and resources meagre; but they had started rudimentary training in firearms and organised political classes in their own houses. In 1902 Aurobindo sent Jatindra Nath Banerji, a soldier in the Gaekwar's` Army to Bengal to impart physical training to the Bengali youth. With that end in view Jatindra Nath set up a society in a house in Grey Street. He also visited the Midnapur society, and advised the adoption of the Western techniques of organising secret societies. Thereafter Aurobindo also met the members of the society when he visited his relatives in Midnapur in the middle of 1902. He even went to the society's secret firing range and tried his hand in firing a shot.[16] During this visit Aurobindo stayed for a couple of days in the Midnapur residence of Hem Chandra. He was such an admirer of Aurobindo, whom he considered as a great scholar and patriot, that he considered the occasion a memorable one and five years later while writing to his wife from France he was lamenting that such a man was not properly looked after in their house.[17]

A few months later Aurobindo once again came to Midnapur and formally initiated Hem Chandra as a member of the secret society observing a quasi-religious ritual, when Hem took the *Gita* in one hand and a sword in another and instead of reciting a verse in Sanskrit, he said it in Bengali. The crucial point in the verse was that he would do every thing for freeing the country from British rule. Jnanendra Nath suggested that the meaning of the *mantra* should be understood by those reciting it and so it was translated by him into Bengali. The oath taken at the time of initiation often created a moral dilemma in the minds of some members, as it enjoined blind obedience to the leader whose orders should be carried out without question, setting aside all moral and ethical considerations. Hem Chandra admits that he was so overwhelmed by a strong desire to free the country by all possible means that no moral qualms about such oath pricked his mind at that time.[18] Due to the efforts of the trio, Midnapur society expanded; but not as remarkably as after the outbreak of the

Swadesshi movement. In due course a *Chatra Bhandar,* an *akhra* and a *Tantshala,* (a weaving centre) were added as a camouflaged shelter for the members. Midnapur society had connection with the Calcutta society of Aurobindo, but it all along, maintained its separate identity...

The revolutionaries of Midnapur secret society joined the *swadeshi* movement because it gave an opportunity for mass contact and propagating revolutionary ideology. Hem Chandra wrote, "Under cover of the anti-partition protest meetings and giving the example of the Russo-Japanese war, we would arrange lectures with magic lanterns and try to convince the people that it would be easy to expel the British by force from India."[19] While Satyendra devoted all his energies to organise the school and college students and recruit suitable of them to secret societies, Jnanendra gave general direction to the growth of the society in the district. Of the new recruits was Kshudiram Bose. Bibhuti Sarkar and Nirapada Ray @Nirmal.[20] Bhupendra Nath Datta (1880-1961) from Calcutta and Chandra Kanta Chakraborty (1882-1974) from Barisal also came and lectured extensively in the district, and the latter "gradually became a powerful preacher"[21]

The wave of patriotism evoked by the *swadeshi* movement motivated a section of the students to join the secret society. As noted above *Tantshala* in Midnapur town under Bibhuti Sarkar as master weaver became a secret shelter and the *Chatra Bhandar* ostensibly openly sold *Swadeshi* goods but clandestinely distributed revolutionary literature.[22] Attempts were made to transform other *Swadeshi* institutions into units of the secret society by converting the office bearers into revolutionary ideology.[23] Veteran Congress leaders supported *Swadeshi* and *Boycott,* agitation, but were critical of the secret society activists and started avoiding them.

According to Police report, four such *Samitis,* in Midnapur, namely (1) *Sakti Samiti* of Chirimarshai, (2) *Swadeshi Samiti* of Paharipur, (3) *Santan Samiti* of Barabazar, and (4) *Basanta Marati Akra* of Mirbazar, propagated the idea of complete independence by driving out the British by force.[24] Kshudiram described the impact of the publication of the *Jugantar* and the change of their attitude towards Swadeshi in his short autobiography, written in jail. "At this time (March,1906) *Jugantar* paper was published. Reading it, I realised that weaving would not lead to freedom of the country. A rhyme in an article impressed me much. The rhyme was: 'To ask for *Swadesh*i after handing over *Swadesh* to the foreigners, is like posting guards outside to protect the house, while thieves have been allowed inside.'"[25] The camouflage of *swadeshi* was however, blown off when in February, 1906 Kshudiram was arrested with *"sonar bangla"* leaflet containing seditious writings during an exhibition. He was prosecuted under section 124A IPC. The case was committed, (to the Court of Sessions) but subsequently withdrawn under order of the Government.[26] At that time Satyendra, was working as a clerk in the District Land Acquisition Department, but to protect a young and courageous member of the society he gave evidence in the court of law in defence of Khudiram and for that he was dismissed by the district magistrate on the ground that the evidence he tendered was false. Khudiram was arrested. Though the leaflet was patently seditious,[27] yet the Government withdrew the case against him on the ground of his age.

The political scenario in Midnapur, like that in the country, was marked by Moderate Extremist conflict. A contemporary intelligence report states: "By the end of 1906 we find that there was in Midnapur a party of men whose ideas were revolutionary, who were collecting other men round them, were begging for money, and were taking an interest in bombs. The outward and manifest signs of the existence of a party were shown by the mysterious *Tantshala,* an unprofitable *Chattra Bhandar,* the support given to open sedition at the time of Kshudiram Bose's case, and the general turbulent character of young men as displayed in picketing, social boycott and the bullying of shop keepers."[28]

Elsewhere in the province the physical culture societies adopted some kind of social welfare activities like relief work, crowed control etc, though their political objectives remained vague except that they would meet force by force. Pramatha Nath Mitra and Bipin Chandra Pal set up a branch of Calcutta Anushilan Samity, at Dacca on 3 November 1905 in the wake of the Anti-Partition and *Swadeshi* movement for "improvement of Bengali youth by the promotion of discipline and physical exercises." Pulin Behari Das, the organizer of the Dacca Samity, showed remarkable skill and in no time he not only strengthened the Dacca unit, but also opened nearly one hundred branches[29] in Dacca district alone and new centres in many other districts of north and eastern Bengal. Initially Dacca *Samity* got some accolade from the official circle as it did not participate in the *Swadeshi* movement and at the same time, on occasions of massive public congregations like *Ardhodayajoga* etc, demonstrated their philanthropic and social service role by mobilising a big number of disciplined volunteers for crowd control and helping the old and the infirm. It continued this way for almost three years till in November 1907 when B.C.Allen, a district magistrate going on transfer was shot at Goalando station.[30]

The *Samiti's* role in Swadeshi was clearly laid down in their charter. "The Samiti has no relationship with any kind of *Swadeshi,* i.e., the boycott of '*belaiti*' articles, clothes, salt, sugar etc. To be mixed up in quarrels and disputes or implicated in litigation about such affairs is entirely against the principles of the *Samity*."[31] It further added that[32] "Unless the foreigners and the foreign king are driven out, it is impossible altogether to drive out foreign goods."

The Calcutta societies too consciously kept off the *Swadeshi* movement although stray members participated in picketing and canvassing *Swadeshi* ideals. Barindra wrote that they in the secret society were pledged "to retrieve the country by sword because they had lost it to sword". That is why they used to despise *Swadeshi* as a movement of the business class (Vaisya).[33]

A major section of recruits in the secret societies came directly from the National Schools and few from the rank of *Swadeshi* volunteers.[34] In the Muraripukur Garden, for instance, no member participated in the *Swadeshi* movement; but at least six young men came from the National Schools and joined the group.

2. In The Trail of A Lieutenant Governor

Aurobindo's secret society unanimously resolved in a meeting in early 1906 in Subodh Mullick's house at Wellington Square, that they should now commence "action", publish a nationalist vernacular news paper to disseminate revolutionary ideas and construct a *Bhowani* temple. Besides Aurobindo and Subodh Mallik, another top leader of the society named Charu Chandra Datta ICS[35] was present. "By the word 'action' we at that time used to understand murder of English officials or plunder of Government treasures or money belonging to Europeans."[36] For the first time the Bengal revolutionaries decided to resort to assassination, although in that meeting no target was fixed. The responsibility for selecting the target was given to a body consisting of Aurobindo, Charu

Datta and Subodh Mullick though the rule was not strictly followed. Lt. Governor Bamfylde Fuller, already notorious for his role in subverting the *Swadeshi* movement, was held responsible by the nationalist press for breaking up the Barisal Provincial Conference and assaulting and humiliating the national leaders in April 1906 by Police action. He was selected for assassination. The landed gentry were also angry with Fuller as he had been trying to make partition a 'settled fact'. Rajendra Mukherji@Mishri Babu, a zaminder of Uttarpara had promised of a reward of one thousand rupees[37] to the assassin of Fuller. Hem Chandra has written, "The committee of the leaders[38] approved of the plan to murder Fuller". Charu Datta wrote afterwards, "Some people earnestly requested to remove Fuller from the scene. The supreme leader agreed."[39]

Kshudiram's name as a probable assassin of Fuller was considered; but either because of the rumour of his connection with a 'fallen woman'[40], or due to his tender age, he was not selected. Hem Chandra was eventually selected. It was resolved that he would start for Shillong from Calcutta when Barin after making necessary reconnaissance would send for Hem Chandra. When the call came Hem Chandra sent his family to Midnapur and left for Shillong with two revolvers.

He was then a middle-aged man (aged about 35 years, with three children) and had passed the age when one could act impulsively in a spirit of adventure. As an intelligent man he was aware of the consequence of the act he was going to commit. He took it stoically; but one thought that really troubled him was the loss and wastage of life, not only of his own but also that of his would-be victim. Like a true revolutionary he loved life and the possible destruction of it anguished him; and yet like a disciplined and dedicated member, he did not raise any question about the propriety or otherwise of the programme of action of the secret society. Though not a confirmed atheist at that time, he did not have much faith in conventional religion. He has recorded the thoughts and emotions that crossed the mind of a would-be assassin who was going to die. A lighter touch was added to his sombre thoughts when his friend Bhupendra Nath Datta[41], who came to see him off at Sealdah railway station, asked him to let him know, by whatever means available, the experience of the 'other world' after death. Hem Chandra promised him to do so!

Hem Chandra has made fun of the futile chase in his memoirs. Was it because the whole episode lost its seriousness and became comical as they did not come close to making a successful attempt on Fuller's life, and they did not have any real brush with death? When Hem Chandra had started from Gauhati for Shillong, the plan of assassination of Fuller in his headquarter town was abandoned as Barin's revolver accidentally went off injuring one person. Apprehending Police enquiry Barin hurriedly left Shillong for Gauhati. He met Hem Chandra on the way and asked him to come to Gauhati where they learnt that the Lt. Governor would go to Barisal by steamer. So Barin and Hem Chandra followed him in another steamer, and reached in time to see Fuller entering the town from the riverside through the cheering crowd. The two intending murderers with bombs and revolvers in their bags looked on. They expected to "find a big secret society" in Barisal, and also an angry mood of the people in view of the police repression only a month ago. There was no trace of either. Frustrated they started enquiring about lesser officials like district magistrate Kemp and superintendent of police Emerson as suitable targets. Barin tried to explain their objectives to one of the leaders of the local *samiti* and sought his help, which was straightway refused. The leader, however, cleverly pressurised Barin, who had to part with a revolver and beat a hasty retreat from Barisal for fear of being arrested by police.

The next attempt was planned at Rangpur. A bomb, planted under the railway track and the fuse of the bomb connected by wire with an electric dry cell, would be detonated as soon as the train carrying the Lt. Governor arrived on the line. But Fuller in stead of travelling that way, went by steamer to attend the farewell function, which was also cancelled at the last moment due to flood. He then proceeded to Sealdah by special train. Being thus frustrated Hem Chandra and Prafulla Chaki—Prafulla Chaki had joined Hem Chandra at Rangpur—resolved to make a desperate bid on Fuller's life at Sealdah station when he would walk from the train to the carriage. They followed the special train in another train and en route found Lt. Governor's Special standing at Naihati station on the outskirts of Calcutta. Having failed to approach the Governor's saloon at the station due to heavy police guard, they waited at the signal hoping to jump into the slow-moving train at that point and to force into the Governor's compartment. To their surprise the train started moving in the opposite direction as Fuller was to go to Bombay[42] after crossing the river at Naihati.

At Rangpur an attempt was made to loot the house of a widow for funds. Hem Chandra rebelled at the thought of committing a dacoity in the house of a widow[43], and refused to participate on the plea that he was sent for assassination and not for dacoity. Barin threatened him that he would be charged with the violation of the order of the supreme leader and the oath he had taken. In consequence he would be declared as a traitor.[44] Hem Chandra joined the group under threat; but the attempt was abandoned when the party on reaching the outskirts of the village learnt that "a police sub-inspector was present in the village with his party on some local investigation. So they had to turn back and were glad to do so".[45] On reaching Calcutta Hem Chandra reported their failure to Aurobindo who accepted the news stoically.

Hem Chandra has ascribed their failure to the inherent weakness of Bengali character. "How terrible it is for a Bengali Hindu brought up in a non-violent and spiritual atmosphere to kill a man without provocation!" So Hem Chandra admitted that lack of opportunity was not really the reason for which they had failed. At least he had moral reservations in his mind about killing a person without provocation. Hem Chandra explains, "The want of requisite frame of mind led to nervous breakdown, as sufficient power of self-control was lacking in the revolutionaries."[46] Hem Chandra suggested that proper training would help overcome such weaknesses. The Western societies inspired the Indian leaders to set up secret societies in India, but, "neither we nor our leaders recognised that it was necessary to receive training in foreign revolutionary methods."[47] Despite their tall talks about revolution, they had remained deficient in mental strength of a revolutionary, and there were no arrangements for training to enhance their ideological conviction and the strength of mind. But in this specific incident of attempt on Fuller's life, it is evident that Hem Chandra himself lacked the strength of mind for man slaughter. If, however, Hem and Prafulla could get a chance of coming close to Fuller, then Prafulla with his energy and zeal for action would have acted as the guiding spirit and was unlikely to let go the opportunity; and in that case Hem Chandra wily nilly would have become an accomplice in the assassination attempt.[48]

During this expedition the relationship between Barin and Hem Chandra soured considerably. Hem Chandra had little patience with Barin's whimsical nature and irresistible tendency towards self-advertisement, much to the detriment of the safety of the secret society. Barin, an egoist, could hardly withstand Hem Chandra's critical and heavily sarcastic remarks. Later on Hem Chandra had admitted that if he could tolerate Barin's idiosyncrasies and patiently make him see his lapses, then he would have perhaps been amenable to reason, and in consequence he might have been able to exercise more influence on Barin. Nevertheless from this experience Hem Chandra had realised that he must prepare himself in a manner so that he could play a significant role in the revolutionary struggle and for that he ought to take military training in a foreign country.

3. Lessons in Socialism and Bomb-making in France

Even "the little knowledge required in indigenously manufacturing a bomb" was not readily available at the beginning when bomb was needed for 'action'. No account of the first bomb is available either in the official records or in the statements and memoirs of the revolutionaries except in Hem Chandra's book which gives an elaborate account of the chase. In his confessional statement in the Alipur Bomb Trial, Barin stated," "After press prosecutions became numerous, we began to think of using explosives; and wherever we went for money we were encouraged to use explosives".[49] Barin evidently withheld the fact of chasing Fuller with bombs and revolvers in May 1906,[50] and CID had no knowledge of it as no overt act of violence was committed in course of the chase. For killing Fuller Barin procured two big cast iron balls and with "the help of a college student in Chemistry, got an explosive from chlorate of potash prepared and this was poured into two big hollow iron balls[51]." Thus the two bombs were made.

Hem Chandra has written, "The bomb has a magical power. Even a rational man becomes spell-bound after seeing a bomb; he will not then ask any question about the revolutionary party or about the power of the bomb. He will accept every thing on the face value."[52] Bombs, unlike guns, were not available in the market anywhere in the world. They were to be made and for that knowledge was needed. Bombs would not only kill, they would destroy too. The bomb was the most mysterious and most romantic weapon of the revolutionaries.

But bomb has further implications in an anti-colonial struggle. "Since the purpose of the bomb is usually to destroy the body. The bomb is also 'modern' not only in the sense of mobility but also in its randomness and amplitude. It is the violent analogue of amplification, the expansion of what a single voice or a single body is able to do. In this sense body and bomb are connected: the bomb is the super-body."[53] The bomb manufactured by Indians had given them a sense of liberation as their aptitude for acquiring the knowledge and capability for manufacturing the bomb would make everyone sit up and listen to them. It was, in fact, a magic weapon; anyone with a bomb in his possession could earn the confidence of the people and create terror in the heart of the opponent. At Rangpur Hem Chandra and Barindra made some experiments "to set off a bomb with electricity"; but they did not get the opportunity of triggering the device. After this experience Hem resolved to learn the science of bomb manufacturing in Europe at his own cost. He declined to take money from his relatives and friends lest they should later on be harassed by the police.[54]

The original idea of taking military training in a foreign country was not, however, given up altogether. During

May-June, 1906, it became abundantly clear to him that their society was secret only in name as the leader himself divulged whatever secret they had at the slightest provocation. Besides, none of the leaders had clear idea of organising a secret society with all its essential apparatus; nor was there any knowledgeable person in the society capable of handling explosives and manufacturing bombs.[55] On his return from East Bengal in June, 1906, Hem Chandra finally made up his mind to go abroad to undergo a course of military training, if possible, and to learn the science and technology of bomb making and with it as a natural corollary, the techniques of organising a secret revolutionary society.[56] Though America was his first choice, the distance and the expenditure involved were discouraging factors. Eventually he chose Paris, as the city, besides being the art capital of the world, had a tradition of revolutionary struggle and many revolutionary leaders of Europe had taken shelter there. Hem Chandra arranged funds by selling a part of his ancestral property and set out for Europe in July 1906. On way to Colombo he tried to take a stock of the secret societies in Cuttack, Madras and Tuticorin; but to his dismay, he found they were almost non-existent. Hem Chandra boarded the ship at Colombo on 13 August, 1906 for Marseilles.

He took from the editor of the *Jugantar* a few letters of introduction to the editors[57] of journals supporting India's struggle against British colonialism such as, H.M. Hyndman of *Justice*, Shyamaji Krishnavarma of *Indian Sociologist*. Hem did not get an opportunity to go to America and as such he could not meet Freeman of *Gaelic American*. Hem Chandra also took a letter of introduction from Aurobindo to Khasi Rao[58] of Baroda, then living in Geneva, in the expectation of getting his help for learning the techniques of war machines.[59] Hem Chandra has not, however, mentioned about the letter or his meeting with Khasi Rao in Geneva in his book.

On reaching Paris he learnt that military training was impossible because no country would admit him to its Military Academy without the permission of the British Indian Government. So he turned to the next best alternative, that is, to learn the techniques of organising underground societies and to learn the science and technology of bomb making.

In a city where there were 25/26 Indians who formed the Paris Indian Society, much help was not expected from the Indians. But its contact with the London India Society brought Hem Chandra in touch with Shyamaji Krishnavarma (1857-1930)[60] who was the editor of "*Indian Sociologist*", a mouthpiece of the Indian Home Rule Society of which Krishnsvarma was the chief. He served as a cook in his India House in London for sometime, but as Krishnavarma disliked revolutionary terrorism, Hem Chandra did not get either suitable contact or adequate finance. He met Vinayak Damodar Savarkar (1880-1966) in India House as a resident and was attracted by his personality and intelligence, but not so much by his political views. Savarkar, however, did not develop stable and convincing political views at that time. He wanted a chain of secret societies covering the length and breadth of India and these societies through incessant propaganda will prepare the ground for an uprising of the people. On Hindu-Moslem issue Savarkar was of the view that those Muslims who would fight side by side with the Hindus against the British or who would help the Hindus in their fight, they would enjoy the fruits of freedom in independent India; others would be treated as enemy. Savarkar persuaded Hem Chandra to join his secret society, which happened to be the first secret society outside India... Later on both met in Andaman as prisoners.

Having failed to make arrangements for funds in London, a dejected and disappointed Hem Chandra came back to Paris. Thus during the first 4/5 months he could not contact any person who would lead him to the underground societies or to the revolutionary fugitives. There were only a few students of whom one was P.M.Bapat, who came for higher study to Edinburgh, but drifted to London and from there to Paris, and joined Hem Chandra with the intention of learning bomb-making.

Hem Chandra also came to know Madam Bhjkaji Cama (1861-1936)[61] the founder member of the Paris Indian Society. Hem Chandra writes, "I had the good fortune of eating my lunch everyday with her for some months. She then knew me as an Art student and not as a revolutionary. She used to discuss very earnestly about India and Indian politics"[62] Madam Cama and S.R.Rana attended the Socialist Conference at Stuttgart in Germany as delegates of the Paris India Society, and in the conference Cama delivered an inspiring lecture and hoisted a flag which she described as India's national flag. This was carried from Paris. Hem Chandra has given a very vivid description of the flag. "The flag was made for independent India. There ware three colours, red, saffron and blue one after another. On the top was red with eight half-bloomed white lotuses, on which in Devnagri script was written 'Bande Mataram'; the bottom was in blue colour with sun on one side and a crescent moon and a star on the other."[63]

After Stuttgart meeting Madame Cama went to America to expose the tyranny of British rule in India and to campaign for India's freedom. It had been a practice with her to wave the flag of Stuttgart at the end of her speech. During her stay in London in November-December 1908

Madam Cama attended meetings at the 'India House', where Bipin Pal delivered a series of lectures on "Indian Nationalism". At the end of Pal's speech Madam Cama "made a very violent speech which was afterwards printed in the *Free Hindustan* and the copies of the speech in the form of a leaflet, purported to have been signed by her, were afterwards sent to India."[64] A paragraph in the leaflet is as follows: "The flag of Bande Mataram which I wave before you was made for me by a noble, selfless young patriot who is standing at the bar of so-called justice in our country."[65] At that time the Alipur Bomb Trial was going on, and the "noble, selfless young patriot" was none other than Hem Chandra Kanungo.

But was the national flag his idea or he got it from elsewhere? As a matter of fact the flag made by Hem Chandra does not appear to be his idea. A 'National Flag' was presented to Surendra Nath Banerjee on 7th August, 1906 at a meeting at Parsee Bagan Park on the occasion of the first anniversary of the Boycott Movement. Contemporary police report and the *Bengalee* dated 8th August, 1906 contain a description of the 'National Flag,' 'in red, green and yellow; the eight half bloomed lotuses stood for the provinces of India, the sun and the crescent moon symbolised the Hindus and the Muslims, while at the centre was inscribed *Bande Mataram* in Devnagri.[66] Hem Chandra, before sailing for Marseilles from Colombo on 13th August must have read a description of the flag in the newspaper and being an artist and an ardent patriot might have made a rough sketch of it, if not on paper, at least in his mind. There was possibility of his reading the description of the flag in Indian news papers either in Paris or in 'India House', London. Bhupen Datta has mentioned that Hem Chandra took a letter of introduction from Aurobindo to Khasi Rao, the revolutionary brother of Madhava Rao, General in

Baroda Army and a friend of Aurobindo. Khasi Rao was then in Geneva with the intention of undergoing a course of training in Western weaponry.[67] Datta further states that Khasi Rao carried a replica of the Parsee Bagan flag to Geneva and gave it to Hem Chandra when he met him there. From this replica Hem Chandra designed and fabricated the flag which Madam Cama displayed in Stuttgart, New York, London and Paris. Fortunately the flag has travelled back to India[68] and is now on display in a library-cum-museum in Pune.

The speech of a 'Hindu' lady in an open conference at Stuttgart holding the flag of 'free India' was widely publicised in the press and created some sensation at that time in Europe. Pleased with their success at Stuttgart both Madam Cama and S.R. Rana were agreeable to stand as surety for Hem Chandra and his two companions namely P.M.Bapat and Mirza Abbas for membership of the socialist party without having to divulge their real objective.

While writing about his days in Paris and London, Hem Chandra, for very understandable reasons, had refrained from narrating many incidents and mentioning many names. He, however, did not know the names of many fugitives who were staying underground in Paris. The American lady who initiated Hem Chandra to an Anarchist party has been identified by Peter Heehs as Emma Goldman[69] from the archival papers in Paris. After attending a few talks on anarchism Hem Chandra left the organisation as the ideology was of no use for India. The American lady then introduced him to a man who was called 'Ph D' for his scholarship by the Indians. He would not, however, disclose his identity, though it was known that he was a socialist and was asked by an underground socialist party to ascertain the genuineness of the students. He informed Hem that to learn the techniques of secret society organisation and bomb making one must be a member of a socialist party and the membership required recommendations of three socialists. Besides the training was also a costly affair. Eventually the ubiquitous Ph D condescended to plead for them with Krishnavarma, whom he had known from before, and succeeded in softening him and making him agreeable to give financial assistance to the revolutionaries. Hem Chandra thought justifiably that it was not merely the Ph D's arguments that melted the heart of Krishnavarma; but the reports of Aurobindo's prosecution for sedition and his writings in the *Bande Mataram* helped a good deal to turn the champion of Home Rule into a supporter of Extremism in politics. S.R.Rana had also helped them in various ways. Ultimately Krishnavarma had agreed not only to give financial help for training but also "became a convert to our cause". Thereafter Krishnavarma financed their stay and training in Paris and also their journey back home.

After being admitted to the membership of a socialist party and to an exclusive training process, the PhD[70] took charge of their training. The party also engaged a former officer of the army, who had worked as a military attaché in India for many years, for their ideological training. Hem Chandra writes, "We were taught many subjects from comparative geography of the world, history, sociology, economics, religion to socialism, communism etc. We were then taught the methods of organising revolutionary secret society, and the techniques of successfully accomplishing various tasks by the members of the society. "But the socialist teachers were very reluctant to teach the techniques of making explosives as from their past experience about the political situation in India they could not believe that India was prepared for revolutionary terrorist activities. They argued that unless a well-managed secret society with an intelligence system more efficient than the official intelligence machinery is set up, bomb manufacturing would be counterproductive, as the possession of bomb would threaten the secret society's existence. The first requirement was to build up the society with all its underground ramifications including a counter—intelligence network to neutralise the police intelligence. Since Hem Chandra was the last to arrive from India, he gave an exaggerated account of the Indian political situation, claiming that India's revolutionary struggle had the prospect of assuming much greater proportion. He was bent on learning the techniques of bomb making from his French teachers as he was convinced that if all political workers try sincerely India would be free within 10/12 years. So the people should be taught mechanism of making weapons and bombs as early as possible. He also believed that a perfectly organised secret society with its elaborate intelligence wing would be a time-consuming affair and it was not really necessary in India. Police there was not as efficient as in Europe and in a country steeped with religion, people could not be as treacherous as they were in Europe.[71] Besides, in Bengal the effective use of sophisticated bombs would solve the problem of funds of the society as a number rich people were eager to donate money in case of successful use of bombs. After prolonged persuasion for months, and at long last "an old engineer belonging to the aforesaid socialist party was appointed to train us in the use and preparation of explosives. He was a fugitive 'political criminal'. The name of the engineer was Nicholas Safranski, a leader of the Maximalist party of Russia. "We, then, relieved the French chemist who was employed by us to teach us explosive chemistry and converted our bed room into a workshop and laboratory and started the course under the new teacher. He for fear of the French Police never used to stir out of the house in day time and even at night he used to go out only in disguise. So we used to work day and night"[72]

Hem Chandra has been honest to admit that he had personal ambition of becoming a hero, like Mahendra in the *Anandamath,* by doing something extraordinary. He was convinced that he had the skill of manufacturing weapons, but as he could not get that opportunity he would learn the technique of making bomb and try to arrange the supply of weapons secretly to India.[73]

All the three students, namely Hem Chandra, P.M.Bapat[74] and Mirza Abbas, used "to take exhaustive notes, which were later on corrected by the teacher himself. Besides he had a big manuscript of elaborate text with drawings and pictures. We had to use tricks and spend lot of money to get it translated and lithographed."[75]

The party which organised the training suggested that the three students should visit Portugal where a revolutionary struggle was then going on; but they were so eager to return home with a view to demonstrating their newly acquired knowledge that they spurned the offer and set out for home, Hem Chandra and Bapat leaving for India and Mirza Abbas for a stop-over in London.[76]

Their dispersal was in fact very timely as otherwise they might have been detected and interned by the police. The news of the attempt to blow up the special train of the Lt. Governor of Bengal at Naraingarh in the night of 6th-7th December 1907 was taken note of by the Paris Police and the French intelligence, which was keeping track of Safranski, received a report from a secret agent that he was teaching a few Indian students the art of preparing bombs. Suspecting linkage of Naraingarh explosion with the training, they informed[77] the British government; but before the British intelligence could be activated, Hem

Chandra and P.M. Bapat had reached India with a luggage which contained a few revolvers and cartridges and huge quantity of political literature including 150-page treatise on organisation of secret societies and a 174-page manual for making bombs.[78] But what Hem Chandra carried in his head was of more lasting importance and that moulded his thoughts and ideas for the rest of his life and made him a revolutionary with a difference. The lessons he learnt from the Bolsheviks in Paris made him a believer in socialism and Marxism.[79] To him freedom struggle became primarily a struggle for freeing the people of the country from the oppressive British rule by force. He, however, did not leave the secret society for a fresh political pasture, as he still retained his faith in terrorism and armed struggle and in Aurobindo's leadership.

It may noted that the CID could not find any direct evidence of Hem Chandra's visit to Europe and his taking lessons in bomb making, except what Barindra said in his confessional statement before the court that Hem Chandra had gone to Europe "to learn mechanics and, if possible, explosives." The CID, however, had seized bundles of letters from his residence and they included his letters to his wife (some of them are printed in the Appendix-A) and others from France, but could find any hint of his objective in the letters. L.Birley, district magistrate, while committing the accused persons to the Court of Session's, wrote in the committal enquiry report, "It is unusual for a man in his position to make a journey to Europe and what is very significant is that in his correspondences I am unable to find any direct reference to any honest purpose for which he went to Europe, while at the same time there is abundant reference to a mysterious mission. The fact combined with Barindra's statement that he went to learn mechanics and, if possible, explosives and with the evidence of what occurred on his return afford very strong evidence that he did actually go to Paris to learn to make explosives."[80]

4. State of the Secret Society

On his return to Midnapur in late January, 1908[81] Hem Chandra spent a few days at home and then went to Calcutta to meet the leaders of the society. Now that he had taken training abroad in the techniques of organising secret society and in bomb making, he had expected that his importance in the party would be duly recognised and his counsel at least in respect of party organisation and bomb making would receive some importance. From Barin's letters Hem Chandra had gathered the impression that he would be provided with enough finance and opportunity for bomb making. No doubt Hem Chandra had some reservation about Barindra, but he had admiration for "some of his sterling qualities."[82] He, therefore, was not averse to work with the two brothers with his knowledge and expertise which he gained abroad.

But what he learnt was not very encouraging. Two top leaders of the society namely Subodh Mullick and Charu Datta who along with Aurobindo constituted the top leadership of the society were critical of the two brothers and their way of running the society. Both Subodh Mullick and Charu Datta advised Hem Chandra not even to see Barin (Aurobindo was out of Calcutta at that time); because Aurobindo would not listen to any one except Barin and it was Barin's nature to act contrary to the suggestions given to him. He further warned Hem Chandra that the way Barin was running the secret society as an open society, he would soon find himself in the clutches of the police, and with him all others would be arrested. He would rather suggest that Hem Chandra should start a new society. For necessary funds he introduced Hem Chandra to two rich men[83] who, he assured, would finance the new society. But after some time none was unwilling to finance a revolutionary party. Disappointed Hem Chandra had to go back to Aurobindo's group. The meeting with Aurobindo frustrated him more as in a dismissive way Aurobindo asked Hem to see Barin. Hem Chandra expected to be treated with due deference because of his experience and training; but it was demoralising when the supreme leader *(badakarta)* of the society sent him to Barin again.

Barin, true to his nature, magnified his own exploits during one and a half years of Hem's absence. It is alleged that Barin was more interested in grabbing the notes especially on bomb making brought from France and Ullaskar[84] was engaged by Barin for that purpose. Hem Chandra parted with all the documents including those on the techniques of organisation of secret society in the fond hope that eventually the members would study them and follow the model, though Barin was not agreeable to reorganise the society on the ground that the Western methods were not applicable in India as India was not a materialist country like Europe.[85] Barin, however, did not raise any such objection while adopting the Western technique of bomb making. Copies of the bomb-manuals were circulated among other terrorist groups and bomb making was taught to the inmates of the Garden too.

Hem Chandra's disappointment further deepened seeing the increasing stranglehold of religion on the secret society movement. Though search for *Guru* was abandoned by the time Hem Chandra rejoined the society, it was mandatory for the inmates in the Garden to attend religious classes every day in saffron robes.[86] Lele's visit to Calcutta in February, 1908 accelerated the pace of Aurobindo's drift towards *Yoga* and spiritualism. In the society Aurodindo was practically unapproachable to all except Barin, who used to covey his instructions to the members, or as Hem Chandra put it more appropriately, Barin used to take Aurobindo's name in order to make his own instructions weighty and inviolable. Aurobindo was the supreme head of the society, but he never visited the Garden during one year of its existence and the inmates hardly knew him.

From the beginning of 1908 Aurobindo was withdrawing himself from politics, particularly from the revolutionary politics, leaving every thing to his egoist and whimsical brother. His close friends like Subodh Mullick and Charu Datta deserted him. The decisions-making body of the party disintegrated. A disappointed Mullick started living most of the time in Benares and Datta, who used to visit Calcutta rather frequently, left for Ahmadabad in February 1908, and did not meet Aurobindo until 1940. After these two had withdrawn, Barin became the top leader while Aurobindo remained a titular head, endorsing Barin's whimsical decisions.

An instance of such condescension may be cited from Abinash Bhattacharya's memoirs.[87] Before the attack on M. Tardivel, Mayor of Chandernagore, Barin went to take the permission of Aurobindo.

> Barin (To Aurobindo): *Sejda,* it is necessary that the Mayor of Chandernagore should be killed.
> Aurobindo: Why?
> Barin: He stopped a *Swadeshi* meeting in Chandernagore and torturing the local people.
> Aurobindo: That is why he ought to be killed? Then how many people you are going to kill this way? I cannot give my consent. Nothing will come out of it.
> Barin: No, *Sejda,* I do not agree. If this is not done the oppressor will never learn the lesson. We must teach them.
> Aurobindo: Very well. If you think like that, then do it."

When Hem Chandra raised objection that the action would be counter-productive as Chandernagore was a safe shelter for the Indian revolutionaries and a convenient place for import of firearms, Barin argued that Tardivel had decided to introduce a bill to prohibit purchase of firearms in Chandernagore. But finally Barin silenced him by saying that Aurobindo had ordered it.[88]

For sometime Barin had been dismissive of the report from his colleagues that the Garden was being watched by the Police. When Aurobindo mentioned about it, he would laugh at such complaints by saying that those were coward's *alibi* for not doing any revolutionary work. Curiously Aurobindo would accept such arguments. Both the brothers remained blissfully ignorant that Manicktala Garden and a few other houses including the residences of Aurobindo had been under the surveillance of the CID and the Special Branch since March 1908. .

Having known his brother's nature Aurobindo should not have left the society in his hands. The imputation of selfish motive to Aurobindo as a political leader by Hem Chandra is no doubt misplaced and untenable; but the imputation of poor leadership of an underground terrorist organisation of which he was the supreme head cannot be brushed aside.

In 1908 when Aurobindo became more and more engrossed in *yoga,* Barindra usurped his authority and would often prevail upon Aurobindo and force him to endorse his whims. Prof.Amalesh Tripathi has written that Aurobindo "acted from behind the scenes and signed all orders as Kali."[89] But in truth Aurobindo had never issued any written instructions to the secret society members who he knew very little. As a matter of fact, he used to sign the letters which he wrote to Motilal Ray of Chandernagore from Pondicherry between 3rd July, 1912 to the end of 1919 as Kali or simple K.[90]

If the decision to assassinate D.H. Kingsford was taken by the three leaders namely Aurobindo, Mullick and Datta, as claimed by Barindra,[91] then the decision must have been taken before February, 1908 when the three met for the last time. Kingsford's murder according to Hem Chandra was ordered by the leaders whom for obvious reasons he has not named but he too meant Aurobindo, Charu Datta and Subodh Mullick. Narendra Gossain, the approver, stated in judicial confession: "Our society decided that Mr. Kingsford was to be killed. Barin, Ullaskar, Hem Chandra Das, P. M. Bapat and I were among those who decided upon this."[92] The persons named by Narendra had presumably discussed about the means of killing Kingsford while the decision to kill him had been taken earlier.

Barindra selected Prafulla Chaki and Hem Chandra brought Kshudiram Bose from Midnapur and they were sent around 20th April, 1906 to Muzaffarpur for assassination of Kingsford. A day or two after the two boys had left, a CID officer also left Calcutta with a letter of warning to Armstrong, local SP that two 19-year old boys were on the trails of Kingsford. In the morning of 30th April the said CID officer was sent back by the Superintendent of Police with a reply that either the information was wrong or the assassins had changed their plans. In the evening the bomb manufactured by Hem Chandra went off in Muzaffarpur killing two innocent ladies.

The post-explosion scenario in Muzaffarpur was marked by an extraordinary spurt of activities on the part of the police and the magistracy, while the two young revolutionaries made mistakes, one after another, and failed to cover up their trails. Besides leaving tale-tell evidence of their identity in the place of occurrence,

Kshudiram was spotted and arrested next morning (1st May) at a railway station 23 mile away in the same clothes in which he was seen by many throughout the day and prior to the throwing of the bomb. He was arrested with two revolvers and made a clean breast of everything as soon as he was questioned. A day later on 2nd May, Prafulla while travelling from Samastipur to Mokamah by train, SP Armstrong wrote in his report, he was "dressed in new clothes, new 'kurta' and wearing a pair of absolutely new patent leather shoes, "and thus he became very conspicuous. He talked too much with his co-passenger without knowing his identity and showed unusual inquisitiveness about the incident at Muzaffarpur to make him a suspect. When attempt was made to arrest Prafulla on the crowded platform of Mokamah Ghat "he ran down the platform pursued closely by sub-inspector Chaturvedi Ramadhar Sharma and a constable Shewsankar Singh. The constable was gaining on him fast and was at his heels when a GRP constable Zameer Ahmed Khan coming up from the opposite direction made a rush for the Bengali, who drew a Browning pistol and fired at him fortunately missing him." The odds were heavy against Prafulla. The two constables "closed on the fugitive and held him with the man's right hand in which he held the pistol was pressed down against his breast, and he was able to direct the pistol against himself before he could be secured. The first shot was high up on the left breast and would not have proved fatal; realising that the man put the pistol under the chin and fired again killing himself stone-dead, apparently shot through the brain."

The dead body was brought to Muzaffarput via Barauni where it was photographed by one accredited photographer from Bankipur. In the waiting room of Muzaffarpur station Kshudiram identified the body in presence of DM Woodman as the body of his companion Dinesh Chandra Ray. Thereafter the body was taken to Muzaffarpur Civil Hospital where Post Mortem was done by the Superintendent Col. T. Grainger, who found two entry wounds. Two bullets were found in the body. "One bullet pierced the upper left side of the chest and went up to be embedded in the left collar bone. The second bullet pierced the chin and went up to the brain. The second bullet caused instantaneous death."

Thereafter the body was decapitated by violating the Government rules. Though Kshudiram had identified the body as that of Dinesh Ch. Ray, and before that photograph of the body was taken, yet the CID in Calcutta had a suspicion that the real name of the dead man was not Dinesh Chandra Ray as no such name had occurred in the secret list of suspects. SP Armstrong thought of sending the dead body to Calcutta for identification and he wired Commissioner of Police, Calcutta on 2nd May "to arrange reception of the body."

But after the Post Mortem was done on the dead body on the 3rd May afternoon, DM Woodman reported, "the head was then preserved in spirit and sent to Calcutta for further identification, necessitated by the discloser that had been made on the previous day in Calcutta of an organised anarchical conspiracy."[93] The news papers also reported that "on the order of the Police Headquarters the head was severed from the body and sent to Calcutta,"[94] though the dead man could have been identified from the photograph. Such an un-called for brutality, however, served no procedural need of identification as Prafulla's mother refused to see the severed head as she had identified Prafulla from the photograph. The decapitation had a pronounced element of vengeance provoked by the mutilation of the bodies of two European ladies in the explosion and a message for the conspirators freshly rounded up in the Garden. The act was strongly criticised in the nationalist press for its unusual barbarity.

Police action was long apprehended but Barin ignored Aurobindo's directives that they should move out of the Garden. He showed no agility to dismantle it even when the Police Commissioner publicly announced that they had full knowledge of the conspiracy. It is really surprising that even in a situation like this Aurobindo failed to prevail upon Barin.

5. Hem Chandra's Bombs

In the first phase of bomb-making Ullaskar Datta and Hem Chandra Kanungo were the pioneers in this field. While Hem Chandra had taken training abroad, Ullaskar first learnt in his father's laboratory how to manufacture a bomb without any one's help. His bombs were used to blow up Lieutenant Governor's trains. But while the Chandernagore attempt failed, the Naraingarh attempt came very close to success.[95] He then manufactured a very sensitive and powerful bomb, but during experiment one of their valuable comrades was accidentally killed.[96] Among Hem Chandra's bombs the book-bomb for Kingsford was a unique one, though it remained a futile endeavour. The bomb for Mayor of Chandernagore did not explode; the other one made for Kingsford did explode but killed wrong persons as the throwers could not correctly identify the carriage. One such complete bomb was seized by the police during the search on 2nd May 1908.

Hem Chandra, like other early bomb-makers, used dynamite and picric acid in making bombs but his techniques were more sophisticated and the products superior in quality. Finding that the Garden was unsuitable for bomb making, he persuaded Barin to hire 78 Russa Road where a bomb-manufacturing unit under his supervision was set up with Kanai Lal Datta, Indu Bhusan Ray, Nirapada Ray and Sushil Sen as assistants. The centre could not be run for long as it came to the notice of the CID. Hem Chandra then hired 15 Gopi Mohan Dutt Lane near his residence at 38/2 Raja Naba Krishna Street for the purpose; but the CID got scent of it in no time.

The first explosive device made by Hem Chandra was the most ingenious one. It was till then unknown in India and not common even among the Western terrorists. This was a book bomb made for Kingsford[97] in March, 1908. As a matter of fact the entire plan of manufacturing and planting a book bomb was conceived and implemented by Hem Chandra with the help of his comrades. He procured a copy of a thick 1075-page book entitled *"A Commentary on the Common Law, designed as Introductory to its Study"* by Herbert Broom, LLD and cut an oblong hole in the book. He then placed a Cadbury Cocoa tin containing picric acid, detonator and a trigger device in the excavated space. The book-bomb was then wrapped in a brown paper.[98] An envelop was kept inside the book in such a manner that a portion of it was visible from outside; but the book was tied with a tape in such a fashion that the letter can not be taken out without untying the tape.[99] The device was intended to be a camouflage and a challenge. The use of a book on Common Law and a Cadbury cocoa tin would evoke the British image while the loud report of explosion and the damage caused would pose a challenge to the British might. As soon as the book is opened the trigger would be activated and the bomb would explode It was neatly packed and sent to Kingsford through Pares Moulik of the Garden dressed in postal peon's uniform, cleverly procured by Hem Chandra himself. Though the parcel was delivered to Kingsford in his Garden Reach residence, he did not care to open it on receipt. As a matter of fact, Kingsford did not open it even later. He moved to Muzaffarpur without vacating his Garden Reach residence. It was detected only after "a well-known revolutionary, when in custody, said that before this outrage[100] a bomb had been sent to Mr Kingsford in a parcel. Upon search being made at Garden Reach library a parcel was found which Mr Kingsford had received but not opened thinking it contained a book borrowed from him."[101] The Sedition Committee did not reveal the name of the informer, but gave enough hints for identification. The Report further stated, " Fifteen were ultimately found guilty (in Alipur Bomb Case) including Barindra Kumar Ghose, Hem Chandra Das and another who made the statement already alluded to and strictly confirmed as to the sending of a bomb in a parcel to Mr Kingsford."[102] It was neither Barin, nor Hem Chandra but someone else who gave the information while in custody.[103] Parcel bomb till then was a novel weapon even to the terrorists of Europe. The society, however, got little opportunity to use Hem Chandra's expertise in more acts of revenge.

Hem Chandra made three more bombs at Gopi Mohan Datta Lane, one of which was used for experiment and found to be satisfactory. The other was made in a hurry as Barin wanted it within a short time though Hem Chandra was sick. He produced a bomb promptly from the materials available in the Garden; but it was not perfect in all respects. This bomb was thrown into the dining room of Mayor Tardivel of Chandernagore in the evening of 11 April, 1908; but the bomb did not explode as at the time of throwing the detonator got detached from the main bomb. Major Black, the Explosive Expert of the Government, who examined the bomb, stated before the Session's Court:

> I found the tin case filled with fused picric acid. In the mass of picric acid there was a small quantity of dark powder, a mixture of sulphide of lead, chlorate of potash, nitrate of potash and traces of picric acid. A depression on the tin case indicates the insertion of a detonator. The dark powder is very readily exploded. I estimated nearly one pound of picric acid is in the tin case, which needs a powerful detonator for explosion. Possibly the detonator was not powerful enough to explode the contents of the tin case. That quantity of picric acid would be sufficient to wreck an ordinary sized room and would probably kill any one who happened to be in it.

Denham of the CID wrote about the composition of the Muzaffarpur bomb: "I am afraid I can not find anything on record regarding the bomb. Smallwood never made any official report, and all he said are in the deposition file of the Alipur case. "My opinion which I believe to be absolutely correct is that the bomb consisted of dynamite with fulminate of mercury detonator. That may account for the absence of any sign on two remnants of the bomb, recovered at Muzaffarpur."[104]

Apprehending search and arrest in the aftermath of any violent incident in Muzaffarpur the bombs and bomb making materials from Hem Chandra's factory in two houses at Raja Naba Krishna Street and Gopi Mohan Dutt Lane were packed in trunks and bags and sent to 134 Harrison Road on way to Shibpur where they were to be safely stored. But the CID was smarter and the removal and storage at Harrison Road house took place under their watchful eye. On 2 May the police found in the trunks one spike bomb with 24 spikes,[105] and two bombs with detonating studs, along with bomb shells, bottles of picric acid and other chemicals and bomb making materials. The notes and books that Hem Chandra brought from abroad were seized from the Garden during search. Major Black the Explosive Expert, examined the contents, and deposed in the court as follows:

> On 2nd May I went to 32 Muraripukur Road with Mr Plowden and Mr Corbet at about 12 o'clock. In my presence a book[106] containing instructions for preparing explosives was found at the Garden. It was in a receptacle, dug up from underground. It was given to me a few days afterwards by Mr Denham. I have read it carefully. It contains detailed information about picric acid and picrates in a language readily intelligible to a layman. It would facilitate preparation of explosives by non-experts. It contains valuable information about explosives. I have no personal knowledge of the source whence the information comes. I have never before seen it to be available to general public.

These notes that Hem Chandra brought from France were cyclostyled and sent to various underground groups from Muraripukur Garden, to facilitate bomb making.

6. Arrest and Alipur Jail

Hem Chandra was arrested in the early hours of 2nd May from his house at 38/4, Raja Naba Kishen Street, Calcutta. The story of the search of the house was narrated in the Sessions Court by C.F.Merriman, Superintendent of Police who led the police party. "At a meeting in Commissioner's office on 1st May, at about 8 PM, I was asked to arrest Hem Chandra Das. No warrant of arrest was given to me but only a search warrant for arms, ammunitions, explosives and incriminating letters. The warrant was in the name of Commissioner of Police and he endorsed it to Mr Macrae, Deputy Commissioner of Port Police. The search was under his supervision. I surrounded and entered the house at about 4 AM. We forced the door open. The witnesses were searched before entrance. Mr. Macrae, S. K. Ghose, and I entered the house. We began the first search shortly after 4 and finished about 7 AM. The house is two-storied facing south. We first went to the east rooms on the first floor: I think there were 8 rooms altogether. I entered all. The first room was closed. We forced open the door. Inside I found a woman and a boy. They remained there. We then forced the rooms adjoining. In it was a man, Hem Chandra Das, asleep in bed. I arrested him at once. Then I entered another room adjoining. A lady and two children were in that. I think the other rooms were unclosed. Immediately after the arrest I proceeded to search the house in Hem Chandra's presence. The witnesses were present. S.K. Ghose wrote the list."[107] The second search was in the afternoon of 2nd May between 2-30 and 4 p.m. During the third search Hem Chandra Dass was present throughout as a prisoner.

It appears from the circumstances of arrest that Hem Chandra was not expecting an imminent arrest and search, as he was in the dark about the Muzaffarpur incident. None from the Garden or from Aurobindo's house informed him about it. When he saw the police in the house in late night, he was unruffled and did not lose his composure even when he was put under arrest and the house was searched. As noted above the house was searched consecutively on three days, and every time he cooperated as enjoined by law. He, however, did not open his mouth about the articles seized, nor did he yield during the next twelve years of his life in prison to the demand of the Police, CID, the Jail authority or the trial court for disclosure.

Chandra Kanta Chakraborty, who was a preacher of revolutionary ideas in Midnapur[108] and a volunteer in Surat Congress met Hem Chandra after his return from France and when asked to get "some pig-iron shells with grooves inside" for bomb making, he left for Kulti to get them manufactured in the workshop there. Chakraborty wrote later on, "I brought them with me in a hand bag and went directly to Hem Kanungo's house in North Calcutta. His daughter told me that her father was taken away by a number of police after thorough search of the house at 3 AM. Immediately I left the place and while crossing Howrah Bridge I slipped the bag into the river."[109] He had left the bomb making instructions given to him with his cousin Bijoy Bhattacharya who was implicated for possession of this in the Alipur case. Chandra had eventually left the country for America.[110]

Hem Chandra, lodged in Lalbazar hajat with *muri* as food and a dirty rug as bed, was interrogated by Samsul Alam, who as a court sub-inspector in Midnapur was known to Hem Chandra, then a 'Pound and Ferry Inspector' under the District Board. Hem Chandra declined to say anything to his 'polite and soft-spoken' old-acquaintance though Alam tried his best for a considerable period of time to extract some information from him. Hem Chandra writes about the usual method of interrogation by the police. "I had previously enquired about the violent methods the police use to make the accused confess. But none of those methods were applied on us. The tricks applied to get information from us were very common and non-violent."[111]

"One of these methods was to deny us the time for taking bath and food for a prolonged period of time. The second was to talk with the accused incessantly for long hours till he became confused and incapable of intelligent reply; and once he divulges something, it becomes difficult to remain tight-lipped". In case of Barin, Inspector Ram Sadai Mukherjee used the techniques of inducement with success.

While Barin wanted Hem Chandra, his *bete noir*, to fall in line with them and confess, Ram Sadai, on the other hand, looked for the confession of a 'hard nut like Hem, as that would be a feather in his cap. So when Hem Chandra was brought to the confessing group which was expected to be a psychological pressure, he remained stubborn and not only declined to confess but even asked others in the group not to do so as that would have dangerous consequences. Realising that the situation was taking an unfavourable turn, Ram Sadai sent Hem Chandra back to Lalbazar. Many years later, while writing his *Atmakahini,* Barin appeared to be still unhappy with Hem Chandra as he made uncharitable remarks about Hem[112] for his stubbornness. Sometime after Hem Chandra was removed from his presence, Ram Sadai showed a paper to Barin and others saying that it was Hem Chandra's confessional statement. Barin readily accepted the words of Ram Sadai on the face value as he was looking for an excuse to implicate Hem Chandra in his confessional statements. It was a ruse. Hem Chandra did not make any statement whatsoever.

Next day (3 May) Hem Chandra was interrogated first by Samsul Alam and then by Inspector Purna Chandra Lahiri. Alam showed him the confessional statements of Barin and others. It appeared to Hem Chandra that Barin had tried to establish that he alone was the leader of the society, and that he and others had no connection with Muzaffarpur murder, and lastly they had named many whom the police would never have succeeded in tracing, but for the information he volunteered. Inspector p.C. Lahiri, whom at one time Hem Chandra thought to be a top CID officer and planned to liquidate him, did not try to get a confession from him. On the contrary, he treated Hem Chandra courteously to an excellent repast.[113]

After their confessional statements were judicially recorded, Barin must have felt in his heart that the grounds he made out to justify making confession was but a thin veil through which his real motive could be seen. He became more anxious to get Hem Chandra's statement for his moral support. So he suggested to Ram Sadai that if he could spend a day with Hem Chandra he might persuade him to change his mind. Accordingly both were taken on police remand for a day (6 May, 1908). This time also Barin failed to convince Hem. To dissuade an insistent Barin, who was dishing out his untenable arguments to justify confessions, Hem Chandra took the name of Aurobindo to convey that he had asked that none should make any statement, not to speak of making any confession, without lawyer's advice.[114] Besides, he had asked Barin to retract his confession as retracted confessions would have less value. Barin ignored Aurobindo's advice saying that Aurobindo had little understanding of law. In reply to Hem Chandra's accusation that by disclosing the names of the comrades he had betrayed them and so he would be known as a traitor, Barin defended his action desperately by saying that like others he was not accustomed to tell lies!

Having realised that Hem Chandra would not confess voluntarily Ram Sadai now thought of using 'other methods' to extract a confession. Hem Chandra writes, "He made me stand in the veranda cuffing my hands from behind in the custody of a sergeant and two constables and began to talk with Barin with loud peels of laughter. Then I was ordered to be taken to the Lalbazar lockup and was marched off to the destination with a rope round my waist. This proved that Rai Bahadur was very angry with me. However, I was taken to the lock up and handed to an old superintendent of police, who looking at me from head to foot began to quarrel with the Rai Bahadur over the telephone regarding his inability to torture me without the order of the higher authority."[115] Hem Chandra spent an anxious, sleepless night in the hajat.

In this context Aurobindo's observations on Ram Sadai, whom he met for a short while, are quite relevant. "In the evening, the redoubtable Ramsadaya Mukhopadhyaya appeared on the scene. He expressed words of unusual kindness and sympathy, told everyone present to be careful about my food and bed. Immediately afterwards some fellows came and took Sailendra and me through rain and storm to the lock-up at Lal Bazar. This was the only occasion when I met Ramsadaya. I could see the man was both intelligent and active, but his words and demeanour, his tone, his gait, all seemed fake and unnatural, as if he was for ever acting a stage. There are men like that whose words, bodies, actions are an embodiment of untruth. They are experts in imposing on immature minds, but those who know men and their ways find them out at once."[116]

Next day in jail Hem Chandra was put in solitary confinement for about a month when he had to spend agonising time as he was not allowed to talk to any one including the warders.[117] Aurobindo wrote about Hem Chandra's solitary confinement.

> I do not know why the authorities were especially afraid of or angry with him. Hem Chandra himself believed that the wrath of the police was explained by the fact that in spite of much effort they had failed to make him admit his guilt. He was confined to a small room in the decree of which even the door would be closed from outside. Since Hem Chandra Das was looked upon as being a greater terror by the CID than I, he had been given this strict regimen.[118]

In his book Hem Chandra has dwelt at length on the Barin's motive in making judicial confession. However much Barin might have tried to justify his action, he knew too well that the arguments were hollow and years later he admitted in his memoirs that by making judicial confession they actually had put their heads on the block.[119] Then why did they confess? Barin has not given any clear answer. Hem Chandra has explained that Barin never expected that he would be caught lock, stock and barrel, and when it actually happened, he disclosed whatever was concealed. It was "the desire to get reprieve in the case" (*obyahotir ichcha*) which was so strong in Barin that he had confessed. Barin's subsequent conduct in the Cellular jail in the Andamans, corroborates Hem Chandra's presumption that Barin had been tricked by the CID to confess using his strong desire to escape punishment.

After spending a month in solitary confinement Hem Chandra returned to the group and soon became popular with other comrades because of his sense of humour, vivacity and culinary skills. He played a crucial role quietly without the knowledge of Barin and many others to plan assassination of Naren Gossain, the betrayer, following which the jail life became much harder than before.

7. Assassination Of Naren Gossain

Naren Gossain alleged that Barin had betrayed him by giving out his name in the attempt on the life of the Mayor of Chandernagore and in the attempted train-wrecking. Barindra admitted : "In an irresistible tendency to glorify our deeds we lost all restraints and named Naren Gossain as one of the accomplices."[120] But this was merely an excuse.

Naren was born in a zaminder family and brought up in an affluent and loyalist environment. His anti-British patriotism was somewhat adventurous and superficial in nature and it promptly evaporated when his influential father and the government officials showed him an escape rout by being an 'approver' in the case. He was also said to have been promised that he would be permitted to go to England with his family and stay there for the rest of his life.[121] It mattered little to him that he would be considered as a traitor to the country. Antagonism against him was so strong that the jail authorities apprehending trouble shifted him to a safe place inside the jail under the protection of two European warders.

But Naren Gossain's fate was sealed. No sooner had he finished giving his statement before Magistrate Birley, the younger section of the prisoners thought of removing him from the mortal world. They consulted Barin as he, in spite of disenchantment of many with his leadership, was still considered as leader. Barin, however, strongly disapproved of the plan, primarily because such an action inside the jail would involve all including Aurobindo as conspirators. Some like Hen Chandra, who had some knowledge of law, contended that if Naren could repeat the same statement in the Sessions' court, then it would be still more disastrous for all. Yet Barin, as was his nature, remained adamant and would not permit it. He found consolation in the thought that 'somebody or some group from outside would do this job (of assassination of Naren): we need not worry about it'.[122] Barin, aware of the loss of his credibility among the followers, wrote in his autobiography in an introspective mood, "Like a new, inexperienced leader I was somewhat self-willed and autocrat type. I had to work with many but used to impose my will on them. I could feel that a section of the boys were angry with me and some were sulking as we were caught before we could achieve something of significance."[123] Yet he could not change himself.

Barin made a plan of breaking jail and escaping to some West Asian countries beyond the zone of British control. But as he could not get the approval of Aurobindo, who opted for facing the trial, undaunted Barin made preparation by asking the revolutionaries outside to send revolvers inside the jail. Both Hem Chandra and Barin wrote in their books that thus they could bring nearly ten revolvers inside the jail taking advantage of the inept jail administration and slack security.[124] The CID also got the information from one of the under-trials. Before jail-break attempt could be made Gossain was killed and the jail security was so tightened that jail break plan was dropped.

Hem Chandra along with Satyendra Nath Bose, who was in jail hospital for a long period and Kanai Lal Datta who worked as his assistant in bomb-making, made plan for the assassination. Hem Chandra managed to send two smuggled revolvers, one to Satyen and another to Kanai, who was admitted in the hospital the day before, on 30th August. Next morning Naren was lured to jail hospital to finalize the confessional statement that Satyendra and Kanai had promised to make before the magistrate for getting pardon. Naren was accompanied by his Anglo-Indian bodyguard and had almost succeeded in escaping but for the agility and determination of Kanai who shot fleeing Naren down. Kanai fired from a big revolver and Satyen from a small one. They surrendered their revolvers.[125] Five bullets from the big one and four from the small one were fired, and according to Captain Daly, who held PM examination on the dead body all the wounds on Naren's body were caused by bullets fired from the big revolver. While Kanai said before W.A.Marr, additional district magistrate, Alipur, "I wish to state I did kill him. I do not wish to give any statement as to why I killed him. No, I do not want to give any reason. It was because he proved a traitor to the country." Satyendra refused to make any statement.[126]

The trial of Kanai and Satyen commenced on 9 September and the five-member jury found Kanai Lal guilty of murder, and the judge forthwith sentenced Kanai to death. As regards Satyen, evidence indicated that the bullets fired from his revolver did not seem to have caused any wound on the deceased's body. So the five-member jury was divided; three held Satyen 'not guilty while other two found him 'guilty'. The judge pronounced Satyendra Nath guilty; but he did not award punishment and sent the case to High Court. Mr. Justice Sarafuddin and Mr. Justice Cox convicted Satyendra for conspiracy to murder Naren and sentenced him to death. While Eardly Norton and Ashutosh Biswas were the prosecuting lawyers in this case as in Alipur Bomb case, P.L.Ray was the defence lawyer. As a matter of fact Satyen was made an accused in Alipur case only on the basis of the statement of Naren Gossain but he could not be brought to Calcutta immediately as he was then undergoing one month's imprisonment for unauthorized use of a gun.

Kanai Lal was hanged on 10 November and Satyendra on 23 November 1908. The day before the hanging the fellow prisoners were allowed to see Kanai in his condemned cell. Upendranath Banerji found his face as peaceful as that of a saint, 'without a line of care or a shadow of despondency' on his face.

The assassination and subsequent executions were significant events in the revolutionary movement. Gossain's statement became legally inadmissible in the Alipur Case, and "much of the evidence particularly against Aurobindo Ghose became invalid". Besides, as F.C.Daly, DIG of the Special Branch wrote," the assassination put an end to a supplementary case which was under contemplation in which such prominent persons as Abinash Chakrabarty, the Munsiff, Charu Chandra Dutt of Bombay Civil Service and Subodh Chandra Mullick of Calcutta would have been placed under trial under section 121A IPC."[127] Even the on-going Bomb case was also weakened from the point of view of the prosecution

All newspapers especially the Anglo-Indian pro-government papers widely covered the proceedings of the Alipur Bomb Case as also of the Muzaffarpur case. The long statement made by the approver in the court was also published in the press. There was very little discussion in public and still less criticism or condemnation of approver Gossain even in the nationalist circle. Gossain's treachery was construed merely as revelation of the unknown facts and not as an act of betrayal. Generally among the people there was an apathy and indifference to the law courts and the legal proceedings therein, not only because of their tortuous and crooked character, but also because the colonial justice system and its periphery were smeared with much deceit, prevarication and falsehood. The statements made in the courts were not generally judged from the standpoints of human values and social morality, but from the point of view of the needs of the legal code. It was as if the legal code introduced by the Raj was so pervasive that it had superseded the code of morality. So Naren's betrayal was initially taken as a part of the inescapable outcome of the legal system having nothing to do with the code of morality and ethics. Hem Chandra was right when he wrote that had Naren Gossain been alive he would have certainly retained his erstwhile social respectability.[128]

Assassination, however, made all the difference. It brought to the fore the fact that something grossly wrong was done by Naren and Kanai's accusation of Naren as a 'traitor to the country' answered that question in public mind and marked his treachery for condemnation. Therefore, the punishment that was meted out to the traitor by the brave sons of the country despite the protection provided by the mighty British government was just and appropriate for him. Naren Gossain was forever condemned as a traitor to the cause of freedom. The heroism of Kanai and Satyendra, who gallantly rose to meet the challenge of a difficult task, shone brighter in the backdrop of the dark deeds of treachery. This explains the massive turnout at the funeral of Kanai Lal.

The government viewed with concern the spontaneous and unprecedented expression of grief and patriotic sentiment in the funeral procession. Kanai's dead body was handed over to his relatives for cremation. Later events had been described by F.C. Daly, the chief of the provincial Special Branch in his 'Notes'. "An extraordinary scene was witnessed at Kalighat at the time of the cremation of Kanai, whose body after execution was made over to his relatives for disposal. Crowds thronged the road, people pushed past one another to touch the bier. The body was strewn with flowers and anointed with oil. Many women, to all appearances, of a highly respectable class, followed the funeral procession wailing, while men and boys thronged round shouting 'Jai Kanai'. This Kanai Lal Datta was a person of humble origin, a weaver by caste. He was a native of Tantipara, Serampur in Hooghly district and was perhaps one of the most daring and cold-blooded of the whole gang. He gloried in the deed and went to his execution without flinching. After the cremation his ashes were being sold in Calcutta as much as Rs 5/ an ounce are paid by some enthusiasts."

The Anglo-Indian papers, particularly 'The Statesman' and 'The Empire' gave a graphic picture[129] of the popular mood. The Statesman editorially commented: 'the crowd paid homage to Kanai Lal on his last journey in a frenzied manner and from their behaviour it might appear to many that he was a great patriot. But they were in fact very deliberately paying homage to one who had committed a crime. It would be clear from the behaviour of the crowd that they were totally in support of the terrorist activities of the extremists'.[130]

There was a craze for the photograph of Kanai Lal taken before cremation, and the authorities banned the sale of it and confiscated the copies of photograph left with the shop. Satyendra was executed on 23 November, and according to the police officer who took him to the gallows, "He walked steadily to the gallows. He mounted it bravely and bore it cheerfully. A brave lad."

But the government, apprehensive of another massive turn out, did not allow the dead body of Satyendra to be taken out of the jail campus for cremation. The colonial government extended its authority even on a lifeless body which symbolized suffering in bondage and supreme sacrifice for freedom, and as such became a rallying point of the people longing for freedom. After Kanai Lal's funeral procession, nowhere in India the government relinquished its authority on the body of an executed revolutionary terrorist and never condescended to hand over the body to the relatives. Such open demonstration of huge public support for the revolutionaries somewhat legitimized their mode of struggle for freedom.

Procurement of revolvers inside the jail by the revolutionaries has remained a mystery. Both Barin and Hem Chandra had asked their contacts outside to send 10/12 revolvers; but how many could eventually find their way into the jail is not known. A departmental enquiry by the prison authority was held in total secrecy. The jail was thoroughly searched, but both the enquiry report and the number of revolver recovered were kept secret. Intelligence reports indicate that apart from two revolvers surrendered by Kanai and Satyen, three more revolvers were found in course of the search.[131]

Following the assassination the jail authority imposed harsher jail discipline in the name of toning up the jail administration. The inmates were not allowed to meet with each other, the shackled prisoners were kept in solitary cells and communication with each other was prohibited. Meeting with the visitors was made so irksome and insulting that jail interview with the relatives became rare. No interview would last for more than five minutes.

Hem Chandra has noted that after the assassination, Barin's vanity as a leader was so badly mauled that he called a meeting of the group and censured Satyen for the act of assassination without his permission and forced Hem Chandra to apologise for disobedience. He spread a canard that Satyen fainted as he was being taken to the gallows[132] Barin had personal rivalry with Satyen from 1902 onwards and he did not spare him even after his martyrdom.

8. Transportation For Life: 'Even This Will Pass'

After nine months' trial in the Court of Session's Judge Beachcroft delivered the judgment on 6th May 1909. As he started reading it out the court room fell silent. Even the dock which was in fact a huge cage of extended metal and which used to remain somewhat noisy, fell silent. After reading the evidence part of the judgment, Beachcroft started reading the punishment part rather slowly pronouncing each word clearly. Everyone in the court room was holding the breath. Barin writes that after pronouncing the punishment on Barin and Ullaskar, both of whom were sentenced to death, "Beachcroft inquisitively stared at us for a moment, expecting perhaps, that we would faint on hearing the order. On the contrary, Ullaskar said to the judge, "Thank you very much." I did not say anything. So the judge proceeded to read out the remaining part."[133] From other accounts too it is known that Barin took the verdict calmly. After the judge finished reading the judgment, Barin muttered, "Sejda has said I will not be hanged." He had deep faith in Aurobindo's power of foreseeing events.

Upendra Banerjee was upset when he heard the sentence of transportation for life. His mind was shattered. He wrote, "I realised my mind is not made of the heroic stuff. Like a bewildered, helpless young boy it lost all directions."

Hem Chandra has not mentioned anything about his state of mind nor has he noted the reactions of other comrades. Barin has written, "The judge was very angry with Hem-da as he did not confess." Barin has, in fact, expressed his own anger while writing this 12 years later. It was known to many including the police and the CID officers that Barin was not at all happy with Hem Chandra for turning down his request. F.C. Daly gave vent to his insensitivity and dislike for Hem in a crude sarcasm in his report to the Government, "Hem Das for the first time looked seriously depressed. It seems he was disappointed at not being sentenced to death."[134] Upendra has, however, recorded Hem's immense optimism expressed in a cryptic sentence: "Hem Chandra commented, "*Kuch paroya nahi. E bhi gujar jayega*" (Do not worry. Even this will pass)."[135] Aurobindo took his release with stoic indifference.

The Session's Court sentenced 19 out of 36 persons facing trial. Barindra and Ullaskar were sentenced to death, ten including Hem Chandra and Upendra to transportation for life and seven others to various terms of imprisonment. The High Court acquitted five more, and reduced the death sentence to transportation for life. Only Hem Chandra and Upendra Nath did not get any redress in the High Court. Ultimately ten persons were sent to Andaman, four with life sentence and six with varying terms of imprisonment. In the early morning of 11th December 1909 seven prisoners[136] including Barin and Hem Chandra, scantily dressed in a winter morning, were taken out of Alipur Jail in a prison van for Calcutta Port where they were put on board the *S.S.Maharaja* bound for Andaman. Three others[137] destined for Andaman left a few days later after being cleared in medical test. Thirty-nine years old Hem Chandra, going to serve life sentence in a distant island prison, retained his cheerful spirit and sang a song of deep love for the country and of burning desire for freedom.[138]

9. In Andaman Jail

Ten convicts in the Alipur Bomb Case were the first batch of political prisoners in the Cellular Jail of Andaman after its construction in 1896. Of the ten convicts Barindra, Upendra and Hem Chandra had spent more than ten years in the Cellular jail, before they were released on royal amnesty in 1920, while the term prisoners had been transferred to various jails in the mainland in 1915. In the Andaman jail they were not called political prisoners, but were known as 'specially dangerous prisoners' and to identify them the letter 'D' was inscribed on a piece of wood and tied round the neck. Shortly after the arrival of the Alipur prisoners, people like Vinayak. Damodar Savarkar and his elder brother Ganesh Damodar. Savarkar, Nanda Dulal (editor of *Swaraj of* Allahabad), Hotilal Varma, Pulin Behari Das and convicts in several conspiracy and sedition cases in Bengal and the Punjab arrived raising the number political prisoner to more than a hundred. The Government of India's instruction was that they should be treated as 'specially dangerous prisoner', and at the same time, "should not be allowed to work with same group with each other or with other ordinary Bengali convicts"[139] Their position was not deliberately defined by the Government and as a result "they were treated very differently by the jail staff. They were denied many privileges enjoyed by the ordinary prisoners. Each of them was kept confined in a solitary cell and strictly forbidden to sit together, to speak to each other and any communication between them "was a punishable offence."[140] As they were not administered by any code whatsoever, the behaviour of the sadistic jailor Barry and superintendent Browning was tyrannical. Filthy abuse, humiliation and inhuman punishment on any pretext made the life of political prisoners unbearable. Some prisoners used to break down. Hem Chandra, however, suffered quietly. In the words of Barin, "I have never seen his strength of mind diminished even by so little. There was none equal to Hem Chandra for bearing pain and suffering with a smiling face. When some of us were so much overwhelmed with suffering that they were up to doing anything, it was he who infused into them his calm strength of mind and kept them back."[141] Two Alipur prisoners namely Indu Bhusan Rai and Ullaskar Datta were totally shattered by the torture of excessive hard labour and humiliation heaped on them. Indu Bhusan committed suicide in April 1912 and in next June Ullaskar, a very sensitive young man, became insane. Ullaskar was eventually shifted to Madras asylum for treatment. It may be noted here that the Alipur prisoners and the Savarkar brothers were also sent out to work in the settlement, but all of them were not given same type of work. Some had to do very strenuous work, while some were given somewhat light work. Indu Bhusan was a sturdy young man who was also sent out to work in the settlement; but finding the work there too hard and insulting, he returned to jail without permission, and for that Barry had chained him and put him to hard labour in the oil mill. Indu Bhusan told his co-prisoners including V.D.Savarkar that he had no desire to live such a life of humiliation and insult. "He was disgusted with life" writes Savarkar who often tried to enliven his depressed spirit with hope and courage. But Indus's depression was too deep and he committed suicide by hanging from the ventilator rod. A suicide note attached to the iron ring round his neck was removed by the jail officials and was not produced in the inquest lest it should disprove the official version that Indu committed suicide as he had gone insane. Two co-prisoners namely Nani Gopal Mukherjee and Nandagopal said in the inquest that due to hard labour and harsh punishment Indu committed suicide. Savarkar was not called as he also wanted to say the same thing. Hoti Lal Varma wanted to make a complaint that Indu Bhusan committed suicide due to hard labour and torture on him in prison.

But strangely two Alipur compatriots of Indu corroborated in the inquest the official version that Indu killed himself in a fit of insanity, thereby exonerating Barry and his staff of the charges of torture and humiliation. Savarkar in his memoirs has exposed the duplicity of the comrades of Indu Bhusan."But even those who flattered Mr Barrie then and deposed that Indu Bhusan killed himself in a fit of insanity, say openly in the history of their prison life that the cause of his death was no other than the very hard condition of jail life in Andaman. Thanks to them because they tell the truth at long last."[142] Though Savarkar has not named the fellow prisoners who told the untruth in the inquest to protect Barry, R.C. Majumdar has identified them. "The two other memoirs written by Indu Bhusan's fellow prisoners were Barin Ghose and Upen Bandopadhaya".[143]

Savarkar has not mentioned Hem Chandra in this connection and so it seems he was not a witness in the inquest.[144] Since both Barin and Upen were 'flattering Barry', presumably from the day the strike had started, they might have advised Barry not to call Hem Chandra as a witness in the inquest. After the inquest Barin[145] and Upen started enjoying Barry's patronage more and more much to the embarrassment of the fellow prisoners.

In June 1912 Ullaskar became insane when he was punished for returning without permission from the settlement where he was put on hard labour in the sun against medical advice. A fatigued Ullaskar with high fever came back to the jail, and immediately thereafter he was abused by Barry who, according to Ullaskar, ordered that" chains should be put upon my hand and I should be suspended by them in my cell for a week continuously".[146] Ullaskar after sometime lost his senses. What happened thereafter is narrated by Savarkar. "Heart-rending cries one after another filled the whole atmosphere. I saw some of them dragging a man from block No.5. There were ten of them trying to lift him up and carrying him to hospital".[147] But jailor Barry would not believe that Ullaskar had become really mad. Four days after the incident Savarkar told Barry, "You had said about Indu Bhusan, you remember, that he had hanged himself because he was mad and not because he had suffered from excessive hard labour in the jail. Why then Ullas has gone mad? Can you give any reason for it?" Mr Barry then changed his front, and said "But who told you that Ullas is mad? He only pretended madness." Eventually, however, Ullaskar was sent to an asylum in Madras on medical advice.

Following Indu Bhusan's suicide and Ullaskar's insanity, the plight of political prisoners engaged the public attention in the mainland when Barin had quietly sent to the press in Calcutta the tales of torture and brutal punishment. The *Bengalee* of Calcutta published leading articles for three days and in the *Tribune* of Lahore dated 3 May, 1912 similar allegations[148] were made. The matter was raised in the Imperial Legislative Assembly too.

As the Alipur prisoners were mostly out in the settlement for work, they remained out of the strike. Nani Gopal continued his protest often with hunger strike and sometimes remaining confined in his cell without any wearing apparel. Nandagopal often resorted to peaceful resistance and suffered punishment. The strike virtually fizzled out.

At this time on 9th August 1913, an extensive search in the jail and outside leading to arrest of a large number of people both inmates of the jail and the residents of the island took every one by surprise. It was rumoured that a section of the political prisoners had a secret plan to blow up the Commissioner. According to Savarkar, "Some (of the prisoners) were manacled, others detained, and many others had their rooms searched. From political prisoners the campaign spread to the houses of free citizens, of Jamadars and Tindels. The search and arrest parties were entirely manned by the European officers, and it did its work with terrible efficiency. It threatened, it shouted, it scolded and it terrorised till whole of the colony was stricken with nervousness and fear."[149]

It was alleged by the prison administration that a group of political prisoners had planned to kill the Commissioner. The information was obtained from a clerk[150] in the Commissioner's office, who had given secret information earlier too to the authority.

But was there really a conspiracy as alleged? Both Upendra and Barin said in their memoirs that it was a hoax. The Government made enquiries, but they failed to find definite proof of it except some brass tubes and brass and copper cylinders. No explosive was found. After examining them the explosive expert opined, "All the articles noted would be most useful in bomb construction." Yet that alone was not sufficient to prove a criminal case.

At this time Charles Tegart, then an Additional S. P in the Intelligence Branch, Bengal, visited the Cellular jail at the instance of the Director, Central Criminal Intelligence to interview certain political convicts with reference to a series of bomb outrages in India. The fact of the matter was that the case of bomb attack on Viceroy Hardinge on 23 December 1912 was till then unsolved though the Government of India had launched one of the biggest man-hunts in colonial India to arrest the culprits and solve the case. But even after that for more than a year the case remained undetected. In the meantime similar bombs exploded elsewhere in the country. One bomb exploded outside the SDO's bungalow[151] at Moulavi Bazar in Sylhet district on 27 March 1913, killing the person carrying the bomb. Another bomb exploded on the road near the Lawrence Hall in Lahore on May 17, killing a *chaprasi*. A similar bomb was thrown at the house of Abdur Rahman an informer in Midnapur town, but it did not explode. Government was worried about the extensive use of such sophisticated bombs throughout north India and the failure of the CID to trace the source. Although nearly eight months had passed after the formidable team of sleuths drawn from different provinces of India was tasked to unravel the mystery of the Delhi Bomb case, there was no positive development. An exasperated Director, central Criminal Intelligence asked Tegart to meet the Bengali prisoners in the Cellular jail in case they could give any clue to the source of the picric acid bomb. Incidentally before Tegart, Geoffrey Denham, then with the Central intelligence, had visited the Andaman prison for the same purpose, but he could elicit little information,

Tegart was clever enough to realise that without inducement it would be difficult to make the prisoners speak. So before his departure he took from the Bengal chief secretary an authorisation letter stating, "that the Government of Bengal are prepared to grant a substantial remission of the sentence to any of the political convicts now in the Andamans, who can give to the satisfaction of the Government true information regarding the places where or the persons by whom picric acid bombs are prepared in India, or who can give to the satisfaction of the Government true information which will lead to the detection of the Midnapur, Delhi, Maulvi Bazar, or Lahore bomb outrages." On return Tegart submitted his report as "Notes on Andaman Enquiry"[152] in the format of an official tour report. Tegart's objectives in meeting the political prisoners were, i) to get clues or information about the source of the picric acid bombs recently exploded in north India, ii) to establish the identity of the young men killed in Maulovi Bazar, and whether he was the untraced revolutionary Sarada Chakraborty, iii) to soften Nani Gopal Mukherji a prisoner in Dalhousie Square bomb case so that he would divulge the source of the bomb, iv) to study and weigh the evidence collected in the alleged "bomb conspiracy" by the prisoners to kill the Commissioner of the Andamans. Tegart was accompanied by a retired Bengali officer of the Intelligence Branch and one elder brother of Nani Gopal. On the first three points Tegart failed to elicit any new information from the prisoners. He could not get any inkling of the source of Picric acid bomb, he could not establish the identity of the man killed in accidental explosion at Moulavi Bazar, nor could he make a dent in the integrity of Nani Gopal even by using his brother as a pawn. It may however, be said in favour of the brother that he did not ask Nani Gopal to betray the cause and that is why

Tegart commented in the note, "I am afraid, Suren (Nani's brother) has not played our game". He did not allow Suren to meet his brother second time. The Government of India's assessment of the report was: "The interesting part of Mr Tegart's notes lies in the frank expression of impertinence on the part of some of the prisoners and the corroboration they afforded of our suspicions against certain of the Chandernagore gang. Otherwise Mr Tegart has failed to elicit any information of great value."[153]

As regards the 'bomb conspiracy' by the prisoners in the Andamans, Tegart, after examining the letters and other documents which he brought from the Commissioner, of the Andamans, telegraphically informed: " Have discussed with Hutchinson (DIG,IB, Bengal). We think it doubtful if the case could be established under section 120-A IPC at this stage." Tegart's opinion was accepted by Craddock, Home Member, who wrote, "I certainly do not contemplate with equanimity an Andaman conspiracy case with the demand for publicity, which will assuredly accrue."[154] Barin and Upen in their memoirs have called the conspiracy as a ploy of the jail authority with a view to tightening the discipline on the political prisoners. But in the prevailing conditions in the Andamans was any excuse necessary to tighten the discipline? Savarkar thinks to the contrary and he hints at some activities involving the residents of the island. There was, no doubt, some effort, which was at a very preliminary stage, was promptly given up when Saha was detected as a double agent.

Tegart's report, however, reveals the true character of some of the revolutionary leaders who are held in great esteem by the people, partly as a result of the clever propaganda they themselves made about them and partly because of the fact that the official classified documents were not in the public domain. Upendra Banerji revealed the names of the Chandernagore leaders like Srish Ghose, Charu Ray, Motilal Ray and many others. These and many more names and their antecedents were, in fact, known to Tegart and the Government as evident from the report[155] that Tegart submitted on 13 July 1913. What Upen did was to connect them with specific secret activities which exposed them to legal liability, besides underscoring their importance in the revolutionary movement. He also divulged certain new names and new centres of secret activities. It may be noted here that while in Alipur jail someone among the under trial prisoners informed the police about the unexploded 'book bomb' in Kingsford's library at Garden Reach. The Report of the Sedition Committee has narrated the story in such a manner that the needle of suspicion would point to Upendra Nath Bandopadhyaya.

About Srish Ghose of Chandernagore, whom Upen identified in a photograph, he said, "He brought and handed over the second or the smaller revolver to Barin in the jail. The other one was brought by Abinash Munsiff and given to Priya Sankar Sengupta @Sasankajiban Ray. Next day he corrected it and named Satish Sarkar. "Srish used to come to the Garden and as many as eight times he came there." Upen further said, "When I went to place a bomb on the railway line near Mankundu, at that time Barin used to visit Srish Ghose at Chandernagore frequently to tie up small details of the arrangement. We collected in the house of Srish Ghose's uncle in the night when the bomb was actually placed." He further said that Srish was angry with Barin because he had made judicial confession. Srish told Charu Ray that the rules of the secret society should be strictly observed and to warn others Barin should be shot dead. Charu, however, did not agree with him. Upendra further disclosed Charu Ray's association with the revolutionaries.

Upen, the closest associate of Barin in the secret society and in the Cellular Jail, told Tegart that Barin's plan of revolution lacked maturity and it was a mistake. He should have started revolutionary activities after properly educating the people. He even told Tegat that Barin through clandestine channel had communication with the main land and in an self-exculpatory tone said that he had asked Barin not to do so secretly. Thus it became clear that the intercepted letters in connection with the 'bomb conspiracy' were really sent by the prisoners.

Upen had often been in a depressing mood in jail as he had taken it for sure that he would have to spend the rest of his life in prison. He expectantly asked Tegart, "If there is any hope of clemency for lifers like myself." Tegart cleverly told him that no real help to the Government to contain violence in the country would remain unrewarded.

But information that Upen gave about Hem Chandra was inspired by spite, because they were not true in all respect. According to him Hem Das forced the secret society to use bombs extensively and to undertake terrorist propaganda. He also informed that Charu Datta was a die-hard revolutionary. Datta had requested Barin that at least one target had to be killed before his leave expired. On being questioned about Delhi bomb, he said that they (the revolutionaries) had many friends and supporters in India who might have taken revenge for not paying any heed to the prayers of the Andaman prisoners. Hem Das, he said, had a society in Midnapur with which he was in regular communication. Prakash Maity of that group was a dangerous person. He further said that the appearance of bomb in Delhi might be the work of Aurobindo's followers.

Under the title "Notes for Reference" written in pencil by Upen was found among his belongings during the search of his cell. It is in fact a hotchpotch of his political thoughts which suggest, inter alia, the creation of an Ascetic Council (*Sannyasi Sangha*) for freedom struggle.

In the second session of interview (29 August, 1913) with Tegart, Upen identified Amarendra Chatterji from a group photograph and revealed his connections with the Garden. Motilal Ray of Chandernagore, Upen informed, was a courier of letters and messages from the inmates of the jail to Abinash Munsiff and Charu Ray and vice versa. About Indu Bhusan's suicide Upen used a convoluted argument to put the blame on Hem Chandra. He stated that Indu was a devoted follower of Hem. He used to treat Nani Gopal with sympathy and compassion. But Hem convinced him that Nani was an informer of the Government and he was in Jail to extract secrets from other prisoners, and therefore Hem had advised Indu not to talk to Nani. At this Indu was so shocked that his depression due to frequent abuse and insult by the low caste criminal convicts was further aggravated, and eventually he committed suicide.

Upendra told Tegart that Hem Chandra had encouraged extensive use of bombs by the underground societies by circulating the bomb manual along with sketches of bombs. He also sent copies of the booklet on how to organise secret underground societies to the revolutionaries outside. When Tegart showed him a copy of the bomb manual, Upen identified that as one brought by Hem Chandra from France, adding that the copies of the manual were distributed from the Garden.

Barindra Kumar Ghose, when interviewed by Tegart, spoke with an air as if he were still the leader of the society. Barin said that he had presently been engaged in broom-making; but at that moment neither bomb making nor broom-making was to his liking. He clearly stated that he would not be a traitor by divulging secrets, because firstly, he did not trust the Government and secondly in case he disclosed some secrets then he would not feel safe anywhere in the world. He strongly criticised the *swadeshi dacoities* though he fully supported political murders. About Delhi bomb he said that it might be the work of an old hand who might be even Aurobindo. He said it was not difficult to make picric acid bombs; but it was difficult to make it with fulminate. He then gave details how they had made picric acid bombs. In Deoghar in the trial of one such bomb Prafulla Chakrabarty was killed. He then said that he did not know much about bomb making. The job was entrusted to two experts, namely Hem and Ullaskar. He also admitted that from the jail he had contacted the friends in Indian mainland.

Tegart met Hem Chandra only once for a short while, because he was very non-communicative. He was shown a photo seized from 15, Jora Bagan,Calcutta . He said he had not seen the photo before. He also said he had very little knowledge in the science of explosive. Whatever little he had learnt was from the deposition of Captain Smallwood in the Alipur Bomb Trial!

Tegart failed in his primary objective of finding some clues to the source of the bombs which exploded from Lahore to Sylhet, yet its source could not be traced for over a year by a formidable team of sleuths drawn from almost all the provinces of India. Tegart tried to reach the source of the bomb by identifying the revolutionary killed[156] as a result of accidental explosion at Moulavi Bazar: but the young man, named Jogendra Chakrabarty[157] of Dacca *Anushilan* samiti, could not be identified by anyone in the jail from the photograph of the mutilated body. As regards the source of the bombs, it may be mentioned that it was not possible for the Andaman prisoners, who had no touch with underground activities for about 5 years to know the source of the bombs except making wild guesses, which they did.

During the period of their absence not only new centres of bomb making had come up but also new and sophisticated techniques had been introduced. As a matter of fact, in Chandernagore Suresh Chandra Ghose and Manindra Nayak, both science students were engaged in making picric acid bombs with fulminate as fuse. Suresh, however, soon left for England for higher studies and the responsibility fell on Manindra, who became the principal bomb maker. As a matter of fact from 1910 to 1916 most of the bombs used in different provinces were made by Nayak. Three bombs made by him were taken to Delhi by Basanta Biswas, one of which was thrown on the Viceroy. A number of bombs were sent for Ghadar uprising in February 1915. The bombs with which Pingley was arrested in Meerut cantonment were made by Manindra Nayak. The Delhi Bomb Case was, however, solved after similar bombs in the process of making[158] were seized in November, 1913 at Rajabazar, and the printing press of some leaflets found in circulation in Delhi was traced in Calcutta. But the Intelligence Branch came to know about Chandernagore as a bomb manufacturing centre only at the end of 1916 from an insider in the *Anushilan* party[159] and Tegart, on 1 December with permission of the French authority, searched various places in Chandernagore and the neighbourhood. Though he could recover from the house of Tinkari Banerji four Mouser pistol stolen from Rodda & Co (August, 1914), he could not trace in Chandernagore any explosive whatsoever.[160]

In the context of press criticism of the treatment of the prisoners in the Cellular Jail and questions asked in the Imperial Legislative Assembly on the subject, Sir Reginald Craddock, Home Member of the Viceroy's Executive Council visited the Jail in October, 1913 to see things for himself. He interviewed some prisoners and accepted their petitions to the Viceroy for redress of grievances. Among the Alipur prisoners who sought interview with Craddock were Barin Ghose, Upen Banerjee, Hrisikesh Kanjilal, Sudhir Sarkar, Biren Sen. Barring Upen all of them submitted petitions to the Viceroy. Barin's verbal submission and written representation[161] are most important as they reveal his true character. Craddock wrote, "Barindra Kumar Ghose's case in some ways was the most interesting of the whole lot. He professed repentance but denied any knowledge of the local plot which led to the incarceration of all the anarchists. His denial was obviously untrue." Barindra was told that the only way to prove his sincerity was to give all the information to the Government. "He at once put it to us could we guarantee his safety if he spoke?" When he was told that he might be sent to Europe, he said that nowhere in the world he would be safe". Then referring to the bounty announced for information about the bomb attack on the Viceroy, Barin said, "Do you suppose that that lakh of Rupees would go begging if safety of the informer could be guaranteed? A lakh of rupees is a very tempting offer." Craddock then gave his own considered opinion about Barin, "I think that Barindra's unwillingness to give any information is due to the knowledge that he would be murdered if he were to speak; and that but for this he would not be unwilling."

In his letter to the Viceroy sent through Craddock Barin promised "I for one shall bind myself down to remain just where His Excellency wishes me to remain, abstain from all movements and obeying his slightest wishes. *More than this I can not say in a petition like this.*"[162] The last sentence appears to be enigmatic; but the context in which the sentence has been written makes the meaning obvious: he wanted to give information to the Government. This might be a surprising revelation about Barin as a revolutionary leader. But if the criticism of Barin made by Hem Chandra from event to event are carefully analysed then it will appear that Barin, though very hard working and often very innovative in his ideas, he was more often than not whimsical and impatient of honest criticism and impervious to sane advice. He was eager to advertise himself as a revolutionary leader. He derived his authority in the secret society from Aurobindo; but he misused, and often, abused the authority. He was neither a capable leader nor a man of strong character.

Hem Chandra did not seek an interview with Craddock, nor did he submit any petition to the Viceroy through him. He was a lone traveller along the difficult path chosen by a revolutionary.

10. A Long and Lonely Evening

On returning from Andaman in February 1920, the prisoners found a change in the political climate. The Congress Party under the supreme leadership of Gandhiji, was determined to pursue the objective of the "attainment of the *swaraj* by all legitimate and peaceful means". The meaning of *swaraj* was, however, kept deliberately vague. Many members of the two prominent underground groups, namely *Jugantar*[163] and *Anushilan,* decided to join the non-violent non cooperation movement, and many were sitting on the fence and watching the developments. While Barindra and Upendra, known for their penmanship, joined Bengali periodicals and started writing about their experience in the Andaman, Hem Chandra went back to Midnapur, where he started photography and painting partly as hobby and partly as a means of livelihood. He did not open a regular photography shop, but carried on the business from his house in the town.

With very little ancestral property left after all these years, Hem Chandra found him in financial distress. The earning from the photography was too meagre. Narendra Lal Khan, *zamindar* of Narajole and a Congress man, gave him a monthly allowance as political sufferer from his estate and in return he asked Hem Chandra to make portraits of the members of his family at his convenience. Hem Chandra made many portraits but few of them have survived today.

Besides portraits, he had a facile brush in watercolour painting, and he used to paint even in the Andaman where Captain Murray, Superintendent, supplied him with paints and canvas at government cost. For photography in those days wooden cameras were in vogue. Sambhu Saha, one of his illustrious students of photography,[164] has said that for seasoned wood he would purchase old pianos in Calcutta and with the wood from piano he would make wooden cameras with such excellent craftsmanship that they were comparable with those imported from England.[165]

Apart from his culinary skill which was acclaimed by his comrades in jail, he was an excellent carpenter and an expert book binder. But the most interesting were the reading and singing sessions. Saha says, "Hem Chandra used to read to us the classics particularly the Russian classical literature of Tolstoy, Pushkin and Dostoevsky. He would read to us from Das Capital too and often lend us books from his rich library".[166]

He did not show much enthusiasm in the social and cultural life of the town where he lived. Midnapur was visited by Gandhi in September 1921 and again from 4th to 6th July 1925 when he stayed and delivered speeches on untouchability in the Narajole house of the Khans. But Hem Chandra chose to remain in the shadow.

He had developed some intimacy with poet Nazrul Islam who during his visit to Midnapur in April 1929 stayed in Hem Chandra's house for two days. He recited his famous poem "Vidrohi" as if as a tribute to Hem's past exploits. Nazrul was the star attraction in the musical soiree organised at the Gope palace in which Hem Chandra also participated. Sambhu Saha took a photograph of Nazrul; but there is no evidence to show that Hem Chandra tried either to take a photograph or to make a portrait of the poet.

He remained aloof from all shades of politics, although during this period from 1922 to 1947 Midnapur was repeatedly rocked by daring acts of terrorism, surging waves of militant mass movement, and also a peasant movement under the leadership of the Communist Party which was gradually gaining strength in the closing years of British rule. Hem turned his back to all of them, except for a brief association with M.N. Ray, which was inconsequential.

Hem started writing his memoirs some time in 1921 and its first instalment was published in the March-April (1922) issue of *Masik Basumati*. Serialised publication continued till January-February 1928. During this period some of his views and observations were strongly criticised and when the account was published as a book in June 1928 criticism became rather harsh. In the preface of the book, he has tried to reply to some of his critics. He promised in his memoirs to write more elaborately about his association and activities in France at a convenient time. Similarly he also said somewhat sarcastically that he hoped to write separately about "our *tales of glory* in Port Blair."[167] But he did not write anything except a small book[168] unrelated to revolutionary movement, though he lived for 30 years after his release and nearly three years after independence. He spent a quiet life which came to an end in his village on 8th April 1951.

11. *Banglaya Biplab Prachesta:* A Memoir with a Difference

Three persons convicted in the Alipur Bomb Case namely Barindra, Upendra and Hem Chandra and two other contemporary Andaman prisoners namely Sachindra Nath Sanyal, and V.D.Savarkar published their memoirs shortly after their release. Troilokya Chakraborty, another contemporary in the prison published his memoirs much later in 1968. All these books contain tales of the plight of political prisoners in the Cellular Jail. Barin's "*Dwipantarer Katha*" was serialised in 1920 in *Narayan,* edited by Chitta Ranjan Das, and was promptly published as a book (1921). In 1921-1922 Barin spent 4/5 months in Pondichery to get his Bengali book translated with the help of Nalini Kanta Gupta and published from there in 1922 as *The Tale of My Exile*" After sometime Barin himself became editor of "Bijali" in which he serialised (1921-1922) once again some parts of his revolutionary life variously styled as "*Bomar Katha*" "*Dwipantarer Pathe*" and they were published as books. In 1922 taking portions of his serialised publications and adding new writings, Barin published '*Barindrer Atmakahini*". This was, in its tone and temper, an apology for his actions till he was sent to the Andaman. It appears from his myriad publications that Barin was in a hurry to tell his version of the story to the people.

Upendra also serialised "*Nirbasiter atmakatha*" in *Narayan* and published it as a book in 1921. As a matter of fact both *Nirbasiter atmakatha* and *Dwipantarer katha* were published almost simultaneously.

Sachindra Nath Sanyal also serialised the story of his prison life in *Narayan* at the request of Hemanta Sarkar who encouraged him to write in Bengali. Being brought up in Benares Sachin was more proficient in Hindi than in Bengali and so he was hesitant to write in Bengali. Eventually his "*Bandijiban*" was published in ten issues from *Agrahayan* 1328 BS to *Bhadra* 1329 BS (Oct.-Nov.1921 to Aug.-Sept. 1922), and soon thereafter in 1922 they were published as a book. Sachin's introduction to the first edition of the book is dated 25th August, 1922.

Sachin has referred to four books of the same genre in the introduction of his book. They are Aurobindo Ghose's "*Karakahini*" (Tales from Prison), Nalini Kishore Guha's "*Banglay biplabbad*" (Revolutionary Cult in Bengal), Upendra Nath Bandopadhya's "*Nirbasiter atmakatha*" (Autobiography of an Exile), and Barindra Kumar Ghose's "*Dwipantarer katha*" and its English translation *The Tale of My Exile*. He has praised Upendra's literary style but criticised his narrative for flippancy. "It is doubtful if there is any writer in Bengal who has such power of using sarcasm and wit. But in his autobiography very serious matters have been discussed in a light hearted manner. He makes fun of every thing. That is why his autobiography has been a pleasant reading, but it does not touch the heart." Sachin is still more forthright about Barindra'a *Dwipantarer katha*."I like that part of Barin Babu's book, which is written by Upen Babu, and more than half of the book is written by Upen Babu." As a matter of fact, as many as three chapters, that is from Chapter X to Chapter XII of *Nirbasiter Atmakatha* have been copied word for word and printed in Barin's *Dwipantarer katha*. Barindra, conscious of his unethical conduct, explained at the very outset," My only hope is that I have Upen behind the curtain, who promises in case of any difficulty to whisper loudly enough to my ears, and I on my side promised to repeat them just what he says and not fabricate anything out of my imagination. Therefore, my readers are kindly requested to consider this tale of the Andamans as the joint utterances of two tongues and to take it from me that whatever I have said is true and pleasant--I have not transgressed the injunctions of our *shastras* by saying either the untrue or the unpleasant."[169] But unfortunately he has copied so extensively and meticulously from *Nirbasiter Atmakatha* that it can hardly be said that he was merely prompted by Upemdranath. There is, however, an element of truth in his statement that he has spoken the 'pleasant things avoiding many truths about him. Sachin has pointed out that Barin Babu has often broken into poetry; but on the whole the heart of the revolutionaries has not found expression in his writing. He also blamed Barin for effortlessly covering up many things that occurred during their stay in the Andamans.

Sumit Sarkar writes about Upendranath and Barindra's memoirs: "They make good reading as adventure stories, but despite some interesting sidelights their flippant style has robbed them of much historical value." Sumit, in fact, has echoed Sachin Sanyal.

"*Barindrer Atmakahini*", published in 1922, is self-exculpatory in character wherein Barindra, aware of the criticism of his actions unlike a revolutionary,[170] has tried to defend them with untenable arguments. The book, in truth, is an apologia for his activities as leader of the Manicktala Society and his conduct after arrest.[171]

Hem Chandra's book was serialised in monthly *Basumati* from Sept.-Oct, 1922 (*Aswin* 1329 BS) to Nov.-Dec. 1927 (*Agrahayan,* 1334 BS) under the title *Banglaya Biplab Kahini*. In 1928 when his book was published, the name was changed to Banglaya Biplab Prachesta. V.D.Savarkar's book was published in Marathi under the title *"Majhi Janmathep"* which was translated into English by V.N.Naik under the title "The Story of My Transportation for Life."

From the above account it will appear that both Barindra and Upendra were in a hurry to tell the readers their side of the story in the Cellular Jail, before any one of their co-prisoners like Schindra Nath Sanyal, V.D. Savarkar and Troilokya Chakrabarty could do so. But both of them are sketchy, vague and evasive in their accounts. Barindra even went to the extent of copying from Upendra Nath's book to avoid any scope of contradiction. But when books by Sachindra, Savarkar and Troilokya Chakrabarty were published and secret official records like Tegart's report on the Andaman prisoners, Craddock's visit notes or the file of petitions of the Andaman prisoners to the Viceroy etc. were not available in the public domain, and as such the facts about their conduct in the Cellular Jail not were known to the people. In his book Hem Chandra stated that he would later on write about "our glorious deeds" "in the Andaman; but he could not do so.

After the publication of Hem Chandra's serialised account, he expectedly faced criticism, first for allegedly denigrating the respected revolutionary leaders like Aurobindo and Barindra, and secondly for disclosing the secrets of the society in his narrative. By doing so he had, it was alleged, betrayed the trust as a revolutionary.

Hem Chandra replied to these charges in the preface of the book. It may be noted that in Alipur Bomb Trial the details of almost all actions were presented before the court. Some secrets were certainly disclosed to the police and intelligence by the Alipur prisoners who almost scrambled for giving information to the intelligence agency. They even debated the 'morality' of such acts of betrayal. There was hardly any actionable intelligence about Alipur Bomb episode of 1907-1908, which was not known to the CID. Whatever remained was more of historical interest than for use by intelligence agency. In Hem Chandra's book the chasing of Banfylde Fuller has been described in details. Naren Gossain in his statement as an approver in May, 1908 disclosed in the court the attempt that failed. It may be stated that Hem Chandra's account did not record any fact which might be of importance to the intelligence or police agencies, nor did the book expose anyone to legal action. His training in explosive in France was also known in details, in more details than what he had written, to the Government. So, the allegation of discloser of secret is without any basis.

After its publication, Nalini Kishore Guha, a revolutionary of the later period, wrote a strongly critical review of Hem Chandra's book, in *Banglar Bani*; and that article was incorporated[172] in the second edition of his book "*Banglaya Biplabbad*' published in 1929. The chapter in which Hem Chandra had delineated the reasons for failure of the revolutionary movement was the special target of attack. It may be noted that Sachindra Nath Sanyal"s *Bandijiban Part-II* has a similar chapter wherein he attributes the failure of the movement to absence of good leadership, lack of adequate preparation and political consciousness of the people etc. Hem Chandra has dwelt on these factors; but over and above his analysis has delved deep into the social and political conditions of the time. Nalini's angry outburst is directed towards Hem Chandra's suggestion that the secret society movement had little prospect in India due to a few basic weaknesses in our national character, for which Hem Chandra blames certain inherent ills in 'our society'.[173] Nalini, evidently with his religious bias in politics, can not accept totally secular approach to political movement. He launches a counter attack by saying that since Hem Chandra did not know about the growth and expansion of the revolutionary movement after 1908 on account of his confinement in jail, he could not perhaps denounce the courage and self-sacrifice of the revolutionaries during this period. So Nalini thinks merely on the basis of his experience of the Maniktala group it will be wrong to conclude that the revolutionary movement was a failure. What Hem Chandra, in fact, wants to say that the movement had the seeds of failure in it, and he has tried to identify the weaknesses of the organisation of which he was a member and an active participant. Nalini has highlighted martyrdom of the revolutionaries in the second phase of the movement, mostly quoting from the Sedition Committee Report to prove that the weaknesses, if any, were in certain individuals and not universal. But Nalini perhaps is not aware of the other side of the picture which has also been highlighted by the Sedition Committee report. When Hem Chandra quoted from the same report the confessional statement of Biren Datta Gupta made on the day before his execution to show how the senior party leaders goaded him to commit the murder, Nalini chided Hem Chandra for relying on the report of an alien government who were out to malign the revolutionaries!

Nalini is very emotional about the revolutionary movement and the sacrifice made by brave young men. But Nalini has ignored that Hem Chandra has questioned the basis of revolutionary terrorism, which, according to him, is derived from the twin impulses of strong hatred against the British and an emotional patriotism derived from fanatical faith in the past glory of the motherland. No revolutionary movement can possibly be built up on such negative and fragile ideas.

He is incensed when Hem Chandra writes candidly about Aurobindo and Barindra for whom Nalini has deep respect. He can not, however, gloss over the fact that while there were instances of indomitable courage and supreme sacrifice, there were many known and unknown examples of betrayals too. Hem Chandra has mentioned the issues like predominance of religion in politics, caste division and disunity in Hindu society, the Hindu-Muslim enmity etc as insurmountable problems jeopardising the strength and potentiality of the revolutionary movement. Nalini is silent on these hard realities in our national life.

It is, however, not correct that the book was not appreciated. As a matter of fact, there were quite a few appreciative articles in the contemporary news papers and journals. In *Bengalee*[174] Charu Roy, Mayor of Chandernagar wrote, "The writer is a keen observer and student of men and things and his analysis of their character and his exposure of their real nature and springs of action could have been easily put down to mischief and perversity if they did not bear the stamp of fearless, dispassionate and outspoken sincerity and genuine love for those who suffered like him." *Anandabazar Patrika*[175] wrote, "No one has so far analysed the weaknesses in the character of the revolutionary leaders and workers and to identify the factors behind such weaknesses; but that is of utmost importance. Srijukta Hem Chandra Kanungo has, in this narrative, borne the responsibility of discussing unpleasant matters. This is a matter of no mean courage." *Manasi O Marmabani*[176] wrote "We may not agree with the author on many issues, even we may feel hurt by the author's views about certain leaders and sub-leaders; but if those views are based on reasons and evidence, then we will have to suffer that agony.

"In this land of devotion, we do not consider it just to determine the duties of the leaders; we feel gratified to obey their orders and advise. As a consequence, irresponsible politico-religious leaders are springing up in the country. In this book we for the first time have seen the author has tried to categorise the leaders and by criticising the mistakes, faults and dereliction of duties of his political guru, has shown great courage in this land of unquestioned devotion."

Hem Chandra's critical comments on other contemporary issues were made not from a narrow nationalist angle but from a true patriotic standpoint. He did not approve of the excessive exhibition of nationalist emotion in the *swadeshi* songs during the anti-partition movement and as the *swadeshi* songs were "too full of idle emotion about past glory, they never inspired the youth to action."[177]

Hem Chandra's contention that the vernacular literature was dominated by the *bhadra-shreni*, and in their writings the joys and sorrows, hopes and aspirations of the *Sudras* or the lower class of people were not reflected, had hit the nail on the head of *bhadralok* Bengali literature of the *swadeshi* period. Such lop-sided literary products were incapable of communicating with the vast mass of the people and were of little help to mass political education.

Hem Chandra was critical[178] of National Education which sought to substitute 'slave mentality' inculcated by the Government education system, by "grandmother's mentality", or backward looking superstitious mind-set. Besides the national education curricula put an excessive emphasis on India's past glory and traditional values. Even in technical and scientific lessons such old and archaic ideas and thoughts were mixed. Hem Chandra, however, ignored the contributions of National Education to the growth and sustenance of the nationalistic and patriotic spirit. It was a bold effort to liberate the education system and the Indian mind from colonial domination. It would have been a constructive measure of far reaching consequences if, however, the Council of National Education could have undertaken, as suggested by Hem Chandra, the translation of the English text books on various subjects into vernacular. No doubt his criticism was directed against almost all aspects of the multi-faceted nationalist endeavours during the *Swadeshi* period; but it cannot be said that his comments lacked merit.

Hem Chandra had an acerbic tongue and his pen, it appears, was no less so. His criticism has often been punctuated by heavy sarcasm and innuendos and the language was sometime, as Sumit Sarkar has said, "extravagant and harsh." His unrelenting criticism and iconoclastic zeal have prompted his critics to call him a cynic, but the accusation does not appear to be quite justifiable.

Though Hem Chandra did not explicitly reject terrorism as a method of freedom struggle, he had, however, come to the conclusion that such methods often led to a dead end. He appealed to the youth to think about new ideals, about new methods, about plan of such actions that would be understood by all. Apparently he was moving away from secretive revolutionary terrorism to a new revolutionary ideal.[179] He appealed to the new generation for relentless self-criticism, learning from past mistakes and an incessant quest for new revolutionary ideals. What he meant by new a revolutionary ideal is obvious but he did not explicitly mention it. Nearly ninety years after the publication of Hem Chandra's book, it still remains as one of the most outstanding memoirs of the revolutionary period, and its author an uncompromising revolutionary.

12. Aurobindo And 'Mixing Religion With Politics'

When in his early youth Hem Chandra was told by his mentor, Jnanendra Nath Bose, that religion had done much harm to the country, he then was a Hindu and had faith in God. The letters that he wrote to his wife, Sarat, from Europe, contain references to God and prayer to Goddess Kali. But his set of beliefs started changing as the study of

Socialism and Marxism progressed in Paris under the able guidance of a person with the pseudonym of 'Ph D'. Gradually he became more materialistic and strongly poised against the use of religion or religious symbols in political movement. After his return from Europe he was not merely a passive non-believer but a staunch critic of religion. According to his newly acquired knowledge, religion acts like opium on the people by inducing a false and unrealistic sense of contentment. Hem Chandra was away from the country for one and a half years and during the period the country did not experience any fresh surge of Hindu revivalism. Yet on his return he started seeing things with a changed outlook. He "found the secret society of Midnapur was abolished and an idol of goddess Kali was installed in a room. *** At our centre at Muraripukur and also in our new centre at Bhawanipur the picture of Kali was hung on the wall."[180] Similarly, he detected religiosity in *Jugantar* emblem[181], although the publication of the paper in the same format had commenced several months before his departure for Paris. In the picture of a *mangalghat* on the top of the editorial column of the *Bande Mataram* he found influence of Hinduism. He described *Navashakti* as a communal journal because it published news about Hindu superstition.[182] In a word, when Hem Chandra returned home he found traces of religiosity in many things which he had not noticed earlier.

Hem Chandra claimed that his patriotism had little emotional content and he did not imbibe it from literature, poems and songs.[183] He criticised Bankim Chandra but about *Vande Mataram* he wrote, "We have got many bad things from him and among the good things *Vande Mataram* is without a parallel. It is the most sublime expression of our national spirit.[184] Hem Chandra could hardly foresee then (1922-1923) that within a decade even *Vande Mataram* would be treated as a symbol of Hinduism and ostracised as a sectarian slogan![185]

Hem Chandra writes that for the first two years or so, the secret society had nothing to do with religion, and Aurobindo himself did not follow any religious practice or ritual.[186] Till his return from abroad Hem Chandra used to consider Aurobindo, "an exceptionally wise and learned person and well versed in politics."[187] He was his political *guru* too. While in France there was no indication that his respect and admiration for Aurobindo had diminished. After his rejoining the party on return, he was not happy with Aurobindo for his *Yoga* and abdication of responsibility of the secret society to Barin. While they were in jail as under-trials, he used to make fun of *Yoga* practices and ridicule those devoted comrades as having lost their way in mist of devotional ideas (*Bhaktitatwa kujhwatika).* But while writing his memoirs he was somewhat unreasonably harsh in criticising Aurobindo.

Hem Chandra has attributed the shift to religion in the secret societies to Aurobindo's ambition to be a popular revolutionary as well as a spiritual leader of the country. He argued that since "the followers were not coming to join the party," Aurobindo Babu, was, therefore, "in search of a spiritual person to teach him supernatural powers." After some futile search "at last one Lele Maharaj was sent for; but he also could not give proof of any such supernatural powers". Aurobindo "grew impatient to drive out the English within a few years and to pass for an *Avtar*". At first he gave a "spiritual interpretation of the revolutionary cult." On account of this Hem Chandra, has accused Aurobindo of "trying to mix religion with politics." He even wanted to make religion an inseparable part of a revolutionary's life and that is why at the instance of

Aurobindo *Yoga*"[188] and religious classes were introduced in the Garden. According to Hem Chandra, Aurobindo had sent scouting parties from the Garden to various probable places in search of a suitable *sannyasi* for imparting spiritual training to the revolutionaries. It was to sub-serve the personal ambition of becoming an unchallenged politico-religious leader and an *avatar*, Aurobindo is alleged to have constructed a revolutionary theory with strong religious overtone. Hem Chandra has also alleged clever use of religious texts by Aurobindo. "After sometime Aurobindo Babu had realised that in Bengal the *Gita* had more influence on the people than the *Chandi*. Besides the *Chandi* could not be subjected to convenient, erudite and philosophical interpretations; but there was no end to philosophical interpretation of the *Gita*. So Aurobindo Babu took to the *Gita* leaving aside the *Chandi*."[189] From Hem Chandra's accusations emerge the image of a totally scheming, designing and extremely selfish person as leader of the underground movement. In this context of such extravagant allegations, an examination of Aurobindo's political writings and a chronological account of his spiritual developments are imperative with a view to clearing the doubts that Hem Chandra and several other writers have created about Aurobindo.

Certain baseless tales circulated by a few friends like Charu Chandra Datta and some of his early biographers created incorrect impression about Aurobindo's connections with religious personalities while he was in Baroda. They have written about his association with Chandot Ashram on the bank of Narmada and its head, Brhmananda Swami whom, it is claimed, he took as a *Guru*. Besides he reportedly had connection with other god-men like Hansha Swarup and Madhava Deva. Datta has even claimed that under the cover of the religious ashram he organised revolutionary societies in the region.[190] Aurobindo discounted such stories by saying that:

> He had known Brhamananda as a *Yogin*, not as a *Guru* only *darshan* and blessings and not beyond that. There was no contact with others.[191]

In fact, Aurobindo had no track with religion till 1905 when he wrote *Bhawani Mnadir* at the behest of his brother Barin, who, being influenced by Debabrata Bose, was determined to use religion as an instrument to attract young men to the secret society. Aurobindo had argued with Debabrata Bose while visiting some districts in 1904 that a patriotic upsurge would rejuvenate the secret societies, but he was disinclined to use religion for the purpose.

As Barin lacked intellectual capabilities to use appropriate tenets of religion to sub-serve the political needs, he was obliged to ask Aurobindo with whom he had been staying at Baroda in 1904-1905, to write a religious tract with which he could rejuvenate the secret society. After *Bhawani Mandir* was published (August 1905), he travelled in the wilderness of the Western Ghat hills in search of a suitable site for the *Mandir* and ended in having contracted hill fever, while Aurobindo in Baroda was urging the Maharaja for a job for his brother.[192] Barindra pursued the *Mandir* plan with tenacity without, however, much result."The idea of *Bhawani Mandir* simply lapsed of itself, Sri Aurobindo thought no more about it, but Barin who clung to the idea tried to establish something like it on a small scale in the Manicktala Garden:"[193]

Sometime in 1907 while Barin was on a mission with Upendra Nath Banerji to find a religious and spiritual guide for the members of the secret society, he found his *Guru* in one Sakharia Swami who ordained him at Chandot Ashram. On return he and Upen, "started practicing meditation every day".[194] They simultaneously started teaching meditation and religious texts to the inmates of the Garden.[195] In the morning the teachers and students, all clad in saffron robes and singing Vedic hymns and practising *Yoga* turned the unkempt garden into a veritable *ashram*. After the first expedition to Western India, a few more futile expeditions went to different places in North India in search of a suitable god-man for the Garden. These were inspired by Barin and Upendra, as the latter had spent as a saffron clad *sadhu* in the Himalayas for more than a year.

When Aurobindo returned to India in 1893, he had no religion, and no mastery over any Indian language. While at Baroda from 1893 to early 1906, Aurobindo learnt Bengali first.[196] Peter Heehs writes, "Aurobindo shifted the focus of his studies from Bengali to Sanskrit around 1900. As one nurtured on Homer and Virgil, it was natural for him to be drawn first to the Indian epics"[197] like the *Ramayana* and the *Mahabharata* and the poems of Kalidasa".[198] He gradually moved on to the *Upanishads* and the *Gita* during 1907-1908. As a matter of fact as an under trial prisoner he carried both the *Upanishad* and the *Gita* to the jail. His articles in the *Bande Mataram* contain references to *Kurukshetra* and the *Gita*.

After the publication of New Lamp for Old (1893), all his writings between 1894 and 1904, were non-religious and non-political writings[199] on poetry, literature and matters of historical interest. As early as in 1894 when he had just started learning Bengali he wrote a literary essay on Bankim Chandra. Evidently he had studied few religious texts because till 1904-05 he was not attracted to religion. Amalesh Tripathi also admits that "there was very little Hinduism in Aurovindo's activities in the early years."[200]

`The *Yoga* that Aurobindo started practising in 1904 was for self development and gaining strength. It was mostly *pranayam*. In Aurobindo's own words "*pranayam* brought me nothing of any kind of spiritual realisation. I had stopped it."[201] After the Surat Congress had ended in pandemonium, Barindra introduced Aurobindo to V.B. Lele at Baroda where Aurobindo was taught a new type of *Yoga*. He found it satisfying to his inner needs and started practising it for long hours. Lele taught him "four fundamental realisations." The first of the four on which his *Yoga* is based was "the realisation of the silent spaceless and timeless Brahman." A few months later, in Alipore jail, he had the second realisation: "the experience of the cosmic consciousness and of the Divine as all beings and all that is." As his *yoga* developed, he made it clear that it was not based on Hinduism or any other religion. The best that could be said was that it was "in consonance with" certain Hindu Scriptures, though "not limited by any Scripture." Later as his Ashram took shape, he wrote repeatedly that it was not a religious organisation, much less a conventionally Hindu one.[202]

Hem Chandra was not alone who had charged Aurobindo of using religion in extremist and revolutionary politics. J.N.Farquhar, the missionary historian, explained that "the old passionate devotion to Hinduism flared up and increased the passion of the anarchist; and his perception of inner antagonism between Hindu and Western culture-ideals at once justified and embittered his hatred.*** Dayananda, the Theosophists, Vivekananda, Sister Nivedita and all that followed them talked in the wildest and the most extravagant way in praise of Hinduism and the Indian civilisation."[203] To the colonial mind-set such mixture of religion with politics was disquieting as it evoked the memories of 1857. *Bhawani Mandir* published in 1905 had little influence on the revolutionary movement, yet the colonial anxiety inflated the threat from it beyond proportion by highlighting that "it contained the germ of Hindu revolutionary movement." It was still more disquieting when political extremism fixed its goal at *swaraj* which was complete independence from British rule. Some apologists for the Empire sought to brand extremism as a regressive ideology by linking it to the Hindu revivalist movement. No doubt the Extremists had used many symbols and metaphors from various Hindu religious texts sometime to elucidate their thoughts and ideas and often to derive mental strength and to refurbish their moral and ethical values. Citing such examples columnist Valentine Chirol, argued that the Bengali revolutionary terrorism was inspired by Hindu religiosity. He, however, wrote simplistically about Arabindo that he was "the most remarkable figure of the Indian unrest, who believes that, by the practice of the most extreme forms of *Yoga* asceticism, man can transform himself into a super-man, and he has constituted himself the high priest of a religious revival which has taken a profound hold on the imagination of the emotional youth of Bengal. It is based mainly on the teachings of Krishna to Arjuna as revealed in the *Bhagvad Gita*."[204] To J.N. Farquhar too, the extremist nationalism was 'religious nationalism' as it was rooted in the revivalist movement of Hindu religion and ancient Hindu civilisation. The missionary in Farquhar overshadowed the historian in him when he wrote, "It is clear as noonday that the religious aspect of anarchism was merely an extension of that revival of Hinduism which is the work of Dayananda, Ramakrishna, Vivekananda and the Theosophists."[205] From their colonialist attitude of racial and cultural superiority, these writers overlooked certain essential limiting nature of the encounter between the West and the Indian society and civilisation. It was not an encounter on equal terms; it could not have been so in a colonial situation. It was hardly an exchange between two equals. It was conditioned by the political relation between the master and the subject race. In this context the strong derogatory tone of the Evangelical criticism of Oriental religions and civilisation was natural, but its impact on the Indian mind was multifaceted and ineffaceable. As a matter of fact, the socio-religious and cultural reform movements in India throughout the nineteenth century, irrespective of their varying intensity and measure of success, bore the imprints of unhappy interface with the religion and culture of the master race.

These critics appear to have missed the main foci of the movements in their analysis as they had an underlying political motive. The basic character of the movements associated with Ramakrishna, Vivekananda and Dayananda were regenerative, pragmatic and nationalistic although outwardly they were often used the idioms and metaphors drawn from the religious texts. Since political extremism and revolutionary terrorist movement had aimed at complete independence of the country, and had drawn inspiration from the leaders of these socio-religious movements, they were also called revivalist and anti-modern, vis-à-vis the Moderates and subsequently the Gandhians who, in their reckoning, were progressive and modern as because they had not asked for complete independence of the country till 1930.

The contemporary colonial officials too, carefully distinguished between the Moderates and the Extremists, and never failed to warn the Government about the deadly combination of religion and politics in the Extremist/ Nationalist ideology and harped on this theme in various reports including the Sedition Committee Report. Consequently they and also British Parliament were careful not to antagonise the Moderate group in India.

Two historians namely, Amales Tripathi and Leonard A. Gordon have targeted the Nationalist/Extremist political ideology with similar arguments for allegedly drawing extensively from Hindu religious doctrine and thus it was construed as backward looking and anti-modern. Amales Tripathi has argued that Aurobindo derived the religious foundation of Extremism and Terrorism in the *Gita* and the *Vedanta*. "When Aurobindo came to the *Vedanta*, love and hatred, good and evil lost their empirical difference, for such seemingly opposed categories were mere illusion of the self. When he arrived at the *Gita* he realised that divine action was not bound by the code of bourgeois morality."[206] Tripathi has likened the war of Arjuna against his enemy to Aurobindo's fight against the British. "God has decreed the destruction of the British and even if Aurobindo refused to act as His instrument He would have His terrible way. Rather than work by his imperfect judgment, he, Aurobindo, should be *nimittamatram*, the agent in the working out of a mighty evolution."[207] Tripathi then concludes, "This explains why the *Gita* was a constant companion of the revolutionaries. In their hand it was a more terrible weapon than the bomb. It stilled them for killing, which was God's will and ordained decree and it assured them of salvation through death in God's service."[208] Tripathi's chain of reasoning follows more or less the pattern used by the present day religious fanatics fighting against the perceived threat to their own religion. It is not premised on Aurobindo's thoughts on the core teaching of the *Gita*. Aurobindo has not explicitly referred to the struggle of the revolutionary terrorists against the British, nor has he likened Arjuna, who could overcome his moral dilemma of fighting and killing the relatives and friends by consigning all such actions to divine will, to the revolutionary terrorists fighting the British. Besides Aurobindo contends that the *Gita* does not merely determine whether a 'pitiless massacre' is a sin if it is done by a soldier doing his duty. "That might be the teaching of a State, of politicians, of lawyers, of ethical casuists; it can never be the teaching of a great religious and philosophical scripture which sets out to solve the problems of life and action from the roots."[209] Aurobindo rejects the generalised interpretation of the *Gita* as "the gospel of human action, the ideal of disinterested performance of social duties." He describes such interpretations as "modern misreading, a reading of the modern mind into an ancient book, of the present day European or Europeanised intellect into thoroughly antique and a thoroughly Oriental and Indian teaching." To him "the *Gita* is a Gospel of work, but of works which culminate in knowledge, that is in spiritual realisation of quietude, and of works motivated by devotion, that is, a conscious surrender of one's whole self first into the hands and then into the being of the Supreme, and not at all of works as they are understood by modern mind;"[210]

Besides the chronology of Aurobindo's political and spiritual career does not indicate that he was well-conversant with the *Vedanta* and the *Gita* when he published his political essays between 1893 and 1908.' As a matter of fact, the "Essays on the Gita" from which Tripathi quotes to prove his points appeared in the monthly review, *Arya,* between August 1916 and July 1918. It was revised by Aurobindo and published as a book in 1922. There was a second series of such articles which were compiled and published in 1928. From 1910 onwards he had been in Pondicherry and had no direct connection with politics nor did he write on political subjects. So when Aurobindo wrote the essays on the *Gita,* the perspective had changed as he had moved to a different world altogether.

After his acquittal in the Alipur trial (6 May1909), he refuted the charge of a bureaucrat, H.H. Risley, who alleged that "the Gita has been misused as a gospel of terrorism". While Aurobindo admitted that "Upendra Bandopadhyaya used to teach the *Gita* in the Manicktala Garden," he, however, refuted Risley in *Karmajogin*[211] by saying, "It is undoubtedly true that selflessness, courage, a free and noble activity have been preached as the kernel of the ethics of the Gita.*** We strongly protest against the brand of suspicion that has been sought to be placed in many quarters on the teaching and possession of the *Gita,* our chief national heritage, our hope for the future, our great force for the purification of the moral weaknesses that stain and hamper our people". Evidently Aurobindo underscored the value of the *Gita* as a book for 'purification' of the moral and ethical values of the people and as such it has continued relevance to the society.

Leonard A. Gordon thinks, "In the later years at Baroda and the first two or three years in Calcutta, Aurobindo placed politics before religion, although he couched his political writings and speeches in religious phraseology."[212] The Baroda period, according to Gordon was the training period when he studied Bengali, Sanskrit and a good deal of Indian culture. In Baroda "Aurobindo participated in séances, searched for a guru and began to practice Yoga."[213] Following J.N.Farquhar's comments on *Bhawani Mandir* Gordon states that "the terms and concepts used by Aurobindo in the pamphlet are drawn in large measures from the *Markandeya Purana,* a Brahmanical text with Tantric influence." He has, however, not tried to measure the influence of *Bhawani Mandir* on the revolutionary movement, nor has he taken into account Aurobindo's own comments on it. He keeps on labouring fruitlessly to find out *Bhawani Mandir* ideas permeating the subsequent writings of Aurobindo. Besides, Gordon has often confused between religion and social and cultural tradition of a civilization. When Tagore stated that Indian cultural tradition did not approve of violence even as a natural course of passive resistance, Aurobindo politely replied, "Aggression is unjust only when unprovoked; violence , when used wantonly or for unrighteous ends."[214] Otherwise aggression and violence are just for righteous ends. When during passive resistance situations develop in such a manner that the people are compelled to take to active resistance and violence is unavoidable, then the violence and aggression are just. Aurobindo draws a parallel from the *Mahabharata* period when the Kshatriyas would resort to aggression to protect the weak on the ground of righteousness and that used to be their social responsibility. The grounds for using violence are, therefore, based on social and cultural tradition, and not ordained by religious code. But Gordon construes Aurobindo's reference to *Kshatriya* and the *Mahabharata* as evidence of drawing from the religious text and using religion in the construction of political principle of Extremism. Thereafter, he draws an amazing lesson from the controversy between Tagore and Aurobindo by saying, "Both men intermingled religion with politics."[215]

Evidently Aurobindo does not appear to have based his arguments in defence of violence in the anti-colonial revolutionary movement on any religious text like the *Vedanta* and the *Gita.* as Tripathi would make us believe. Nor his writings during the period from 1905 to 1908 contain anything on the basis of which he can be called a "religious nationalist." Aurobindo's nationalism is derived from his deep understanding of the predatory nature of the colonial rule in India from a totally non-religious standpoint and so the methods he suggested to end colonial domination were also devoid of any religious bearing. Colonialism being inherently oppressive and dehumanising, he wrote, "There are certain moral qualities necessary to self-government, which have become atrophied by long disuse in our people and can only be restored by the healthy air of a free national life in which alone they can permanently thrive or by the vigorous exercise in the intensity of a national struggle for freedom." In this struggle against colonialism (Aurobindo could not have written more explicitly in 1907 about the techniques of anti-colonial struggle.) he has not invoked any divine *shakti* or supernatural power. And the objective of the struggle was to attain "the inalienable right of the nation to independence."[216]

Aurobindo's critics rely on his celebrated Uttarpara speech[217] to prove that Aurobindo had indeed mixed religion with politics. It is likely that Hem Chandra had also read the Uttarpara speech and the description of Aurobindo's vision of Krishna in the Alipore courtroom and jail. In any event, the passage with which Aurobindo concluded the speech reads as follows: "This Hindu nation was born with the *Sanatana Dharma,* with it it moves and with it it grows. When the *Sanatana Dharma* declines, then the nation declines, and if the *Sanatana Dharma* were capable of perishing, with the *Sanatana Dharma* it would perish. The *Sanatana Dharma* that is nationalism." This passage is often quoted as the final proof to establish that Aurobindo was a follower of traditional Hinduism, and a proponent of Hindu nationalism. But a careful study of the speech would reveal that Aurobindo has not used some crucial terms in the sense in which they are popularly used. While the expression *Sanatan Dharma* generally means an orthodox Hindu religion, Aurobindo has accepted the true etymological meaning of the term *sanatan* as 'eternal' not confined in time and space. Therefore *sanatan dharma* is eternal religion and not orthodox religion, nor is it confined to a specific geographical area or country. The term *sanatan* here connotes 'timelessness' and not 'changelessness' or 'orthodoxy' as in popular understanding. He made it clear in the speech itself that the Hindu religion, which he here equated with the *sanatana dharma,* was "the Hindu religion only because the Hindu nation has kept it" in "the seclusion of this peninsula," but that it was "not circumscribed by the confines of a single country." He further states that it "is really the eternal religion, because it is the universal religion which embraces all others. If a religion is not universal, it cannot be eternal. A narrow religion, a sectarian religion, an exclusive religion can live only for a limited time and a limited purpose". He went further to explain in an essay published in the same issue of the *Karmayogin* in which the speech was published, that the "Hinduism" of which he spoke was "not a dogma or combination of dogmas but a law of life," not "a social frame-work but the spirit of a past and future social evolution." This *sanatana dharma* had, he said, "many scriptures, *Veda, Vedanta, Gita, Upanishad, Darshana, Purana, Tantra,* nor could it reject the *Bible* or the *Koran;* but its real, most authoritative scripture is in the heart in which the Eternal has His dwelling." It basis, in other words, was not any particular belief or practice but inner experience that was available to all humans. It was this experience-based "Hinduism" that might become, he thought, "the basis of the future world-religion."[218]

From the above discussion it will appear that the charge against Aurobindo of mixing religion with politics is not sustainable. Evidently Hem Chandra was overwhelmed by a strong personal dislike for both Barindra and Aurobindo in making such random accusations. Yet the real state of affairs on the ground and the impression created in the minds of the members of the secret society and of the Extremist faction about their hallowed leader were of considerable relevance in an on-going political movement. In early 1908 Aurobindo had emerged on the national scene as a top leader of the Extremist faction in the Congress party and the supreme leader *(badakarta)* of the secret society. When all these political responsibilities rested on his shoulders, Aurobindo got deeply engrossed in prolonged *Yoga* practices for his personal salvation, ignoring his public duties. In this scenario lie the seeds of allegation of mixing religion with politics. Besides he was not a consistent and effective leader of the secret society as it appears from the day to day account of the society. He delegated all the authority to his brother Barin, more out of blind affection than after due deliberation. Barin was not really guided by the *badakarta;* he often used to act according to his own whims. Aurobindo was so indifferent to the society that he had never visited the Garden during one year of its existence, nor did he care to know as the head of the secret society as to what exactly was going on there. Even when his two close friends had deserted the society in February, 1908 on account of Barin's arrogance, Aurobindo remained unmoved. He could not have been unaware of the legal consequences of bomb-making and attempts to kill the officials for which plans were made in the Garden. He must have known-- he himself had faced the charge of sedition only a year ago-- the danger to which the young boys were exposed. Yet he did not try to streamline the loose organisation and discipline his brother. Aurobindo's blind reliance on Barin was the weakest point in his leadership of the secret society, and it eventually led to disastrous consequences. As one of the secret society members who had suffered for the lapses of the leaders, Hem Chandra, no doubt, targeted Aurobindo and Barin in exclusion of other leading members for his strong criticism. Judging in the context of lackadaisical internal functioning of an underground organisation which had challenged the might of the British Empire, his criticism of Aurobindo's leadership of the secret society cannot be brushed aside as extravagant or biased.

Notes & References:

1. Sachindra Nath Sanyal : *Bandi Jivan;* The story was serialised in *Narayan* in ten issues, from *Agrahayan* 1328 BS to *Bhadra* 1329 BS (Oct.-Nov.1921 to Aug.-Sept. 1922), and soon thereafter in 1922 the book were published.
2. Sachindra Nath Sanyal: *Bandi Jivan Third Part,* p. 29
3. Out of ten convicts of Alipur case sent to the Amdamans, only three, namely Barindra. Upendra and Hem Chandra were in jail in early 1920. Of the rest Indu Bhusan Ray committed suicide, Ullaskar became insane and was removed to asylum in the mainland. Remaining five namely Hrishikesh Kanjilal,Sudhir Sarkar, Birendra Ch. Sen, Bibhuti Sarkar and Abinash Bhattacharya were transferred to mainland prisons by 1915.
4. Bijoy Bandopadhyaya: *Biplabi Nayak: Sachindra Nath Sanyal,* Quoted from Sanyal's *Bandi Jiban,* P119-120
5. Troilokyanath Chakraborty: *Jele Trish Bachar O Pak-Bharater Swadhinata Sangram,* Calcutta, 1981. p. 124.
6. Hem Chandra: *Account of the Revolutionary Movement in Bengal,* 1928; pp. 9-10. The book is an English translation of Hem Chandra's writings serialized in *Basumati.* . Henceforth it is referred to as *Accoun*t.
7. *Ibid;* pp. 4-5.
8. Barindra Kumar Ghose: *Dwipantarer Katha (1921);* The English translation made by the author is entitled, The Story of My Exile (1922); Upendra Nath Bandopadhayaya, *Nirbasiter Atmakatha* (1921), Hem Chandra Kanungo, *Banglaya Biplab Prachesta (1928)* Hem Chandra's book will henceforth be referred to as BBP in the footnote.

9. Sardarsinh Raoji Rana belonged to the princely family of Marvi , Kathiwar. He arrived in London in 1898 and became an associate of Krishnavarma and thereafter he started a jeweler's business in Paris. He attended the Stuttgart Socialist Congress in 1907 with Madam Cama and financed the publication of *Bande Mataram* and *Talwar* .
10. Deposition of J.K. Naug, P.W. No. 126 in Alipur Bomb Trial
11. Peter Heehs: Bomb in Bengal, pp. 262-263.
12. Hem Chandra: *BBP*, pp. 4-5.
13. *Ibid*: pp. 6 and 8.
14. Hem Chandra: *Account*, p. 4 .
15. Hem Chandra: BBP, pp, 6-7. In it Aurobindo is camouflaged as "K" Babu.
16. Hem Chandra : BBP, p.43. From the manner of handling the gun Hem Chandra thought that both Aurobindo and Barindra had not touched a firearm before.
17. Hem Chandra's letter to his wife from France. Exhibit No. 364 of Alipur Bomb Trial.
18. Hem Chandra: *BBP*, p. 23.
19. Hem Chandra: *BBP*, p. 48.
20. Both Bibhuti and Nirapada were accused in the Alipur Bomb Case.
21. Hem Chandra: *Account*, p. 20 and *BBP*, p. 49.
22. It was established during Alipur Bomb Trial that *Chatra Bhandar* was a camouflaged organization of the revolutionaries.
23. Hem Chandra: *BBP*, p. 49.
24. Alipur Bomb Trial Records, Statement of PW. 88, Inspector N. Chakrabarty.
25. Terrorism in Bengal, Vol. IV, p. 1386.
26. The Government dropped the case as prosecution of a 17-year old lad for sedition would be scandalous.
27. Records of Alipur Bomb Trial. Deposition of PW. 88
28. Godfrey Denham's report on "*Midnapur Revolutionary Conspiracy*". See Terrorism in Bengal, Vol. III, p. 529.
29. Terrorism in Bengal, Vol. II, pp. 754-756.
30. F.C. Daly: *Notes on the Growth of Revolutionary Movement in Bengal (1905-1911)*, reproduced in Terrorism in Bengal, Vol.I, p. 20.
31. *Ibid*, p. 16.
32. Terrorism in Bengal: Vol II, p. 132.
33. Barindra Kumar Ghosh: *Barindrer Atmakahini*, p. 14.

34. Terrorism in Bengal, Vol. II, p. 284.
35. Charu Datta (1877-1952) claims in his *Purano Katha* that he first met Aurobindo at Baroda station sometime in 1901, but from 1904 onwards he was in regular contact with Aurobindo. *Purano Katha*, *Upasanhar*, pp. 16-17.
36. Hem Chandra: *Accounts*, p.24 and BBP, p. 63.
37. Statement of Narendra Gossain, approver in Alipur case. See Court Records. It may be mentioned that Barin had to return the money as he failed to fulfill the contract.
38. *Ibid*; p. 25 and p. 64.
39. Charu Chandra Datta: *Purano Katha Upasanhar*, 1952, pp. 21-22.
40. It was Hem Chandra who had reported the rumour to the leadership in Calcutta. Later on, however, Hem Chandra admitted that he had made a mistake about Kshudiram, *BBP*, p. 74.
41. Bhupendra Nath Datta (1880-1961) was the youngest brother of Swami Vivekananda. He was working on the editorial group of *Jugantar*. In 1907 he was convicted for publishing seditious articles in the paper.
42. Fuller was leaving India for good after laying down office as desired by the Home Government.
43. This action was ordered by Aurobindo and communicated through Naren Gossain. See the statement of the Approver in Alipur case.
44. Hem Chandra: *BBP*, p. 104.
45. Hem Chandra: *Accounts of the Revolutionary Movement in Bengal*, p. 37.
46. Hem Chandra: *Account of the Revolutionary Movement in Bengal*, pp. 39-40.
47. *Ibid*, p. 40.
48. Charu Mazumdar (1914-72), the ideologue of the Naxalites wrote that to be a true revolutionary one must smear one's hand with the blood of class enemies. He directed that each member of the guerrilla squad killing a class enemy should strike the enemy even if he was dead. Thus they should overcome their middle-class inhibition of committing murder.
49. Alipur Trial Records. See Barin's confessional statement in Appendix-A.
50. Intelligence or any other official records have not mentioned this incident as the first unsuccessful attempt at *swadeshi* dacoity.

51. Hem Chandra : *Account*, p. 28.
52. *Ibid*, p. 77.
53. *The Body and the Bomb:Technologies of Modernity in Colonial India* by Chritopher Pinney in Picturing the Nation : (Ed) Richard Davis' 2007, pp. 51-52.
54. Terrorism in Bengal, Vol. III, p. 528.
55. Ullaskar Datta (1885-1965) joined the society much later in September 1907.
56. Hem Chandra: op.cit., p. 115 and Account, p. 40. "The more I participated in the activities of the secret societies, the more I was disillusioned about our leaders."
57. Hem Chandra: op.cit , p. 113.
58. Khasi Rao was the brother of Madhava Rao, General in the Baroda Army and a friend of Aurovindo. Both the bothers were in favour of expelling the British from India by force.
59. Bhupendra Nath Datta: *Dwitiya Swadhinatar Sangram* , p. 32.
60. Shyamaji Krishna Varma.studied in Oxford and Inner Temple. During 1885 to 1897, he worked in the princely states but could not please the British Residents and consequently had to leave India in 1897-In England in 1905 he set up India House for Indian students, published *Indian Sociologist*,and founded Home Rule Society. In 1907 had to leave London for Paris on account of some questions raised in Parliament. In 1914 on the outbreak of the War he left for Geneva and died in Geneva in 1930.
61. Madam Bhikaji Cama was a rich Parsee lady from Bombay. While travelling in Europe she became an ardent nationalist. She spent most of her days in exile, as the British did not allow her to return home. In 1931 an ailing Madam Cama was permitted to return to India and in 1936 she died.
62. Hem Chandra: *op.cit.*, p. 128.
63. *Ibid*, p. 129.
64. *Memorandum on the Anti-British Agitation among Natives of Indiain England and Continent of Europe. Circular No. 8.* Terrorism in Bengal Vol. V, pp. 425-429.
65. The leaflet was named as *Bande Mataram* leaflet, as on the top "Bande Mataram" was printed. In it the speech of Cama was printed under the heading *"A Message to the People of India."*
66. Sumit Sarkar: The Swadeshi Movement in Bengal, p. 307.
67. Hem Chandra is silent on this as Madam Cama was still (1922-28) a suspect in the eyes of the British and was denied permission to return to India.

68. When an ailing and bed-ridden Madam Cama could get permission to return to India in Nov. 1935 after giving a pledge that she would not take part in seditious activities, she had left the flag with Madhava Rao in Paris. Rao passed it on to Indulal Yagnik who brought it back to India and handed it over to V.D.Savarkar. Savarkar publicly displayed it in Poona on 26th October, 1937.
69. Peter Heehs: *op.cit.*, p. 90.
70. Peter Heehs has tried to establish the identity of the "PhD", but he remains elusive. The name of the second man teaching formation of secret society has also remained unknown.
71. A few months later when Hem Chandra urged to reorganize the secret society, then ensconced in the Maniktala Garden, on the European model, Barindra used the same argument for not doing so.
72. Hem Chandra: *BBP*, p. 132.
73. Hem Chandra: *op.cit.*, pp. 133-134.
74. Pandurang M Bapat (1880-1967) known popularly as Senapati Bapat assisted Hem Chandra in making bombs in Calcutta and when warrant of arrest was issued in his name, he absconded.. In 1913 he surfaced and joined Tilak's *Maratha* as a journalist and later on joined the Congress and participated in satyagraha movement. After independence he was given the honour of hoisting the national flag in Poona. Streets have been named after him in Mumbai and Pune.
75. This bomb manual has been mentioned in the report of the French Intelligence, and at least a part of it was seized from Manicktala Garden.
76. Hem Chandra did not publish separate account of his activities in Paris.
77. J.C. Ker: Political Trouble in India: 1907-17; p. 144. Ker has quoted the report sent by the French intelligence, which runs as follows:"1. That there was in Paris a Russian anarchist named Safranski, an ex-officer of the Engineers, who was in touch with the Hindu students in the city, supposed to be Bengalis. 2. That Safranski possessed a manual on the manufacture and use of explosives, and that he was instructing the Hindus with the object of bringing about a change of rule in India by acts of terrorism, 3. That Safranski, being unable to communicate with the Comrades except through an interpreter, was learning Hindusthani at the Ecole des Langues, Orientales, and 4. It was suggested that the

recent attempt to wreck the train of the Lt. Governor was an outcome of this connection between Safranski and Hindu students."

78. Hem Chandra: *BBP*, p.138. At the Customs House in Bombay he had a providential escape from customs check. He brought a few Browning pistols, and several other firearms, literature on bomb-making and on firearms, and books on Marxism and Socialism evading the Customs. While going to Muzaffarpur Prafulla Chaki was given one with which he eventually committed suicide.
79. Hem Chandra arguably was one of the first Indians to profess Marxism and Socialist thoughts and to become the member of a Socialist party abroad. He retained his faith in Marxism throughout his life, though after his release he was politically inactive. He named his grand son as Lenin.
80. Report of the committal enquiry in Alipur Bomb Case Trial, 1908-1910.Case records of the Trial.
81. He landed at Bombay in the first week of January, 1908, and spent a few days in visiting the secret societies in Bombay, Nasik and Nagpur before arriving at Midnapur.
82. Hem Chandra: *op.cit.*, p. 94.
83. Hem Chandra: *op.cit.*, pp. 146-147. Hem Chandra tells us of one financier, but Binoyjiban Ghose tells us of two, namely Brajendra Roy Choudhury and the Raja of Narajole.
84. Hem Chandra *op.cit.*, p. 147. Ullaskar was a simple and noble soul. He possibly wanted to know what new things Hem Chandra had learnt in France.
85. Hem Chandra adduced the same argument to his teachers in Paris when they refused to teach bomb-making on the ground that India had no well-organized secret society protected by a capable intelligence net work.
86. Ex. 257 in Alipur Bomb Trial. At least ten saffron robes were seized by the police from the Garden.
87. Abinash Bhattacharya: "*Aurobindo*" A short memoirs in a Bengali journal "*Galpa-Bharati*" 1357 BS, pp. 829-850. Incidentally Abinash stayed continuously with Aurobindo from the middle of 1907 till he was arrested with Aurobindo on 2 May, 1908, except for three months when he was in jail in connection with another case..
88. Hem Chandra: *BBP*, p.149.
89. Amales Tripathi: The Extremist Challenge, p. 135.
90. Sri Aurobindo: Autobiographical Notes and other Writings of Historical Interest, Pondicherry, 2006, pp. 175-234. When

Aurobindo left for Chandernagore in March 1910, he went unannounced to the house of Motilal Ray, "who made secret arrangement for my stay."There was an image of Kali in the room where Aurobindo stayed. That is why he used to sign as Kali.

91. Barindra Kumar Ghose:, '*Agnisishu Kshudiram*', *Jugantar*, Autumn Number, 1354 B.S; (Sept.-Oct. 1947) "Three leaders of our secret society namely Aurobindio, Charu Datta and Subodh Mullick ordered the killing of Kingsford".
92. Alipur Bomb Trial Records: Statement of the Approver.
93. Home Departments Notes Nos. 112-150,DM's letter to the Chief Secretary, Bengal, p. 52.
94. *The Statesman*, dated 8th May, 1908.
95. The bomb used at Naraingarh in the night of 6-7 December, 1907 to blow up Lt. Governor's train.
96. While experimenting a newly manufactured bomb at Dighiria Hills near Deoghar on 29th January,1907, Prafulla Chakra borty was accidentally killed.
97. According to Naren Gossain's (Approver) statement "Barindra, Ullaskar, Hem Das, P.M. Bapat and I were among those who decided upon this. "Barin wrote later in 1948 that Aurobindo,Subodh Mullick and Charu Datta selected the target.
98. Christopher Pinny: *The Body and the Bomb: Techiologies of Modernity in Colonial India.* An essay in Peter Davis (Ed) Picturing the Nation, p. 53.
99. Hem Chandra, *BBP*, p. 163.
100. Muzaffarpur blast took place on 30 April, 1908.
101. Report of the Sedition Committee, 1918, p. 32.
102. Hem Chandra: *BBP*, pp. 210-211; The scramble for giving information to CID became so wide spread that a question about the moral justification of such acts was discussed, and Aurobindo's verdict was that the sin of the informer would be washed off if, on release he dedicated himself to country's work more vigorously!
103. When the Sedition Committee wrote the report in 1918, Ullaskar was in lunatic asylum in Madras. Besides a man of Ullaskar's nature could not have done it. Upendra Bandopadtyaya, who was next to Barindra in the leadership of the society had disclosed planting of the book-bomb. Incidentally Upen had divulged a lot of unknown information to Tegart in 1913 and even spoke against his friends in the Cellular Jail.
104. IB's Note; *Account of the Revolutionary Movement in Bengal*, p. 65.

105. Ex. No. 610 and 614. Major Smallwood, the explosive expert decommissioned the bombs at Park Street PS.
106. Ex.738 in Alipur Bomb Trial.
107. Ex.8/1 to 8/3 in Alipur Bomb Trial.
108. G.C. Denham: writes in "Revolutionary Conspiracy in Midnapore" "While Abinash Chakrabarty (Munsiff-revolutionary) was still in Midnapur another prominent member of the anarchist party arrived there; that was Chandra Kanta Chakrabarty one of the 60 dismissed clerks in Barisal. He quickly made himself conspicuous by his inflammatory and seditious speeches and became one of the select band under the leadership of Satyen Bose. He was a fast friend of Hem Chandra." *Terrorism in Bengal*, Vol. III, p. 527.
109. Chandra Chakraborty: *New India*, p. 9.
110. Chandra was an accused in the San Fransisco Conspiracy Case, 1917-1918. He confessed in the case and escaped with a very light punishment.
111. Hem Chandra: *BBP*; p. 172.
112. Barindra Kumar Ghose: *Barindrer Atmakahini*, p. 54 " *se paka,jhanu jib., anekkal pound-inspector rupe police charaiye kheache.* (He is a seasoned, crafty animal, who as Pound Inspector lived on tricking the police.)
113. Hem Chandra: *op.cit.*, p. 175.
114. Hem Chandra took the name of Aurobindo only to stop Barindra from pressurizing him to confess. In fact he had no conversation with Aurobindo on this issue. But Barin was so much under the spell of Ramsaday that he retorted in anger, "What does Aurobindo know about these things"?
115. Hem Chandra: *BBP*; p. 178.
116. Aurobindo: *The Tales of Prison Life*, p. 19.
117. Hem Chandra: *BBP*, pp. 178-179.
118. Sri Aurobindo and the Freedom of India, Pondicherry, p. 208.
119. Barindra K. Ghose: *op.cit.*, p. 56.
120. Barindra Kumar Ghose: *Barindrer Atmakahini*, 1329 BS, p. 55.
121. Hem Chandra: *BBP*, pp. 191-192.
122. Barindra Kumar Ghose; *Op.Cit.*, p. 87.
123. Barindra K.Ghose, *Op.Cit.*, p. 87.
124. Hem Chandra, *BBP*, pp. 196-197.
125. *Ibid*, p. 199.
126. Special Branch File No. 662/1908: W.A. Marr, magistrate Alipur held judicial enquiry into the murder of Naren Gossain and

committed the accused to the court of sessions. He started his enquiry at 7.55 AM on the same day and examined the witnesses. His report is to be seen in the file. Marr's report was substantially published in contemporary news papers as the incident created sensation in the country.

127. F.C. Daly Notes, p. 23.
128. Hem Chandra, *Op.Cit.*, p. 191.
129. *The Statesman*, dated 14 and 15 November, 1908.
130. Editorial comment in *The Statesman* dated 14 November, 1908.
131. Annotation by the Intelligence Branch, CID, Bengal ; Hem Chandra: *Account*, p. 65.
     Also see *The Statesman*, dated15 September, 1908
132. Hem Chandra: *BBP*, pp. 200-205.
133. Barindra: *Atmakahini*, p. 106.
134. Peter Heehs: *op.cit.*, p. 209.
135. Upendra Nath: op.cit., p. 64.
136. Seven prisoners were: Barin Ghose, Ullaskar Datta, Hem Chandra Kanungo, Hrishikesh Kanjilal, Indu Bhusan Ray, Bibhuti Sarkar and Abinash Bhattacharya.
137. Three others were Upendra Nath Banerjee, Sudhir Sarkar and Birendra Chandra Sen.
138. Binay Jiban Ghose: *Agnijuger Astraguru Hemchandra*, 1952, pp. 155-156.
139. Home Department Political Proceedings A February, 1915, No. 68-160.
140. R.C. Mazumdar: *op.cit.*, p. 153.
141. Barindra K. Ghose: *The Tale of My Exile*, p. 78.
142. Quoted by R.C.Mazumdarin "The Penal Settlement in the Andamans" ,GOI. pp. 180-181, from V.D.Savarkar's memoirs entitled, "The Story of My Transportation for Life," English translation by V.N. Naik from Savarkar's Marathi original.
143. R.C. Mazumdar: *op.cit.*, pp. 196-197.
144. Hem Chandra: op.cit. P120-122 Savarkar had known Hem Chandra in London in 1907, when he organized secret society there. Savarkar would have mentioned Hem Chandra's name if he were a witness in the inquest.
145. Barin is said to have called a few Brahmins from among the jail inmates and treated them with good food. Tegart has called this a feast. Possibly he arranged something like *sradh* ceremony of Indu Bhusan.

146. Ullaskar Datta: "Twelve Years of Prison Life, 1924, p. 63.
147. R.C. Mazumdar: *op.cit.*, p. 191.
148. *Ibid*, p. 171.
149. *Ibid*, p. 192.
150. Barindra K. Ghose: *The Tale of My Exile*, p. 92. The name of the clerk was Lal Mohan Saha. This is corroborated by Savarkar. See R.C. Mazumdar, *op.cit.*, p. 192. Saha was a double agent. The prisoners failed to realize that in time.
151. Moti Lal Ray; pp. 96-97. Ray has however described the target as Police Commissioner, though SDO of Maulovi Bazar was the target..
152. See I.B.File No. 1032/1913 in the West Bengal State Archives and also Home (Political) Department File No. 293 of 1913 of the Government of Bengal, available in the State Secretariat Library.
153. Government of India, Home Department(Political) A February, 1915 No 68-160.
154. R.C. Mazundar: *op.cit.*, p. 195.
155. Terrorism in Bengal, Vol. I, pp. 278-307.
156. Moti Lal Ray: *Amar dekha biplab O biplabi*, 1957, pp. 96-98.
157. Terrirism in Bengal, Vol. V, p. 857. Chakraborty was on Intelligence and Police record for his involvement in a mail dacoity case in 1911, in which he was given 8 months imprisonment.
158. Terrorism in Bengal, Vol. III, p. 274; Nayak used to teach the making of picric acid bomb to Sasanka @ Amrita Hazra,, principal accused in the Raja Bazar Bomb Case (Nov. 1913).
159. Moti Lal Ray: op.cit, p. 158.
160. Terrorism in Bengal Vol.III, pp. 271-307, Tegart has written in great detail about the search. See also M.L.Ray: *op.cit.*, pp. 157-164. Ray also has given an interesting account of the search of his house by Tegart.
161. Home Department (Political), File A, February 1915. No. 68-160. Craddock kept a record of the conversation with the political prisoners. These records and the prisoners' petitions are available in the file noted above. R.C.Mazumdar has given extensive extracts from the file, in his book. *op.cit.*, pp. 197-198.
162. Home Department. Poll. A. Feby. 1915, Nos. 68-160. Appendices to Honourable Member's Note dated 23rd November,1913. Reproduced in R.C. Mazjumdar's "Penal Settlement in the Andamans", GOI,1975, pp. 207-208.

163. Terrorism in Bengal, Vol II, pp. 653-673. Note on the *Jugantar* Gang, subsequent to the search of the Manicktala Garden" by G.C. Denham, This was for the first time (1909) that the name *Jugantar* was used for a group of revolutionaries, though by that time the Government confiscated the press and stopped publication of the paper.
164. Sambhu Saha was a reputed photographer of his time. He is credited with some of the best photographs of Rabindranath and Santiniketan.
165. Sambhu Saha: *Ekti Sakshatkar* (Sambhu Saha: An Interview), *Ekshan;* Seet-Grishma, 1392-93 BS, pp. 52-72.
166. *Ibid*, p. 54.
167. Hem Chandra: *BBP*, p. 219. He revised *Banglay Biplab Prachesta* in 1949 for a new edition. I have seen the revised copy. But it appears no new fact or incident was added to it.
168. Hem Chandra: *Anagata Sudiner Torey* Renaissance Publishers, 1945, Total Page: 226.
169. Barindra Kumar Ghose: The Tale of My Exile, First published in 1922, Second reprint by Sri Aurobindo Ashram, Pondicherry, 2011, p. 2.
170. Some people like Srish Ghose of Chandernagore toyed with the idea of killing Barindra for his betrayal by making judicial confession.
171. The titles of the chapters such as "Why did I Confess?" and "What Led to Our Arrest?" clearly convey to the reader the apologetic nature of the contents.
172. A chapter entitled *"Banglaya Biplab Prachesta" in the Parisista* (Pages from 238 to 265) has been added to *Banglay Biplabbad*.
173. *BBP*, Chapter IV. Hem Chandra has discussed as to why the revolutionary movement failed with reference to the Maniktala Society alone. He has made some general observations from which it may appear that he lost faith in the revolutionary movement by secret societies.
174. *Bengalee*, dated 29 August, 1928
175. *Ananda Bazar Patrika*, 7th *Sravan*, 1335 B.S.
176. *Manasi O Marmabani*, *Agrahayan*, 1335 B.S.
177. Hem Chandra: *BBP*, p. 54.
178. Sumit Sarkar: *op.cit.*, p. 174.
179. Preface to *Banglaya Biplab Prachesta*, p. VI.
180. Hem Chandra Kanungo: Account of Revolutionary Movement in Bengal, Govt. of Bengal, 1928, p. 58. It may be noted that the

Bhawanipur Center was started at the behest of Hem Chasndra and he was in charge of the bomb-making center.

181. The Jugantar emblem was cross sword and trident , traditional weapons of Hindus and Muslims and crescent moon and lotus on either side.
182. Hem Chandra: *BBS*, p. 157.
183. It is significant that in his more than 300-page memoirs he has not for once mentioned the name of Rabindranath, "who sang Bengal to a nation."
184. Hem Chandra: *Accounts*, p. 47.
185. Sabyasachi Bhattacharya: *Vande Mataram: The Biography of a Song*, p. 3.
186. Hem Chandra: *op.cit.*, p. 37.
187. Hem Chandra: *BBS*, pp. 156-157.
188. *Ibid*, p. 153.
189. *Ibid*, p. 67.
190. C.C. Datta: *Purano Katha*, Part III, pp. 37-43. He writes that Aurobindo set up Ganga Nath Pathshala in Charodi Ashram in the model of *Bhawani Mandir*, that Aurobindo sent him to Sakharia Swami with a plan to set up Bhawani Mandir there. According to Datta Bhawani Mandir was written in 1903-1904.There are many such stories like a plan to kill Curzon on his way to Bombay o that he set up many secret societies in Western India. They are often incorrect and some are lacking corroboration.
191. Sri Aurobindo: *Autobiographical Notes*, p. 108.
192. *Ibid*, Aurobindo's letter dated 29th March, 1905, pp. 164-165.
193. *Ibid*, p. 75.
194. Baindra Kumar Ghose: *op.cit.*, pp. 10-11.
195. Barindra Kumar Ghose: *Atmakahini*, pp. 10-11.
196. Autobiographical Notes: pp. 43-44, Dinendra Kumar Ray a Bengali novelist was not exactly his teacher. "Dinendra lived with Sri Aurobindo as a companion and his work was rather to help him to correct and perfect his language and to accustom him to conversation in Bengali than any regular teaching."Yet Aurobindo could never muster sufficient confidence to address meetings in Bengal from 1906 to 1910.
197. Peter Heehs: *Sri Aurobindo: A Short Biography*, p. 33 .
198. Peter Heehs: *Sri Aurobindo: A Brief Biography*, 1989, p. 33.
199. Some of his writings during this period are: *The Harmony of Virtue*, *Bankim Chandra Chatterji*, *Essays on Kalidasa* and the *Mahabharata*,

The National Value of Art, Conversations of the Dead, the songs of Myrtilla (Poems) Vide Vol.I of Sri Aurovindo's Writings, published by Sri Aurobindo Ashram Pondicherry.

200. Amalesh Tripathi: *op.cit.*, p. 64.
201. On Himself; p. 77.
202. Peter Heehs: *Sri Aurobindo and Hinduism,* (2008). A lecture delivered on 9th December,2006 at Hyderabad in the 12 th Annual Conference of the Sri Aurobindo Society, Andhra Pradesh.
203. J.N. Farquhar (1861-1929): *Modern Religious Movements in India,* 1915, p. 21.
204. Valentine Chirol: *Indian Unrest,* 1910, Chapter VII, The Storm in Bengal, p. 123. Presumably Hem Chandra based his criticism on such writings.
205. J.N. Farquhar: *op.cit.,* Quoted by C.R. Cleveland. Vide Ker's Political Troubles in India : 1905-1917, p. IX.
206. Anales Tripathi: *op.cit.*, pp. 135-136.
207. *Ibid*, p. 136.
208. *Ibid*, p. 137.
209. Sri Aurobindo: *Essays on the Gita,* Sri Aurobindo Ashram, Pondicherry, 2006, pp. 33-34.
210. *Ibid*, pp. 20-31.
211. Karmajogin, 12th February, 1910.
212. Leonard Gordon: Bengal: The Nationalist Movement,1876 -1946, p. 111.
213. *Ibid*, p. 110.
214. Sri Aurobindo: *The Morality of Boycott*, Bande Mataram, p. 134.
215. L. Gordon: *op.cit.*, p. 121.
216. Sri Aurobindo : The Doctrine of Passive Resistance, *Bande Mataram*, p. 125.
217. The speech was delivered on 30th May, 1909 and published in *Karmayogin* in June, 1909.
218. Peter Heehs: Sri Aurobindo and Hinduism, (2008). A lecture delivered on 9th December, 2006 at Hyderabad in the 12 th Annual Conference of the Sri Aurobindo Society, Andhra Pradesh.

Account of
Revolutionary Movement in Bengal

Chapter - I

Foreword

I do not remember when I first read the *Anandamath* by Bankim Chandra. I saw the *Anandamath* on the stage before the year 1902. I do not think that any particular impression struck me at the time. I do not know whether anybody had even suspected that the song *Bande Mataram* had so much inspiration and so much power hidden in it. It is said that before a gathering of authors and poets at the Shovabazar Rajbati, Bankim Chandra prophetically told that his *Anandamath* would actually take place and bring about a great revolution in Bengal. Such stories are often circulated on big occasions. Who knows whether this one is like that or not?

I read the *Anandamath* once again after 1902 and realised that, besides giving the pleasure of reading fiction, it unconsciously left a living and earnest impression on the mind. Other novels by Bnakim Chandra left similar impressions, but I could not then realise, as I do now under the influence of a series of incidents, what that impression really was. So I am trying to narrate the story of the so-called revolutionaries of Bengal trying unawares to enact '*Anandamath*' on the political stage.

Inception of the Secret Society

In my boyhood no *jatra*, play or mythological story pleased me, unless there was some incident of warfare in it. The

Basumati, Aswin, 1329 B.S. (September and October 1922)

newspaper is never so widely circulated, as when it contains news of war. From this it appears to me that all persons old, young, male and female are more or less fond of warfare. It is now often said that warfare is unfair and unspiritual, and so uncivilised. But in October 1899, when news of the Boer War reached Bengal it was received, not with that feeling of terror and disgust which we now feel towards it in this country, but with an almost imperceptible pulsation of the heart, with a suppressed feeling of satisfaction and with a feeble sense of hope.

At that time I became acquainted with a colleague of mine, who had previously been the sub-editor of English journals, and who could not be said, therefore, unversed in politics. In fact, Jnanendranath Babu[2] was probably far more advanced in politics than the country's political leaders of the time. He was intolerant of all those who differed with him, and thus felt the want of a companion in his leisure hours. Under the circumstances he had no alternative but to select some one and to train him in his own views, a matter of some difficulty. Perhaps he had been unsuccessful in this and, therefore, as a last resort picked on me. This he did without notice and probably not even after due deliberation. Everyday we do such things, the significance of which is not apparent at the time.

Everyday he used to read me the news of the Boer War and to explain the politics in such a way that thinking failure to understand him would be discourteous, I pretended to grasp his arguments. My reason for this was that I had an extraordinary regard for the late Rajnarain Basu,[3] of whose greatness I had heard from my maternal uncle in my boyhood. Jnanendranath Babu was an ardent disciple of Rajnarain Babu, and our uncle had great respect for Jnanendra Babu. How could I, therefore, be discourteous or disrespectful to such a person?

Of all the wonders of the Boer War, the one which struck me most was the fact that a handful of uncivilised (I thought them so at the time) Boers could have routed the English, enormously powerful as they were. Jnanendra Babu made it clear by citing examples from history that secret societies alone made this possible.

I inherited to some extent from my parents the instinct for doing, knowing and thinking about something new. But that instinct could not develop on account of the stereotyped 'petticoated' method of my life. I cannot but be despondent about the condition of the country whenever I think of how this 'grandmotherliness' has frustrated the attempts of hundreds of buoyant and industrious persons in the past, and will continue to do so for ages to come. But then I found no such cause for pessimism, rather I hankered more after novelty. At last the question as to why we should not adopt the ways of the Boers became the subject of frequent discussion.

Before the Boer War, Italy suffered a defeat in Abyssinia and there were other instances of the defeat of the white race by the black. But few of our countrymen remembered such things, and there was an impression in their minds that the dark-skinned people could never conquer the white-skinned ones. This impression was rather upset by the Boer War. Although the Boers are also white-skinned, yet we took them to be illiterate and barbarous in comparison with ourselves. By the loud speeches we can lower a nation in the public estimation, and this can evade the hard and troublesome process of becoming great ourselves. This characteristic is not peculiar to us— Indians in general, are perpetual slaves indeed—but all nations imbibe it as long as they remain in subjugation. I have digressed far from the main point in issue. To return to the point. In an auspicious moment we decided that the Boer method was quite suited to our cause or in short we were determined to form secret societies.

We feel some diffidence or disinclination to do something which has neither precedence nor the sanction of past history. This is another feature of the slave nature. The question of providential inspiration did not occur to us, so our minds sought for and obtained precedence. The Italians, who were a slave nation like ourselves, have recently secured their freedom through the medium of secret society. By similar methods, Russia has been increasing her rights and privileges and entertains the hope of securing absolute freedom. Such was the case with China too. When the idea was supported by so many precedents, an embarrassing question as to whether we were really in a position to form secret societies or not, did not occur to us.

The formation of the secret society began. The programme included target practice, walking fast in the sun without an umbrella, and riding on a pony from which there was no fear or falling, but which was more likely to fall senseless down . The chief task was the recruitment of members, and the information that we had started a secret society was whispered to as many people as possible with the request that the matter should be kept secret. Several months passed in this way. The Boer War considerably increased the desire for freedom in almost all subject nations, and after this war a struggle for freedom began, after a long period of inactivity, in various countries—our country, of course, not excepted. But our desire for freedom was somewhat different from that in other countries.

Our desire for attainment of freedom

In 1902 the Boer War was just drawing to a close, and with much effort three or four members and seven or eight half-members had been recruited. Satyendra Nath Basu, who murdered Naren Gossain[4] inside the Alipore Jail, was a member. He was the nephew of Rajnarain Basu. Many had been privately sounded about our secret society. The word 'sounding' bears a special meaning, that is to say, the mentality of the person 'sounded' used to be tested by conveniently introducing, after long preliminaries, the real subject in an allegorical manner. If it was thought desirable the whole scheme was disclosed to the man without reserve. Many took fright on hearing of it, and we took much pleasure in characterising them as cowards and ourselves as heroes. A most noticeable feature was that practically none protested against it as something wrong, but rather regarded it as a hopeful sign as might be judged from the cautionary instruction which they imparted like wise men. In consequence the impression that the whole country was prepared for securing independence was firmly rooted in our minds. Let me disclose here somewhat more fully the nature of this preparation.

The want of freedom in our country was not and is not to-day acute enough to be compared with the hunger of a famished man who snatches away and swallows a mouthful of food from his own children who are themselves dying of hunger, or who is compelled to stuff his stomach with human flesh in order to soothe the pain of privation. When the perception of misery becomes sufficiently acute, a man takes his own life in order to get rid of it and feels a sort of uneasiness in sacrificing it. But we had no such feeling up to that time, nor had we any means of realising it; but a superficial or fanciful desire for gaining freedom was lurking in the hearts of certain individuals, although realisation of the pleasure of freedom was an impossibility for us. Had anybody any conception even of that happiness? Had anybody any idea as to what is meant by the real power of shaking off one's yoke? Then, again, the question of our capacity for maintaining freedom, should we acquire it, had not occurred to anyone. To-day when I think how we could take a whole country as it was then as being ready for the attainment of freedom, I cannot help a feeling of contempt for us rising within me. To speak the truth I pity those leaders who, without making us expert swimmers, threw us into the fathomless water.

I can see how the desire for gaining independence crept into our minds. We thought that we had learnt through the Congress leaders almost all the miseries that accrue from absence of freedom, but because of our inability to realise our misery, the yearning for freedom was not properly roused within us. Perhaps our leaders never thought of arousing such a desire, believing as they did that this country could never be totally free. But although these leaders made no attempt to excite the desire for complete independence, yet long before the birth of the Congress, the great poets, inspired by contemporary European agitation, sang songs and poems as their first sign of grief caused by the want of freedom, and these songs and poems surpass all comparison.

In spite of all this, we felt only one kind of misery, and it was this which gave us our desire for gaining freedom. This freedom meant relief from English subjugation.

In spite of the fact that from time immemorial the people of this country have been oppressed under the merciless tyranny of various types of domination, yet we Indians never felt that we were a subject nation. But under the present English rule, public opinion has helped the development of the perception of the misery, that we are under foreign domination. It is this pain that we feel in the depth of our heart caused by the hatred and slanderous accusations of the foreigners. We cannot deny, of course, that these accusations are not wholly untrue; but our misery becomes more acute when we are forced to admit that the slanderers are superior in all respects to those who are slandered. It is natural that along with the intense perception of misery and pain, a desire for its removal should arise. There are only two alternatives for getting that relief. The first is to remove the cause of accusation. This work was commenced in a quiet but firm manner by Raja Ram Mohan Roy, Vidyasagar and others. But conservatism and public opinion, which clung to the old order characterised this attempt as an imitation of the foreigners who hold a different religion, and held it to be inconsistent with self-respect. Since then getting support and help from certain Western people who, out of some motive, became lovers of the East; imitation of the West became an object of panic and terror in the country. The result of this reaction well-nigh succeeded in frustrating the first attempt for removing the causes of the accusation.

Then the second and the easier method of alleviating our misery was adopted. It was nothing but renouncing everything foreign and clinging boldly and without shame to whatever foreigners hated. The people with Western education were deployed for proving that whatever belonged to our country and culture was better than those of the foreigner. The idea of superiority of things Indian considerably developed the literature of our country.

Among the hundreds of foreigners, one or two speak or have spoken ill of themselves for some particular purpose, and one or two businessmen who are professional Orientalists do speak well of India with some motive or other. When we accept their testimony as infallible in order to prove the aforesaid truth, we do not pause to think about the other side. In this way since the passing of the Ilbert Bill, anti-British feeling has begun to increase. The Congress has continued to pour forth its offering of *ghee* into the flame of that anti-British feeling. Eventually this feeling of hatred has taken the name of patriotism. As a result of this anti-British feeling, our sympathy towards the Boers, who were enemies of the English, increased, and the same idea as was in their minds permeated our minds too; in other words we imbibed the desire for independence. In order to satisfy that desire, we adopted only one of their methods – the secret society.

The argument which promised us success, was that if several lakhs of barbarous Boers could defeat such a nation as the English, then why should not we – 32 crores in number – be able to defeat a handful of English. Bankim Chandra in his *Anandamath* had shown us the line of action. When Santi, one of the Bengali ladies who are proverbially weak and timid creatures, was able to snatch a rifle from the hands of an English Captain, then what is there on earth which we male Bengalies cannot accomplish? And when it was not only Santi, but many other heroines of Bankim Chandra did the same, could there be any doubt of our success?

If the expression 'Indian freedom' is given its correct interpretation, this desire of ours could not be called yearning for it, but it might rather be said to be a desire to rid ourselves of the hatred, calumny and disgrace to which we were subjected by the foreigners. If the English could, by dint of generous treatment, have soothed the acute pain which this hatred, calumny and disgrace inflicted, then the desire for political freedom would not perhaps have been awakened in us even to-day. Such is the case in the French colonies. It cannot be too emphatically stated that it is for such reasons that the love of the East sometimes swells in the hearts of white men.

Easy means of awakening patriotism

One day in the middle of the year 1902 I heard from Jnanendra Babu that Aurobindo Babu was trying to organise secret societies in Bengal; that such societies existed throughout India, except Bengal, and that many important men of Calcutta had joined them. I was overjoyed at hearing all these strange tidings, and my own worth appeared to me to have much increased.

A few days later a tall, bulky man, an assistant[5] of Aurobindo made his appearance. He was Jatindranath Banerji. His talk was inordinately long matching his sturdy features. What he said was mostly absurd and strange, and I give a summary as far as I remember of what he gabbled : The whole India was ready to drive out the English. The native States and millions of soldiers of every province were sharpening their swords. Even the Nagas, the Garos, the Bhils and other such savage tribes were marking time. Everyone was waiting for Bengal. It was for this reason that Aurobindo Babu had sent him as a messenger. Bengal must be ready within a year. There was no trouble whatsoever about guns, rifles and other weapons. The generals and captains were also in readiness; but Bengali commanders and captains were wanted. Those who joined the movement first would have prior claim to these posts.

I much regret that I cannot reproduce exactly all the strange stories which he poured forth from his life. But what was stranger still was that I myself accepted all these tales as truth.

We learnt from this gentleman more about the object, *modus operandi*, and duty of the secret society. Training in *lathi* and sword-play, wrestling and boxing, etc., were to be included, and in order to become a member, one had to touch the *Gita* with a sword. None but the authorised and initiated preceptor was empowered to enlist members and that after a rigid test. The *mantra* (incantation) of initiation was composed in Sanskrit. Before this, we had no *mantra* nor any connection with religion or God.

The evil effects of our servility which this gentleman gave us were, to the best of my memory, no more than those given by the Congress, *e.g.*, the non-separation of the judicial and executive functions, the exorbitant salt-tax, income-tax, Home-charge, the holding of the I.C.S. examination in England, the monopoly of high Government posts by the English, the decline of our industry and commerce, the growing poverty in the country, the rise in the price of commodities, famine, the spread of epidemics, the Arms Act, the Press Act, etc.

It is only since the time of the Ilbert Bill that a section of the Indian people had lost their faith in British administration as a result of Congress agitation. The success of the Congress lies in having infused deeply into the minds of the majority of educated Indians, that the English have not come to govern India in order to acquire spiritual righteousness.

But there were many other reasons which influenced the spread of this faithlessness among the illiterate laymen. Although the police *zulum* and the inhuman and unjust tyranny of autocratic rajas, zamindars and kazis were of everyday occurrence in the past, yet as a result of Western education as well as of the free exchange of views, the general public has learnt to think and to raise its voice against all unjust oppression as unendurable. It has also learnt to pay heed to what others will think of them if they do not treat the oppressors with contempt and hatred instead of fear and regard as in the past. Then again there was an outbreak of plague in Bombay; and many illiterate people were under the impression that, in order to send the peace-loving black natives of this country to the land of eternal peace, the English had imported this disease, and that they used to infect the wells with its germs and, thereafter, as soon as any symptom of any kind of fever appeared, declared the victim to be attacked with plague and dragged him and the inmates of his house to the segregation camp to be put to death. In this connection the famous Chambakar (Chapekar) shot Mr. Rand.[6] On account of this plague, there was terrible riots in other provinces as well, and during the first outbreak, there were serious incidents in Calcutta too. Shortly before this, there was some loss of life in a riot over the dismantling the Talla Mosque, and afterwards there was a great sensation in the country over the nasty incident of the judgement [7] of Mr. Pennell, the District Judge of Noakhali.

Previously the people felt that English law and justice were preferable to the Hindu and Moslem judicial systems, and for that reason they had some regard for the British people. The last named incident, however, firmly sowed the seeds of faithlessness and hatred for the English in the minds of the people of Bengal. The tactics to which Aurobindo resorted were meant, so it seems to me, only to stimulate that hidden grudge against the English and to cultivate a popular desire for revenge.

Jatindranath went away after giving us assurance that Aurobindo would come and initiate us.

However false or hollow a hoax it may have been, it inspired us with a feeling of strong excitement. I well remember the state of my mind at that time. The English would leave the country in four or five years! The country would become absolutely free, and we should have a king of our own. After that each of us would be worshipped in free India by our free countrymen as the rescuer of the land. (Till then we had no idea that we might not reap what we had sown, the doctrine of which is preached in the *Gita.*) This one idea appeared before our eyes like the living truth. I could not even imagine that there was the least flaw in it.

But what is the condition now? About 20 years (1902 to 1923) have rolled by since then and what changes have been brought on this earth! Thoughts, impressions, ideals and methods everything has advanced with great speed. But alas! during these years there has been in Indian thought the same want of vigour, in ideas the same laziness, in ideals the same illusions and in our work many farcical actions have been evident. Others learn by experience or by self-exertion or by failure, but as for ourselves in spite of experience, self-exertion and repeated failures we have become inured to failure. It is for this reason that both in great and small undertakings we fail every day. But the reason for our failure never occurs to us even by chance. And so in the sure hope of winning the Moon, we recline to-day spell-bound in grandmother's arms listening to the song, "Come, come oh Moon, come, come, come, and touch the forehead of my ruby son."

Annotations :

1. This account was published in serial in the *Basumati*, a monthly magazine published in Calcutta. It was subsequently published as a book under the title of *An Attempt at Revolution in Bengal*.
2. 'A' Babu is probably Bepin Chandra Pal of Sylhet, a journalist, who was one of the prime movers of the revolutionary movement in Bengal. He was one of the editors of *Bande Mataram* and the editor of *New India*.
   Editorial Note : The Intelligence Branch is wrong. A Babu was Jnanendra Nath Bose. Peter Heehs has also made similar mistake.
3. Rajnarain Basu (deceased) was the father of Arabinda Ghosh's mother.
4. Narendra Gossain, an approver in the Alipore bomb case, was shot by Kanai Datta and Satyen Basu, under-trial prisoners in the same case, on the 31st August 1908.
5. From Mr. Daly's "Note on the Growth of the Revolutionary Movement in Bengal" (*vide* page 6) it will appear that in 1900 Arubindo Ghosh sent Jatindranath Banarji of Chana, police-station Galsi, district Burdwan, who was then in the Baroda Army to Bengal as a missionary. Jatindra, on arriving in Bengal, joined P.

Mitter's association and started an athletic club. After sometime there was a quarrel between Jatindra and P. Mitter, the result being that the original party was broken up into two divisions, viz., Arubindo's party directed in Bengal by Jatindra and P. Mitter's party which founded the *Anushilan Samiti* and its many branches. Jatindra subsequently quarrelled with Barindra Ghosh, dropped out of the movement and became a *sadhu* as 'Niralamba Swami'.

6. On the 22nd June 1897 the Chapekar brothers murdered two Government officers Mr. Rand and Lieutenant Ayerst, who were engaged in the evacuation of plague-infected houses in Poona. (Rowlatt Committee Report, page. 2)
7. This judgement is in the Bengal Secretariat.

Editorial Note :

* Hemchandra's *An Attempt at Revolution in Bengal* was published in June, 1928, and the last instalment of serialised narrative was printed in January-February 1928. This translation of the serialised narrative was printed in October 1928.

Chapter II
Initiation and the Guru

The course we adopted was so strange that, in order to define our aims and to make our scheme workable, we needed the help and advice of an expert. Every country requires such a leader under similar circumstances.

In spite of Jnanendra Nath's accomplishments, the manner of his teachings was like that of a schoolmaster, and his selection as our guide did not meet with the party's approval. We wanted and were pleased with the idea of getting a new leader in Aurobindo Babu.

Leaders may be classified as follows :

i) Leaders with no knowledge of the subject in which they have to give the lead. Such leaders possess a kind of supernatural power or are well-equipped with the etiquette of righteousness and puritan formalities. Such leaders attract their disciples, who become blind to their lack of knowledge in the matter in which they seek their guidance. Aurobindo Babu was not a leader of this nature.

ii) Leaders who emerges in consequence of a change of circumstances in the society. Those who pander to public opinion in order to attain fame or for selfish reasons or who utilise some social weakness for such a purpose are generally accepted as leaders of a country.

Basumati, Kartik 1329 BS, October-November, 1922

It is this class of leader which is much esteemed in this country and this class accordingly predominates. Aurobindo Babu did not belong to this class.

iii) Thoughtful leaders who realise social evils and introduce some new line of thought in order to rid their country of them. Their ultimate object is to bring about a revolution. As the result of introduction of new thoughts and ideas, there appears the spirit of indomitable activity. If there be any individual, at such a moment, who can notice the change and can direct such activities along the right lines, he automatically becomes a leader. This class of leader is still wanting in this country.

iv) Those who take the lead for personal reasons to maintain their self-respect or to gratify their revenge when some ambition of theirs is shattered. This class of leader can achieve impossible things on this earth, although their patriotism originates from a sense of revenge and hatred. The term 'revenge' may not find favour with some in these days of non-violent agitation, but in the *Gita* we have instances of Sree Krishna himself exciting the spirit of revenge in his disciple Arjun and inducing him to kill his nearest and dearest. Moreover who can vouchsafe that at the root of non-violent agitation there does not lie the instinct of hatred and revenge?

I can now see that Aurobindo Babu was a leader of this class. Jnanendra Babu knew him from his very boyhood, and we heard from him that Aurobindo Babu was an exceptionally wise and learned person, and that he was well versed in politics. So we decided that there was nothing to be done but to obey the orders of our leader.

One evening I found that Jnanendra Babu had taken Aurobindo Babu to our Midnapore house. I felt honoured that such a man should pay me a visit, should consider me fit for the work of liberating the country. In consequence I became attached to him at the very outset.

Satyen and Barindra[1] were also in the company. Barin was a nephew of Satyen. We all thought of target practice with a gun, and went to a big ditch in a field wherefrom the sound of firing would not be audible at a distance. From the manner of Aurobindo Babu and Barindra holding a gun and taking aim I realised that it was the first time they handled such a weapon.

Aurobindo Babu suggested that Bengal should be divided into six centres, each of which should be subdivided into smaller centres. Midnapore was to become a centre. The principal centre in Calcutta had not at that time been established. We heard that many influential men of Calcutta had joined Aurobindo Babu, and that arrangements were being made to open a centre there.

Aurobindo Babu left assuring us that as soon as the *mantra* for the initiation was composed, he would come back and initiate us.

Towards the end of the year 1902, Aurobindo Babu returned alone. Meanwhile we had induced many persons to be initiated, but not more than four appeared on the evening fixed for the ceremony, and one of these disappeared on hearing the meaning of the Sanskrit *mantra*. A lively discussion took place between Jnanendra Babu and Aurobindo Babu as to whether the *mantra* should be composed in Bengali or not. In later days, when we ourselves conducted our initiations, we experienced similar difficulties. Many gave their consent at the time of proposal, but withdrew at the time of initiation. They were not wholly unjustified in doing so, because the oath of initiation enjoined very strict duties.

The following were some of the obligations of the oath[2] of initiation:

Failure to obey all orders issued by the society would involve the punishment of death. To commit murders without provocation, and to commit dacoity even at the risk of getting killed. To commit forgery, swindling and theft, if needed, and if caught in all these crimes there was the punishment of hanging, transportation, or long term of imprisonment like an ordinary criminal. Everything will have to be staked for the sake of the country, that is to say, none will have any personal interest in his property, when required all such property would have to sacrificed for country's cause, and so on.

When thought over all those things, it certainly produced a sort of wavering attitude in the minds of many people. But still there were others who, without caring for anything, took the initiation only to share the pride of freeing the country before long.

However, I went through the ceremony by touching the sword and the *Gita*, but instead of citing the Sanskrit *mantra*, I swore in Bengali that I would do everything for the salvation of India.

I had no reason to think about the utility of formal initiation at that time, but I realised the necessity when I myself was compelled to do things against my conscience. Even under ordinary circumstances human beings will abandon the course of their duty as soon as they meet with any obstacle in the way, but as the nature of work of the secret society was so very terrible, any member might at any moment have felt inclined to deviate from that path on the plea of conscience without any compunction for breaking the oath.

Instances of such deviation from the avowed path of duty are to be found in the character of Devi in *Devi*

Chaudhurani by Bankim Chandra, and of Satyananda in the *Anandamath* by the same author. Such instances are not wanting in the characters of Bankim Chandra's other novels as well as in those by many other Bangali novelists. It is not unlikely by that the influence of all those novels had affected the character and mentality of many of our leaders, famous or otherwise.

For all these reasons the members of secret societies had to be bound by some oath, the penalty for the violation of which was *death.*

In practice one would be threatened with such punishment. Unfortunately I never heard whether anybody considered what the punishment would be if the initiating preceptor violated the vow, and who would administer that punishment.

Annotations :

1. "Barin Da" is Barindra Kumar Ghosh, an accused in the Alipore bomb case.
2. Similar terms of oath will be found in Mr. Daly's "Note on the growth of the revolutionary movement in Bengal" in the statement of a revolutionary Lalit Mohan Chakrabartti of Diamond Harbour, recorded by the Magistrate of Howrah on the 24th March 1910.

Chapter III

Before the Partition of Bengal

Satyen and Jnanendra Nath were in charge of the secret society at Midnapore. We spread disaffection by discussing with all – peasants, police officers and even Deputy Magistrates – the miseries which the English had brought to the people. On one occasion a Deputy Magistrate took exception to such discussions on the ground that they were seditious. We found *mufassal* students more eager than those in Calcutta; new thoughts appealed to them more.

The more enterprising of these boys were taught shooting, and hunting excursions were arranged for them. Some of them displayed keenness in getting enlisted as members of secret societies when they came to hear of them. The leaders received a certain amount of response from Government servants and even from police officers, but very little from zamindars.

We had sympathisers amongst all classes who were, however, not willing to be initiated. There was cause for disappointment, but Jnanendra Nath and Satyen never knew the word 'despair'. Satyen succeeded in winning over many students, of whom some five or six were faithful to the last. In two years we succeeded in procuring one horse and one bicycle and about a dozen leaders.

Basumati, Pous, 1328; December 1922-January 1923

We knew of Debabrata Basu[1] who was well informed about secret organisations the world over. He told many, exaggerated stories of those societies. It does not appear he deliberately used to tell such highly exaggerated stories. This was his nature. This can be called pious or honest fraud. If someone points out the inconsistencies, then the raconteur will take shelter behind the plea that such things do happen and might as well happen in future. This is called truth in anticipation, and Debabrata Babu used to defend himself with this argument. When it was found that the recruitment to the society was at a stand-still we had recourse to disseminating political nostrums in the guise of religion. Barin, who was primarily responsible for gradual erosion of the party in Calcutta was advised by Debabrata to take recourse to religion. He also tendered the same advice to Aurobindo. Debabrata was a religious person and after the Alipur trial he joined the Ram Krishna Mission.[2]

In 1903 Sister Nivedita[3] went to Midnapore and stayed there for five days. She delivered lectures on politics through the medium of religion and the attendance at these meetings grew from day to day. She encouraged the society by personal demonstrations of sword-play and other athletic exercises and presented the works of Mazzini and a copy of Prince Kropatkin's book to them.

One old barrister[4] was the president of the chief centre of the secret revolutionary society in Bengal. He had learnt the theory of secret organisations while in England. I was introduced to him in Calcutta by Jnanendra Nath. There was another experienced and highly-educated England-returned leader, who was an intimate friend of Aurobindo. He was Charu Chandra Dutta[5], a civil servant of Bombay Presidency.

When Jatindra Nath Banerjee was the leader of the Calcutta Centre at Circular Road, Barin was an organiser under him. Jatindra used to stay there with his family. Barin and a few other workers also used to live there. Barin made efforts to start district centres of the secret society and was successful to some extent though adequate new recruits were not available after initial enthusiasm. It was a matter of concern to all of us as to why the ideals of the secret society movement was not striking roots in the minds of the people. I discussed with Jatindra Nath, Debabrata Babu and a few others as to how we could make the younger generation accept our ideals. From discussion with them we had realised that they had also been facing the same problem.

Probably at 1903-end the Calcutta Centre was shifted from Circular Road to Grey Street, and during my visit to the centre I found it in a disorganised state. In early 1904 the centre was closed mainly due to conflict among the leaders for supremacy over the society. Jatindra Nath was very hard working and disciplined, but he was very authoritarian too.

Our Barin was not born to follow the path shown by others; he was destined to show the path to others. Many a time he used to boast like this. In course of time this turned out to be the reality in the society. Gradually Aurobindo started seeing through the eyes of Barin, to hear through the ears of Barin and even he spoke through the mouth of Barin. So long Barin was compelled to abide by the authority of Jatindra Nath; but soon to drive away Jatindra Nath became his principal task. He got an opportunity when a woman came to live at Circular Road house. Barin reported to Aurobindo about suspected illicit relationship of Jatindra with the woman; and since Barin had the ears of Aurobindo, he gave one-sided verdict and ordered Jatindra Nath to be driven out of the society. Consequently the centre at Circular Road was closed. Under Barin's leadership a new centre was set up at Grey Street. Separation with the aged barrister P.N. Mitra and his *Anushilan Samiti* was also complete as Barin was impervious to any control by Mitra. Jnanendra and Satyendra found it difficult to submit to the authority of Barin, who possibly apprehended that Satyendra might come up as his rival to claim the leadership of the society. He did not hesitate to use the same woman as weapon against Satyendra. At that time Satyendra was staying in the same office. So, Satyendra had also to leave for Midnapur. The members of the Midnapur Society were disappointed at these developments; still they did not severe their connections with Barin and his society due to their deep respect for Aurobindo.

Barin was wanting in two great qualities of an inspiring teacher. First, his physical appearance might be befitting a lover, a poet, a *yogi* or a *sadhak*, but it was quite unsuitable for a would-be general in India's fight for freedom. Secondly, he was not sharp witted. To be a good speaker one has to be knowledgeable about the events around the world. For these and many other reasons the Grey Street society gradually waned and then by early 1904 was closed. Barin left for Baroda to live with his *Sejda* and carried with him the advice of Debabrata Babu. The revolutionary ideas should be given to the people in an attractive cover and the cover was religion.

Aurobindo had travelled to the districts of East Bengal and had realised the difficulties the secret societies had been facing for want of new recruits. He also failed to avoid influence of Debabrata Basu who had been harping on the theme of religion as a means of attracting new members. When a new idea used to come to Aurobindo's mind, he would try his best to act in pursuance of it. He started collecting materials for using religion as an instrument in the secret society movement.[iii] The leaders of the other secret societies, however, continued to strive for new members and did not desert the secret societies.

I have mentioned about Bhupen Babu. He was then touring various places to preach revolutionary ideas. Having failed to create any impact he used to abuse the people of the country to his heart's content. He was a great devotee of Aurobindo Babu. He did not aspire to be a leader. I have taken him to very poor villages in the interior and he was given very wretched food. Although he was born and brought up in Calcutta, he never grumbled.

Influence of the Partition of Bengal and Russo-Japanese War

The resolution to partition Bengal was adopted on 3rd December,1903 and the anti-partition agitation became stronger from the middle of 1904.The Russo-Japanese War broke out on 8th February,1904. We however, felt the impact of the war from the middle of 1904. Had not these two events, namely the Russo-Japanese War and the Partition of Bengal, taken place, our secret society movement would have ended there only.

During two years prior to 1904 the propaganda for independence through armed struggle had, by and large, ended in failure. To put it in simple language no leader was aware that unless a revolutionary change in the mentality of the people could be brought about no revolution was possible. It did not occur to any of the leaders that to prepare the people for freedom their mindset had to be changed and modified at the very root. It should be set on a higher moral and ethical code conducive to the needs of the revolution.

These two events—the Russo-Japanese War and the Partition of Bengal—provided great impetus to the secret society movement and without that the secret societies would have been extinct. As a matter of fact we had been kept awake and active by impulses from outside from time to time. Such state of inertia was not special to the Bengalis, similar lack of initiative was noticed in all other places in India.

When a man slips into deep drowsiness after consuming more than the usual dose of opium, then efforts are made to keep him awake by causing pain, by pulling his hairs and ears or poking him violently so that physical pain does not allow him to pass into a state of coma. Our condition was also like that. We came back to temporary consciousness only when strong impulses came from outside.

Opium has poisonous effect on an addict; we will try to find out whether religion has similar effect on the people.

Now we will discuss why we failed to inspire our countrymen into action with the ideals of freedom.

Annotations :

1. Debabrata Basu was an accused in the Alipore bomb case.
2. Some of the members of Ramkrishna Mission were sympathisers of the revolutionary movement. Bhupen Datta, brother of Swami Vivekananda, the founder of this Mission was prosecuted and convicted for writing seditious articles in the beginning of the movement.
3. Sister Nivedita (or Miss Margaret Noble), an American lady*, was a disciple of the late "Swami Vivekananda". She is dead.
4. This is P. Mitter (deceased).
5. 'Ga Babu' and 'G Babu' ** are apparently identical. He is not known.

Editorial Notes :

i. She was an Irish lady.
ii. 'Ga' Babu was Charu Chandra Dutta. IB failed to identify him.
iii. Aurobindo did not accept the suggestion of Debabrata Basu that religion should be used to rejuvenate the secret society. On the contrary he argued that a patriotic upsurge in the country would inject life into the society. Hem Chandra was, however, harped on the ineffectiveness of the leadership and their effort to combine religion with politics led to the failure of the revolutionary movement failed.

Chapter IV

Why the Secret Societies Failed

Although our secret societies aimed mainly at securing India's political liberty, there are many short-comings in our very national character which make us unfit for any kind of liberty. Even if at that time we could reasonably conceive the possibility of liberty, the very idea has become impossible since the Great War. We are, as a nation, unable to accept and assimilate anything new or, in other words, the masses of our country have altogether lost the faculty of feeling any wants and acute sensitivity to pain and pleasure. This is the primary reason why our secret societies met with such signal failure.[i]

All attempts in our country to introduce a new idea or to start a new movement have met with partial success, if at all, especially with regard to the masses. This total loss of the perception of want is one of the chief causes that has all along obfuscated the realisation of the idea of liberty. The causes why we have not this faculty sufficiently developed, are many. The first is that we are taught that the consummation of existence lies in callousness to material needs. This training has deprived us of any desire to better our lot.

We have been further taught to think that all our miseries in this world consist in the multiplication of our material wants, and that we should therefore try to shun them as far

---

Basumati, Sravan, 1330; July-August, 1923

as practicable. A third factor is our rooted belief in the doctrine of predestination. This fatalism has deprived us of all incentive to self-improvement. Belief in astrology has also converted us into so many puppets being trapped in the greatness of our own past. So engrossed are we in enumerating our past exploits that we have not the leisure or inclination to think for the future. And finally, all the doors to the temple of knowledge are securely shut against us. It is said that all that is knowable and worth knowing, is to be found in the scriptures and the texts of our ancient sages and that we have therefore to confine all our attention to them and them alone. The key of this temple, however, is in the hands of the priests, and the domination of this priestly caste has left us devoid of all powers of initiative and free and rational thinking. I may be asked why all these artifices were used to keep human minds in permanent bondage? The Aryans, being a conquering nation, tried their utmost to keep in eternal subjection the aboriginal Sudras who greatly exceeded the Aryans in number. And it is for this that all these elaborate artifices were invented and introduced into society. But although these artifices had been originally meant for the Sudras alone, with the lapse of time the victors themselves came to be caught in their meshes.

It is, of course, true to some extent that under the sway of our present rulers, the English, we have of late begun to feel some kind of want. But they are few and are of no moment. Our present conquerors do not differ much from the Aryan conquerors of the Sudras in as much as they, too, aim at keeping us in permanent chains. They know that they cannot exterminate us as the aboriginal tribes of America and Australia have been by the white colonists from Europe, nor is India a suitable place to plant a colony in for the Britishers. Hence their aim in keeping India under permanent subjection has been to derive as much pecuniary profit out of us as may be thought consistent with their purpose. They want to pass their manufacturers upon us as much as they can, and to achieve this they have been trying to enkindle in our minds some feeling for wants. But they know full well that we shall not be able to shake off their yoke as long as the relation between the masses and the classes remains as that between the devourer and the devoured. The upshot of all this has been that we have become a do-nothing ease-loving people, afraid of innovation and rational thinking.

Chapter V

Political Liberation Through Religion

It was in 1902 that an attempt to form secret societies in Bengal was seriously undertaken. Shortly before this, secret societies had been established in the Mahratta country, but we heard that their ideal was not very exalted. Nevertheless the Mahratta secret societies were not void of religious associations. Rumour has it that before the commencement of the formation of secret societies in Bengal Aurobindo Babu had come in touch with the Mahratta secret societies. But for two years after his attempt to form secret societies in Bengal, Aurobindo himself never used to perform any religious observance and except touching the *Gita* at the time of initiation, the societies had nothing to do with religion either in their deeds or ideas. Amongst other leaders, Debabrata Babu had been preaching religion seriously from before. Certainly, Aurobindo did not find any lapse on his own part or on the part of his fellows or assistant leaders in preaching ideals of freedom to the people. Still they failed to impress the people. Consequently it was easy for him to conclude that it was beyond any temporal power to infuse the ideal of freedom into the mind of the people. But then he had a whole-hearted desire to

---

Basumati Kartik, 1330 BS; October-November 1923

drive away the English form his country. Such being his temperament Aurobindo had no other alternative but to believe in the existence of supernatural powers of the so-called *Sidha Yogis* of Debabrata Babu, and to rely on them. This method of achieving the freedom of the country for salvation of the ancient civilisation and religion of India through supernatural power or religion, was borrowed wholly from the *Anandamath*.

Our leaders were aware that our blind faith and ignorance were primarily responsible not only for our political dependence, but for all other forms of misfortune and degradation as well. The foundation of all knowledge in this country has been on the cult of devotion. Hence argumentation or freedom of thought is despised. In one matter alone, a certain amount of scepticism has become deep-rooted. The issue is whether it is for our good or for subserving the interests of their own countrymen that the British Government are running the administration of the country.

The two great problems, which cannot but stand like the insurmountable Himalayas in the way of liberation of India from the clutches of the English, did not become matters of concern for Aurobindo Babu as well as for other leaders, or at any rate they failed to appreciate their seriousness. These two issues are the Hindu-Moslem problem and the caste distinctions amongst the Hindus themselves. One day, in a meeting of the secret society, means to solve the Hindu-Moslem problem was discussed. It was resolved that if the Moslems joined this revolution it was all to the good; because when the country became free, privileges in proportion to the extent of their help would be conferred on them. But if they did not join they would be classed as enemies and were to be put in the same category with the English. Needless to say, the idea of a solution of this type indicates lack of serious thought on the issue. On the contrary, the Moslems might have indulged in bragging of the past domination over the country.

The Moslems need no explanation to understand the plain fact that the liberation of India through Hindu religion meant establishment of supremacy of the Hindus. This meant that the Moslems would not only abstain from joining this movement, but they were sure to become more bitter enemies of the Hindus than the English. In the circumstances, if the Moslem leaders thought that to rely on the Sultan or the Amir was the only way of emancipating India from her subjection to the English or if they could join the Pan-Islamic agitation with such purpose, they would not certainly be held guilty of committing any serious wrong.

If for argument's sake it is accepted that both the Hindus and the Muslims have equal interest in freeing the country from the British, and so there might be a unity of both the communities on the basis of common interest. But when the communal hatred and enmity are so strong between the two religious denominations, it will be self-deception to believe that even a working atmosphere of friendly relationship may be created.

For a religious community the best way to protect itself was to generate hatred and enmity against contending religions. The religion that fails to attract people from other religions by the wealth of its thoughts and practices or fails to hold on to its own followers, that religion adopts mean methods to protect itself from erosion. Our *sanatan* Hindu religion has done much in this regard, because in Hindu religion there is no conversion but there is excommunication. So for the sake of self-preservation the Hindus have been accustomed to hate and bear animus against followers of other religions so much that even animals are not treated in like manner.

To make communal harmony feasible emphasis should be on scientific reason and patriotism which should put religion on the back-burner. In the light of reasoning the mist of religion will disappear. But our leaders will not be able to tolerate that. Because they belong to the aristocratic class in the upper layer of the Hindu society. Their aristocracy and leadership are protected by religion. So they are incapable of banishing religion from politics.

As in the ancient period so in the present day situation, religion protects the upper aristocratic strata at the cost of those who are in the lower rung of the religious community. So, religion is a hindrance to the development of man in the lower strata of the society. Nationality which in many countries has marginalised the influence of religion, has been accepted as the alternative ideal for the unity and development of all sections of people. In Hindu community a small section of upper caste people through their hereditary right has kept a vast majority under subjugation on the plea of religious sanction. The large majority has silently accepted their all round domination as ordained by God. The talk of religious or spiritual nationalism will be detremental in context of Hindu-Muslim animosity.

We have two types of freedom to choose from : one is the ever-increasing sense of want by the lower class of people and the continuous endeavour to meet those wants. Thus by bringing them up, they become strong enough to be part of a strong nation. This is called Western nationalism and freedom of the nation. The other freedom would imply retrogression to the 'golden age' or to primitive uncivilised condition. It is this type of independence which is the aim of our leaders in "achieving the salvation of the country through religion." In other words, those who are determined to govern the people, using religion as the administrative machine, are the very persons who want to drive away the English masters and to monopolise that mastery themselves. As a proof of this we have now got an inkling of their intention from the withdrawal of several Bills, laid before the legislature, purporting to increase the rights of the comm....... people, according to the proposals of the Congress for the uplifting of the untouchable castes. This was opposed by the *Hindu Sabha* and *Sanatan Darma Sabha.**

Annotations :

1. Sedition Committee's report records (page 67); "The combination of the religious, political and social views is clearly brought out in the rules by which the new order was to be governed. Generally speaking a new organisation of political sanyasis was to be started, who were to prepare the way for revolutionary work. The central idea as to a given religious order is taken from the well-known novel *Anandamath* of Bankim Chandra. It is an historical novel dealing with settling the sanyasi rebellion in 1774 when armed bands of sanyasis came into conflict with the East India Company and were suppressed after a temporary career of success.

Editorial Notes :

* The Tenancy Act (Amendment) Bill and Inter Caste Marriage Bill were drafted on the basis of Congress resolution. They were withdrawn in view of the protest of the *Hindu Mahasabha* and the *Sanatan Dharma Sabha.*

Chapter VI
Anti-Partition Movement

Exciting events from various parts of the world used to give impetus to our revolutionary work. This was the state of affairs before anti-partition agitation. Though Aurobindo Babu had left Bengal, the secret societies in Calcutta and Midnapore managed to somehow drag on through the efforts of Jnanendra Babu, Satyen and others.

Though the proposal for partitioning Bengal had been first mooted in December 1903, it was towards the end of 1904 that the agitation against it took serious shape. The victory[1] of Japan over Russia at this time also had had a very striking effect on us. It dispelled from our mind the belief that Westerners were invincible, and that the blacks could never become equal to, or defeat, the whites. It imparted a new life into dying and decaying Asia. It is in this sense that this victory of Japan over Russia constitutes important event in the history of the world. It instinctively led us to believe that were we ever to win our independence, we must follow the path of Japan.

The agitation against the partition having failed to achieve its end, it, by way of retaliating the wrongs thus inflicted, took a new turn in the shape of the *Swadeshi* and boycott agitation and led to the final but inevitable appearance on the scene of the bomb and the revolver.

Basumati, Chaitra, 1330 BS; March-April 1924
Jaistha, 1331 BS; May-June 1924

This desire to retaliate the wrongs done to the country, even at the sacrifice of our lives, was quite a new thing in this country, specially among the Hindus.

In the first chapter I have described how the awe and reverence for the British Government were gradually transformed, first into distrust and lastly into positive hatred. The failure of the partition agitation gave a strong fillip to this feeling. Though very few people could be found who dared oppose and assault a European openly, yet there was hardly any man at the time who did not at heart feel gratified when a European was assaulted. This condition of the country arrested our notice, and we were fondly led to believe that the country, as a whole, was ripe for revolution and needed but a push from us.

This was a mistake; but not only we ourselves but veteran diplomats of Germany also were guilty of it.[1] The fiery speeches delivered at the *Swadeshi* meetings and the inflamatory writings in our periodicals and the press led them to believe that India was ripe for a revolution and would at once plunge into it as soon as Germany had declared war against England. As a matter of fact, we, too, on our part, were anxiously longing for 'action', which word was, with us, synonymous with the murder of Englishmen, plunder, dacoities, etc. Such 'action', though ultimately a failure, commenced by the middle of 1905.

Our first duty was to utilise the partition agitation for the spread of the revolutionary cult. Protest meetings were organised all over the district and were addressed by our own men who so magnified the Japanese success, as to encourage Indians to believe that they could easily throw off the English allegiance.

Bhupendra Nath Datta, late editor of the *Yugantar*, was one of our chief preachers, and his enthusiasm in this direction knew no bounds.[2] Though Debabrata Babu had no party of his own, he was the life and soul, as it were, of all the societies then existing, and it was the endeavours of persons like these that rejuvenated the dying samitis in Calcutta and strengthened their faith in revolution.

At Midnapore Jnanendra Babu and Satyen were carrying on their activities vigorously. Satyen utilisd his energies in organising school and college students in secret societies and Khudiram joined one of these.

In Midnapore the cult of revolution was spread in the villages by means of magic-lanterns and homeopathic dispensaries served as shelters of the revolutionary preachers. It was at this time that Chandra Kanta Chakrabartti (now Dr. C.K. Chakrabartti)[3] joined us and gradually became one of our most powerful preachers. Nirapada Ray *alias* Nirmal[4], of Nadia, and Bibhuti Bhushan Sarkar[5] also joined the revolutionary society at about this time. Nirapada possessed the virtues of a revolutionary to an extent not approached by anybody else I knew of.

A secret society in the guise of a weaving institution had been opened at Midnapore and joined by all those who had left their hearth and home and plunged themselves into the service of the country. There was a loom here and Bibhuti acted as the weaving master.

The destruction by the Muhammadans of the image of *Durga* and oppression upon the Hindus at Jamalpur, are said to have been chiefly responsible for the change in the aims and objects of the Dacca Anushilan Samiti, which now took to organising the Hindus[ii] against Muhammadan oppression.[6]

Full advantage was taken of this agitation to put forward the cause of *Swadeshi* and boycott. School and college students were organised; weaving institutions and athletic societies were started. Cart-loads of foreign goods were looted, shops dealing in foreign articles burnt to ashes, assaults took place and heads were broken. The fury of the police was much in evidence, and many were arrested and sent to jail. Punitive police forces were stationed in various places and the country as a whole was astir. The other provinces of India as well took to *Swadeshi* in imitation of Bengal.

The revolutionaries started, under the name of *Chatra Bhandar*[7], a *Swadeshi* shop in Calcutta and a branch was opened at *Midnapore*. Attempts were made in every district to bring the local *Swadeshi* institutions under the control of the revolutionaries, and to initiate the leaders thereof to the cult of revolution and thereby to convert them into so many secret centres of revolutionary activities.

The *Sandhya*[8], edited by the late Brahmabandhav Upadhyaya, was, at this time, a very highly popular newspaper. It was second to none in holding up Englishmen in contempt and deriding them; but it was no organ of the revolutionaries. The tone of many of the newspapers managed by the people of the country had largely changed by this time.

It was at about this time that the book *Desher Katha*, by the late Shakharam Ganesh Deushkar, was published. Shakharam Babu was a leading man, though he had no party of his own. It was he alone who was at this time preaching revolution through literature. Although his writings contained little or nothing to awaken the sense of nationality, yet the mere perusal of his *Desher Katha* converted many a reader into an inveterate enemy of the English.

Besides *Desher Katha*, revolution was sought to be preached through the works of Jogendra Nath Vidyabhushan and some other authors. We collected and distributed as many of them as we could.

This is how revolutionary ideas were preached in those days through speeches and writings : the Hindu regime was totally free from the famine and poverty and the Muhammadan period too was no less so; it was the British subjection of India which had brought in its wake all the ills we were suffering from; and if we were to be happy and prosperous once again, we must put an end to British rule; the taxes would then be reduced and prices would fall and so on.

We have now realised the innate fallacy of these stock arguments; but at that time, not only we, but most of our leaders as well, took them to be gospel truths.

Compared with many other people our people undoubtedly are very poor at present, and we can certainly ameliorate their condition to a very large extent if we are really so determined. But it would not be true to say that poverty was unknown in the Hindu or Moslem regime. On the contrary, the nature of poverty in those days was as extreme as it could be, only the masses were incapable of feeling it.

It is this incapacity to feel the pangs of want which is really at the root of our troubles, and indeed our own religion is responsible for it than either British subjection on foreign imitation.

It was at this time that thousands of *Swadeshi* songs were composed and replaced the earlier ones. But one thing about them is to be particularly noticed. They all dilated upon the past glories and beauties of the country and dwelt on the insults, wrongs and indignities heaped on us by the foreigners, as though our country should be loved and served only because once she was great. The result was that those who, inspired by such writings and songs, plunged themselves into revolutionary activities were active only so long as it brought fame and glory. But at the very first sight of danger and misery they turned approvers and informers.[iii]

During the days of the *Swadeshi* an attempt was made to set up a National Council of Education in Bengal. At that time is was popularly believed that the system of education that had been introduced in the country by Government, was primarily responsible for our slave mentality, and it was to eradicate this evil that attempts were now begun to be made to impart education prevailing in the Government institution was blindly imitated with slight modifications, and the whole thing therefore came to be a failure. The best thing that the leaders of this movement should have done was to publish translations of standard works from foreign languages, but this they neglected. Another movement, calculated to benefit the country, was, however, started at about this time. The association for the cultivation of science was started and, in imitation of Japan, hundreds of young men were sent to foreign countries under its auspices for scientific and technical education. But, for want of proper and judicious selection of suitable candidates, this laudable attempt too bore no fruit. One thing, however, must be credited to the account of the *Swadeshi* movement and it was this. Before the movement had broken out, the people of the country were, politically speaking, divided into two groups those who kept aloof from politics altogether and those who took to it as a profession. At the time of the *Swadeshi* movement this second group was further subdivided into what came to be henceforth known as Extremists and Moderates.[9]

Failing to secure the repeal of the partition by petitions and prayers, some people lost all faith in their efficacy and began to try to force the hands of the English by hitting them through their pockets. These people subsequently became known as Extremists.

It was out of this Extremist group that a third party emerged known as the revolutionary secret societies. It was the revolutionary party and it aimed at the complete overthrow of the present system of Indian administration. Most of the members of this party had had no connection whatever with secret societies and many disliked them even. Then, again, there were men among them who, though they ourwardly professed to be Moderates or Extremists, were nothing but revolutionaries at heart. But there was hardly any difference in the aims and ideals held by them as well as by the secret societies. Both aimed at driving the English out of India and putting the administration of the country in the hands of some capable Indians. Some of the most influential leaders of the time joined this party. Differences among the political groups led to the emergence of a host of orators and writers and the one effect of all these was that the people in general began to lend their support to *Swadeshi*, though most of them could hardly realise what it really meant.

This so-called *Swadeshi* spirit was mainly confined to the Hindus. The Moslems sided with the Government and, in many cases, were even hostile to the *Swadeshi* movement. This intensified the hatred of the Hindus towards Musalmans. But the then leaders did nothing to bring about a unity between the two rival communities with the result that the whole movement gradually tended to be and ultimately became a movement to assert Hindu superiority. The Musalmans, in their turn, commenced, by way of retaliation, molesting Hindus in their religious observances and practices.

Such was the state of the country on the eve of the commencement of revolutionary activities.

Annotations :

1. Sedition Committee's report (page 12) : "But neither the religious teachings of Vivekananda nor the exhortations of Sri Krishna in the 'Bhagvad Gita', would have afforded so moving a text to preach from, had not the whole world, and especially the Asiatic world been electrified and amazed by the victories of Japan over Russia at a time when within this country circumstances occasioned by certain Government measures specially favoured the development of Barindra's plans."
2. This fact was substantiated in a case in the court of the Presidency Magistrate, Emperor *vs.* Bhupendra Nath Dutt, under section 124A, Indian Penal Code, in which the accused was convicted and sentenced to one year's rigorous imprisonment on 24th July 1907. It was held that the articles 'Sway with fear' and 'Stick medicine', written by the accused, were such as to excite not merely feelings of disobedience to the authority of the Government, but an inclination to defy and subvert it by open acts of violence; and the accused was held to have circulated the articles with that intention. "The accused is appealing not to any particular class, but to his countrymen in general, and that no less than 7,000 copies were ordered to be printed, and that the price brings it within the reach of the poor."
3. A well-known revolutionary of Barisal.
4. An accused in the Alipore Bomb Case.
5. An accused in the Alipore Bomb Case.
6. In this connection it will be found at page 43 of Mr. Beachcroft's judgement in the case Emperor *vs.* B.K. Ghose and others, that Paresh Chandra Mullick was bound down to keep peace in the Mymensingh district in 1907. "In that case about the time of the Jamalpur disturbances, apparently after the breaking of the image of a goddess by the Muhammadans, Paresh Mullick was found in company with Indra Nath Nandi and others, who were national volunteers, wandering about in Jamalpur disguised as Muhammadans, and one or more of the party were armed with revolvers. This fact is also corroborated by the statement of Bibhuti Bhusan Sarkar, an accused in the Alipore bomb case, recorded by Mr. Birley on the 4th May 1908 (*vide* page 5), in which Bibhuti Bhusan Sarkar said, 'I did this (Narayangarh train wrecking) because the Muhammadans oppressed the Hindus at Jamalpur and Comilla and I learnt that it was done on behalf of the English.

7. It will be seen at page 48 of the Alipore Sessions Judge, Mr. Beachcroft's judgement that Nirapada Ray and Satyendra Nath Bose were the prime movers in the starting and management of the 'Midnapore Chhatra Bhandar'. Mention is also made of this 'Chhatra Bhandar' or students' stores in Mr. Beachcroft's judgement in the Alipore bomb case, pages 4 and 79. "The prosecution sought to extablish the fact that a company was started, called the Chhatra Bhandar, Limited, which, under the guise of a general trading company, devoted itself chiefly to the circulation of seditious literature in which it was assisted by various agencies in different parts of the country". (Page 4) But the learned Judge dissented from the prosecution story and held that although one of the provisions in the articles of association was that 30 per cent of the profits was to be given as grants for the general good of the country and the welfare of the people, but as this provision was inherited from the concern, before it was formed into a company, there seems no reason to think that that concern was intended to assist in promoting a revolution. (Page 79)
8. This fact was substantiated in Mr. Beachcroft's judgement, page 81. "Of the papers other than *Yugantar*, the *Sandhya* was the worst. Its main object appears to have been personal vituperation of the grossest character. It is not shown to have been connected with this conspiracy by any association with persons connected with the conspiracy".
9. This fact was substantiated by Mr. Daly's "Note on the revolutionary movements of Bengal", page 5, where it is stated that at the Congress which was held in Calcutta in December 1906, a definite line was drawn between the extremists and moderates. The moderates wanted a measure of self-government within the Empire. The extremists of which Arabinda Ghosh and Bepin Pal were organisers, aimed at nothing short of complete freedom from the British and all other foreign rule.

Editorial Note :

i. Hem Chandra had in mind count Bernhard's work entitled *Germany and the Next War*, 1911, wherein Indian revolutionary situation was considered as convenient for strategical use by Germany. J.C. Kar wrote about the visit of the German Crown

Prince to India and other officials on 6th March, 1914 the *Berliner Togeblatt* stated in an article that the day of reckoning for England would far sooner.

ii. *Dacca Anushilan Samiti* was of the view that Hindu-Muslim riots were engineered by the British and not the Mohammadans.

iii. Such presumptions are highly lopsided and biased.

Chapter VII

Revolutionary Actions

It was towards the beginning of 1906 that Aurobindo Babu returned to Calcutta. He was soon followed by another leader named Charu Babu.[1] The two, together with a few others, convened in Calcutta a meeting of the secret society wherein it was decided, among other things, to at once commence 'action'[2], to establish 'temples of Bhawani' at suitable places and to publish an organ of the revolutionary party. By the word 'action' we at that time used to understand murders to English officials and plunder of Government treasures or money belonging to Europeans. The idea underlying it was that any one such act, if successful, would draw the attention of the public and thereby facilitate the diffusion of revolutionary ideas among them. Another motive was that murders of Englishmen and frequent commissions of dacoities would eventually enable us to throw off for ever our habitual and inborn aversion to manslaughter, cruelty, etc., and invest us with war-like qualities. Besides, it would also help us in collecting funds for carrying on the revolutionary propaganda, as many of the big men of the time promised to pay large sums in return for the murder of one single Englishman of name and position. The then leaders seemed to have taken very little note of the obstacles that might

---

Basumati, Sravan, 1331 B.S. (July and August 1924)

naturally stand in the way of carrying out their idea. Many of them were no doubt well-read in the revolutionary histories of other lands but unfortunately failed to profit by their experience, owing, *inter alia,* to their ignorance of the mentality of the people and their own mental inertia and lethargy. The result was that the whole country was utterly demoralised when Government met the revolutionary activities with rank oppression. The leaders also do not seem to have fully realised the true significance of the term 'revolution' as it is understood in Europe and America, their only idea being to replace the British Government in India by one of their own countrymen.

A little before this Debabrata Babu[3] seemed to have been obsessed with the idea of establishing 'temples of Bhawani' in imitation of *Anandamath.* His idea seems to have been to erect temples in mountains or jungles, far away from human abode and to install therein images of the goddess *Kali.* Agricultural farms were to be started, in order, first to supplement the income of the temples, and secondly, to throw dust into the eyes of the police. Arms and ammunition were to be collected and stored therein, so that in case war broke out against the English, these temples might serve as so many impregnable forts. A book was also published under the title *Bhawani Mandir* 'The Temple of Bhawani', wherein it was sought to foreshadow these ideas. It was from this time that pamphlets and booklets breathing hatred towards the English began to be published and sent by post to schools, colleges, bar libraries, etc.

A little while after, some lands were taken at 'Phulkushama' or 'Chhenda-Pathar', somewhere between Bankura and Midnapore, with a view to establishing a temple of *Bhawani* there. A few boys too were sent there to cultivate the lands, but as they had to struggle with insurmountable difficulties for their bare living they were, one by one, forced to leave the place and no more similar attempt was made hereafter.

By this time Aurobindo Babu had seriously taken to the study of the *Chandi*, perhaps because in his opinion the slaying of the *Asuras* as depicted in the *Chandi* might be likened to the murder of Englishmen. But soon after he gave up *Chandi* and took to the *Gita*.*

By this time Barin had come back to Bengal and was trying hard to revive the old secret societies. His chief aim at this time was to start an organ of the party. A house was rented in Champatola, and a weekly the famous *Yugantar* was published from this place. The first set of writers in the *Yugantar* were no experts, and their writings had to be touched and retouched by Debabrata Babu, Sakharam Babu, Bhupen Babu and others.[4] The first two, however, were themselves clever writers.

The articles advocating revolution soon succeeded in catching the popular fancy and thereby contributed to the numerical strength of the party inducing fresh recruits to join it. The aim of the *Yugantar* was more to excite hatred against the English than to inculcate love of the country. It was first published either in March or April 1906. By this time most of the other secret societies in the country had more or less joined Aurobindo Babu's party, but before a year was out, Barin's excessive love of power and hauteur soon succeeded in annoying and scaring away most of these leaders. The *Yugantar*, however, became very popular and began to bring in a decent income, but soon changed hands. It was taken over by a group experienced in business matters.

It was in the *Yugantar* office that meetings of secret societies used to be held. The ground floor of the office was occupied by the press. There was a wooden safe in one of the small rooms on the upper storey which was believed to contain arms. A very young boy, hardly out of his teens, was placed in charge of the room. Once I went there to buy a revolver and was shown one of an old pattern. I offered to buy three or four such, but they could not supply me with them at that time. I deposited the price thereof, but after a few months got, one, and one only. It was here in this *Yugantar* office that I first made the acquaintance of Naren Gossain.

Annotations :

1. Charu Chandra Datta, ICS, a friend of Aurobindo and posted in Bengal Presidency.
2. 'Action' means murder of English officials and looting of Government money.
3. It will be found from the confession of Narendra Gossain that Debabrata used to write the editorial column for the *Yugantar*, and that Bhupendra Nath Datta was the Manager and Debabrata Basu and Barindra Ghose were the leaders, but as Narendra Gossain was murdered prior to the trial, his confession was useless, and the Sessions Judge of Alipore did not think the finding of seditious literature, viz., 'Bhawani Mandir', 'Mukti-kon Pathe' etc., in the house, sufficient to show conclusively that Debabrata was a member of the conspiracy. Barindra K. Ghose's complicity was however firmly established from his own statement, which runs as follows : "I then returned to Bengal, convinced that a purely political propaganda would not do for the country, and that people must be trained us spiritually to face dangers. By that time the *Swadeshi* and boycott agitation had begun. With my friends Abinash Bhattacharji and Bhupendra Nath Datta I started the *Yugantar*. We managed it for nearly 1½ years and then gave it over to the present managers, and I took again to recruiting. I collected together 14 or 15 young men from about the beginning of 1907 till now (1908). I educated the boys in religious books and politics. We are always thinking of a far off revolution and wish to be ready for it, so we were collecting weapons in small quantities. I have collected 11 revolvers, 4 rifles and 1 gun."

It will also appear from page 21 of Mr. Beachcroft's judgement in the Alipore bomb case that Barindra Kumar Ghose's complicity has been correctly estimated. It is as follows : "The passages which I have quoted from the *Yugantar* exhibit a burning hatred of the British race, they breathe revolution in every line, they point out how revolution is to be effected, no calumny and no artifice is left out, which is likely to instil the people of the country with the same idea or to catch the impressionable minds of youths, etc."

4. Bhupendra Datta (now Dr.), brother of Swami Vivekanda.

Editorial Note :

* Prosecution of a boy of 16 years for sedition was ridiculous. So the case was withdrawn.

Chapter VIII
Kshudiram

An agricultural industry exhibition was held at Midnapore in February, 1906, when a pamphlet entitled '*Sonar Bangla*' containing abuses and words of racial hatred was circulated. Its English version was published in the *Pioneer* creating a stirr in the European community. Satyendra printed one thousand copies in Bengali and when Kshudiram was distributing them near the gate of the exhibition, he was arrested by a head constable. Satyen intervened to get Kshudiram released by calling him a deputy's son. The policeman released Kshudiram, but before that Kshudiram gave a blow on his nose and absconded. Satyen was a clerk in the collectorate and as such he was asked to explain his conduct. The authority dismissed him for his discourtious manner. A case of sedition was registered against Kshudiram the first of a series of cases of sedition against the revolutionaries in Bengal.

After evading arrest for sometime, Kshudiram surrendered before the court. Before surrender the seriousness of the charge U/S 12L and 124 IPC, and the implications of the sections were explained to him, and was warned of torture in police custody for confession and long years of imprisonment. Kshuduram was fearless and undaunted. We had no hesitation to trust him. After

---

Basumati, Bhadra 1331 B.S. August-September 1920

surrender he did not disclose anything in spite of much effort by the police. The case was committed to the Court of Sessions. A number of pleaders and barristers stood to defend him in the court on compassionate grounds. But eventually the case was withdrawn for unknown reasons. *

A little introduction of Kshudiram is necessary here. A few months before the aforesaid incident I first came to know Kshudiram. One evening I was passing through a lonely street in Midnapur, when one of several boys sitting a few yards away from the roadside came running towards me and said straightway that he wanted a revolver. He was Kshudiram, aged about 14 years, but looked only 12 or 13. He looked small and thin, but gave the impression of being strong and firm.

I was annoyed at the thought that since the boy had the knowledge of our having revolvers, many more people must be knowing about it. I scolded him for such unusual request. Undaunted, he repeated his request with so much candour and earnestness that I was compelled to ask him as to what he would do with the revolver. His frank reply was that he would kill a *sahib*. With considerable excitement he said that he would take revenge for unjust oppression over India. I was excited seeing his attitude and determination; but keeping a stern face I had to tell him that I had no revolver.

Soon I came to know all about Kshudiram from Satyen. Since then through small tasks which I asked him to perform I observed some of his uncommon traits of character. One of them was, he could not tolerate any unjust oppression not only on himself, but on others too. This quality is lacking among the Hindus. Instead of punishing the oppressor, or when unable to do so personally, at least to hate and despise him, we pretend to show forgiveness and compassion for him, taking the plea that such compassion and forgiveness are characteristics of Hindu religion. Thus we glorify the self-deception.

Again, depending on the quantum of oppression either we supplicate before the oppressor or remain totally inactive out of fear, except occasionally expressing verbal sympathy for the oppressed. We have never been taught by our ancient grand mother that we have some responsibility in such situations. But one who forgives an oppressor instead of trying to punish him, may be regarded as God, but actually he is devoid of humanity and is not really a human being. A society which does not resist oppression either by its own members or by outsiders, is dead. The leaders, either political or of the society, who act and advice against the most natural human reaction to oppression, are, in fact, enemies of the people. Lest Jesus Christ should be regarded as enemy of the people for his preaching of forgiveness for all oppressors, Christ's followers ignore this lesson all over the world.

Any way, good or bad whatever, it may be, there was no compassion and forgiveness in Kshudiram's character. He was proud of being a Hindu, yet, as an exception, he was an embodiment of revenge in Hindu Society. *

Kshudiram grew up in the family of his relatives as he lost his parents in his childhood. The property that he inherited was just sufficient to pay off his father's debt and to give his youngest sister in marriage. Thereafter as it happens in majority of similar situations, Kshudiram was brought up in relations' house when he was made to work as a servant with accompanying harassment and insult. Even that was not enough; he had to give some property to the relatives in whose house he used to live. Kshudiram, instead of putting up with such insult with gratitude, he rebelled against it and his rebellion was variously described as boisterousness, unmannerly, disobedient, haughty, naughty etc. Consequently he was often harassed, oppressed, abused and beaten up. But his relatives cannot be blamed for that; our society in responsible for it. There is, however, no doubt that because Kshudiram was brought up in such a social ambience that he became a rebel. One hates the wrong doer as much as he sympathises with the oppressed. Same was in case with Kshudiram.

A woman who was forced to be somewhat wayward because of torture in the family was living for long in a house close to the house of Kshudiram's elder sister's husband. As the woman was a regular visitor to the house of Kshudiram's sister, she witnessed the humiliation and torture that the young boy used to suffer. Overwhelmed by the sympathy for the boy he would often call him to her house and would feed him with kindness and sympathy. This intimacy with a 'fallen woman' gave rise to suspicion about the moral character of Kshudiram. It is a matter of great regret that the writer was also one of those who blamed Kshudiram for the undesirable intimacy. But none of the family of Kshudiram's sister had ever thought of any illicit relationship. We, however, made many enquiries to disabuse our minds about Kshudiram's character. The cruel treatment that he used to receive in the family and the society in which he grew up made him a rebel and so it was natural for him to ignore the prevailing social norms and popular views is such matters. Despite the environment in which he grew up he had no meanness in his character, and he was impervious to either public acclaim or public criticism for his deeds.

He used to do daring acts spontaneously without caring for danger or even death. Since extra ordinary courage becomes meaningful if two other associated qualities accompany such courage. Kshudiram's *guru* Satyen had the ability to decide on the correct course of action in a critical situation; it does not appear Kshudiram had that quality. But the other quality, that is the tenacity of purpose, Kshudiram had in abundance. Once he had resolved to do something, nothing, not even death could deter him from doing that. During a game of *Kabadi* short and slim Kshudiram ignoring the chances of being badly hurt, would catch a much bigger and stronger opponent and would never let him go. In that tender age he would jump from the roof of a house or take a plunge into the strong current of the river without caring for consequences.

Kshudiram was not a great man or an angel. He was one of many thousand Bengali youths. He had many failings too. Kshudiram is the embodiment of courage and determination to fight against injustice, torture and oppression without caring for consequences; and that Kshudiram survives even beyond his martyrdom.

Annotations :

1. The incident is true. On 21st February 1906, an exhibition was held at the old Midnapore Jail, and it lasted for 6 days. The local student community objected against the opening of the exhibition on the ground of their being in a state of mourning for the partition of Bengal. On 26th and 27th February seditious leaflets were distributed at the gate. On receipt of sanction of the Government, the Superintendent of Police, Midnapore, filed a complaint under sections 124A and 505, Indian Penal Code. The case was withdrawn under the order of the Government of Bengal on 20th April 1906.

Chapter IX
The First Attempt at Revolutionary Murder

After the partition of Bengal, Sir Bampfylde Fuller became Lieutenant-Governor of Eastern Bengal. He used to be annoyed if people failed to do him obeisance wherever they met him. In certain districts it became punishable to utter *Bande Mataram*, while in others students were prohibited from joining in any political agitation. In connection with such minor matters various oppressive measures were enforced in Assam and in Eastern Bengal.

In the memorable incident, which occurred during the Barisal Conference in April 1906, Sir Surendra Nath was arrested while other leaders and delegates, such as Messrs. Bipin Chandra Pal, Bhupendra Nath Bose, Upadhyaya, Kabyavisarad etc, were beaten or threatened to be beaten. Many had even to scale walls and seek shelter in gutters to save their lives. Further, a punitive police force was billeted there for a long time with the result that immediately after this even many respectable Moderates came to believe in the revolutionary cult.

For these reasons Sri Bampfylde Fuller incurred the serious displeasure of many people; several respectable

---

Basumati, Pous, 1331 BS; December 1924-January 1925
Chaitra, 1331 BS; March-April 1926

persons even promised a reward of a few thousand rupees to anybody who might kill him. Barin was not the man to let this opportunity slip. A certain person had paid him a thousand rupees in cash as earnest money for this purpose.

Rumour has it, that there was a Bengali head craftsman in the arms and ammunition factory of the Maharaja of Nepal. Barin used to say that he had learnt all his art by enlisting him in his party. The truth is that Barin succeeded with the help of a college student of chemistry in preparing an explosive from chlorate of potash, and this he poured into two big hollow iron balls, and gave out that they were bombs! If urgently required, he used to take out a little powder from these balls and hold a lighted match to it, whereupon, the powder used to explode; seeing this and hearing his bombastic talk, rich people used to think that the end of the British was near at hand. Anyway, there was a stipulation that Barin would have to refund the one thousand rupees if he failed to murder the Lieutenant-Governor.

After receiving the money, Barin started for Shillong with two revolvers and the so-called bombs for reconnoitring purposes. It was arranged that a person who would execute the murder would be despatched from Calcutta on receiving his wire.

At that time leaders and pseudo-leaders were in abundance, but business-like men were wanting. It used to be said that there were big centres of the secret society not only in various places in Bengal but also in Bombay, the Central Provinces, Orissa, Bihar and Madras. Afterwards it transpired that nowhere except in Bombay was there anything worthy of being mentioned. Whereever the authorities found traces of one or two persons having sympathy with the revolutionaries, they would presume that the place was a big centre.

At first a revolutionary consented to go to Shillong from Midnapore, but as he failed to go there for certain reasons, the name of Kshudiram was suggested. For some reason—it may be either for his connection with a fallen woman or his tender age—the opinion was against sending him. After that another member of the Midnapore Committee consented to go, and it was then decided that he would have to go to Shillong on receipt of Barin's wire.

Being a man with a family, he had taken long leave from his service to employ himself fully in revolutionary work.* At this time, owing to his son's illness, he had to stay in Calcutta with his family for a long time, and hence he used to frequent the committee of the leaders where the conspiracy to murder Sir Bampfylde was being hatched. As a result of this he was selected for executing the murder of Sir Bampfyldde, and so he took his family to his country home and left them there. After waiting for four days a wire came from Shillong to send him.

He started that very day for Goalundo by the evening train. It was perhaps in the first week of May 1906. He had taken with him two revolvers, a European costume and one or two articles necessary for the journey. Babu Bhupendra Nath Datta went to Sealdah Station to see him off. Immediately before the train started Bhupen Babu made a very strange request to that pilgrim on the path to death. He made the latter promise that he would let him know if there was anything beyond death. The promise has not yet been fulfilled because the man is still alive.

It took him another five days to reach Shillong. He was certain that within 24 hours after his arrival at Shillong, he would either have to die or become a culprit awaiting the gallows. Barin would get everything ready. He would show the place to the appointed man, tell him the time, acquaint him how to identify the Lieutenant-Governor, and hand him over the bomb. The Lieutenant-Governor would be visible after an hour at the most, and then bang! The thought that he after the murder was committed would perhaps be shot dead by his pursuers or be condemned to be hanged from the gallows, recurred to him again and again. Bhupen Babu's strange request in connection with a life after death gave a new direction to his thoughts, and he was determined that if there were anything beyond death, he must be a martyr there also.

On the day following he arrived at Goalundo and took up his residence in a hotel. The curries here being highly spiced, he wanted plainly cooked food, and was bluntly told by the hotel keeper that there was no use of his coming to Eastern Bengal if he was unable to take spiced food. This served him as an eye-opener, for he thought that if he would not put up with this inconvenience, how was he to accomplish the serious task he had undertaken? So he hastily swallowed his food and boarded the steamer for Gauhati. He did not get any companion to talk to, nor did he have inclination for conversation. In the evening he was attacked with blood dysentery, but began to feel better after taking a few doses of chlorodyne.

The would-be assassin had no faith in a life hereafter, but owing to the thought that he was to die very soon, he could not resist the temptation of believing that there was such a life. Nevertheless the desire to live made him afraid of death. The work of the revolutionaries is fraught with very serious dangers such as imprisonment, banishment and death. So when danger becomes imminent, they show a natural tendency to save their lives, but as that entails serious disrepute amongst the people, they try to resort to such a course as would heighten their reputation instead of destroying it. The best way to do so is to turn metaphysical. But our man disliked hypocrisy and was determined never again to turn his thoughts to matters of life beyond death.

At this juncture he remembered the text of the *Gita* which enjoins people to do their duty heedless of consequences. But he presently understood that the maxim only held good in theory and not in practice, and that people worked only to make a name for themselves.

After this his thoughts turned to another direction, viz., that if he succeeded in assassinating Sir Bampfylde Fuller, he would be able to create a sensation throughout the world. He remembered that he had already made such arrangements as would prevent the police from identifying him if he were arrested in connection with the murder. Was he then to make such confession to them as would give a wide circulation to his name? That might bring his relatives to harm and give a death-blow to secret societies. There were two sides of the question. His action might injure some, but there was at the same time the possibility that his example would inspire others to perform nobler deeds. His views were, however, changed shortly, and he felt convinced that it was on the maintenance of strict secrecy that the success of the revolutionary societies and the achievement of the freedom of the country rested. At last he made up his mind to assassinate Sir Bampfylde Fuller, but regretted that he had not taken an adequate farewell from his relatives.

On the morning of the sixth day his steamer arrived at Gauhati. His bowel complaint having partially subsided in the meantime, he took a hearty meal and started for Shillong at 9 a.m. The beautiful natural scenery of the place delighted him very much, and while he was thus engaged in admiring the landscape and thinking of spiritual matters, he recognised the face of Barin in the *tonga* which was coming from the opposite direction. He asked Barin the reason of his return, and was told that the attempt should be made from Gauhati and not from Shillong, and was informed that he must also retrace his steps to the former place. This reduced him to a state of hopeless perplexity. A strong desire to live and an apathy for murders again took possession of his mind, and being a Bengali and consequently of a non-violent disposition he perceived that it would be most difficult for him to execute the assassination of the Lieutenant-Governor as days passed by and the excitement wore away.

The man appointed to murder[2] the Lieutenant-Governor arrived at Shillong the same afternoon. He met the man described by Barin after a little enquiry who received him so eagerly and with such friendliness that his first impression was that he might be a spy. In the course of conversation it came out that the latter knew all about his object of coming to Shillong.

He went with him to another gentleman's place, where several others joined them. They told him all about Barin's doings there. Sir Bampfylde Fuller was in the habit of riding out every day. There was a point of vantage in the road taken by him from where a bomb could be thrown on him and the murderer might make good his escape without being espied by anybody. But one day while Barin and his companion were cleaning a loaded revolver, it went off accidentally, the bullet piercing the palm of the companion. He had to be sent to the hospital and the incident became known. Nobody of the place, where Barin and his companion had put up, knew anything about the conspiracy, and as the incident was regarded as quite suspicious, they had to leave. Sir Bampfylde Fuller also left for Gauhati at the same time. Barin was compelled to come to Gauhati for these reasons.

The abovementioned gentlemen of Shillong had heard about the horripilating activities of the revolutionary secret society from Barin, but they wanted to learn more from the aforesaid murderer. He had, at first, some suspicion of these people, and besides he was resolved not to divulge any fact about the secret society, but he could not keep his resolve up to the last. To maintain the secrecy of counsels according to the rule of the secret society, he ought to have declared as false all that those gentlemen of Shillong had heard from Barin. Though he did not speak out anything personally and on that account congratulated himself on obeying the rule of the secret society, he gave them to understand by means of gestures and hints that what they had heard was quite little in comparison to what had happened. This circumstance raised a doubt in his mind abort the correctness of his estimate of Barin as a first class revolutionary worker. He felt a doubt whether it was proper to take so many people into confidence with regard to such a serious conspiracy as that of murdering the Lieutenant-Governor. He argued, however, that this step was necessary in order to secure the help of the local people without which the perpetration of a murder of this nature was not possible. It was, moreover, an easy way of pushing revolutionary propaganda and of securing the sympathy and regard of the people to the revolutionaries. At a subsequent period he gained this experience that by divulging conspiracies of this nature, it was easy to secure immediate regard and sympathy of the people with the effect that ultimately this, instead of the perpetration of a revolutionary murder or the fulfilment of any glorious undertaking, becomes the main objective of the revolutionaries.

He returned to Gauhati the next evening. He had been accorded such a reception at Shillong before carrying out his mission of murdering the Lieutenant-Governor that his ambition of achieving lasting fame by performing the deed had considerably weakened.

At Gauhati also he found that the secret had been divulged by Barin to many men. There, too, a little powder was taken out of a bomb, and it was put to fire to show how it exploded with a hissing noise. The same cordial reception was given him there as at Shillong. He got his first opportunity here of coming into close contact with and knowing Barin during his four or five days' stay with him.

By trying to make a few modifications in the plan of murdering the Lieutenant-Governor, he discovered that Barin was not a man to tolerate any such thing, although he himself lacked in energy to take action on any plan already decided upon by him. His general plan was that the bomb should be placed on the path frequented by the Lieutenant-Governor in such a way as to burst when coming into contact with him, while they might hear from a safe hiding place that he had been killed by means of their bomb. For this purpose a two-hundred cubit long fuse was required. During the time the fuse would burn and the fire reach the bomb they might escape to a safe distance.

A gentleman was listening to the discussion of such plans. He went away in silence and came back with a heap of things which we never expected to be able to procure. He was not given to much talking. Whenever he heard that anything was wanted during such discussions, he procured it, however, rare it might be. It was through his help that we were able to maintain our prestige up to the last.

Barin was prevailed upon to make an experiment with the bomb and a few other things and to go for that purpose to a distant part of the neighbouring jungles, so that the police at the town might not hear the explosion of the bomb. The party had to go to a distance of five to six miles, but after the party had proceeded two miles, somebody said that herds of wild elephants often came out in those jungles. It was held to be unwise to risk death by being trampled down by elephants, and the party returned after expressing their regrets.

Other plans were subsequently taken into consideration. From all this Barin's companion came to realise that the murder of the Lieutenant-Governor was not the main object of Barin, his main object, was revolutionary propaganda and self-advertisement along with it. The propaganda was carried on in something like this style: They have come to murder Lieutenant-Governor Fuller; they have bombs, revolvers and many more things with them; there are many big men in their party and many terrible things have been done by them; the people ought to understand from all this and after reading the *Yugantar* edited by them that they are not ordinary men and so to offer them homage and become their disciples, etc.

He could foresee that there was very little chance of carrying out the plan of murdering the Lieutenant-Governor. But to protest against Barin was to make it impossible to carry on with him.

After three or four days Barin and his party came to know that the tour programme of the Lieutenant-Governor which was made known to the public was not generally acted upon. It might be guessed from this that the Lieutenant-Governor had some suspicion that there might-be an attempt to murder him. In any event, they saw from the information they received about the secret tour programme that they might catch him at Barisal. So they started for Barisal and, on alighting from the steamer, saw that the Lieutenant-Governor's special steamer *Brahmakundu* was lying at anchor and police constables were lined up on both sides of the road leading from the steamer ghat. There were also large numbers of people waiting for interview with him. At the end of reception ceremonies on board the steamer he entered Barisal. The intending murderers looked on with regret as the Lieutenant-Governor went out of their reach.

Expressing their sorrows for missing such a fine opportunity, they went to the town with two bags containing revolvers and other articles and, failing to find a suitable safe private room in any hotel, went to the house of a *Swdeshi* leader who welcomed them when he heard who they were.

Barin had come to Barisal with the hope that he would find there. a big secret society, or that he would be able to organise one quite easily. The reason was that the insult on all the big leaders of Bengal at that time at the Provincial Conference at Barisal had been witnessed by the local students and they had also suffered more than others from the oppression of the punitive police. After the Barisal incident, the people could not but show new sympathy to the revolutionary work and, in fact, the mention of it in the course of propaganda for getting recruits for revolutionary work was an infallible weapon for the attainment of the object. Barin was afraid on this account that Barisal might finally take the lead in revolutionary work, He mingled with the crowds at the meetings to discover what was the underlying motive of these. When after a week he saw that there was no revolutionary spirit anywhere, he commenced propaganda in his usual style. It made such impression on the audience that they were for the time being inspired by the revolutionary ideal.

There was at the time a man at Barisal who commanded the undivided allegiance of the local students. It was decided to win him over, and for that purpose Barin and his party went to his house with their bags and showed him the bombs, etc., and employed their usual propagandist method. But this produced the reverse of the desired effects.

Sir Bampfylde Fuller safely departed from Barisal a day or two later. Barin's party stayed there for some time longer on the pretext of taking steps to murder the Europeans (Messrs. Kemp and Emerson, the DM and SP respectively) responsible for the Barisal outrage. For the purpose of getting information about the residence, the club and the whereabouts of these Europeans a few men had been acquainted of their plan, and in this way it became known that they were trying to commit some murders. Learning this news probably from the abovementioned leader of the students, the leader of Barisal had issued his prohibition order against the revolutionary movement. But encouraged by the response from the young men Barin and his friend went to him to persuade him over to their side. On the subject of the necessity of secret societies, he like the other Bengali leaders, at once replied that he had neither the strength nor the desire to follow a new course in lieu of the one adopted by him.

That very day he played such a trick about handing Barin and his friend over to the police, that they hurriedly got off from the place the next morning.

There was not a single revolver with any man at Barisal. The party left a superior quality revolver with the abovementioned leader of the students, hoping that it might be utilised at some moment of excitement, if any opportunity came to them. They received their due punishment a few days later when the said leader bravely endured the harassment by the police and earned the respect of the students, by sending a letter to the press and informing the Magistrate about it.

During the conference at Barisal a boy did not stop crying *Bande Mataram* in spite of incessant beating with *lathis* by the police, and even when he fell into a tank near by, he continued the *slogan* under showers of blows. A crowd had gathered around the place and were silently watching feeling proud of the boy's heroism. Every Bengali admired him and felt proud of him for being a Bengali when he read about this incident in the Indian newspapers.

From the incidents mentioned above, it will appear that the creed of non-violence is not something new in Bengal. This spirit is ingrained in the Bengali character and is a matter of pride to him. It is for this reason that the Bengalis cannot persuade themselves to enlist in the army and sufficient recruits cannot be found even for the University Corps, although there are no immediate prospects of bloodshed in this case.

Barin's party started again for Gauhati, stopping for a day at Chandpur on the way. At Gauhati they came to know that the Lieutenant-Governor would stop at Rangpur. After two or three days they started for Rangpur. No place to stay in the town. The *Swadeshi* agitation was running high there and a secret society had also been formed. Lathi-play-fencing, wrestling, running, target-practice with air-guns were carried on. A few gentlemen had devoted themselves to these things whole-heartedly with a number of young workers.

The society at Rangpur had become impatient like the Midnapore society at the 'excessive interference' of the central society at Calcutta. Inexperienced boys or young men came down from Calcutta, told that they were inspectors or propagandists sent by the central society, and asserted themselves oppressively over experienced local leaders and tried to get money. Some of the old gentlemen at Rangpur were severely displeased with the Calcutta leaders. They gave a lecture to Barin on this subject. He could not give battle to so many men at the same time, nor could he get any opportunity to use his usual tactics. He informed them finally that if a particular gentleman from among them was sent to him, he might tell him the grave reason for their coming to Rangpur and also how the local leaders might help them. They sent one gentleman, and the conversations began in the old style in the evening on the bank of a lonely tank, the requisite paraphernalia of the two bags containing bombs and revolvers being ready at hand. The experiment with gun-powder taken out of a bomb was made, and it was described how the attempt on the life of the Lieutenant-Governor had miscarried for a revolver accident, and how they had come to Ranger on the same mission. The gentleman was highly delighted with all this, and excellent arrangements were at once made for our lodging and boarding. The local leaders agreed to give all assistance they could. After this, plans were made to carry out the mission.

It was decided to place some bombs under the rail line attaching thereto some electric dry cells, so that as soon as the train came on that line the bombs would explode blowing up the train. The companion of Barin was sent .to Calcutta to buy dry cells. He laid bare the plan to Aurobindo Babu and asked for money. He handed over to him Rs. 25 which was all he had at the time. The companion bought three or four dry cells, some insulated wire, a wrench and a boring instrument and went hack the same day to Rangpur.

Aurobindo Babu had been written to for more money. As he could not get any more money, he sent Naren Gossain to Rangpur to procure money by means of dacoity.

Naren Gossain was taken to be the cleverest man in committing dacoity. The financial condition of our secret society, particularly of our headquarters, can be guessed from this fact.

An experiment had been made as to how a bomb bursts automatically under the rail line by means of the electric battery. A man was sent to Dhubri to wire as soon as the

Lieutenant-Governor started for Rangpur by special train. It was planned that on receipt of that wire, a bomb attached to an electric battery would be placed under the rail line one mile up the station an hour before the time when the train was due. It was further planned, in case the bomb did not burst, to post this companion of Barin and Prafulla Chaki of the Muzaffarpur bomb-case fame, a mile down the station with red lanterns in their hands. The Lieutenant-Governor's special train would stop at the signal and they would *get* into his compartment and open fire on him.

The latter plan was not taken seriously into consideration perhaps there was in it a greater chance of success and equally greater risk of being hanged if caught. The question of murdering the Lieutenant-Governor became, as time passed, a secondary matter while propaganda and self-advertisement were the first concerns.

After the plan had been laid down, arrangements for dacoity were made, as still there was some delay in the coming of the Lieutenant-Governor.

Annotations :

1. This fact is substantiated in Mr. Daly's "Note on the growth of the revolutionary movement of Bengal", paragraph 5, where it is said that the trouble in Barisal in 1906 was the result of a deliberate effort on the part of the agitators led by Mr. S.N. Banarji to defy the executive authority. One or two young men received blows from the police, out of which enormous capital was made in the press and by public speakers, and it became the fashion to swear by the blood split at Barisal to serve one's country with one's life, if necessary.
2. No mention is made in any official report of the several unsuccessful arrangements made by Barindra Kumar Ghose and his companion to murder the Lieutenant-Governor of Eastern Bengal at the various places mentioned in this chapter.

Editorial Note :

* In this chapter Hem Chandra has mentioned himself in the third person as Barin's companion. In the published book one paragraph was added by the author, in which Barin was called Don-Quixote and Hem Chandra as Sancho Panja. Although he has tried to redicule Barin and his plans by calling him Don-Quixote, he, at the same time, wrote, "he was charmed by many unexceptional qualities of Barin."

Chapter X

The First Attempt at Revolutionary Dacoity

The first attempt at *Swadeshi* dacoity was made in Rangpur. Plans to this effect had been made before, but no attempt had hitherto been made to put them into action. Dacoity was the most important among the means adopted at the beginning of the organisation of secret societies to collect funds. This plan was borrowed from the novels of Bankim Babu like many other things, and an emphatic sanction to it was derived from a similar procedure alleged to be adopted by the Russian revolutionaries.

Nobody enquired whether the Russian procedure had any speciality. At first our plan was to seize the money of Government or the railway companies or foreign merchants. We did not take into consideration the fact that the money of Government was but the money of the people. Some among us encouraged even the idea of note-forgery, but I am not aware that it was ever tried.

Consultation were held with Rangpur leaders about the selection of victims. Jute-traders who moved about with large sums of money, the railway station, post office and some wealthy local men were passed in review, but none of these was considered to be safe. Finally an information

---

Basumati, Jaistha, 1332 BS; May-June 1925

reached the party about a widow living some twelve to thirteen miles away from the town who had a thousand rupees in cash and no male relation to help her. Arrangements were made to commit this non-violent dacoity, and the help of some local young men and a professional dacoit was secured for the purpose.

The present writer felt many a scruple to take part in such a ridiculous and ignoble business, namely, stealing of a paltry amount from a helpless widow. Experience showed that ultimately many educated *bhadralogs* committed ordinary dacoit in the name of *Swadeshi* dacoities, and indeed much of the money secured by dacoities committed by genuine revolutionaries, is also known to have been despicably misused. Anyway, his objections were overridden, and he was compelled to join the party by Barin who threatened him with denunciation as a backslider in case of refusal.

The party was divided into two batches — one led by the writer and the other by Naren, and the two batches started after 9 P.M. for the destination at short intervals. Barin remained at quarter, claiming the right of the commander.

The batch under the writer arrived at 11 P.M. at the appointed place, but did not find Naren and his men who should have arrived before. After searching for an hour, they were found, but news came from the local informer that the police Sub-Inspector was present at the village with his party on some local investigation.

So they had to turn back and were glad to do so. They returned to the town and related the matter to Barin who expressed that he was satisfied that an honest attempt had been made.

After a few days, another plan was made. But the writer was anxious to get away. Barin might have been equally anxious to get rid of him, and probably this was why he allowed him to go to Goalundo along with Prafulla Chaki to make a fresh attempt on the life of the Lieutenant-Governor who had started for the same place on board his steamer *Brahma Kundu* from Guahati.

Annotations :

1. About this incident, Narendra Gossain made the following statement before Mr. Birley, before he was murdered : "Arabinda Ghose told me that I should have to go to Rangpur to loot a widow's money. He gave me Rs. 12 and some cartridges. I was to go to the house of Ishan Chandra Chakrabartti at Rangpur, where the other people would be present. I had a revolver, which Abinash had given to me. I went to the house of Ishan, where I found Barindra Ghose, Hem Das and others. All started for the place armed with revolvers, except Barindra Ghose, who stayed at the *cutcherry*. We arrived at 9 p.m. One said that the Sub-Inspector of Police had been to the village that day in the morning, and that therefore we oculd not loot that day and returned to Rangpur".

Chapter XI
Second Attempt to Kill the Governor

The train started from Rangpur, and on the next morning halted at some station without proceeding up to Goalundo. I heard that Goalundo was under water owing to a heavy flood. I ascertained that the proposed reception to the Lieutenant-Governor was postponed on account of the flood, and that he was going to Calcutta by a Special. I and my companion bought tickets for Calcutta and reached Naihati at 6 P.m. We saw that the station platform was packed with constables and learned on enquiry that the Lieutenant-Governor's Special was shortly due. Our plan was to reach Sealdah before the arrival of the Special, to wait there and use our revolvers when the Lieutenant-Governor would alight from the train. From the precautionary arrangemnets at Naihati we could easily conclude that at Calcutta these arrangements were not likely to be less elaborate, so both, Prafulla and I decided to get down at Naihati and make the attempt then and there.

The police were dispersing the crowd from the platform. A few school-boys were waiting outside the fencing; nevertheless the police searched their persons. So we feigned to be frightened by the sight of the police, and without going out by the platform entrance, followed the railway line south to the platform and sat down at some

Basumati, Aswin, 1332 BS; September-October 1925

distance. We thought that when the Special would go along the line in front of us, it would, of course, move at slow pace, and taking advantage of it, we would climb into the Lieutenant-Governor's compartment and open fire on him. With this plan in our head, we took out a revolver each from our pockets and waited.

After some time the Special arrived and lights were switched on in the Lieutenant-Governor's compartment. We were attentively looking at the compartment and were rehearsing the whole scene in our minds, how we would jump into it and fire away without being overcome by nerves in the least. The only reason why the police did not take any notice of us was perhaps the ignorance of the police of that time of such matters. From our appearances the police undoubtedly took us to be slow-witted rustics, because we had no shoes on, our dress was dirty and shabby, we had no shave and wash for many days and above all want of regular diet, and terrible anxiety and oppressive thought had made frightful scarecrows of us, whom none but experts could suspect of harbouring any dangerous plan. But two years after this incident, the police had grown wiser, for, Sub-Inspector Nandalal arrested Prafulla, suspecting him because of his strange appearance.

While we were thus contemplating, the starting bell rang out and the Special steamed away before our eyes to the same direction from which it had come. We were taken by surprise. We learned later that the Lieutenant-Governor would cross the Hooghly Bridge to catch the Bombay Mail. Prafulla broke down as soon as he got the information, I, too, was not in a better condition. However, we went to Calcutta and told the whole story to Aurobindo Babu. He listened to it calmly and told us to go home.

During nearly two years after it, numerous such 'honest attempts' at action were made and all of them failed. Why?

The reason is that the kind of war in which a man derives satisfaction from slaying a man has been almost unknown in this country for many years. We are not accustomed to hear that any member of the society amidst which we live has killed a man in war or even taken part in any fighting. We do not conceive such a situation in our minds nor do we feel encouraged to conceive it. In our country even males, not to speak of females, shudder at the mention of war, which they consider to be nothing better than an homicidal affair. We are all spiritual beings, and the men and women of any other country do not compare with us in that respect. We cannot, therefore, with our spiritual excellence, approve of war which entails destruction of human life.

For generations in the past the cult of non-violence has so profoundly taken hold of us that among the Hindus to shudder at the sight of killing or even the report of killing an animal for the purpose of food, has come to be regarded as a significant indication of pious mindedness.

So it is easily to be guessed how terrible a matter it is for a Bengali Hindu, brought up amidst such non-violent and spiritual atmosphere, to kill a man without provocation. I do not say that the Bengalis do not commit homicide in any way. It is to be noticed, however, that the majority of the Bengali criminals convicted of this crime, kill women. In any case murder committed on sudden provocation is quite a different thing from revolutionary murder. No doubt revolutionary murders have taken place in Bengal, but their number is insignificant in comparison with the number of failures. The public do not know to what extent mental weakness was responsible for it. In Bengal, of all countries, the strength of mind required for unavoidable murder for the welfare of humanity or of the country is most lacking. This want of the requisite frame of mind led to nervous breakdown when sufficient power of self-control was lacking among the revolutionaries undertaking murder for a revolutionary purpose. I believe a different atmosphere has got to be created, and training for generations in that new atmosphere has to be undergone in order to enable the Bengalis to overcome such weakness. We accuse the English of having neglected to give us training for *swaraj* during 150 years, but it is the English who have made whatever little attempt there has been made to lift this curse from us by forming a Bengali regiment. The Bengalis, in particular, ignore entirely the importance of the power of self-defence to national self-existence, and it has become our aim to show the world a new way of achieving the same purpose by the application of soul-force.

This aspect of the problem was neglected by us at that time, and being persuaded that we must fight, *we* adopted the method of secret organisation which was the usual method. We firmly believe that if we could work for five or six years in that method, the war for independence in India would break out automatically. Neither we nor our leaders recognised that it was necessary to receive training in foreign revolutionary methods for the purpose.

I entertained a desperately ambitious scheme in my mind two years before this. It was to go either to America or to Italy to learn the art of war thoroughly like our legendary Suresh Biswas or like Garibaldi, and then to return with all materials of the prospective war and cause veritable rivers of blood to flow in the country. The plan, in short, was to organise an Indian legion with Indians abroad and to sail for India with a fleet of war-vessels loaded with the best materials of war, displaying national colours, to occupy the Ghoramara Island and to declare suddenly the war of independence to the noise of grapeshots. The more I participated in the activities of the secret societies, the more I was disillusioned about our leaders, about their ability to make India free, and at last I came to doubt whether they had any real capacity for organising secret societies. My ambition, too, had died with my increasing experience. I believed even a year previously that the revolutionary secret societies in Maharashtra were doing solid work, but subsequently I was convinced that these activities were only make-believe.

I had heard that there was a vast organisation of secret societies in Russia with ramifications in other European countries. My decision to go to America was taken, because I thought that it was impossible to become a member of any such society after learning the language of the countries in which the society was located.

Some of my relatives volunteered pecuniary assistance which I refused, considering that though they were ignorant of my mission, if I was arrested, they might be subjected to harassment. Subsequently, a part of my apprehension proved to be true.

Towards the end of July 1906 I booked my passage for Marseilles. My plan *was* to proceed to Europe from Colombo and thence to America.

At that time the *Yugantar* was received in exchange by the *Justice,* edited by Mr. H. M. Hyndman, leader of the Social Democratic Federation, by the *Indian Sociology* of Shyamji Krishna Varma, and by the *Gaelic American.* The editors of the three papers were reported to be highly sympathetic with the aims and ideals of the *Yugantar.* I had also heard that the editors with the exception of the Pandit were in favour of complete independence of India. Just a year after, I personally heard from Mr. Hyndman that India might aspire at best to self-government under England. However, I considered myself very fortunate in having secured three introduction letters to these gentlemen.

I was told by our leaders that there were revolutionary centres at Cuttack, Madras, Coimbatore and Tuticorin. On the way to Colombo and securing letters to the leaders of those centres and some other gentlemen, I bought a ticket for Tuticorin.

I stayed for two days at the house of my maternal uncle after taking leave of the members of the Midnapore society.

At Cuttack I searched in vain for two days for the secret society. The person to whom I had a letter of introduction was an extremist. I was introduced to a few students and gentlemen having the same views as he, some of whom were ardent readers of the *Yugantar.* I was pleased with the hospitality offered to me by some liberal-minded students and repaid it by lecturing them on the method of organising secret societies and on excellence of patriotism.

I halted for one day at Madras and for one day at Tuticorin, but could not find out the men to whom I had letters of introduction. From Tuticorin I went to Colombo by steamer, and after staying there for four or five days, started for Europe probably on the 13th August 1906.

It is not yet time to make public what happened in Europe, so shall only briefly refer to my doings there. **

Annotations :

1. Barindra Ghose in his confession states : "In the meantime another friend of ours, Hem Chandra Das of Kandini in Midnapore district, after I think selling part of his property, went to Paris to learn mechanics, and, if possible, explosives." The news of 'Hem Das' visit to France has been also alluded to in Mr. Daly's 'Note on the growth of the revolutionary movement in Bengal', at page 8, paragraph 3, where it is stated that one Hem Chandra Das of Midnapore had been sent to France in 1906, nominally to study mechanics, but in reality to learn the art of making bombs.

2. Lieutenant-Colonel Suresh Chandra Biswas, who had gone to Brazil and settled there.

Editorial Note :

* Hem Chandra wrote at the end of the chapter that "it was not yet time to make public what happened in Europe." But when he published these writings as a book in June 1928, chapter XII was expanded to include more details about Krishna Varma, S.R. Rana, French Socialist and Anarchist parties and also Madam Cama, about whom he is totally silent in *Basumati* Publication. But whatever was added to *Banglaya Biplab Prachesta* has been incorporated in Ib's translation, as this was published four months after the publication of Hemchandra's book in June, 1928.

** Hemchandra revised the book after independence. .... had occasion to see the revised manuscript, which does not contain any new addition to the Chapter XII.

Chapter XII
Joined A Revolutionary Party in Europe

I reached Marseilles in France, the land of patriotism, and bowed my head and saluted the tricolour, the symbol of equality, fraternity and liberty, the sight of which overwhelmed Raja Ram Mohan Roy, the father of Indian nationalism, with joy. I had to wait in the port city for 4/5 days and during that period, a French gentleman, who had working knowledge of English, acted as my guide free of charge. I, however, ultimately could not make out if he had any ulterior motive for being so kind-hearted towards a 'Kala Admi'.

With the help of this gentleman I saw many places and learnt many things. I saw an old dilapidated fort called Chateau d'if in a small rocky island. In the olden days the fort was used as a prison for political offenders and revolutionaries. At present the visitors are allowed inside for an entry fee. The inside was dark and cold. By carving the stones on the floor small caves were made for the prisoners. It is a matter great surprise how some prisoners could survive as long as 25 years in these dark, cold and moist pits. Later on I saw terrible instruments of torture on human being in Paris, Rome and Naples.

Basumati, Chaitra, 1332 BS; March-April 1926
Baisakh, 1333 BS; April-May 1926

One day while imagining the prospect of being confined to a jail, I imagined the terrible fate of being confined in a jail in Sakotra Island. I almost fainted. I had a glimpse of the island south of Aden while coming to Europe. It was an island of rocks of grotesque shapes, all black and bare without any sign of vegetation. I thought that if I could escape the gallows, then I might be deported to Sakotra or the Andamans.

Now-a-days, I think, the prisoners are fortunate that they were not likely to experience the hell of a life in yester years. It was impossible to guess what punishment would be meted out to the persons who defied the Raj and conspired to overthrow it. During the Hindu and Muslim period inhuman punishment used to be meted out to the offenders. But seeing the terrible nature of punishment awarded in the countries of Europe, I could not dare to believe that the English rulers would not do the same thing to the 'Kala Admi' if the situation arrived.

I was about to go mad thinking how I would withstand such terrible punishment. It also crossed my mind that I should bid good bye to the revolution and devote myself to painting or such other fine art. I remained in two minds for quite some time. I even thought of committing suicide in case I was caught and sentenced to long imprisonment in a prison. Then the question arose in my mind how would I procure the articles necessary for committing suicide!

I went to Paris via Switzerland, the ideal democratic country. On the way I met with one of my own countrymen. This gentleman professed great sympathy for my aims, and made very large promises, but when the time came for me to leave him, he gave me nothing by way of help, except an introductory letter to a distinguished gentleman in Paris. At Paris, I saw this gentleman. He had full sympathy for my mission, but refused to help me in any way. At that time there was a society at Paris named "The Paris-Indian Society." It was composed of some of the Indian gentlemen, numbering about 25 or 26, who were then living in Paris. It was associated .with the London Indian Society which was under the leadership of Pandit Shamaji Krishnavarma, M.A.[1], an inhabitant of Gujrat. He was probably the first man to conceive the idea that the freedom of India could be easily achieved by the adoption of the policy of passive resistance. His notion of passive resistance was derived from a movement in 1902 among the students of a certain English University against the teaching of the Bible. In 1903, he started a Home Rule League and a newapaper named *Indian Sociology* as its mouthpiece. His policy was on the whole this home rule under the British *raj* is the ideal system of administration for India. The right hand man of this Panditji was Srijukta Vinayak Damodar Savarkar, an inhabitant of Nasik in Bombay Presidency. Vinayak Savarkar graduated from the Bombay University and came to England probably in June 1906 with the object of reading for the Bar. In London, the aforesaid Panditji had several houses, at one of which he had opened a hotel, so that Indian students might live there at a small expense. This hotel was called " India House." It was here that Savarkar lived.

About five years ago, Ganesh Vishnu Savarkar, the elder brother of Binayak had organised a society at Nasik, named *Mitra Mêla,* in the model of *Anushilan Samiti* at Dacca. The ostensible object of this society was to give physical training to Indian youths, while its real object was probably to train up youths in such a manner that they might come to attain the mentality which would prepare them to fight with the English when the convenient time arrived. While in India, Binayak was connected with this society and had also made some name as a political leader. This is also probably the reason why, on reaching London, he set himself to organising a secret society. Vinayak was handsome and had a very winning personality. He could easily charm anybody he came in contact with. It is very difficult to say what his idea about the achievement of freedom of India was. From what I heard about it from others, it appears to have been on the whole somewhat like this : a second revolution like the Sepoy Mutiny would not be possible unless intense hatred of the English could be generated in the public mind. The Sepoy Mutiny failed for lack of educated leaders. No endeavour was then made to spread the revolutionary sentiment all over the country. But India would now have to be honeycombed with secret societies with the object of creating revolutionary literature and impregnating everyone with revolutionary feeling. Only those of the Musalmans who would assist in this coming revolution and would turn Hindu would have a share of the freedom that would be achieved. All others would be classed with the English as enemies of the land. When India would thus again become a country of the Hindus, that one among the feudatory chiefs or princes who would render the largest measure of assistance to the accomplishment of the revolution would be, like Immanuel II of Italy raised to sovereignty, and all the other provinces under him would form either republican or monarchical states agreeably to their convenience. It does not appear that the Panditji kept himself informed about the secret organisation contemplated by Vinayak. I do not know what Panditji thought about the Hindu-Moslem problem; but, as we have said before, Home Rule was, according to him, the only ideal system of administration for India.

The leader who strongly craves for name, fame and devotion of the people, needs to follow the double political line. One is an open forum for public appearance to seek popular support and the other is a secret one. Since this line is violative of law it is frought with danger. As a result the prospect of name, fame and popularity becomes remote. So the line is gradually neglected and finally abandoned.

Such leaders pursuing two political lines are responsible for destroying the revolutionary society. They became so greedy in their lust for public worship that they do not hesitate to do all kinds of bad deeds detrimental to the interest of the country.[i] Be that as it may, Panditji was not such a leader with two political lines, I will cite two examples here.

When after four or five months *in* Paris, I could not establish contact with any organisation of anarchists or revolutionaries, a desire grew in me to learn explosive chemistry. Fortunately, in a few days, an experienced French chemist came in my way. It was settled that we would put up a small laboratory where he would' give us thrice-a-week practical demonstrations on how to prepare explosives. His remuneration was fixed at twenty francs per day. But where was the money to come from? I sought the help of Panditji, but when he came to know why the money was needed, he refused any help because what I intended to do might most probably (according to him) shatter all possibilities of Home Rule. A few days afterwards I learnt that a man was wanted to serve as both manager and cook at the "India House " already referred to. I went to London and got the appointment. But as it was known to Panditji that I had gone to London with a view to joining some revolutionary party or the other in Europe, many unpleasant quarrels arose, and I was driven out. There was at this time another Indian gentleman[ii] in London. He had a small jewellery business there. Though his business was on a small scale, he had, however, a very large heart. It was through his kindness that a small laboratory could be constructed, and I began the experiments with the help of the French chemist mentioned before. I got hold of another Indian [iii] also and made him my associate. At about this time, I read in a newspaper that Monsieur Liberta, one of the greatest pillars of anarchism, had been sentenced to one week's imprisonment for having violated some law. The address of this man was given in the newspaper. I went and saw him. He expressed much sympathy with my aims and said such assuring things that I thought all our objects would be realised through the help of his party of anarchists. But I did not then know what anarchism meant—I did not know that anarchism implies a state of things in which every man's will is law. I did not know that the path to the realisation of this state of things was as dark as the path to the realisation of our spiritual *swaraj*. I had then an idea that the words 'anarchist' and 'revolutionary' were synonymous. I joined this society which I found to consist of people belonging to almost all the other countries of Europe except England. The reason why the English were absent from this society was, so far as I could ascertain, that they were very poor and besides had no great hatred towards their own system of administration. After about a month, I found out that this society had little to give me. It could teach me nothing with regard to the formation of secret societies. So gradually I stopped frequenting it.

In the meanwhile an American lady anarchist introduced us to a man who was a leader of a socialist party in Paris. His name was unknown to us and we used to call him Ph. D. He was a student of Hindu philosophy at a European university and had studied at Benares and attained fame later as an Orientalist. Our Panditji had already left London and come over to Paris and settled there in consequence of some adverse comments made about him in the House of Commons. We cleverly arranged a few meetings between Panditji and the Ph.D. with the result that the former became a wholesale convert to our ideas about the emancipation of India. The *Bande Mataram,* under the able editorship of Arabinda Ghosh, with its plea for full independence for India, along with the arguments of the Ph.D., was mainly instrumental in bringing about this change in Panditji's views. We rented a house in a deserted quarter of Paris. The charge of our training was taken over by the Ph.D. and an ex-military officer, who had been an attaché in India, belonging to his party. We were taught at one and the same time comparative geography, history, sociology, economics, religion, socialism, communism, etc. At least we began to note down in our books instructions, as to how to organise secret societies and to carry on their work.

Four or five months went by in this manner. Then we dismissed the French chemist from whom we had so long been learning explosive chemistry. At our earnest request, an old engineer, belonging to the aforesaid socialist party, was appointed to train us in the use and preparation of explosives. Our *gurus,* however, did not at first approve of our training in the chemistry of explosives. They did not believe that India was ripe for revolutionary terrorism. They tried to dissuade us. I, however, managed to bring them round to the conviction that India was quite ready for terrorist work. That I could do so was to some extent because their minds were predisposed to such a view by some events (such as the severe criticism of the Government by the press, the arrest of Bhupen Babu, the editor of the *Yugantar,* and of Arabinda Ghosh, the editor of the *Bande Mataram,* on charges of sedition, the deportation of Lala Lajpat Rai, Sardar Ajit Singh and Shufi Amba Prasad, the agitation created in Bengal by the so-called *Swadeshi,* movement which happened about this time in Bengal, etc.). Huge preparations for a revolution were then, so we were told, in progress in Portugal, and we were asked to go there and acquire practical experience. But none of us was agreeable, so it was at last settled that we should for the time being return to our native land and make use of our newly-acquired knowledge in forming secret societies all over India, and return to Paris after a year, when a secret institution -would be set up there for giving the men sent out by the Indian secret societies a thorough revolutionary training. The specialists of the aforesaid socialist party would act as teachers free of charge. Then the companion who was sent to us by the London secret society went back to London for a short stay there, while we two boarded a ship for India from Naples about the middle of December, 1907.

Annotations:

1. Shamji Krishna Varma of Kathiawar and Vinayak Damodar Savarkar of Nasik are well-known revolutionists whose history corresponds with the history given in page 4 of the Sedition Committee's report, where no mention of their connection with Hem Das is made. Hem Das, training in the art of preparing explosives, with the help of a lady anarchist will, however, be found in page 8 of Mr. Daly's "Note on the growth of the revolutionary movement in Bengal." It is as follows : "Hem has lived with a Russian anarchist woman during his stay in Paris, and through her he had become acquainted with a number of foreign anarchists from whom be acquired a certain amount of skill in the art of preparing explosives. It was he who prepared a bomb contained in a book and sent it to Mr. Kingsford by one Paresh Mallick, disguised as a peon."

Editorial Note:

i. Although Hem Chandra has not named anyone here, when he wrote these lines he had Aurobindo in mind. While in Europe he had deep respect for Aurobindo as evident from his letters to his wife Sarat.

ii. The gentleman was S.R. Rana, a jewellery merchant from Gujharat. Hem Chandra learnt the business from him. He also helped Hemchandra financially. After the outbreak of war he was interned by the French police.

iii. His name was Pandurang Mahadev Bapat (1880-1954) who also became a bomb-expert. But he left the revolutionary party later on.

Chapter XIII
Secret Societies in Maharastra

When it was decided to return home from Paris, I put into a trunk along with clothings a good many things necessary for the purpose of revolutionary activity and sent it to the address of a Calcutta friend by a cargo boat. This particular friend was a convenient one for me, for I had received the news of his death just a few days back and he had belonged to the police service. Besides the trunk, I took with me a small bag in which I put things, the loss of which would in my opinion at that time mean the loss of half the requirements for the emancipation of India. If the Customs Office could discover them, hanging or transportation for life would have been my certain fate. There was every chance of both the trunk and the bag being found out; nevertheless the atmosphere of a free country had made me bold enough to run the risk.

But the more we came nearer Bombay from Naples, the more did our fear, which is the result of slavery for generation after generation, increase. The fear, in particular, that we might be the chief and first cause of such a great misfortune as the discovery of a serious thing like a revolutionary effort for the liberation of India, oppressed our minds more than anything else.

Basumati, Kartik, 1333 BS; Ocotber-November 1926

We reached Bombay at 12 in the noon on a certain day in the first week of January in 1908. I and my companion had decided, since there was so great a chance of getting arrested, that we should not go together, and he passed beyond the Customs Office and waited for me. I went to the Customs Office with the luggages of both along with the agent of a European hotel. I carried something or other on my person from head to foot. The bag contained many things, and one of the pillows too contained a lot.

I experienced the greatest, difficulty in retaining a natural and fearless face, and I was feeling that the more I tried to do it, the more distorted did my face grow. Luckily for me there happened something which turned away all attention from me.

The Customs officer who was quite innocent of Italian was trying to explain something to two Italian missionaries who did not know English to the intense amusement of all the company present. Overcoming my stiffness, and seizing this golden opportunity, I approached the two Italians who as it turned out knew French. I explained to the officer what they wanted. He felt quite relieved, and requested me to ask them to fill up the forms and inform him whether there was any of the prohibited articles within their heap of luggages. I submitted my own form after filling it up along with theirs. Needless to say that there was no enquiry in my case; on the contrary I was the blessed recipient of many thanks.

My companion went in search of some charitable rest-house, while I argued that it was not safe to go anywhere and everywhere with such dangerous things as we had with us and went straight to a big hotel.

At Bombay we had two important items of business in hand. The first was to establish communication between the Bengal Secret Society and the Bombay Secret Society, and thereby to establish an All-India Central

Organisation and subsequently to build up branch societies under it throughout India.* The second was to make personal enquiries into all that we had heard about the Maharastra Secret Society since the commencement of the Bengal Society.

According to the arrangement previously made, we had no difficulty in finding out that society. We were introduced to some leaders and workers. The substance of what I heard from them is that there were branches of the revolutionary society at all the places in India which had Mahratta inhabitants. In addition to these, there were central societies at Nasik and Poona. We were told that some of their leaders had tried to organise societies in other Indian provinces. Though this attempt had failed, they were quite willing to work again in co-operation with the Bengalis. They said, however, that it was necessary to come to an understanding on this subject with the authorities of the chief centre. They agreed to send revolutionary workers or apprentices from Bombay to Bengal and to receive in their society workers from Bengal.

We were invited to the house of a rich leader of theirs a few miles off Bombay. We had expected to see there a lot of things collected by the Maratha society. During the last five or six years since the foundation of secret society in Bengal, members had been told about the extensive preparations of the Maratha secret society. But they were found to be untrue.

We were received and feasted there in a style befitting an All-India leader. It tickled our vanity and also checked our desire to criticise them for the complete absence of things which we had expected to see.

I would have been happy if I could give a full list of their implements and a full account of preparations for the future Indian revolutionary insurrection. I am not able to give a full list because what I found there I counted as good as nonexistent. Consequently I directed my attention to other business without looking carefully into those things. We remained there for a day and half, and the whole time was spent on showing and explaining all the things we had with us to our admiring audience with the object of making them admit that we were provided with all the materials and skill required for the immediate liberation of India.

With regard to the arms, so far as I remember, there were not more than five or six rifles and revolvers. Even these were antiquated, and I think they were lucky that they had even so much; cartridges of various kinds numbered nearly two hundred.

We undertook to supply them with whatever they might require for the work of revolution. Then we returned to Bombay.

After a week, my companion went to Poona, and I left Bombay with the object of looking at the work of the Nasik and Nagpur societies *en route* to Bengal. A member of the Mahratta secret society who was at once a leader and the chief worker thereof, was waiting at Nasik station. I put up with him for two days. While I was on one hand charmed by his sincerity and amiability, on the other all my hopes cherished so long were dashed to the ground on the receipt of a correct, general account of the activities of the Mahratta secret society. I was driven to the conclusion that we Bengalis must take up the work of organising revolutionary societies throughout India. At Nasik I had the good fortune of making the acquaintance of some extremist leaders.

Anyway, I noticed there a remarkable thing which was absent in the other Indian provinces and which was calculated to prove of service to the political uplift of India in distant future. The Mahratta ladies have no *purdah;* what is more I found some ladies who took an equal part with us in the discussion of political matters.

From enquiries made by me, it appeared that no arms and ammunition had as yet been collected there for the liberation of India. From their manner when they saw the things we had with us and heard about their uses, it appeared that they had never realised that they might be required even for the work of revolution if not for the war of liberation of India. And yet they had no conviction that revolution by violent methods would not succeed in this country, and that it would succeed only by spiritual efforts. Nor had they thought over the matter and come to the conclusion that considering the state of the country a revolutionary society would not require any arms at all for the next ten or twenty years.

Of course they had been preaching revolutionary doctrines for a long time, and they said that they were educating public opinion for a revolution.

But from what I saw and heard there, I came to the conclusion that they called it a revolutionary propaganda to rouse hatred against the English. On the other hand they explained that it meant an awakening of patriotism to teach the people to feel pride for their past achievements and to intensify their religious fanaticism amongst Hindus.

I do not intend to say that these two things were wanting in Bengal. In any case, the new literature which came into existence as the vehicle of preaching patriotism and revolutionary doctrine contained *Swadeshi* songs, poems, articles, the history of the rise of the Mahrattas, biographies of Sivaji, Ramdas and other famous Mahratta heroes and those of Mazzini, Garibaldi, the history of the mutiny, etc. I gratefully acknowlege here that I received some of these writings as presents, and I also received a coloured picture representing Mother India and the photographs of the Chapekars.

On the whole the main idea behind the Mahratta secret society was the re-establishment of Hindu supremacy in India. But I was not aware at the time that Hindus desired to re-establish Mahratta supremacy.

From Nasik I went to Nagpur and remained there for two days. I noticed the sincerity of the Mahratta students and their enthusiasm for revolutionary movement. I also made the acquaintances of some of the leaders. I felt that the political opinions of the educated community at Nagpur had become somewhat warm under the influence of the speech which Arabinda Babu had delivered at Nagpur on his return from the Surat Congress. The speech dwelt on the need of full independence for India. Just as at the beginning of the revolutionary movement, we in Bengal thought highly of the Mahrattas as revolutionary leaders similarly the Nagpur revolutionaries and extremists thought highly of the Bengalis.

My friends lost their faith in me to some extent when they noticed my reluctance to offer obeisances to Hanuman whom they worshipped on the occasion of a visit to a wrestling club of the revolutionaries. In consequence of this, I had to forego my wish to show them the live implements of revolution I had in my bag.

I left Nagpur after arranging that they would send some of their members to Bengal to have a training in the work of revolution.

Next day I reached Midnapore. I tried the tricks I had learnt in Paris to find out whether I was being shadowed, and concluded that I was free from suspicion.

Annotations :

1. Narendra Gossain, the approver in the Alipore bomb case, stated that there were societies in touch with their society in Bombay, Guzrat, Satara, and he did not remember others.

Editorial Note :

* Hem Chandra was not aware that in December, 1907, Barindra had tried to co-ordinate the activities of the secret societies in India, but failed.

Chapter XIV

The Beginning of Bomb in Bengal

A few weeks before an attempt[1] was made on the 6th December 1907 to blow up the train carrying Sir Andrew Fraser quite near my house. I had become a little afraid when I received this news at Bombay. I heard now the details of the incident from my revolutionary friends of Midnapore. This was also another "honest attempt" made by Barin. He sent Sriman Bibhuti to put a few pounds of dynamite under the railway line at a solitary place ten or twelve miles off Kharagpur. The Lieutenant-Governor's train is said to have been damaged. Government had declared a reward of Rs. 1,000 and the Bengal-Nagpur Railway Company Rs. 5,000 for the apprehension of the culprits.

The Bengal Police had no idea at that time that this thing could be done by revolutionaries or that they existed in Bengal at that time. They found out a number of Nagpur coolies whose guilt was duly established according to the law.

On the 7th December the Bengal Provincial Conference met at Midnapore. The police stated in their deposition in the Midnapore bomb case which came up some seven months later that they and the Calcutta Police had smelt the existence of the secret society at Midnapore from the angry speeches made at the conference by the extremists. If this

---

Basumati, Kartik, 1330 BS; October-November 1926

were true, the innocent coolies would not have been punished, giving eternal shame to British Justice. On the 23rd December some unknown persons shot[2] Mr. Allen, Magistrate of Dacca. Although all the revolutionary parties claimed the honour of this achievement, none was found out or punished therefor.

From what happened at the Surat Congress a week later, it might have been clearly noticed that the Bengalis were acting under a new inspiration. But that the police had not any information of the existence of the secret society or even that they did not suspect the existence as yet is proved by the fact of the punishment of the Kharagpur coolies.

I came to Calcutta feeling quite assured and saw Debabrata Babu. I heard that the Calcutta revolutionaries had become divided into many parties. Four or five of them were important. Aurobindo Babu was absent from Calcutta. I requested Debabrata Babu to inform Barin and went to see a big leader, of whom I have already spoken, named Charu Babu It was under his inspiration and with his sympathy and advice thatI had gone abroad to find out a mature method of making the country free. He used to put up with another leader. [i] They requested me with great importunity at the outset not even to see Barin, that is, not to have anything to do with Barin's party. They did not give me any strong reason for not doing it, but only said that Aurobindo Babu listened to none except Barin. And they added that it was Barin's nature to do the opposite to what he was advised to do and that he was carrying on work of the most confidential nature of the secret society in a manner as though his object was to make them public in consequence of it, he was sure to fall into the hands of the police very soon, and all those who worked with him would similarly fall into their hands. It appeared that they had lost faith in Aurobindo Babu in respect of the secret society.

I have already said how I had lost faith in Aurobindo Babu before I went to Europe. At that time I looked upon Charu Babu as a more competent leader. But at Paris I forgot all that, and used to sing the praises of Aurobindo and laud him to the skies. My displeasure with Barin as being of quixotic nature also disappeared because I found that it was Barin alone who of all the revolutionary leaders in Calcutta was trying to take some revolutionary action (subsequently styled as 'honest attempts'). Moreover while at Paris I received a letter in which Barin wrote to me amongst other things that on my return he would find all the money required for beginning 'action'. In spite of my determination not to ask for anything of anyone so long as I had a single farthing of my own, I saw that a lot of money was needed for spreading a network of revolutionary societies throughout India, and that a financier must be found if any part of my object was to be realized. Of course I could not see in the midst of my new found enthusiasm for Barin that his assurance was quite empty. One more thing, I had nursed enormous expectation; the technique that I had learnt to crown the activities of the secret, revolutionary society with success would please Aurobindo and his special assistant Barin so much that to fulfill my ambition they would give me every help. That was the reason why I thought of first seeing Barin and Aurobindo Babu on coming to Calcutta.

On the advice of the two big leaders,[ii] however, I decided not to see Barin for the time being; but the next day Barin appeared at my house.

Barin gave me long accounts of the many types of work done by him during my absence of one year and a half. He told me of the bomb factory opened in the Muraripukur Garden[3], at Manicktola where cases for bombs were being prepared. A similar factory had been opened at Deoghur or some other place.

I had also heard from the abovementioned two leaders that hitherto more than one hundred failed plans were made by Barin to kill the aliens and to commit dacoity. I tried to please him by giving him an account of my works, but it did not appear that he was much happy. I was a bit surprised at the want of enthusiasm shown by him on the subject of organizing revolutionary societies on the European model.

After this, I sounded the leaders of many of the secret underground parties; but they appeared to me to be unwilling to introduce any change in their own methods of organization. This was a disappointment to me, and more so because I was still unaware of the fact that all Indian leaders resent outside counsel.

Confronted by such difficulties, I decided to organise a separate party according to the advice of Charu Babu. I intended to exclude both Barin and Aurobindo. Finally arrangements were made to persuade some members belonging to other parties to come out and join my party. Charu Babu placed me in the hands of a wealthy leader and left Calcutta. The gentleman who had earned a reputation for generosity was frightened when I put up before him my programme in detail. For a fortnight I waited on him, but he never spoke once of giving me money for the work I proposed. He used to speak a lot, much of which was criticism of Aurobindo. I had then realised, he was, as Barin said, an armchair leader who hoped to make India free while sipping tea.

This discovery effectively dampened my enthusiasm. I had to give up for the present my plan of organising a new party as I was unable to collect funds for the purpose even by borrowing from others.

Nearly a month I had spent in Calcutta on these useless matters and also for making arrangements for some sort of business. In the meantime Aurobindo Babu returned to Calcutta and I called on him to pay my respects. I looked on him as my last resort. I was surprised when he dismissed me after exchange of a few words only. I learnt from Abinash Bhattacharya that he was always engrossed in meditation and contemplation and did not speak much with anyone from outside.

Any way, Aurobindo Babu advised me to see Barin when I asked him what I was to do. So I had nothing else to do but to join Barin who had, however, taken away from me all the books and papers necessary for the work of revolution and which I had brought from Europe. Barin had also sent Ullas to acquire all that I had learnt in Europe. I had hoped that as a result of the study of these books, etc., Barin would reorganise his party on the Western model. It did not come to pass. He preached among his disciples that everything Western, even the methods of organising the revolutionary party, were unnecessary for and even positively injurious to this country with the single exception of the science of manufacturing bombs. According to him all such things which came from the materialistic West were unsuitable for spiritualistic India. It seemed that it did not occur to them that the whole revolutionary endeavour was due to Western inspiration. Possibly I might have persuaded him to accept the European method, if I could become a blind supporter of his.

Barin had many reasons for regarding me with disfavour. From the incident of the failed Rangpur dacoity he came to realise that I was unfit to become a blind admirer of his. He had further come to know of my attempt to organise a party with those who were against him. Moreover I really belonged to the Midnapore Secret Society, and Satyen Bose, who was its leader, was an eyesore to him although they were blood relations. Satyen disregarded Barin's claim to respect as one of the main section leaders of the Calcutta committee and freely abused him to others. Barin was not accustomed to put up with such treatment. Satyen was a competent leader and had shown great ability in working individually or collectively, and accomplishing the task. It was due to his efforts and due to the confidence that the volunteers and the revolutionary workers had in him, the extremist activity in Midnapore met with such success at the Midnapore Conference. Though Barin was present there, Satyen did not show him the respect due to his superior position. Similarly Satyen displayed in the presence of Barin superior skill and energy in the matter of breaking up the Congress at Surat. Naturally Barin was not fond of either Satyen or me. He was only anxious to learn from me the techniques of making bombs, because he had been receiving promises from many quarters of getting thousands of rupees as soon as a bomb is targeted on an Englishman. But bomb was not ready and so the promised money did not come. The scarcity of fund was acute.

A few months previously, Ullaskar, who had assaulted a sahib in the Presidency College, fell somehow into Barin's hands. We became intimate friends at our first meeting. I have no doubt it was highly foolish and reprehensible to have decoyed a young man of his noble nature to the revolutionary path.

Shortly after my acquaintance with Ullas, I made the acquaintance of Srijut Upendranath Banerji[4] and after a little conversation, I was compelled to admit he was the fittest person in Bengal to become the member of a revolutionary secret society.[iii]

None of the revolutionary societies in Calcutta cared much for practical work. Barin alone tried heart and soul for terroristic deeds. He did not, perhaps, remember that there were many other important things which it was necessary to do immediately for the success of the revolutionary endeavour, and these escaped the notice of Aurobindo as well. Or perhaps they thought that what was to be done must be done right in the *Swadeshi* spiritual method, and had, therefore, arranged for the moral and spiritual instructions of the workers at the Muraripukur Garden, and Upen had been appointed to act as spiritual guide. This system had been made compulsory.

Anyway, there was no indication that Barin had any desire to make his terroristic attempts successful. He held that we were only entitled to make 'honest attempts' in the middle of 1907. The Muraripukur Garden, chosen for doing the most secret works of the society, was in such a locality as was bound to attract the notice of all new comers who went there. There were other disadvantages. Moreover all the things which they wanted to manufacture subsequently turned out to be useless. For these reasons with great difficulty we persuaded Barin to transfer to a densely populated locality the bomb factory or the school for learning to make bombs.

While we were looking out for a house, Barin ordered a bomb for killing the Mayor of Chandernagore.[5] At first I could not understand how a man like Aurobindo could think of killing anybody for the purpose of revolution before organising our society on the new model, training a sufficient number of men for terroristic work, founding similar secret societies by educated men throughout India and enabling all the provinces to take up terroristic work simultaneously. I think now that they had not as yet acquired the knowledge that such things were quite impossible in a spiritual country like India. If they had, they would not have been possessed by a mania for bombs. A few months after, they however came to see the truth.

Secondly, why had the choice fallen on the French Mayor? I think that I protested at that time, but still I gave my help because the desire of advertising my newly acquired knowledge was too strong to resist and obliterated all other considerations from my mind. It was, moreover, unthinkable of disputing the authority of Aurobindo, who had as it was given out received a 'message' to that effect and had delivered it through Barin.

Though I was suffering from fever at the time, I made a bomb. The materials were not readily available; yet the bomb was to be delivered by the evening. So with the materials available at Muraripukur garden and the rest purchased from M/s. D. Waldie's shop a bomb was made. But the objective was not achieved and consequences were just the opposite.

Enquiries into the Narayangarh Bomb incident had been finished, and some coolies were punished as culprits. The Government of India did not accept the finding of the Bengal Police, and after the Chandernagore incident,**** deputed a Police Inspector named Sasi Bhusan Dey for special investigation. He kept his eyes on the extremist leaders. A fellow named Rajani Mitra or something like that was sent to Aurobindo for dedication to the service of the country. He was sent to Barin at Muraripukur.

At this time all the Calcutta societies were full of leaders and deputy leaders, and they were eager to recruit workers. Barin welcomed the said Rajani, and in order to impress him, showed him all the places where bombs and revolvers were kept, bomb cases were manufactured and spiritual practices were performed. Rajani did not show himself up again in the garden, but since that time all those who frequented the garden began to be shadowed.

A house[6] was ultimately found at Bhowanipore, and a school for bombs was opened about the middle of March

1908. At first there were five students among whom were Kanailal, Indu Bhusan Roy who later committed suicide at Port Blair and Nirapada *alias* Nirmal Roy. There were no servants, and the students cooked their own food. I went there now and then.

I wanted one or two young men from Barin to teach them the skill of throwing bombs at people. First the authorities sent Sushil who was ordered to murder Mr. Kingsford, probably because he used to punish *Swadeshi* offenders and also Srijut Purna Chandra Lahiri whom we looked upon as the real head of the Intelligence Branch. Sushil was a very promising boy, and I did not understand why Barin had deputed him for a work which meant certain death. I came to learn the reason later. Nirmal Roy who was an old member of the Midnapore Society and was then an active worker of the Muraripukur centre was appointed by me a spy to watch[7] over the doings of the members of the secret society. He told me that Sushil had been chosen because he did not join in the spiritual practices held at Muraripukur, and was therefore considered unfit for revolutionary work.

Annotations :

1. The details of the attempt to wreck the Special train of His Honour the Lieutenatn-Governor at Narayangarh were first obtained from the confessions made by Barindra Kumar Ghose, Bibhuti Bhusan Sarkar, Ullaskar Dutt, Upendra Nath Banarji and Hrishikesh Kanjilal, accused of the Alipore bomb case, after which the coolies who were wrongly convicted in this case were released. The statement of Barindra Kumar Ghose is as follows : "I, Profulla and Bibhuti left the train at Kharagpur at 10 a.m. In the afternoon we went by train to Narayangarh where we waited on the road which is parallel to the railway line. When it was dark, we went to the railway line and waited till 9 p.m. We waited at a spot about a mile from Narayangarh on the Kharagpur side. Here I shall give minute details because innocent people have been

punished for this offence. We had with us a mine made of 6 lbs. of dynamite charged in a thick iron vessel with a lid at the top. The lid had a nob in the centre. We had a fuse made of picric compound and picric compound powder was placed in a paper tube; we used a leaden pipe in case it should get choked by ballast. We had a dark lantern with candles. We placed the mine there between 11 and 12 at night. I alone went back to Narayangarh. I left behind the 2 boys, and they placed the fuse on the line when the Special came. (Bibhuti Bhusan Sarkar, Hrishikesh Kanjilal.) They said they were about 1½ miles away when the explosion took place. We took no assistance from any cooly or any one else." This was corroborated by Bibhuti Bhusan Sarkar, Upendra Nath Banarji and Hrishikesh Kanjilal.

2. Regarding this incident, we have the following in page 8 of Mr. Daly's 'Note on the growth of the revolutionary movement in Bengal': "On 23rd December 1907, Mr. B.C. Allen, I.C.S., was shot with a revolver on the platform at Goalundo Railway Station. This act is believed to have been committed by some youths of the 'Dacca Anushilan Samiti' regarding whose doings Mr. Allen had been making enquiries."
3. Regarding the Muraripukur Garden bomb factory and its branch at Deoghur, we have the following statements and records

   a) "In the beginning of 1908 Ullaskar Dutt wanted to come among us as he had learnt the preparation of explosives. He had a small laboratory in his father's house. With his help, we began preparing explosives in small quantities in the garden house at No. 32, Muraripukur Road. In the meantime Hem Das went to Paris to learn mechanics and explosives in the middle of 1907. When he came back, he joined Ullaskar in preparing explosives and bombs." Barin's statement.

   b) "A very important part of the evidence as against Sudhir Kumar Sarkar concerns his connection with Sil's lodge. It is about 3 miles from Deoghur Railway Station between the village of Raidi and Ghoslas. Sil's lodge was searched on 28th May and some articles were taken into custody. We thus have material objects found at Sil's lodge, indicating a connection with the Muraripukur Garden and 134, Harrison Road, and we have the correspondence and map found at No. 134, and the sketch in the book and the gunny bag found in the garden indicating connection with Sil's lodge." *Vide* page 73 of Mr. Beachcroft's judgement in the Alipore bomb case.

c) "According to Barin Ghose, he himself began to organise the Manicktola Garden Society at the beginning of 1907 with 14 or 15 young men and educated them in religious books and politics. Among the young men was Ullaskar Dutt, a chemist, who had a small laboratory in his house." *Vide* page 9 of Mr. Daly's 'Note on the growth of the revolutionary movement in Bengal."

d) "I thought it necessary to found a sort of religious political society for the cause of Indian regeneration. I joined Barin and engaged myself in teaching the boys about the state of our country and the need of independence, and that the only way left us is to fight for independence and to start secret societies to propagate ideas and collect arms and rise in rebellion." Upendra's confession, page 9.

e) "Indubhusan Roy told Birendra Nath Ghose of an Asram at Manicktola where Upendra Nath Banarji taught *Gita* and Indian philosophy. He went to the garden. Upen asked him to read certain books, and after an interval of about a week, he again went to the garden and stayed day and night for 5/6 days. He was told there was a regular class for the *Gita* and other philosophical books, Upendra being the teacher." *Vide* page 58 of Mr. Beachcroft's judgement in the Alipore bomb case.

f) "I see the book. I remember it by its contents. It is a treatise on explosives. I read parts of it. I have seen people copying and dictating about explosives; whether it was this book or another that they were working, I cannot say. This copying and dictation was in the Manicktola Garden. There used to be conversation about getting firearms from foreign countries. Barindra Ghose and Upendra Banarji used to talk about this in the garden. While I was at the garden, I used to see revolver practice. We all practised with a small rifle. There was conversation about revolution. Barin and Upen took the leading part in the discussion. ... While I was at the garden, Ullaskar Dutt lectured in the manufacture of explosives. Barindra taught the mechanical part of the explosives. The training in the garden consisted of religious training, political training and physical training. Revolutionary knowledge was also imparted, *vide* approver Narendra Gossain's confession.

4. An accused in the Alipore bomb case and an *ex-dètenu*.
5. The attempt to kill the Mayor of Chandernagore is alluded to in the following statements and records

a) "After that there was a bomb outrage at Chandernagore. Hem Chandra Das prepared the bomb. Indubhusan Rai of Jessore, myself and Narendra Gossain of Serampore went to Mankundu. Indu undertook to throw the bomb. The bomb did not work. We crossed the river at Telinipara Ghat." Barindra Ghose's statement, page 3.

b) Indu Bhusan Roy, an accused of the Alipore bomb case, corroborated Barindra regarding the throwing of the bomb at the Mayor of Chandernagore. *Vide* page 8 (confession)

c) Narendra Nath Goswami also corroborates the above *in toto*. *Vide* page 16 (confession)

d) Hrishikesh Kanjilal corroborates the major part of the story. *Vide* page 15 (confession)

e) "It was in the beginning of 1908 that the Bengal C.I.D. first obtained information that led to enquiries at No. 32, Muraripukur Road. Watch was organised and some members were followed out to Chandernagore. They were lost sight of there, and the following day the news of the attempt to murder the Mayor of Chandernagore by throwing a bomb through his window, betrayed the object with which they had gone there." *Vide* "Mr. Daly's report on the growth of the revolutionary movement of Bengal," page 9.

f) "On the 10th April 1909, Barindra and two other men were followed from the garden, No. 32, Muraripukur Road, to Howrah, and thence to Mankundu by rail and thence to Chandernagore by road. On the 11th April 1909 (night) an attempt with a bomb was made on the life of the Mayor of Chandernagore." *Vide* Mr. Beachcroft's judgement against B.K. Ghose and others, page 1.

6. This house is probably 78, Russa Road, as mention is made of this in the confession of Hrishikesh Kanjilal, *vide* page 15, confession : "That night Barin took me to 78, Russa Road, Bhowanipur, and Upendra accompanied us. I found there 4 or 5 boys whose names I did not enquire." It will be also found in Mr. Beachcroft's judgement, page 27, that Hem Chandra Das was followed to this house on 2 occasions.
7. It will be found from the confession of approver Narendra Gossain how both of the above individuals were shadowed by men of their party. It is as follows :

a) "Our society settled that Kingsford was to be killed. Barindra, Ullaskar, Hem Das, P.M. Bupat and I were among those who decided upon this, because he had had Sushil whipped and sent Bhupendra Dutt and 2 other printers to jail, and was trying the

'*Bande Mataram* case'. Khudiram and Profulla Chaki were chosen to do it. Profulla was present at the meeting."

b) "I know Police Inspector Lahiri. I have shadowed for shooting him. I did this under orders of Abinash Chandra Chakrabarti whom I have frequently mentioned. Abinash told me to do it, because he (Inspector Lahiri) made arrests in cases about newspapers in which Arabinda and others were arrested. I followed him for 3 or 4 days. Abinash arranged to have him shot by another man, but he wanted to ascertain his habits and movements first. *Vide* Narendra Goswami's confession.

Editorial Note :

i. This leader was Raja Subodh Mullik, known for his donation of One lakh rupees to the National Council of Education. The three member council which used to take crucial decisions consisted of Aurobindo, Charu Dutta and Subodh Mullik.

ii. The big leaders were Subodh Chandra Mullick and his brother in law Charu Chandra Datta. Even they were disenchanted with Aurobindo on account of Aurobindo's indulgence to Barin in disregard to the safety and security of the society. Charu Datta left for Bombay and had no connection with the society. Thereafter, Mullik also lost interest in it and lived in Benaras.

iii. In the book Hem Chandra added a few more sentences about Upendranath by way of making fun of his saffron dress.

iv. At that time both the Central and Provincial intelligence used to work in perfect co-operation. Dey was an officer of Bengal Police, deputed to the Central Criminal Intelligence. Till February 1908 none suspected the existence of secret terrorist group in Bengal. Hem Chandra is correct that Sashi Bhushan Dey of Central Intelligence for the first time detected the existence of a secret society in the Muraripukur Garden in February, 1908.

Chapter XV
Hindu Conservatism

When' even after two years of the formation of the secret society, the spread of revolutionary cult did not catch on, Aurobindo took to religion and wanted to give a religious[1] look to the revolutionary movement. Thereafter when the *Swadeshi* movement assumed huge proportions, he tried to take advantage of it to spread his revolutionary cult. The work of spreading the cult, though comparatively satisfactory this time, it was still far below the desired level. Differences of opinion, quarrels for leadership among Barin[2], Jatin[3] and other sub-leaders and workers and undue partiality of the leaders and their lieutenants gave rise to a bitter factional feeling[4] among them. The 'Barrister Sahib'[5] who had so long been the nominal president of the Bengal Revolutionary Society had his Anushilan Samiti completely separated. The other leaders and deputy-leaders, such as Indra, Chandra, Nikhil, Satis, etc., formed several secret societies under different names, of which the *Anushilan* Samiti of Dacca is worth mentioning. Their object at that time was to make 'honest attempts' to commit dacoities, and their only work was to tightly bind their followers in the fetters of the rules and regulations they famed.

As a result of the *Swadeshi* movement, societies under diverse names were started in every district for the sale of

---

Basumati, Chaitra 1333 BS; March-April 1927

indigenous articles, and under them a large number of *Swadeshi* stores and shops were opened. The leaders tried to turn these institutions into so many revolutionary societies.

Barin was the foremost worker in Aurobindo Babu's party at that time. Aurobindo Babu was said to have been practising *yoga* to attain spiritual powers. But still followers were not coming to join the party; the few that came, did not stick long; one or two that still remained refused to be fully subservient. Aurobindo was, therefore, in search of a spiritual person to teach him supernatural powers. After some fruitless search, at last one Lele Maharaj was sent for. But he, even, could not give evidence of any such supernatural powers, as would hypnotise trains of people into joining the revolutionary party and obeying any and every behest of the leaders. [i] Be that as it may, on hearing all the accounts of our revolutionary movement, he expressed the opinion that no warfare would be required to free India from the hands of English. There would happen such events in the world as a result of which India would be free without any warfare.

Although the leaders were disappointed with the followers were not permitted to be so. An account of *sadhus*, the progress in religious training in the Garden was taken every morning as to how much progress each had made. It was also circulated among these disciples that Aurobindo had received 'message'. Aurobindo grew impatient to drive out the English within a few years and to pass for an *Avatar*. So, at first he gave a spiritual interpretation of the revolutionary cult. The result was that, in trying to mix religion with politics, he created much smoke. This too did not produce any effect. Aurobindo then realised that unless he could display supernatural powers, people would not obey him blindly.

On returning from Paris, I found that the secret society of Midnapore had undergone changes and an idol of goddess *Kali* was installed in a room, which was named *Anandamath* near the house of Satyen. When I asked for its reason, Satyen replied, "Everyone wants something like this. The whole country has suddenly become full of reverence for *Kali*. I do not know why." Khudiram said, "If nothing else, we get enough goat's flesh to eat through the mercy of *Kali*. But then only white goats are sacrificed." At our centre at Muraripukur and also at the new centre in Bhowanipur the picture of *Kali* was hanging up. At other centres and in the houses of many, such pictures were daily worshipped with flowers and sandal paste.

Now we hear of *swaraj* and then of independence. No attempt has ever been made either to give a logical interpretation of these two terms or to give to the people a clear idea of what the condition of the country will be if we attained any of the two. They have failed to put up before the country any such ideal as might tempt the people to sacrifice their all, even their life, in obeying the leaders; nor has any reasonable ground ever been shown for so doing. This much about the leaders.

Now about the workers. The number of workers at the Muraripukur Garden at that time was not more than 15 or 16. Besides them, there were some others in other places. Although in the rules there was no gradation of rank among the workers, the workers, they however were divided into two classes. Those engaged in religious practices belonged to the spiritual class. And it is they that were regarded as best entitled to perform terrorist actions. They were said to belong to the men of the idealistic or spiritualistic world. In matters revolutionary, save manufacturing and throwing bombs, everything else was of the spiritual realm. It is perhaps for this reason that I have found some to participate in the so-called political dacoities, and others to court jail for it and many to become informers! Generally speaking their behaviour was very amiable; they were known everywhere as good and gentle lads. They were in the habit of considering themselves superior to others. A convict, sentenced for fraud, managed to get his *charash* and opium through the warders by posing himself to be a *sanyasin* possessing knowledge of palmistry. Our leaders saluted the man as one belonging to the spiritual plane, and presented him with a rupee. This will give an idea as to what sort of spiritual *swaraj* we would have had if the country, after being freed, had passed into the hands of these leaders.

Be that. as it may, although these disciples were sentimental and more or less devoid of sense, their allegiance to their *Guru* was unflinching and their highest pleasure in life consisted of carrying out consciously or unconsciously – any and every instruction and wish of the *Guru*. They had to make "confession" before their *Guru*. Among those who joined this party by making "confession", Naren Gosain was one. Many of the workers left their parents, wives and children, got initiated to asceticism and actually went to forests and mountains. They, however, returned at last to Bengal and whole-heartedly joined the *Swadeshi* movement. They had not to wait long to get the scent of the revolutionary parties. [ii]

All of them who were thus drawn to the Manicktola Garden, had, at first, to engage themselves in religious practices and meditations. Those who found it agreeable to them and could show expected progress to the leaders were given the honour of the higher rank. There were many among them who could not show much progress and failed to understand the connection between the attainment of liberty of the country and such *yogic* practices. These people came to sacrifice their young life full of hopes in order to attain immortality in the future history of India. These lads had to suffer much humiliation. It was these boys who were considered as unspiritual persons belonging to the lower rank; and hence they were thought to be unworthy of doing higher work for the emancipation of the country. This led some to leave the party. The five persons mentioned in the previous chapter, who were sent to the new centre[6] at Bhowanipur to learn bomb-making, were also of the lower rank. Even the famous Kanailal was one of that rank, because he did not himself practise those *yogic* exercises, nor did he like others to do so.

Annotations :

1. Barindra Kumar Ghosh, accused in the Alipore bomb case, in his confession admitted that when the *Swadeshi* and boycott agitation had begun, he came to Bengal convinced that a purely political propaganda would not do for the country, and that the people must be trained up spiritually to face dangers.
   In the judgement of the Alipore bomb case, Mr. Beachcroft remarked : "But what was the basis of Barin's action? We have it from himself that it is the idea of independence. He found that a purely political propaganda would not stir up the country, so he appealed to religion, the most dangerous factor of all, especially in the case of an Oriental people, when used to obtain political ends." (Page 13 of the judgement.)
2. Barin is Barin Ghosh (accused in the Alipore bomb case).
3. Jatin is Jatindra Nath Banerjee *alias* Niralamba Swami who was arrested in connection with the Manicktola case, but was discharged by the Committing Magistrate (*vide* Mr. Daly's note). *See* also note 7, Chapter 1.
4. Mr. F.C. Daly writes in his "Note on the growth of the political movement in Bengal" regarding the party feeling in the revolutionary camp :
   "In the year 1900, Arabinda (Ghosh) sent Jatindra Nath Banerjee, who was then in the Baroda army, to Bengal as a missionary. On arriving in Bengal, he joined P. Mitter's association and started an athletic club. After sometime, however, there was a quarrel

between Jatindra Banerjee and P. Mitter, the result being that the original party was broken up into two divisions; Arabinda's party directed in Bengal by Jatindra Banerjee and Barin Ghosh and P. Mitter's party which founded the Anushilan Samiti and its many branches all over Bengal." (page 6).

5. The barrister sahib is apparently P. Mitter, Barrister-at-Law (since deceased).
6. The Bhowanipur centre was situated at No. 78, Russa Road.

Editorial Note :

i. Hem Chandra has written this about twenty years after Lele's visit to Aurobindo and the garden on the basis of hearsay and surmise from a hindsight to suit his scheme of analysis of the events of the post. In his analytical frame religion was the villain of the piece and his bête noires were responsible for ushering in religion into the society.
ii. Hem Chandra has accused Aurobindo of preaching Yoga with a motive of hypnotising young men and recruiting them as members of secret society. But these charges are not borne out by facts. Aurobindo started practising *Yoga* at Baroda in 1904, "not to clarify his ideas, but to find spiritual strength which would support him and enlighten his way." (Autobiographical Notes, p. 107) It was confined at first to the assiduous practice of *Pranayam* (at one time for six hours or more a day). "There was no conflict or wavering between *Yoga* and politics; when he started *Yoga* he carried on both Aurobindo went to Baroda where Barin introduced him to a *Yogi* named V.B. Lele who initiated Aurobindo to a new type of *Yoga*. Aurobindo had practised it for his self-development and not for any public purpose. He never tried to impose the practise of *Yoga* on no one even when he was in jail with other members of the group. In this context Hem Chandra's allegation appears to be unsubstantiated. This is an extravagant criticism, if not out of malice as Hem Chandra was not properly treated and his merit was not given due recognition by both Aurobindo and Barindra.

Chapter XVI
Before Arrest

Why Sushil was selected to throw a bomb upon the Presidency Magistrate, Mr. Kingsford, has been described in the previous chapter. A few months before, Arabinda Babu was prosecuted[1] for a seditious article in the *Bande Mataram*. Bipin Babu[2] also was prosecuted for his refusal to give evidence in that case. On the day of his trial, a European Inspector was using the cane upon the crowd in front of the Lal Bazar Police Court. Sushil[3], a lad of 14 years, was punished by Mr. Kingsford for having boxed that Inspector as a protest against this wrong and received 15 stripes. In as much as the matter would have been received in a different light if the Magistrate who had sentenced him were killed by Sushil, he was let off, and a worker of the lower rank was brought from the Manicktola centre. But Sushil was not till then allowed to know anything about the (contemplated) murder. Otherwise, it would have been very difficult to avoid him. The first bomb that was manufactured[4] for murdering Mr. Kingsford, was kept in a big book by making room for it therein in such a way that it would explode with the opening of the book. The book was bound with a piece of tape. A long envelope was protruding from within the book in such a manner that it could not be taken out without untying the tape. It was learnt that

---

Basumati, Chaitra 1333 BS; March-April 1927

Mr. Kingsford used at that time to put up at Mrs. Monk's Grand Hotel and go to court in his office cab after 9-30 A.M. Going to hand over that book to him when he would enter the cab, it was learnt that just the day before he had left that house and gone over to a house at Tollygunge. Then the house at Tollygunge was found out, and on another day the book was handed over to him. But he was so lucky that he kept the book in an almirah without opening it. It was strange that he did not feel any inclination even to see what the envelope contained. Then, when we were undertrial prisoners at Alipore, upon one of our leading men having informed a police officer about it, the book with the bomb was recovered from Mr. Kingsford's almirah at Muzaffarpur. In this connection the Report of the Rowlatt Commission records : "The police had received information 10 days before that the murder of Mr. Kingsford was intended and during the next year a well-known revolutionary, when in custody, said that before this outrage a bomb had been sent to Mr. Kingsford in a parcel. Upon search being made a parcel was found which Mr. Kingsford had received but not opened, thinking it contained a book borrowed from him. The parcel did contain a book; but the middle portion of the leaves had been cut away and the volume was thus in effect a box and in the hollow was contained a bomb with a spring to cause its explosion if the book was opened."

"Fifteen were ultimately found guilty of conspiracy to wage war against King-Emperor, including Barindra Kumar Ghose, already mentioned as one of the most active founder of the criminal revolutionary movement in Bengal, Hem Chandra Das, the manufacturer of the bomb which killed Mrs. and Miss Kennedy, and another who made the statement already alluded to and so strikingly confirmed as to the sending of the bomb in a parcel." (Sedition Committee Report, p. 24, para 38)

In any case, our centre at Bhowanipur for manufacturing bombs had soon to be abolished. Some seven days after we had started the centre, we came to know that the C.I.D. were after us. Whenever during the day time we went to Bhowanipur[5] and returned from there, we invariably noticed following us either a man of the appearance of an opium-smoker in a most ordinary dress or an elderly woman in the garb of a female *sanyasi*. Who this elderly woman was, I have not yet been able to know. That gentleman was the well-known police Inspector Babu Purna Chandra Biswas.[6] He used to watch my movements from a miserable tiled hut in front of our house in Shovabazar from morning till evening. Besides him, there were two others on the other two sides of the house. Similarly there were arrangements for spying on other centres as well.

After a vigorous search, a suitable small house was found in Gopi Mohan Datta Lane in Syambazar. We decided to shift our bomb factory there. We were so irresponsible that those who were escorting the bullock carts carrying our articles from Bhowanipur to Syambazar, lost the cart while they went to take their tiffin in the way. Searching from 10 in the morning, the cart, however, was at last found in the evening near Syambazar Bridge.

With those articles and after considerable effort, we started our centre at Gopi Mohan Datta Lane two days later. Kanai, Nirapada[7] etc., and two apprentices from other provinces used to reside there. We came to know within a few days that the C.I.D. were watching this house also from morning till evening. The C.I.D. of those days, though not endowed with much skill and ability, possessed common sense more abundantly than we did. They could not be found after evening. They used to attend the Sealdah and Howrah stations at night in batches of two or three at a time.

One evening, while seeing a Marhatti gentleman off at the Howrah Station, I noticed two spies on the platform. I could understand that they knew us. Both of us entered an Inter class compartment and got down by 'the opposite door and changed our garments and our appearance. Then, returning to the platform through a third class compartment, we noticed them vigorously searching- for us. Then from their evidence at the court, we came to know that they had gone as far as Raniganj searching for us in the compartments of the train and returned disappointed from there.

On many other occasions at night we threw dust into the eyes of the police in this way. One of the three bombs first manufactured in Gopinath Dutt Lane, was examined and found to be quite effective. Mr. Kingsford was then the Judge at Muzaffarpur. Lest the attempt[8] this time should turn out to be a mere "honest attempt" as on previous occasions, it was decided, after much deliberation, to send two persons. If two persons from two distinctly different parties and unacquainted with each other, could be sent, then the possibility of their returning without finishing the work on a false excuse would be less. So the leader of a different party was asked to supply a murderer. The following day when he was seen at the Beadon Park with the leader, he appeared to be a worker of ability. Intending to bring him with me finally, I asked the leader to bid him the last farewell. The leader felt much embarrassed and asked for 2 days' leave for him. The meaning was that he should be photographed in a hero's dress and a farewell feast should be given in his honour in the company of his friends and relatives before he was sent out as a sacrifice. I felt with regret that day, that the hope to bring about a. revolution in this country was far remote. Be that as it may, it was I who had to take the last leave by severing my connection with them.

Finally Khudiram was brought in without the knowledge of any one of the Midnapore Society. He was instructed for a week and then sent to Muzaffarpur along with the above mentioned Prafulla Chaki. It became apparent from their attitude and their words at that time that they felt much grateful for being entrusted with that work. The police had no scent of it as they set off in the evening. * It was settled that when all preparations would be complete, they would send us an information in our code words before performing the deed. And we should at that time stay away from our houses and go into hiding.

Meanwhile we began to prepare ourselves. It was decided that we should remove from our respective houses and also from our centres all incriminating articles, so that the least trace suspicion might be found. Till then I could not convince Barin that the police were on our trail. As a matter of fact he had not the least fear on that score. He was very often heard to say"Police were merely paid servants. Had they possessed the capacity to understand our business, they would not have then come to serve in the Police Department. Just see, for instance, the veteran C.I.D. officer Purna. Lahiri came to search the *Yugantar* office, and before his very eyes they went out of the office with highly incriminating papers in the disguise of *kulpi* vendors thus throwing dust into his eyes," etc. Aurobindo Babu also warned Barin to be careful, to which Barin is said to have replied, "Don't you see there is no truth in these words? Because these people do not want to put their hands to any difficult work, they see visions of the police," etc. Aurobindo Babu accepted these words as quite reasonable.

At the Muraripukur Garden, all things were kept where they were. The two foreigners at the Gopinath Dutt Lane, moved away like good boys. Only Kanai and Nirapada stayed on. Instruments and all suspicious articles were put into 5 or 6 boxes. Ullash was given the charge of carrying these articles after dusk in a boat to be hired at Koilaghata, to his father's laboratory at the Shibpur Engineering College. In two of those boxes such instruments and materials had been placed as would not cause any suspicion whatsoever if found in any laboratory. And it was so arranged that excepting those two boxes, the others should be thrown into the Ganges. Nothing of the sort happened. Barin's fearlessness infected others also to some extent. So many more things were left in the house at the Gopi Mohon Datta Lane. Four or five boxes were taken in day time, in a hackney carriage, and kept under a bedstead in a roadside room of the house of an innocent Kaviraj, a relative of Ullash, in Harrison Road.[9] The police too followed the carriage to the spot and began to secretly keep watch over the place from that day.

Nearly a week passed in great anxiety. No code news came from Muzaffarpur. All on a sudden the news was published in the *Empire* of 1st May 1908, that at 8 o'clock in the evening of 30th April, at Muzaffarpur, while entering the gates of the house of the Judge Mr. Kingsford, Mrs. and Miss Kennedy had been killed by a bomb. Immediately on receipt of this news, our leader gave orders to Barin to convey this news to all the members of our party and to send them away from the centre at once. But it was not in his nature to carry out any orders. So, without informing anyone about it, he went, to the Manicktola centre and gave orders to bury all the guns, revolvers, etc., in a pit.[10] In compliance with this order, some earth was put upon those things till 12 at night. It is said that at that time some one from the police gave hints to the effect that the police would raid the house the following morning. But those boxes, full of incriminating articles, deposited in Harrison Road[11], were not removed. Not receiving any intimation till 12 at night, I went to sleep.

Annotations :

1. Arabinda Ghosh was prosecuted under section 124A, Indian Penal Code, for a seditious article in the *Bande Mataram*, but was discharged.
2. Bipin Chandra Pal was prosecuted for his refusal to give evidence in the case against Arabinda Ghosh, and was sentenced to 6 months' simple imprisonment under sections 178, 179, Indian Penal Code, on the 10th September 1907.
3. On the 27th August 1907 Sushil Sen of Sylhet was convicted and sentenced under section 332, Indian Penal Code, to 15 stripes for assaulting a police officer at the time of Bepin Pal's trial.
4. In Mr. Daly's note it is stated, "It was he (Hem Das, the writer) who prepared a book containing a bomb and sent it by one Paresh Maulik (convicted in the Alipore case), disguised as a peon, to Mr. Kingsford who was then living at Garden Reach. The book was hollowed out, and in the hollow was a cocoa tin containing about a pound of picric acid with three fulminate of mercury detonators. It was so arranged that on the parcel being opened, a spring would be released and would strike on a nail inserted in one of the detonators, which would cause the bomb to explode. Fortunately, however, Mr. Kingsford, taking the parcel to contain a book which he had lent to a friend, did not open it. It was packed among his other books and taken to Muzaffarpur where it remained unopened until the beginning of 1909, when on information received from one of the under-trial prisoners in the jail, a communication was made by the Sub-divisional Officer to Mr. Kingsford and the book-bomb was discovered in his library."
5. The Bhowanipur centre was situated at No. 78, Russa Road, where Hem Das was followed on two occasions by Sub-Inspector Suresh Chandra Ghosh (*vide* his deposition in the Alipore bomb case). The writer mentioned before (Chapter XII) that they had a bomb school at Bhowanipur.
6. It was not Inspector P.C. Biswas, but Sub-Inspector S.C. Ghosh who followed the wirter to and from Bhowanipore (*vide* the deposition of Inspector P.C. Biswas in the Alipore bomb case).[i]
7. Kanai in Kanailal Datta, who was subsequently hanged, and Nirapada is Nirmal Roy, an accused in the Alipore bomb case. The two apprentices from other provinces were two Madrassis[ii] who were living at No. 15, Gopi Mohon Datta Lane. Both of them left before the house was searched. On the 27th April 1908, one of

these Madrassis was followed to Sini (*vide* the deposition of Inspector P.C. Biswas in the Alipore bomb case).

The following is found in the deposition of Inspector Purna Chandra Biswas:

"On the 26th April, I paid Rs. 5-8 to Sibokali Das for a room in Hem Chandra Das's house, and Sibokali Das gave me a receipt for the rent. Exh. 854 is the receipt.

"On the same day I hired another house in front of No. 15 Gopi Mohon Datta's Lane. I paid Rs. 3 and some annas. It was hired in the fictitious name Amritolal Das (page 245 of depositions).

8. Mr. Daly writes in his note regarding Muzaffarpur affairs:

   "At the end of April, the C.I.D. received intimation that two members of the conspiracy had gone to Muzaffarpur with the intention of murdering Mr. Kingsford." (Page 9).

   In the confession of Barin Ghosh (in the Alipore bomb case), the following occurs:

   "There is one more incident that at Muzaffarpur, and I shall explain it. Profulla Chandra Chaki insisted on going with a bomb to do away with Mr. Kingsford because he had tried the case against the national papers. The people in the country demanded his death.

   "Hem Chandra and Ullaskar prepared the bomb at No. 15, Gopi Mohon Datta's Lane—it was made of dynamite put in a tin case with a wooden handle ... Hem Chandra recommended Khudiram ghosh (?) of Midnapore; he was also allowed to go. I gave them two revolvers because they wanted to kill themselves if they were caught."

9. Regarding the removal of incriminating things to Harrison Road:

   On April 26, Sub-Inspectors S. Banerjee and S. Ghosh and Head Constable Balai Chand reported to Inspector Purna Chandra Biswas that they had seen a man carrying 2 trunks and a hand-bag from No. 15, Gopi Mohon Datta's Lane, to 134, Harrison Road, in carriage No. 494. (*Vide* page 245 of depositions in the lower court of the Alipore bomb case.)

   Sibokalli Das, one of the watchers deposed in the said case that under orders he kept watch over the house numbering 134, Harrison Road, in order to see if the trunks which were brought there from Gopi Mohon Datta Lane were removed from the house.

   This house was then in the occupation of Kaviraj Nagendra Nath Gupta.

10. Barin Ghosh admitted in his confession that many things were buried, and he pointed out two of them to the police when they went to search the grden.
11. It is a fact that the boxes brought to 134, Harrison Road, from No. 15, Gopi Mohon Datta Lane, were not removed. They were recovered when the house was searched.

Editorial Note :

i. Police (CID) came to know that two young men aged about 19 had left for Muzaffarpur from an internal source. A CID officer with a letter from commissioner of police went to Muzaffarpur and stayed there for more than a week. SP sent him back on 30th April, 1908 after with the letter, that "The most thorough and searching enquiries have been made but with no result. The CID appears to have been misinformed or the plot was abandoned." When the CID officer was in the train to Calcutta, the bomb exploded in Muzaffarpur.
ii. They were not Madrasis but Maharastrians. One was P.M. Bapat and the other was Balkrishna Hari Kane. Kane was arrested and put up for trial in Alipur case and acquitted by the High Court. Bapat could never be arrested. Known as 'Senapati' Bapat later on joined the Congress Party.

Chapter XVII
May, 1908

It was on the 30th April ,that instead of killing Mr. Kingsford, Khudiram killed Mrs. and Miss Kennedy at Muzaffarpur. A week prior to that date, Khudiram and his companion set off from Calcutta after dusk successfully eluding the police. Both of them were members of the old secret society, more active and clever than others, and obeyed orders like Casabianca. They were advised to dress themselves like men of some other province before going to throw the bomb and to assume Bengali costume after performing their mission. But they did not follow that advice. They were also taught to throw away their revolvers when the bomb burst, but they did not do that either. All along Khudiram had a strong desire to secure a revolver, but no revolver was given to him for fear of misuse of the weapon. Nevertheless, both he and his friend took one revolver[1] each, and an extra one was taken by Kshudiram without informing me on the day on which they started for Muzaffarpur. On the day following the bomb outrage, Khudiram was arrested[2] at the railway station while he was taking refreshments with both hands, and two revolvers were dangling from the pockets of his shirt which was of a fine stuff. That very day, Sub-Inspector Nanda Lal Banarji

---

Basumati, Bhadra 1334 BS, August-September 1927
Aswin 1334 BS, September-October, 1927

seeing the haggard looks of Profulla in a railway compartment[3] and growing suspicious of him, wired to the police authorities at the next station regarding him. At Mokama Station, the Sub-Inspector also alighted from the train with Profulla, and when the police, who were ready beforehand, came to arrest the latter, he committed suicide with his revolver.* Khudiram was carefully instructed not to make any statement whatever in case of his arrest without properly consulting his pleader. But he did not follow that instruction. He made one statement before the Magistrate and another before the Sessions Judge. In his confession, he implicated none but Profulla[4] and as he was not aware of the latter's real name, he mentioned him as Dinesh.[5] In his first statement, Khudiram said that he had met Profulla for 'the first time at the Howrah Station, and having expressed his determination to kill the *sahib*, was supplied with bombs, etc., by the latter and was also escorted up to Muzaffarpur by him. In his second statement, learning that Profulla had committed suicide, he shifted much of the blame to the former in the hope that his own punishment might be lighter.

Be that as it may, the bomb experts of Government gave out their opinion that the Muzaffarpur bomb was prepared with picric acid, but that was wholly erroneous.[6] The bomb outrage occurred on the 30th April, and on the 1st May it was decided in a meeting of the Calcutta Police that everybody who had come in contact with Barin should be arrested. Early in the morning of the 2nd May, the police raided the following places[7] and arrested the following persons:

1. Manicktola Muraripukur Garden. Here they arrested Barindra Kumar Ghosh, Bibhuti Bhusan Sirkar, Upendra Nath Banerji, Indu Bhusan Roy, Ullaskar Dutt, Nalini Kanta Gupta, Paresh Moulik, Bijoy Nag, Sachin Sen, Sisir Ghosh, Naren Bakshi,

Kunjalal Saha, Purna Sen, Hemendra Ghosh, fourteen in all. Besides these, one gardener of a local garden and the two sons of a gentleman were also arrested, but they were let off after 15 days.

2. At No. 15, Gopi Mohan Datta's Lane, Kanailal Dutt and Nirapada *alias* Nirmal Roy were arrested.
3. Two Kaviraj brothers, viz., Nagendra Nath Gupta and Dharani Nath Gupta, and one Asoka Nandi were arrested at 134, Harrison Road.
4. Arabinda Babu, Abinash Bhattacharyya and Sailendra Ghosh were arrested at No. 8, Grey Street.
5. Hem Chandra Das *alias* Hem Chandra Kanungoi was arrested at No. 38/4, Raja Nava Krishna Street.
6. Satyendra Nath Bose was arrested at Midnapore. Other persons who were arrested one after the other on the strength of the statement of Barin and others as well as from written records found in the garden, were as follows: Narendra Nath Gossain, Hrishikesh Kanjilal of Serampore, Sudhir Sirkar of Khulna, Birendra Nath Ghosh of Jessore, Krishto Jiban Sannyal of Malda, three brothers, Hem Chandra Sen, Birendra Chandra Sen and Sushil Kumar Sen of Sylhet, and Bal Krishna Hari Kane of Nagpur.

On the basis of information received from us as well as from subsequent enquiries, the following were arrested after a few weeks: Debabrata Bose, Indu Nath Nandi, Jatindra Nath Banarji, Prabhas Chandra *alias* Manik Dev, Bijoy Chandra Bhattacharyya, Nikhileswar Roy and Professor Charu Chandra Roy of Dupleix College, Chandernagore.

Besides these many innocent persons were arrested and sent to prison for a few days, and amongst them was Panchanan Tarkaratna.[8] Barring only two places, where domiciliary visits were made, nothing incriminating was found excepting one or two letters. But in the Muraripukur Garden were found the requisite machinery for casting bomb-shells, revolvers, rifles (six or seven in all), Noble's dynamite, several electric batteries fuse, etc., two English books for the preparation of explosives, one huge manuscript in hand-writing containing the mode of preparation of bombs and instructions for using them, documents relating to the formation of secret societies as well as several other books, note books and papers.

At Harrison Road, several boxes full of bombs and machinery for the preparation of explosives were found. In the afternoon of the 2nd May, persons arrested from different places were all brought out from their respective cells and collected on the courtyard of the Police Court. We were then taken aback on seeing each other. On the following morning we were all packed in hackney coaches and were taken, under a strong escort, to the Kyd Street C.I.D. Office. Here in separate rooms different police officers undertook to extract confessions from each different party.

The Muraripukur party consisting of Barin, Upen and others fell to the lot of Deputy Superintendent Rai Ramsaday Mukharji Bahadur. I was allotted to Maulvi Shamsul Alam, but I do not remember to whom the other prisoners were consigned. A desperate attempt to make us confess was made till the night had far advanced. I learnt afterwards that Barin was fed like an honoured guest and slept in that office comfortably Arabinda Babu was not perhaps so lucky, and I was thrust into the lock-up of the Lal Bazar Police Court, was given fried rice for supper and a blanket to sleep on. In trying to wring out a confession from us, the police did not adopt any violent method, and the tricks they applied were most commonplace and non-violent.

At first we were not permitted to take bath or food, then we were not allowed to sleep at night by being subjected to incessant questions till our reasoning power was confused. Almost all of us were subjected to this, excepting Barin, because the Rai Bahadur had perhaps understood that a treatment, quite the reverse of this, would be productive of better results in his case. It was perhaps for this that a European warder one morning offered me some tea without milk and bread. Coming to see me, he asked me to hand over to him any money or valuables that I might possess, promising to deposit them with Government, whereupon I made over to him my gold buttons; ring, two precious stones and my purse, containing a few rupees. As a result the warder gave me tea and bread and tried to humour me saying that revolutionary activities once started could never be suppressed. The cause of this man's kindness however became clear to me at the time of my transportation to Port Blair, because out of all that I had handed over to him, I only got back a set of brass buttons and my ring!

I had to pass that night munching fried rice, and no serious attempt was made to keep us awake till late hours because we were not allowed to sleep on two preceding nights. It was on that day that for the first time the Maulvi Sahib advised me to follow his directions if I wanted to be exculpated from all guilt. The truth is that going without food or sleep for days together and being subjected to continual sallies of questions by the police makes one lose one's head, and one cannot but make some admission in such a case, and admission once made, the whole thing comes out.

Be that as it may, the Rai Bahadur adopted a novel trick in respect of Barin and others. He expressed every sympathy with their aspirations, adding that he was himself a revolutionary at heart and invited them, in the name of his wife, to his own house where they were sumptuously fed and were treated with so much cordiality that they were cheated into the belief that he was their most sincere friend. They had already made some confessions in the Muraripukur Garden, but the Rai Bahadur considered the confession to be too scanty and advised them, as their well-wisher, to make a clean breast of the whole affair before the Magistrate to ensure their release. Thus cozened, Barin, Upen and Ullas gave out the names, and the whereabouts of others and their confessions were published in the newspapers on the day following. On the 3rd May another attempt was made to keep us talking incessantly from morning till 12 or 1 at night, one police officer taking the place of another when exhausted. Many had scanty meal that day and some had no food at all. I kept silent for a long time when the Maulvi Sahib handed me a copy of the *Statesman* wherein the confessions of Barin and others were published in the hope that it might also encourage me to make a confession.

About 4 in the afternoon Mr. Purna Chandra Lahiri, who was then an Inspector of the Criminal Investigation Department, and was the author of all mischief, appeared on the scene. On telling him that I would answer his questions if he could give me ice-cold water to drink, some refreshments and water were given to me which I highly relished. However, he did not say anything to us with a view to secure a confession. As in the previous night, each party was housed in separate places. In the lock-up of the Fenwick Bazar Police Station, I found myself amidst nauseating smell on an old and torn blanket. There were in the room myself, Abinash and two carters who were almost dead through intoxication. Next to them was placed a huge pot wherein the inmates eased themselves, a wooden bedstead in the middle of the room serving as a barricade. On the other side, sat the poor innocent Nagen Kaviraj half-dead through fear, while in front of him stood a sentry.

On the 4th May, we were all taken to the police court at 10 A.M. without being given food or permitted to bathe. After some time spent in confessions or statements before the Commissioner, we were all produced before the court of Mr. Birley, District Magistrate of Alipore. Most of us here made some confessions,[9] the only exceptions being Arabinda Babu and a few others while Upen, Barin, Ullas and others made special confessions. After that we were all sent to the Alipore Jail. Hitherto those who had not made a confession were kept separate, and separately they were sent to jail also. But Arabinda Babu was kept entirely separate from them. Before admitting us into the jail, we were made to bathe in conformity with the custom in vogue. In the evening we enjoyed hot Rangoon rice, a soup of pulses, fish and a vegetable curry, and found that the jail arrangements were better and more sanitary than those obtaining in our secret societies. Myself, Sailen, Nirapada, Abinash and Kanai spent that night in a big room.

Towards evening on the day following, I[10] was again taken to the C.I.D. Office where I found that the Rai Bahadur was listening, apparently with rapt attention, to the cock-and-bull story of Barin describing how he was spreading revolution in the country by establishing through his own effort, revolutionary centres in every district and subdivision. Later on I learnt from Barin the reason why I had been summoned that evening to the C.I.D. Office. Barin had given his word to the Rai Bahadur that if he were allowed to spend a night with me, he would prevail upon me to make a confession. Sitting with Barin, I helped myself to various edibles and heard many things in praise of me. Barin's manner of talk and his nonchalant behaviour led me to think that he was himself not only convinced of the Rai Bahadur's assurance of release, but that he was trying to convince me of it also.

Ramsaday Babu, however, gave way to despair at my attitude, and so asked Barin, half an hour or so after my arrival at the C.I.D. Office, to pump out of me, somewhere out of hearing, whether I should be of any use or not, adding that he would allow us to spend the night together only if I seemed promising. I tried to make Barin understand that there could be no privacy in the C.I.D. Office, but this he would not understand. So our conversation began, and the gist of what Barin said was, that I too should make a confession for the good of the country. I was at a loss what to reply. At last thinking that he might obey the instruction of his elder brother Arabinda Babu, informed him that I had met the latter, and was advised by him that every one of us who had made a confession, ought to retract it. But that too produced no effect on Barin. So I tried another expedient, and told him that he should first of all consider whether his confession could be looked upon as blame-worthy, that is, his confession might be considered as treachery. Barin was sorely put out at this, and replied that neither his brother nor anybody else had the intelligence to understand what service he had rendered to the country by making a confession, adding that we were all cowards. On being asked why he had divulged the names of others, he replied that he was not accustomed to tell lies like ourselves. The Rai Bahadur was seeing and enjoying all this. So thinking that it would not be wise to allow the matter to proceed further, he made me stand in the verandah, cuffing my hands from behind, in the custody of a sergeant and two constables and began to talk with Barin with loud peals of laughter elsewhere. Shortly after, I[11] was ordered to be taken to the Lal Bazar lock-up and was marched off to that destination with a rope round my waist. This proved that the Rai Bahadur was also very angry with me. However, I was taken to the lock-up and was handed over to the custody of an old Superintendent of Police, who looking at me searchingly from head to foot began to quarrel with the Rai Bahadur over the telephone regarding his inability to persecute me without the orders of the higher authorities. I was shut up in the lock-up and spent the night in great anxiety. Next morning I was again taken to the jail and lodged in a solitary cell a sepoy and a constable always mounting guard over me. Even those who brought me food were not allowed to speak with me, and I remember that I spent about four or five weeks in this manner.

Barin's confession[12] has a great historical value because it was on the basis of this that many historians have written and may write in future, about the genesis of the revolutionary movement in Bengal. The Rowlatt Commission also accepted this confession as gospel truth. The very next moment after his arrest at the Muraripukur Garden, Barin exclaimed "my mission is over" and began to show to the police everything that was kept hidden. For some time past, the leaders and pseudo-leaders of our society, such as Upen, Barin, etc., had begun to attach spirituality to revolutionism, and hence they did not care to take the most necessary precautions for their own safety. Nevertheless, the motive which inspired Barin to make a confession and divulge the names of those who had not yet been arrested was the hope held out by the Rai Bahadur that he would be released. Barin being a member of a sentimental race, it was no wonder that he should take the Rai Bahadur at his word, and as he was wholly unprepared for arrest, he believed that confession was the only means of his salvation.

After the assassination of Gossain, many of us began to supply information to the police arguing that on being released as a result of their information, we would amply atone for our guilt. After our deportation to Port Blair, Messrs. Denham and Tegart[13] were deputed to us, one after the other, to collect informations regarding the revolutionary murders, etc., that had been taking place in the country. They talked with each one of us separately, and we asked each other what questions and answers were exchanged between each of us and the *sahibs*. Barin however replied that he had supplied no information at all in as much as Government had treated him most shabbily for all the help rendered by him to the police. Barin many times opposed the proposal of murdering Gossain within the jail on the plea that Arabinda Babu would be implicated thereby, but when he formed the plot of breaking loose from the jail, he not only tried to prevail upon those who had taken exception to it to agree, but also lost sight of the fact that it too would implicate Arabinda Babu.

Egged on by the police, I, too, felt a strong desire to regain my liberty by making a confession and same was the motive which inspired others[15] of our set to supply information to the police, of their own accord, after the jail murder. Others again took to reading the *Gita* in the hope of securing immunity from punishment. Be that as it may, towards the close of our case, many of us, in imitation of Debabrata Babu, tried to exert will-force or hypnotic suggestions on the European judge who was trying us. The long and short of the whole story is that every one of us was swayed more or less with the desire of securing liberty. Barin really believed that while being marched off to the Alipore Court, he would be rescued from the custody of the police, and thereby gains his liberty. Upen, Ullas, etc., were not at first prepared to make a confession of his own initiative, the latter informed the police that the persons arrested in the Kaviraja's shop at Harrison Road were innocent, and that he himself was responsible for all the deadly articles found there. It was on the ground that their confession would act as an incentive to the spread of the revolutionary cult in the country that Upen and Ullas agreed[16] to make confessions. In fact, Ramsaday Babu touched the vanity of Barin to such a degree that in his confession he not only held back nothing, but on the contrary added many things that had no foundation in fact!

A few months before our case came up for hearing, Babu Bhupendra Nath Dutt[17], the then editor of the *Yugantar* newspaper, was prosecuted for sedition, and the leaders of our society were at great pains to make Bhupen Babu admit his guilt fearlessly which being done, the latter was sentenced to one year's imprisonment[i] and thereby became almost a popular hero. But a few weeks after this, Arabinda Babu[18] being prosecuted on a similar charge for writing an article in the *Bande Mataram* took a quite different attitude[ii] and also created great public sensation. Such is the unreasonableness of public opinion in this country! As in the case of ordinary criminals so also in our case the desire to give away the names of our fellow revolutionaries was generated in our minds. Many instances are to be found where a revolutionary immediately before being hanged betrayed his leaders.[iii] However, Barin helped to throw suspicion off the real leaders of the movement by declaring to all the world that he was the sole leader and was responsible for everything.

Annotations :

1. Barin Ghosh in his confession said that he gave Khudiram and Profulla two revolvers because they wanted to kill themselves if they were caught (*vide* page 3 of confessions).
   Actually three revolvers were found with them; one with Profulla Chaki (with which he committed suicide) and two with Khudiram Bose when he was arrested.
2. Khudiram Bose was arrested on the 1st May 1908 at Wani Railway Station by two constables, and two revolvers were found with him (*vide* deposition of Mr. Armstrong, Superintendent of Police, Muzaffarpur, in the Kennedy murder case).
3. The fact of Profulla Chaki journeying by train in a compartment with Sub-Inspector Nandalal Banerji up to his committing suicide by means of a revolver was corroborated by a report of Superintendent of Police, Muzaffarpur, dated 18th May 1908, to this department.
4. Khudiram Bose actually changed part of his confession and blamed Profulla Chaki for inducing him to commit the murder.
5. In the Alipore bomb case Mr. Beachcroft remarked thus : "That the bomb which killed them (Mrs. And Miss Kennedy) was intended for Mr. Kingsford, there can be no doubt. It was thrown just outside Mr. Kingsford's gate, and the unfortunate ladies were riding in a carriage like Mr. Kingsford's. Khudiram Bose was hanged for the murder, and his accomplice, who went by the name of Dinesh Chandra Ray, committed suicide on the Mokama platform when about to be arrested." (*Vide* page 24 of the judgement).
6. Regarding the composition of the Muzaffarpur bomb, Mr. Denham wrote in a letter to Mr. Barnard, C.I.E. : "I am afraid I cannot find anything on record regarding the Muzaffarpur bomb. Smallwood never made any official report, and all he says you will see in his statement in the book of depositions in the Alipore bomb case. My opinion, which I believe to be absolutely correct, is that the bomb consisted of dynamite with fulminate of mercury detonators. This may account for the absence of any signs on 2 remnants of the bomb which were recovered at Muzaffarpur."
   "Khudiram Bose also stated that the above was the composition of the bomb." (Letter dated 26th January 1911.)
7. Regarding the searches after the Muzaffarpur outrage, Mr. F.C. Daly says in his note at page 9 :

"A conference was held in the house of the Commissioner of Police on the night of the 1st May and the searches commenced on the morning of the 2nd. Barindra Kumar Ghosh and a large number of young men were surprised in their sleep and actually arrested in the Manicktola Garden, a search of which revealed the storage of a large quantity of explosives, of bomb shells ready to be filled with explosives and of revolvers, rifles and ammunition. Barindra Kumar Ghosh, for his own reasons, actually assisted the police in the search and indicated the whereabouts of the store of arms."

The places and persons named by the writer were actually searched and arrested by the police. 48, Grey Street, and not 8, Grey Street (as written by Hem Kanangore), was searched.

Four persons, two of whom were Oriya gardeners, were arrested in the Manicktola Garden on suspicion and were subsequently released.

8. Panchanan Tarkaratna was not arrested in connection with the Alipore bomb case as written by Hem kanango. He was arrested with the Kankinara bomb case.
9. The arrested persons were produced before the District Magistrate, Alipore, on the 4th May 1908, and Barin Ghosh, Ullashkar Datta, Upen Banarji, Indu Bhusan Ray and Bibhuti Bhusan Sarkar made confession before the Magistrate Mr. L. Birley which were recorded by him. (*Vide* order sheet of the Alipore bomb case.)

Regarding the confession, Mr. Beachcroft says in his judgement (Alipore bomb case):

"It is also argued that the confession of Barin is not admissible in evidence as not being voluntarily made. Mr. Birley has started with regard to this confession as well as the others, that he was satisfied that they were voluntary, etc., etc.

"Mr. Banarji's case is that it was prompted by his 'desire to save the innocent on the inducement of Ram Sadai that that would be best for them.' Now strictly speaking such an inducement would not make a confession inadmissible, etc., etc.

"I do not, however, desire to base my decision on this technical ground, for I have no doubt whatever that the confession was quite voluntary.

"Made on the 4th may it was not retracted till the trial began in this court on the 19th October, in spite of the fact that in the Magistrate's court he had legal advice, and that on the 13th

August the Magistrate expressly invited him to affirm or deny the confession." (Page 10 of the judgement.)

10. Regarding Hem Das' going to the C.I.D. Office from jail custody, the following is found in the order sheet of the bomb case:
"7-5-1908 Accused Barindra and Hem Chandra were remanded to police custody yesterday, and have been brought back today and remanded to *hajat* till May 18th Sd. L.B."
From the above it appears that Barin and Hem Das (the writer) were taken to the C.I.D. Office once on 6th May 1908.
11. Accused Barindra Kumar Ghose and Hem Chandra Das were remanded to police custody on 6th May 1908 and brought back to *hajat* on 7th May 1908 (*vide* order sheet of the Alipore bomb case).
Hem Chandra Das did not make any confession.
12. Mr. Beachcroft, Sessions Judge, who tried the Alipore bomb case, held that the confession of accused Barin Ghosh was quite voluntary.
Regarding the motive of his confession, Barin Ghosh stated in his confession, "Please take down my motive for disclosing these facts. Our party was divided as to the property of disclosing these facts. Some thought they would deny everything and take the consequences, but I persuaded them all to give written and oral statements to Inspector Ram Sadai Mukharji because I believe that as this band was found out, it was best not to do any other work in the country and because we ought to save the innocent." (Page 4 of confession.)
Barin Ghosh did not implicate Arabinda ghosh and others intentionally. Their names transpired in the statement of approver Naren Gossain. Barin actually tried to shield Arabinda and took the whole responsibility upon himself (*vide* Barin's confession in the Alipore bomb case).
The Sedition Committee took into consideration the confessions of Barin Ghosh and several others. The Committee remarked thus : "It is important to note that the confessions from which the above statements have been extracted were held by the Chief Justice of Bengal to be free from "the slightest apprehension of sinister influence of pressure." (Page 15 of the Sedition Committee's report.)
Sir Charles Tegart went to Port Blair on 28th August 1913 and interviewed the political prisoners there. Among other things Barin Ghosh told him that he was unwilling to play the part of a traitor as he distrusted Government's promises. (*Vide* page 8 of

"Notes on Andaman enqairy.")

13. Naren Gossain was made approver in the Alipore bomb case. He was murdered within the jail by Satyen Bose and Kanailal Datta (accused in the same case).
14. Regarding the plan of escape from the jail, one of the prisoners gave the following account:
"A month after our admission into the jail, there was a proposal amongst us that we must make some plan for escape. Barin said that without help from outside and without firearms inside we cannot succeed. One day B.C. Chatterjee, Bar-at-law, interviewed Barin and said 'that some plan must be devised for your escape. I can help with men and arms.' Barin came back and called out five of the accused and told them of his conversation with B.C. Chatterjee. He said that we cannot all escape and only four selected by ballot shall escape, so that we can do some work outside." (*Vide* page 13 of Mr. F. C. Daly's " Note on the growth of the revolutionary movement in Bengal.")
15. After the murder of approver Narendra Nath Gossain in the jail, detailed information regarding the outrage was given to the police, in strict confidence, by one of the prisoners. (*Vide* pages 13-14 of Mr. F. C. Daly's note.)
16. Ullashkar Datta made a statement to the police in which he said that he kept the articles in the house of his friend, Kaviraj Nagendra Nath Gupta at Harrison Road, who was innocent and was not a member of their party.
In regard to the motive for their confessions, accused Upendra Nath Banerjee and Ullashkar Datta stated as follows:
Upendra said : "I have made this statement because we agreed to tell the truth, if arrested, that the innocent might not suffer, and that our successors may use greater caution." (Page 10 of confessions in the Alipore bomb case.)
Ullashkar Datta said : "I wish to add that the object of my confession is that innocent persons shall not suffer," (Page 7 of confessions.)
17. Bhupendra Nath Datta was prosecuted and sentenced to one year's rigorous imprisonment under section 124A, Indian Penal Code, on 24th July 1907. In his judgment, the trying Magistrate remarked: "The accused has filed a written statement in which he acknowledges full responsibility for the publication of these articles, and the crown has accordingly adduced only formal evidence."

18. Arabinda Ghosh was prosecuted under section 124A, Indian Penal Code for a seditious article in the *Bande Mataram,* but was discharged on 23rd September 1907. The defence was that Arabinda was not the editor, but that he had been employed as a member of the editorial staff, his sole duty being to supply contribution to the editorial columns of the paper.

Editorial Note :

i. Bhupendra Nath Dutta admitted before the police that he was the editor of the *Jugantar*. Aurobindo told later on, "When the police searched the office of the news paper, he came forward and in a spirit of bravado declared himself the editor, although this was quite untrue." (*Sri Aurobindo: Autobiographical Notes,* p. 77) In a written statement before the court he acknowledged full responsibility. It is not correct that the secret society asked him to take the responsibility as editor of Jugantar.
ii. Aurobindo was not prosecuted for writing an article, but for publishing a sedition writing as Editor of Bandemataram. He was not formally declared as Editor and so his culpability could not be established. Hem Chandra was away in Paris when Bhupendra and Aurobindo were prosecuted.
iii. Hem Chandra refer to the confession of Barindra Nath Dutta Gupta who killed Inspector Shamsul Alam in Calcutta High Court. The day before his execution he made a statement in which he implicated Jatindra Nath Mukherjee as instigator of the murder. Following the comments of the Sedition Committee on the issue, that 'The real criminal responsible for the boy's act was Jatin Mukherjee', Hem Chandra also blames the old and new leaders and sub-leaders who are not now engaged in spiritual *sadhana*. But how would Hem Chandra explain his own mole in quietly bringing Kshudiram from Midnapur and sending him to Muzaffarpur to murder Kingsford?

Chapter XVIII
In Alipur Jail

About three weeks after our arrest, we learnt that the police *sahib* and his staff had been holding discussions *in camera* with Naren Gossain and his father, daily for three or four hours. It then became clear to us that Naren was going to turn King's evidence against us, and hence our wrath[1]; and hatred were all focussed on Naren and his rich father. We little thought that treachery was one of our national characteristics. The leaders, when starting revolutionary societies, ignored the fact that those who supported Clive or the Bengalis who showed keen insight during the Sepoy Mutiny were all our countrymen. Indeed public opinion here is not sensitive to the enormity of treachery to one's party. Thus when Naren began to make disclosures against the secret society, in the role of an approver, in the court of Mr. Birley, no sensation was created in the country. He was the first approver so far as the Bengal revolutionary movement was concerned, and he received great inducement to become so. He was not only promised a pardon, but was also given to understand that he and his family would be maintained in England in a rich style. He used to say that he had turned approver in order to avenge himself on Barin, who had out of jealousy got him

---

Basumati, Kartik 1334 BS, October-November 1927
Agrahayan 1334 BS, November-December 1927

and others arrested. But subsequent approvers had no such opportunities nor do they enjoy them now. Still, seeing the huge number of men who turn approvers, informers, agents provocateurs, etc., I am sometimes led to think that two precious lives, viz., those of Satyen and Kanai were sacrificed uselessly and without any justification for committing a horrible murder. In the jail, in spite of strict surveillance, we used to get paper and pencil and could communicate with any person within or without the jail by exchange of letters on payment of small tips. Many convicts again prided themselves on exhibiting the bravado spirit by doing hazardous and specially punishable acts without hope of reward. "How much paper and pencil do you want?" asked a certain lamp trimmer.

"One sheet for the present and a little pencil lead." "Very well Babu, I will get them for you. But keep them carefully."

"Would you carry a letter to so and so?"

"Let me have it. You will get a reply either in the evening or tomorrow."

If we gave him a reward, he used to take it, if not, he never asked for anything. In this way we began to receive and transmit letters to and from the jail, using two or three codes.

At this time, Satyendra Kumar Bose, who had been sentenced to two years' rigorous imprisonment[2] for using his brother's gun without license, by the Midnapore Court, was brought over to the Alipore Jail to stand his trial for complicity in the conspiracy case. He was lodged in the hospital from the very beginning as he had been ailing from various maladies, such as dysentery, asthma, etc., and it was easy at that time to be booked for the hospital on spending a paltry sum.[3]

Learning everything about Naren, after his arrival at the Alipore Jail, Satyen wrote three letters to a revolutionary desiring to know whether there was any other amongst us of the type of Naren, for the names of those who could be thoroughly trusted and added that it was necessary to keep us informed by way of precaution of everything that Naren had been disclosing to the police. He further suggested that if there was no other way of so doing, one of us should pretend to turn a fellow approver, and lastly turned to the question of devising means for murdering Naren. After a good deal of discussion, it was at first settled that the task of murdering Naren should be entrusted to our revolutionary friends outside the jail, and Satyen afterwards undertook to enact the part of the corroborator, little thinking that he would ultimately become the murderer of Naren. The man with whom Satyen discussed the matter, himself undertook to perform all unimportant things such as the formation of a detective branch with the help of a handful of trustworthy and clever boys, watching the trend of others' opinions, keeping Satyen informed of it, and lastly keeping up the spirit of self-sacrifice for the country in the minds of all. Almost all of us with only one or two solitary exceptions, such as Arabinda Babu, Debabrata Babu, etc., sincerely desired that Naren should pay the extreme penalty, and Barin entrusted this task to all the revolutionary secret parties in the country, but none could see its way to comply. Three or four parties gave almost the same reply, and the party of Midnapore was one of them. The gist of what they said was that their hands were full of more weighty matters than the murder of Gossain, and that we ourselves should see the matter through. In other words they had disbanded and were ready to thank their stars if they escaped detection. Hoping that the two or three parties, which had made no reply, might hazard an attempt, they were supplied with a lengthy plan to enable them to understand where and in what way the attempt should be made. In the meantime, all of us were one day thrust into a narrow place called the "Six degree" with the object that Naren would be able to collect any secret that might be lurking in us and communicate it to the police. Naren did not then know that we had found him out, but he understood this a few days later. So the attempt of the police was baffled, but they perhaps scented that Naren might be murdered by us. In fact he was regarded with such a strong hatred by us that he was shortly after lodged in a separate place near the hospital and two Eurasian convicts were appointed to guard his person, the rest of us being all put into Ward No. 23 which was a very big room. During the few days of Naren's stay with us, Debabrata Babu and Barin treated him in a most friendly manner and tried to win him over, the former by exerting will-force and the latter by love. Satyen who was still an inmate of the hospital began to cultivate acquaintance with Naren, and it gradually became known even to the public that the former was going to become the corroborator of the latter. As arranged, Satyen began to pretend that he was terribly upset in anticipation of the heavy punishment that would be meted out to him and earnestly entreated Naren to find him a way out. The latter carried the matter to the head of the police, who after testing Satyen for a. few days, was at last satisfied with him and granted his prayer. He also gave various instructions to Naren to tutor up Satyen who in his turn began to send every information to the proper quarter. This continued for three months.

In Ward No. 23, we 35 or 36 of us began to have a very merry time of it. New forms of amusement were daily devised, and everybody made to participate in the fun. Nor were bickerings, fightings, party spirit, etc., lacking, and even religious instructions, austerities, etc., were carried on with great gusto. When Naren began to make his deposition before Mr. Birley, the wicked boys in their excitement resolved that they would secure firearms by rifling the contents of a box, produced as an exhibit and supposed to be full of such weapons, and also by snatching away the revolvers of the two sergeants on duty and then kill Naren, leap over the window and make good their escape as best they could. But Barin stood in the way on the ground that Arabinda Babu would be implicated thereby. Nevertheless, in spite of this possibility, Barin was the first to formulate the idea of breaking loose from the jail. Most of us being admirers of Barin, all objections were overruled. We heard that one or two of the secret societies outside were ready to help us in our enterprise. A plan was also got ready setting forth the route through which we must reach Persia and a list of the articles to be required *en route* was also sent to those societies. Many of us even went so far as to "rehearse " running within the ward and got fever and pain in consequence. The party outside was asked to smuggle 15 revolvers within the jail, and gradually the proposal of murdering Naren was shelved. Learning all this, Satyen filched the first revolver that arrived to us within the jail, and without saying anything to anybody for fear of being hindered, determined to kill Naren with his own hands. It was indeed inexplicable, why being a recognised revolutionary leader, he himself undertook that responsibility instead of shirking it, as the leaders used to do. Satyen knew how restless Sushil had become in order to murder Naren and had many times found that it was the custom with secret societies to send youngsters forward to such undertakings while the leaders kept themselves at a safe distance. He was the chief inaugurator of the memorable Midnapore Conference in the previous year, and it was through his cleverness that the extremists scored a victory in it. In the famous Surat Congress also his presence of mind and moral courage saved the prestige of the Bengal extremists.

It was very easy at that time to import revolvers into the jail from outside because no great strictness then used to be observed[4], and that is why I had no desire to know how the first revolver arrived. One of Satyen's* friends was entrusted to keep it safely. It was a large weapon of the old type, rusty and with a jammed trigger. When its very existence was almost forgotten by us, the friend referred to handed it over to Satyen. But he too could not use it, and had to wait till the arrival of a better weapon. Satyen tried to bring over some revolvers from Midnapore, but learnt that the leaders there had all become inactive. At that time Government was labouring under the impression that the revolutionaries had a great centre of activity at Midnapore, and that they were very practical, and hence unlimited powers were delegated to the local authorities to cow down the inhabitants of the place with the result that 30 or 40 persons were arrested. The friend of Satyen, referred to above, was one day turned out of the hospital for going there without permission. On the other hand, Satyen used to see Naren almost every day at the hospital and to recite, by way of testing his memory, all the statements made by the latter, wilfully perverting them, while Naren in his turn used to make the former read the depositions he had made and warned him against making a contradictory statement himself. At last Satyen asked permission of the police *sahib* to file a written statement and his prayer was granted. Hence he began to write it before Naren in the dispensary for some days. The cases[5] of Debabrata Babu, Indra Nath, etc., who were arrested later were still pending at the court of Mr. Birley, but we had already been committed to the sessions.

Naren Gossain was to have begun his deposition on the 1st September and Satyen learnt that many new names would be given out and many persons would be arrested in consequence. It was in the wind that at least twenty highly respectable persons[6] would be arrested. Hence Satyen's endeavour was to kill Naren on the morning of that eventful day, and so he sent word to his friend to that effect and the latter, unable to come personally, sent him a revolver[7] through Kanai, wrapping it up in cloth so dexterously that even Kanai did not know what it really was. It was only when Satyen asked Kanai to take the bigger revolver back with him that the latter learnt the whole truth and at once volunteered to help the former with the bigger weapon. Satyen would not at first, it is said, agree to Kanai's proposal without the permission of his friend. Having received the permission, they settled amongst themselves that Satyen would make the attempt first and, if he missed, Kanai would see the matter through.

On the 1st of September, Naren, accompanied by two Eurasian warders, came up the stairs and took his seat, as usual, in the dispensary before Satyen. Satyen first aimed at Naren keeping the revolver within his coat. There was a click, but the cartridge missed fire, whereupon he drew the revolver out and was again aiming when one of the Eurasian warders came up and was trying to wrest away the weapon from him when it went off fracturing the warder's wrist. In the meantime, Naren slipped out of the room, but was fired at by Kanai, who was pacing in front of the staircase. The bullet hit Naren on the leg, nevertheless he descended the stairs, passed through the hospital gates and entered a long and narrow alley flanked by high walls, Kanai closely following at his heels in hot chase. After coming out of the dispensary, Satyen met a convict, and learning from him where Naren was, ran up to Kanai and both began firing their weapons at him.

Then everything customary happened. An alarm was given, officers began to run here and there, Satyen and Kanai were arrested, and the wards were locked up and searched. The investigation[8] of the murder and the trial were finished as usual. Kanai made an admission without giving out anybody's name or telling where the revolver came from, while Satyen denied everything.

The quarrel[9] between Satyen and Barin originated in 1902, when the secret society was first started in Circular Road.[10] At that time as a result of a quarrel amongst us as to whether it was justifiable on the part of the members of a secret society to make admissions, two parties were formed in the jail. One was headed by Barin and the other by Satyen.

As a result of this party spirit, many ceased to acknowledge the leadership of Barin, and so all his wrath was turned upon Satyen with the result that there had been serious passages at arms between the two in that connection. Barin's vanity was further wounded by the fact that Satyen murdered Gossain without letting him know[11] anything about the matter beforehand.

The Magistrate did not allow Naren to be cross-examined after his deposition on the ground that much delay had already occurred. One of our pleaders, however, got a petition granted to the effect that Naren's evidence would not be considered as proof until he was subjected to a cross-examination[12] at the Sessions Courts. But for this the murder of Gossain would have been in vain and Arabinda Babu would not have got off. No pleader in the court of Mr. Barley could then understand the importance of this, and the plan was devised and got up by Satyen himself.

Be that as it may, both were condemned[13] to be hanged, and Kanai was hanged first because he was not prepared to make an appeal. Satyen would not at first agree to prefer an appeal, but at last I prevailed upon him to do so on the pretext that it would be conforming to the rules of the revolutionaries, little thinking that Satyen would incur odium thereby. Five or six days after Naren's murder, we too were placed in the interior of the jail room called "44 degrees" where Satyen and Kanai had been shut up, and in spite of strict surveillance we used to receive and transmit letters in codes through the *mehtar*.[14]

After the execution of the sentence on Kanai, his dead body was cremated with great *eclat* and a serious agitation and excitement[15] were created in Calcutta. Hence the date on which Satyen was to be hanged (23rd November) was not made known[16] to the public, but a few relatives were allowed to be present on the spot and cremate his body there. Satyen's anti-party, however, snatched this opportunity to spread calumny against him to the top of their bent. They went so far as to say that Satyen had fainted when the noose was put round his neck and so on. But we learnt the real facts later on from those who were actually present at the time of Satyen's death. Let me quote a letter from a highly respectable gentleman who was present there

"27, Samavaya Mansion, Calcutta,
2nd July 1924.

Dear Hem Babu,

One day, I do not remember the date or the year, Satyen's mother (since deceased) came to my house and asked me to undertake the heavy responsibility of cremating Satyen as his elder brother was down with fever and nobody else could be found. I assented and sought the aid of my friend Babu Premtosh Bose[17], who was a new patriot and was the first leader in the history of strikes in this country. I presented myself before Mr. Bompas (?), Magistrate of Alipore, and he gave me permission to cremate the dead body on these conditions, viz., that cremation outside the jail was not allowable, there should be no pomp or demonstration, no mementoes were to be taken away, the cremation should be done within the jail before the eyes of the authorities, and there' should not he more than 14 or 15 persons present.

"Early in the morning of the day appointed for the execution, we presented ourselves at the gate of Alipore Jail. We were not prepared to witness the cruel scene, but when it was over, a white Superintendent of Police came to us and said, 'You can *go* now. The thing is over. Satyendra died bravely, Kanai was brave, but it seems Satyendra was braver.' At that very moment a sergeant put in, When I went to his cell to get him to the gallows, he was wide awake, 'when I said, Satyendra, be ready,' he answered 'Well, I am quite ready' and smiled. He walked steadily to the gallows. He mounted it bravely and bore it all cheerfully. A brave lad!

"Myself and my wife visited him on two occasions before his death. He talked with us with a cheerful countenance for about an hour and remarked, 'My death or Kanai's death alone will not do, the country will not be freed and awakened unless thousands like us die.' When informed that his mother was anxious to see him in jail, he replied, 'I will see her only on condition that she does not weep,' and his mother shed not a drop of tear! Asked whether he had any hand in the murder of Naren Gossain, he indicated by a gesture that he had.

"I was sorely pained to notice the condition he had been placed under. His cell was only 4 cubits by 3 cubits. It was winter, and he wore a blanket. and had a blanket to lie down upon. In one corner of the cell was placed a wicker basket only a cubit and a half from the bed covered with earth, which served the purpose of a commode, and it was in the same cell that he had to take his food. We had to talk under strict police guard, and Mr. Emerson, the Jail

Superintendent, used to be present there. The *Empire* published a distorted account of the affair, but we published a contradiction. —A.C. Rai.

Annotations :

1. Mr. F.C. Daly at page 13 of his report writes : "They received a rude shock when one-of the leading members of their party, Narendra Nath Gossain, appeared one day in the witness box as an approver, and it was soon decided amongst them that Narendra Nath Gossain must be murdered."
2. Satyendra Bose was prosecuted and sentenced to rigorous imprisonment for one month and not two years under section 19 of the Arms Act *(vide* Midnapore P. S. case No. 8, dated 9th June 1908).
3. The following account by one of the prisoners will give an idea of the state of affairs at the Alipore Jail at that time :
   "A month after our admission into the jail, there was a proposal amongst us that we should make some plan of escape. Barin said that without outside help and without firearms inside, we could not succeed. One day B.C. Chatterjee, Barrister-at-Law, interviewed Barin and said that some plan must be devised for our escape. He could, he said, help us with men and arms. At the time of this interview Arabinda Babu was in hospital. Barin came back and called out five of the accusedSailendra Nath Basu, Upendra Nath Banerjee, Hem Chandra Das, Nalini Kanta Gupta, Sudhir Sarkar and some others, and told them of his conversation with B.C. Chatterjee. He said at the time that we could not all escape, and that only four selected by ballot would be able to escape, so that we can do some work outside. Kauai, Nalini, Kunjalal Shaha and another were selected. Barin sent intimation of this selection to Arabinda in hospital on a slip next morning. Barin wrote a letter to B.C. Chatterjeean ordinary letterand that letter was sent by post through the Senior Hospital Assistant. The letter stated that four men had been selected, and asked him to collect men and to supply arms. Barin also wrote letters to Sudhangshu Jiban Rai, Preo Sankar Rai, and Srish Chandra Ghosh of Chandernagore and Basanta Banerjee of Chandernagore telling them to see B.C. Chatterjee at his house in Bhowanipur. These letters were posted by the same doctor. B.C.

Chatterjee replied that he had arranged men and weapons and had sent a man to Dacca. At this stage the code was communicated to all these persons, and all subsequent communications were in code language. These letters were received through the same doctor generally after 11 P.M., and they (the outsiders) also used to come to the doctor's place at that hour to receive letters. B.C. Chatterjee wrote asking Barin to suggest a plan of escape and means for the introduction of firearms. Barin consulted Sailendra Nath Basu who made a sketch of the wards and the jail surroundings and ward No. 23. Barin and Hem Das made a plan of the north wall showing the jute godown, etc. It was first suggested that seven revolvers should be introduced packed in pillows. This was communicated to Basanta. Banarji of Chandernagore. ... On the 23rd August (Sunday) several of the prisoners were taken to the gate for interview. It had been arranged that a revolver should be brought in that day by hand and not packed in a pillow. Barin wore a *dhosa;* he gave eight annas to the warder to keep off other interviewers. Sudhangshu Jiban Rai and a fat boy of fair complexion (name not known) had come to interview Barin, and they and Barin stood close together at the bars. Sudhangshu Jiban Rai handed a packet to Barin and the fat boy gave him a wax ball. The packet was kept among the blankets and cloth until 10 A.M. the next day when Hem Das took it to the hospital. Hem had decided that the very first thing to do was to shoot Naren Gossain (who, though still kept in the Alipore Jail, had been removed from close contact with the other prisoners). When Hem Das came back from hospital, he said that Satyendra Nath Basu, who was in the hospital, said that he could not utilise such a big revolver against Naren. This was on the 24th. Kanailal Datta then volunteered to manage it.

4. Regarding jail discipline at that time, Mr. F. C. Daly writes at page 13 of his note "The undertrial prisoners in this case were at first allowed all the liberties to which undertrials could ever be entitled. They mixed freely with one another in the jail. A large number of visitors were permitted to visit them, and from all accounts great freedom and laxity were allowed at the time of these visits."
5. Debabrata Bose, Indra Nath and several others were committed to the Court of Sessions in a second batch.
6. Regarding the arrest of respectable persons on the statement of Naren Gossain, Mr. F.C. Daly writes thus : The mischief. however,

had been done and the assassination of Naren Gossain put an end to a supplementary case which was under contemplation, in which, had it been proceeded with such prominent persons as Abinash Chakravarti, the munsif, Charu Chandra Datta of the Bombay Civil Service and Subodh Chandra Mallick of Calcutta would possibly have been placed on trial under section 121A."

7. One of the prisoners gave the following account of the incident (*vide* page 14 of Mr. F. C. Daly's note):
"Barin wrote to Srish Ghosh of Chandernagore to send in a small revolver. On Sunday, the 30th, Srish Ghosh came to interview Barin. All the prisoners were taken to the jail gate. The jailor took Arabinda and Barin inside the office and gave a chair to Arabinda and another man who had come for an interview. Barin was-talking with several boys at the corner of the jailor's table. Srish arrived at this time. The jailor asked whom he wanted to see. He said " Barin." Srish, Barin and the three boys moved on and stood near an almirah. There was no warder near them, Srish handed to Barin a small packet packed up in a cloth and Barin kept it under the *chadar*. After the interview, the prisoners returned to their wards and Hem Das took the packet and gave it to Kanailal Datta. It was about noon. That evening Kanailal Datta pretended to be sick and was taken to the hospital. The revolver had been received loaded."

8. Mr. W. A. Marr, District Magistrate, Alipore, held a judicial enquiry into the murder of Naren Gossain and committed Satyen Bose and Kanailal Datta to the Court of Sessions for trial.
During the trial, it transpired that on the morning of 31st August 1908 (not on the 1st September as the writer states) Naren Gossain went to the jail hospital upstairs along with one European prisoner named Higgins, in the hope of obtaining some confession from Satyen Bose. Suddenly Satyen and Kanai began to shoot at Naren. There was a struggle, and the European prisoner Higgins in attempting to protect Narendra was shot through the wrist by Kanailal Datta. Another prisoner Linton came to the place with the jailor and some of his assistants, but they were threatened by the accused with revolvers. Naren Gossain was then shot dead. In the course of trial, Kanailal stated that he had fired at Gossain "because he proved to be a traitor to the country" Satyen denied everything. (*Vide* file 662/1908 of S.B.)

9. In his confession Barin Ghosh stated, "Our party was divided as to the propriety of disclosing these facts. Some thought they would

deny everything and take the consequences, but I persuaded them all to give written statements, etc., etc."

10. Regarding the secret society in Circular Road, Mr. F. C. Daly writes in his note thus: "According to Barindra, he started his propaganda in Bengal between 1900 and 1903 and visited every district and subdivision in Bengal preaching the cause of independence."
11. It is not a fact that Barin did not know anything about the murder of Naren Gossain. Barin himself smuggled the revolver into the jail and sent it to Satyen in the hospital through Kanailal. (Vide Mr. Daly's note, page 14.)
12. Accused Sailendra Nath Basu filed a petition through his pleader, Narendra Nath Basu, praying for cross-examining the prosecution witnesses in the lower court before commitment, on which Mr. Birley, the enquiring Magistrate, passed the following orders : "The petition is rejected. There was recently a case of this kind in which the High .Court allowed a refusal to allow cross-examination. In this case, I have already carefully considered the evidence offered, and I have decided that there are sufficient grounds for committing this man. To recall the witnesses for cross-examination would probably cause all 31 of the accused to be unnecessarily detained in jail for two months."
13. In the Court of Sessions the jury found Kanailal Datta guilty of murder and Satyen Bose not guilty by a majority of three to two. The Sessions Judge sentenced Kanailal to death and referred the case of Satyen to the High Court. Both of them were sentenced to death by the High Court on 21st October 1908.
14. Regarding the smuggling of letters to and from the jail, there is information that the prisoners did it through a jail hospital doctor.
15. Regarding the agitation and excitement over the funeral of Kanailal Datta, 11r. F. C. Daly writes in his note : "An extraordinary scene was witnessed at Kalighat at the time of the cremation of Kanai, whose body after the execution was , made over to his relatives for disposal. Crowds thronged the road, people pushing past one another to touch the bier. The body was strewn with flowers and anointed with oil. Many women, to all appearance of a highly respectable class, followed the funeral procession wailing, while men and boys thronged round shouting 'Jai Kanai'! This Kanailal Datta, was a person of humble origin, a weaver by caste. He was a native of Tantipara, Serampore in the Hooghly district, and was perhaps one of the most daring and cold-blooded of the whole gang. He gloried in

the deed he had committed and went to his execution without flinching. After the cremation, his ashes were being sold in Calcutta as much as Rs, 5 an ounce being paid by some enthusiasts."

16. On account of the public demonstration and agitation, the body of Satyen Bose was cremated within the jail premises by his relatives or friends (six in all) on 21st November 1908.
17. Premtosh Bose was a strike leader. (*Vide* page 7 of Mr. F.C. Daly's note.)
18. A.C. Rai is Abinash Chandra Rai of Dacca, formerly editor of the *Regeneration*.

Editorial Note :

* It was Hem Chandra, who jointly with Satyen and Kanai hatched the conspiracy to assassinate the traitor.

Chapter XIX

Our Morale

Nearly a week after Naren Gossain's murder, we were all kept in a solitary part of the Alipore Jail, which was known as "the degrees". The name of this "44 degree" strikes terror into the hearts of the prisoners in Alipore Jail. It is to be remembered that Tikendra Jit, the independent Hindu ruler of Manipur, along with his Minister and generals were put here after their trial.

Quite elaborate arrangements for keeping guard on us by European and Gurkha soldiers were made. There was nothing of this before the murder .of Gossain. From Government's previous attitude to us, it did not appear that any heavy punishment would be awarded to us. But from our experience in the "44 degree " it seemed to us that all the leaders would be hanged and the rest deported for life.

How terrible the jail discipline is, we came to know from our personal experience in the "44 degree". In addition to the tyranny of the jail regulations and rough treatment of the warders, we had to feel the want of decent food to which we had become accustomed previously. What we felt to be more intolerable than anything else was that we were not allowed to speak. We found out the device of communicating with our neighbours by rapping on the

---

Basumati, Magh 1334 BS, January-February 1928

wall, but at first much could not be made of this discovery as it was a difficult experiment.

Our mental condition was terrible at this time. The hardships of jail life were enough to depress the heart of any one with the exception of those patriots who felt pleasure in suffering for the welfare of the country. In these circumstances those men alone who posed as the leaders of the revolutionary movement were to be held responsible for the conduct of those who turned out to be traitors to the party in the hope or even the mistaken hope of buying release for themselves at the price of treachery.

Our traditions are incompatible with patriotism. Our leaders have been guilty of many inconsistencies in their effort to harmonise these two contradictory elements. An instance may be cited. Nearly three weeks after Naren Gossain's murder, Jogen Babu, our jailor, came to us and complained that someone amongst us had asked to see a particular police officer in order to disclose some of our doings within the jail, and he requested us to dissuade him from this, so that he (meaning Jogen Babu) might not suffer. I mentioned the matter to our leaders when we met in the prison van on the way to the Judge's court. They replied that they knew of the matter, and it was their opinion that it should be hushed up, for if they denounced him that would exasperate him to go to greater length before the police. The result of this conciliating policy was soon in evidence. Mr. Denham, Shamsul Mian and others of the C.I.D. began to put in their appearance quite frequently, and there was a sort of competition as to who could give more information.

In January 1909 the Lieutenant-Governor Sir Edward Baker paid a visit to four of us amongst whom were Arabinda Babu, Indranath Nandi and Balkrishna Harikaney. Leaving those who were with him at a distance, he came to the cells and spoke to the men to the effect that our duty as educated and respectable men was to help Government in the suit against us.

The European warders at first regarded some of us with extreme hatred and contempt. One of them was nicknamed "the Ruffian" by us on account of his roughness. But the "Ruffian" and a few others like him had very noble hearts. They cordially hated those who gave information to the police and tried to overhear what the informers said to the police and later on disclosed it to us and gave us news about our case and sympathised in various ways with those of us, who did not act as informers.

A few days after the Lieutenant-Governor's visit, it was rumoured that Arabinda Babu had been given paper and pen to write something. This matter attracted our notice on account of the effort made to conceal it. On asking Arabinda Babu about it when we met in the prison van, he replied that he had written something. As he did not belong to our party, I could not understand why so much secrecy was observed about this petty matter. Anyway, a few days after, this writing business became quite contagious. The fathers and guardians of many of us also insisted on their sons and wards writing something. The barristers advised us not to undertake to write anything without consulting them but in vain, Our morale was gone. On the other side the press went on proclaiming our heroism.

At the Sessions Court we found that six men out of the eight belonging to the second batch having been committed to the sessions[1], were placed along with us. Of the other two, one was Claru Chandra Roy[2] of the Dupleix College and Jatindra Nath Banerjee[3] who was acquitted of all charges. He became a sannyasin on account, it is said, of difference of opinion with Barin. All others of the batch except these two had been arrested on the charge of being leaders of the revolutionary movement.

Altogether there were 36 of us, who had been committed to the sessions. Lawyers had been engaged for the defence of the majority of these. Amongst those who could not engage any lawyer for want of money were the two brothers Nagen and Dhiren Kaviraj, who were wholly innocent but were arrested because some boxes[4] containing materials for manufacturing bombs had been kept in their shops by Ullashkar. They did not even know what the contents of these boxes were, but they were, nevertheless, sentenced[5] to seven years' rigorous imprisonment, each under the Arms Act. The police had on receipt of information from the leaders arrested Balkrishna Harikaney[6] at Nagpur and placed him along with us. He was acquitted on appeal to the High Court.

On the 6th May 1909, was delivered the judgment of the Sessions Court, 17 amongst us were acquitted of all charges. Of the rest Barin and Ullashkar were sentenced to be hanged, Upen, Hrishikesh, Biren Sen, Indranath, Bibhuti, Sudhir, Indu (committed suicide in the Port Blair), Abinash, Sailen and myself were sentenced to transportation for life with forfeiture of property; Nirapada (subsequently dead), Sisir and Paresh for 10 years, Sushil, Bal Krishna for 7 years and Krishnajiban to one year's rigorous imprisonment. Ashoke Nandi died of phthisis during trial.

On returning to the "44 degree", we had to put on the convict's dress which brought us to a sense of the reality of the convict's life.

In December 1909 was delivered the judgment of the Appeal Court. Barin and Ullashkar were sentenced to transportation for life. In the case of myself and Upen the sentence of the Sessions Court was not altered. Convicts sentenced to penal servitude started for Port Blair on the 11th December 1909.

Annotations :

1. Seven out of ten of the second batch were committed for trial.
2. Charu Candra Roy was committed for trial, bus the charge against him was withdrawn under orders of the Government.
3. Jatindra Nath Banerjee was discharged for *want* of evidence. He became a sanyasi and adopted the name of "Niralamba Swami." He left Barin Ghosh's party on account of differences of opinion (ride notes by Mr. Daly).
4. Actually some boxes containing materials for manufacturing bombs. etc were recovered from the house of Kaviraj Nagendra Gupta at 134, Harrison Road. The boxes were brought there by Ullashkar Datta *(vide* judgment. page 2).
5. This is correct. They were sentenced on the 7th August 1908. This individual's name was obtained from Barin Ghosh. He surrendered on the 20th July 1908, and was sentenced to seven years' transportation by the Sessions Judge, but acquitted by the High Court.
6. The judgment of the Appeal Court was delivered on the 23rd November 1909.

Conclusion

As no revolution has taken place in Bengal, there cannot be any story of the revolution. The narrative should have been named " The Attempt at Revolution in Bengal." There were many aspects of this attempt of ours. The aspect which the public has seen or which has been shown to them is the exterior aspect, in respect of which we Bengalis feel pride and cherish the cheap hope that the deliverance of our country will soon take place. The object of this narration is to show the other aspect of the thing though it may be painful and to remove false and misconceived ideas about this episode from the minds of the public.

APPENDIX

Appendix-A

Photocopies of eleven letters, nine of which were written to his wife Sarat Kumari and one to his aunt by Hem Chandra from abroad and another letter written by Sarat to Hem Chandra, are printed here. The Police, however, seized no less than 60 letters from his residence at 15 Gopi Mohan Datta Lane in May, 1908, though only a few of them had some marginal relevance to the charges levelled against him or the Manicktala group. Nevertheless, the prosecution got all the letters translated into English. Six such letters in official translationthe Bengali original of only one is reproduced here--- are reprinted. Most of the original Bengali letters are so badly damaged that their reproduction will not serve any purpose. As a matter of fact, some of the letters are so brittle that they could not be microfilmed.

Majority of the letters were written to Hem Chandra's wife and as such they contained matters primarily relating to the family. It appears that Hem Chandra was very anxious about the health and education of the children and would often give elaborate instruction on this to his wife. Notwithstanding the inescapable undercurrents of mischief and jealousy in a fairly large middle class family, Hem Chandra insisted upon his wife to maintain good and friendly relations with all, and even disapproved of the conduct of his wife when she had visited her relatives without taking permission from the head of the family. Hem Chandra, true to his nature, was critical of the lapses of his wife, who it appears, was not prepared to accept an absentee husband's criticism without protest. Consequently there was occasional cessation of correspondence between them.

Hem Chandra might appear to be harsh at times to his wife, but he was frank and truthful. He wrote about the girls, about free mixing but at the same time he assured his wife that he never felt any attraction towards them. He admitted candidly that he had felt some sexual urge a few months after his arrival; but he could overcome it as he busied himself with the task for which he had come to the foreign country.

Letters reveal that even after selling a part of the property for passage money, Hem Chandra's estate had a moderate income. When during the first few months, he was badly in need of money he would fall back upon the income from the property. He was determined to do something unique for the freedom of the country. His single-minded devotion to the work he had been doing abroad is reflected in the letters, although he had never revealed what the work was.

It is evident from the letters that Hem Chandra was a believer in God when he had left for Europe. As he set sail for Marseilles in France from Colombo, he wrote to his wife, "Pray to Mother Kali that my hopes be fulfilled" In his letters from Europe, there is ample evidence that till then he had faith in God. His faith, however, gradually started weakening after his study of Marxism and Socialism as a member of a Socialist Party in France. Another significant point to note is his deep respect for Aurobindo whom he used to call Guruji at least till early 1908. He has severely criticised his wife for somewhat desultorily treating Aurobindo and serving the most ordinary food, when he had stayed in his house as a guest in 1902. Remembering the occasion nearly six years later, he wrote to his wife just a few days before his departure from Paris, " I am glad to hear that you are reading news papers. Have you now been able to make out who Aurobindo Ghose Mahashaya is? He put up for 3 or 4 days in a room on the upper floor of our house at Midnapur; he whom you did not properly feed, and with whom you used to be annoyed for putting up in a room on the upper floor, is the high-souled Aurobindo Ghose. On being reminded of what happened then tears come even now into my eyes, through shame and grief." (See letter No. 6 below) On his return to India when he came to know about the state of Manicktala Society and its leadership, his high hopes dashed to the ground and he started revising his opinion about Aurobindo.

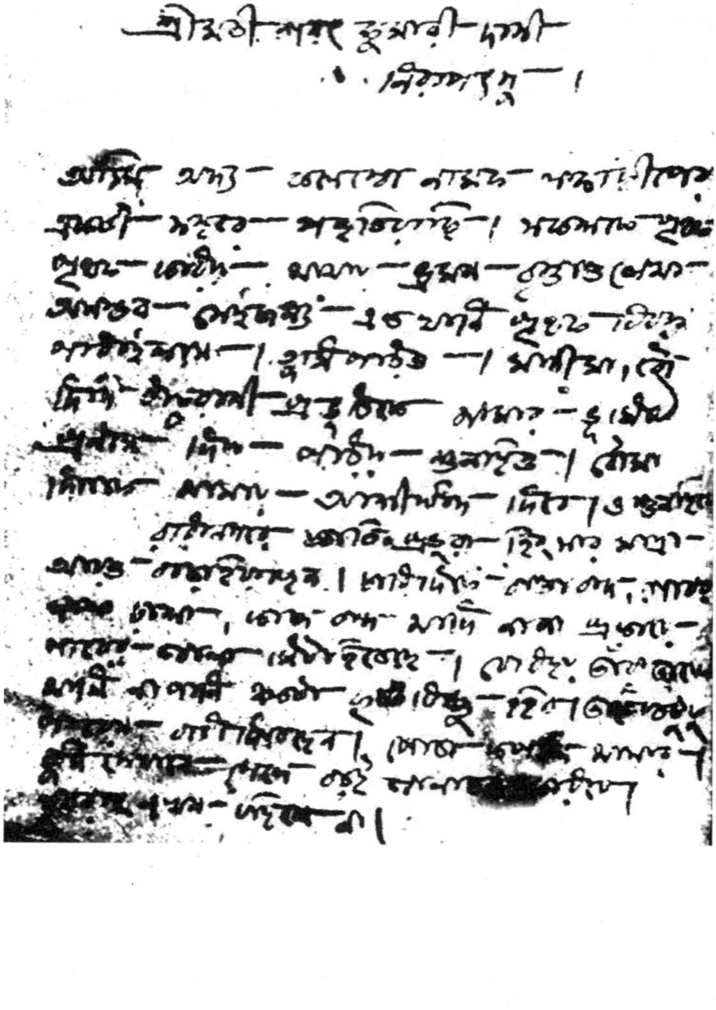

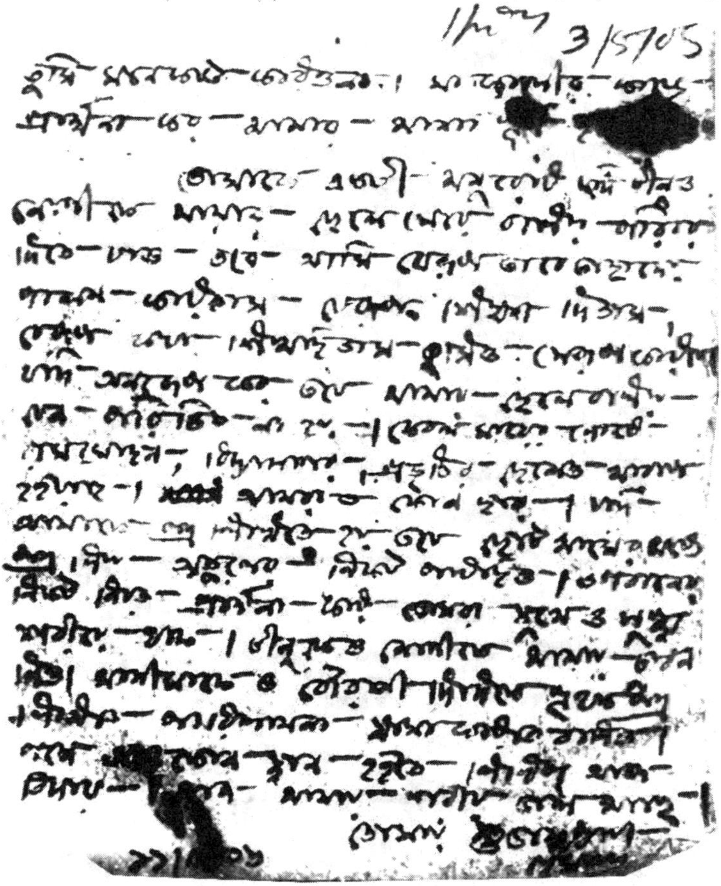

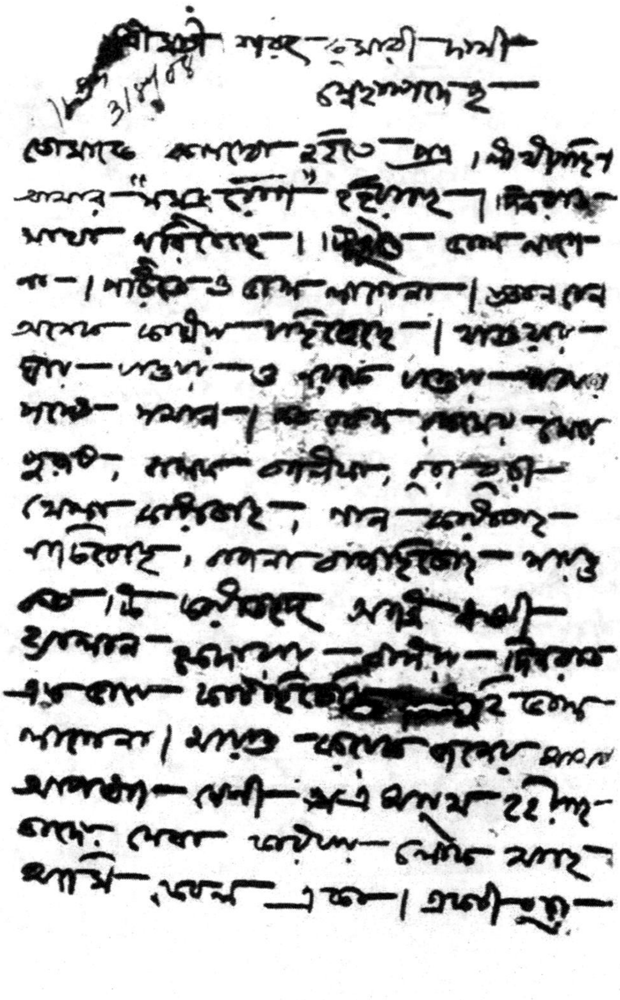

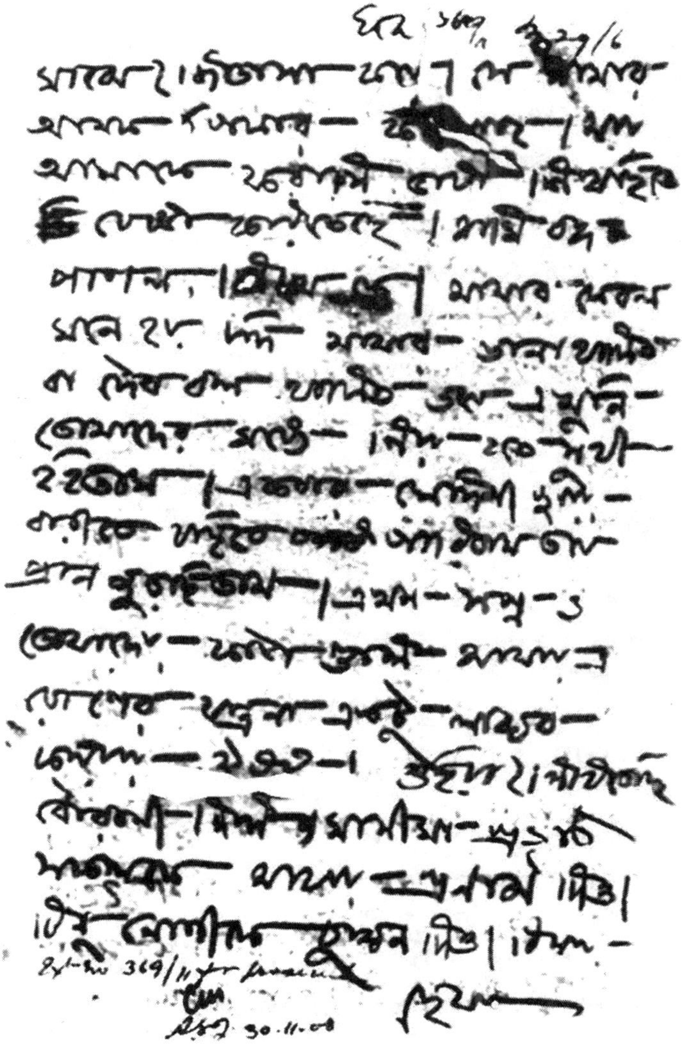

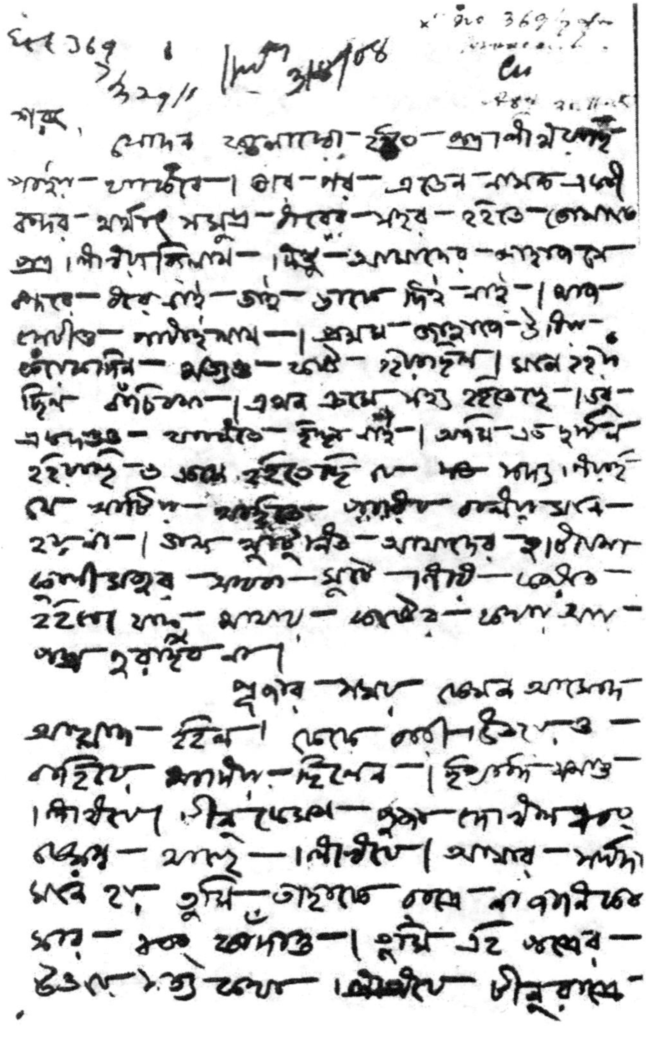

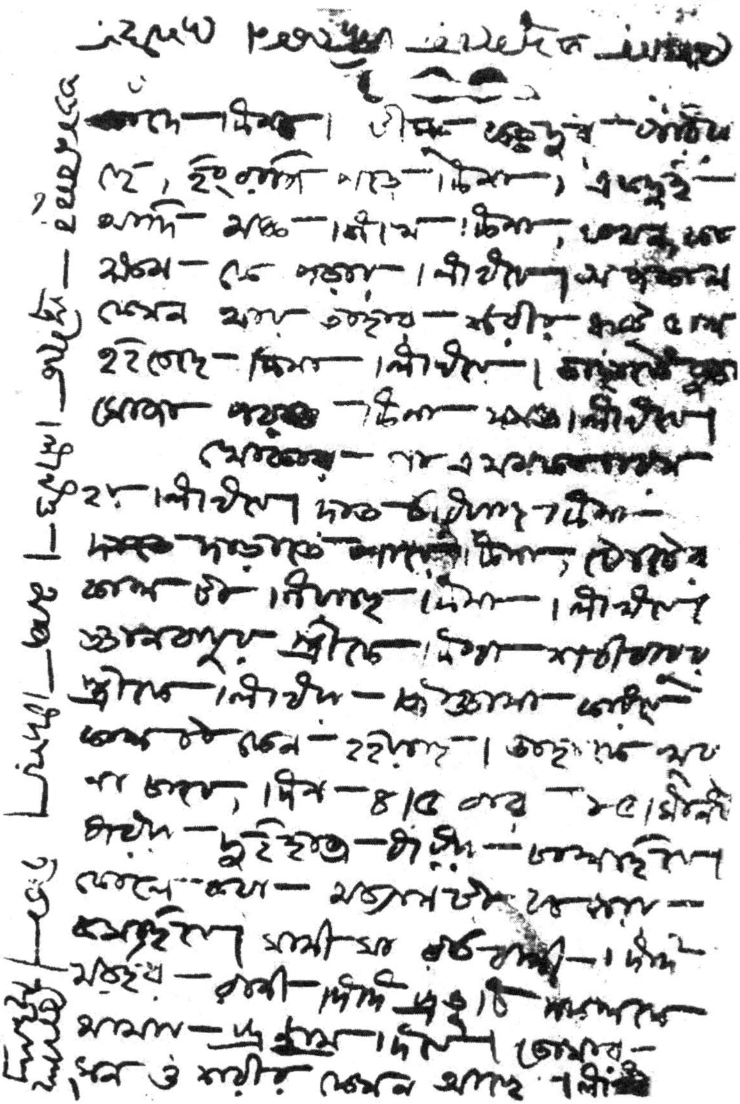

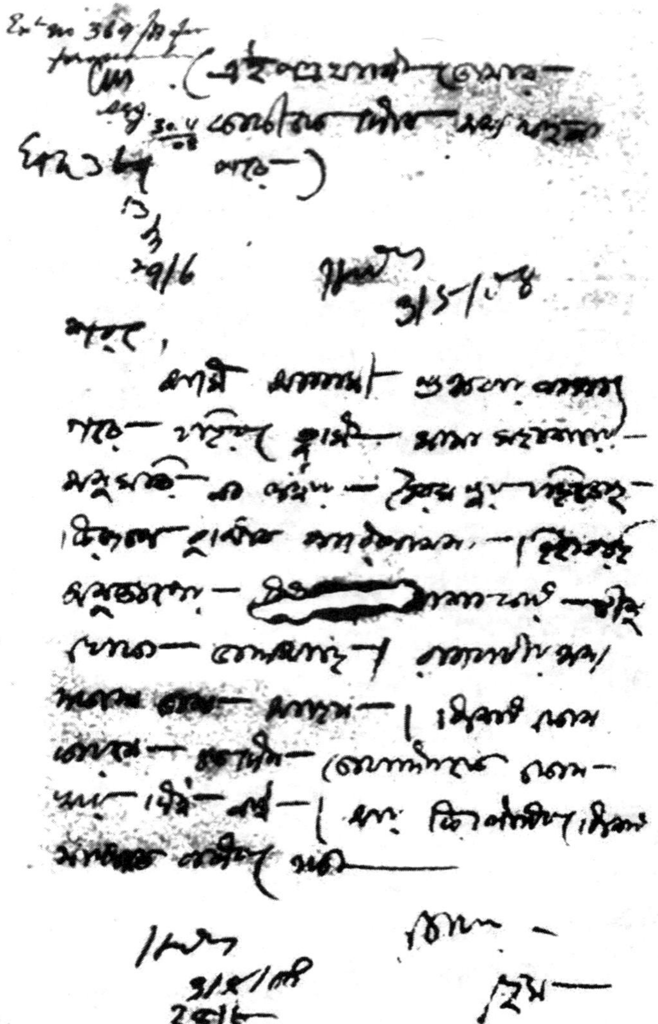

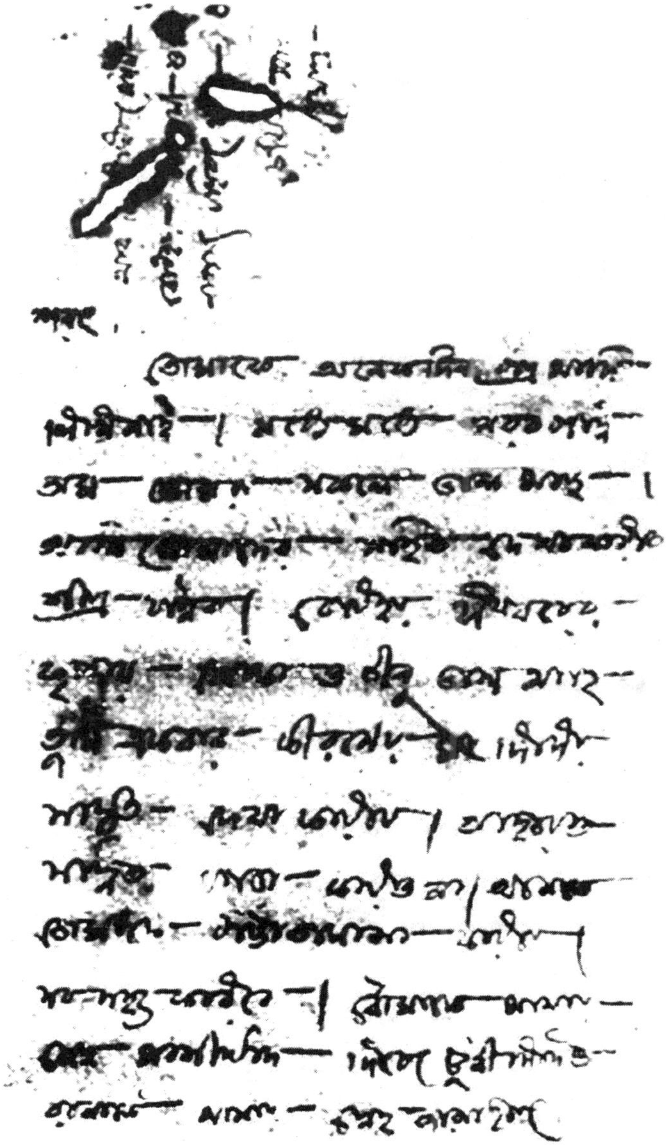

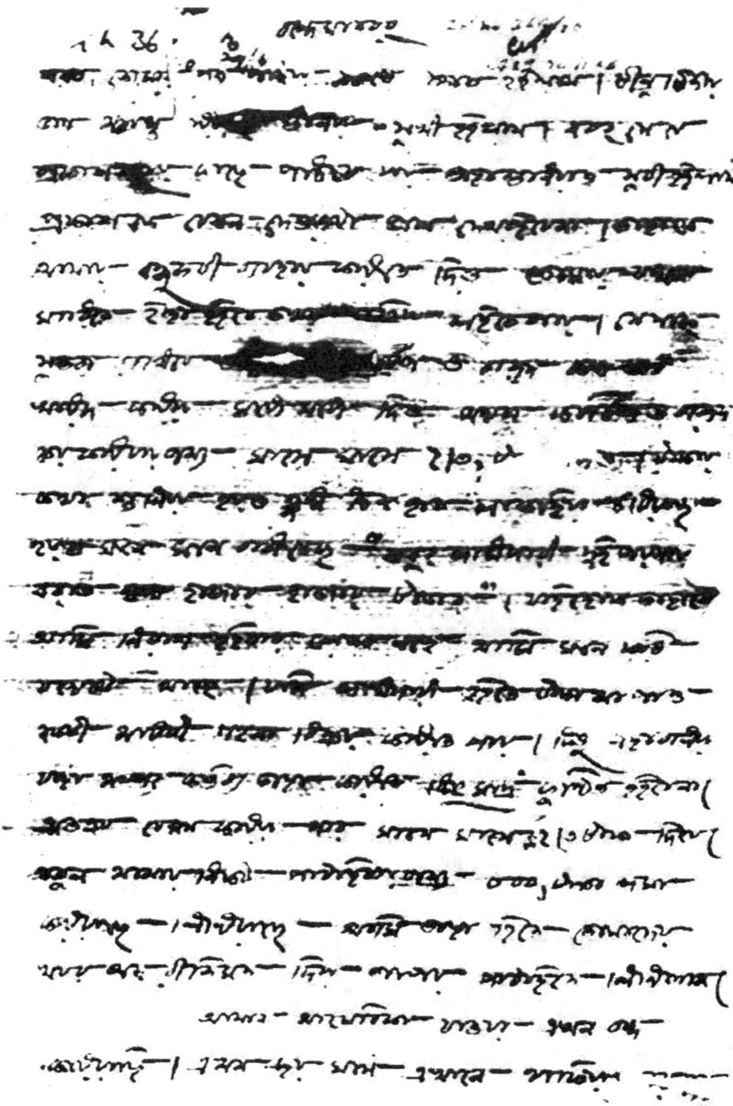

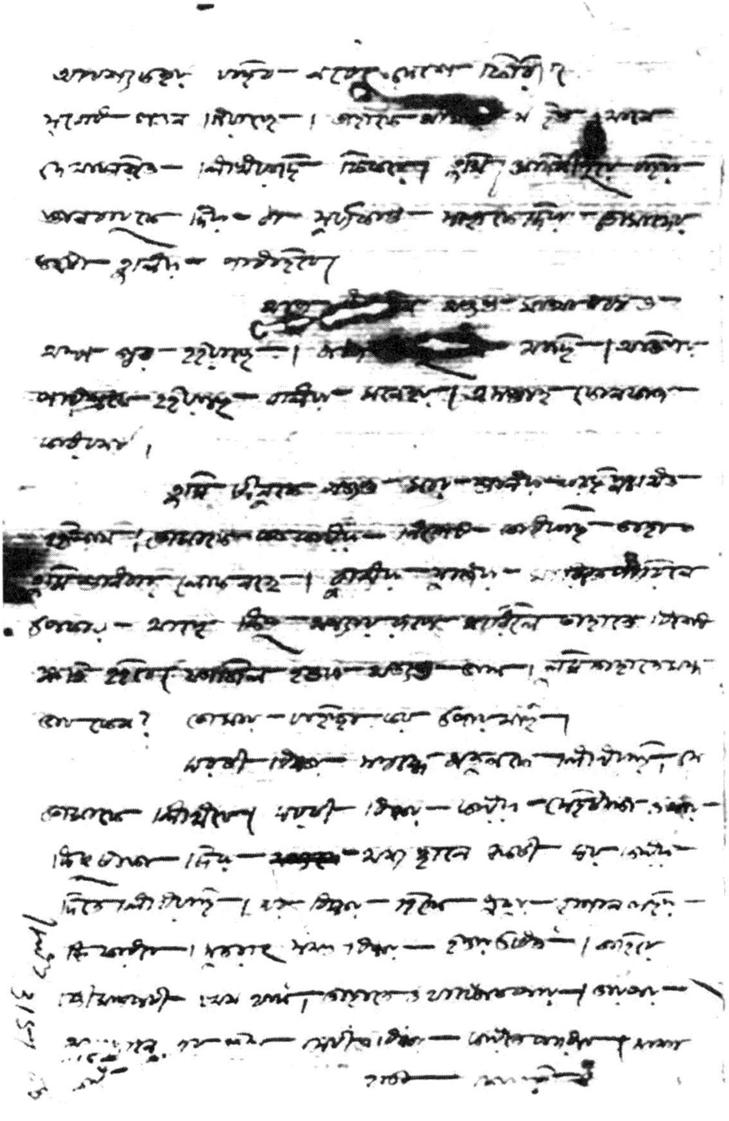

বন্দে মাতরম্।

[illegible]

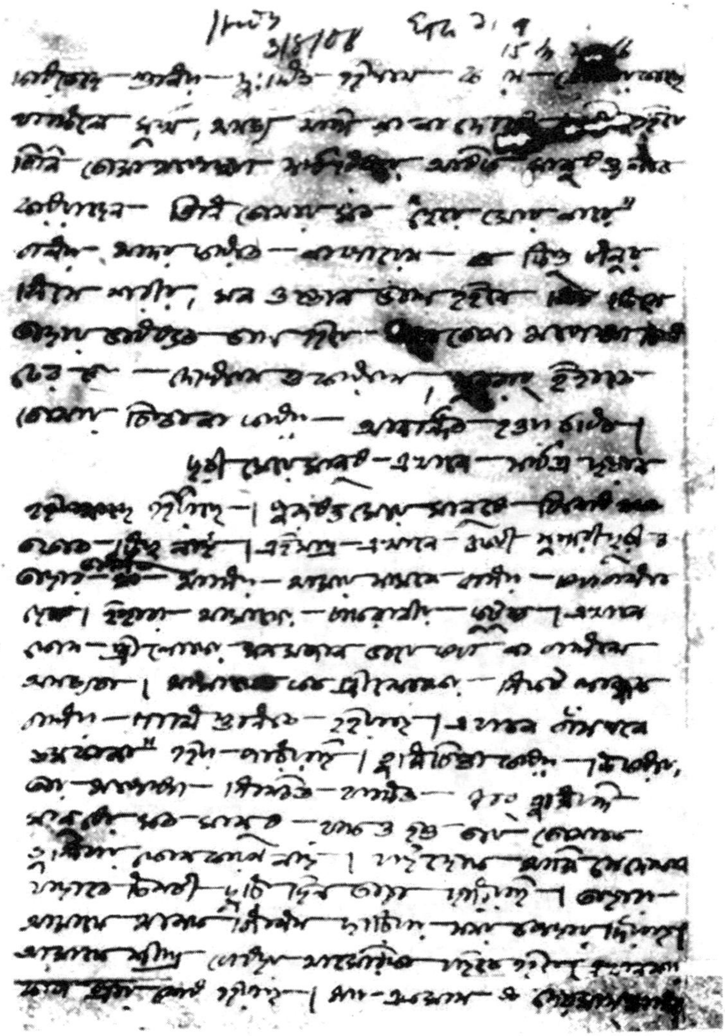

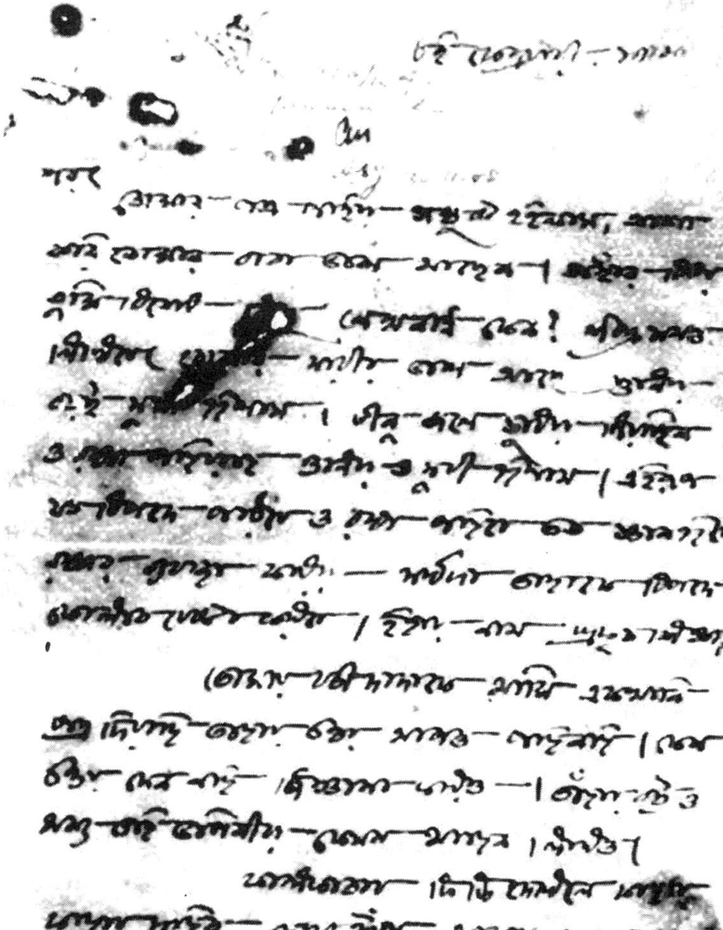

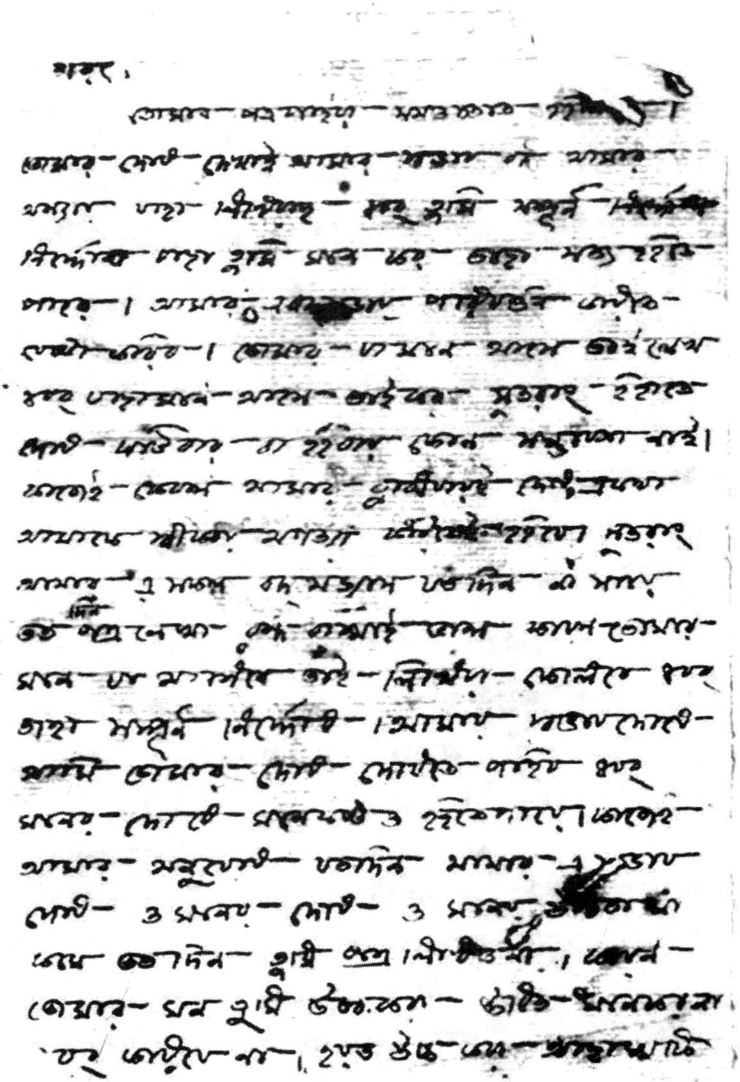

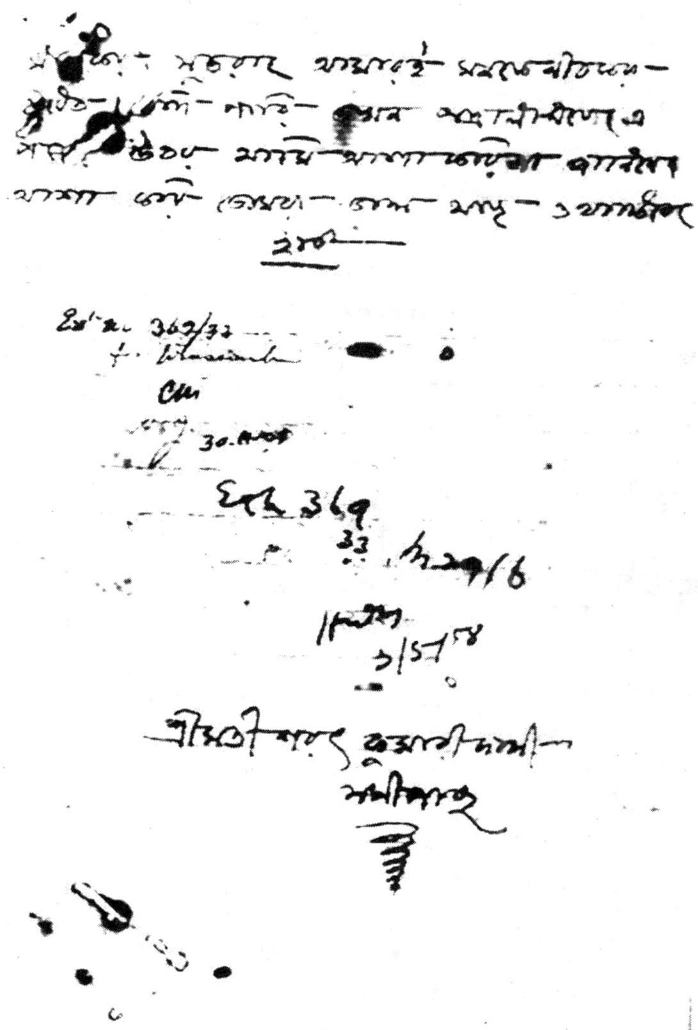

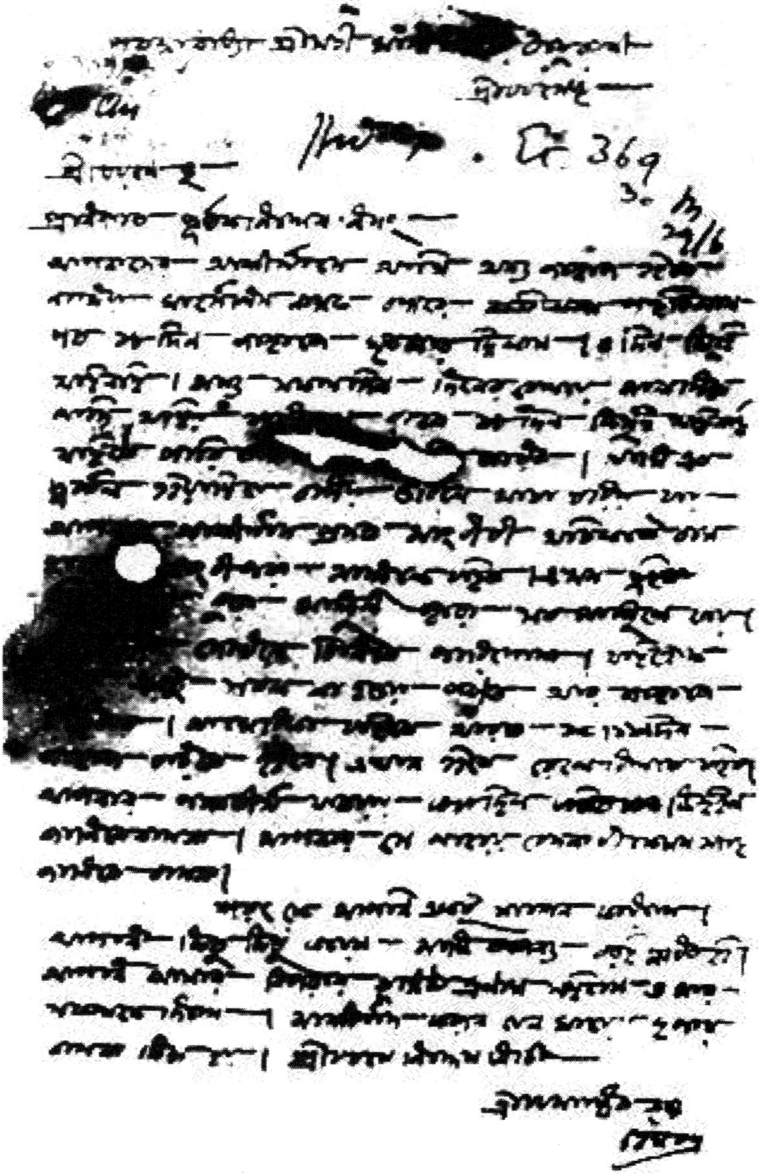

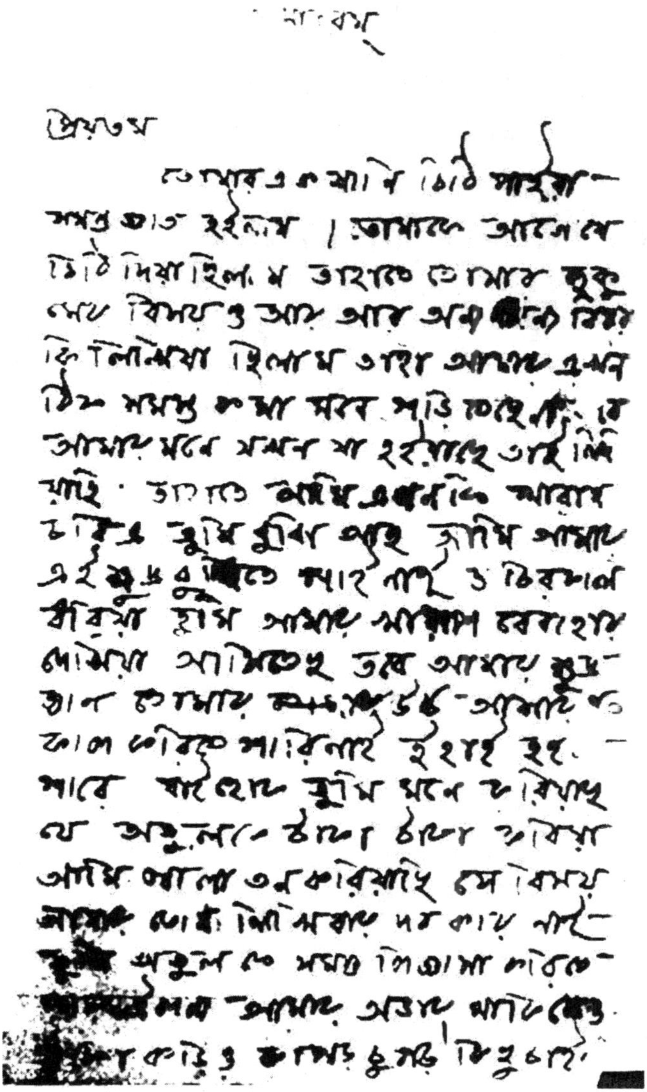

প্রিয়তম

তোমার এক খানি চিঠি পাইয়া—
অত্যন্ত প্রীত হইলাম। তোমাকে আগে যে
চিঠি দিয়াছিলাম তাহাতে তোমার [illegible]
শেষ বিষয় ও আর আর অনেক [illegible]
তে লিখিয়া ছিলাম তাহা আমার এখন
ঠিক সমস্ত কথা মনে পড়িতেছে না। যে
আমার মনে যখন যা হইয়াছে তাই লিখি
য়াছি। তাহাতে আমি [illegible] আবার
চাই যে তুমি বুঝিবে [illegible] আমি আমার
এই [illegible] ও চিরকাল
[illegible] তুমি আমার [illegible]
তোমরা [illegible] তবে আমার [illegible]
জান তোমার [illegible]
[illegible] পারি নাই [illegible]
পারে [illegible] তুমি মনে করিয়াছ
যে [illegible]
আমি [illegible] করিয়াছি সে বিষয়
[illegible] কারু নাই
[illegible] সময় জিজ্ঞাসা করিতে
[illegible] আমার [illegible]
[illegible]

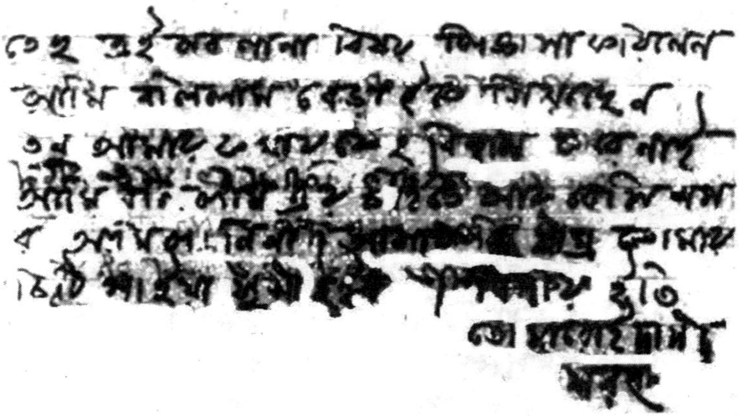

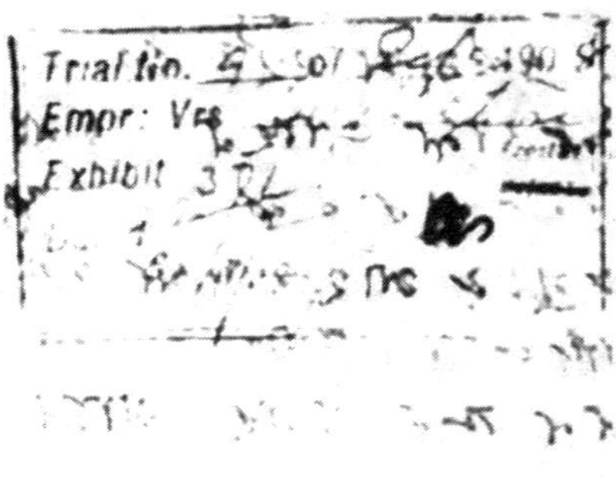
Trial No.
Empr: Vs
Exhibit

To
Sreemuti Sarat Kumari Dasi
Free from all misadventure,

To-day I have arrived at Columbo, a town in the Island of Ceylon. It being impracticable to send a narrative of my travels to every one separately. I enclose a separate narrative herewith. Read it yourself read it over to dear aunt (মাসিমা), sister-in-law (বৌদিদি) and others, and tender my humble bow to them. Tender my blessings to Banmas and read this narrative over to them as well.

Our august cognates at Radhanagore have increased the degree of their malicious mischief. They are satisfying their grudge by closing, the pathway, throwing cow-dung, obstructing works and in various otherways. Perhaps, they think that I shall turn out a great personage like Kristo or Bishnu. And so they are trying to thwart me as best they can. Fie to my luck! Thy will tease you if you go there. So do not go there now. Don't take it to heart. Pray to mother Kali that my hopes may be fulfilled.

This is my request to you. If you wish Tinoo and Nogee to be known as my children then you should bring them up and train them on the same lines and teach them the same things as I used to do. If you do otherwise, let them not to be known as my children. The sons of so great personages as Ram Mohon, Vidyasagar, and the like, not to speak of us, have been spoilt simply on account of their mother's fault. When you write to me, send the letter in a smaller envelope to Atul. My constant prayer is that God might preserve you in health and make you happy. Kiss Tinoo and Nogee for me. I am unable to write separately to aunt (mother's sister) and to Bawranididi (sister-in-law). Ask them to pardon me. I shall write from port another on my way. Good-bye today. I am keeping well to-day.

Dated 11-9-1906

Your well wisher,
Hem Chandra

Note: Adapted from the existing printed translation with corrections.

(Sd.) J. Bagchi,
Translator

Exhibit No. 364

Sarat,

On receipt of your letter I have come to know all. I am glad to hear that Tinoo is going on with the readings in Protham Bhag (first book) you should send him to school everyday for 2 to 3 hours he will not be spoilt, if he associates with the boys of the neighbourhood. The greater the variety of characters he associates with the more he will improve, Tinoo is a little shy. He will get over his shyness if he goes school every day and he will get accustomed to going to school. Tell the teachers at school to teach him English. It is better (to learn) something than nothing at all. Further you too should teach him. You should make him get by heart good poems and good verses.

If you do not find poems, you should make him get by heart the Swadeshi (national) songs. Further try to teach him tunes from time to time with the help of a Harmonium. Teach Nagi to walk repeatedly by holding her hand, and always repeat Ka, Kha, Ga, Gha (the first four letter of Bengali alphabet) to her and she will learn Ka, Kha, Ga, Gha as she learns to speak. If you are in Calcutta, you get a photo taken of Tinoo and Nagi by Sarat Baboo's sons or send a photo of each including that of yourself through Sarat Adhikari or Atul as may be convenient.

I am much distressed to hear that you are not well, both in body and mind. It is a pity you have not written to me any thing about the cause. This is, indeed, very bad you should certainly disclose everything to me, I will try my best to prevent it. I am sorry to hear that your pain in the chest has not yet cured. Write to Jnan Baboo's wife. Do as she advises. If Mashima agrees, she and you may put up for a few days, in Midnapur or Calcutta. I have written to Atul and he will make the arrangement as soon as (sufficient) money is in. Write to me in detail the cause of your distress. Write to me whether you are able to read my hand writing. I am anxious to know what has happened to Kantiri. It would be well if you could send away all for a few days.

The cold here was intense (for some time). It is now a bit warmer for the last 4 or 5 days. I keep very well in cold. The urinary disorder has altogether disappeared. Let me know whether you suffer from it. It being very cold I feel no desire.

Further, in the beginning, while conversing with females, now and then, my mind used to get a little excited. But now I feel exactly the same with females as with males. Even now, I daily take wine in small doses, but I did not get drunk for a single day. Write to me the news of Tamlook, Bahirberiah? And Tilantapura, Mayna and other places. I have written letters to all of tamlook, Bahirberiah, Tilantapura, Mayna and other places, but I have not received any reply from any. Tender my bows to Mashima, Bowrani didi, Rani Didi of Kharai and others.

Tender my affectionate benedictions to the Bowmas. I am now getting gratis "Jugantar", Medini Bandhab and various others papers. Kartik of Santipur, who was with us at Midnapur for a few days, has been sentenced to imprisonment for 6 months. Did you read about it? Send him some present the day he is released, taking the money necessary from Jnan Baboo's wife. The present of a pair of clothes would be the best. Bear this in mind and do this, you should give what ought to be given to (torn) and relations when they return from a pilgrimage. Write to me in reply about your distress.

Ever yours,
Hem Chandra

I am exceedingly sorry and anxious to hear of your father's serious illness from your letter today. I wrote to you long ago to go once to Tamlook. You must go if you so desire. Moreover, you must go, when your father is ill. Communicate my consent to Mashima, uncle. I am writting you every week. Only for 2 weeks I sent them to the Calcutta address. I am very sorry to hear of the death of Kontiri. Finis Hem]

Exhibit No. 369/4

Dated 3rd May 1907.

Sarat,

I have received two letters from you. I am very sorry to hear of Khoka's and Tinu's fever. I am sorry to hear that you too are unwell. What more can I do from here? I pray to God that He may grant you His blessings. Why don't you arrange for the supply on credit of two seers of milk, as you did before? I request you especially to take 3 seers of milk on credit. Pay what that would cost. If that would necessitate the sale of ornaments do it. I am writing to Atul, and he will certainly send you Rs. 6 a month, as the price of milk (at 3 seers). You should give to Tinu one seer of milk with *Mudi* (parched rice) morning and evening, one seer of milk to Nogi with *Soojee* (Semolina), Sago, and Barley, morning and evening, and you yourself should take one seer, morning and evening, (see) that it is not creamed. Take it simply hot with sugar in the morning. I write to Atul to send Rs. 8 per month. I also write to him to make arrangements for milk. The food taken is certainly insufficient, and for this reason there have been frequent relapses of fever. Fever cannot attack when the body is (well) nourished. You may give Tinu a half-boiled egg every day. It will do him much good.

Who told you that the income of my family does not come up to Rs. 5 even? I can make arrangements for you to live separately, but it is doubtful whether you have the capacity to live alone (apart). For you cannot make the man and maid servants work in harmony. You do not know how to keep the bazar account. You do not know what should be done and what should not be done when one is ill. You do not know how to live in *pardah*. For this various reasons, I dare not let you live independently. But then, I hope it might, to some extent, be convenient to do so, when the children grow a little older. However don't be impatient. Let things take their course. All the days (of one's life) do not run alike. Even troubles and miseries are the precursors of happiness. Don't you feel vexed (but) always think of finding out the means of relief. Bear in mind that whatever Providence does, He does for the good. You have written to say that having left you in difficulties, I am living here unconcerned. But it is exceedingly improper for you to think in this way. Never entertain such (a thought) in your mind. If you reflect, you will find that it is you who live unconcerned. You cannot even form an idea as to what a dangerous task I have taken in hand. What an agonising situation I am in. However, be not annoyed, or do not torment yourself with the thought that I am living unconcerned. This is not the end of our sufferings and miseries. The miseries and sufferings I have prepared myself to undergo, have not begun even now. You will be stunned if you (but) think of them you shall have quietly and patiently to bear all that is passing before your eyes and within your hearing. It will not do for you to grow so impatient so soon. But happiness is never attained without suffering. You should not mind the little pain that is caused by the illness of children and living in a state of dependence in the house of a friend or relative as pain at all. Harden your heart like a stone; then you will feel happy even in dire distress. Let them pass.

You need not spend a pice in going to Mayona, Tamlook. Whoever may invite you to any place, you should let him know that you are poor and unable to spend money. You should ask them not to make any customary presents to you, nor should you make any to them. It is they who will pay the travelling expenses. There is no particular necessity for spending money herein.

I do not know whence Atul and Jati Babu came to know of your distress. They simply touched upon it in their letters. However, that does not matter. I have not received any letters from your father. I wrote three letters, but did not get reply to any of them. I often get affectionate letters from Mohendra Babu. I have not received any more letters from Jati Babu. I had a slight misunderstanding with Jnan Babu (Bose) in (our) correspondence. That is why I think his wife did not write to you. I hear from Naren. The letter you gave to Nalin was sent to me. That letter was well written. I am sending to-day a photo for you. The man standing by my side, is a Madrassi Mahomedan friend. The man who is seated is Varma Shaheb in whose house I am putting up. Shew the photo to all, send your photo, if you can manage.

For various reasons I have not even now been able to settle

when I shall leave for America. America is eight day's journey from this place. If Atul can manage to send me some money, that is, if I am not obliged to earn my living there, I shall be able to return home within a year.

However, you should regularly read newspapers, and write to me what fresh news you get therein or what new things you learn (therefrom). Get Tinu to learn the national songs by heart. Do not chastise him. Teach him the song (commencing with) 'Bande Mataram' (Hail Motherland) and "Katu Kala Pare" (after what length of time), what more shall I write? Tender my bow to your elder sister and my affection to the *bowmas* (daughter-in-law or wives of younger brothers). I will send a *noloke* (a pendant for the nose-ring) for *Bara Bowma*. What do you say to that?

Ever yours,
Hem Chandra

Translated by D.C. Chatterjee
Examined by S. Paul.
Exhibit No. 369/5

The 5th July, 1907

Sarat,

On receipt of your letter I have come to know everything. I am extremely sorry to hear of Nogi having got a relapse of fever. I feel inclined to write many things by way of instruction but it is no use doing so. There is nothing left for me to do than to pray to God.

I hope you have by this time arrived at Midnapore. I think you will largely benefit by the change. Let me know which room you occupy at Midnapore. How are the plants doing? Send Tinu to school. The habit of going to school is good, no matter whether he learns anything or not. See Sachin Babu's wife. Sachin Babu being displeased with me has dropped all correspondence. You can once go from Midnapore to Panchberia now, if you can manage. I think you will not be allowed to go before *Barabowma's* delivery. Do as you think proper. I have received Mahendra Babu's letter. They are all doing well. Your father, too, is doing a little better.

I am very glad to hear that you are now reading newspapers. You should read *Sandhya*, you will be able to understand it easily. Unless you read every day you will not be able to understand the connection between the events that have gone before, with those that follow. Try to read *Jugantar* too. You will be able to understand it easily after you have read it for some time. There is not in India, another newspaper as admirable. Enquire and write to me who read *Jugantar* there. Write to me which of the two, Lala Lajpat Rai and Ajit Sing, is superior, and which of them has done better work, in your opinion. Don't you feel a desire to imitate the wives of Lala Lajpat Rai and Ajit Sing? So long as the world should endure, their names shall be recorded in History in sacred letters. All the well-known newspapers throughout the world are not singing their praise. How many newspapers are publishing their portraits in numbers! We got the news of their arrest much sooner than you did. I have cleared a large amount by selling the portrait of the Lala Saheb. I have not as yet received a good portrait of Ajit Sing.

You should take my letter in hand before you sit down to write a reply. Read and answer bit by bit. Write to me whether Atul has paid you money and what boarding arrangements he has made for you. I do not feel well. Write to me whether you have received (any) letter from Naren's wife. I have not received letters from them for a long time. Write to me how you feel in body and mind. Write to me whether *Mashima* (mother's sister) has come or not. Tender my bow to all. Kiss Tinu and Nogi for me. *Finis*.

Ever yours,
Hem

Translated by D.C. Chatterjee
Examined by S. Paul.
Exhibit No. 367

Sarat,

I am really very happy to get a letter from you to-day. This is, perhaps, the first time in (your) life that you admit (your) faults. I do not remember whether you did so even before. I do not know whether you write so, thinking of whose particular faults that you have committed, or upon a (general) recollection of them. Had you done so, I would have been more glad. But it is now too late. What is the use of watering a tree after it has been out root (are branch) (completely). Had you been so disposed a few days before, I would not perhaps have been able to take the highly sacred vow of renouncing the world.

Now, it can't be helped any more. Now do not stand in my way any more. Let me work out God's benign well. Do not write so any more.

You have not written anything as to what sort of pain you feel and in which part of your abdomen and when. Write to me the particulars. Bring it to the notice of the maternal uncle, no matter what he might say. I am much surprised to hear that you feel different to write to maternal uncle. Your modesty has something very strange about it. I could never prevail upon you, by requesting you a thousand times to feel modest in matters in which you ought to do so; you feel modest only when you ought not to do so. Do what you think proper. It way my duty to point out (and) I have done so. I wonder that *Khoka's* (male child's) dysentery has not left him (yet). Do you give him lime-water? Do you give him goat's milk? Did you forget that the matters on which you were to give (your) answers, were given by me under 12 heads? Why did you not give your answers with those 12 numbers noted? Are these matters of small regret? What more shall I write? I have written to you to write to me a letter every day, so long as I should remain here. But even that I am not fortunate enough to get. There are not many days remaining. Rub *Khoka's* body from time to time (with a wet napkin). Rub *Khoka's* body at interval of 2 or 3 days except on wet days. Write to me if *Khokal* is still as fat and plump, as before. What more shall I write? *Finis.*

Ever yours.
Hem Chandra

Translated by D.C. Chatterjee
Examined by S. Paul.
Exhibit No. 366

Dearest Sarat,

I have come to know everything on receipt of your letter last week. I could not write a letter for (pressure of) work. I have been much worried by repeated intimation of the various ailings of Tinu and Nagi; what else have I got to do other than praying to God? Write (to me) whether or not you have ceased beating Tinu.

I am glad to hear that you are reading newspapers. Have you now been able to make out who Arabinda Ghose Mohasaya is. He put up for 3 or 4 days in a room on the upper floor or our lodging house at Midnapur. He whom you did not properly feed and with whom you used to be annoyed for putting up in a room on the upper floor, is the high souled Arabinda Ghose. On being reminded of what happened them, tears come even now, into my eyes, through shame and grief. Can't help; in this world, we cannot have everything to our liking and to everything as we please. However, I shall be happy if you should be careful for the future.

My business here is almost finished. I am preparing to return home soon. Write to me whether or not you have made separate arrangements for milk for yourselves. If you have not (already) done so, then you should make a separate arrangement for pure milk at least 1½ seers per day, you should make arrangements for goat's milk for Nogi, if cow's milk does not agree with her (or him). Do not look upon all this as Nababi orders on my part and remain indifferent. It does not matter if maternal uncle gets displeased. You must make the arrangement in spite of this displeasure. You should do what is necessary in order that the children may get good nutritious food in sufficient quantities. This will certainly save them to some extent from getting ill or unwell. If you do not do this, do not write to me any longer, or do not send me any news about the illness of children any more.

The old Parsee lady, named Mrs. Cama who used to love me just like her son is shortly leaving for America. My mind is much depressed on that account. Tender my bow (with the head) touching the ground to masima (mother's sister) as also to your didi (elder sister). Write to me how they are doing. I hope I shall get news of your welfare this week. Finis.

Yours
Hem Chandra

Exhibit No. 369/3

APPENDIX-B

Barindra Kumar Ghose voluntarily made a confession before District Magistrate Leonard Birley in the Alipur Bomb Trial. At the time of search of the Garden in the night of 1-2 May,1908, he volunteered to show the places where he had concealed the weapons which, on being shown, were seized by the police. From the point of view of evidence his action and statement were as important as his subsequent confession. Barindra's confession recorded by Birley and signed by Barindra is reproduced below in original. It was marked as Exhibit No. 12 in the trial. A type copy is also printed for convenience.

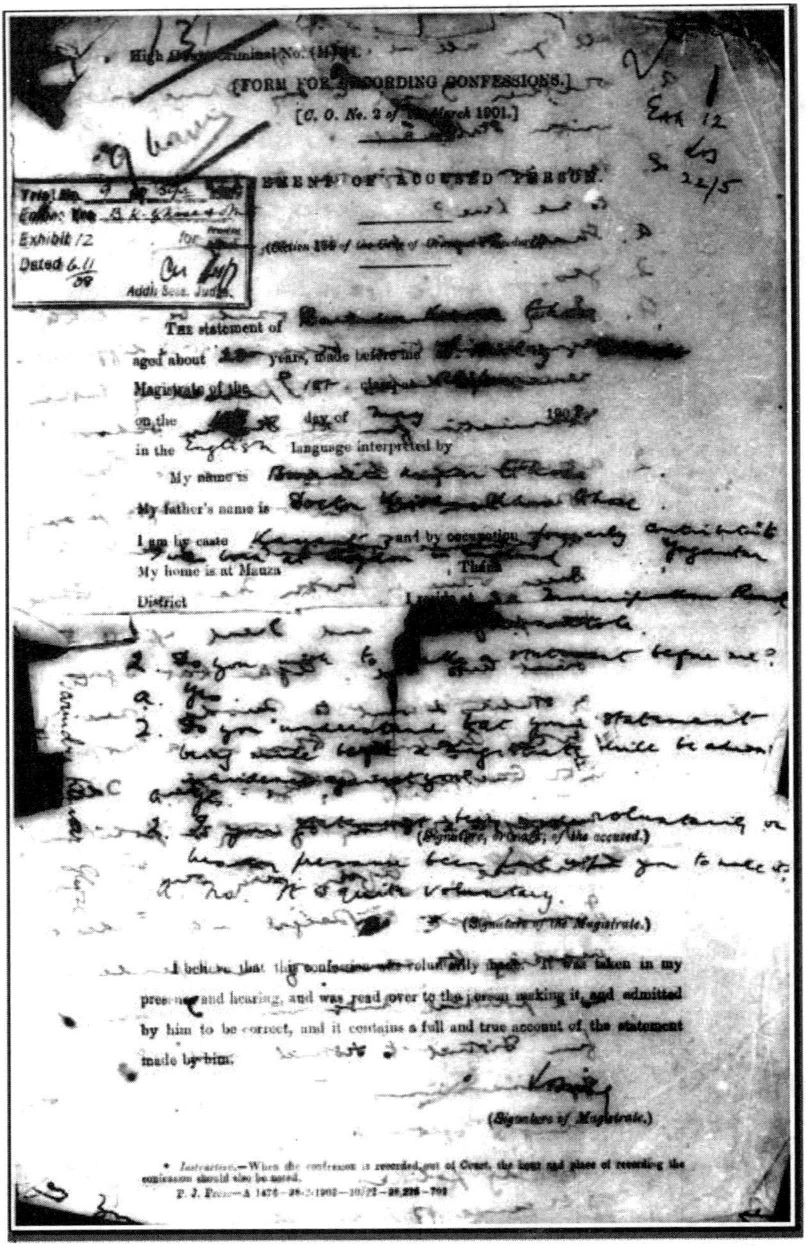

High Court Criminal No. (H)

[FORM FOR RECORDING CONFESSIONS.]

[C. O. No. 2 of March 1901.]

STATEMENT OF ACCUSED PERSON.

(Section 164 of the Code of Criminal Procedure.)

Trial No.
Exhibit 12
Dated 6.11.08
Addl. Sess. Judge

The statement of
aged about years, made before me
Magistrate of the 1st class
on the day of 190
in the English language interpreted by

My name is

My father's name is

I am by caste and by occupation

My home is at Mauza Thana

District I reside at

(Signature, or mark, of the accused.)

(Signature of the Magistrate.)

I believe that this confession was voluntarily made. It was taken in my presence and hearing, and was read over to the person making it and admitted by him to be correct, and it contains a full and true account of the statement made by him.

(Signature of Magistrate.)

* *Instructions.*—When the confession is recorded out of Court, the hour and place of recording the confession should also be noted.

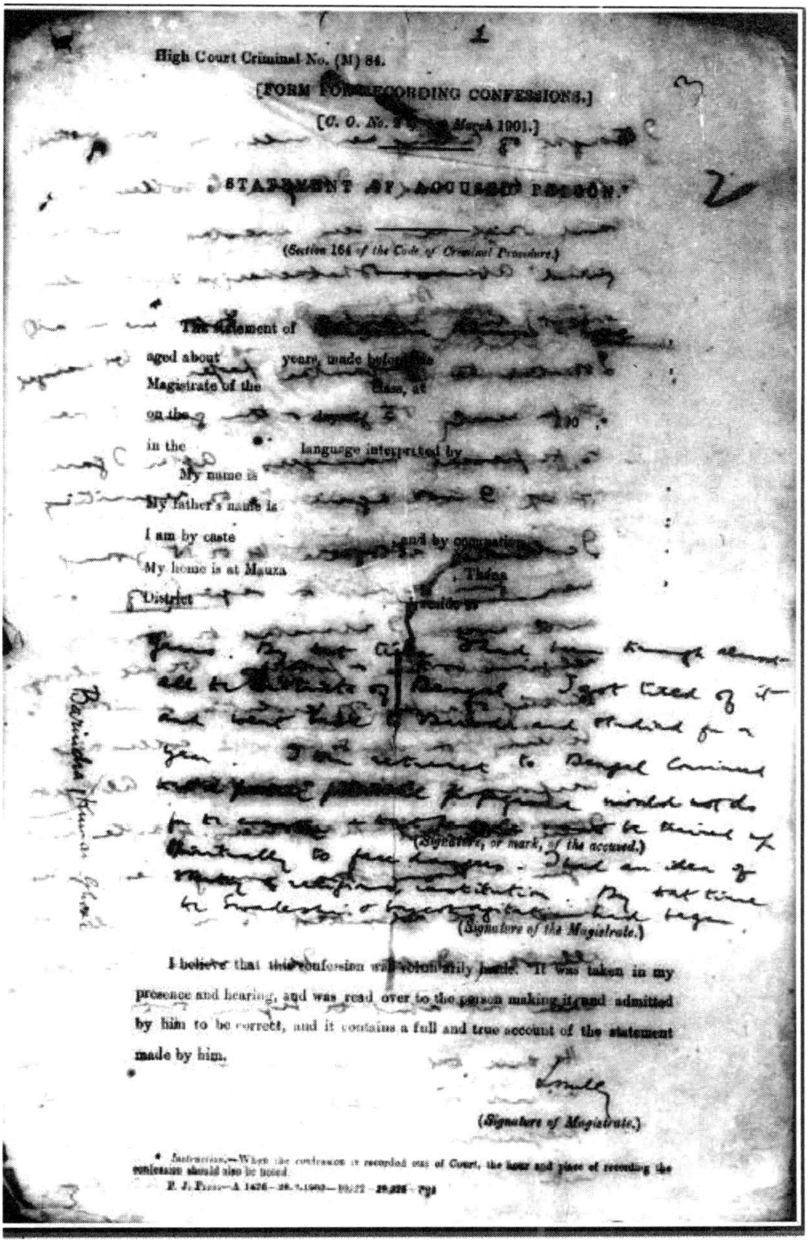

High Court Criminal No. (M) 84.

[FORM FOR RECORDING CONFESSIONS.]

[C. O. No. ... March 1901.]

"STATEMENT OF ACCUSED PERSON."

(Section 164 of the Code of Criminal Procedure.)

The statement of ... aged about ... years, made before the Magistrate of the ... class, at ... on the ... day of ... 190 ... in the ... language interpreted by ...

My name is ...

My father's name is ...

I am by caste ... and by occupation ...

My home is at Mauza ... Thana ... District ... I reside at ...

(Signature, or mark, of the accused.)

(Signature of the Magistrate.)

I believe that this confession was voluntarily made. It was taken in my presence and hearing, and was read over to the person making it and admitted by him to be correct, and it contains a full and true account of the statement made by him.

(Signature of Magistrate.)

* Instruction.—When the confession is recorded out of Court, the hour and place of recording the confession should also be noted.

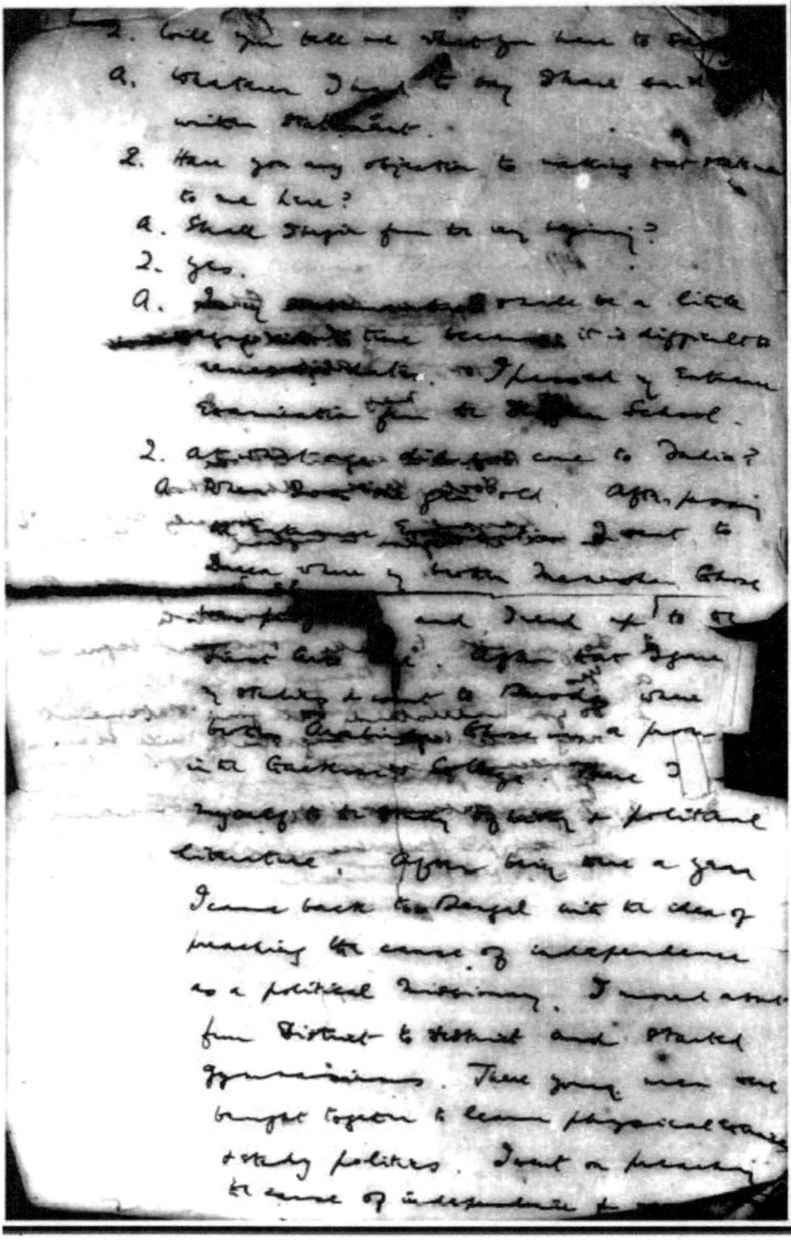

Q. Will you tell me what you have to say

A. Whatever I had to say I have said in the written statement.

Q. Have you any objection to making that statement to me here?

A. Shall I begin from the very beginning?

Q. Yes.

A. [illegible] would be a little [illegible] time because it is difficult to [illegible]. I passed my Entrance Examination from the [illegible] School.

Q. [illegible] come to India?

A. [illegible] After passing [illegible] I went to Baroda where my brother Manmohan Ghose [illegible] and I read up to the First Arts. After that I gave up studying & went to Baroda where my brother Aurobindo Ghose was a professor in the Gaekwar's College. There I [illegible] myself to the study of history & political literature. After being there a year I came back to Bengal with the idea of preaching the cause of independence as a political missionary. I moved about from District to District and started gymnasiums. There young men were brought together to learn physical training & study politics. I went on preaching the cause of independence [illegible]

10

8. Nidhi Uria
and (under arrest) before.
9. Panu Uria

My motive for disclosing these details is simply to save the innocent who has been arrested by the police and principally to place the details of our workings before the country so that others may follow in our footsteps. I do not believe that such political murder will bring about our desired regeneration of our motherland. It is a means to educate the people up for facing death and daring anything for their country's sake. I am the organiser and author of this secret society. There was a wide and persistent demand all over India for one successful political murder in order to stiffen the back of the people and satisfy their spirit of vengeance. We were, though unwilling, compelled to take up the task and work it out to its bitter end. We had taken a vow to serve the nation at the cost of all that we consider dear including life and so like obedient slaves we carried out the behest of the nation.

Barindra Kumar Ghose.

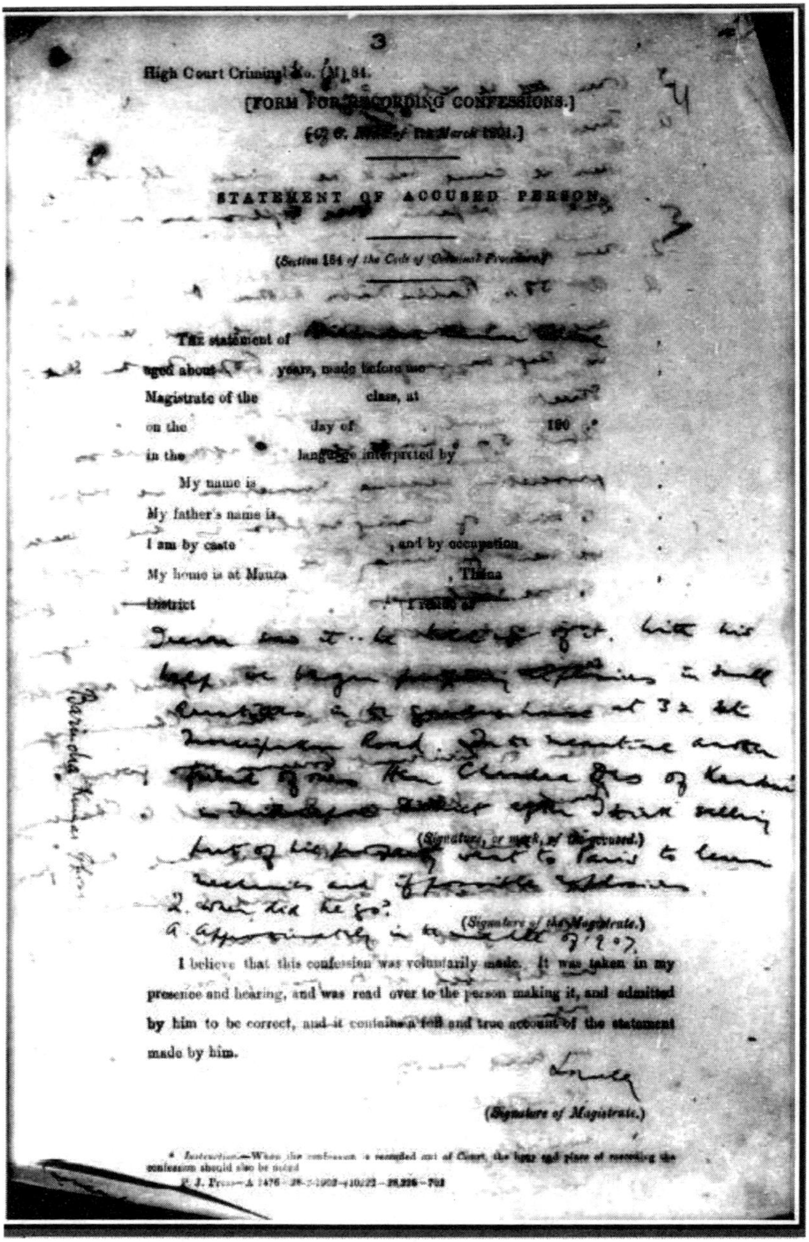

3

High Court Criminal No. (M) 84.

[FORM FOR RECORDING CONFESSIONS.]

STATEMENT OF ACCUSED PERSON.

(Section 164 of the Code of Criminal Procedure.)

The statement of

aged about years, made before me

Magistrate of the class, at

on the day of 190

in the language interpreted by

My name is

My father's name is

I am by caste , and by occupation

My home is at Mauza , Thana

District I reside at

... Paris to learn ...

Q. When did he go?

A. Approximately in ... 07.

(Signature, or mark, of the accused.)

(Signature of the Magistrate.)

I believe that this confession was voluntarily made. It was taken in my presence and hearing, and was read over to the person making it, and admitted by him to be correct, and it contains a full and true account of the statement made by him.

(Signature of Magistrate.)

* Instruction.—When the confession is recorded out of Court, the time and place of recording the confession should also be noted.

Ex. 12

(Sd.) L. Birley

22nd May

Statement of Accused Person

The statement of Barindra Kumar Ghose, aged about 28 years, made before me, L. Birley, Magistrate of the first class at Alipore, on the 4th day of May 1908 in the English language interpreted by . My name is Barindra Kumar Ghose. My father's name is Doctor Krishnadhan Ghose. I am by caste Kayast and by occupation formerly contributor to *Jugantar*. I was born at Croydon in England. My home is at Mauza , Thana , District . I reside at 32, Moraripukur Road, Maniktolla.

Q. Do you wish to make a statement before me.

A. Yes.

Q. Do you understand that your statement being made before a Magistrate will be admissible in evidence against you?

A. Yes.

Q. Is your statement being made voluntarily or has any pressure been put upon you to make it?

A. No. It is quite voluntary.

Q. Will you tell me what you have to say?

A. Whatever I had to say I have said in .... statement.

Q. Have you any objection to making the document to me here?

A. Shall I begin from the very beginning.

Q. Yes.

A. In my statement I shall be a little vague about time because it is difficult to remember dates. I passed my Entrance Examination from the Deoghur school.

Q. At what age did you come to India?

A. When I was one year old. After passing the Entrance Examination I went to Dacca where my brother Manmohan Ghose was Professor, and I read up to the First Arts there. After, that I gave up my studies and went to Baroda where my brother Arabinda Ghose was a Professor in the Gaekwar's College. There I devoted myself to the study of

History and Political Literature. After being there a year I came back to Bengal with the idea of preaching the cause of independence as a Political Missionary. I moved about from District to District and started Gymnasiums. There young men were brought together to learn physical exercises and study politics. It went on preaching the cause of independence for nearly two years. By that time I had been through almost all the District of Bengal, I got tired of it and went back to Baroda and studied for a year. I then returned to Bengal convinced that a purely political propaganda would not do for the country and that people must be trained up spiritually to face dangers. I had an idea of starting a religious institution. By that time the Swadeshi and Boycott Agitation had begun. I thought of taking men under my own instruction to teach them and so I began to collect this band which has been arrested. With my friend Abinash Bhattacharjya (now under arrest) and Bhupendra Nath Dutt (now in jail) I started the *Jugantar* paper. We managed it for nearly 1½ years and then gave it over to the present managers. After I gave it up I took again to the recruiting. I collected altogether 14 or 15 young men from about the beginning of 1907 until now. I educated the boys in religious books and politics. We are always thinking of a far off revolution and wish to be ready for it, so we were collecting weapons in small quantities. Altogether I have collected 11 revolvers, 4 rifles and 1 gun. Among other young men who came to be admitted to our circle was Ullaskar Dutt; I don't remember exactly when but about the beginning of this year. He said that as he wanted to come among us and be useful he had learnt the preparation of explosives. He had a small laboratory in his house without his father's knowledge and he experimented there. I never saw it, he told me of it. With his help we began preparing explosives in small quantities in the garden house at 32, Moraripukur Road. In the meantime another friend of ours, Hem Chandra Das of Kandrui in Midnapore District, after I think selling part of his property, went to Paris to learn mechanics and, if possible, explosives.

Q. When did he go?

A. Approximately in the middle of 1907.

Q. When did he return?

A. Three or four months ago.

When he came back he joined Ullaskar Dutt in preparing explosives and bombs.

Q. Where did he do it?

A. At 38/4, Raja Nabakrishna's Street, Calcutta, and at a house which he had rented in Bagh Bazar, viz., 15 Gopi Mohun Dutt's Street.

About 5 or 6 months ago, that is after press prosecutions became numerous, we began to think of using explosives; and wherever we went for money we were encouraged to use explosives. Thinking that to be the voice of the nation, we submitted and began serious preparations. The first attempt which we made was in French Chandernagore when the Lieutenant Governor was going to Ranchi. Ullaskar Dutt went to Chandernagore with a small dynamite mine and some fuse and detonators and tried to place it on the line just before the special came, he was disturbed at the first place where he began by people coming out of their houses. He tried another place and could not place it properly and the special train came and speedily dropt 2 to 3 cartridges and went away, there was a futile explosion.

Q. What is your authority for this statement?

A. I sent him. I, Ullaskar and Upendranath Banerji used to do these things in consultation. I heard the account from Ullaskar.

When the Lieutenant Governor was coming back from Cuttack two others started with a similar object, viz., Profulla Chandra Chaki of Bogra and Bibhuti Bhusan Sarkar (of Santipur I believe) I went with them. We thought he would come back via Asansol. We went to Chandernagore.

Q. What had you with you?

A. A mine and fuse.

We waited but he did not come that way.

Q. Did you lay the mine?

A. Yes.

Q. Where?

A. Between Chandernagore and Mankundu Stations. As he did not come we picked it up and brought it away; we enquired at Chandernagore Station and we were told that the Lieutenatn-Governor was not coming that way.

The third time we went on a similar errand to Khargpur.

Q. Who went?

A. The same 3, I Profulla and Bibhuti. We left the train at Khargpur at 10 a.m. In the afternoon we went by train to Narayangarh where we waited on the road which is parallel the Railway line. When it was dark we went to the Railway line and waited till 9 p.m. We waited at a spot about a mile from Narayangarh on the Khargpur side. Here I shall give minute details because innocent people have been punished for this offence. We had with us a mine made of 6 lbs. of dynamite charged in a thick iron vessel with a lid at the top. The lid had a hole in the centre. We had a fuse made of picric compound and picric compound powder was placed in a paper tube; we used a leaden pipe in case it should get choked by ballast. While we were placing the mine the leaden pipe was found too long so we cut a piece off and threw it down there. We had a dark lantern with candles. We had various things wrapped up in paper and we had copies of the *Englishman* and of the *Bande Mataram;* we also left them behind. They had a cardboard shoe box which we left behind. We put cotton in the cardboard box and then fuse and then cotton over it. We left the pieces of cotton behind. We ate sweets there near some bushes below the line; we left some sal leaves with the remnants of the food. We placed the mine there and between 11 and 12 at night 1 alone went back to Narayangarh and went by the last down passenger to Calcutta. I left behind the 2 boys and they placed the fuse on the line when the special came. They said they were about 1½ miles away when the explosion took place. We took no assistance from any cooly or any one else.

After that there was a bomb outrage at Chandernagore. Hem

Chandra Dass prepared the bomb. Indu Bhusan Rai of Jessore and I and Narendra Nath Gossami of Serampore went to Chandernagore together : we left the train at Mankundu Station at sunset. We went straight to Chandernagore Strand and waited till 10 p.m. We did not see the Mayor that night. We went and stayed the night under a tree near the Station and the next morning Indra and Narendra went to Serampore to Narendra's place. Naren is the son of Nando Lal Gossami, Zamindar.

I returned to Calcutta. We 3 went to Chandernagore again the same evening.

I left the train there and Indra and Naren left at Mankundu. We met in the Strand and Indra undertook to throw the bomb. He went to the window of the dining room where the Mayor was dining with his wife : that was on the ground floor in a bye lane. He threw the bomb through the window gratings. We three went to Telinipara Ghat and crossed the river to Shamnagar and thence to Calcutta. The bomb did not work; we came to the conclusion that the picric acid was bad. I was at a little distance when Indra threw it.

There is one more incident, that at Mozafferpore, and I shall explain it. Profulla Chandra Chaki insisted on going with a bomb to Mozafferpore to do away with Mr. Kingsford because he had tried the cases against the Nationalist papers. The people in the country demanded his death.

Hem Chandra and Ullaskar prepared the bomb at 15, Gopi Mohun Dutt's Lane, it was made of dynamite put in a tin case with a wooden handle. Upendranath and Khudiram Ghose of Midnapore; he was also allowed to go. I gave them two revolvers because they wanted to kill themselves, if they were caught. Khudi Ram Ghose was an outsider. He did not know of the garden house or of 15, Gopi Mohun Dutt's Lane. He was staying with Hem Chandra Das. I took Profulla from the garden house, No. 32, Moraripukur Road to 15, Gopi Mohun Dutt's Lane and there he packed the bomb in a canvas bag and revolver with it.

Q. Where did you get the revolvers?

A. I do not wish to say.
I took Profulla to Hem's place and left him with Khudi Ram. I was told that they started the same night.
Q. When were you arrested?
A. The day before yesterday early in the morning.
Q. Where?
A. At 32, Moraripukur Road.
Q. Who else was there?
A. Ullaskar Dutt.
Upendra Nath Banerji.
Indra Bhusan Rai.
Bibhuti Bhusan Sarkar.
Pares Chandra Mallik.
Nalini Kanta Gupta.
Kunjo Lal Saha.
Sachindra Nath Sen.
Purna Chandra Sen.
Hemendra Nath Ghose.
Sisir Kumar Ghose.
Bijoy Chandra Nag and others.
Q. What were they doing there?
A. They are being instructed by me and Upendranath in religious and political books.
Q. Do they live there?
A. Yes, they were staying there with us.
Q. How was this household supported?
A. I collected money from different people for supporting them. The object was to teach them and sent out missionaries and for this anarchical work.
Q. What did the Police find?
A. They found the weapons which I have mentioned and a quantity of dynamite and some bottles of nitric acid, sulphuric acid and picric acid. These things were buried in two iron tanks in the ground and in an earthen pot.
The police found one and I pointed out the other two. There is one other thing which I can't tell you, viz., the supporters' names.

Q. Are any people out now on similar errands?

A. No.

I also want to say that we are not responsible for shooting Mr. Allen nor for the Kustia shooting case.

Q. Have you planned to destroy any one else?

A. No. We have discussed destroying the Viceroy and the Commander-in-Chief but the plans took no practical form. We never believed that political murder will bring independence

Q. Then why do you do it?

A. We believe the people wanted it.

(Sd.) L. Birley
4-5-08

Please take down my motive for disclosing these facts. Our party was . . . as to the propriety of disclosing these facts. Some thought deny everything and take the consequences, but I persuaded them, give written and oral statements to Inspector Ramsaday Mukerji, because I believe that as this band was found out, it was best not to do any other work in the country, and because we ought to save the innocent.

(Sd.) L. Birley
4-5-08

(Sd.) Barindra Kumar Ghose
(Signature of the accused)

I believe that the confession was voluntarily made. It was taken in my presence and hearing and was read over to the person making it, and admitted by him to be correct, and it contains a full and true account of the statement made by him.

(Sd.)L. Birley
(Signature of Magistrate)

The statement was recorded in open Court between 3 and 5

p.m. The accused was guarded by 2 constables of the Bengal Police and not by the Calcutta Police Constables who brought him. No other Police Officer was in Court.

(Sd.) L. Birley
4-5-08

True Copy
W. Islam
Pr. Dy. Magte,
Alipore
7-5-09
Trial No. 9 of Sept. 1908.
Emp. *vs.* B.K. Ghosh and others
Ex. 12 for prosn.
6-11-08
(Sd.) C.P.B.,
A.S.J

Appendix --C

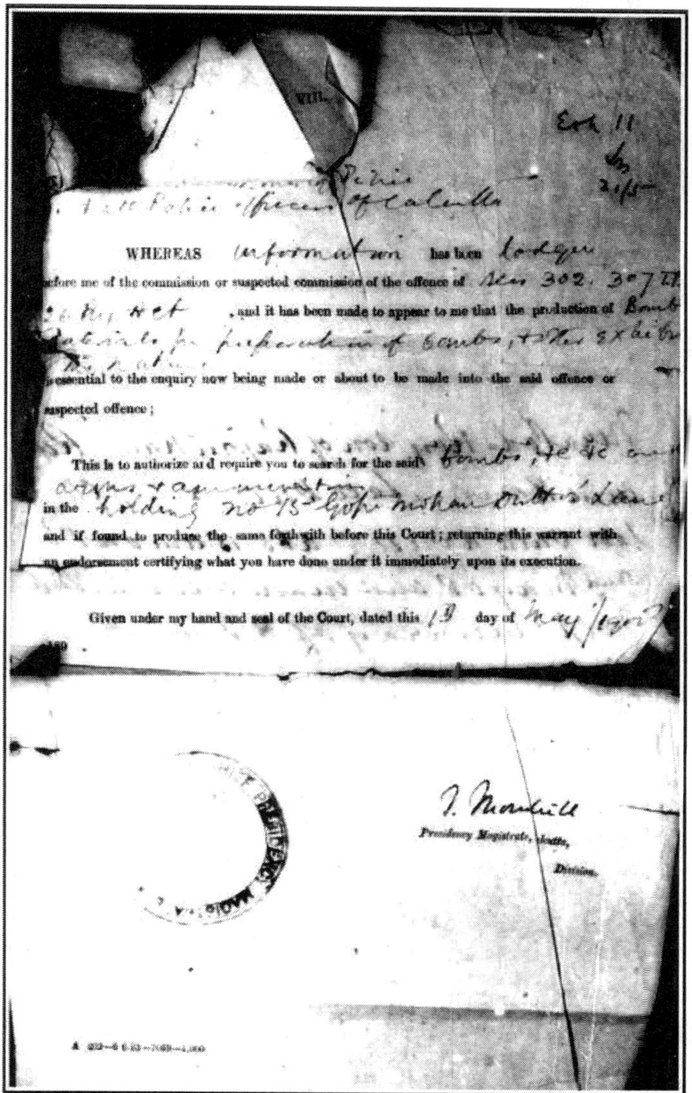

VIII.

All Police Officers of Calcutta

WHEREAS information has been lodged before me of the commission or suspected commission of the offence of Secs 302. 307 I.P.C. Ex. Act, and it has been made to appear to me that the production of Bomb materials for preparation of bombs, & other explosive materials is essential to the enquiry now being made or about to be made into the said offence or suspected offence;

This is to authorize and require you to search for the said bombs, &c &c and arms & ammunition in the holding No 15 Gopi Mohan Dutt's Lane and if found to produce the same forthwith before this Court; returning this warrant with an endorsement certifying what you have done under it immediately upon its execution.

Given under my hand and seal of the Court, dated this 19 day of May 1908.

Presidency Magistrate, Division.

Search warrant issued for
the search of Hem Chandra's house

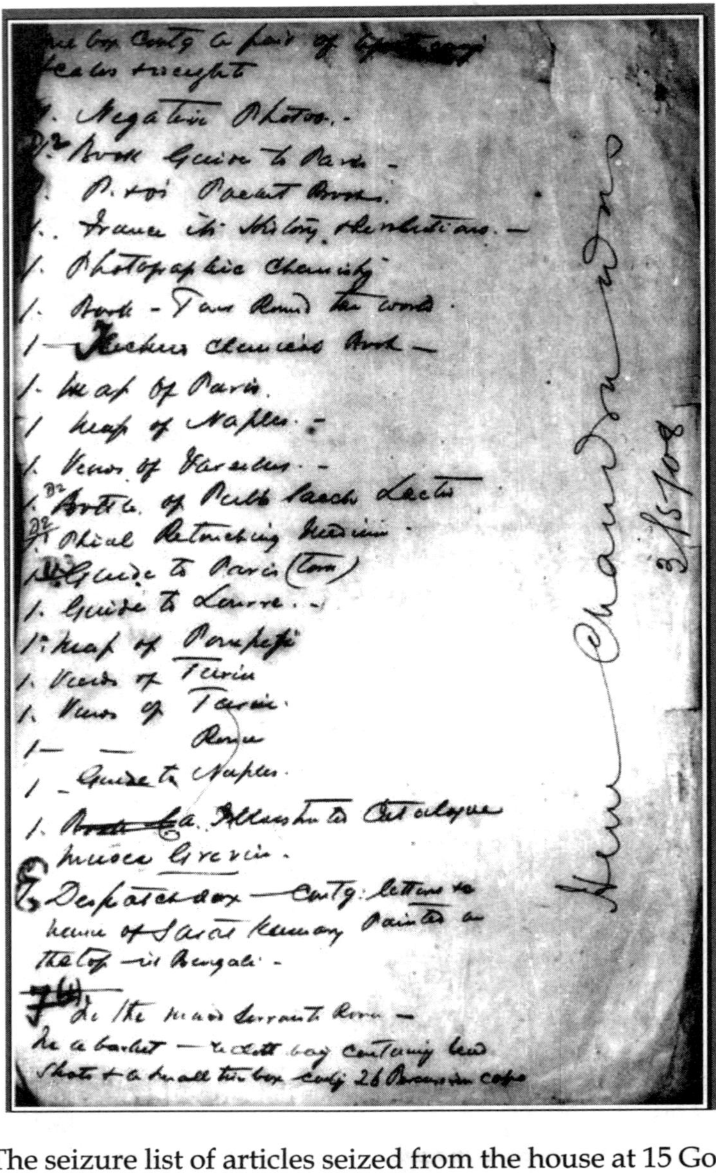
One box contg a pair of [illegible] scales & weights
1. Negative Photos.-
1 Book Guide to Paris -
1. P. & O. Pocket Book.
1. France in History Revolutions.—
1. Photographic Chemistry
1. Book - Tour Round the World.
1 — Hecker's Chemical Book —
1. Map of Paris.
1 Map of Naples.-
1. Views of Versailles.-
1. Bottle of [illegible]
1 Phial Retouching Medium.
1 Guide to Paris (Com)
1. Guide to Louvre..
1. Map of Pompeii
1. Views of Turin
1. Views of Turin.
1 — — Rome
1 - Guide to Naples.
1. ~~Book~~ Ca. Illustrated Catalogue Musea Greveii.
E3 Despatch box — Contg. letters & name of Sarat Kumar Painted on the top - in Bengali -
F(4) In the main Servants Room —
In a basket — a cloth bag containing lead shots & a small tin box contg 26 Brunswick caps
Hem Chandra Das
3/5/08

The seizure list of articles seized from the house at 15 Gopi Mohan Datta Lane on the third day of the search and signed by Hem Chandra :

The bigger revolver was used by Kanailal as Satyen being a sickly person wanted to use the lighter weapon. Hem Chandra writes, "Satyen asked Kanai to take the bigger revolver." In the committal enquiry held by W. Murray, ADM, Alipur and according to his own admission, Kanai was carrying the bigger one According to Captain Daly,who held the PM examination, all the wounds on Naren's body were caused by bullets fired from the big revolver.

This was used by Satyen Bose. Four rounds were fired. One bullet mis-fired. One hit the wrist of Gossain's bodyguard. One grazed passed the body of Kanai as he was also chasing Naren and was behind Kanai. One bullet went astray .

Parcel bomb was till 1908 was a novel weapon even to the terrorists of Europe. It was prepared at Hem Chandra's residence, neatly packed and sent to Kingsford through Pares Moulik of Manicktala Garden dressed in postal peon's uniform, cleverly procured by Hem Chandra himself. But Kingsford did not care to open it on receipt.The information about the bomb was given to the Police by one of the undertrials in Alipur case. The Sedition Committee did not reveal the name of the informer, but gave enough hint. The needle of suspicion indicates Upen Bnaerji.

Charlea Augustus Tegart as Commissioner of Calcutta Police. In 1908-1909 he was deputy commissioner of the newly created Special Branch of Calcutta Police.

Leonard Birley as Chief Secretary, Government of Bengal.
In 1908-1909 he was officiating DM, 24-Parganas.

This is one of the shells (Exhibit No. 614 in Alipur Bomb Case) of the three live bombs seized from 134 Harrison Road in the early hours of 2nd May,1908. One of them had 24 spikes. The bombs were de-commissioned at Park Street Police Station after seizure by Major Smallwood, Government Inspector of Explosives.

Aurobindo spent about a week in seclusion with Vishnu Bhaskar Lele from the end of December, 1907 up. to the end of the first week of January, 1908 for training in Yoga. This photograph was taken at Baroda before departure from Baroda.

This photo was taken when Satyendranath was a clerk in Midnapore Collectorate. He lost the job in 1906, when he refused to depose against Kshudiram Bose in a sedition case.

Smasane Kanai This photograph was taken by a private photographer at the burning ghat. There was a craze for Kanai's photograph and hundreds of copies of this photograph were printed and sold .. The Government banned the sale of the photo and all the copies were seized and destroyed. This copy survives in the file of the State Archives, West Bengal.

Hem Chandra - in the evening of his life

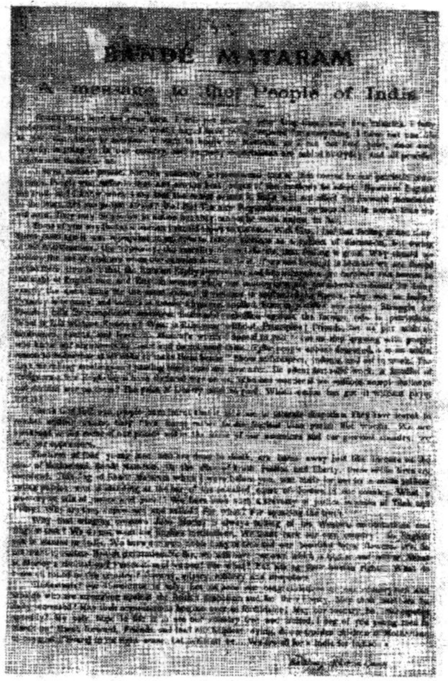

BANDE MATARAM

A message to the People of India

Left : *Madame Bhikhaji Rustom Cama (1861-1936) with the Indian National Flag which was unfurled at the International Socialist Congress, Stuttgart. p. 39*

Right : *Madame Cama's message to the Indian people*

Madam Rustomji Cama

In this message she clearly stated that the flag in her hand "was made for me by a rebel self less young patriot who was standing in the lear of so called justice in our country." She meant Hem Chandra Kanungo.

Aurobindo with the students of the English Department of the College in Baroda.

Aurobindo when he was touring western India.

Bhupendra Nath Datta at the time of his association with *Jugantar*.

Barindra Kumar Ghose at the time of Alipur trial.

Hem Chandra Kanungo at the time of Alipur Trial.

A group taken in 1908 at India house, Highgate, London

No	Name	Father's Name	District or Town
1	Kashi Prasad Jayaswal	Mahadeo Prasad Kalwar	Mirzapore
2	Madan Lal Dhingra	Rai Saheb Ditta Mall	Amritsar
3	Varaganeri Venkatesa Subramania Aiyar	Venkatesa Aiyar	Triochinopoly
4	M. A. Rashid		Aligarh
5	Tillastanam Sesha Sundam Rajan	Madathu Sesha Aiyangar	Tanjore
6	J. D. N. Dass		
7	Waman Vishnu Phadke	Vishnu Vasudeo Phadke	Miraj
8	Pala Singh		
9	Bajan Lal Dhingra	Rai Saheb Ditta Mall	Amritsar
10	Umiashankar Lakshimidas Joshi	Lakshmidas Joshi	Mandvi (Cutch)
11	Mamidi Devendruedu	Rajahmundry	
12	Narayen Vinayek Kirtikar	Vinayek Putoba Kirtikar	Bombay
13	Master Rana	Sirdarsinghji Revabhai Rana	Bhoika State Kathiawar
14	Govind Amin	Javerbhai	Kaira (Bo. Pres.)

This photograph was obtained by the Scotland Yard from an insider in the India House group, and a copy was sent to the Indian Central Intelligence at Simla along with their report on the agitation of the Indians in Britain. Often they used to invite the visiting Indian political leaders to address the meetings. A number of them belonged either to Free India Society or Savarkar's underground *Avinava Bharat* society.

A group taken on the 25th April 1909 at the India House, Highgate, London.

1 2 3 4 5 6

7 8 9 10 11 12

No.	Name	Father's name	District or Town
1	Asutosh Mitra		
2	M. P. Tirumala Chari	M. P. Narasunha Iyengar	Madras
3	Harnam Singh	Sardar Aya Singh	Amritsar
4	Haidar Raza	Ahmad Raza of Muzaffarnagar District (U.P.)	Delhi
5	Tillastanam Sesha Sundara Rajan		Tanjore
6	Gopal		Surat
7	Varaganeri Venkatesa Surramania Aiyar	Venkatesa Aiyar	Trichinopoly
8	Gyan Chand Varma		Jodhpur
9	Vinayak Damodhar Savarkar	Damodhar Savakar	Nasik
10	Naraujan Pal	Bepin Chandra Pal	Sylhet (E. B. and A.)
11	Rafik Mahomed Khan	Khan Bahadur Sardar Wali Muhammad Khan	Nabha
12	Govind Amin	Javerbhai	Kaira (Bo. Presy.)

Another group photograph taken sometime before 1st July,1909, because Madal Lal Dhingra is present in the group. He killed Cuezon Wyllie on 1st. July.

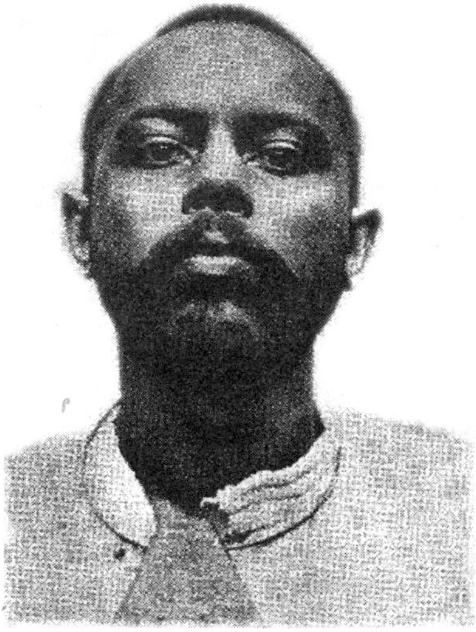

Ullaskar Datta as an undertrial prisoner.

Upendra Nath Bandopadhyaya as undertrial prisoner.

Khudiram Bose : The photo was taken by the polic at Muzaffarpur jail

1st row from left : Himangsu Roy , Gour Hari Mitra
2nd row from left : Friend of Sarat Chandra, Bijoy Krishna Khan, Sarat Chandra, Khitish Chandra Dutta, Manmatha Nath Das,
3rd row from left : Tinkori Sen, Binoy Dasgupta, Chandra Sekhar Dutta, Sudhamoy Bandopadhay, Hemchandra Kanungo, Bibhuti Bhusan Das, Sibomoy Bandopadhay, Shantimoy Bandhopadhay

Hem Chandra Kanungo with Sarat Chandra Chattopadhyay during the latters visit to Midnapore

A Swadeshi post Card. After affixing postage stamp it was used as a regular post card. The recipient of this post card was sushil Sen who was awarded 15 stripes of cane by Kingsford after Sushil had assaultd a sergeant, who while controlling crowd, used his lathi indiscriminately. This and the photos of Swadeshi movement and of Lal, Bal and Pal were exhibits in the Alipur Case.

The Photo was Raksha-bandhan. After taking bath in the Ganga on 16th October, 1905 the day the Partition of Bengal came into effect, people are seen tying rakhi.

The second photograph is of the crowd at the foundation stone laying ceremony at a field called *Pantir math.* The alling Ananda Mohan Bose laid the foundation stone in presence of the elite of Calcutta. Present day Federation Hall is located at that site.

Photographs of the famous trio, Lal, Bal and Pal. It was a very well known photograph in contemporary India.

Bipin Chandra Pal's photograph was widely circulated

Lala Lajpat Rai emerged as a national leader after his deportation in 1907 for participation in a peasant movement.

Aurobindo as an undertrial prisoner. While in custody he and other Alipur Case prisoners were photogrphed by the CID.

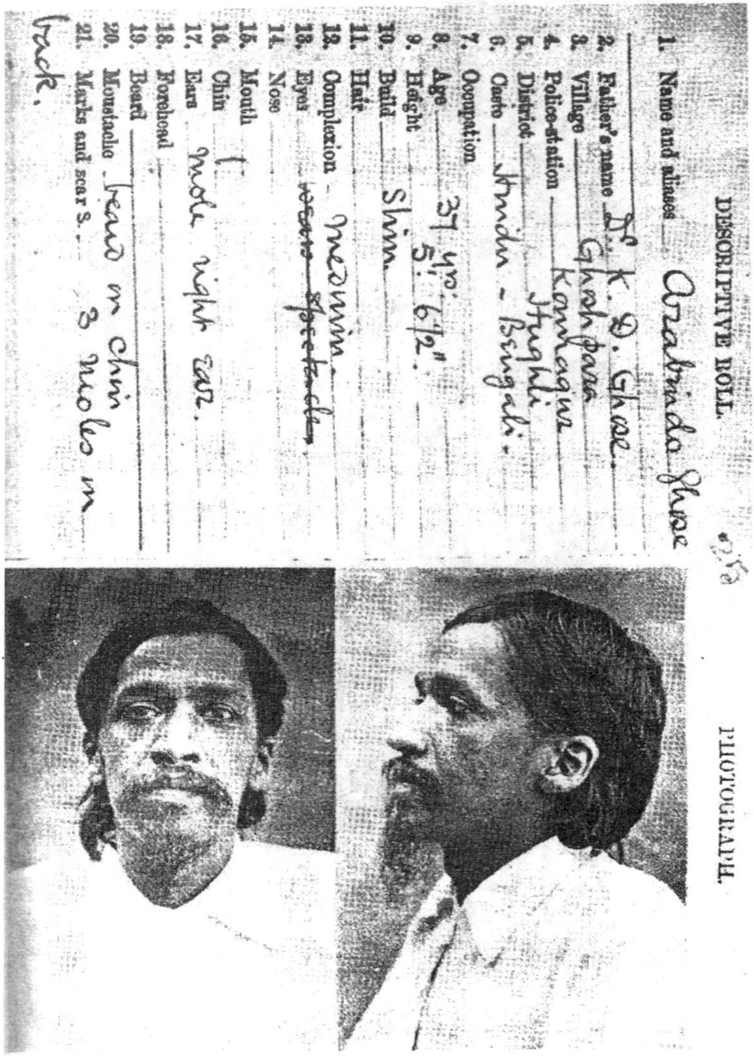

Alipore Jail, Calcutta

Aurobindo's descriptive roll prepared by the CID.

Satyendra Nath Bose (left) and Kani Lal Datta with specs. (right) as accused in the murder case of Naren Gossain.

Kshudiram Bose at the railway station flanked by two constables and Armed Reserve Force Inspector Haden, who with SP Armstrong went to Saini to bring Kshudiram to Mazaffarpur.

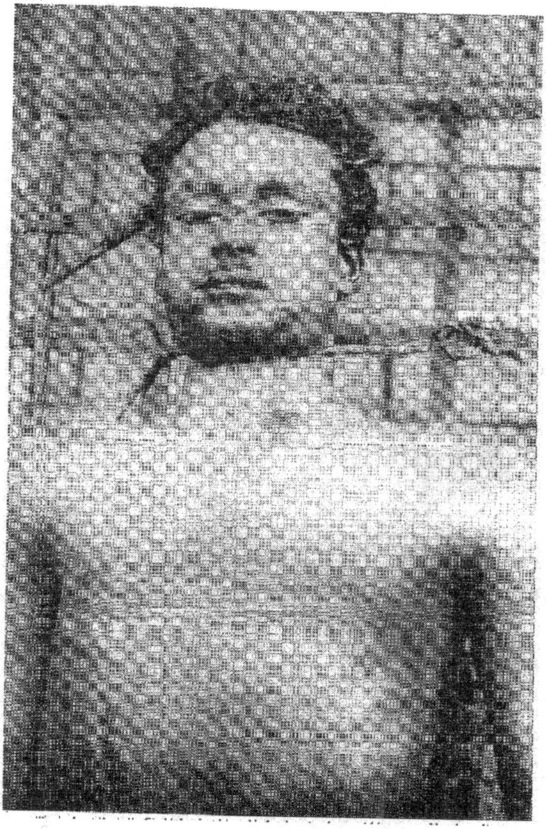

34. The dead body of Prafulla Chaki, who killed himself at Mokamaghat railway station, was brought to Muzaffarput via Barauni where it was photographed after sundown by one Shew Presad of Bankipur. As the photos did not come up very well the body was again photographed (front and profile) in the morning at Muzaffar pur, where Kshudiram identified the body in presence of the DM as the body of his companion Dinesh Chandra Ray. Thereafter Post Mortem which was done by the Superintentendent of Girl Hospital Col. T. Grainger, who found two bullets in the body.
The CID at Calcutta was not satisfied with Kshudiram's identification as according to their information there was none by that name in the revolutionary group. On their insistence a most gruesome act was committed. The head was severed from the body and sent to Calcutta.

Hem Chandra Kanungo in Midnapur.

Aspects of Tourism

THE TOURISM AREA LIFE CYCLE

Applications and Modifications

Volume 1

Aspects of Tourism

THE TOURISM AREA LIFE CYCLE

Applications and Modifications

Volume 1

Edited by
Richard W. Butler

Viva Books

New Delhi | Mumbai | Chennai | Kolkata | Bangalore | Hyderabad | Kochi | Guwahati

First Indian Edition 2010

VIVA BOOKS PRIVATE LIMITED

- 4737/23 Ansari Road, Daryaganj, New Delhi 110 002
  E-mail: vivadelhi@vivagroupindia.net, Tel. 42242200
- Plot No. 76, Service Industries, Shirvane, Sector 1, Nerul, Navi Mumbai 400 706
  E-mail: vivamumbai@vivagroupindia.net, Tel. 27721273, 27721274
- Jamals Fazal Chambers, 26 Greams Road, Chennai 600 006
  E-mail: vivachennai@vivagroupindia.net, Tel. 28290304, 28294241
- B-103, Jindal Towers, 21/1A/3 Darga Road, Kolkata 700 017
  E-mail: vivakolkata@vivagroupindia.net, Tel. 22836381, 22816713
- 7, Sovereign Park Apartments, 56-58, K. R. Road, Basavanagudi, Bangalore 560 004
  E-mail: vivabangalore@vivagroupindia.net, Tel. 26607409, 26607410
- 101-102 Mughal Marc Aptt., 3-4-637 to 641, Narayanguda, Hyderabad 500 029
  E-mail: vivahyderabad@vivagroupindia.net, Tel. 27564481, 27564482
- First Floor, Beevi Towers, SRM Road, Kaloor, Kochi 682 018, Kerala
  E-mail: vivakochi@vivagroupindia.net, Tel: 0484-2403055, 2403056
- 232, GNB Road, Beside UCO Bank, Silpukhuri, Guwahati 781 003
  E-mail: vivaguwahati@vivagroupindia.net, Tel: 0361-2666386

Published by arrangement with

Multilingual Matters Ltd.
Frankfurt Lodge, Clevedon Hall
Victoria Road, Clevedon BS21 7HH
England

ISBN : 978-81-309-1229-5

Published by Vinod Vasishtha for Viva Books Private Limited, 4737/23, Ansari Road, Daryaganj New Delhi - 110 002. Printed and bound by Raj Press, R-3, Inderpuri, New Delhi - 110 012.

DEDICATION

To my wife, Margaret, and my children, Caroline, Richard and Antonia, who have lived with 'the cycle' and its demands and been there with support and encouragement over the last three decades, and:

IN MEMORIAM

To my father, Sgt. Pilot Richard Butler, RAF (VR), 106 Squadron, whom I never had the privilege of knowing, and the more than 55,000 men of Bomber Command, who like him, were killed in action in the Second World War.

'When you go home, tell them of us, and say:
For your tomorrows we gave our today'

Contents

Acknowledgements

There are many acknowledgements that have to be made for the publication of any book, but in the case of edited works there are inevitably more needed than for a single authored work. In the first place I must thank most sincerely the authors whose writings appear in this and the accompanying volume. They have done most of the academic work in terms of their contributions, and it is a truism to say the books would not have appeared without their efforts. Of all the people I approached, some old friends, some former students (and hopefully still friends), some recent acquaintances and some known only to me by their writings, only one did not reply, and only one was finally unable to contribute a chapter. Some responded early (5.00 am in one case), others performed more like myself, cutting it rather fine. Virtually all wrote exactly what was asked of them, sometimes at rather short notice, all took my comments and suggestions in good spirit and some have even yet to take me up on the offer of a beer. Perhaps above all, I wish to thank them for finding the TALC of interest and using it in the first place.

Second of course, there are those involved in the publication of the books. At the University of Surrey, my long-suffering secretary Margaret Williamson and at various times, Malcolm Thompson, for assistance with Word and word processing, and Paul Fuller and John Briggs for rescuing various items from faulty laptops and illegible files on more than one occasion. At Channel View Publications, first and foremost, Mike Grover, for his support, particularly as this project grew from one book of 80,000 words and 15 chapters to one book of about 20 chapters, and then to two books of nearly 40 chapters and over 200,000 words in total, and to his family team, whose efforts I appreciate greatly.

Third, there is the general support team. Conceptually in its creation the TALC owes a great deal to Jim Brougham, the nearest person to a Renaissance man I have ever come across in person. Many good arguments, parties, football matches and above all, incomparable folk singing (on his side) contributed greatly if tangentially at times, to the final product. He was one of many former students at the University of Western Ontario, including Brian Keogh, Peter Keller, James Strapp, Colin Harris, Dave Weaver, Winston Husbands, Dave Telfer, Stephen Boyd, Tom Hinch and Bryan Smale, all of whom helped develop, test and refine the model in various ways. There are also many more graduate and undergraduate students, unfortunately too many to list, at Western and at the University of Surrey who have used the model and also helped in its development. Peter Murphy (once English, then Canadian and now Australian) should be acknowledged (or blamed) particularly for TALC seeing the light of day in terms of publication, first by nagging me to produce a paper for the Canadian Association of Geographers' meeting in Vancouver, and then by persuading the Association to publish the first ever special edition of *The Canadian Geographer* (24 (1), 1980) (which he edited), one devoted to papers on tourism and recreation.

Since 1980 in particular, many colleagues have assisted greatly, either by using the model (including all those featured in these volumes), or by just being there to talk, and to share ideas and good times. Some legitimately might feel their research should be included (or may be relieved it is not!), Gareth Shaw and Allan Williams in the UK in particular, but I do have one representative from the south west at least included, who was influenced by their work. Klaus Meyer-Arendt, Paul Wilkinson, Ngaire Douglas and Gerda Priestly especially are also owed apologies for apparently being ignored, but only by noninclusion of papers I can assure them. There are also a vast number of other writers who have used the TALC, most, if not all, included in Lagiewski's bibliography, and an even larger number of students at universities around the world who have probably driven their supervisors mad by using the model. (Arriving at an Australian university on sabbatical in 1992 I was greeted at coffee by a staff member there, with the comment, 'So you're the bugger that wrote that, I've just had to mark 20 reports using it!') Finally there is the family support team, to whom these books are dedicated, who have been hoping to heaven 'it' is finished soon and doing their best to make sure it is. They have eventually won and I am very grateful, not only for their support and encouragement, but for the ideas, suggestions (mostly) and willingness to lose sandpits, rooms and furniture buried under TALC-related material for far too long.

More formally and finally, I should also like to thank the Canadian Association of Geographers, not only for publishing the article in *The Canadian Geographer* in the first place, but also for giving me permission to reproduce the original article (Chapter 1, this volume). I trust this book will relieve some pressure on their office at McGill University by reducing the number of requests for copies!

Contributors

Names and e-mail addresses of Contributors to TALC Books.

Book 1

Richard 'Rick' M. Lagiewski, Rochester Institute of Technology
Rick.Lagiewski@rit.edu

K. Michael Haywood, retired, at time of writing University of Guelph
Michael.Haywood@sympatico.ca

Gary Hovinen, retired at time of writing
ghovinen@yahoo.com

Jan O. Lundgren, McGill University
jan.lundgren@mcgill.ca

Jigang Bao, Sun Yat Sen University
eesbjg@zsu.edu.cn

Chaozi Zhang, Sun Yat Sen University
No e-mail, use Bao (above)

Stephen Boyd, currently University of Ulster (Coleraine Campus)
sw.boyd@ulster.ac.uk

Antonio Paolo Russo, Erasmus University
russo@few.eur.nl

Jane Malcolm-Davies, at time of writing University of Surrey
jane@jmdandco.com

David B. Weaver, University of South Carolina
dweaver@gwm.sc.edu

Charles S. Johnston, Auckland Institute of Technology
charles.johnston@aut.ac.nz

Jerry D. Johnson, Montana State University
jdj@montana.edu

David J. Snepenger, Montana State University
dsnep@montana.ed also dsnepenger@earthlink.com

Bonnie Martin
bmartin@mail.wcu.edu

Juanita Marois, University of Alberta
Juanita-marois@aol.com

Tom Hinch, University of Alberta
thinch@ualberta.ca

Sanda Corak, Institute of Tourism, University of Zagreb
sanda.corak@iztzg.hr

Charles Stansfield, retired from Rowan College, New Jersey
ruthig@rowan.edu

Bill Faulkner, deceased at time of writing, Griffith University

Carmen Tideswell, Auckland Institute of Technology
carmen.tideswell@aut.ac.nz

Brian Wheeller, at time of writing NHTV Breda, Netherlands
wheellerbrian@yahoo.com

Book 2

Tim Coles, University of Exeter
T.E.Coles@exeter.ac.uk

Andreas Papatheodorou, at time of writing University of Surrey, now University of Aegean
academia@trioptron.org

C. Michael Hall, University of Otago
cmhall@business.otago.ac.nz

Rosslyn Russell, Royal Melbourne Institute of Technology
rosslyn.russell@rmit.edu.au

Sabine Weisenegger, University of Muenchen
weizenegger@bwl.uni-muenchen.de

Stephen Wanhill, at time of writing Bournemouth University, now University of Limerick
Stephen@Wanhill.force9.co.uk

Sven Lundtorp, as Wanhill (above)

Neil Ravenscroft, University of Brighton
neil@ravenscroft.fsnet.co.uk

Ion Hadjihambi, KPMG Services (Pty) Ltd.
ion.hadjihambi@kpmg.co.za

Chris Cooper, University of Queensland
c.cooper@mailbox.uq.edu.au

Sheela Agarwal, University of Plymouth
S.Agarwal@plymouth.ac.uk

Mara Manente, CISET, University of Venice
mtourism@unive.it

Harald Pechlaner, Catholic University of Eichstatt-Ingoldstadt, Bavaria
Harald.Pechlaner@ku-eichstaett.de

Ted Berry, Lower Kuskokwin School District, Alaska
Tedberry_aus@yahoo.com

Introduction

C. MICHAEL HALL

It is an indication of the significance of a concept that it starts to attract not only articles but entire books as to its nature. And, as the reader will find in going through the various chapters in the two volumes of this book, the Tourism Area Life Cycle (TALC) is one of the most cited and contentious areas of tourism knowledge. Even as Butler (this volume), himself notes 'there was nothing devastatingly complicated or original in the data or facts on which the model is based'. The TALC has gone on to become one of the best known theories of destination growth and change within the field of tourism studies.

As the second volume highlights, there is a substantial body of contested theory and concepts that surround the TALC. Although 'Butler put into the realistic cyclical context a reality that everyone knew about, and clearly recognised, but had never formulated into an overall theory' (Lundgren, 1984: 22), the TALC is arguably one of the most significant contributions to studies of tourism development because of the way it provides a focal point for discussion of what leads to destination change, how destinations and their markets change and, even, what is a destination. Moreover, the two volumes together highlight the manner in which theory informs the development and generation of tourism knowledge, the importance of understanding the intellectual history of tourism ideas, and the disciplinary dimensions of tourism studies. These come from a number of different areas of knowledge, are applied at different scales, and often seek to tackle different dimensions of understanding destination change. Nevertheless, they highlight the importance of the intellectual history of ideas in tourism, and of the intellectual heritage of the TALC in particular. Some of these issues are discussed at the outset of this volume in terms of the foundations of the TALC, however readers seeking to gain a wider appreciation and understanding of the TALC will need to read this section in conjunction with the discussions of the second volume. Nevertheless, it is readily apparent that the TALC remains one of the most oft-cited works in tourism studies even if many people have never read the original article and have instead only read interpretations of it in textbooks or journals.

This particular volume looks at the means by which the TALC has been applied in particular situations and settings. It commences with a reproduction of the original article from *The Canadian Geographer* and is followed by a chapter by Butler on the origins of the TALC. Being able to easily access the original article will be helpful to many students of tourism but the opportunity to read Butler discussing its background will be especially welcome. As noted in the introduction to the second volume, being able to encounter such a variety of insights into the TALC helps readers gain an appreciation not only of the significance of the TALC but also its intellectual history. In the case of Butler revisiting the origins of the TALC we see the significance of authors active in the 1960s and 1970s rarely cited in contemporary tourism studies, such as Roy Wolfe and Charles Stansfield, as well as even earlier authors from the 1930s and 1940s. Significantly, we also learn of the extent to which personal travel experiences, particularly in Scotland, may have influenced Butler's understanding of tourism destinations, as well as the role of his work with Jim Brougham, then a graduate student at the University of Western Ontario. These reflections highlight that in tourism research, as in other fields of knowledge, the generation of ideas rarely occurs in isolation and instead needs to be understood in relation to its personal and intellectual context.

The first section also includes a chapter by Lagiewski that provides an overview of some of the writings that have utilised the TALC and a chapter by Haywood that seeks to relate the TALC to understandings of destination change. The Haywood chapter in particular should be read in conjunction with the chapter by the same author in the second volume, which notes the extent to which concepts of life cycle and change have been poorly understood and appreciated by the tourism industry itself. As the introduction to Volume 2 notes, such a situation reflects the need for a broader understanding of the processes of the diffusion of tourism knowledge that the various contributions to the two volumes partly illustrate.

The second section of this volume deals with examples of the implementation of the TALC. Hovinen discusses the relationship between TALC and concepts of sustainability in Lancaster County, Pennsylvania. The reflections by Hovinen are particularly welcome as he was the first person to empirically apply the TALC to a specific location (Hovinen, 1981, 1982). Indeed, there are a number of chapters in this volume that illustrate the value of reflection on previous work and reconsiderations of its application. Similarly, Lundgren provides an empirical examination of TALC with respect to the eastern townships of Quebec, locations in which he has previously undertaken substantial research. The section is concluded with a case study of the role of TALC in tourism planning in China by Bao and Zhang.

The third section of the volume deals with the application of specific setting, that of cultural and natural heritage. The first chapter in the section is by Stephen Boyd, a former graduate student of Butler, who applies the TALC to Canadian national parks. Russo provides an appraisal of the TALC at a different scale by examining its relationship to heritage cities, while the final chapter of the section, by Malcolm-Davies, shifts the scale of analysis even further by dealing with its potential role at a site level.

One of the main points of debate that has emerged out of consideration of the TALC is its implications for the social and political dynamics that exist within a destination as it changes. Some of these issues are discussed in the fourth section of the volume, which discusses the TALC in relation to local involvement. Weaver and Johnston examine some of these concerns with respect to island destinations, examining the Caribbean and the Hawaiian islands respectively. Johnson and Snepenger discuss residents' perceptions of tourism development in a longitudinal investigation of Silver Valley, Idaho, with Marois and Hinch (another former graduate student of Butler) examining the links between TALC and sustainable tourism in Northern Thailand. The remaining chapter in the section, that of Martin on tourism and politics, discusses the significance of the political aspect of the growth that occurs as tourism progresses through the different stages of the life cycle. Martin provides a case study of Hilton Head, South Carolina to illustrate his general arguments regarding the politics of tourism growth.

The final section of the volume examines empirical studies of the rejuvenation stage of the TALC. Ideally, these should be read in conjunction with the chapters on conceptualising restructuring and rejuvenation in the second volume. Corak discusses the reinvention of a destination in terms of the Opatija Riviera in Croatia while Stansfield examines the rejuvenation of Atlantic City. Both locations have significance for the development of the TALC: Opatija in that it was the first continental destination visited by Butler; and Atlantic City, and the work of Stansfield (1972, 1978), because of the substantial insights it provided into the processes by which resorts rise and fall in popularity. Indeed, the length to which some of these ideas have now been circulating is reflected in Stansfield's chapter in which he refers to the recycling of the resort cycle. The final chapter in this section is by Faulkner and Tideswell and focuses on the rejuvenation of the Gold Coast, Australia.

The conclusion to this volume is an insightful and provocative chapter by Brian Wheeller who successfully managed to integrate issues of authenticity, sustainability and TALC with wildlife ecology, eco-lodges and Elvis Presley. Nevertheless, Wheeler's chapter has a serious message in that it seeks to bring together a number of significant concerns in contemporary tourism studies as well as question some of the assumptions made with respect to ethics, morals and tastes in tourism. The Wheeller chapter also provides a suitable springboard to some of the more theoretical and conceptual dimensions of TALC that are discussed in the other volume, particularly as it seeks to illustrate the manner in which empirical observation and experience and theory are interwoven.

This volume therefore provides a welcome overview of some of the ways in which the TALC has been applied and some of the implications of those applications for further theoretical and conceptual developments in understanding destination change. The second volume goes on to investigate some of these changes in further detail and the contested theoretical terrain that is the TALC. However, as noted above, it is important to realise that the contents of the two volumes are interwoven and ideally need to be read together in order to gain a wider appreciation of TALC, its intellectual history and its contribution to tourism studies, as well as understanding the processes of destination change.

References

Hovinen, G. (1981) A tourist cycle in Lancaster County, Pennsylvania. *Canadian Geographer* 15 (3), 283–286.

Hovinen, G. (1982) Visitor cycles: Outlook in tourism in Lancaster County. *Annals of Tourism Research* 9, 565–583.

Lundgren, J.O. (1984) Geographic concepts and the development of tourism research in Canada. *Geojournal* 9, 17–25.

Stansfield, C. (1972) The development of modern seaside resorts. *Parks and Recreation* 5 (10), 14–46.

Stansfield, C. (1978) Atlantic City and the resort cycle. Background to the legalization of gambling. *Annals of Tourism Research* 5 (2), 238–251.

Part 1

Foundations of the TALC

RICHARD W. BUTLER

This first section of the volume serves to introduce the TALC and review in general terms its origins and uses. It begins with a reproduction of the original article. While this may be felt redundant given the frequency with which it is still quoted, in fact it appears to be an elusive publication. As noted below (Butler, next chapter), the journal, despite its quality, is not commonly found in the holdings of a considerable number of institutions focusing on tourism, unless they also have departments of geography. This has meant over the years that a number of potential readers have, or appear to have had, considerable difficulty in obtaining access to a copy and have relied on summaries in other sources. It seemed appropriate, therefore, to republish the original article in its entirety to increase availability, as well as to enable readers of this volume to have a copy to hand should they wish to refer to it.

The chapter that follows traces the origins of the concept, including a fair amount of reflexive comment by the author, in order to provide a context for the model. It was felt necessary to point out the limited nature and scale of tourism research in the decades before 1980, as well as taking the opportunity to acknowledge the contribution to the theoretical and conceptual development of tourism of authors whose works are, unfortunately, relatively unknown to many of the present day's tourism students and scholars. As is the case of many models, the original focus and purpose was somewhat different to what finally emerged, and the spatial emphasis explicit in the original model had become implicit at best in the final version.

Lagiewski's chapter presents a review of several of the major initial applications of the TALC, and some of the authors whose work is reviewed have contributed chapters in this and the accompanying volume. Of particular value is the table listing applications of the model and the extensive bibliography resulting from it. While no bibliography is ever likely to be complete, this one would appear to have more references to the use of the TALC than any other single piece of work, and is in itself a valuable reference tool for other potential users of the model.

Finally in this first section of the book is the chapter by Haywood, who was one of the first to write a detailed full critique of the model once it had been published. His chapter in this volume focuses particularly on aspects of the model that need addressing in order to improve its potential value for application in areas such as destination development, policy and strategy formulation, and destination management. His comments are particularly valuable in identifying issues that still have to be resolved, some of them coming from the same points that he raised in his original review in 1986. In the section on Configuration and Transformation he discusses in detail issues such as the unit of analysis and unit of measurement most applicable for application of the TALC. He concludes by linking the TALC to sustainability, a theme dealt with in several chapters in this volume (Hovinen, Marois and Hinch, Russo, and Wheeller in particular).

After this the book proceeds with chapters applying the TALC in a variety of situations and locations, at different scales, and through different approaches. Hopefully this introductory section provides sufficient detail on the background and foundations of the TALC for the reader to be able to place these later chapters in an appropriate context.

Chapter 1

The Concept of a Tourist Area Cycle of Evolution: Implications for Management of Resources*

R.W. BUTLER
University of Western Ontario

There can be little doubt that tourist areas are dynamic, that they evolve and change over time. This evolution is brought about by a variety of factors including changes in the preferences and needs of visitors, the gradual deterioration and possible replacement of physical plant and facilities, and the change (or even disappearance) of the original natural and cultural attractions which were responsible for the initial popularity of the area. In some cases, while these attractions remain, they may be utilized for different purposes or come to be regarded as less significant in comparison with imported attractions.[1] The idea of a consistent process through which tourist areas evolve has been vividly described by Christaller:

> The typical course of development has the following pattern. Painters search out untouched and unusual places to paint. Step by step the place develops as a so-called artist colony. Soon a cluster of poets follows, kindred to the painters: then cinema people, gourmets, and the jeunesse dorée. The place becomes fashionable and the entrepreneur takes note. The fisherman's cottage, the shelter-huts become converted into boarding houses and hotels come on the scene. Meanwhile the painters have fled and sought out another periphery – periphery as related to space, and metaphorically, as 'forgotten' places and landscapes. Only the painters with a commercial inclination who like to do well in business remain; they capitalize on the good name of this former painter's corner and on the gullibility of tourists. More and more townsmen choose this place, now en vogue and advertised in the newspapers. Subsequently the gourmets, and all those who seek real recreation, stay away. At last the tourist agencies come with their package rate travelling parties; now, the indulged public avoids such places. At the same time, in other places the same cycle occurs again; more and more places come into fashion, change their type, turn into everybody's tourist haunt.[2]

While this description has most relevance to the European and, particularly, to the Mediterranean setting, others have expressed the same general idea. Stansfield, in discussing the development of Atlantic City, refers specifically to the resort cycle,[3] and Noronha has suggested that 'tourism develops in three stages: i) discovery, ii) local response and initiative, and iii) institutionalized 'institutionalization).'[4] It is also explicit in Christaller's concept that types of tourists change with the tourist areas. Research into the characteristics of visitors is widespread, but less has been done on their motivations and desires. One example is a typology conceived by Cohen, who characterizes tourists as 'institutionalized' or 'non-institutionalized,' and further as 'drifters', 'explorers,' 'individual mass tourists,' and 'organized mass tourists.'[5] Research by Plog into the psychology of travel, and the characterization of travellers as allocentrics, mid-centrics, and psychocentrics, substantiates Christaller's argument.[6] Plog suggests that tourist areas are attractive to different types of visitors as the areas evolve, beginning with small numbers of adventuresome allocentrics, followed by increasing numbers of mid-centrics as the area becomes accessible, better serviced, and well known, and giving way to declining numbers of psychocentrics as the area becomes older, more outdated, and less different to the areas of origin of visitors. While the actual numbers of visitors may not decline for a long time, the potential market will reduce in size as the area has to compete with others that are more recently developed. Plog sums up his argument thus: 'We can visualize a destination moving across a spectrum, however gradually or slowly, but far too often ineroxably toward the potential of its own demise. Destination areas carry with them the potential seeds of their own destruction, as they allow themselves to become more commercialized and lose their qualities which originally attracted tourists.'

While other writers, such as Cohen,[7] have warned against the problems of unilinear models of social change, there seems to be overwhelming evidence that the general pattern of tourist area evolution is consistent. The rates of growth and change may vary widely, but the final result will be the same in almost all cases.

A Hypothetical Cycle of Area Evolution

The pattern which is put forward here is based upon the product cycle concept, whereby sales of a product proceed slowly at first, experience a rapid rate of growth, stabilize, and subsequently decline; in other words, a basic asymptotic curve is followed. Visitors will come to an area in small numbers initially, restricted by lack of access, facilities, and local knowledge. As facilities are provided and awareness grows, visitor numbers will increase. With marketing, information dissemination, and further facility provision, the area's popularity will grow rapidly. Eventually, however, the rate of increase in visitor numbers will decline as levels of carrying capacity are reached. These may be identified in terms of environmental factors (e.g. land scarcity, water quality, air quality), of physical plant (e.g. transportation, accommodation, other services), or of social factors (e.g. crowding, resentment by the local population). As the attractiveness of the area declines relative to other areas, because of overuse and the impacts of visitors, the actual number of visitors may also eventually decline.

The stages through which it is suggested that tourist areas pass are illustrated in Figure 1.1. The *exploration stage* is characterized by small numbers of tourists, Plog's allocentrics and Cohen's explorers making individual travel arrangements and following irregular visitation patterns. From Christaller's model they can also be expected to be non-local visitors who have been attracted to the area by its unique or considerably different natural and cultural features. At this time there would be no specific facilities provided for visitors. The use of local facilities and

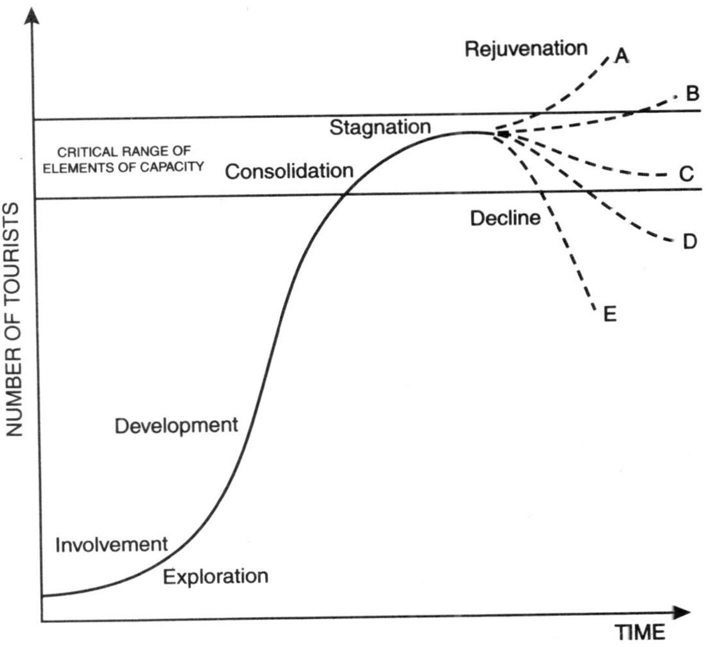

Figure 1.1 Hypothetical evolution of a tourist area. (For explanation of A–E see 'Implications.')

contact with local residents are therefore likely to be high, which may itself be a significant attraction to some visitors. The physical fabric and social milieu of the area would be unchanged by tourism, and the arrival and departure of tourists would be of relatively little significance to the economic and social life of the permanent residents. Examples of this stage can be seen in parts of the Canadian Arctic and Latin America, to which tourists are attracted by natural and cultural-historical features.

As numbers of visitors increase and assume some regularity, some local residents will enter the *involvement stage* and begin to provide facilities primarly or even exclusively for visitors. Contact between visitors and locals can be expected to remain high and, in fact, increase for those locals involved in catering for visitors. As this stage progresses, some advertising specifically to attract tourists can be anticipated, and a basic initial market area for visitors can be defined. A tourist season can be expected to emerge and adjustments will be made in the social pattern of at least those local residents involved in tourism. Some level of organization in tourist travel arrangements can be expected and the first pressures put upon governments and public agencies to provide or improve transport and other facilities for visitors. Some of the smaller, less developed Pacific and Caribbean islands exhibit this pattern, as do some less accessible areas of western Europe and North America.

The *development stage* reflects a well-defined tourist market area, shaped in part by heavy advertising in tourist-generating areas. As this stage progresses, local involvement and control of development will decline rapidly. Some locally provided facilities will have disappeared, being superseded by larger, more elaborate, and more up-to-date facilities provided by external organizations, particularly for visitor accommodation. Natural and cultural attractions will be developed and marketed specifically, and these original attractions will be supplemented by man-made imported facilities. Changes in the physical appearance of the area will be noticeable, and it can be expected that not all of them will be welcomed or approved by all of the local population. This stage can be seen in parts of Mexico, on the more developed Pacific islands, and on the north and west African coasts. Regional and national involvement in the planning and provision of facilities will almost certainly be necessary and, again, may not be completely in keeping with local preferences. The number of tourists at peak periods will probably equal or exceed the permanent local population. As this stage unfolds, imported labour will be utilized and auxiliary facilities for the tourist industry (such as laundries) will make their appearance. The type of tourist will also have changed, as a wider market is drawn upon, representing the mid-centrics of Plog's classification, or Cohen's institutionalized tourist.

As the *consolidation stage* is entered the rate of increase in numbers of visitors will decline, although total numbers will still increase, and total visitor numbers exceed the number of permanent residents. A major part of the area's economy will be tied to tourism. Marketing and advertising will be wide-reaching and efforts made to extend the visitor season and market area. Major franchises and chains in the tourist industry will be represented but few, if any, additions will be made. The large numbers of visitors and the facilities provided for them can be expected to arouse some opposition and discontent among permanent residents, particularly those not involved in the tourist industry in any way, and to result in some deprivation and restrictions upon their activities. Such trends are evident in areas of the Caribbean and on the northern Mediterranean coast. The resort cities will have well-defined recreational business districts,[8] and, depending upon the length of time involved, old facilities may now be regarded as second rate and far from desirable.

As the area enters the *stagnation stage* the peak numbers of visitors will have been reached. Capacity levels for many variables will have been reached or exceeded, with attendant environmental, social, and economic problems. The area will have a well-established image but it will no longer be in fashion. There will be a heavy reliance on repeat visitation and on conventions and similar forms of traffic. Surplus bed capacity will be available and strenuous efforts will be needed to maintain the level of visitation. Natural and genuine cultural attractions will probably have been superseded by imported 'artificial' facilities. The resort image becomes divorced from its geographic environment.[9] New development will be peripheral to the original tourist area and the existing properties are likely to experience frequent changes in ownership. The Costa Brava resorts of Spain and many cottage resorts in Ontario manifest these characteristics. The type of visitor can also be expected to change towards the organized mass tourist identified by Cohen and the psychocentric described by Plog.

In the *decline stage* the area will not be able to compete with newer attractions and so will face a declining market, both spatially and numerically. It will no longer appeal to vacationers but will be used increasingly for weekend or day trips, if it is accessible to large numbers of people. Such trends can be clearly seen in older resort areas in Europe, such as the Firth of Clyde in western Scotland. Miami Beach would also appear to be entering this stage. Property turnover will be high and tourist facilities often replaced by non-tourist related structures, as the area moves out of tourism. This latter factor, of course, is cumulative. More tourist facilities disappear as the area becomes less attractive to tourists and the viability of other tourist facilities becomes more questionable. Local involvement in tourism is likely to increase at this stage, as employees and other residents are able to purchase facilities at significantly lower prices as the market declines. The conversion of many facilities to related activities is likely. Hotels may become condominiums, convalescent or retirement homes, or conventional apartments, since the attractions of many tourist areas make them equally attractive for permanent settlement, particularly for the elderly. Ultimately, the area may become a veritable tourist slum or lose its tourist function completely.

On the other hand *rejuvenation* may occur, although it is almost certain that this stage will never be reached without a complete change in the attractions on which tourism is based. Two ways of accomplishing this goal can be seen at present. One is the addition of a man-made attraction, as in the case of Atlantic City's gambling casinos. Obviously, though, if neighbouring and competing areas follow suit, the effectiveness of the measure will be reduced; a major part of Atlantic City's anticipated success is the element of uniqueness which it has obtained by the change.

An alternative approach to rejuvenation is to take advantage of previously untapped natural resources. Spa towns in Europe and the summer holiday village of Aviemore in Scotland have experienced rejuvenation by a reorientation to the winter sports market, thus allowing the areas to experience a year-round tourist industry. The development of new facilities becomes economically feasible, and simultaneously serves to revitalize the older summer holiday trade. As new forms of recreation appear, it is not impossible that other tourist areas will find previously unappreciated natural resources to develop.

In many cases, combined government and private efforts are necessary, and the new market may be not the allocentric section of the population (which would suggest a recommencement of the complete cycle), but rather a specific interest or activity group. Ultimately, however, it can be expected that even the attractions of the rejuvenated tourist area will lose their competitiveness. Only in the case of the truly unique area could one anticipate an almost timeless attractiveness, able to withstand the pressures of visitation. Even in such a case, human tastes and preferences would have to remain constant over time for visitors to be attracted. Niagara Falls is perhaps one example. Artificial attractions, such as the spectacularly successful Disneyland and Disneyworld, may also be able to compete effectively over long periods by adding to their attractions to keep in tune with contemporary preferences. Many established tourist areas in Britain, the United States, and elsewhere attract visitors who have spent their vacations in these areas consistently for several decades, and the preferences of these repeat visitors show little sign of changing. In the majority of cases, though, the initial selection of the area to be visited by these people was determined by cost and accessibility rather than specific preferences.

Implications

Although a consistent evolution of tourist areas can be conceptualized, it must be emphasized again that not all areas experience the stages of the cycle as clearly as others. The establishment of what has become known as the 'instant resort' is a case in point. The process whereby areas for development, such as Cancun in Mexico,[10] are selected by computer from a range of possibilities allowed by certain preselected parameters has meant that the exploration and involvement phases are probably of minimal significance, if they are present at all. Under these circumstances the development phase becomes the real commencement of the cycle. Even here, however, it can be argued that, at the national scale, Mexico is experiencing the cycle illustrated in Figure 1.1. Perhaps the later stages of the cycle are more significant, then, because of the implications which they hold for tourism in general and for the planning and arrangement of tourist areas in particular.

The assumption that tourist areas will always remain tourist areas and be attractive to tourists appears to be implicit in tourism planning. Public and private agencies alike, rarely, if ever, refer to the anticipated life span of a tourist area or its attractions. Rather, because tourism has shown an, as yet, unlimited potential for growth, despite economic recessions, it is taken for granted that numbers of visitors will continue to increase. The fallacy of this assumption can be seen in the experience of older tourist areas, such as those of southern Ontario, over the past two decades.

The process illustrated in Figure 1.1 has two axes representing numbers of visitors and time. An increase in either direction implies a general reduction in overall quality and attractiveness after capacity levels are reached. In the case of the first visitors, the area may become unattractive long before capacity levels are reached and they will have moved on to explore other undeveloped areas. It can be anticipated also that reaction to the visitors by the local population will undergo change throughout this period, a process suggested by Doxey in his 'irridex' (index of tourist irritation); the scale progresses from euphoria through apathy and irritation to antagonism.[11] More recent research has shown that resident reaction to tourists is not necessarily explained by increasing contact with visitors or increasing numbers of visitors alone. It is a more complex function, related to the characteristics of both visitors and visited, and the specific arrangements of the area involved.[12]

The direction of the curve after the period of stabilization illustrated in Figure 1.1 is open to several interpretations. Successful redevelopment, as for example in Atlantic City, could result in renewed growth and expansion as shown by curve A. Minor modification and adjustment to capacity levels, and continued protection of resources, could allow continued growth at a much reduced rate (curve B). A readjustment to meet all capacity levels would enable a more stable level of visitation to be maintained after an initial readjustment downwards (curve C) Continued overuse of resources, non-replacement of aging plant, and decreasing competitiveness with other areas would result in the marked decline (curve D). Finally, the intervention of war, disease, or other catastrophic events would result in an immediate decline in numbers of visitors (for example, Northern Ireland from 1969), from which it may be extremely difficult to return to high levels of visitation. If the decline continues for a long time, the area and its facilities may no longer be attractive to the majority of tourists after the problem is solved.

To date, the arguments put forward in this paper are general and are only now being substantiated in terms of quantifiable data. A major problem in testing the basic hypothesis and modelling the curve for specific areas is that of obtaining data on visitors to areas over long periods. These are rarely available, and it is particularly unlikely that they will date back to the onset of tourist visits. However, those data which are available for a few areas for periods in excess of thirty or forty years substantiate the general arguments put forward in this paper.

At the same time, the shape of the curve must be expected to vary for different areas, reflecting variations in such factors as rate of development, numbers of visitors, accessibility, government policies, and numbers of similar competing areas.

It has been clearly shown, for example, that each improvement in accessibility to a recreation area results in significantly increased visitation and an expansion of the market area.[13]

The development of health resorts in Britain, France, the north United States bears witness to this process.[14] If development of facilities and accessibility is delayed, for whatever reason (e.g. local opposition, lack of capital, lack of outside interest), the exploration period may be much longer than anticipated. In the case of new 'instant' resorts, where tourist facilities are established in an area in which there has been little or no previous settlement, the first two stages in Figure 1.1 may be of minimal significance or absent, a situation noted by Noronha as particularly applicable to some developing nations.[15] The classic, well-established tourist areas of the world (i.e. those which have been popular over several decades), frequently reveal evidence of having passed through all of the postulated stages.

The resort areas of the northern Mediterranean, Britain, the north-eastern seaboard of the United States, and parts of Florida have moved steadily through an evolutionary sequence. Other areas, such as Hawaii, the Caribbean and Pacific islands, and the resort areas of north Africa, are in earlier stages of the cycle, but the pattern of visitation strongly approximates the curve illustrated in Figure 1.1.

These observations also suggest that a change of attitude is required on the part of those who are responsible for planning, developing, and managing tourist areas. Tourist attractions are not infinite and timeless but should be viewed and treated as finite and possibly non-renewable resources. They could then be more carefully protected and preserved. *The development of the tourist area could be kept within predetermined capacity limits, and its potential competitiveness maintained over a longer period*. While the maximum number of people visiting an area at any one time under such arrangements may be less than most present policies of maximum short-term development, more visitors could be catered for in the long term. In a few localities already, limits to the growth of tourism have been adopted, chiefly because of severe environmental damage to attractions (e.g. the erosion of Stonehenge in England, or the damage to prehistoric cave paintings in Spain and France). Unless more knowledge is gained and a greater awareness developed of the processes which shape tourist areas, it has to be concluded, with Plog, that many 'of the most attractive and interesting areas in the world are doomed to become tourist relics.'[16]

Acknowledgements

I would like to acknowledge the valuable discussions and contribution of J.E. Brougham, International Centre for Research on Bilingualism, Laval University, to the ideas expressed in this paper.

Notes and References

* This article was first published in *The Canadian Geographer* 24(1), 5–12 (1980), and is reproduced by permission of the Canadian Association of Geographers.

1. R.I. Wolfe, 'Wasaga Beach-the divorce from the geographic environment,' *The Canadian Geographer,* 2 (1952), pp. 57–66.
2. W. Christaller, 'Some considerations of tourism location in Europe: the peripheral regions-underdeveloped countries-recreation areas,' *Regional Science Association Papers,* 12 (1963), p. 103.
3. C. Stansfield, 'Atlantic City and the resort cycle,' *Annals of Tourism Research,* 5 (1978), p. 238.
4. R. Noronha, *Review of the Sociological Literature on Tourism* (New York: World Bank, 1976).
5. E. Cohen, 'Towards a sociology of international tourism,' *Social Research,* 39 (1972), pp. 164–82.
6. S.C. Plog, 'Why destination areas rise and fall in popularity,' Unpublished paper presented to the Southern California Chapter, The Travel Research Association, 1972.
7. E. Cohen, 'Rethinking the sociology of tourism,' *Annals of Tourism Research,* 6 (1978), pp. 18–35.
8. C.A. Stansfield and J.E. Rickert, 'The recreational business district,' *Journal of Leisure Research,* 4 (1970), pp. 213–25.
9. Wolfe, op. cit.

10. F.P. Bosselman, *In the Wake of the Tourist* (Washington, DC: Conservation Foundation, 1978).
11. G. Doxey, 'Visitor-resident interaction in tourist destinations: inferences from empirical research in Barbados, West Indies and Niagara-on-the-Lake, Ontario,' Unpublished paper presented to the Symposium on the Planning and Development of the Tourist Industry in the ECC Region, Dubrovnik, Yugoslavia, 1975.
12. R.W. Butler and J.E. Brougham, *The Social and Cultural Impact of Tourism–A Case Study of Sleat, Isle of Skye* (Edinburgh: Scottish Tourist Board, 1977); J.E. Brougham, 'Resident Attitudes Towards the Impact of Tourism in Sleat,' unpublished PHD dissertation, University of Western Ontario, 1978; and P.E. Murphy, 'Perceptions and preferences of decision-making groups in tourist centres: a guide to planning strategy,' in *Tourism and the Next Decade: Issues and Problems* (Washington, DC: George Washington University, 1979).
13. C.A. Stansfield, 'The development of modern seaside resorts,' *Parks and Recreation,* 5: 10 (1972), pp. 14–46.
14. E.W. Gilbert, 'The growth of inland and seaside health resorts in England,' *Scottish Geographical Magazine,* 55 (1939), pp. 16–35; D.G. Pearce, 'Form and function in French resorts,' *Annals of Tourism Research,* 5 (1978), pp. 142–56; R.I. Wolfe, 'The summer resorts of Ontario in the nineteenth century,' *Ontario History,* 54 (1964), pp. 150–60; and Stansfield, 'Atlantic City.'
15. Noronha, op. cit., p. 24.
16. Plog, op. cit., p. 8.

Chapter 2

The Origins of the Tourism Area Life Cycle

RICHARD W. BUTLER

Introduction

The origins of the Tourism Area Life Cycle model have been discussed before in a number of academic papers, both by this author (Butler, 1990, 1998a, 2000) and others (see contributors to this and the accompanying volume). It is felt appropriate at this point to expand further upon those origins in order to place the model and its development in a clearer context. This is done partly to correct what may have been misperceptions of the real origins of the initial (1980) article (Hall, personal communication, 1996), and to elaborate upon comments made by this author in the earlier papers referred to above. As well, it is felt necessary to re-emphasise the importance of understanding from whence the academic literature on tourism, of which the TALC paper is a part, has evolved. All too often, in this writer's opinion, current students of tourism are led to believe, or come to the conclusion themselves, that tourism is a recent phenomenon, and that relatively little had been written on it before the 1990s. Such misperceptions have partly contributed to the still relatively low academic reputation which tourism has as an academic subject, and the all too familiar occurrence of scholars in more established subjects venturing into publication in tourism on the faulty assumption that it is a 'new' area waiting to be discovered and 'enriched' by their often somewhat limited contributions.

The TALC model as it initially appeared in its 1980 form had a distinct gestation period and was based on, and integrated within it, several strands of research and conceptual development. Although it may not appear overly so in its published form, it was inherently based in the geographic literature, reflecting the author's training and interests in geography. It is not by accident that several of the contributors in these two volumes (in particular Coles, Hall and Papatheodorou, all geographers themselves) draw attention to this linkage in their own chapters. The 'facts' on which the model is based are fairly obvious to any would-be observer of tourist resorts (as shown in the Postscript to this chapter), just as people were generally aware that apples appeared to always fall to the ground before one hit Newton on the head, resulting in the explanation of gravity. Before any reviewer draws the erroneous conclusion that the TALC is being compared to, or thought equal in significance to the theory of gravity, let me dispel any such arrogance of thought. The point that is being made is that there was nothing devastatingly complicated or original in the data or facts on which the model is based. Lundgren (1984: 22) summed up the situation very aptly when he commented 'Butler put into the realistic cyclical context a reality that everyone knew about, and clearly recognised, but had never formulated into an overall theory.' As noted below, at the time of its development, while it seemed to make good sense, the future wide application of the model was not anticipated. The chapter proceeds first by emphasising the reflexivity inevitably involved in the formulation of any model or concept.

Reflexivity and the TALC

Just as 'we are what we eat', our knowledge and understanding of the world around us is, to a large degree, based on what we observe first hand. My initial interest in tourist destination development came from personal experience with a number of British holiday resorts and destination areas from the 1950s onwards. Living in Birmingham, the major town in England that is furthest from the sea, meant that family holidays were not confined to the nearest resort linked to the home town by the railway, as was the normal pattern in that time period, because many resorts were equally distant and thus equally inaccessible. During my formative years holidays were spent in locations as varied as Rhyl (North Wales), Weston-Super-Mare and Skegness on the west and east coasts of England respectively, and Stonehaven, St Monans and the Isle of Arran in Scotland. A good sampling of classic railway-dominated resorts, mass tourist destinations and small fishing communities using tourism to support their traditional economic activity. Arran was an interesting and somewhat different example, because it could only be reached by boat, at that time by several of the fleet of steamers (some still paddle-wheelers then) that serviced the resorts of the Firth of Clyde. Some of my abiding favourite memories are of spending 10 days of a summer holiday on the Clyde steamers, setting out from Glasgow on the train to railheads such as Gourock and Wemyss Bay, to catch the steamers and visiting different resorts each day. By the time I began doctoral studies at Glasgow University in the mid 1960s, the fleet of steamers was rapidly diminishing and being replaced by roll-on roll-off car ferries, catering efficiently to a new breed of tourists but about as interesting to sail on as a modern day Ford car is to drive compared to a pre-war convertible Jaguar.

It became apparent that the resorts of the Clyde, as well as those elsewhere, were beginning to change significantly, in appearance, in accessibility, in tourists, in economic health and in attractivity. Like most Northern European resorts they were, for the first time, facing competition from Mediterranean resorts for the mass tourist market. Whereas in earlier years they had been shielded from such competition by continental conflict, relative inaccessibility, cost and what Plog (1973) might call 'pyschocentricity', from the 1960s onwards attitudes, accessibility and affluence had all changed dramatically. The old resorts were no longer as attractive to potential tourists, nor catering to the same market as effectively as in the past. Working alongside a colleague who was undertaking his own doctoral research on the Clyde resorts (see Pattison, 1968), these changes were frequently discussed. During the course of my doctoral research the same patterns became evident in other smaller resorts in the Scottish highlands and islands (Butler, 1973). In particular, the changes taking place in the Spey Valley, with the development of winter sports, meant that villages such as Aviemore and Grantown on Spey, previously quiet Victorian summer destinations, were now being developed or redeveloped to cater to a very different winter market. The physical, as well as social and economic changes were very obvious.

My first experience of continental Europe in 1966 included a visit to Opatija (see Corak, this volume), providing further visual evidence of changes taking place in well established resorts. A subsequent visit to Mallorca provided first-hand experience of why Mediterranean resorts were attracting a sizeable segment of the traditional British holiday market from British holiday resorts. Thus by the end of the 1960s I had witnessed very clearly the dramatic changes that were taking place in tourism in Britain and parts of continental Europe. At that time few people realised what might be the full extent of these changes and their implications, and extremely little had been written on the subject. In the 1960s and earlier the tourism literature was very limited, although publications such as those by Gilbert (1939, 1954), Ogilvie (1933), Pimlott (1947), House (1954) and Barratt (1958) had all discussed and analysed aspects of resort development, markets, morphology and dynamics. Their contributions today go almost unnoticed and uncredited, although they laid the foundations for much of the later work on resorts and tourist destinations. Barratt's model of resort morphology predates the work of Stansfield and Rickert (1978) on Recreational Business Districts, for example, but is rarely mentioned unless in the context of the citation in Mathieson and Wall (1982). The model Barratt produced is as valid in the 21st century as it was some five decades earlier when he first produced it. It is against this backdrop of personal experience and limited references that the resort cycle began to take shape.

Antecedent Literature and Concepts

In an earlier review of the TALC (Butler, 2000), two major bases for the model were identified, the Product Life Cycle and models of wildlife populations. While these were major influences, other specific writings predate these concepts in terms of influence on TALC establishment, in addition to those noted above. The first of these were articles relating to the flows of tourists and their patterns of movement, both at the micro (destination) and the macro (global) scales. This author's interest in modelling these flows and accounting for their patterns owes a very great deal to discussions with and contributions from Jim Brougham, then a research student at the University of Western Ontario. A paper produced jointly (Brougham & Butler, 1972) is, in reality, the first version of the TALC. Entitled 'The Applicability of the Asymptotic Curve to the Forecasting of Tourism Development', it was presented at the annual meeting of the Travel Research Association, held in Quebec City in 1972. To say that it did not set the audience on fire would be somewhat of an understatement, and despite a continuing interest in the ideas contained in the paper, neither author felt the topic practical to pursue much further at that time, mainly because of the perceived nonavailability of the data that would have been required.

That paper does deserve some attention, however, in the context of the origins of the TALC, as it introduced many of the key points of the 1980 model and appears to have been the first time 'the resort cycle' appears in print. (This is contrary to what I had stated in a paper and subsequent chapter (Butler, 1998a, 2000), where I mistakenly credited the origin of the phrase to Charles Stansfield in his 1978 article on Atlantic City.) The 1972 paper argued that much more attention should be paid to flows of tourists, building on the work of Williams and Zelinsky (1970) and Yokeno (1968). We stated that 'from the point of view of prediction of flows of tourists, and consequent growth of tourist destination areas, the need is greatest to explain the choice of specific locations and the process of movement from one location to another over time' (Brougham & Butler, 1972: 1). The second section of the paper was headed 'The Resort Cycle', and it utilised data from the resorts in the Firth of Clyde from 1949 to 1966 to illustrate (not tremendously convincingly it must be admitted) an asymptotic curve. It also made reference to the fact that an article in the Nice Matin (1971) suggested other areas were at 'this state in their cycle' and made reference to Christaller's (1963) article and the pattern of resort development described therein. We concluded that section by suggesting 'that a point will be reached, however, at which the rate of increase of visitors begins to decline, and may even, as in the case above, become a decline in numbers. Such a trend may be due to a number of factors, such as increasing pollution, increasing land values limiting expansion of facilities, congestion of facilities, and the availability of alternative areas' (Brougham & Butler, 1972: 6).

Most of the rest of that paper was taken up by attempting to model a hypothetical pattern of development of a tourist destination. It was suggested that the process 'may be satisfactorily approximated by the solution of the logistic equation:

$$\frac{Dv}{Dt} = kV(M - V)$$

where V is the number of visitors, T is time, M is the maximum number of visitors and K is an empirically derived parameter representative of the telling rate, or the spread of knowledge of the resort from tourists to potential tourists' (Brougham & Butler, 1972: 6).

The solution was proposed as:

$$V = MV \quad \frac{O}{V + (M - V) - Mkt}$$

where V is the number of tourists at time t. The resulting curve is shown in Figure 2.1.

It should be emphasised that the main focus in the 1972 paper was the prediction of where tourist development and flows would be in the future, not the resort cycle per se. Undoubtedly reflecting the authors' geographical roots, we referred to the 'shifting rule' of Garrison, as cited in Bunge (1966: 27).

> Where capacity increases require physical expansion, where the expansion cannot be in the vertical dimension and where the new space is made more 'expensive' by the presence of the phenomena itself, a shift is likely during times of capacity strain and the shift will probably occur to a new location as near to the old location as the area of induced expense will allow.

It was argued in our paper that when relocation to a new development took place in the same general location or region as the original tourist development, the pattern of development would be as illustrated in Figure 2.2.

The paper concluded with a brief discussion on the way that such a curve might be used for predicting the future patterns of tourism development (see Marente & Sheclader, and Berry, other volume, for examples of how the TALC can be used in a predictive manner). It suggested sufficient empirical regularities might illustrate patterns, assuming tourists would opt for nearby alternative developments,

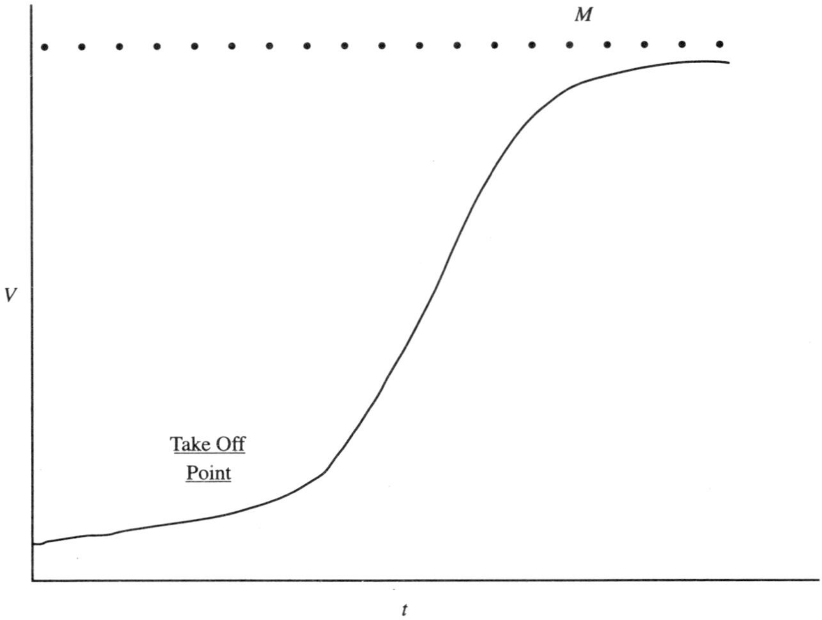

Figure 2.1 A theoretical asymptotic curve

although this was recognised as being a dubious assumption. An alternative approach suggested involved manipulating potential surface maps of migrant populations of specific regions, an idea not pursued in the context of tourism flows. A tentative pattern of tourist development matching the 'shifting rule' was suggested in the Mediterranean, beginning on the French Riviera, spreading to the Italian Riviera, then to Spain, the Adriatic coast and to North Africa. At this point, perhaps puzzlingly with the advantage of hindsight, Malta and Cyprus were overlooked, and Turkey not anticipated.

Contemporary Literature

(In this section contemporary is used in the context of the development of the TALC, not the present day.) Reference has already been made to Christaller (1963) and his seminal work, although it is interesting to note that the key comments in that article on the development process of tourists resorts are not the main focus of the article, but like that by Brougham and Butler (1972) were on explaining the flows and patterns of tourists. Christaller's contribution was significant, not least because, coming as it did from someone who was generally regarded as one the

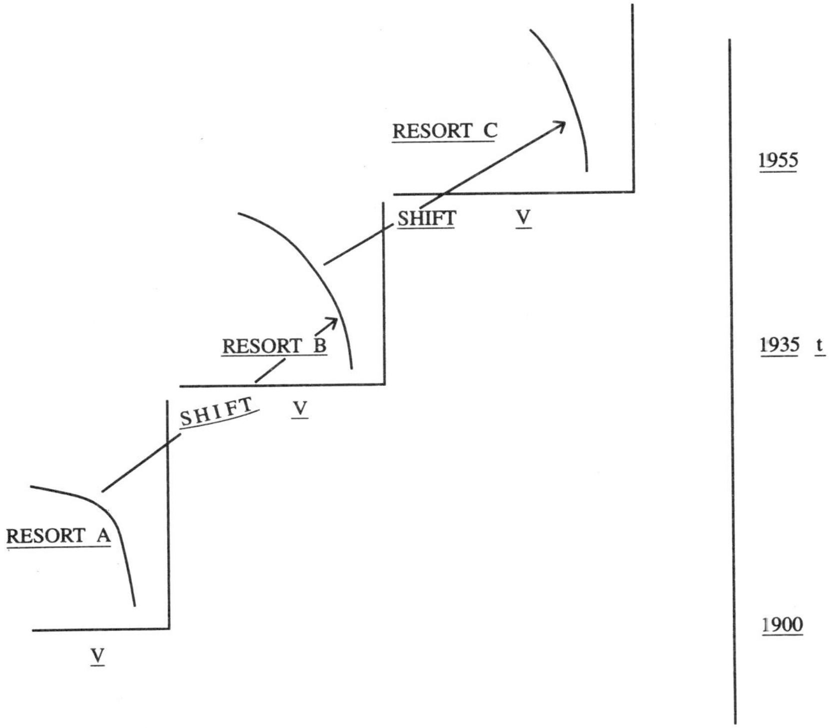

Figure 2.2 Modelling resort development in space and time

greatest contributors to theory in geography, it gave added gravitas to a tentative paper in a fledgling subject by young researchers.

Of equal importance in the development of the 1980 article was the frequently cited paper by Plog (1973) on the psychographics of tourists. It was titled 'Why destination areas rise and fall in popularity', and again, the title of this article does not really reflect the empirical work on which the article was based. This was a survey of American travellers to determine why some people were prepared to fly and others not. Perhaps ironically, it had been presented first at a meeting of the Los Angeles chapter of the Travel Research Association the preceding year, the same time and to the same association as the Brougham and Butler article had been presented. What made Plog's article of particular relevance and importance to the TALC model was that it put forward a suggested model describing how changes in the tourist market were related to subsequent changes in the destinations visited. It also included Plog's oft-quoted statement about destination areas carrying with them the seeds of their own destruction, making it one of the few articles at that time to even raise the topic of the decline of destinations. The points made in Plog's article fitted in extremely well with the ideas germinating from the 1972 paper and with Christaller's description of changes in visitors to destinations over time.

Three other papers were of particular relevance also. The first (although last in chronological order of publication) was Stansfield's (1978) article in the then recently established *Annals of Tourism Research*, titled 'Atlantic City and the Resort Cycle'. In this paper Stansfield discussed and analysed the rise and decline, and then rebirth of Atlantic City through the legalisation of gambling there. In doing this he supplied support in the academic literature for the concept of a cycle and a convincing example of the process of rejuvenation of a tourist destination. Stansfield has been one of the major contributors to the literature on resorts, and his earlier articles (1972) on the Recreational Business District (1970) were both highly insightful and innovative.

A second paper of considerable importance was that by Doxey (1975), yet another paper that was first presented at a meeting of the Travel Research Association. His well quoted 'Irridex' proposed a process of change in resident attitudes towards tourists in destinations. It suggested, in line with the adage 'familiarity breeds contempt', that over time residents of tourist destinations would move from a positive to a negative attitude towards tourism. While it has been argued (Butler, 1975) that such a view is probably too simplistic, the overall proposition of the article, that destinations and the attitudes of their residents change as tourism development takes place, clearly complemented well the other literature on resorts available at the time. Subsequent research on resident impacts (see, for example, Johnson and Snepenger, this volume) has shown how much more complicated this subject is, but such research was not available in the 1970s.

Finally, the third paper, which helped throw additional light on the process of change in tourist destinations, was one of several invaluable publications by Roy Wolfe (1954). Acknowledged as the 'Dean' of Canadian, and perhaps North American researchers in the 1950s and 1960s in outdoor recreation and tourism, Wolfe and his contributions are far less cited and well known in the tourism literature than they deserve to be. His epic study on second homes in Ontario (1948) provided a key link between 'old' and 'new' studies of tourism, and his works with the Ontario government on highway travel models are far in advance of most academic work in this area being published at that time. Wolfe's article on Wasaga Beach (1952), the classic Canadian 'honky tonk' resort, discussed its 'Divorce from the Geographic Environment' and traced its development from a quiet second home location to the major tourist and recreation destination in Ontario. In this he confirmed the importance of location, the way that development changes the role and importance of natural features in a destination's attractivity, and the influence of exogenous factors on tourism patterns. It was published in *The Canadian Geographer* almost three decades before the original TALC article.

To this rather limited number of references on resort development processes and related research should be added an even shorter list of writings that pertain to the other 'leg' or foundation of the TALC, that dealing with wildlife ecology and populations. This literature and its influence were not, in fact, cited in the 1980 article, although they have been referred to in subsequent discussions of the TALC (Butler, 1990, 2000), and Haywood (1986) also drew attention to such an analogy with wildlife population cycles. The comparison with wildlife populations was key to the development of the asymptotic curve in the 1972 article discussed earlier but the links were somewhat more tenuous and less profoundly academic than might be imagined. Again, my personal background intervenes. I had for a long time been a keen bird-watcher, and thanks to an excellent school library, had become familiar with the writings of the late Frank Fraser Darling, a naturalist and scholar. His books *Island Farm* (1943) and *Island Years* (1941), read in lieu of assigned school material, encouraged me to read more of his work, including *A Herd of Red Deer* (1936) based on his PhD research. Some of my apparently misspent afternoons in the school library proved useful eventually, and Darling's comments on the population fluctuations of 'his' herd of deer obviously remained in my memory. When writing the 1972 paper and looking for support and assistance in drawing the development curve, his comments proved invaluable:

> Mathematicians have helped ecology enormously by their analysis of data of experimental animal populations... We know now the nature of the asymptotic or S curve applied to animal populations, that after a slow start of increase in a population in an ample habitat there is a sharp rise in increase or productivity until near saturation of the habitat, whereafter the curve flattens out, making the numbers of the population more or less static. The animal manager gets ready for a catastrophic fall if he has read the signs. (Darling, cited in Thompson & Grimble, 1968: 47)

The analogy to a tourist destination, growing rapidly, without apparent regard for the future or the preservation of its resources, of a wildlife population increasing with a natural lack of regard for the future and the ability of the environment to sustain the increased population was a strong one to us, even if a little peculiar to others at the time. It has been interesting to read of support from others for an analogy between TALC and wildlife ecology and natural systems (Haywood, 1986;

Ravenscroft, other volume), especially as this was not discussed in the 1980 model.

Final Comments

This chapter has been intended to provide more detailed background to the development of the TALC model than had hitherto been available in order to provide a context for the chapters in this and the other volume. It may be pretentious to argue that the old generation have an obligation to interpret the past for future generations, but it is surely better for those who were working in the past (even if we occasionally appear to still live there) to take on that task rather than to leave it to those who were not. Admittedly we may at times be guilty of putting a more favourable gloss on developments and processes to hide our ignorance and embarrassment, but we are the only ones in a position to know how and why particular ideas emerged at specific times and others did not. What we cannot do is explain *why* particular ideas take hold and remain popular when others disappear.

There remain a few items to address. One is why a tourism article should appear in a journal such as *The Canadian Geographer*, which did not have a strong record of publishing articles on tourism. Excellent journal though it is, its relative obscurity outside the field of geography and thus absence from libraries in institutions that do not offer geography (the author's current university is a case in point!), mean that increasing numbers of students and others working in tourism do not have easy access to the original article. It is clear from citations appearing in the literature that some writers citing the TALC are doing so 'second hand', and its all-too familiar curve is taking on more variations than Paul McCartney's 'Yesterday'. This inaccessibility of the original publication was one of the reasons for reproducing it in this volume, and I am most grateful to the Canadian Association of Geographers for giving permission for this. *The Canadian Geographer* was the vehicle of publication because the original paper was presented at the annual meeting of the Canadian Association of Geographers in Vancouver, 1980. At the urging of Peter Murphy, for the first time in its history, the journal produced a special issue, one devoted to tourism and recreation, containing some of the papers presented at the annual meeting, reviewed and edited by Murphy.

A second point that needs addressing and is much more difficult to explain, is why the TALC has received the continued attention and application that it has over the past two decades. It is unusual, as all academics know, for any article to remain popular and apparently relevant for two decades, especially in social science. One of the authors in this volume, on being asked to contribute a chapter based on an article he had written, commented to the effect that he was somewhat surprised to hear from someone who had actually read the article as he never took it for granted that one's journal articles were actually read (Snepenger, personal communication, 2001), a feeling I imagine most academics share. One might conclude that the TALC has remained accepted because, as Wall (1982: 18) commented, it is 'elegant and useful'. But long-time friend and colleague though he is, he did go on to note a number of difficulties and gaps, some of which have since been addressed, but many of which are still causing researchers problems, as noted in many of the chapters in these two volumes. The reasons probably lie in a few simple realities including that noted by Lundgren earlier. First, the model is simple and easy to use, and able to accept a variety of forms of data. It is intuitively appropriate and provides a conceptual 'hook' on which case studies of specific destinations can be 'hung', a rather valuable aid, especially to students undertaking thesis research and to other researchers examining a specific location. Second, it appeared at a time when concepts and models were lacking but being eagerly sought in tourism as research in the subject moved beyond simple description towards interpretation and analysis. Finally, it has proved capable of modification and adaptation, as shown by the chapters that follow, and as discussed later (Butler, other volume) still has some relevance in the context of concepts such as sustainable tourism and appropriate development.

Postscript

Although it may appear from the previous discussion that Brougham and Butler (1972) coined the term 'resort cycle' before Stansfield (1978), the concept of a consistent process of resort development and change, with recognisable phases or stages, is in fact almost a century older at least. In 1990 I received copies of several articles and letters from Dr Bill Clark of the Graduate School of Geography at Clark University in Massachusetts. They ranged in date from 1883 to 1914 and are rather devastating in terms of their implications for supposed academic originality! While too long to reproduce in their entirety, some selected quotations are revealing. The earliest piece, and the initiator of the correspondence which followed, was, according to Clark (personal communication, 1990) an editorial in *The Nation* on July 19, 1883, entitled 'Evolution of the Summer Boarder' by E.L. Godkin, the editor of the paper (Godkin, 1883: 47–48). Godkin notes that 'The growth of the American watering place, indeed, now seems to be as much regulated by law as the growth of asparagus or strawberries and is almost as easy to foretell. The place is usually first discovered by artists...or a family of small needs in search of pure air...'. He goes on to describe a process of development beginning with the provision of informal accommodation, followed by advertisement, the conversion of farms to hotels and boarding houses (a stage lasting up to 30 or 40 years according to Godkin), followed by visitation by 'crowds of people'. After this comes the 'cottager' (second home owner), building on land sold by the original farmer, and the boarder moves on to find other 'unsophisticated' farmers. Godkin talks of the 'great summer tragedy of American life', referring to the loss of opportunity for the lower income boarder because of the development of cottages by the more affluent second home owners.

His editorial clearly hit a nerve among residents of the northeast of the USA. The following month a reader sent a letter (C.P., 1883) arguing that Godkin's process was based on a fallacy and that 'The evolution of certain perfidious boarders into the baleful cottager is merely a phase of the phenomenon of this annual migration. The evolution of the summer resort is not necessarily toward cottage life. Saratoga is, quite as logically as Newport, the outcome of this evolution' (as Wolfe, 1952 noted). C.P. goes on to state that 'The tragedy, the phenomenal fact, is the influx of large numbers into all the secluded summer nooks, and the consequent destruction of their rural picturesque aspects.' Dislike of the second home owner was stated again in a letter a week later by A.R. (1883) from Bar Harbour, who wrote, on the habit of locals selling property to cottagers, 'each is so busy frying his own little fish that he does not see that the fire on which all depend is already going out.'

The discussion begun by Godkin continued for several years in the pages of The Nation, as evidenced in a letter by A.G. Webster in 1914. He wrote in support of Godkin's description of the evolution of resorts, noting that 'The original discoverers have long since had to move on because of the rising scale of prices and the original simplicity of the place is lost. . .different villages on the island are now showing the successive stages of the development of Bar Harbour.' He discusses the declining fortunes of such settlements, ending with 'automobile weekenders or extreme transients' and concludes that 'while Bar Harbour is in its senescence, Northeast Harbour is in its full maturity.' A few years earlier George Street, in a publication *Mount Desert – A History* (1905: 328) pointed out that 'The development of popular summer resorts on the New England coast has followed a curiously uniform law', supporting the description of Godkin. Finally, in 1915, in an article in the *Worcester Magazine*, Conrad Hobbs (1915: 35) began with the statement 'Lake Quinsigamond is now passing rapidly through a history of gradual degradation, which has been the lot of many similar pleasure resorts owned by private individuals and subject to no comprehensive scheme of control.' Hobbs comments that 'the evolution of all the other pleasure resorts of the State confirms me in this belief' (p. 35).

He describes this process in this manner:

> The story of each is roughly, this:
>
> (1) Quiet enjoyment by a few.
> (2) Increasing popularity and the appearance of symptoms of abuse.
> (3) Rapidly increasing abuse and degradation, leading to
> (4) a fuller appreciation of its latent but diminishing value and a public demand for its conservation, which, if strong enough and persistent enough, ends in
> (5) its final reclamation and protection under strong and efficient control. (Hobbs, 1915: 35)

It is both encouraging and depressing to find such statements. Encouraging because they provide evidence and support for the ideas expressed in the TALC about the nature of the process of resort development, the idea of stages, of a consistent pattern or trend, and the inevitability of this process without the intervention of control and regulation. Depressing, or at best, salutary, in the sense that ordinary observant individuals had noted and recorded in print the same process that academics assumed to be their own discovery some half to a full century later!

Postscript to Postscript

In concluding this volume I reviewed the literature cited one last time and to my embarrassment realised that the idea of a pattern of development of tourist resorts is even older than the postscript above suggests. In their article *A Theoretical Approach to Tourism Sustainability*, Casagrandi and Rinaldi (2002) refer to Gilbert's (1939) article on English holiday resorts. They note that Gilbert cites an article from *The Times* dated 1860 discussing the process of resort development:

> Our seaport towns have been turned inside out. So infallible and unchanging are the attractions of the ocean that it is enough for any place to stand on the shore. That one recommendation is sufficient. Down comes the Excursion Train with its thousands – some with a month's range, others tethered to a six hours' limit, but all rushing with one impulse to the waters' edge. Where are they to lodge? The old 'town' is perhaps half a mile inland and turned as far away from the sea as possible...But this does not suit visitors whose eyes are always on the waves, and so a new town arises on the beach. Marine Terraces, Sea Villas, 'Prospect Lodges', 'Bellevues', hotels, baths, libraries and churches soon accumulate, till at length of the old

borough is completely hidden and perhaps to be reached by an omnibus.

Perhaps fortunately for me the author of *The Times* article did not discuss further development and relocation of resorts, and I end this introductory chapter before I discover how the Romans developed their coastal resort settlements, no doubt following the pattern of the ancient Greeks!

Chapter 3

The Application of the TALC Model: A Literature Survey

RICHARD M. LAGIEWSKI

Introduction

This chapter categorizes and documents a selection of major works relevant to Butler's 1980 article on the TALC. The goal is to present a simple, yet informative chapter that helps scholars find and select appropriate works and commentary pertaining to the TALC model. It is important to note that this chapter is not meant to be a literature 'review' of the original 1980 article, but rather a literature 'survey' that documents the works of others who have solidified this work as an academic classic in the field of tourism. This chapter does not take into consideration the new contributions to the volume in which this chapter is found, but rather looks back in order to document previous literature. The author has made every attempt to include a bibliography for this chapter that contains all works pertaining to the 'application' of Butler's concept of a tourism area life cycle. These works were generated between the year 1980 and 2002. Because of the nature of the volume in which this chapter appears, it is the author's judgment that it would be redundant to include a review and description of Butler's original work and its origins, as it can be gained from the previous chapter in this text. Again, this chapter is meant to be a resource based on works addressing Butler's destination life cycle model and judgments of the usefulness and appropriateness of such works are left for the reader to assess.

For the sake of clarity, the concept described in Butler's 1980 work will be referred to generically throughout this chapter as the 'Tourism Area Life Cycle' (TALC). The length of coverage of any one piece of research covered in this chapter should not necessarily be correlated with the relative importance of either the work covered or this author's personal interest. Rather, the depth of coverage reflects the amount of information deemed necessary to provide those interested in Butler's destination life cycle model with the right background, understanding, and direction, so they may choose and explore these original works further as they apply to their current interests and needs.

All of the works covered here clearly provide much more value when read in their entirety, yet the mission here is not to tell their whole story in detail, but rather to lead the reader in the direction relevant to their current interest in the TALC. While Table 3.1 attempts to capture the majority of major works and authors concerning the TALC, the text that follows can only provide a glimpse into these works and authors that have challenged, supported, and expanded Butler's work over the last 20 plus years.

How to Categorize and Divide the Works

How to provide a useful overview of the literature pertaining to works surrounding Butler's original work is not an exact science. One could just discuss each work as it appeared over time. Works could be split between those that support the premise and those that do not. Additionally, works could be broken down by methods employed or stages of the cycle addressed. One could also look at simplifying access to the major works visually. Argwal (1997) proposed that research into the TALC should focus on either one of two aspects: assessing the applicability of the model; and redeveloping the model to incorporate different issues. In the end, a combination of these strategies, along with a broad division of the work based on broad themes is used.

Literature Survey

'The first test and the first proposed changes'

Gary Hovinen's (1981) work on Lancaster County, Pennsylvania is likely the first use of Butler's model. In using Lancaster County as a 'test case', Hovinen (1981, 1982) concluded that the destination departed significantly from the TALC in the later stages, yet the model does remain useful. Two critical conclusions arise from Hovinen's (1981, 1982, 2002) work on Butler's TALC (see also Hovinen, this volume). The first is that his case site (Lancaster County) is characterized by the coexistence of growth, stagnation, decline, and rejuvenation – a stage he terms 'maturity'. The maturity stage begins when rapid growth in the number of visitors has ended (Hovinen, 1982: 573). According to Hovinen, during this stage a diverse destination will see a complex coexistence of the consolidation, stagnation, decline, and rejuvenation in and among the tourist attractions and services. At this point he noted that outside investors invest in new ventures, while original enterprises decline. Some attractions begin to lose their drawing power while new attractions flourish. The issue here is that Lancaster County is deemed a diverse destination where the tourism product is not 100% comprised of a single tourist resource.

This leads into the second outcome of his application of Butler's model concerning the decline stage. While carrying capacity is Butler's premise for decline, Hovinen poses three 'interrelated factors': relative

Table 3.1 Summary of major tourism life cycle studies following Butler's model (modifications and update of Table 2-1 from Berry, 2001)

Author, date	*Region*	*Aspect tested/method/ special emphasis*	*Results*
Hovinen, 1981	Lancaster County, PA	Butler's theory in total. Uses visitor numbers, otherwise a perceptual/historical approach.	Substantially consistent with model. No sign of a decline in region.
Oglethorpe, 1984	Malta	Uses visitor numbers, number of beds, hotels and % foreign ownership. Emphasizes dependency on foreign tour operators.	Accepts relevance of TALC and makes the point that dependency has led to rapid decline in the tourism industry.
Brown, 1985	Weston-super-mare	Historical account, perceptive approach.	Rejuvenation attempted.
Meyer-Arendt, 1985	Grand Island, Louisiana	Emphasis on cultural processes and environmental degradation. Uses building activity, maps at 5 different stages visitor-days, & capacity.	Strong support for TALC which indicates onset of 'decline' stage.
Butler, 1985	Scottish Highlands	Historical account from early 1700s to early 1800s. Emphasis on fashion, tastes and transportation improvements. Uses maps and historical evidence.	Complies with TALC model.
Keys, 1985 (Masters thesis)	Some Queensland resorts compared, with Noosa in depth	Comparative, cross-sectional study of a number of Queensland resorts using TALC as an analysis framework and a time series study of Noosa. Data used is from Australian Bureau of Statistics, Queensland Travel and	The Noosa case substantially complies with Butler's model with some outstanding differences. The comparative study of the other resorts showed that they are at different stages of development.

Table 3.1 (*Continued*)

Author, date	***Region***	***Aspect tested/method/ special emphasis***	***Results***
		Tourism Commission, press reports, interviews and observation.	
Haywood, 1986	Not region specific	Emphasis on making Butler's model useable by suggesting more rigid criteria & a method involving the use of standard deviation for stage identification.	Concluded the TALC model was not sufficient *on its own* to use for planning and marketing purposes even with the proposed changes.
Richardson, 1986	Galveston & other urban water fronts	Emphasis on revitalization of historic buildings and the use of product life cycle models as tools for managing resort evolution. Uses tax receipts, employment, population and dollars spent on works.	Using TALC theory, Galveston is in 'decline' stage but it may be possible to rejuvenate using historic buildings as an attraction. Work is being done in the area.
Wilkinson, 1987	Caribbean islands of Antigua, Aruba, St Lucia, & US Virgin Isles	Focuses on the later stages of Butler's model and Lundberg's (1980) model.	Essentially a comparative analysis, which found a high level of compliance with both models. Other conclusions related to the tourism industry rather than the TALC model.
Keller, 1987	Canada's NW Territories	Emphasis on importation of capital and management leading to possible dependence on non-locals. Leakage of tourism dollars back to core regions. Uses arrival types (business, fishing, sightseeing,	Does not question the applicability of TALC and concludes that no further development possible without large injection of outside capital.

Table 3.1 (*Continued*)

Author, date	***Region***	***Aspect tested/method/ special emphasis***	***Results***
		education etc) and where from. Also uses staff turnover in tourism.	
Strapp, 1988	Sauble Beach, Ontario	Emphasis on the transition from a tourism resort to retirement center as previous holiday makers buy holiday homes and then retire there. Uses visitor numbers.	Proposes using 'average length of stay' to calculate 'total-person-days' rather than visitor numbers to overcome the change of status of tourists who eventually become retirees.
Cooper and Jackson, 1989	Isle of Man	Butler's theory in total. Visitor numbers and other tourist statistics going back 100 years.	Exemplifies the utility of Butler's model, emphasizing dependence on management decisions and resort quality. Also introduces some suggestions for rejuvenation of region.
Cooper, and 1990	Isle of Man, European 'cold water resorts'	Uses passenger arrivals etc.	Most resorts in this category are in serious decline.
Debbage, 1990	Paradise Island, Bahamas	Combines the use of TALC with Markusen's (1985) 'profit cycle' and the influence of oligopolistic tourist suppliers.	Concludes that Butler's model does not take into account organizational behavior as the cycle matures (i.e. mergers and acquisitions).

Table 3.1 (*Continued*)

Author, date	***Region***	***Aspect tested/method/ special emphasis***	***Results***
Martin and Uysal, 1990	No specific region	Expands the concept and importance of carrying capacity for the TALC.	Each stage will reveal different carrying capacity levels and require separate policy responses.
France, 1991	Barbados	Mainly a perceptional approach but also uses visitor numbers, number of establishments, number of rooms, etc.	The Island is split into different market segments, which are at different stages in TALC. One area is in decline, another is still in the growth stages.
Weaver, 1988, 1990, 1992	Grand Cayman and Antigua	All aspects of TALC but emphasis on outside ownership and control, particularly in Antigua. Grand Cayman has little outside ownership and control. Uses arrivals, cruise ship statistics. Emphasis also on planning. Uses arrival numbers, building, bed numbers and Tourist Board Budget.	Found substantial compliance with Butler's model. Concluded outside ownership & control affected stability of cycle. Grand Cayman is planned and has low outside ownership and is stable but Antigua is unplanned with high degree of outside ownership and control and is in danger of decline. Referred to as a new type of plantation economy (dependency).
Cooper, 1992	Coastal resorts	Talks about the three uses of TALC (as a conceptual framework, for forecasting and strategic planning) and then goes into detail about the strategic planning process.	Strategic planning process consists of: defining the mission statement; business portfolio analysis; and growth strategies. Also talks about types of growth strategies.

Table 3.1 (*Continued*)

Author, date	***Region***	***Aspect tested/method/ special emphasis***	***Results***
Ioannides, 1992	Cyprus	All aspects but emphasized the role of government and dependence on foreign tour operators. Used visitor numbers, number of beds, type of accommodation, tourism receipts, tourist type, arrivals.	TALC used to make the point that govt is steering towards 'consolidation' (intentionally) and that destinations follow a predictable cycle through identifiable stages.
Getz, 1992	Niagara Falls	Examines carrying capacity and planning aspects. Uses historical data, existing statistical data, interviews, field observations, maps and questionnaires.	'Exploration' and 'involvement' stages correspond partly with Butler's model but there are many points of divergence and no dating of stages is possible. Niagara Falls appears to be in a long 'maturity' stage similar to Lancaster County.
Johnson and Snepenger, 1993	Greater Yellow-stone region	Variables used are visitation trends, the growth of the service economy, host resident's perception of current tourism development and current biological indicators of the ecosystem.	Tourism in the region is more intricate than the TALC theory suggests and the region is at no specific stage of the cycle. The TALC concept incorporates alternatives for future directions within the Yellowstone region.
O'Hare and Barrett, 1993	Sri Lanka	Considers the effect of the civil war on tourism using tourism numbers. Also discusses the effect of cheap airfares based on stop-overs in Sri Lanka.	Accepts relevance of TALC and concludes that there have been two distinct cycles in the country, one before the civil war and one after.

Table 3.1 (*Continued*)

Author, date	***Region***	***Aspect tested/method/ special emphasis***	***Results***
Choy, 1993	Pacific Island destinations	All aspects of Butler's model, but only with reference to visitor numbers.	Very little compliance with Butler's model reported. 'At best the model can be used after the fact as a diagnostic tool'.
Williams, 1993	Minorca, Spain	All aspects but emphasis on dependency theory through external ownership and control. An 'expanded' model of 8 stages was suggested. Uses tourist numbers, employment, number of hotel rooms.	High level of external ownership and control. Existing industries declined as tourism expanded. The region has yet to reach its peak.
Wang and Godbey, 1994	Lancaster, Poconos, America's Ind. Heritage Project (AIHP)	Emphasis on measuring growth in tourism activity and what is the ideal rate of growth to year 2000 using surveys and expert perceptions of future growth.	AIHP is in the early stages of TALC. Lancaster is in the mature stages and Poconos is in decline.
Cooper, 1994	Not applicable	Overall review of the TALC body of knowledge to date.	Found Butler's model to be a useful framework for analysis and stated that with every study the body of knowledge increases suggesting further research. He suggested some more criteria.
Bianchi, 1994	Not applicable	Compares TALC and a number of other theories and models.	TALC fails on many grounds and what is needed is a concept of tourism development which is integrated into a sociological framework.

Table 3.1 (*Continued*)

Author, date	***Region***	***Aspect tested/method/ special emphasis***	***Results***
Agarwal, 1994	UK generally. The resort cycle revisited	Discusses the usefulness of TALC for analysis and planning using anecdotal and perceptual methods.	Suggests that TALC be modified to include a 'reorientation' stage before 'decline/ rejuvenate'. States that as it stands, TALC cannot be usefully applied.
Prosser, 1995	Not applicable	TALC in general. Progress and prospects as well as some suggestions for future research.	Finds that TALC is a handy framework for analysis.
Opper-mann, 1995	Not applicable	Life cycle concept used to analyze the travel life cycle of individuals.	Successful application of general life cycle theory to individual's lifetime travel patterns.
Harrison, 1995	Swaziland	Used Butler's TALC as an 'ideal' or 'expected' model and analyzed the difference between it and the situation in Swaziland.	The cycle in Swazi-land consisted of 'exploration', 'inactivity', 'transition', 'truncated development' and 'decline & attempted rejuvenation'.
Braunlich, 1996	Atlantic City	Success of rejuvenation program using casinos. Statistics include amounts invested, tax receipts, social services for the elderly, urban redevelopment.	TALC accepted as an appropriate framework for analysis. Atlantic City has successfully entered the 'rejuvenation' stage.
Russel, 1996	Coolan-gatta	All aspects of Butler's model, uses visitor numbers & a perceptual/historical approach for the period of the resort's existence.	Found substantial compliance with the model. The region was found to be in the 'decline' stage.

Table 3.1 (*Continued*)

Author, date	***Region***	***Aspect tested/method/ special emphasis***	***Results***
Meyer, 1996	Waikiki	Emphasis on rejuvenation plans. Uses reports etc.	Concludes that the area is entering the 'decline' stage and suggests rejuvenation.
Agarwal, 1997	Torbay region (Torquay, Paignton and Brixham)	Tests the validity and applicability of TALC. Justifies this work by, stating that the universal applicability of TALC is not yet proven. Among other things, the author stresses the importance of the 'unit of analysis'.	The application of TALC is reasonably consistent with Butler's (1980) model except for the post 'stagnation' stage which requires more research. The author assumes that the original model specifies that 'decline' is inevitable (p. 72).
Prosser, 1997	Gold Coast, Coffs Harbour (NSW)	Uses time series (census) population figures, employment in tourism, unemployment etc. Also relies on a perceptual approach.	Both regions are at different stages in TALC. Finds that TALC is a handy framework for analysis.
Douglas, 1997	Melanesia, (PNG, Solomons & Vanuatu)	Historical picture using Butler's model as a framework. Uses largely perceptual methods.	Each country is at a different stage. A major influence is the colonial past of each country.
Tooman, 1997	3 regions in the Greater Smoky Moun-tains	Emphasis on the long-term, from 1900 to present and socioeconomic effects using unemployment and food stamp figures etc. Also looks at the number of 'Mom & Dad' hotels and motels verses chain companies as an indicator.	Concludes that TALC can be used to avoid the negative impacts of tourism.

Table 3.1 (*Continued*)

Author, date	***Region***	***Aspect tested/method/ special emphasis***	***Results***
dá Conceição Gonçalves and Roque Águas, 1997	Algarve, Portugal	Analysis using TALC with demand, supply, distribution and competitors within each stage. Fits a 3rd degree polynomial to overnight data.	Identifies stages and links them to regional strategies (cause and affect). Concludes area should plan for a long period of stagnation and stabilization.
Russell and Faulkner, 1998	Coolan-gatta	All aspects of Butler's model, also use of visitor numbers & a perceptual/historical approach.	Found substantial compliance with the model.
Priestley and Mundet, 1998	Catalan Coast, Spain (3 resort towns)	Assumes away the early stages of TALC and concentrates on the poststagnation stages in response to Agarwal's (1994) challenge that there is not enough work in this area.	All three resorts (Lloret de Mar, L'Estartit & Sitges) are in post-'stagnation' stage and have implemented 'reconstruction' strategies in an attempt to rejuvenate. Uses hotel capacity as core data.
Oppermann, 1998	No specific region	Main thrust is to attack Agarwal's (1997) article on Torbay. Says there has been too much testing of TALC.	Finds Butler's model good but suggests that there should be more testing of other models and theories.
Agarwal, 1998	No specific region	Defends her 1997 article against Oppermann's 1998 attack.	States there is a need to apply TALC to different tourism products in a variety of contexts.
Baum, 1998	No specific region	Proposes the idea that abandoning tourism altogether can be a theoretical extension of TALC.	Abandonment can be seen as an Exit Stage when tourism becomes impossible to sustain.

Table 3.1 (*Continued*)

Author, date	*Region*	*Aspect tested/method/ special emphasis*	*Results*
Knowles and Curtis, 1999	European mass tourist destinations	Study of second generation (Mediterranean but mainly Spanish) resorts. Ultimately, there is no avoiding decline for these resorts.	The authors generally find that the TALC model is a good fit up to the post 'stagnation' stages after which they postulate three new stages.
Johnston, 2001	No specific region	Integrates ontological & epistemological elements into the TALC debate.	That 'we have not yet learned everything' there is to know about the TALC.
Lundtorp and Wanhill, 2001	Data sets from: Isle of Man & Danish island of Bornholm	Uses mathematical process to form the 'ideal' TALC.	The TALC curve can only be representative if all tourist arrivals are repeat tourists.
Agarwal, 2002	Three mass tourism coastal resorts: Minehead, Weymouth, Scarborough	Integrates the theory of the TALC and the restructuring thesis.	Relating the two concepts provides insights into destination decline and a more in-depth understanding is needed of resort restructuring.
Hovinen, 2002	Lancaster County, PA	Revisits his early work and also considers chaos/complexity theory as a complement to the TALC.	TALC would be more useful by recognizing a "maturity" stage. Also the model has value by its premise that without appropriate planning, management & development, destinations will see decline.

location, diversity of the tourist base, and effectiveness of planning to alleviate problems that arise. The first two factors point to why the decline stage may be less significant at the time of Hovinen's first work on Lancaster County. The first is that the destination's close proximity to major cities in the eastern USA give it the ability to draw from a large population base. Additionally, the reasons for visiting the county are not solely reliant on the Amish community, but rather are supported by other cultural aspects and attractions, like the rural landscape itself.

In Hovinen's (2002) article in which he 'revisits' the issue of the TALC in Lancaster County, he proposed that the 'chaos/complexity theory' provides a useful alternative and complementary perspective to Butler's life cycle model. This is based on Russell and Faulkner's (1999) idea that changes in tourism at a destination can be 'viewed in terms of tension between entrepreneurs (who are agents of change) and planners (who seek to control change)'. In this hypothesis, entrepreneurs are the chaos makers while planners seek to establish certainty and predictability (see Russell, other volume). It is argued that entrepreneurial instincts are crucial, because to avoid the decline stage, innovative responses are needed to meet the complexities that a destination faces as it reaches this stage. Overall, his early work on Lancaster County is likely most recognized for proposing the idea of a 'maturity stage' to the TALC.

'Major criticism or major advancement?'

Haywood's (1986) work, 'Can the Tourist-Area Life cycle be made operational?' is often cited as being critical of Butler's tourist-area life cycle model, yet it has likely done the most to make the tourist-area life cycle model an operational research concept. Haywood's (1986) 'test of importance' for Butler's TALC is, 'its possible use as a tool for planning & management of tourist areas'. Six issues or questions are raised as requirements to make Butler's model a useful tool in destination planning. Many of the answers to these issues have gone on to provide a framework for researchers as they applied Butler's model (see also Haywood, this volume and the other volume). The following are considered operationally important for the usefulness of Butler's model (Haywood, 1986: 155):

- unit of analysis;
- relevant market;
- pattern and stages of the TALC;
- identification of the area's shape in the life cycle;
- determination of the unit of measurement;
- determination of the relevant time unit.

The first issue revolves around defining the tourist area under question. For example, is the tourist 'area' a town, a hotel, an attraction? Haywood (1986) states that defining the unit of analysis for the 'tourist area' is the crucial first step in using Butler's life cycle model. The next point addresses the issue of the number of tourists used as the 'Y' variable in the life cycle curve. The concern presented is that the total number of tourists over time may represent different markets, and it may be more helpful to consider them by different market segments. The reason is that a different market type, say 'domestic versus international tourist', may interact differently with the tourist area.

In the third operational requirement, Haywood (1986) questions whether the pattern of the s-shaped logistic curve is the only useful curve and suggests looking at other evolutionary curves. The fourth operational requirement is determining the stage of a tourist area and when an area has moved from one stage to another. He then questions whether using the change in the number of tourists to determine these changes will provide appropriate answers. Haywood (1986) provides one possible approach based on the total number of tourists occurring at the tourist area on a year-to-year basis and then plotting these changes as a normal distribution with a zero mean.

Based on the premise that as the number of tourists grow they negatively impact the carrying capacity, Haywood (1986) suggests the need for a clear unit of measurement. This is due to the fact that not all tourists have the same impact on the carrying capacity of the tourist area they are visiting; not all tourists are created equal. Some stay longer, some visit in different seasons, and some are more and some are less conscious of the local cultural and natural traditions. Therefore, the use of pure arrivals as a determinant of a tourist area carrying capacity is questioned along with whether there exists one variable that represents carrying capacity for the whole tourist area.

The last operational question is whether the traditional use of annual data to track tourists over time is necessarily the best relevant time unit. Here Haywood (1986) notes that if there is a 'major shortcoming' in the use of the tourist area cycle of evolution it is the 'lack of empirical data' available about the tourist area in question. Haywood (1986) also concludes that a 'natural use' of the tourist area is as a forecasting tool (see Butler, this volume; Manente and Pechlaner and Berry, other volume).

'Changes to later stages and the vertical axis'

As Hovinen's (1981) work first suggested, changes and discussion of the TALC's later stages has been a common theme in the literature.

Additionally, Butler's use of the 'number of tourists' on the vertical axis has also received great attention.

Strapp's (1988) study of Sauble Beach, Ontario, Canada contributes to the TALC through its recognition of second homeowners as tourists. The claim is that this type of tourism had been neglected by researchers in generating tourism models while Butler's model premises that without adequate planning, destinations are likely doomed to decline. In Strapp's (1988) work, 'conventional' tourism is showing a decline while 'residential development' and 'cottage conversions' are experiencing a revival. He suggests that this refinement to Butler's decline stage be termed a 'stabilization reaction'. Therefore, after stagnation, tourist areas may experience growth in a nontraditional tourism market, thus stabilizing an otherwise anticipated decline in the number of visitors. Strapp also provides two interesting 'discrepancies' or proposed departures to Butler's original model. These are that population and community changes are just as crucial as a tourist change in the resort cycle, no matter how dominant tourism may be as a segment in the local economy.

Here it is proposed that instead of measuring pure numbers of visitors over time, the use of a 'person-day' concept be used. The idea is that the person-day concept takes into consideration visitors and residents and their length of stay. This leads to the proposal that the most 'appropriate way' to 'graphically portray' Butler's tourist area curve is to use the average length of stay instead of the number of tourists. (See Figure 3.1) Using this model, Strapp (1986) proposes an illustration where in the early stage of Butler's TALC the length of stay is at its greatest and declines toward the stagnation stage over time. This argument, based on Sauble Beach, is that early in the life cycle of a tourist area it is difficult to access the destination, therefore it 'necessitates a long stay'. Strapp (1986) states that, 'as development increases, improvements in access makes shorter trips possible and overall length of visits decline'. Within his case, the ease of potential day trips increases near the stagnation stage.

Three options are presented at this point. The first is the length of stay declines to the point where the tourist area basically 'becomes more of a recreational area or rest stop'. The next option relates to rejuvenation. By exploiting or developing the area's resources, 'visit time regains its length'. The last option pertains to the evolution of a year-round community based on his case in Sauble Beach. Here a tourist becomes more like a resident. As tourists transition to homeowners, the tourist season increases beyond its traditional confines.

In Foster and Murphy's (1991) work on the connection between the TALC and retirement, they construct a case study of Parksville and Qualicum Beaches located on the east coast of Vancouver Island, Canada. Their goal was to determine if these destinations follow Butler's premise and whether retirement is a 'successor or parallel activity with regards to

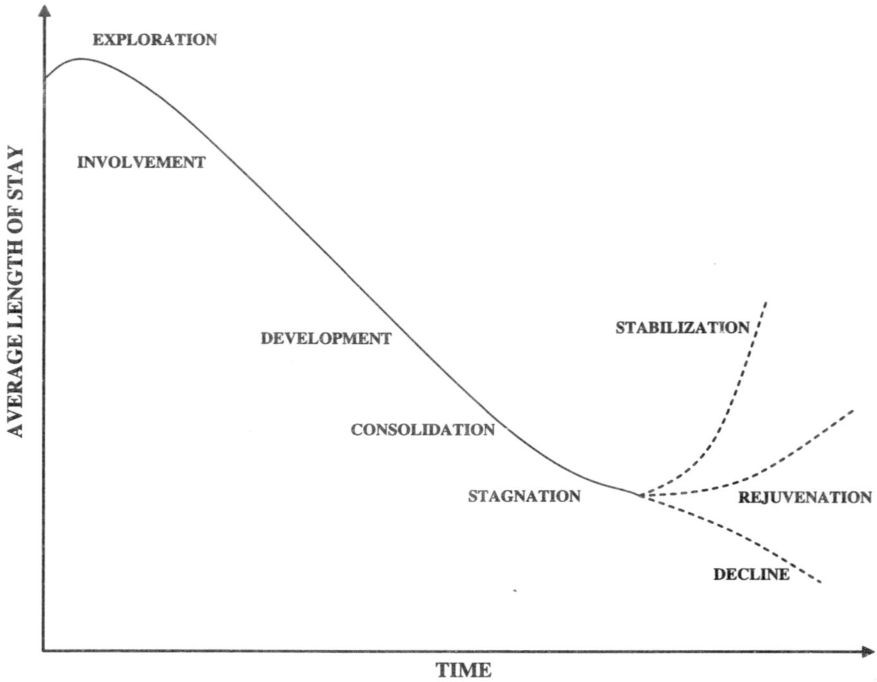

Figure 3.1 Associated changes in length of stay (Strapp, 1988)

tourism'. They conclude that their research supports Hovinen's (1982) suggestion that Butler's stages of consolidation and stagnation be replaced with an extensive maturity stage. In terms of retirement, Foster and Murphy (1991) provided a mixed review of its connection with Butler's later stages. They also point to the bias that the TALC has toward the supply-side characteristics of the market. Specifically, this pertains to the use of data of the supply of accommodations versus the use of actual visitation numbers (demand). This issue supports the critical challenge of applying the TALC; the lack of actual long-term visitor data over the life of a destination.

Douglas' (1997) application of Butler's life cycle model addresses its ability to explain tourism development in colonial and postcolonial societies. Specifically, she uses the model to develop a comparative study of tourism in three island nations: Papua New Guinea, the Solomon Islands, and Vanuatu. These tourist destinations are collectively known as Melanesia. Through this case study, the rate of tourism development is said to be significantly influenced by the pre- and postindependent government of the three island nations. Another contribution to the destination life cycle model concerns the use of the term 'locals' and

Butler's premise that in the involvement stage, contact between visitors and locals will remain high. The assumption is that while Butler didn't specifically define locals in his concept, the implication is that he was referring to persons indigenous to the tourist area. In the historic development of tourism, these former colonies' expatriates have often played the role of 'locals'. Specifically, Europeans visiting these tourist destinations preferred to interact with the European expatriates and not necessarily with the Melanesians.

Douglas (1997) also addresses three types of visitors who have influenced tourism development in the colonial period of these islands: 'excursionists', 'pilgrims', and 'planners'. Excursionists refer to the early cruise passengers and later air travelers who arrived seeking sun, sand, and sea. The 'pilgrims' were the Allied and Japanese soldiers who established the foundations of both the tourist attractions and later on the attractions in the form of military cemeteries and battlefields. The last group, the 'planners', refers to the organizations that attempted to establish the institutional foundations to manage the tourism system. These included all of the various tourism marketing and promotional boards, along with the chambers of commerce.

In the article, *The Resort Lifecycle Theory Generating Processes and Estimation*, Lundtorp and Wanhill (2001) examine the theory behind use of the number of tourists as the 'measure of the time path' of the destination. The authors formulate a demand model of the resort cycle that considers the segments of various tourist markets and their levels over time, related to Butler's tourist area life cycle. Specifically, two general types of tourist are considered: 'repeat' and 'non-repeat'. Using the logistic curve to model the relative demand at each stage, the authors conclude that the life cycle curve can only be representative of the destination if all visitors to that destination are 'repeaters'. By adding data concerning nonrepeaters (those who only visit a destination once but never visit again), the life cycle model becomes only an 'approximation or caricature' of reality. According to the authors, as more and more market segmentation occurs in the tourist data, the observed effect will result in a scatter diagram, 'from which it might be impossible to discern anything'.

Lundtorp and Wanhill (2001) present a mathematical process and formula to formulate the 'ideal' expected tourist volumes over the stages of Butler's model (see also Wanhill & Lundtorp, other volume). They test this concept on a data series for the Isle of Man in Britain and for the Danish Island of Bornholm. They find that Butler's concept fits the destinations 'tolerably well' during periods when domestic tourists dominate the market and return year-after-year. Therefore, for the data to support Butler's model it must be made up of repeat visitors. In later years, in the tourist area evolution they point to 'too many shift factors'.

That is to say new markets are drawn to visit the area while old tourists are drawn elsewhere. Demand or decline in demand to visit the destination may not be so much a function of exceeding a 'carrying capacity', but rather because 'the market is exhausted, as all tourists wishing to visit the resort "have been"'.

Getz's (1992) case study of Niagara Falls, Canada–US is considered unique in that this destination 'has evolved into a permanent state of maturity in which aspects of consolidation, stagnation, decline, and rejuvenation are interwoven and constant'. It is acknowledged that Hovinen's (1982) conclusions about Butler's later stages is a more appropriate way to view a destination's later life. The author states that for old destinations like Niagara Falls, the maturity stage will likely be a permanent condition. The rationale is that those in charge of resort areas will never allow tourism to disappear and will use every attraction they can to maintain it. Getz (1992) concludes that the destination life cycle does not fit Niagara Falls and therefore has very little usefulness for local tourism planning. Another departure from Butler's original model pertains to carrying capacity. Instead of carrying capacity being linked to a destination's ability to sustain change without environmental decline and loss of attractiveness, Getz sees it as a planning and management concept. This idea of capacity in a 'mature' destination is based on a tourist area's constant practice of mitigating the adverse effects of tourism while also pursuing destination enhancements. Agarwal (1994), like Getz (1992) and Hovinen (1982), suggests that the later stages of the TALC need modification. Her issue pertains to poststagnation, specifically 'decline'. She argues that dramatic and total decline of tourism is likely unacceptable both economically and politically. Therefore she proposes a 'reorientation stage' (see Agarwal, other volume). In this stage one would observe the constant efforts a destination makes to adjust to changes before decline occurs.

'New contexts and variances'

Much of the literature over the last 20 years has attempted to apply the TALC to new destinations to test its relevance. Additionally, many works point to particular departures from Butler's original TALC. Weaver (1990) states that his empirical research on Grand Cayman Island 'largely conforms to the stages' of Butler's TALC. He discerns one 'significant deviation' from Butler's original work. In Butler's TALC, it is stated that over time local control and ownership will shift to nonlocals. However, in viewing Grand Cayman, 'a non-plantation culture', and Antigua, 'a plantation culture', Weaver (1990) concludes control has been maintained by locals in the development of Grand Cayman's tourist sector (see Weaver, this volume). However, Antigua's tourist sector suffers from a high degree of external control associated with its former plantation economy.

Tooman (1996) uses Butler's model as a framework to explore the economic impact of tourism in the Smokey Mountain region of Tennessee and North Carolina. Specifically, he looks at first-, second-, and third-order economic effects. This discussion is based on tourism's roll as an economic development tool. From this perspective, Tooman (1996) discusses the theoretical economic outcomes that would be expected throughout Butler's life cycle stages. The author concludes that tourism is likely to be most beneficial from the economic perspective if it is not the dominant sector of the economy. Tooman (1996) points out that according to Butler's TALC, tourism should not dominate until the consolidation stage. However, in his case study, one local economy was dominated by tourism in the development stage and another in the involvement stage.

According to Tooman (1996), 'under conditions where tourism becomes the dominant economic sector (regardless of the particular stage), social welfare indicators failed to show significant improvement'. From the context of tourism and the economy, the involvement stage (where tourism does not dominate the economy) can produce desirable effects. These benefits have the potential for greater local economic linkages, economic diversity, and more time to establish the utility to manage the growth of the tourism sector.

Wilkinson (1996) supports Cooper's (1994) conclusion that while the life cycle concept has weaknesses, it does provide a useful tool for comparing tourism development among different destinations and provides one with an organizing framework to do so. Wilkinson selects six destinations in the Caribbean (Anguilla, Bahamas, Barbados, Cayman Islands, Dominica, and St. Lucia), to compare using the life cycle model proposed not by Butler, but de Albuquerque and McElroy (1992). This version of Butler's model proposes three general stages of tourism growth: (1) emergence or initial discovery, (2) transition to rapid expansion, and (3) maturity.

Another unique context for the application of Butler's TALC is by Johnson and Snepenger's (1993) to a 'federally managed resource'. In examining the Greater Yellowstone Region, the authors concluded 'that development is a not a specific stage in the cycle'. This work is based on the use of four factors to track the tourist destination over Butler's TALC: visitation trends, growth of the service economy, resident perceptions (see also Johnson & Snepenger, this volume), and ecosystem indicators. This work is based on the reconceptualization of the life cycle carrying concept by Martin and Uysal (1990). Their concept is based on the notion that there are many components that make up the resources in a tourist area. Within these different components, differing destinations will likely have different carrying capacities. For example, the physical infrastructure of a tourist area may have one carrying capacity while the environmental resources may have another. Martin and Uysal (1990) contend that this will require 'distinct policy responses' for each resource capacity. This being the case, Johnson and Snepenger concluded that, in fact, different resources in the Greater Yellowstone Region exhibit characteristics of different stages concurrently, depending on which resource is being measured.

'Destination drivers'

In Butler's original work, changes within a destination were attributed to 'preferences and needs of visitors' and the 'gradual deterioration' of manmade and natural attractions and services. Many authors applying the TALC as a framework for analyzing a destination have identified other issues that drive change within a destination and thus influence the 'evolution' of the resort.

In Klaus J. Meyer-Arendt's (1985) work, *The Grand Isle, Louisiana resort cycle*, he explores the issues pertaining to the factors causing the barrier island of Grand Island, Louisiana to move through all of the stages, ending in the stagnation stage. These issues relate to settlement patterns, changes in environmental perceptions, and efforts to fix a dynamic shoreline. Special emphasis is placed on the settlement patterns of residents over time to this coastline and the natural and manmade impacts on the shoreline. Here, the model is considered from the perspective of resident population growth over time versus Butler's growth in number of tourists (see also Martin, this volume). Therefore, Meyer-Arendt (1985) concluded that the settlement of Grand Isle and the manmade battle to secure the natural resource against storms and erosion help demonstrate the evolution of this resort through the stages of Butler's TALC.

Cooper and Jackson (1989) emphasize that the TALC provides, 'a useful descriptive tool for analyzing the development of destinations and the evolutions of their markets'. In their use of a case study on the Isle of Man, UK, they conclude that the TALC is, 'dependent upon the actions of managers and the settings of the destination'. The authors address Butler's model from its utility as both a prescriptive and descriptive tool. They conclude from the prescriptive point of view that the model encounters many problems, and that, 'Butler's original conceptualization of the tourist cycle did not envisage its use as a prescriptive tool'. However, as a descriptive tool, the life cycle is very useful in, 'understanding how destinations and their markets fall'. Their case study on the Isle of Man proposes that the unique setting of the island and the reliance on the UK market has presented challenges that have driven the destination along the life cycle curve. Additionally, the leadership decisions of private and public institutions, both directly and indirectly involved in tourism, have had substantial impact on the island's move through the tourist area life cycle.

Debbage (1990) provides an alternative to Butler's decline paradigm. Instead of decline being the outcome of a tourist destination exceeding its carrying capacity, thus resulting in the degradation of the resources in which the area relies on, he argued that outside influences destroy competitiveness. Specifically, stagnation and decline are influenced by oligopoly. This results in decline, because in this case, tourism suppliers are 'gaining market share' and maintaining 'competitive stability'. This is achieved at the expense of innovation and diversification. Debbage's (1990) argument, based on Paradise Island, Bahamas, is that declining visitor numbers were traditionally viewed as changes in tourism trends, and declining destination attractiveness may be better viewed as a result of the control and influence transnational corporations have at the destination level. Here, Debbage (1990) argues that Butler did not give appropriate emphasis to the role of imperfect competition and oligopoly, but put more weight on a detailed discussion of the internal dynamic of resort areas. This case is based primarily on the role of Resorts International in influencing both the tourist distribution chain and the composition of tourist products on Paradise Island.

Ioannides' (1992) case study of the island of Cyprus provides insights into the role the tourist area's government and external transnational firms have in destination change over the life cycle of a destination. Historical data for Cyprus demonstrated that the island's tourism area followed Butler's exploration, involvement, and development stages. During these earlier stages, the government played an important role in the growth of tourism. First there was the recognition that tourism should be used to increase foreign exchange earnings and to diversify the economy. That was followed by the government's efforts to stimulate tourism sector growth through economic incentives and loan programs. Additionally, the Cyprus Tourism Organization was formed to supervise tourism development. At this time, modern airport tourism facilities were also built.

During the development stage on Cyprus, the government helped the island recover from the 1974 War through Emergency Action Plans that gave a high priority to tourism (p. 721). The government also sponsored action plans in the late 1970s that provided financial incentives (low interest loans and free government land) to the private sector with the goal of making Cyprus an international tourist destination.

Besides identifying the influence of government on the TALC, the role of tour operators was also addressed. This influence of foreign tour operators from Cyprus's primary inbound markets (Britain, Germany, and Sweden) are acknowledged as supporting Debbage's (1990) point that dominant suppliers have a significant role in the TALC. In the case of Cyprus, this was shown specifically through the impact and influence of charter flights and preference for 'cheaper self-catering' accommodations, and inclusive tour packages targeting lower income mass tourism. These are seen as negatively impacting the environmental and cultural resources of the island. Additionally, the dependence on a few large tour operators has left Cyprus marketed as a 'could be anywhere' destination with little competitive market power. While Ioannides (1992) acknowledged that the growing power of foreign tour operators supports Butler's premise that external influences would increase over the life of a tourist area, he believes that the tourist area is not an actorless development path. The State was not only shown to have been a catalyst to developing tourism on Cyprus, but also to have reacted to its negative impacts. Specifically, the government enacted efforts to reduce the tourist growth rate and balance the geographic distribution of lodging development. Ioannides (1992: 731) concluded that 'Cypriot government has intentionally steered the island's resort cycle towards Butler's "consolidation" stage'.

'Theoretical foundations and integrations'

Agarwal (2002) relates Butler's TALC to the 'restructuring thesis'. Her motivation to 'inter-relate' these two works is based on the insights this would provide into the causes and consequences of destination decline. The 'restructuring thesis' referred to in this work pertains to the process of change in capitalist economies and societies, along with significant shifts in the strategy by which capital seeks expanded accumulation. Agarwal (2002) includes a discussion into the way in which industries have responded to competitive and consumption challenges. These are categorized into three main forms and strategies: product reorganization, labor reorganization, and spatial relocation and product transformation. These strategies are then defined as they relate to the 'structural process of change' in the context of tourism. Therefore, the key elements in the relation between the restructuring thesis and Butler's model are the application and insights into responses to decline. Agarwal (2002) acknowledges that a number of problems are associated with and encountered when using both Butler's model and the restructuring thesis to provide understanding into how destinations can respond to decline (see also Agarwal, other volume). However, it is concluded that that they do provide two useful theoretical links; both concepts may be related to the causes and consequences of resort decline, and to the responses of resorts to decline.

The premise is then discussed in the context of three English seaside resorts of Minehead, Weymouth, and Scarborough, all of which have been categorized as currently in the poststagnation stage. Here it is concluded that the integration of the restructuring thesis helps overcome the failure of the destination life cycle model to consider the role of external factors in the changes that occur at a tourist destination. The point being that decline in a destination is the outcome of interactions between internal and external forces. Thus, the responses to decline likely are responses to external changes.

While much of the literature has focused on the 'concept' of Butler's TALC model, Johnston (2001) has attempted to 'shore up the model's theoretical foundations'. His paper focuses on the ontological and epistemological aspect issues surrounding the model (see also Johnston, other volume). The methods used in this work were a modified form of 'grounded theory'. From this ontological and epistemological perspective of Butler's model, the author presents a redrawn version of the life cycle curve with two notable differences from the original (Figure 3.2). First, the original model is divided horizontally over time, by three eras. These are the 'Pre-tourism', 'Tourism-era', and 'Post-tourism era'.

Based on this discussion of ontological considerations, Johnston concludes that it would be reasonable to claim that Butler's model is based on a basic geographic process. He identifies a set of epistemological elements through a variation of the constant comparative method applied to four other types of process research. These elements are: human life

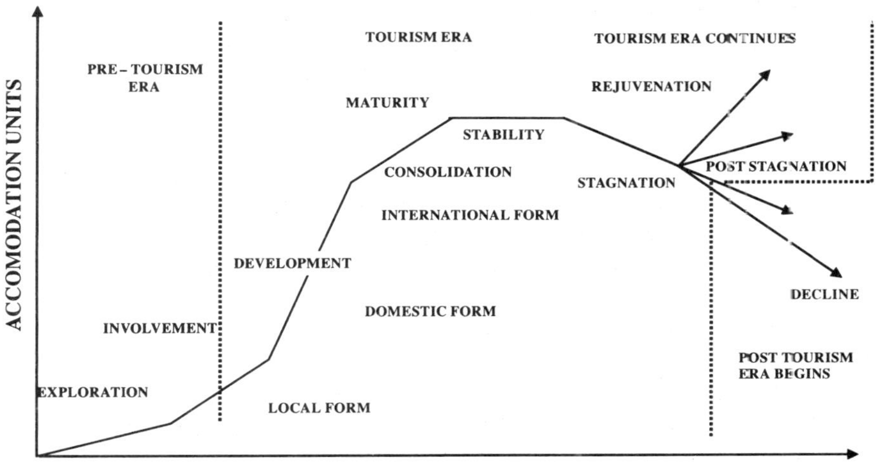

Figure 3.2 A revised version of Butler's (1980) 'classical' sequence of stages (Johnston, 2001)

cycle, product life cycle, port development, and ecosuccession. Following extensive discussion of the ontological and epistemological discussions, Johnston then revised the TALC, incorporating three eras. These are a pretourism era, from before the exploration phase extending into the involvement phase; a tourism era, which could carry through the maturity stage and may include a poststagnation phase; and a post-tourism era when a new institution dominates at the local level. Johnston also replaces growth in visitor numbers with growth in number of accommodation units. He applies this model (see Johnston, this volume) to the case of Kona, Hawaii (Johnston, 2002).

Final Comments

While not all the works cited below have been discussed in detail, every attempt has been made to include all relevant works pertaining to Butler's (1980) article in the bibliography. As mentioned in the introduction, works that pertained to the creation of Butler's original work have been listed, as they were important to the generation of Butler's concept, but only published works specifically using Butler's model have been discussed in detail. Works relating to the general theory of a product life cycle have been omitted (some are discussed at length in Coles, other volume, editor's note). Apologies go out to any authors whose works were not recognized in this chapter. This was not intentional; however, the literature survey was heavily biased toward both published works and works printed in English. Any and all errors pertaining to the representation of works covered here are completely unintentional and the fault of this author.

(Editor's note: Since the completion of this chapter yet another article using the TALC has been published (Moss *et al*., 2003), and is included in the Bibliography.)

Chapter 4

Evolution of Tourism Areas and the Tourism Industry

K. MICHAEL HAYWOOD

Introduction

This chapter reviews some of the conditions and concerns necessary to make TALC studies and research of greater value to those individuals whose tasks and responsibilities necessitate the following: creating legitimisation for, and direction of, tourism development in specific areas or destinations; crafting and implementing industry policies and strategies; leading the development process; and managing destination management organisations or other types of tourism and hospitality enterprises.

As an industry paradigm, TALC has proven valuable in articulating the evolution of tourism region, and in confirming the mimicking of the predictable pattern of lifecycle stages – introduction, expansion, consolidation and contraction – associated with all forms of organisation – genetic, biological, cognitive, ecological, cultural and economic. As Butler (1980) and other tourism researchers seem to urge, a particular characteristic of a destination's evolution is that it is influenced and yet confounded by the nature, politics, demands, use and experience of place. Place gives substance and meaning to the tourism product being offered. Tourism is place-sensitive; not only are regional landscapes and cultures fragile and rarefied, but visitors and tourism developers are attracted to certain locales simply because of their attractiveness and appeal (a major and complex factor determining the growth and sustainable competitiveness of destinations). Tourism is also place-demanding and place-exhausting; that is, the development process and the usage of a locale (natural and cultural resources) by a typical, seasonal insurgence of users, mainly visitors, has a tendency to undermine attractiveness of an area if activities are not managed or if capacity limits become stretched or exceeded. Even citizens are susceptible. They grow weary of the stress, as characterised initially by Doxey (1975); and their behaviour may compromise a destination's hospitable characteristics if they are denied or do not realise promised benefits. If tourism's impacts are ignored and not acted upon, the movement into stages of maturity, and eventually decline, is exacerbated.

Identification of stages in life cycles of destinations with particular reference to the 'place' concept is concomitant with tourism development; that is, destinations are repositories of organisations in service to the needs of visitors. Because the speed, process and extent of tourism developments differ from one locale to the next, no two tourism life cycles are alike. The range and diversity of tourism developments (Bianchi, 1994), variations in growth patterns (Choy, 1992) and the scale of tourism developments (Gosling, 2000) have to be taken into account when determining the impacts of tourism development. The magnitude of tourism's impacts, however, has to be put into context. Consider the name – 'tourism area life cycle'. What actually constitutes a tourism area? A review of the literature suggests that it is any place that attracts visitors or represents a primary tourist gathering spot. It could be as large as a country and as small as a development site. Included are cities, rural areas, world heritage areas, parks, historic and cultural sites, fairs, theme parks, resort towns, and the like, as discussed in other chapters in this volume. Once an area is defined, then it is necessary to determine what constitutes a capacity limit for development, and/or for the number of users (not necessarily tourists) at one time or a prolonged period. This is a topic that has stirred considerable debate (Martin & Uysal, 1990; Prosser & Cullen, 1987), and determination of capacity limits for many tourism areas and the existing infrastructure remains a challenging and imposing task. Indeed tourism may be only one of many activities responsible for various impacts. It is inappropriate for the tourism industry to shoulder blame when other local industries, and normal commercial and resident behaviours, contribute significantly to the unattractiveness and demise of an area.

Fortunately an appreciation of the dynamic and diverse set of changes wrought by tourism on 'sense of place' (Hiss, 1990; Hough, 1990; Wilson, 1991) is beginning to awaken a sense of responsibility within the industry. As tourism destinations and organisations become 'place conscious', sustainable environmental practices – environmental codes of ethics, environmental impact studies and ecoefficiency programmes – are being considered and implemented. The determination and use of appropriate metrics and perceptual measures for measuring impacts is also moving forward. But should society be comforted by the current responsiveness and ways in which nature- and cultural-based resource issues are being addressed? There is doubt in some quarters as to whether transformational activities, and the ways in which they are currently conceived and implemented, are sufficient and appropriate. Hawkin *et al*. (1999) argue that conventional wisdom is mistaken when priorities in economic, environmental and social policies compete. They challenge industries, such as tourism, to find solutions based not on trade-offs or 'balance' between competing objectives, but on design integration, achieving all of them together at every level of the industry. Obviously, this challenge suggests that most destinations would have to alter the ways in which they think about and manage tourism. At the very least, more broadly based results-based objectives and strategies would have to be factored into the equations, while taking into account relations among the organisations responsible for tourism, the quality of tourism products and the dynamics of regional economies (Russo, 2002 and this volume).

Visualising the big picture or contemplating a different future for tourism is easily forestalled when destinations and tourism organisations operate on a demanding economic treadmill. Whether they are at the starting gate, capitalising on growth opportunities, or witnessing erosion of their success by successive tides of technological, demographic and regulatory change, the industry is in a constant state of anxiety, and sometimes flux. Hotels and attractions are examples of organisations with high breakeven points, and an inability to place products into inventory for sale at some future period. Fixed capacities have to be filled daily; hence preoccupation with marketing and the delivery of high-quality services. Furthermore, competitiveness problems are inescapable as increasing numbers of places hitch to the tourism bandwagon. In fact stagnant growth, declining margins and falling market share are not characteristic simply of the mature phase of the cycle, but of too much supply chasing demand or the not-too-uncommon disruptive phases of business cycles (Haywood, 1998). Factor in seasonality, climatic irregularities, market orientations, integration of global economies and the dynamic organisational interlinkages within the industry, and the complexities intensify. Regardless of which stage of the life cycle a destination might be in, the challenge is ever-present. Every destination and tourism organisation is being challenged to improve their understanding and anticipation of the underlying dynamics of change, not only within the industry, but particularly within the destination (Bianchi, 1994; Haywood, 1986, 1992).

While the study of life cycles in many destinations continues to provide interesting historical representations of cyclic activity (based on available, though often unreliable, statistical data), it is as if these studies examine tourism from the wrong end of the telescope: what is nearby seems far away, and so the details melt into amorphous blobs. Destinations viewed from afar can't help but succumb to the characteristic life/death pattern; yet when viewed closely the tourism organisations and the people could be observed making choices continuously. To be truly effective as a pragmatic paradigm, TALC studies must consider, not simply the existence of choice in reaction to change, but the conditions that both underlie change, and enlarge or restrict choice. Destinations and the tourism industry operate within a rich and nuanced world, full of surprises, a world that favours imaginative action. Tourism researchers must get closer to, and understand, the details.

Fortunately the life cycle can be employed in such a way as to explain some of the details associated with the emergence and development of tourism within a region; but serious gaps exist. For example, glimpses into the development of local entrepreneurship (Din, 1992) and small businesses (Beverland, 2001), and preconditions for urban destinations in determining investment and industry growth (van de Borg, 2000) provide useful information about the start-up phase, yet little is known about the activities and behaviours associated with the conceiving, incubator or predevelopment phase. This omission might not have occurred if methodological approaches for studying teleological (strategic) and dialectical (power) actions associated with developing a new industry had been employed. With literature on how to go about developing a tourism industry, particularly the importance of taking a community approach to development intensifying (Haywood, 1988), tourism leaders and decision makers need to know which processes work, or not, when, where and why. Wisdom and knowledge needs to be shared about the influencing factors inherent in the preformative years, and the ways in which tourism development needs to be legitimised – not only in this stage, but during every stage of the life cycle.

Early stages of development represent periods in which industry champions come forward (Weaver, this volume). Commitment from a community is sought. The enthusiasm of developers and their initial supporters and beneficiaries is infectious; promises are made; vision and goals are articulated; tourism master plans may be prepared; negotiations are entered into; feasibility and environmental studies conducted; sites selected; and projects designed. Gradually fantasies are translated into realities, and the inherent risks quickly translate into day-to-day responsibilities. Getting an infant industry and/or organisations started is an exhausting and emotional endeavour, so there is a tremendous need to understand the characteristics and behavioural patterns of young and emerging destinations. For example, what are the repercussions when destinations and tourism organisations are undercapitalised, and basic infrastructure lacking? Is inadequate planning, and development of appropriate systems and procedures problematic? Can the possibilities of premature death be avoided (the bankruptcy rate for many independently owned businesses is extremely high during the first few years of operation). What occurs, or doesn't, shapes the industry and affects the transition to subsequent stages in the life cycle for years to come.

Similarly, the factors that make the emergent and early growth phases of tourism development into a virtual honeymoon have not been explored in the TALC literature. Because the tourism development process is primarily supply-led, developers are courted and romanced, and investment incentives provided. Job creation is a high priority. As demand materialises, money pours in; everyone appears happy and content. But, misperceptions as to the benefits and beneficiaries abound. For example, profits and return on investment take considerable time to be realised. Sunk investment costs may not be recouped for decades (at which time, considerable reinvestment may be required), and demand may not be sufficient to exceed breakeven points. Attention, obviously, is focused on marketing and branding to build demand (fill capacities) and attract further investment. Yet, it is ironic that TALC researchers feel the urge to be extremely critical of developers and investors, and the focal relationship-building pursuit necessary to make the industry viable. Increasing numbers of visitors, tourist activity and large-scale tourism development projects are said to set the stage for decline. The ideal scenario is tourism without visitors and development! Given the improbability of this occurring, the notion that tourism activity may be merely symptomatic of problems, rather than being the underlying cause, needs further investigation.

Whether an organisation fulfilling its mission through capacity maximisation, or a tourism area protecting itself from reaching limits to capacity (see Boyd, this volume), there exist diverse views and interests in capacity research. The extent to which differing concerns about capacity utilisation are seen as overlapping, however, depends on the degree to which the dominating forces (natural, organisational, political, economic, etc.) can be unified and/or are seen as affecting each other's concerns, mandates or goals. Unfortunately, the impact that these forces have on each other, and on tourism within a destination as a whole, may not be readily apparent, to even the most knowledgeable of people. A primary reason is that insufficient time has been spent learning how destinations or tourist areas function from a structural point of view. TALC research needs to become better attuned to discovering the interplay of the dominant forces that cause a destination to advance or decline, particularly in respect to capacity management. Study of structural dynamics might reveal interesting information as to appropriate mixes or diversity of tourism segments, activities and programmes. Relationships among the various players could be better understood. The delicacy of managing the development and growth of the industry through the emergent and subsequent phases needs to be highlighted. The key questions are: how are destinations or tourism organisations being managed throughout the lifecycle, and what are some of the dominant characteristics of successful and unsuccessful tourism areas?

Some TALC studies characterise some destinations as being rudderless. Sucked in by the dogma of growth, and fuelled by a booster spirit and visions of 'bigger and better', tourism development is portrayed as (greedy?) economic salvation writ large. Multinational lodging organisations and tour operators become sought-after partners. Their brand power is considered catalytic in propelling growth. But what may not be appreciated is that many of these large, more mature organisations may be quite focused on linking their brand integrity with sustainable development. If, as corporations mature, they become more socially responsible (Swanson, 1999), then concern over growth-fuelled development may be ill founded. Inevitably, more knowledge is required as to how tourism organisations alter their values and behaviour over time. Certainly failure to meet a community's noneconomic needs is cause for considerable concern, but appreciation for the cause and effect relationships in relation to the evolution of the industry needs to be contextualised and improved.

Worrisome side effects and outcomes during phases of tourism growth suggest other concerns that need to be addressed. For example, there is misdirection lurking in commonly accepted measures of growth. Impact studies have revealed that growth is a complex, multidimensional process; therefore, visitation rates, visitor expenditures and market share may be inadequate measures in determining a destination's stage in a life cycle. Researchers might want to learn how astute corporations are building 'balanced scorecards' in order to align individual, organisational and community initiatives; achieve healthy growth; and broaden their base of leading indicators (Kaplan & Norton, 1996, 2001). Then there are the perils associated with forcing growth (for example, through tax incentives), and exacerbating the imbalance of supply in comparison to demand. Tourism areas, by focusing on a singular industry, are inherently vulnerable when they tie their fortunes to a cyclical industry. Moreover, ill-conceived development and improper management of the growth process can result in places becoming 'displaced' – out of favour commodities in an industry of sameness.

Achieving tourism growth has been characterised as a difficult, if not perilous, journey. For example, industry development can be either fostered or curtailed by numerous factors and influences – historical influences on development (Douglas, 1997); external events (di Benedetto & Bojanic, 1993); influence of business, investment and real estate cycles (Haywood, 1998); prevalence of market or state-managed capitalism (Bacon, 1998); relationships between travel personalities and destinations (Plog, 2001); the ability to satisfy visitors and build demand on repeat visitation (Oppermann, 1998); difficulties in branding and building awareness (Beverland, 2001); recognition that no local industry operates in isolation and that national institutions and transnational firms can foster or undermine development (Ionnides, 1992); involvement of both informal and formal sectors of local economies (Kermath & Thomas, 1992); proactive planning initiatives (Knowles & Curtis, 2000); the influence of corporate strategies (Debbage, 1990, 1992; Tse & Elwood, 1990); and the increasing complexity of decision making and investment at various life-cycle stages (Keller, 1987).

The importance of innovation and diffusion cannot be ignored, as they are instrumental in reinvigorating growth and diversity (Getz, 2000). The evolution of tourism's structural and dynamic properties over a lifetime cannot be ignored. For example, Schumpeter (1939) observed that after the introduction of a major product innovation, a strong 'band-wagon' effect often appears, followed by the entry of many new firms into the rapidly expanding sectors, attracted by the high profits associated with innovations (see Stansfield, this volume). However, the entry of new firms leads to an erosion of profit rates, and as the industry matures and its product becomes standardised, a shift to cost-saving (process) innovations then occurs. The exploitation of scale economies becomes important, and correspondingly this leads to a reduction in the number of firms in the industry. On the basis of these observations one might anticipate that future TALC studies could capture issues on the innovative efforts of destinations and tourism organisations, the importance of scale economies, and the shift from product innovations to process innovations. Klepper (1996) provides an appropriate general, dynamic model, and has explained why these and other parameters change over the life cycle of an industry.

While innovative behaviour is presupposed to occur during latter stages of growth, and during mature or stagnant states, in actual fact it can be prevalent during all stages of the life cycle. Most visitor-focused enterprises need to be rejuvenated every decade or less (Malcolm-Davies, this volume). During these times there can be major reinvestment in facilities and equipment. Similar changes also occur as hotel properties, for example, change brands or flags. Buildings that are poorly maintained decline in value and move 'down-market'. These might be replaced with new facilities, many incorporating environmentally friendly systems. While addition to the stock of tourism facilities may stem from corporate decisions, prudent or otherwise, they can also be spurred or denied through competing political priorities (Voase, 2002). So, there are multiple reasons and numerous actors involved in reconfiguring and restarting the cycle (Baum, 1998). Indeed, due to the fact that there are numerous types of tourism activities taking place within a tourism area, as well as variations or differentiation within a given activity or sector of the industry, it is possible to discover the coexistence of various stages of the life cycle within a destination (Hovinen, 2002). While this reinforces the notion that there can be numerous variations in the dominant design or states of tourism development (Weaver, 2000 and this volume; de Albuquerque &

McElroy, 1992), it challenges the ease in which stages can be identified and measured.

The possibility of dominant designs of destinations and/or organisations in accordance with various life-cycle stages is also worthy of investigation (Weaver, 2000). In the business world Abernathy and Utterback (1975, 1978) have made important contributions in studying relationships among firms. In a similar vein, Miles and Snow (1978) classified corporate behaviours into four broad categories, which they labelled *defenders*, *prospectors*, *analysers* and *reactors*, each with their own unique strategies for relating to their chosen markets. Another example of dominant design research is represented by the work of Mintzberg and Waters (1982). They identified five stages in the development of a firm's strategies – development, stability, adaptation, struggle and revolution – and suggested that stages were sequenced in accordance with four main patterns – periodic bumps, oscillating shifts, life cycles and regular progress – and probed into the periods of major change in organisations. In moving this research forward, Miller and Friessen (1984) went on to identify archetypes of organisations, that is, states of strategy, structure situation and process, and transitions between archetypes, and thereby noted that strategic and structural change are quantum rather than incremental. In other words, there are benefits in tracking the behaviours (actions and outcomes), as well as thought processes (intentions and perceptions), associated with the leaders and managers of destinations and the tourism organisations. Our understanding of how they learn and drive strategic change is strengthened; and our ability to recognise stages or states of change is sharpened. If tourism areas go into decline then it becomes vital to understand why destructive strategies and structures emanate from constructive ones. In his book, *The Icarus Paradox*, Miller (1990) suggests that all positive trajectories suffer from built-in faults. So cycles of success and failure, growth and decline, seem to be an inevitable part of the natural, human and organisational condition.

The inevitability of stagnation and decline is a common occurrence for homogeneous products and services, and among organisations that fail to adapt. This inevitability of tourism area decline is also being manifest by a widening chasm between expectations for growth and its realisation. Economic and geopolitical problems always have the industry on edge. Add to this list recognition that some markets are increasingly mismatched with demand; that not all growth is healthy; that social disintegration, cultural degradation and exhaustion of resources are possible outcomes; and the obvious signs of decay become worrisome. In any event there is a need to appreciate the options when growth prematurely halts or when nongrowth occurs. What does rejuvenation entail? is it possible? how can it be accomplished (see Cooper, other volume, editor's comment)? Life-cycle research has made some inroads, but the greater attention has to be focused on belief and behavioural change.

During the so-called saturation or mature stage, tourism areas cannot help but face an age of triage (Rubenstein, 1983). Successful tourism areas will be those that can deal with the threats (internal as well as external), and sift out genuine opportunities from the illusory. Important questions concerning management in nongrowth situations will have to be answered. Indeed, survival and sustainability for all tourism areas and organisations may hinge less on the possibilities of rejuvenation, and more on learning to recognise and avoid the traps waiting to ruin destinations and organisations that make desperate grabs for growth that should never happen in the first place (Knowles & Curtis, 1999).

Configuration and Transformation of Changing Tourism Areas

Sustaining the economic, environmental and cultural vibrancy of tourism areas are primary goals of every industry stakeholder. If the life-cycle concept is to gain validity and relevance as an evaluative framework, with mutually dependent goals in mind, it must become a more effective learning model capable of (1) discovering and representing the dynamic and inter-related qualities of the industry, those that are both self-reinforcing (for example, reinforcing development) and self-correcting (for example, limiting development due to imbalance with carrying capacity), and (2) facilitating evaluation of the consequences of new policies, strategies and structures that might be proposed. Legitimisation of the life cycle cannot occur, however, until a stop is put to attributing the demise of the industry solely to individuals and organisations, rather than recognising that systems structure is the prime shaper of behaviour. By discovering the leverage points brought about by system structure redesign, particularly if each stage of the life cycle has its own structural and dynamic qualities, researchers will become capable of identifying the actions and behaviours that lead to significant, sustained and beneficial improvements to industry and organisational performance.

Most attempts to identify the imminent change as reflected in the TALC have been based on sequential, open-loop views of change. As such suggestions as to how to make the lifecycle model useful and operational required addressing major conceptual and measurement concerns such as unit of analysis, relevant market, pattern and stages of the tourist area lifecycle, identification of the area's shape in the life cycle, determination of the unit of measurement and determination of the relevant time unit (Haywood, 1986). Tourism systems, however, react to development and to the interventions of all players. The resulting feedback defines the situations to be faced in the future, given the inadvertent time delays, the accumulation, usage and dispersal of tangible and intangible resources, attribution errors and false learning. In overcoming the limitations of the lifecycle in accounting for change, and based on the assumption that the lifecycle could become an appropriate nest for alternate theories of change resulting in the configuration and constant transformation of tourism areas, it is now recognised that a broader set of issues need to be resolved. Each of these is introduced under a label, by a question, and as a dilemma.

Unit of analysis

What is the appropriate unit of analysis – the tourism area, or change itself? If it is the 'tourism area', how is it defined? Tourist area life cycle research focuses on regions in which tourism is considered to be the prime activity or industry. But what constitutes 'prime' if tourism represents only, let's say, 25% of a region's gross product? Because life cycles of regions are influenced by a multitude of commercial, government, human and other activities, attributing cause and effect just to tourism seems foolhardy and misleading.

Just as confusing is: What constitutes tourism activity? As a modern phenomenon, tourism is in a constant state of evolution through the 'convergence of industries', and the growth of varied leisure activities pursued away from home. New relationships between tourism, recreation, cultural, educational, leisure and even work activities are developing constantly. Not only is there a merging of industries, but a merging of consumer groups or markets in search of 'experiences' (Pine & Gilmore, 1999). Many businesses find it virtually impossible to differentiate between local residents and visitors. Despite the prevalence of definitional distinctions, the current state of tourism market research and visitation and activity data in many locales may make the distinction moot.

Determining the unit of analysis is also confounded by the fact that life-cycle theories are only considered relevant to single, rather than multiple entities. If a defined geographic area is considered as a singular entity (a cluster or network of organisations in a defined space), then it seems appropriate to suggest that its development and growth (the function of potentials that are likely to occur within a given territory) is beyond the control of a single entity. That is, development decisions are made by a multitude of different organisations, each responsive for and to their own lifecycles. For example, if tourism is largely based on convention activity, the rejuvenation of conference and meeting facilities may not occur unless hotels participate in the process. A supply-side appreciation of those organisations that comprise and affect the industry, and their relationships with each other, is crucial in determining the industry's health and wellbeing. Indeed, a community-based approach may be totally ineffective in determining life-cycle changes if so-called destination management organisations are concerned only with marketing. Even government organisations that provide necessary infrastructure, or control over the development process, may be ineffective in managing the life cycle if they have limited appreciation for the dynamics and intricacies of tourism.

The fact that the TALC concept has been strongly based on product life-cycle research is quite evident as market performance measures dominate. Usage of visitation rates and the associated expenditure levels suggest that researchers consider the industry life cycle as being market-driven, rather than organisationally driven (Simon, 1991). As tourism areas are 'place-based', it seems reasonable to require that performance during the life-cycle periods be determined on the basis of sustainability measures. If the essence of a tourism area is its attractiveness, scenic beauty, natural and cultural heritage, then these attributes should be taken into consideration. There are a wide variety of industry stakeholders interested in place-based performance, but they need the requisite information to detect problems and progress, as well as institute preventative measures. Indeed, it can be argued that the creation of tourism's economic value is a process that involves the best or most appropriate, combinational use of all resources.

Being precise as to delineation of what constitutes a tourism area or geographic region also presents a conundrum. Tourism areas tend not to conform to jurisdictional boundaries; sometimes they are better determined through typical patterns of visitor or tourist activity. Even when the subject area is proscribed – a national park, for example – consideration should be given to visitation and development activity in peripheral areas (see Boyd, this volume). The 'park gate syndrome' represents distinctive and dense forms of development that may have profound impacts on tourism areas even though they may not be precisely located in the region under consideration. Another concern is the possible expansion and contraction of tourism areas over time; when this occurs it confounds and destabilises the notion of carrying capacity.

Particular attention also has to be given to those regions that are on the verge of becoming tourism areas. Sometimes tourism is introduced as a benign industry capable of overcoming place-related damage caused by other industries (usually in decline), or as a preferential form of industrial development. Then there exist those resource-rich tourism/recreation areas recognised for their potential, but which have yet to be developed in accordance with their potential. In each case the challenges associated with tourism development and growth need to be better understood. The obstacles to overcome are decidedly different if development and growth are to succeed.

As discussed in detail elsewhere (see Haywood, other volume, editor's comment), there is considerable merit in moving beyond discrete tourism areas as units of change, to the unit of analysis becoming change itself. If, as suggested, there are different explanations for stability and change then it becomes important to determine the degree to which these explanations are nested in each other. Research is required to determine the relationships among these explanations, the macro–micro links, their timing, temporal shifts and degree to which they complement each other.

Unit and mode of change

Is tourism development a linear or cyclical activity – a biological progression of life-cycle events? The tendency has been to treat seemingly random patterns as stochastic processes. Observed change and development processes within tourism areas, however, are more complex than the life cycle suggests. As such, conditions may exist to trigger interplay among several instigators of change and produce interdependent cycles of change. For example, change and development goes on at multiple and hierarchical levels – a geographic level (place and space), an industry level (groups of organisations), organisational levels, stakeholder group levels and individual levels. This classification suggests that there are two different angles for studying development and change – the internal processes of change, adaptation and replication of individual entities, and the interactive processes of competition, cooperation and conflict among entities (Baum & Singh, 1994).

Application of life-cycle theory to explain change and development has made occasional reference to teleological theories, either in attributing blame to tourism organisations or in proposing positive or ameliorating mechanisms (policy making or tourism planning) through government or nongovernmental organisations. Because the dynamics of tourism systems arise from the interactions of all these organisations, the impact of their relationships needs to be better understood. With evolutionary and dialectical theories operating at the level of multiple entities, their application in this regard should be invaluable.

Different approaches for examining and explaining development and change in tourism areas also require that recognition be given to variations in the sequence of change events. For example, sequencing could be either prescribed *a priori* by either deterministic or probabilistic laws, or could progress and emerge in a constructive manner as the change process unfolds. Lifecycle and evolutionary theories of tourism area development rely on the prescriptive in that the imminent form is realised through steps or stages that provide an underlying continuity of form. Appearance of radical or sudden change is extremely rare, and in reality tends to be explained as a statistical accumulation of small individual events that gradually change the nature of the tourism area or industry. Radical change or breaks with the past, however, are identifiable within the industry and in tourism areas. The accompanying change based on new goals (teleological) and resolution of conflict (dialectical) tends to be described as constructive as it produces unprecedented, novel forms that, in retrospect, are discontinuous and unpredictable departures from the past.

With tourism areas developing and changing over space and time, it is likely that more than one of the theories will come into play on any occasion. The development process is influenced by different organisations and individuals. The spatial dispersion of organisations and individuals also means that different influences may be at work simultaneously, each imparting their own particular momentum to the development process. Development and change also take time to occur, and may not exert any influence until noticed. In other words the patterns and impacts of tourism development and change processes is multilayered and complex.

Unit of measurement

If the health and wellbeing of tourism areas are of fundamental concern in TALC studies, why are visitation and expenditure data pre-eminent in determining the progression of cyclical stages? Understandably destinations or tourism areas are dependent on visitors, but should the inherent stages of the life cycle be determined and based solely on growth trends associated with the number of visitors and their expenditures? Furthermore, if these are measures of growth, are they not rubber yardsticks – uncertain indicators of that which is being measured? As TALC studies point to growth as a highly complex social, economic and environmental process, why is growth not considered more often from a multidimensional perspective?

In industry circles the growth drumbeat is so pervasive that it is hard to imagine tourism development without growth. But not every kind of growth leads to development, let alone progress. Not only has the management guru Peter Drucker (1973) admonished growth as an objective, but the ambiguities of growth prevent various definitions and measures of growth from serving as valid indicators of achievement. In fact most constituencies within tourism areas have their own preferences as to which measures of growth (development) should be emphasised. Arbitrarily imposed growth targets and rates, however, are likely to favour the interests of some constituencies in the short term at the expense of other constituencies over the long term. And here is an intriguing paradox. Of all the stakeholders, visitors not only have the least interest in any form of growth, but may avoid places where growth is rampant and destroying the essence of place. As such, some tourism areas and industry partners are learning that performance can be enhanced by actually catering to fewer visitors.

Because tourism areas pursue tourism development to accomplish societal purposes, not solely economic ones, progress and performance need to be measured in aesthetic, environmental, social, cultural, as well as economic and monetary terms. To date, measurement has been narrowly focused on traditional performance areas, which tend to look at visitation and expenditure data. These measures are quantitative, relatively abundant and precise, though historical or lagging in nature. Present and future requirements, however, require non-traditional, less well defined and emerging measures. These measures need to be more predictive in nature and sufficiently robust to deal with today's changing marketplace and resource environment. However, if researchers are to answer sophisticated measurement questions as ...

- How can measures be identified that are linked to critical success factors, to industry/business risks, and to policy and strategic objectives?
- What are the key predictors of performance that relate to policy and strategic objectives; programmes, outputs, initiatives and limits; and contributions to desired results?
- How are the cause and effect of policy, strategic and other decisions to be measured?
- How do you benchmark a tourism area's ability to adapt to changing industry/business decisions or social/cultural/environmental conditions?

... there should be knowledge and awareness of key objectives, policies, strategies and capacity limits. This may be a challenge in that few tourism areas have a clear idea as to tourism's mandate, the strategic approaches used to operate effectively in the tourism industry or marketplace, and how value is created now or into the future for visitors and other stakeholders.

Because tourism policies and strategies set direction, measures are required to stay on track. By linking measurement to policy and strategy, researchers can identify and implement measures in the context of where tourism is headed, or what is expected from its development (leading indicators), rather than simply on where it is today, where it has been, or what has occurred (lagging indicators) (see Berry, other volume, editor's comment). This differentiator is critical in resource and community settings in which tourism challenges sustainability. Moreover, tourism areas and organisations that remain nimble and alert to the need to change their policies and strategies (and thus their measures) to meet evolving needs and requirements are more likely to be successful in environments increasingly characterised by change. The expanding use of nonfinancial and intangible measures, such as the Balanced Scorecard (Kaplan & Norton, 1990, 2001), environmental and community sustainability indexes, and quality of life measures, is indicative of a desire to find ways to enhance industry and corporate governance, meet stakeholder requirements, and reflect community and visitor value to be derived from tourism.

A tourism area's ability to optimise its return from tourism ultimately depends on whether it has the trust of its stakeholders. A key challenge is to identify which issues different stakeholders care about and to develop mechanisms for communicating with them in a timely manner. The goal is not to report on what stakeholders currently demand; it is also to supply information they need if they are to gain a better understanding of the area's strategy and performance. Promoting dialogue and engagement with stakeholders will help the tourism area obtain the information it needs in order to become more effective in managing through various lifecycle stages.

Cycle and pattern determination

Sustainability, defined in its broadest sense, is predicated on the clear expression of societal (community, organisational, individual) choices regarding the management of tourism areas and organisations for their intrinsic values, and tangible and intangible benefits they confer. Given the dynamics of change, varying spatial and temporal scales, and lag effects, the critical question is how can the TALC analysis become more useful in achieving goals and objectives, while anticipating and avoiding the inevitable barriers, behaviours and mistakes in achieving sustainability? Are there particular forces that influence the complex development process in tourism areas during different times? What are the typical characteristics and behaviours associated with various stages in the life cycle, and can these be determined *a priori*?

Acceptance of deterministic modelling of change is currently being critiqued as managers and planners broaden their utilisation of both prescriptive and constructive models to explain the patterns of stability and change in tourism areas and organisations. Improvement in learning about and managing such complex systems as tourism areas requires tools capable of capturing all the sources of dynamic complexity. Such tools as causal mapping and simulation techniques (made accessible through modern system dynamics modelling software) could be of tremendous value in capturing past events or in anticipating future events (Morecroft & Sterman, 1994). Their application to life cycles, as nests of change, could be profound if tourism areas and organisations are to influence the speed and means of the evolution they set in motion.

A first order priority is to pay attention to changing patterns of behaviour. It has been proposed that growth and ageing of organisations are primarily manifested in the inter-relationship between two factors, flexibility and controllability (Idizes, 1988). This observation runs counter to the importance *size* and *time* are afforded in TALCs. In other words, young tourism destinations or organisations tend to be quite amenable to development and change, although what they may do is likely to be unpredictable because there is little controllability. On the other hand more mature tourism areas and organisations tend to be far less flexible and pliant when it comes to change or managing transitions. This is due to a greater degree of calcification or controllability of behaviour. Understanding the differences in behaviours during cycles of change adds to the poignancy of intensified commoditisation among tourism areas and organisations, increased competition, product obsolescence and customer power. Recognising that there is no such thing as long-term sustained competitive advantage, and that operating margins are constantly being squeezed, tourism areas and organisations are anxious to learn how to manage through the necessary transitions; that is, they must demonstrate the most effective actions and behaviours.

Typically the inflection points in TALCs have been associated with significant increases or declines in tourism volume, thereby giving credence to the rather outmoded importance of market share as the driver of profitability. Paradoxically, TALC studies, while recognising that volume growth is important, have emphasised that *how growth is achieved* is much more important. Yet lacking are the convincing studies that point to why, when, where and how high growth, with poorly conceived tourism designs, destroys value and profitability. With fundamental shifts occurring in both business and tourism area landscapes, there is a need for tourism life-cycle research to improve understanding of how and when tourism areas and organisations, if they are to remain sustainable and profitable, must change their designs so that, as living entities, they can continue to function in coherent and mutually reinforcing ways over time. So, if the inflection points are to be anticipated, they need to be based on a new set of metrics associated with value capture and value loss using a Balanced Scorecard approach (Kaplan & Norton, 1990, 2001), and market, financial, social and environmental measures or performance data must be incorporated.

Determination of life-cycle stages, therefore, requires a multicomposite set of leading and lagging indicators that will identify value migration patterns of importance to key constituents in the tourism area – citizens, businesses, governments, NGOs – and throughout tourism's value chain or network/constellation (Norman & Ramirez,

1998). As life-cycle patterns really are graphic portrayals of the realisation or destruction of value, it can be argued that life-cycle stages need to be represented through value configurations. Based on Porter's value chain framework (1985), which is presently the accepted language for representing the logic of organisation-level value creation, it is possible to configure tourism areas (the unit of analysis) as value networks – the creation and reinvention of value achieved through the relationship of organisations within and affecting the sense of place. Subjecting this value network/constellation to analysis would then require decomposing tourism areas into a range of strategically important activities and then measuring and understanding the impacts of these activities in terms of cost and value (creation, capture or loss). If the unit of analysis were to be a tourism organisation, however, value configuration could be based also on the value chain (the creation of value through the transformation of inputs into performances, products or services). At a lower level of hierarchical analysis the notion of value shop could be employed (the creation of value by mobilising resources and activities to resolve particular problems associated with visitors or particular interest groups) (Stabell & Fjeldstad, 1998). For example, work is already proceeding in developing environmental chain analysis (Ishii & Stevels, 2000); the relevancy for tourism areas is significant

Because tourism areas are configured as networks/constellations, value creation, capture and loss will need to be derived from a mix of activities, capacity levels and opportunities. Unfortunately, little work has been conducted, to date, in identifying and modelling these activities, and in measuring value, or changes in value, over time. Likewise, identification of corresponding life-cycle stages has yet to be determined. However, as previously stated, these stages should be in accordance with goals, capacity limits and boundary constraints that need to be identified *in situ*. As such, much of what is currently known about the pattern and stages of tourist area life cycles needs to be rethought.

The complexity of achieving truly sustainable tourism areas is in balancing various demands that reveal themselves at different points in the evolution of tourism areas. Supply-side and resource-based considerations definitely need to play a predominant role in value determination, as do behavioural patterns. For example, as organisations age they tend to become oblivious to the incompatibility of their current business models with changing operating conditions (Slywotzky, 1996). Different stages of the lifecycle also alter the resource requirements of organisations and the responsiveness to the demands of various stakeholders if they are not considered critical to their survival or needs at a given time (Jawahar & McLaughlin, 2001). On the demand side, visitor value can be compromised if ignored or if competing demands from other stakeholders take precedence. The result: repeat visitation and the development of loyal, visitor-centric relationships may not be realised; growth in tourism arrivals may cease; length of stay may diminish; and the TALC may prematurely slide into decline.

Conclusion

TALC research typically has been dominated by interesting, though synoptic, accounts of change and patterns at different points in time that normally escape perception. The industry, however, requires more sophisticated performance accounts of change, simply because they are more directly connected to the 'lived experiences', and actions and behaviours of practitioners. Indeed change, which is synoptically explained *ex post facto*, is experienced in tourism areas and organisations as an unfolding process, a flow of possibilities, a conjunction of events and open-ended interactions occurring in time. To understand how change is actually accomplished, it must be approached from within, not as an abstract concept, but as performance enacted in time.

As a nested theory of change, for example, the life cycle has the potential, not simply to clarify exogenous influences, but to further our awareness of how tourism areas and organisations respond to these influences. It is the endogenously conditioned responses, however, that cannot be anticipated. There is a world out there that causes tourism authorities and managers to respond, but the pattern of response depends on self-understanding – the historically created assumptions and interpretations of the community, the organisation, and the individuals, along with the perception of place, the importance of the environment, and the visions, goals and limits that exist for the industry. The responses to exogenously generated pressure over time are complex, multilayered and evolving, rather than simple, fixed and episodic.

The relevancy and pragmatism of TALC studies, therefore, will be enhanced when more is known about the motors of change – the degree to which they are nested at different stages of the life cycle, and whether they act simultaneously, at different times and complement each other. While the complexity of the theoretical relationships between constructive and prescribed motors of change is likely to play a major role in explaining patterns of stability and change in tourism areas, there will be a requirement to develop more dynamic systems models. If sustainability of tourism areas is the ultimate goal, then TREC studies need to focus on gaining a better appreciation of each of the major stakeholders, their beliefs and habits of action in response to local circumstances, and pressures to survive; as well as the influence and interventions of these stakeholders into the stream of actions that are manifest in various stages of the TALC.

As living entities and clusters of tourism-focused enterprises and human action, tourism areas are subjected to a barrage of change. The view expressed here is that if TALC researchers avail themselves of the opportunity to capture and make sense of the dynamics of this change, the myriad of issues and questions regarding sustainability have a greater chance of being resolved. In the process, TALC research needs to become more theoretically integrative, as well as demonstrate its relevance to practitioners, who require the knowledge and tools to (re)configure and continually transform tourism areas and their organisations in accordance with their independent quest for survival and their mutually dependent goals for enhancing the quality of the places or communities in which they live and operate.

Part 2
Implementation of the TALC

RICHARD W. BUTLER

This first section contains chapters that discuss the application and implementation of the TALC in rural settings in North America and the People's Republic of China. The first application of the TALC model appeared, as did the original article, in *The Canadian Geographer*, a year later in 1981, and was the first of three articles by Hovinen (1981, 2000, 2002), which have applied the TALC to Lancaster County in the USA. This is the setting made famous in the movie 'Witness', which helped to increase the visibility of the area and is partly responsible for making it more widely known to a more international audience. In the first chapter in this section, Hovinen discusses the process of the tourist development of this rural location and its distinctive cultural milieu. The changes brought about by tourism in this setting are perhaps, in some ways, more significant than in many other American tourist destinations because of the conservative and private nature of the Amish who populate this area. Hovinen notes how they have adjusted to tourism, utilising it in some situations and avoiding or minimising contact with it in others. He goes on to examine the TALC and tourism in Lancaster County in the light of attempts to move the tourism industry there to a more sustainable form, a topic which is discussed later in this volume by Marois and Hinch, and by myself in the final chapter of the accompanying volume.

The following chapter presents a second North American application of the TALC, in this case to another rather distinct cultural setting, that of the province of Quebec. While Quebec is predominantly French in language and to some degree culture, the Eastern Townships, the area to which Lundgren applies the model, is mostly English speaking. It has a long-established tourism industry as he notes, and one which has adjusted consistently to changes in transport innovations and accessibility. The tourism industry has taken several forms, including the traditional North American cottage development, winter sports (particularly downhill skiing), and most recently, a more varied focus on local community attractions, including festivals, art and gastronomy. Lundgren illustrates the cycles within cycles that affect a region and the way in which a region can constantly revitalise its tourist and recreational appeal.

The final chapter in this section, by Bao and Zhang, discusses the specific application of the TALC to tourism planning and development in the People's Republic of China. While China is relatively new on the international tourism scene, its massive population means that it has a large domestic tourism industry, and as general levels of affluence rise, it can be expected to emerge as a major player in international tourism in the years ahead. It is already a significant international tourism destination, and the 2008 Olympic Games will certainly increase its international visibility in tourism. Bao and Zhang's paper demonstrates a particularly pragmatic solution to some of the problems with applying the TALC, particularly the bounding problem noted by Johnston (see other volume) and others. They reveal how the decision to designate a specific feature as an addition to the attractions of a declining tourism destination can successfully, if possibly only temporarily, revitalise the appeal of, and increase the visitation to, the area. This is a theme returned to in the last section of this volume.

Chapter 5

Lancaster County, the TALC, and the Search for Sustainable Tourism

GARY R. HOVINEN

Introduction

Lancaster County, Pennsylvania, an important diversified tourism destination in the Northeastern USA, was the location of the first application of the Tourism Area Life Cycle (TALC) model (Hovinen, 1981). In a second, expanded article, Hovinen (1982) confirmed the general usefulness of the model while noting some of its limitations for this particular destination. A much more recent study (Hovinen, 2002) of Lancaster County revisited the TALC model after two decades of additional development and again evaluated its usefulness.

This chapter will first summarize the results of these previous applications of the TALC model. As the model emphasizes the potential for tourism destinations to experience significant decline if appropriate planning efforts are not undertaken, the author will then discuss the prospects for avoiding such a decline in Lancaster County. The county has in recent years begun to pursue elements of a sustainable tourism strategy. How has sustainable tourism been defined thus far and how may the definition be further refined in the future? What have been the successes up to now in the tourism planning approach? What setbacks have occurred and what challenges remain? Can a lasting form of tourism be devised which is economically successful while being judged by county residents as enhancing their quality of life? In the final analysis, how useful is the TALC model or suggested revisions thereof in assessing the future of Lancaster County tourism?

Previous Applications of the TALC Model to Lancaster County

The first applications of the TALC model to Lancaster County (Hovinen, 1981, 1982) dated the postulated exploration stage to the pre-World War II period. No organized tourist industry existed, visitor facilities were few, and the number of visitors was very small. Lancaster's highly accessible location meant that most early visitors were likely traveling through the county on their way elsewhere. An incipient cultural attraction was the large population of 'plain people', including the country's oldest settlement of Amish. By the 1930s these plain people, who had chosen to remain to a high degree culturally and socially separate from the rest of society, were becoming a curiosity to outsiders (Hovinen, 1982).

Butler's proposed involvement stage, characterized by local people investing heavily in tourist facilities and the establishment of a formal tourist organization, can be usefully applied to Lancaster County during the period from the end of World War II until about 1960. The Amish were the principal tourist attraction, so it is not surprising that tourist facilities developed rapidly to the east of Lancaster City in the direction of the major concentration of Amish. Heavy promotion of the Amish attraction by local businessmen and eventually by a formal tourist organization (henceforth called Visitors Bureau) helped generate growing awareness and resulted in a rapid growth of visitors from nearby urban centers along the Atlantic coast (Hovinen, 1982).

The development stage of Butler's model clearly characterized Lancaster County from 1960 to about 1975. The growth in the number of visitors was huge, and Lancaster County was being touted as one of the top tourist destinations in the USA. Although the Amish, with their horse and buggy transportation, distinctive conservative clothing, and homes without electricity, were certainly the principal attraction, the county was also becoming a more diversified destination. One example was the construction of the Dutch Wonderland amusement park with its castle façade along a major traffic artery east of the city. As Butler has suggested, the development period saw major investment in capital facilities such as motels and restaurants by external organizations, which had by now recognized Lancaster's business potential. The initial positive attitude of many local inhabitants and the media towards tourism, given its economic impacts, turned more critical during this stage. There was growing concern about garish commercialism as exemplified by Dutch Wonderland, about increased traffic congestion along the two principal tourist arteries, and regarding the perceived exploitation of the Amish as unwilling tourist objects. The Amish themselves complained about invasion of privacy. Two noted Amish scholars expressed concern that tourism was beginning to destroy Amish culture (Hovinen, 1982). Thus tourism had become much more controversial.

The next two stages in Butler's model, consolidation and stagnation, are difficult to apply to Lancaster County's tourism cycle as the tourist industry has become ever more diversified and the conditions of tourism ever more complex since the mid-1970s. For example, Butler's assumption in 1980 that few, if any, additional investments are made by franchises and chains from the consolidation period onward is contradicted by evidence in Lancaster County. A lodging and restaurant construction boom occurred in the 1990s, financed heavily by external chain and franchise organizations, during the same time that there was growing concern in some elements of the tourist industry about stagnation or even decline in visitor numbers and revenues. Lancaster County has never been a conventional resort destination and is now comprised of a number of different tourism elements with varying degrees of strength and weakness. Whereas the Amish were the principal attraction into the 1980s, that has not been true of the period of the 1990s and beyond. Instead new attractions such as factory outlet malls and theaters have come to the forefront (Hovinen, 2002).

The empirical evidence suggests that there has been no simple shift from a development stage to the postulated consolidation and stagnation stages in Lancaster County. Rather than a gradual slowing of tourism growth during a consolidation stage, there was an abrupt and dramatic decline in visitor numbers in 1979 because of a combination of internal and external factors (Hovinen, 1982). That decline was followed by a renewed growth of tourism through the mid-1980s, although possibly not to the level of the record high visitor numbers of the mid-1970s. The new growth was attributable partly to a brief renewed interest in Amish culture because of the impacts of a popular Hollywood film ('Witness'). By the 1990s, the Amish were no longer the principal attraction for a visit; instead shopping had become the single most important reason for coming to the county. Visitors flocked to large new factory outlet malls or to antique shops. Another example of a new and highly popular attraction was Sight and Sound, a theater that offered plays with religious themes. At the same time, owners of older attractions were complaining of stagnation or even decline and an air of crisis seemed to pervade the tourism industry (Hovinen, 2002). Thus there appeared to be a mixture of growth, stagnation, and even decline during the 1990s, making it difficult to discern a clear progression from Butler's proposed consolidation stage to stagnation and then decline.

Given the initial evidence used in testing Butler's model in Lancaster County, the author proposed replacing the consolidation and stagnation stages with a new maturity stage (Hovinen, 1982). Such a stage might be partly characterized by either a slowing of growth or the existence of stagnation, but also might have short periods of renewed growth or even decline. Further evidence from the 1980s and 1990s seemed to support this alternative maturity stage (Hovinen, 2002). Perhaps Butler's model is most successfully applied to certain conventional resort destinations that undergo cycles of evolution. A cycle is certainly discernible in Lancaster County, but the highly diversified nature of tourism that currently exists and the fact that there are different elements of the tourist industry which are at different stages of the cycle makes it difficult to distinguish between consolidation, stagnation, and decline. Growth, stagnation, decline, and even revitalization through new investment may in fact coexist (Hovinen, 2002).

Table 5.1 sheds further light on the growing complexity of tourism trends in the county. It includes annual percentage change figures for either visitors or sales calculated for five individual large businesses. Operators of these businesses had records dating back many years from which the author was able to calculate annual percentage changes. Although not representative of the entire industry, a partial picture of long-term trends thus emerges. The author agreed to respect the confidentiality of the businesses whose operators agreed to supply figures.

The attraction represented in Table 5.1 is one of the longest-lasting features of the tourism landscape and thereby contrasts with the newer types of attractions that date from the late 1980s and 1990s. This earlier attraction experienced rapid growth in visitors during the county tourist boom of the 1960s and much of the 1970s period. In the major downturn in county tourism of 1979, the attraction suffered almost a 30% decline. The next year, however, saw an equally rapid percentage rebound. Most of the remainder of the 1980s and the beginning of the 1990s were also strong, but then five of the next six years saw declines in visitors. The attraction is somewhat representative of trends in the older parts of the attractions sector during the 1990s period and gave rise to a perception among operators of these businesses that county tourism was facing a crisis.

The two large restaurants and the lodging facility included in Table 5.1 provide a more complicated picture, as visitor total percent changes do not exhibit a consistent pattern of growth or decline in most years of the 1990s period. Only in 1991 and 1993 did all three of these businesses experience decline together. In every other year of this decade, one or two suffered decline while the remainder had growth. This variability in growth or decline in individual years was also apparent in the overall industry during the decade, as reflected in trend figures for a much larger sample of businesses surveyed by the author (Hovinen, 2002). In contrast to the development stage of county tourism, this 'maturity' stage is characterized by greater variation in success or failure among individual businesses rather than the earlier tendency of all to prosper or (on rare occasions) to suffer together in a given year.

Results for the large shopping facility included in Table 5.1 further confirm the preceding generalization. In contrast to the other four businesses, this especially well managed establishment experienced no declines (in sales) during any year of the past two decades. The manager of this shopping facility told the author in a meeting in June 2002 that a number of tourism operators succeeded in the boom years of the 1960s and 1970s 'in spite of themselves'. At that time, favorable economic

Table 5.1 Percent change in sales or visitors for five individual businesses

Year	*Attraction (visitors)*	*Shopping (sales)*	*Lodging (visitors)*	*Restaurant (visitors)*	*Restaurant (visitors)*
1960	596.5				
1961	51.8				
1962	36.1				
1963	22.8				
1964	1.7				
1965	22.0				
1966	3.4				
1967	2.9				
1968	4.7				
1969	8.5				
1970	24.2		10.1		
1971	12.6		6.6		
1972	– 1.9		5.6		
1973	12.2		0.9		
1974	– 2.1		– 0.9		
1975	5.2		10.5		
1976	– 0.7		2.9		
1977	3.4		7.3		
1978	– 5.7		– 2.2	4.8	
1979	– 29.4		– 10.5	– 12.3	
1980	29.3		2.6	7.2	
1981	9.3	25.0	1.8	3.4	
1982	– 2.0	11.0	0.0	3.6	
1983	– 6.8	9.0	0.4	– 0.7	
1984	6.2	14.0	2.8	– 2.0	
1985	5.6	20.0	2.6	– 0.7	9.6
1986	1.7		1.3	0.5	1.9

Table 5.1 (*Continued*)					
Year	*Attraction (visitors)*	*Shopping (sales)*	*Lodging (visitors)*	*Restaurant (visitors)*	*Restaurant (visitors)*
1987	– 0.8	14.0	4.9	0.3	5.4
1988	2.9	14.0	– 1.2	0.7	0.8
1989	5.4	9.0	– 3.6	3.2	– 3.7
1990	10.8	5.0	2.5	– 3.4	1.0
1991	8.3	11.0	– 6.0	– 0.4	– 10.3
1992	– 4.2	5.0	1.3	– 2.7	5.3
1993	– 5.5	4.0	– 4.5	– 2.9	– 3.0
1994	– 10.7	4.0	– 0.1	2.0	2.3
1995	– 4.9	4.0	1.8	– 2.6	2.3
1996	4.2	5.0	– 0.3	6.0	8.2
1997	– 9.2	3.0	6.8	– 1.8	– 4.0
1998	13.6	14.0	– 1.3	2.8	7.4
1999			0.5		

The large attraction included is one of 104 Visitors Bureau member attractions in the county The large shopping facility represents one of 98 shopping members, accommodation one of 186, and restaurants two of 63

trends in the overall industry virtually guaranteed success. Now success or failure is influenced more by the management or business planning skills of the individual operator than was true previously. In a mature industry, how to prevent decline therefore becomes a greater concern.

The decline stage of the TALC model

One of the most useful aspects of the TALC model is its emphasis on the potential, if not the inevitability, of significant decline if appropriate long-range planning strategies are not pursued for a particular destination. The author's previous studies of Lancaster County have not shown any evidence of significant overall decline up to now, despite clear evidence of decline among some individual businesses, especially including older attractions. Nevertheless, the potential for future decline was a matter of concern among some tourism operators during the 1990s (Hovinen, 2002).

The 1990s saw the emergence of a new proactive and longer-range planning approach at the same time that the dominant approach of the

Visitors Bureau and individual tourism operators continued to be reactive and short range with a strong annual marketing emphasis (Hovinen, 2002). The first example of the new proactive approach, in the mid-1990s, was a new heritage tourism program financially supported by the state and county governments; it also involved a public–private partnership, as it was sponsored in part by the private Visitors Bureau and the National Trust for Historic Preservation. The partnership produced a heritage tourism plan for Lancaster County by the beginning of 1998. Then, in the year 2001 another state-supported partnership resulted in the creation of a new Lancaster–York Heritage Region including the neighboring county to the west of the Susquehanna River. A long-range management action plan was completed in 2001, prepared with the assistance of a heritage tourism consulting firm from the Washington DC area.

Theoretical alternatives to the TALC's decline and rejuvenation stages

Agarwal (1994 and other volume, editor's note) argues for a reformulation of the poststagnation phase of the TALC model with its suggested alternatives of decline versus rejuvenation. Restructuring efforts may be initiated before decline sets in. In contrast to Butler's suggestion in proposing the TALC model that rejuvenation to avoid decline involves a complete change in the attractions on which tourism is based, Agarwal contends that this may not be financially or politically acceptable. Therefore, efforts are concerned with renewal and with encouraging growth and market maturity rather than with accepting decline. She proposes a reorientation stage after the TALC stagnation stage and before eventual rejuvenation or decline to reflect these restructuring efforts. Such a reorientation stage has some relevance to circumstances in Lancaster County although there has been no clear stagnation stage for the overall industry. As one example where 'reorientation' may better describe current efforts at renewal than 'rejuvenation', no complete change of attractions in Lancaster County is likely as long as the Amish remain in the county as one of the continuing attractions.

In a study of restructuring theory, Agarwal (2002) points out that restructuring involves both product reorganization and product transformation. 'Specific product reorganization strategies include investment and technical change, centralization and product specialization. Product transformation strategies include service quality enhancement (improving the quality of service delivery), environmental quality enhancement (improving key areas of the resort), repositioning, diversification, collaboration, and adaptation.' (Agarwal, 2002: 36–37). Some of these strategies are part of Lancaster County's restructuring efforts as will be evident from the discussion of further trends.

The Search for Sustainable Tourism

The potential for a tourism destination to avoid the decline stage can also be related usefully to the theme of sustainable tourism. Butler (1998b) has previously noted how popular this theme has become in the academic discipline of tourism. From the perspective of managers in the tourism industry, economic sustainability of tourism is without doubt the primary interest. But sustainable tourism is also defined on the basis of environmental, social, and cultural considerations. Butler (1998b: 28) has argued that 'it is clearly illogical and unrealistic to contemplate sustainability in any one sense alone, such as economic sustainability.' Furthermore, according to Butler (1998b: 29), 'calls for sustainable tourism to be developed irrespective of whether other, interrelated, segments are to be sustainable or not is inappropriate and contradictory.' That is, the tourism sector is related to and dependent upon other sectors of the economy and society, so any definition of sustainable tourism must consider the overall system and not simply tourism alone. The difficulty of implementing sustainable tourism therefore becomes apparent. Perhaps it is best to view sustainable tourism as a set of idealistic principles that may be useful as a basis for long-range planning rather than a condition ever likely to be fully achieved.

The first consideration of sustainable tourism principles in Lancaster County occurred as part of the preparation of the 1998 Heritage Tourism Plan. A basic premise of the heritage tourism program was that there is a need to maintain a strong balance between the economic benefits of tourism and the preservation of natural and cultural resources. After discussion and input from county tourism and development representatives, the following eight principles of sustainable tourism were adopted for the plan.

(1) The natural and cultural environment has intrinsic value, and its protection and preservation is [sic] essential to the long-term success and viability of tourism in Lancaster County.
(2) The relationship between tourism and the environment, both natural and cultural, must be managed so that it is sustainable in the long term.
(3) Tourism should enhance and complement the unique natural and cultural features of Lancaster County.
(4) Tourism activities should respect and accurately reflect the scale, nature, and character of Lancaster County's unique places.
(5) Carrying capacity should be a prime consideration in managing and protecting the natural and cultural heritage of Lancaster County.

(6) A balance should be sought between the needs of the visitor, the place, and the residents of Lancaster County.
(7) Tourism should communicate appropriate cultural and environmental sensitivity.
(8) Local involvement in sustainable tourism planning processes is essential in promoting harmony between tourism and the residents of Lancaster County. (Lancaster County Planning Commission, 1998: 18–19)

Development trends and issues in the county

Sustainable tourism, most appropriately defined, depends not only on achieving positive impacts from tourism itself, but also on what happens in other sectors of the economy and society. Therefore, it is necessary first to consider briefly some of the broader development trends and issues in the county that have implications for the success of sustainable tourism.

In 1998 the Hourglass Foundation, a private nonprofit citizens' group in Lancaster County, hired the Polk-Lepson Research Group of York to do a random scientific telephone survey of the Lancaster County population. The research firm asked a variety of questions about issues affecting the county, including what respondents considered to be the biggest threats to the quality of life in the county. Over one half of the sampled population cited overdevelopment, urban sprawl, loss of farmland, or unlimited growth as the biggest threats to the quality of life in Lancaster County; a much smaller percentage mentioned environmental concerns or traffic as the chief threats. Furthermore, a large majority of respondents said they considered sprawl a serious problem rather than a minor problem or no problem and agreed that something should be done to stop or slow down sprawl (Rutter, 1998).

The Hourglass Foundation commissioned a second survey of the county population by Polk-Lepson, with an even larger sample, in the year 2000. Results revealed that what more than half of respondents liked best about Lancaster County was the countryside, farmland, open space, and the rural way of life. This survey revealed an even greater concern with perceived threats of overdevelopment, sprawl, and loss of farmland to quality of life than found in the previous survey. Furthermore, a third of respondents said they felt the quality of life in Lancaster County was worse in 2000 than it had been five years earlier (Hourglass Foundation, 2001).

As further reflections of the challenge that sprawl development presents to quality of life in Lancaster County, the county has been designated on two different endangered places lists. In September 1997 the World Monument Watch included Lancaster County on its list of the 100 Most Endangered Sites in the world along with the Taj Mahal and

Angkor Wat. This listing was effective for the period 1998–2000 and later was renewed for the period 2000–2002. In a separate action, in June 1999 the National Trust for Historic Preservation designated the county as one of the 11 Most Endangered Places in the USA. The latter listing generated a great amount of discussion and debate in the county, and both the Pennsylvania Builders' Association and the National Association of Home Builders expressed objections and mounted a public relations counteroffensive.

Efforts to restrain sprawl development and to preserve farmland and the rural countryside for the future enjoyment of both residents and visitors are reflected in the goals of the Lancaster County Comprehensive Plan that dates from the 1990s. To implement the goals of the plan, the county has used such techniques as the establishment of urban and village growth boundaries and the purchase of easements on farmland. Despite the partial success of these and other techniques, sprawl development continues to be a problem in various parts of the county.

Whereas the UK and other European countries have a top-down planning system that gives government considerable authority over private land use decisions and makes it easier to prevent unwanted sprawl, the US system reflects more individualistic values and also emphasizes more of a bottom-up planning approach. Therefore, in order to implement the county comprehensive plan, county government must depend heavily on the cooperation of local governments, which have zoning and subdivision authority, and of private organizations, businesses, and individuals. Consensus building is an inherent part of successful implementation of a plan.

In 2001 Lancaster County announced a new Smart Growth initiative to help build the necessary coalition for implementing further the goals of the comprehensive plan. Smart growth is defined by the county government as growth that sustains the local economy, that enhances the livability of the community, that maintains or improves the quality of the environment, and that thereby enhances the quality of life. One of the stated themes of the Smart Growth initiative is the reduction of the sprawl development that is causing concern among many county residents.

Sprawl, overdevelopment, and loss of farmland were also mentioned as concerns in the author's late 1999 survey of tourism operators as well as in follow-up focus group meetings (for further discussion, see Hovinen, 2002). Although tourism development has contributed to overall development and to loss of farmland, it is clear that most of the sprawl and other development has taken place in other sectors of the economy. Nevertheless, if limits are not placed on such development, one of the principal reasons for visitors from large nearby metropolitan areas to choose Lancaster County as a destination will be diminished and tourism might suffer in the long run. In discussing sustainable tourism, one must therefore recognize the relationship between tourism and other sectors.

The transformation of the Amish attraction

In a diversified county tourism industry, the Amish are no longer the principal attraction as they were into the mid-1980s period. Most people who now visit on short getaway vacations or on day trips from nearby metropolitan areas have been to the county before and have experienced the Amish already. Nevertheless, the Amish and a pleasant rolling countryside of small farms still comprise important elements of the county image. The Amish and rural scenery are parts of the general environmental context of the tourist experience even as tourists today primarily undertake other activities, such as shopping, attending theater performances, and dining.

During the tourism growth years of the 1960s and 70s, there was much concern expressed about the exploitation of the Amish as unwilling tourist objects and the harm this might do to their conservative culture (Hovinen, 1982). In the past, some Amish religious leaders also expressed concern about tourism's potential to undermine authentic Amish agricultural heritage (Hovinen, 1995).

One tourism strategy that eased some of the pressure on the Amish themselves while providing opportunities for mass tourists to satisfy their curiosity about Amish lifestyles was the establishment of staged attractions such as the Amish Farm and House and the Amish Village along the main highways. These attractions gave many tourists a quick front stage experience of some aspects of Amish culture without the Amish themselves being present. They were criticized by scholars, however, as violating standards of authenticity (Hovinen, 1995). One staged attraction, the Amish Country Homestead in Bird-in-Hand, did win approval as an authentic heritage site in the 1990s county heritage program. Although the house tour does not use a building constructed or ever owned by Amish, a member of the Amish community verified that the interpretation provided an accurate view of how Amish now live. By contrast, the Amish Village is a particularly egregious example of lack of authenticity, as the Amish do not live in villages.

Even with these staged attractions helping to separate many tourists from the Amish, other tourists engaged in insensitive and offensive behavior on guided bus tours, while roaming the countryside in their own cars, or on encountering Amish conducting business in communities such as Intercourse. Not surprisingly, many Amish developed an aversion to tourism. It is therefore ironic that growing numbers of Amish in the main tourism district have not only accommodated themselves to the realities of tourism but have become active participants in it during the period of the 1990s on. Their psychological carrying capacity towards tourism has in effect been altered. Although the preferred Amish occupation is still agriculture, the shortage and high cost of land together with the natural increase of the Amish population has forced some Amish out of economic necessity to select nonagricultural occupations. Producing and selling farm products and craft items to tourists has become a means for some Amish to earn a livelihood and to remain in Lancaster County. These Amish, who generally practice a boundary maintenance strategy towards the outside world, have been pragmatically experimenting in recent years and have been cautiously shifting the boundary line in order to survive economically. Nevertheless, more conservative Amish outside the main county tourist district cling to the preferred agricultural lifestyle and frown on practices of their more liberal brethren elsewhere. What the ultimate outcome will be for tourism and for the Amish culture remains unclear (for further discussion of this issue, see Hovinen, 1995, 2002).

Some visitors to Lancaster County desire a more authentic backstage experience with the Amish, and the increasing Amish participation in tourism has accommodated them. In addition to interacting briefly with Amish children or adults selling fresh farm products or craft items such as quilts at their farms, tourists may be able to eat home-made ice cream on Amish farms or even to partake of a meal in an Amish home for a cash 'donation'. Some tourism operators and local elected officials regard eating in an Amish home as an important cultural exchange opportunity, especially for foreign visitors. In early 2002, one Amishman estimated that about 15 local Amish families provided such meal services in their homes (Smart, 2002). Often operators of bed and breakfast establishments arrange for such in-home experiences, and demand for them is growing. Certain Amish bishops have given the practice a tentative endorsement as a way for Amish farm families to supplement their income. However, state health authorities have pointed out that Amish families must be licensed to serve such group meals, just as regular restaurants are. To receive a license, an inspection of kitchen conditions must occur. Amish are unwilling to subject themselves to such government authority and intrusion of their privacy. So generally such arranged meals have been handled rather secretly. The issue came to a head in the summer of 2001 when a group of tourists who had just left Lancaster County became ill and some had to be hospitalized with a bacterial infection. To avoid a major fine, the Amish family in question had to promise not to serve home-based meals again. Despite this, some local elected officials argue that in general Amish kitchens are very clean and that the importance of the cultural exchange is a strong argument for excluding the Amish from the licensing requirements (Smart, 2002).

The tourism industry and sustainable tourism

In order for a tourism destination to remain competitive and thereby to support the goal of achieving sustainable tourism, the tourism industry should emphasize unique attractions rather than relying mainly on standardized and 'artificial' attractions imported from the outside. One long-term strength of county tourism has been the unique Amish population with their distinctive culture. But to sustain tourism at a high level of visitation it is necessary to develop additional unique attractions. This has been one of the goals of the Lancaster County heritage tourism program since its inception in the mid-1990s.

Two recent examples of attempts to foster new unique heritage attractions may be noted. The first involves rediscovering Lancaster's role in the planning of the Lewis and Clark expedition across the North American continent from 1803 to 1806. The second involves the proposed designation of a new historic site in the center of Lancaster City to emphasize the role of a prominent pre-Civil War era congressman as an early civil rights advocate. Neither one alone is likely to make much difference in county tourist numbers or revenues, but together with other existing and potential attractions each could help sustain tourism. The Visitors Bureau has been invited by private nonprofit organizations, as part of an evolving public–private partnership arrangement, to help promote the first of these initiatives, whereas a private nonprofit organization is the sponsor of the second.

Captain Meriwether Lewis, an aide to President Thomas Jefferson, spent three weeks in Lancaster in the spring of 1803. In Lancaster he received training form Andrew Ellicott, Secretary of the State Land Office and one of the country's foremost mathematicians, astronomers, and land surveyors, in the use of scientific instruments for accurately determining latitude and longitude on the journey of discovery to the Pacific Coast. Lancaster was the capital of Pennsylvania at this time.

The Bicentennial of the Lewis and Clark expedition will be held from 2003 to 2006 and will involve communities from the Atlantic to the Pacific. Given Lancaster's important role in the initial planning of the voyage, a public–private partnership of organizations is planning a series of exhibits and events, including one in the house where Lewis and Ellicott worked. By publicizing the planned activities in brochures and on a web site, the Visitors Bureau and the county government hope that visitors will come and learn more about this colorful part of American history. At the same time, they may also be exposed to the variety of other heritage attractions that the county has to offer.

The proposed Thaddeus Stevens and Lydia Hamilton Smith historic site in the center of Lancaster would educate visitors about an abolitionist attorney and later congressman who helped finance a spy network to infiltrate slaveholder groups that tried to track fugitive slaves escaping the South. His housekeeper and confidante, who lived in an adjoining house to the Stevens law office (both proposed for restoration), assisted escaping slaves. She also encouraged Stevens' efforts as a congressman to ratify two important amendments to the US Constitution granting full rights of citizenship to newly freed blacks after the Civil War. The Historic Preservation Trust of Lancaster has commissioned an economic impact study that estimates annual visitation to a proposed museum and revenues that it might generate. As of September 2002, the Trust anticipated that the historic site would complement a planned convention center adjacent to it and would generate some visitors therefrom. In 2001 the Lancaster County Convention Center Authority, which is planning the convention center, had thought it easier simply to remove the historic buildings in question from the site. However, the Historic Preservation Trust eventually succeeded in signing an agreement with the convention center authority to preserve the historic buildings. In September 2002 new plans for the convention center were in preparation, emphasizing respect for the existing streetscape and incorporation of historic structures. An architectural design firm also hopes to incorporate elements of the indigenous architecture of downtown Lancaster into the appearance of the planned convention center facility.

The planning process for the new Lancaster–York Heritage Region can also help make tourism more sustainable. One of the most important heritage resources of Lancaster County and neighboring York County that tourists find attractive is their agricultural landscape and the related farming activities. Of five heritage themes identified in the plan for the two-county heritage region, one is 'foodways: from farm to table' (Mary Means & Associates, 2001: 28–37). A grant from the state of Pennsylvania and contributions from the two counties' visitor bureaus are helping to finance an agritourism initiative. The Lancaster County Planning Commission is coordinating the effort. In August 2002 representatives of public and private organizations from both counties, working in a collaborative partnership, approved plans for a regional interpretive and informational guide and corresponding website. The guide and website were completed by 2003 and interpret regional agricultural heritage and list farm markets, historic downtown markets, roadside market stands, pick-your-own operations, wineries, and other sites where homegrown fresh or processed food can be purchased directly from the farmer.

Agarwal's (1994, 2002) proposed reorientation stage and restructuring alternatives are relevant to the tourism planning efforts noted above. There is recognition in Lancaster County that tourism is a mature industry and that a certain amount of renewal is necessary to prevent overall decline and to sustain moderate growth. Restructuring alternatives evident in the efforts discussed so far include new investment and product specialization (proposed downtown Lancaster convention center), repositioning by emphasizing unique heritage and environmental attributes, further diversification, preservation of the built and natural environment, and collaboration (initiation of joint public–private sector ventures).

In contrast to the aforementioned state-supported heritage planning programs where the initiative for a public–private sector venture has come mainly from government, the impetus for yet another potential tourism planning effort has come from within the tourism industry itself. As this is the first time a proposal for a long-range proactive planning process has originated from within the tourism industry, it is especially significant.

In early 2002 a secret task force, consisting of a half dozen members of the tourism industry with a long-range perspective, emerged. The task force was initiated by a local tourism operator who is very familiar with the TALC model and who is concerned with the potential for future decline in county tourism if strategic long-range planning and restructuring do not occur. This businessman contacted one of the elected county commissioners to attempt to gain his support for a collaborative tourism planning effort.

In June 2002 the author was invited to attend a meeting of this task force to discuss the TALC model and the need for long-range strategic planning. One prominent topic discussed at this meeting was how to achieve a more sustainable tourism. The author presented various ways of looking at sustainable tourism and tourism planning and advocated a planning approach based on broad-based community input and recognizing the interdependence of the tourism sector and other economic sectors. Members of the task force, including the county commissioner and the president of the Visitors Bureau, generally expressed support for the ideals espoused at the meeting. In a succeeding session held in July 2002 a tourism consultant from outside the local area met with the task force to help lay the groundwork for a tourism planning effort.

At the time of this writing, the success of this venture is uncertain. There are considerable political and economic risks to such a plan. The current intention of the task force is to announce the proposed tourism plan to the media and to members of the Visitors Bureau at a later date. It is possible that some tourism operators might then question the need for such a tourism plan. Overall political support for the plan from within the tourism industry and from other sectors of the economy would be important, as would be some financial support from the county government. Considering the county government recently announced cutbacks in budgets for 2003, whether it will be able to provide the financial support desired is questionable. Other sources of funding will have to be explored, including the willingness and ability of the Visitors Bureau to finance part of the planning effort.

Obstacles to sustainable tourism within the tourism industry

Despite the evidence that parts of the tourism industry have begun to show support for long-range tourism planning efforts, major obstacles to sustainable tourism remain within the industry. Most tourism operators have little understanding of the role of long-range tourism planning and remain focused on their short-term business operations supplemented by the Visitor Bureau's annual marketing campaigns. The author's study of Lancaster County tourism at the end of the 1990s (Hovinen, 2002) revealed considerable divisiveness within the industry. Tourism owners have widely varying viewpoints about a number of issues affecting tourism growth. Owners often disagree with Visitors Bureau staff about the causes of stagnation or decline of individual businesses. The former tend to blame ineffective marketing and promotion by the Visitors Bureau, whereas the latter point to the reluctance of many operators to reinvest in new products or in improved facilities and service quality. Therefore, developing a consensus within the industry for a long-range tourism plan will be a major challenge.

A recent example of bitter divisiveness within the tourism industry is the legal battle between 11 hoteliers and sponsors of a new Marriott Hotel and associated public convention center in downtown Lancaster. The proposed hotel–convention center project is an example of a public–private partnership in an attempt to revitalize the city's downtown and to make the city and its important heritage resources a stronger tourism destination. Plans call for the hotel to occupy space in a former department store and thereby preserve century-old architectural heritage. Sponsors hope the project will attract a new, more affluent market segment of convention visitors to spend money in the city and become aware of its attractions. The Visitors Bureau has officially supported the project, which is financed in part by a new hotel/motel room tax that began in January 2000. The Visitors Bureau and its members had for many years opposed such a tax, but a portion of the tax collected now helps support the Bureau's annual tourism marketing.

In March 2000 the 11 hoteliers began a legal challenge to the fairness of the tax, claiming that it in effect subsidized their potential competitors. The Marriott Hotel that would be developed by a consortium of three private businesses would share some space and facilities with the public convention center financed by the room tax and a potential $15 million state grant, lawyers for the hoteliers have argued in court. Therefore, they maintained, the private hotel would in effect be subsidized with public funds and would compete unfairly against hotels and motels in suburban locations. The fact that several of these suburban hotels had conference facilities was the basis for another claim of unfair public subsidies of a public convention center that would compete against private facilities.

The complicated and often bitter legal battle has dragged on for 2½ years. Sponsors and supporters of the public convention center project have often complained in the local media that the hoteliers who have filed legal challenge after challenge are simply trying to kill an important project. The Marriott Corporation has threatened to withdraw from its agreement to manage the privately built hotel if construction cannot begin by March 2003. The large state grant for construction of the convention center cannot be tapped until the legal challenges are resolved. In July 2002 the Pennsylvania Supreme Court rendered an important decision in favor of the public convention center by declaring that the disputed room tax for financing the convention center was constitutional. Such room taxes for public purposes are in fact common in the USA. The Supreme Court sent two other issues of fairness back to a lower state court for resolution, and lawyers for the hoteliers filed additional arguments against the project shortly thereafter. So the future of this project, which exemplifies several of Agarwal's (2002) suggested restructuring alternatives, remained unclear at the time of writing.

Conclusion

This case study has shown that a tourism cycle has been progressing in Lancaster County, although not always in the ways Butler hypothesized in his 1980 TALC model.

Earlier stages of exploration, involvement, and development with many of the characteristics suggested by Butler in his 1980 formulation are clearly discernible. But the county tourism industry is now mature and highly diversified, and problems arise when trying to fit the tourism trends of the past quarter century to Butler's assumptions of a progression to later stages of consolidation, stagnation, and then either possible decline or complete rejuvenation.

In the diversified and essentially culturally based tourism destination of Lancaster County, different sectors of tourism (older versus newer attractions, variety of accommodations, shopping alternatives, chain versus local restaurants) have combined to create what is now a mature industry where growth, stagnation, decline, and revitalization through reinvestment or new investment coexist. One tourism sector, or a portion of a sector, may have results in a given year that contrast with those of another sector. The different elements of tourism can be said to have their own individual life cycles. Some individual businesses thrive in a given year while others stagnate or even decline. An owner of an accommodations facility, for example reported to the author record results for the first six months of 2002 at the same time that some traditional attractions experienced stagnation (personal communication, August 2002). The overall industry may exhibit fluctuating growth patterns year to year based on a complex combination of internal and external factors. A temporary decline, for example, may be followed by a growth spurt as happened when the major attraction Sight and Sound was destroyed by fire and then rebuilt. A number of county tourism businesses apparently benefited in the first half of 2002 from the tendency of many Americans to prefer destinations that they could easily drive to in the new age of terrorism. Such are the characteristics of what the author has termed the 'mature' stage of county tourism.

Butler's TALC model suggests the potential for overall decline of a tourism destination exists if effective long-range planning to address problems and competitive challenges does not take place, thus the prospects for creating a more sustainable tourism in Lancaster County through long-range planning have been discussed in this chapter. The creation of several existing or potential public–private partnerships for long-range planning since the mid-1990s suggest the partial applicability of Agarwal's (1994) proposed reorientation stage as well as at least one of her proposed restructuring alternatives. However, the possible emergence of such a stage in Lancaster County has not followed a clearly defined stagnation stage as Agarwal suggested.

Chapter 6

An Empirical Interpretation of the TALC: Tourist Product Life Cycles in the Eastern Townships of Quebec

JAN O. LUNDGREN

Introduction

Tourist development has been a major focus of scholarly research for over two generations. Contributions have come primarily from environmental and social sciences, basically starting with W. Hunziker's famous, and interdisciplinary 'Tourism Doctrine', published in 1942, and W. Christaller's 'Beiträge zu einer Geographie der Fremdenverkehr' in 1955. Over the decades since, the writings have become both more voluminous and diverse, hardly surprising considering the consistent and vigorous growth in tourism after 1950. Some 60 million international tourist arrivals were recorded in 1960. Today, at the start of the Second Millennium, international travel volume stands at around 700 million, an 11-fold increase (WTO, 2001). In addition, recognising the dominant and massive domestic tourist travel volumes predominantly found in the countries of the Western world pushes the aggregate annual global (tourist) travel volume to levels between 2.5 and 3.0 billion.

Given the above, there is no surprise that the relationship between aggregate tourist travel demand/tourist destination area system (TDAS) is often strained, resulting in detrimental impacting consequences for many TDAS (Turner & Ash, 1974), and, more importantly, to their respective tourist attraction(s) – the geographically definable tourist product (Smith, 1994). The saying '. . .die Zerstörung der Turismus durch Turismus. . .' (Krippendorf, 1975), coined in the mid-1970s, when tourist travel volumes were much smaller, still holds.

Placing the Tourist Development Process in a Conceptual Context

Negative environmental consequences of modern tourism were recognised in the early 1970s – in overvisited national parks and popular nature reserves, mushrooming seaside resorts along the Mediterranean coastline (Ambio, 1977), in packed winter resorts – especially in Europe, and in popular small resort islands, notably in the West Indies (Ambio, 1981). Through the skilful pedagogical conceptualisation of TDA development dynamics by Butler (1980), the implications of unfettered tourism-based TDA development were brought to the forefront of the debate and the 'Tourism Area Life Cycle' (TALC) model was born (Figure 6.1).

Simplified, the TALC model pits two principal variables against each other: the open-ended, market-driven 'growth' factor, slowly rising, then quickly accelerating, but eventually stagnating *a la* W. Rostow's stages-of-economic-growth concept (1960); or the typical marketing/product life cycle (Kotler & Turner, 1993). The 'exploitation-of-limited-resources' variable demonstrates how the development reaches a 'critical range of elements of capacity', which initiates the decline in the capability of the TDA to 'handle'/'absorb' additional tourist influxes (Butler, 1980). This stage often activates secondary and third-rate under-used attractions, which invariably set the TDA on the road toward an increasingly destructive marginality. As the aggregate TDA components face diminishing returns, the development grinds to a halt and usually enters a stage of decline.

The critical factor in the TALC model centres on tourist resource depletion through excessive use. Viewed in the context of today's debate on the pros and cons of tourism-based development, it brings us to concepts not properly parlayed by scholars in the early 1980s. 'Sustainable (tourism-based) development', as emphasised in the Brundtland Commission report on Our Common Future (1987), and 'ecotourism' or

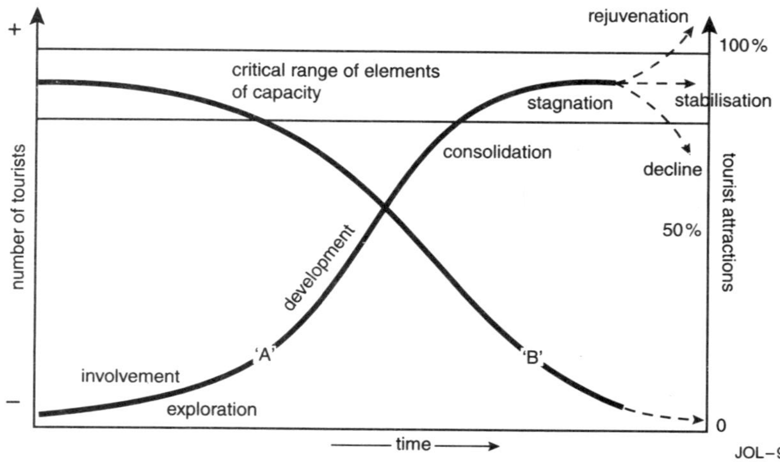

Figure 6.1 Tourist area cycle of evolution (modified from Butler, 1980)

'soft' tourism development were concepts still waiting in the wings (Smith & Eadington, 1994; see also Butler, this volume).

Product Life Cycles and their Spatial Consequences

Butler's model is not a complicated conceptualisation, and therein lies its beauty. Almost a quarter-century old, the TALC is still applied in tourism development case studies, sometimes as a benchmark device, sometimes as a conceptual framework for a more detailed tourism development study, invariably resulting in further fine-tuning of the model, or adding new aspects to the original. The model can easily be complemented with the notion of sequential tourist product (TP) developments (Figure 6.2), which would better reflect the innovative spirit of emerging 'new products', which is frequently stressed in marketing research (Kotler & Turner, 1993; see also Coles & Hall, other volume, editor's comment). In the typical physical production enterprise an 'older', well established on-line product (1) and a 'nascent' new product development cycle (2) often operate side by side. The dynamics of the auto industry, the fashion industry or the hectic consumer electronics company provide examples of this 'parallel' strategy of continuous product development/marketing and ongoing, new product development. Overlapping product cycles interact (Figure 6.2), with the activation of Product 2 dependent upon the duration of successful sales/profit performance of Product 1.

The 'product parallelism' described above also happens in tourism development, where new TDA complementary 'attraction products'

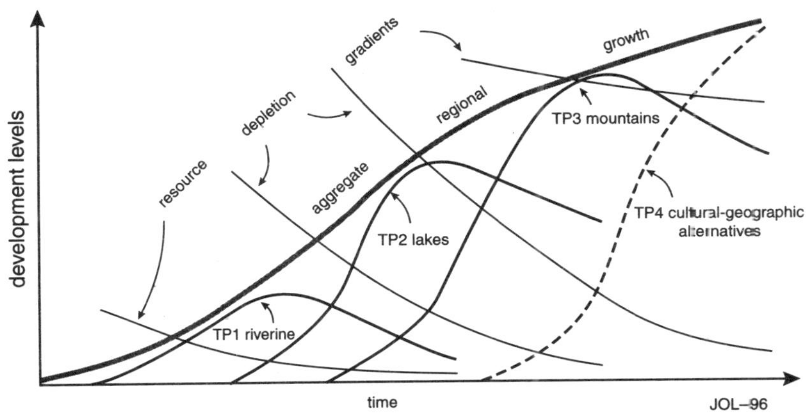

Figure 6.2 Multiple tourist product evolution/exploitation cycles (modified from Kotler & Turner, 1993)

often are grafted onto a well established older one. This has been the case at alpine ski centres that often broaden their market appeal by providing for cross-country skiing, as can be seen at Mt. Orford (Quebec), Stowe (Vermont) or Jasper National Park (Alberta). In a similar vein, the recent construction of a snowboarding 'half pipe' at Owl's Head and many other ski resorts may attract more of the younger snow boarder market clientele. Adding mountain biking during the summer season would obviously represent a 'third' TP cycle, thus making the same mountain destination a profit source even during the hitherto quieter summer season.

Objectives of Study

Sometimes, however, completely new, extra-regional 'tourism products' having little, if any, obvious local affinity with existing tourist attractions emerge, sometimes by accident, and succeed over time in countering stagnating trends experienced by the older attraction. The new TP often has different location characteristics, and therefore produces major shifts in the region's overall tourist geography. The phenomenon of successive new TP cycles in the Eastern Townships (ET) region of Quebec constitutes the principal focus of this review, especially as they relate to the modified TALC model (Figure 6.2). Thus, within the overall regional tourist development, we should be able to observe sequentially layered product cycles *a la* Kotler and Turner, representing diverse, new forms of tourism entering the region.

As a consequence of the introduction of new products, we should also be able to observe a successive and healthy regional TP diversification, which in turn should strengthen regional economic stability, reduce seasonality and partly lower excessive visitor pressures at already developed TP destinations. A final aspect relates to the layers of spatial impacting brought about by the new product cycles that tend to be much less dependent upon specific landscape features. Instead of a TDA having a comparative competitive advantage based on the effective verticals in the topography – typical for alpine ski hill sites – the 'new products' may rely upon completely different factors – unique individual talent, person-to-person interaction, idyllic geographic settings with local ambiance, cultural appeal, a sense of place, local history or combinations thereof. Consequently, to anticipate impacting patterns of new TPs becomes difficult, as they usually are spontaneous rather than planned creations.

Geographical Characteristics of the Study Region

Before analysing the specifics of the different TP life cycles, we must recognise some general landscape characteristics. Basically, the area being discussed is a subregion of the ET in southern Quebec, which broadly encompasses a west-to-east rectangular area. It is bound in the West by the Richelieu River, in the South by the USA/Canada border, and stretches some 100 km eastward to the Sherbrooke–Coaticook–USA border line. The northern limit follows the 140 km long Eastern Townships Autoroute (Figure 6.3), the principal road artery linking Montreal (3 million) to the City of Magog (15,000) and Sherbrooke (100,000).

The region features a gentle downward tilting, northbound extension of the US Appalachian mountains consisting of parallel mountain ridges separated by valleys and elevated plateaus. Starting east of Farnham, the terrain softly rises from the St. Lawrence Plain and becomes more dramatic. CLICOR (Canada Land Inventory Capability for Outdoor Recreation 1971) diligently registers this in the identified landscape scores, that stretch from an omnipresent Class Six (Low Capability) on the Plain via typical Class Five (Moderately Low) to more numerous patches of higher scores, Class Four (Moderate Capability), eventually reaching terrains with Class Three (Moderately High Capability) as well as a few Class Two/One (High/Very High) sites.

Three top-scoring locales demonstrate distinct tourist potentials: the Mt. Sutton and Mt. Orford Station-de-Ski areas and Provincial Park, and the spacious beach strip west of Magog; all are Class One. Impressive mountain topography (800 m elevations) and stretches of fine lakeshore

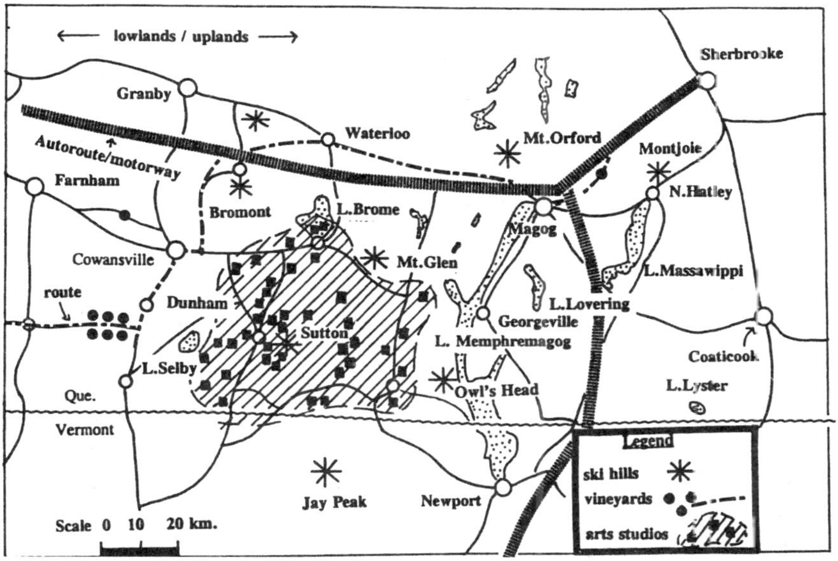

Figure 6.3 Eastern townships tourist resources

always produce top scoring sites – and attract developments. The central part of the study region features numerous mountain peaks with the essential effective verticals of 400–500 m, which would automatically condition their present vocation as alpine ski centres (Figure 6.3).

The climate is 'typical' for southern Quebec – continental, with pleasant winters in its more easterly part, notably east of Granby-Bromont-Cowansville-Dunham, where the 'stable' snow line begins. This guarantees good ski conditions for the seven alpine ski centres (see Figure 6.3), with a business season starting around Christmas and closing in early April. Summers are warm with July day temperatures in the 20–25°C range, usually including two or three week-long heatwaves with temperatures around 30°C. Cooler night temperatures compensate for the daytime heat.

The landscape characteristics also relate to settlement history. The study region has a long settlement history dating back to the 1790s, when United Empire Loyalists moved north, away from republican USA, settling most of the region (Bullock, 1926). This has ensured a particular regional distinctiveness: substantial forest areas alternate with extensive tracts of rolling meadows and cultivated lands; rural New England styled villages and farms invitingly dot the landscape; small but diverse industrial (mill) towns at the edge of rivers with manageable, modest waterfalls offer an interesting industrial cultural heritage; the original predominance of English-speaking settlers and their descendants has diminished in the past century – today's regional population is mostly francophone, but the historical anglophone ethnic/cultural heritage is strong and comes through as a distinct tourist attraction; the region is uniquely and comfortable bilingual, the latter further reinforced by cross-border interaction with neighbouring USA.

Development Characteristics

The background to this review rests on observations by those that have closely followed the region's tourist history. In principle, the traditional bases for early tourist development were in most cases more or less fully exploited, in an accelerating tempo, only in the last 25 years (Fritz-Nemeth & Lundgren, 1996; Lundgren, 1988; Nadeau, 1989). However, reviewing the historical and regional application of the modified TALC tourist development concept, one can observe a clear succession of distinct TP life cycles. It is this regionally based spatial TP succession that constitutes the interpretative part of this study. Thus, below follows a discussion of the TP life cycles experienced by the region, and the extent to which their respective development dynamics relate to the TALC model.

Traditional TP cycles: Riverine and lakeshore tourism developments

Certain types of tourism were responsible for carrying the overall development process over long periods of time. Among these, riverine- and lakeshore-based tourism were early initiators, with their cycles starting in the 1840s, when transport access saw some improvement, but also when a more substantial wealthy urban market segment started to emerge in major urban tourist-generating locales – Montreal in particular. Steamship services along the Richelieu River corridor in the West already operating in 1845 helped to bring in the first tourists. This aided both riverine cottage development and the establishment of commercial tourist resort operations in the foothills of Mont St. Hilaire and at the Fort Chambly rapids (Tulchinsky, 1977). The Lake Memphremagog basin, some 110 km further east, an area hardly accessible at all until the arrival of the railway in the 1850s (to Sherbrooke) and the early 1860s (to Newport, Vermont) also saw major facility developments. The lakeshore Mountain House Hotel at Owl's Head Mountain (1847) catering to the US market was followed three years later by the private Hermitage Club located halfway between Magog and Georgeville on the eastern shore – still thriving 150 years later.

Steamship services gradually integrated otherwise small lakeshore settlements more effectively (Story of Magog, 1951) starting already in the 1850s, with major economic consequences. Thus, both the resorts above, and the two principal urban centres on the lake, Magog, Quebec at its northern tip, and Newport, Vermont in the South, became hubs in a dynamic 'lake economy', with tourism traffic being an important, albeit seasonal, component.

However, a more modern transport infrastructure was needed before the lakeshore-based cottage TP2 cycle (Figure 6.2) could take off. The main bottleneck problem disappeared with the 1859 inauguration of the Victoria Bridge, spanning the St. Lawrence from Montreal, plus an energetic eastbound railway construction programme (Booth, 1982; Briere, 1967). The 1870s saw strategic southbound rail connections effected with the New England rail network (Meeks, 1986, see Figure 6.4). As a result, the US market emerged as an important player in Eastern Townships' tourism development. Thus, well before the turn of the century, the tourist development could forcefully converge upon numerous appealing lakeshores – Brome Lake and Selby Lake, the Mt. Orford Lakes, Lake Massawippi further east – but above all, upon the magnificent Lake Memphremagog.

For each lake, where rail access played an important role, a powerful market-driven 'lake shore cottage subdivision encirclement process' was initiated (Bullock, 1926), a linear land/cottage occupancy process similar

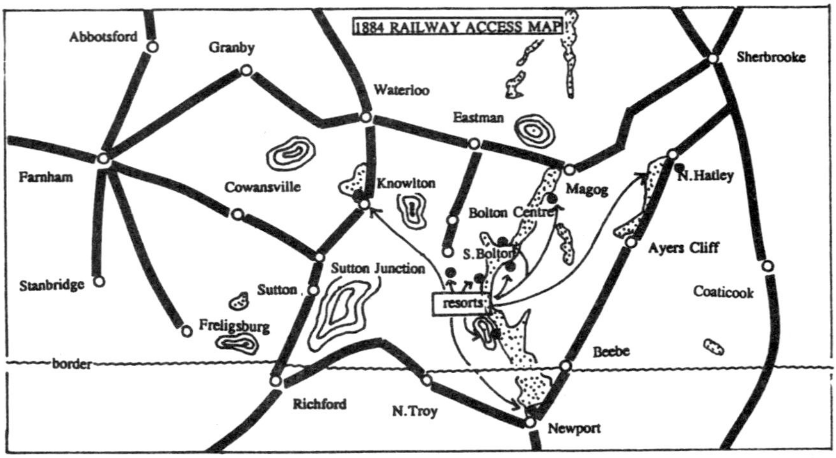

Figure 6.4 1884 Railway access map

to modern urban sprawl roadside subdivisions. It started in earnest in the 1870s but reached its conclusion a century later, between 1975 and 1990 (see Lake Memphremagog 1:50,000 Topographic Map Sheets, 1917–2000 editions). With the final stage in the lakeshore cottage exploitation concluded, the encirclement had succeeded in effectively closing the earlier informally functioning para-public lake access for the larger year-round residential populations. Only occasional fortunate compensations partly remedied the situation, notably for the City of Magog, which in the 1980s secured land for an extensive, new municipal public beach complementing the older public town beach. However, for most lakeshore municipalities, public access to their lakeshore was usually reduced to a few points around the lake. The most popular of summer pastimes – 'going to the public beach' – was practically history. The same extra-regional tourist demand resulted in the advent of steamship services on the lake. Influential outsider Sir Hugh Allen of Allen Steamship Line of Montreal initiated this crucial enterprise, which more than any other transport provision contributed in integrating the 'lakescape' as a major tourist attraction (Potton Heritage Association, 1993, North Troy, Vermont, Public Library Historical File).

As a consequence, small and large commercial lakeshore resort facilities sprang up in strategic locations, sometimes in beautiful lakeshore sites, and sometimes near the two major urban centres on the lake (Wall & Marsh, 1982). Time and fire, however, seem to have been the common destructive agents at work for many of these large wooden encampments. With few exceptions they are now all gone. What remains in terms of concentration of resort facility development can best be seen at the North Hatley end of Lake Massawippi, which to this day retains a reputation as a high-quality resort tourist village, probably one of the most idyllic in Quebec, and gastronomically one of the finest. Hatley Inn, Hovey Manor and Ripplecove Inn are principal magnets for this part of the region.

The final stage of cottage-derived market pressures occurred quite late in the development cycle, primarily in the 1980s and early 1990s, with the introduction of major capital-intensive 'high density' lakeshore cottage/ condominium projects. These exploitations often originated with discreet partial acquisitions by the developer of agricultural properties with substantial shoreline frontage, which, after zoning bylaw modifications had been secured, were developed in a large scale. Villa de l'Anse on the eastern shore of Lake Memphremagog, halfway between Magog and Georgeville, as well as the Owl's Head condominium and hotel project on the lake's western shore, are typical. Similar high density projects are common elsewhere as well: outside Magog, adjacent to the large Plage Municipal, also with a wide range of direct and indirect impacting consequences; and at other lakes in the region, notably the Inverness development on Brome Lake.

Presently, the cottage-based lakeshore TP life cycle has reached its physical carrying capacity limits on most lakes as the encirclement process has run its course. The rate of exploitation has dropped. However, lakeshore property is frequently changing ownership, which often triggers large-scale urban-styled rebuilding projects of older, quaint cottage residences, which suggests that lakeshore cycle dynamics are not completely dead.

Nodal tourist resources: The mountain locales

In contrast to the lakeshores, the TP3 life cycle is based on site-specific characteristics in the physical landscape – the 'mountainscape' and its topographical dimensions. Thus, we deal with a nodal resource, both in appearance and in touristic usage. The Clawson and Knetch (1966) classification of outdoor recreational lands comes to mind, with its differentiation between 'user-oriented resources' and 'resource-based' outdoor recreational areas. The former defines multipurpose outdoor recreation terrains such as sports fields or certain types of (urban) parklands while the latter tends to rely upon some outstanding physical landscape attributes that predetermine one or two kinds of specific outdoor recreational usage. 'Landscape specificity', then, is the key. This gives the TP3 cycle a good fit with the 'ski hill development process', a relatively late arrival on the tourism scene, in the early 1960s.

The CLICOR (1971) landscape differentiation of the study region identifies numerous 'above average' mountains with adequate slope angle, good orientation and effective verticals (calculated from base elevation to mountain summit), that usually have attracted ski hill developers and the establishment of fully fledged alpine ski centres. The existence today of seven ski hill operations – eight including nearby Jay Peak in Vermont – attests to the excellent site potentials for such developments (see Figure 6.2). The cycle as such, however, hides a much longer incubation time than that which meets the eye.

Prior to the advent of modern alpine skiing, which developed around 1930 in the Austrian Alps, Canadian mountain tourism was a summer pastime involving fresh air, nature discovery, hiking and mountain climbing. Any change over to ski-based mountain winter tourism required, out of necessity, a lengthy introductory learning stage, as skiing hardly was an indigenous winter sport. Therefore, even with the first integrated alpine/downhill ski centres opening up and demonstrably being successful in the mid 1930s in the Montreal Laurentians, it took time to activate the market. In fact, the ET region was 30 years *behind* the Laurentians in discovering and launching alpine skiing. This delayed start is remarkable and can only partially be explained by the fact that the Laurentians had access by autoroute and passenger rail services around 1960, however, the first alpine ski centres were established already before WWII, even the least accessible of them all, Mt. Tremblant, which opened for the winter season of 1938/39. The ET region had good access, with railways crisscrossing the landscape well before WWI (Railway Access Map, 1884), to no avail for ski resort development, which did feature early, but hardly in a commercially viable form (an alpine ski facility was established at Mt. Orford in 1938 (Nadeau, 1989).

The true start of TP3 and the full-scale commercial alpine ski development cycle is well known. The year was 1959 and the place was Sutton. The reason was to develop a complementary winter season income for the Belanger family's very seasonal dairy business. The rapid succession of ski centres that followed was remarkable: Mt. Orford (1962), Mt. Glen (1963), Bromont (1964), Mt. Echo (1964), Owl's Head (1965), Jay Peak, Vermont, USA (1956) – the latter functioning with its own, unique cycle – an overall almost explosive regional capital investment and development sequence within a geographically quite confined area; the centres are a half hour's car drive from each other. Except for Mt. Echo, all centres still operate, admittedly sometimes saved through opportune refinancing actions. By virtue of survival, they have now for over 40 years been impacting both their respective mountains and their surroundings, physically, economically and socially. To the above seven should be added two modest places – the recently renovated Montjoie ski centre outside North Hatley, and the equally neighbourhood-oriented centre at Shefford Mountain across the autoroute from Bromont, equidistant between the towns of Granby (45,000 inh.) and Waterloo (5000 inh.).

The convergence of major tourist traffic flows toward the centres have resulted in major local impacting due to the service multiplier factor, almost immediately triggered in order to make each centre properly equipped to meet the service demands from the ever-increasing visitor volumes (Nadeau, 1989). These include trail maintenance and artificial snowmaking, base lodge facilities with food, beverage and after-ski services, ski rentals and ski schools, sports boutiques, and, given the above-average site quality, diverse accommodation: hotels, condominiums, chalets and smaller pensions.

Further, if locations possess summer potential, the opportunity has existed for 'diversifying out' of winter season dependency by converting the locales into year-round resort operations. This has been done at Mt. Orford with the lakeshore city of Magog and its waterfront a 10-minute drive away, and at Owl's Head, with its all-important lake access, apartment hotel and an 18-hole championship golf course. But places deficient on the important point of lake access have diversified also – Bromont and Mt. Sutton today offer mountain biking, tennis, golf and spa services, while others such as Montjoie (North Hatley) and Mt. Glen (Knowlton) benefit from nearby, picturesque village services. The same applies to a degree also for Mt. Sutton with Sutton village in the valley below.

Since 1959 the TP3 cycle has run its course, responding to the seemingly inexhaustible alpine ski demand generated by the metropolitan Montreal market area, and the more distant Lake Ontario urban conglomeration, as well as smaller local towns on both sides of the Canada/USA border. Today, little remains in terms of expansion potential of the basic TP3 phenomenon, although mountains with the essential effective vertical minimum of 500 m still exist. However, the increasingly unreliable winter season may make investor-developers hesitant. Extra-regional competition is greater – from the Laurentians in the North with Intrawest's massive Mont Tremblant expansion, from the Canadian Rockies, and snow-rich Quebec City and Charlevoix in the East. Also, snow boarders do not necessarily need a big mountain-challenging obstacle – designed half-pipe courses do the trick. The threat of global warming might also drive the market northward to more reliable winter seasons (Wall, 1998). Also, the physical impact of mountain developments may be less acceptable in our modern era of environmental–ecological concern. Therefore, any new alpine ski centre developments in the region must be considered unrealistic. The growth dynamics of the TP3 cycle are over.

The Contemporary Era, New TPs, New Cycles

The break with past TP cycles and the injection into the region of new sets of TPs hardly occur at a revolutionary tempo. Rather than the gradual consolidation and stagnation of the resource-based TP3 cycle, regional economic restructuring and a quickening demise of more traditional regional economic sectors – agriculture, and the historically famous regional industrial sector with roots in the small-scale industry developed in the early 1800s – have assisted the easing in of the new. TP2 and TP3 were both spent forces lacking in dynamics toward the end of the 1970s. Hence, if any new tourist-derived regional dynamics were to occur in the TALC model (Figure 6.2), alternative tourism ventures had to emerge. Three new TPS have been selected for analysis in order to demonstrate how new TP cycles become reality and how they differ from the older, more resource-dependent cases discussed so far.

Institutional facilities as tourist attractions

Some embryos for new tourism and new TPs have been regionally rooted for many decades, but their presence was on a very minor scale – diverse cultural institutions, often historical museums, usually supported by enthusiastic local historical societies. The official 2000 Eastern Townships Tourist Guide and the Repertoire de la Societe des Musees Quebecois list some 15 museums, among which the historical museums stand out as the most serious and most resilient enterprises, some not even new, as they date back to the 1920s.

Mississquoi Historical Society Museum (in Stanbridge East), Brome County Historical Society Museum (in Knowlton village) and the Stanstead Historical Society's Colby-Curtis Museum in Stanstead belong to the historical group, all three located in quaint villages. Geographically, their locations are interesting as no deliberate act of planning has been at work, but rather individual local initiatives – and 'luck'! Hence, they can only benefit from proximity to other, popular tourist attractions: near Dunham's popular vineyards ('the Mississquoi'), in idyllic and historic Knowlton village ('Brome County'), and in the urban core of well established and historically stylish Stanstead next to a very busy US border crossing. In contrast, and in addition to the 'historical' institutions, is the modern entrepreneurial/industrial snowmobile inventiveness, the forte behind the Musee Bombardier in off-beat Valcourt, the birthplace of inventor Armand Bombardier, some distance north of the ET autoroute.

Industrial cultural heritage milieus (Fritz-Nemeth & Lundgren, 1996) have in many cases constituted a different basis for the development of outdoor attractions – The Gorge and waterfalls in downtown Coaticook, the renovated turn-of-the-century industrial milieu on the St. Francis river rapids section in central Sherbrooke, and the Stanbridge East mill pond complex are examples of how early regional industrialisation outside the major Canadian urban centres have been 'redesigned' into touristic lures.

The tourist attractions discussed above have very few linkages to the previously discussed TP1-2-3, except for the fact that they cohabit regionally, and consequently benefit from overall convenient access for the touring excursionist.

Rural agricultural attractions

The bucolic ET landscape is constantly referred to in guide books and in conversations with tourists as the principal tourist asset, offering distinctly different seasonal attractions. The rapid post-WWII development boom brought increased societal prosperity which boosted car ownership, which in turn improved spatial mobility for the population at large (CORD Surveys 1969–72). In a regional context, the role of the Montreal population as a tourist-generator and the upgrading of the road system increasingly benefited the whole of the ET region. Touring and day excursion travelling into the region is very much a function of the natural assets. These include apple blossom trips in springtime toward Freligsburgh on the US border, vineyards visits (see Figure 6.3) in Summer and Fall to the popular Dunham area and the recently promoted 150-km long vineyard route (Chemin des Vignobles pamphlet), popular back road bicycling, lake/beach outings in provincial parks, early-Fall U-pick orchard visits or glorious foliage tours, and in winter the design-sharp scenic winter landscape and winter sports.

In this multiseasonal way of recreational/touristic opportunities, the vineyards stand out, for two reasons. First, they represent the beginning of a distinctly new TP cycle, suddenly initiated in 1979, in the Dunham area, basically an apple orchard district south of Cowansville. Second, from at first being a seasonal (harvest-time) attraction, they have extended their appeal to most of the year, winter being the exception. With a three-season spread, the annual visitor volume has grown fast; today's estimate is close to 100,000 (conversations with Dunham vineyard owners, 2000), proof enough of the popularity of the Dunham area as a weekend- or day-excursion destination.

The economic impacting process is spatially very concentrated – the vineyard area is just a 3–4-km country road stretch offering a diverse range of visitor services, wine tasting, restaurant services, picnicking, food/wine boutiques, and crafts and souvenirs, with considerable vertical business integration. Calculating only the basic $5 expense for a wine tasting at the five or six establishments produces only some $500,000 in annual gross sales, but there is clearly more than bottled wines sold, such as foodstuffs and lunches. Economic leakages exist, but still a large portion of the first, second and third round of expenditures remain in the vineyards area and adjacent Dunham village. The vertical integration and local entrepreneurship assure this.

The vineyards seldom operate as a single destination; they are 'stops-en-route', together with many others, all often part of a systematically organised day of touring featuring historical museums, fine art exhibitions, a local summer festival or a theatre matinee, and walking tours.

The artist: A dispersed persona attraction

The fact that the landscape appeal of the ET has manifested itself in the Canadian arts world for almost 200 years leads to the most recent TP development cycle – the artist's studio/the artist's world/the artist's products. The famous historical landscape etchings by W.H. Bartlett date back to the 1830s and early 1840s (JETS, Spring, 1996). Thus, already then, the artist's visual sensuality had discovered the dominating grandeur of Lake Memphremagog with its string of quaint shoreline settlements. Later, in the 1870s, other Canadian painters like E.A. Edson and J.A. Fraser produced panoramic landscape art of still recognisable scenic vistas.

Thus, the artists' local presence is hardly a 'new' TP (Christaller, 1964). However, today's presence is not just of occasional artists, but of coteries of painters, who, together with skilful and talented arts-and-crafts professionals, represent an interesting case of a spontaneous, unstructured recent TP development. Through the formation of loosely organised associations, they have become major tourist attractions and have, jointly, instigated an intensive and vigorous new TP cycle.

The oldest coterie is that of the 'Tour-des-Arts' (TdA), started in 1988, with some 40 artist members (TdA 2002 pamphlet), all opening the doors of their studios/ateliers to the general public during a hectic 10-day period each July. The membership is spatially quite concentrated (Figure 6.3). With few exceptions, the TdA members, when moving into the region, have tended to avoid high-priced lakeshore locations. Rather they have tracked down more low-priced rural cottages, old farm buildings and adjacent barns in back road locations, in the foothills of mountains, or in unassuming locations in the outskirts of villages. Thus, they have successfully avoided areas where property and land have become more directly affected by local tourism development. TdA members also have the privilege of being the first 'past the pole' each Summer (TdA 2002 pamphlet), usually a 10-day period in the second half of July each year, nicely timed for the peak of the tourist season. The financing of the summer programme comes from the membership and local sponsors. The other two organisations – the Circuit-des-Arts (CdA, 1993) centred on Magog and the northern end of Lake Memphremagog, and the Freligsburgh Festiv'art (1996) south of Dunham – are more recent and they also function differently. The CdA usually mobilises over 100 artists, half of them being local and seasonal Fine Art practitioners, for a 10-day summer exhibition programme starting at the end of July, combining open-house studio visits for the public with indoor art shows in strategic locations – in Magog, Georgeville and the famous Elefant Barn, south of Georgeville (CdA 2002 pamphlet). In contrast, the Freligsburgh Festiv'art is an outdoor Fine Art village street market with some 150 participants (culled from 300 applications but including only a few local resident artists. The majority comes from a wider region, particularly metropolitan Montreal, only an hour's car drive away.) Among the three, only the CdA receives government funding.

The aggregate impacting of the fine art TP is difficult to gauge. Visitor statistics for the individual studios are notoriously unreliable. However, a 1995 TdA survey of studio guestbooks recorded 20,000–25,000 visitors. The 2002 Freligsburgh Festiv'art supposedly attracted over 50,000 during its Labour Day weekend programme. Close proximity to Montreal is a vital factor behind the large number (Lavasseur interview).

Given the above, the economic multiplier is hard at work, and in the Freligsburgh case strongly concentrated on the village. Economic leakages are substantial, however, due in part to the many extra-regional artists participating. To the purchases of art objects can be added many other visitor expenditures, including parking, dollar expense among village-based service actors, which in turn pumps the tourist dollar back into the village economy. Studio visits, visits to exhibition halls or walks through a Fine Art street market represent the principal TP attraction, at least the pretext for the visit – while the intricacies of the multiplier are place created and offered beyond the Fine Art experience per se.

Summary and Conclusions

The purpose of this review has been to relate tourist-based regional development dynamics to the cycle concept expounded in the TALC model. Hence, the review covers a section of the ET area in southern Quebec well suited for the exercise, as the region has been exposed to tourist development dynamics over the past 150 years. This means that the region has experienced typical Canadian tourism development characteristics of both earlier eras and new, more recent TP cycles. Looking back on the empirical material presented, certain characteristics deserve emphasis.

First, apart from the recent and new attractions, one can undoubtedly recognise a chronological sequence of TP life cycles already beginning with the exploitation of the very first tourist resources, subsequently creating the distinct development cycles of the 1850–1900 period, and repeated with the activation of subsequent attractions. The successive TP cycles are an unmistakable reality and should be an equally realistic phenomenon in many other tourist regions.

Second, the duration of TP cycles is difficult to establish as is when they start, and when they have they run their full course. In these examples, beginnings can be undistinguishable, but endings finite. This is for instance the case with the TP2 cycle which starts as access improves in the 1850–60s, but does not seem to realise that by now it has reached its end as the prime lakeshore locations are fully occupied. Cottage and condominium development projects may still occur, but the particular lakeshore sitings of the past have now sometimes been replaced with manmade attractions – golf course developments and locations along ski runs up the ski hills, both locations appealing to the active sportsperson and to the active retired individual.

Third, TP cycles often start 'with a bang' – as the ski hill development did. In less than a decade the development cycle, in terms of facility investment, was completed. The cycle still contains dynamics which keep it going, and which should also maintain the cycle on a fairly stable business level for years to come – unless global warming makes the operations uneconomic.

Fourth and finally, modern TP cycles can be quite unpredictable phenomena. In this study, this is true both for some museum-related developments and for the vineyards – but above all for the Fine Art phenomenon. To predict their beginnings is hard, to simulate their development likewise. When their developments start, they are explosive, and location patterns are quite accidental. No tourist development expert working in the 1950s or 1960's ever foresaw their true beginnings and growth, but this may be a common problem in many tourism destinations.

Chapter 7

The TALC in China's Tourism Planning: Case Study of Danxia Mountain, Guangdong Province, PRC

J. BAO and C. ZHANG

Introduction

Danxia Mountain, located in Guangdong, China, is one of the important scenic spots designated by the central government in 1982. Well known for its temple, it is also one of the four famous mountains frequented by tourists in Guangdong. In the early 1990s, the resort experienced a decline in the number of visitors. Tourism experts were invited to tackle the problem in 1993, and they agreed that the resort had fallen into the decline stage of its life cycle because of the declining image of Danxia Mountain. Applying the life cycle model (TALC), they planned a new attraction, Yangyuan Scenic Spot, in order to rejuvenate tourism at Danxia Mountain. Five years later, the mountain came to the rejuvenation stage. In the mean time, some new problems arose. This paper studies and applies the life cycle model theory to this case.

Literature Review

Since the life cycle model was put forward by Butler in 1980, it has been widely accepted around the world, though many arguments have arisen at the same time (Haywood, 1986; Prosser, 1995; Wall, 1982). Different case studies show that different tourist destinations have different characteristics at different stages of their life cycles, especially at the stages of decline and rejuvenation. Nevertheless, Prosser concludes in his review of empirical case studies that the concept of the life cycle provides a useful framework for research that seeks to enhance understanding of development processes and their implications, but the model is not operational enough (Haywood, 1986; Oppermann, 1995). Some scholars argue that these case studies are not credible because the data used for research did not exhibit the properties of uniformity and replication of tourists (Lundtorp & Wanhill, 2001). Moreover, another method for analysing the tourist area's stage of life cycle, the Travel

Balance Approach, was discussed with the aim of replacing Butler's life cycle theory (Toh *et al*., 2001).

The life cycle model was first introduced to China by Jigang Bao in 1993. Since then, various scholars have used it as a descriptive tool for specific case studies. For example, Bao (1994, 1995) analysed the life cycle of large-scale theme parks and karst caves. He found that a karst cave has no obvious exploration and involvement stages, and that shortly after its development stage, visitation to such a cave will decline. Lu (1997) took the famous Huangshan Mountain as an example to examine the life cycle of the mountain resort. He found that most famous mountains had already moved into the development stage, and action was needed to be taken in order to avoid a decline in popularity.

The first application of the life cycle model in tourism planning in China, as noted above, was by Jigang Bao in 1993. He found that Danxia Mountain was in the stagnation stage, and considered that the best way to solve the problem was to develop a new tourist attraction there. After all related factors had been considered, Yangyuan Stone Scenic Spot was chosen as the new attraction and subsequently developed. Danxia Mountain was quickly rejuvenated. Bao (1998) also discussed some other issues of the life cycle, taking the Summer Palace and Seven-star Cave as examples.

As Western scholars had done, Chinese scholars questioned and refuted the theory of the tourism life cycle when it was introduced. In 1996, a paper entitled 'Doubts About the Life Cycle Theory' was published in the journal *Tourism Tribune.* The author (Yang, 1996) argued that the life cycle model was neither convincing in theory nor operational in practice. Yang's discussion was followed by a series of discussions in the academic circle. Yu (1997) put forward a double cycle theory, the long cycle indicating the decline process, the short one indicating the fluctuation caused by external factors. A number of other scholars also contributed to the discussion (Chen, 2001; Li, 1997; Xu, 1997; Yan, 2001).

Based on the analysis of the stage variation in a tourist area, Xie (1995) suggested approaches for controlling the fluctuation of the life cycle curve. Other scholars have used the system dynamic approach to demonstrate the theory of the life cycle model (see, for example, Xu, 2001). The descriptive function of the life cycle model theory has been widely accepted in the West, but some scholars argue that the true test of any theory in applied social sciences is whether it is operational. The main argument is that the criteria for stage identification and criteria for turning points are difficult without hindsight, and different units of analysis lead to different results because of the problem in market homogeneity (Cooper, 1994). The situation is different in China: the data used to analyse the life cycle in a tourist area are the numbers of admission tickets; therefore, the geographic boundary of the research is clear and market homogeneity is guaranteed. This makes study of the life cycle relatively easy in China.

Different Types of Life Cycle Models in China

Life cycle of theme parks

Because the history of theme parks is short in China, it may be still somewhat premature to discuss the life cycle of theme parks now, however, some characteristics of theme parks' life cycle can be concluded (Bao, 1998).

Large theme parks usually need big investment and mass advertisement. Tourists are normally given massive amounts of information about a new theme park and become anxious to see it for the first time. As a result, thousands of tourists tend to swarm into a newly opened theme park. According to a market survey (Bao, 1996), about 30% of the tourists visiting a certain theme park during its opening period had their entrance tickets paid for by their own enterprises or companies. All they wanted was to have 'the first look' and to see 'something new'. Thus the theme park reaches the culmination of its visitation in the first year, and its business slows down from the second year on.

This phenomenon has been demonstrated by many theme parks in China. Generally, the number of visitors at a theme park will fall to the lowest level within 2–5 years. Although it is not convincing to say that this is the decline stage of a theme park, it has been true that a theme park will have to close soon if no new product is developed.

Karst caves

According to many cases studies (Bao, 1995), the life cycle of a karst cave is very special. They usually have no exploration and involvement stages, and their first stage is usually the development stage. Normally, caves isolated from other tourist destinations go directly to the development stage after they are open. They then will experience a short consolidation and stagnation stage, and subsequently come to a close soon afterwards. If a cave is close to a famous tourist destination, the situation will be different.

Because it is dark and dangerous in the karst cave before it is open, only a few local residents would go to it after its initial discovery. When it is better known, tourists tend to flood in. Because there are so many karst caves in China, they can only attract tourists from nearby. The number of tourists normally falls quickly after the initial influx, as shown in the cases in Guangdong and Yunnan Provinces (Bao, 1995). However, if the cave were close to a famous tourist destination, such as Ludi Cave in

Guilin city, tourists to such caves would fluctuate in numbers with those going to the famous tourist destination.

International Level Tourist Destinations

Tourist destinations that attract international tourists usually enjoy very long consolidation and stagnation stages. The Summer Palace can be taken as an example. It has one of the best royal gardens in China, and has been listed as a World Heritage Site since 1998. It is considered to be a must-go place for international tourists. From the available data (the entrance tickets), the number of tourists fluctuated with the economic development of the country during the period 1949–2001. After 1985, The Summer Palace entered into its consolidation stage, but because it is irreplaceable, it will stay in the consolidation stage for a very long time. Similar cases are Huangshan Mountain and The Great Wall (both also World Heritage Sites) (Bao, 1998).

These kinds of international level tourist destinations usually enjoy good business under the right economic circumstances. All the manager has to do is to control the carrying capacity and maintain their images and quality to ensure sustainable development.

Applicability of the Life Cycle Model in China

Stage identification

Although tourism in the modern sense only began in China no more than 30 years ago, the phenomena of travel and sightseeing have been around for more than 1000 years. There was some government involvement in tourism, and although the number of travellers was not recorded, aristocrats and politicians did travel a great deal at the public's expense in historic times. However, virtually all industries, including tourism, were destroyed during the last 100 years in China; therefore, taking this period into account would be irrelevant to life cycle research. It was only after 1949 that China's economy began to prosper and the tourism industry started growing.

After the major political, economic and social reforms in 1978, the government began its involvement in scenic spot development. This marks the development stage in the current research. During the late 1990s, most of the scenic spots in China were crowded with tourists. Some of the facilities were in very poor shape, and their environment was spoiled. These are indications of the stagnation stage and the decline stage. However, mass tourism was only in its early stage, with demand increasing rapidly from the market. Therefore, the stagnation stage in the Chinese context may be temporary and caused by external factors rather than internal developments or policy. Improving and strengthening the management of the attractions involved could rejuvenate them.

Data collection

Another issue with the life cycle model is that the theory is difficult to calibrate because of the lack of long-term data on visitor numbers and sales. Many of the studies in the past have been based on island tourism. The number of visitors was obtained from traffic tolls. This makes the data reliable but also causes a problem in market homogeneity. The tourists who reach an island by vehicle may go there for different purposes. Some may do sightseeing; some may be taking a holiday. In China, only the tourists who purchase a ticket can enter a scenic spot. For a very long time, a Chinese tourist's purpose in going to an attraction was to sightsee. As a result, ticket counts guaranteed both the accuracy of the number of visitors and market homogeneity. This makes the ticket count a reliable source of data for the analysis of a destination's life cycle. On the other hand, as China's tourism industry develops, the purposes of the Chinese tourists will become more varied, which will create a problem with respect to market homogeneity.

Unit of analysis

In terms of research on the life cycle of an attraction, the level of aggregation is problematic and must be clearly addressed. Geographical scale is of considerable importance for a tourist destination's life cycle, because in the Chinese context each destination has a single product rather than having different hotels and other facilities as well. Depending on the scale taken, a destination may be seen to be at a different stage in the cycle. The unit of analysis is, therefore, crucial. As noted earlier, some scholars argue that life cycle assumes a homogeneous market and a perfectly logical stance would be for different scales of a destination to contain different market segments. Some scholars argue that using different units of analysis will lead to different conclusions and will affect the reliability of the life cycle model. In the case studies in the literature, some experts took a county as the unit of analysis (Haywood, 1989; Lundtorp, 2001), while others took an island as the unit of analysis (Cooper & Jackson, 1989; Weaver, 1990). Different scales may bring about different tourist products, and different tourist products may vary a great deal over the long term, making the life cycle model of a destination much more complicated (Hovinen, 2002), thus increasing the difficulty in research. However, in China, every scenic spot has a distinct boundary, and the number of admission tickets sold shows the number of visitors within that boundary, thus variations in the numbers sold reflect the real situation in that tourist area. This is a system that facilitates the life cycle research.

The Application of the Life Cycle Model in Danxia Mountain

Danxia Mountain and Red Stone Park

Danxia Mountain is one of the most popular scenic spots and geological parks in China. It is located in northern Guangdong province, 9 km south of Renhua County. It is 56 km away from Shaoguan City, its main area being about 180 km^2. Red stone and hills are typical characteristics of the Mountain. It is where the term 'Danxia Landform' originated, thus giving the developed tourist attractions in Danxia Mountain the recent new name Red Stone Park. Before the new attraction was developed, the area opened to tourists was about 3.5 km^2. About 1200 years ago, a temple was built in Danxia Mountain. Later, this became one of the most famous temples in Guangdong. As a result, Danxia became an important pilgrimage destination, as well as a place for sightseeing and watching the sunrise.

The decline and rejuvenation of Danxia Mountain

People started to visit Danxia Mountain as long ago as about 1000 years. For the convenience of this research, the period of the late 1970s is taken as the beginning of the development stage in Danxia Mountain. Inadequate management and competition from other resorts eventually caused visitation to Danxia Mountain to decline. The number of tourists stopped growing and overnight tourists decreased in numbers. Although efforts were made to counteract this trend (including sales promotion in Hong Kong and special express train service between Shaoguan and Shenzhen), the number of visitors remained low.

In 1993, Professor Jigang Bao was invited to work on improving the old tourist attraction in order to revive its popularity. Bao decided that the decline was the result of an image crisis at Danxia Mountain caused by poor management of the resource, and that the way to solve the problem was to plan a new attraction to improve the image of the Mountain and then rejuvenate it. Reflecting the situation of Danxia Mountain, and taking into account factors such as the state of the facilities, and the uniqueness of the resort, the planners chose to feature the Yangyuan Stone as the main attraction. The Yangyuan Stone is a stone that is 28 m in height and 7 m in diameter, and is in the shape of a phallus.

Red Stone Park includes both the old and new attractions in Danxia Mountain. It began to receive tourists in 1995. The number of tourists has climbed steadily since it was opened (Figure 7.1).

It should be pointed out that after the development of the Red Stone Park, the new scenic spot (represented by the Yangyuan Stone) and the

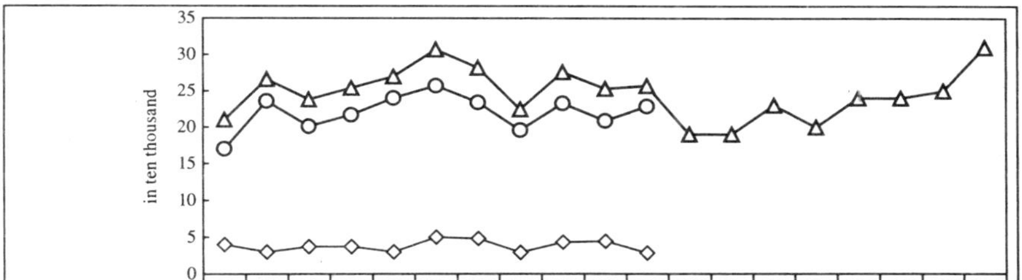

	1982	1983	1984	1985	1986	1987	1988	1989	1990	1991	1992	1993	1994	1995	1996	1997	1998	1999	2000
Domestic tourist	17	23.6	20.1	21.7	24	25.7	23.4	19.56	23.28	20.87	22.87								
Overseas tourist	4	3	3.7	3.7	3	5	4.8	2.91	4.3	4.42	2.82								
Total	21	26.6	23.8	25.4	27	30.7	28.2	22.47	27.58	25.29	25.69	19	19	23	20	24	24	25	31

Figure 7.1 The number of tourists to Danxia Mountain (old scenic spot) from 1982 to 2000
Source: Danxia Mountain Administrative Bureau

old one (represented by the temple) sold admission tickets separately. Therefore, Figure 7.2 does not show how many tourists the new scenic spot brought to the old one. However, it does indicate that the increase of tourists to the old scenic spot is closely related to the new scenic spot.

A search was made on the Internet to examine the material and information about the destination in order to confirm the rejuvenation of Danxia Mountain. The tourism industry has been one the first industries in China to take advantage of the convenience of the Internet. Almost all big travel agencies, scenic spots and hotels have their own web pages. Most of the commercial websites have special columns to promote tourist products. In order to make the web page more attractive, the best part of a destination and the best designed products would be advertised. These become the selling points of the destination, and the key component of the destination's image, which can be taken to reflect the demands of the market.

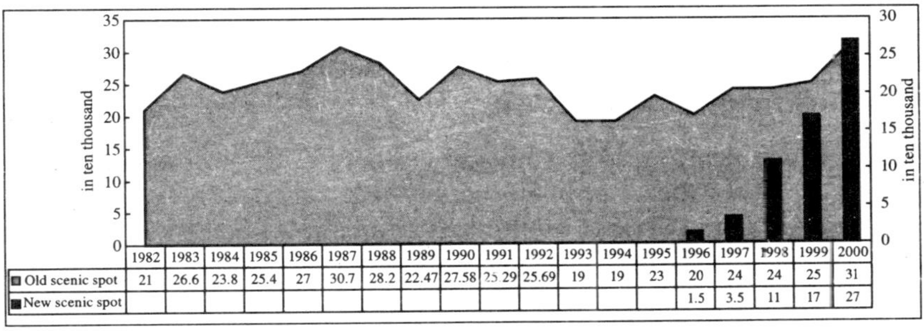

	1982	1983	1984	1985	1986	1987	1988	1989	1990	1991	1992	1993	1994	1995	1996	1997	1998	1999	2000
Old scenic spot	21	26.6	23.8	25.4	27	30.7	28.2	22.47	27.58	25.29	25.69	19	19	23	20	24	24	25	31
New scenic spot															1.5	3.5	11	17	27

Figure 7.2 The number of tourists to the old and new scenic spots
Source: Danxia Mountain Administrative Bureau

Table 7.1 The selling points of Danxia Mountain on the commercial websites

Searching key words	*Results*	*Percentage (%)*
Tourism + tourist itinerary + Shaoguan + Danxia Mountain	497	100
Tourism + tourist itinerary + Shaoguan + Danxia Mountain + Yangyuan Stone	18	3.62
Tourism + tourist itinerary + Shaoguan + Danxia Mountain + sunrise	24	4.82
Tourism + tourist itinerary + Shaoguan + Danxia Mountain + Biechuan Temple	10	2.01
Tourism + tourist itinerary + Shaoguan + Danxia Mountain + sightseeing	77	15.5
Tourism + tourist itinerary + Shaoguan + Danxia Mountain + taking holiday	46	9.26
Tourism + tourist itinerary + Shaoguan + Danxia Mountain + meeting	46	9.26
Tourism + tourist itinerary + Shaoguan + Danxia Mountain + recuperating	8	1.61

Searching time 19:31 – 19:47, 1 January 2002

A search of the Internet showed that the rejuvenated old scenic spot is still the most important selling point of Danxia Mountain. The new scenic spot is also one of the important selling points of the tourist area (Table 7.1), and this coincides with the authors' assumption. It is clear that the old scenic spot in Danxia Mountain is still favoured by tourists. It also explains the decline that was experienced in the 1990s: some factors negatively affected its image but it was rejuvenated after the image improvement through the development of the new scenic spot.

Conclusion and Discussion

Since it was introduced to China, the theory of the Tourist Area Cycle of Evolution has been applied widely. Its successful application in tourism planning in Danxia Mountain demonstrates that the right unit of analysis can identify the right stage of the tourist area if the admission ticket count is used as research data. The model can also be used for the tourism planning of an attraction.

When the theory of the life cycle model is used in China, it is inappropriate to take into account the period before 1949. The period after the reform and open policy in 1978 is a suitable point from which to benchmark the development stage for life cycle research. Recently, some scenic spots have begun to show signs of deterioration. This may be the result of the negative effects of an image crisis caused by external factors. Under these circumstances, the image of a tourism destination can be amended through exploiting new attractions that are appealing to tourists.

Resorts that are newly exploited are likely to come into the development stage quickly because their external condition is relatively mature, but they may soon face stagnation and decline if there is lack of good planning and management, confirming the original argument of Butler's model.

Part 3
The TALC in Heritage Settings

RICHARD W. BUTLER

As discussed earlier, the concept of carrying capacity was, from the beginning, an integral part of the TALC and the process of resort development discussed in the model. While all destinations have some inherent merit and warrant appropriate management, including even those created specifically for the tourism industry, for those destinations whose attractiveness is based on some aspect of heritage, the importance of operating within the limits of their capacity is particularly important. Not only does their existence as a tourist destination depend on the existence and quality of their heritage resources, but perhaps more importantly, the heritage resources themselves need to be safeguarded from overuse or misuse and subsequent degradation (see Butler, other volume). The importance of preserving the heritage aspects of destinations is crucial, whether these be natural or cultural in nature, and the chapters in this next section examine the application of the TALC in a variety of heritage situations.

Boyd discusses the issues involved in applying the TALC to national parks, using the specific case of national parks in Canada. Many of Canada's national parks are significant tourist destinations, none more so than the oldest park, Banff, and they provide good examples of how tourism use and development, over more than a century in some cases, can impact on the parks' natural resources and require continual evaluation of and changes in policy and management. The significant shifts in the policies practised by Parks Canada and its predecessor agencies are reviewed and the contemporary policies examined in the light of the processes outlined in the TALC and the concept of sustainable development. While Boyd's paper is not the first to discuss the TALC in the context of parks, it provides by far the most detailed and extensive discussion on this topic. (A discussion of the conceptual issues raised in applying the TALC to a wider range of protected areas is contained in Weizenegger, other volume.)

The second chapter in this section, by Russo, builds on his earlier work in discussing what he terms the 'vicious circle' of essentially negative feedbacks in the tourism development process in a variety of locations, whereby the negative effects of tourism upon destinations results in a reduction in attractiveness that in turn results in a range of other problems, ending in a downward spiral of investment and quality. He uses the case of Venice to illustrate this process, thus providing an example of the application of the TALC to both a heritage situation and a traditional urban settlement which operated for much of its life as a 'normal' urban centre. While Venice has a long history of attracting visitors, its rise as a modern tourism destination is relatively recent and the problems which Russo analyses can be seen as very contemporary in their nature and cause. The problems that Venice faces, an old infrastructure, a declining population, decreasing tax base and an increasing proportion of day to overnight visitors, are common to many historic urban centres. While Venice has unique problems in addition because of the physical nature of its setting, these are only compounded by the pressures of tourism. The implications which can be drawn from Venice have application to a considerable number of other tourism heritage destinations.

The final chapter in this section deals with the application of the TALC with respect to heritage sites and properties, and in particular with the issues of marketing such attractions in a manner that maintains both their heritage qualities and their tourist attractiveness. Malcolm-Davies discusses the basic problems resulting from the differences in approach to the marketing and development of heritage sites in the public and the private sectors. Whereas the private sector is willing to renovate and rejuvenate its product, the public sector is often either unwilling or unable to provide the necessary funds to allow the site to avoid a decline in attractiveness and quality to visitors. She reviews the marketing approaches and their relevance to the TALC process in the context of the future roles of heritage sites in tourism.

Chapter 8

The TALC Model and its Application to National Parks: A Canadian Example

STEPHEN W. BOYD

Introduction

This chapter differs considerably from the majority of chapters in this book as it addresses how Butler's (1980) Tourism Area Life Cycle (TALC) model can be applied outside of the tourism context. The focus of the chapter is on national parks, with a case study presented on the development of the Canadian national park system and how Butler's model may be applied in this specific context. While national parks are a relatively recent phenomenon compared to protected areas in general, it is well acknowledged that they are important spaces for leisure, recreation and tourism (Butler & Boyd, 2000). While their location remains constant, the purpose of use varies between those making use of national parks as a local recreation venue and those entering the parks as domestic or international tourists. In many cases, local recreation users make up the majority of visits, Banff National Park in Western Canada being a good example of this. Regardless of whether visits are for recreation or tourism, the concern that many parks face today is pressure from visitors and therefore the distinction between the nature of users becomes meaningless. An argument to be put forward in this chapter is that the TALC model has applicability as a useful guide to trace park development, measure the extent of development and to avoid overuse. The author, therefore, has undertaken three tasks. First, the extent to which the evolutionary elements of the Butler model can be used to describe how individual parks and entire park systems are developed is examined. Second, visitor data for Canadian national parks between 1993 and 1997 and information on impacts, threats and the condition of parks are used to locate individual parks along the curve of the TALC model. And third, a general discussion is presented that explains the mechanisms that are available for park management to avoid parks moving towards the latter stages of the model and numbers overreaching the zone of critical limits of capacity.

The Lack of Application of TALC to Other Leisure Environments

The TALC has probably been the most written about model developed within tourism research, and the contributions in these two edited volumes of works are testament to this fact. One of the reasons for its popularity is the relative simplicity of the model itself, demonstrating that destinations evolve, change and in doing so may pass through a number of identifiable stages (exploration, involvement, development, consolidation, stagnation, decline or rejuvenation). Based on two very different principles, those of the product life-cycle and animal population growth, the pattern of development resembled that of an S-shaped curve where growth was finite and dependent upon recognition that there existed capacity limitations beyond which growth could not be sustained. It is argued that this capacity would vary according to type of setting and that stagnation or possible decline in tourism would result if capacity limitations were indeed exceeded (see Butler, this volume). The latter feature is often less discussed when the model has been reproduced and critiqued by other researchers. Butler himself, in a review of his model in 1990, noted that the majority of the discussions concerning the model had been focused on applying it in various locations from which the findings have been compared and contrasted with the original postulations made by Butler in 1980.

While the literature on the model and its application within specific contexts is vast, commentary has been generally supportive of the model. Wall (1982) and Haywood (1986) were perhaps the first to raise some issues such as the ability to identify actual stages of development as well as the use of the product life-cycle itself. Despite early criticism, the model has been applied and presented in case study form for destinations as diverse as Lancaster County, Pennsylvania (Hovinen, 1982), Canada's Northwest Territories (Keller, 1987), the Bahamas (Debbage, 1990) and the Grand Cayman Islands (Weaver, 1990), and has been the topic of update and review (Agarwal, 1994; Cooper, 1994). Butler (1990), in his own review, talked of the applicability of extending the model beyond that of a particular tourism destination to tourism development in a broad regional context and to applying the model to specific types of tourism in a region such as heritage tourism in a developing world destination (see Butler, 1997). While the model was developed primarily for tourist destinations and for tourism in a region in general, there have been relatively few applications in other leisure-oriented settings such as national and provincial parks, although the contributions by Eidsvik (1983) and McKay (1990) should not go unnoticed. This is relatively surprising, given the comments offered earlier in the chapter that national parks more than provincial or other parks are increasingly been sought out by tourists, and are becoming increasingly reliant on revenue from tourism to justify their existence. In many cases national parks, particularly those being inscribed with World Heritage status, are emerging not just as tourist attractions and part of the overall tourism experience but rather specific tourist destinations and the entire tourism experience in their own right. This latter development is a consequence of many national parks emerging as leading ecotourism and natural heritage destinations.

Historical Review of the Development of the Canadian National Park System: The TALC as Chronology Descriptor

National parks owe their origin to the emergence of a preservation/conservation ethic that permeated North American society in the mid-19th century and it is not surprising that Canada was one of the earliest of the New World nations to set aside tracts of land for its people (see Boyd & Butler, 2000 for a detailed discussion). Banff and the original area around its hot springs were set aside as Canada's first national park in 1885 to be free from sale, settlement or squatting (Lothian, 1977). While this would establish a precedent which other national parks would follow, Banff was to develop in an atypical manner compared to other parks that would be declared later, as it would become Canada's most 'developed' national park. According to researchers like Nelson (1982), Canada's national parks were developed on the basis of three threads of interest, first that of preservation; second, the potential that parks offered for tourism; and third the role that the parks may play as poles around which economic growth would occur. Alongside these three threads, there existed a myriad of institutional arrangements that would both encourage as well as prevent national park development from taking place. The historic chronology of national parks in Canada resembles a series of flows (or possible curves) when numbers of parks and park developments are plotted against time. And therefore in a relatively tangential manner, it may be loosely argued that the chronology of national parks in Canada resembles a Butler curve that repeats itself.

The 'exploration' stage could be summarised in the creation of other parks in Western Canada around Banff the following year (Glacier and Yoho) to be quickly followed by three more by 1907 (Waterton Lakes, Elk Island and Jasper). Many of these parks occurred alongside railroad development in Western Canada and the beginning of early forms of tourism to the parks and tourist-related developments in the parks. The early parks were individually managed but in many cases they were noted for their absence of management (Boyd, 1995). Only one national park was established in eastern Canada by 1907, namely St Lawrence Islands, established from federal crown land that had been initially under Indian ownership. Aspects of park development that could be labelled as constituting the 'involvement' stage comprised further national park establishment in both Western and Eastern Canada up until 1929, a date which saw the park count rise to 14 in total. As for institutional developments, the Dominion Parks Branch was set up in 1911 and became the world's first national park service. Established under the Dominion Forest Reserves and Parks Act, it placed all existing parks under the jurisdiction of park service, and in essence was the start of a 'national parks system' (Eidsvik, 1983). Its first commissioner was James B. Harkin, who was to hold the office until 1936. It was under his leadership and vision that the recreation and tourism potential within the parks was realised, balanced with the need to ensure preservation and a state of wilderness, but where the revenue to be gained from use within the system would provide the means to further develop the park system.

It is possible to argue that Canada's national parks entered the 'development' stage between 1930 and 1978. A stop–go policy existed regarding park establishment owing to legislation, which prevented the federal government having control over public land across the Prairie Provinces, allowing park creation in only Eastern Canada. The post-war years and subsequent travel and leisure boom that followed created a demand for travel for recreational purposes in natural places, supported by a new phase of park establishment between 1969 and 1972. This period saw 10 new parks being added to the existing system, both in the West, East (where parks were established to act as regional economic growth poles) and for the first time in the North. Park attendance was recorded to have increased threefold between 1960 and 1972 from 5 to 15 million, with the majority of that increase being absorbed by a few Western parks (Boyd, 1995). Towards the end of the 1970s it was clearly emerging that institutional arrangements were needed to safeguard parks from overuse and abuse. Early forms of institutional arrangements had developed as early as 1930 with the passing of Canada's first National Parks Act. The wording of the Act stressed 'unimpairment', 'enjoyment' and 'benefit' and was an early example of the principles of sustainable development. Other evidence to suggest Canada's national parks had reached the 'development' stage includes the first national parks policy tabled in government in 1964. While this had strong development-use tones, it helped greatly to establish the preservation of significant natural features in national parks as its 'most fundamental and important obligation' (Eidsvik, 1983). This was followed in 1970 by the development and approval of the first systems approach to national parks planning and development in Canada. An early iteration of the systems plan was based on broad physiographic regions (see Eidsvik, 1983). The systems plan approved by government was based around the concept of 'natural regions'. Canada was divided into 39 terrestrial (natural) regions based on biological, physical and geographic features, and it was based on these regions that further development of the park system would be developed to ensure that each region had national park representation.

In terms of features that could suggest a 'consolidation' stage, the following argument is made. Between 1979 and 1992 few new parks were added to the existing system. By 1993 Canada had 34 national parks, with new parks added in North and Eastern Canada. Visitation had levelled across the entire system to around 20 million. Institutional arrangements were well established with a revised national parks policy coming out in 1979 that introduced ecological integrity as the guiding principle in parks as a prerequisite to use. This development saw a formal amendment to the National Parks Act in 1988, which formalised the principle of ecological integrity. Other developments in this time period include the establishing and tabling of State of the Parks Reports and the establishment of a co-management agreement between the federal government and the Haida Nation over the management of Gwaii Haanas in 1993. An additional revision of national park policy in 1994 further stressed that priority be assigned to ensuring the ecological integrity of parks.

It would be difficult to establish a case that after 1994 a 'stagnation' phase followed. Rather it would be fair to suggest that increasing evidence was emerging that parks were coming under increasing threat and, if this was not addressed, could stagnate and become less attractive and lose their unique natural and commemorative integrity. This concern had been stated a decade earlier in a study undertaken on external perspectives and future strategies that Parks Canada (the title of the national park service then) should embark on up to 2001 (Nelson, 1984). But the first comprehensive study of human use in national parks would not be commissioned until 1994 when the Banff–Bow Valley Study was launched over concern about the montane region of Canada's first national park (Parks Canada, 1997). The study reported its findings in 1996 and brought into focus the need for ecological integrity to be established as the first priority. The implications of the study were to have a wider application to the entire national park system by establishing and making clear that the 'stagnation' threatening the system could be avoided in parks if integrity received priority over use (including tourism, which was a major component of use). Another action taken to avoid stagnation and decline was the announcement in 1998 of a moratorium placed on commercial development outside of park communities within national parks (Parks Canada website, 2002).

There is evidence since 1998 to imply that Canada's national parks have entered a stage of 'rejuvenation'. Much of the legislation that was passed since 1979 and the related institutional arrangements that were put in place were directed at attempting to keep use levels within the parks system within the zone of the 'critical limits of capacity' or at worst, to avoid capacity limits being severely overreached. The chronology of national parks since 1998 reflects concern over use levels and the pressures placed on parks by users. A report by the Panel on the Ecological Integrity of Canada's National Parks was released in 2000 and stated that the ecological integrity of the parks was under threat from many sources and for many reasons. Action that was taken included the passing of the Canada National Parks Act in 2001 that shifted priority to beyond just ensuring ecological integrity to maintenance and restoration of ecological integrity through the protection of natural resources and natural processes. The Act helped set new standards for park management plans where the primacy of ecological integrity is enforced. Other developments within the Act that could promote a base for rejuvenation were the requirement of legal designation of wilderness areas within parks and the placement of commercial development in national park communities. The Act heralded in the recycle of the cycle as it saw the establishment of seven new national parks. This was then followed up in 2002 when the government declared its intentions of establishing what it called the 'most ambitious expansion of national parks in over a hundred years' by aiming to establish 10 new parks by 2007, increasing the size of the Canadian national parks system by almost 50% (Parks Canada, 2002). In so doing, national parks will be present in all of Canada's 39 terrestrial regions and thereby complete the system. In addition, the 2002 announcement stated that action would be taken to restore the ecological health of all Canada's 39 existing national parks based on an integrated strategy. This strategy has three key elements: to improve understanding about what is changing in the parks, to understand why these changes are taking place and to take action to address the changes. The focus will be on scientific understanding of the parks, involving active monitoring and research into gaining a better understanding of human use of the parks and their surrounding ecosystems. Other efforts will include enlisting the help of Canadians as active partners through the development of partnerships to address stresses originating outside the parks, and encouraging and strengthening partnerships particularly with Aboriginal peoples. Such actions will go a long way to ensure that Canada's national park system will enjoy a rebirth or rejuvenation.

Application of the TALC to Individual Parks

Although the concept of sustainable development had not been 'coined' when Butler produced his model, implicit within the curve is the notion of limits and what possible scenarios may result if these are exceeded (see Butler, other volume). Figure 8.1a outlines the model as it was first developed in 1980 and how it may be modified to include issues of sustainability (Figure 8.1b), where a number of types or stages of sustainability may exist. These types or stages may be discernible on the basis of the ability of parks to cope with pressures, economic, environmental, or social, that are placed upon them from the mix of activities present and the various functions of the parks themselves. In the context of parks, the modified model implies that for both the 'exploration' and 'involvement' stages, initial sustainability is evident with an emphasis on maintaining ecological integrity (for an example of applying the TALC to other types of protected areas, see Weizenegger, other volume, editor's note). User levels are low and no noticeable impact occurs on the environment. Between the 'development' and 'consolidation' stages, it may be argued that conditional sustainability exists. More specifically, the nature of this sustainability is perceived as, first, moving in the direction of achieving economic sustainability with an emphasis on growth and, second, returning to maintaining ecological integrity as decreasing tolerance and stress placed on parks from both greater development (use) and continued high visitor counts may lead to exceeding the capacity limits of some parks. Parks placed between the

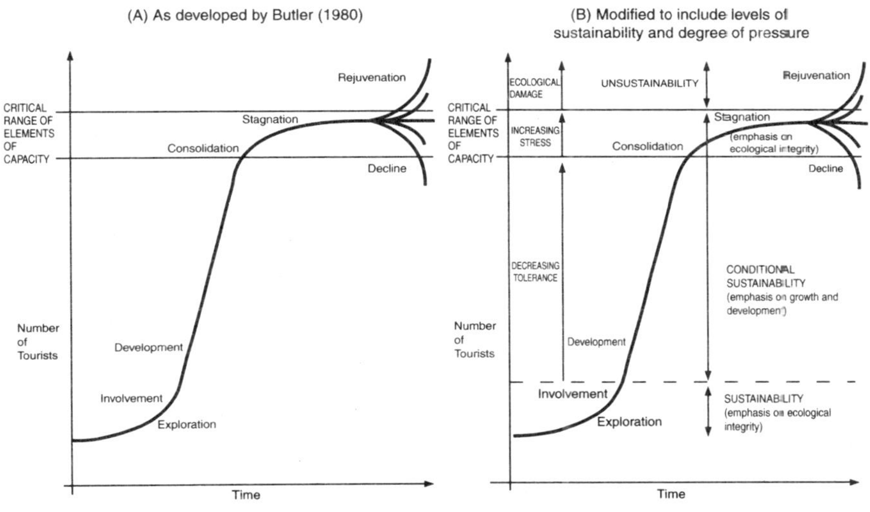

Figure 8.1 Modification of the TALC of evolution model

stages of 'consolidation' and 'stagnation', thus falling within the critical range of capacity, may be perceived as having a focus placed on maintaining ecological integrity as the increased stress, threats and impacts on parks may result in carrying capacity being exceeded. Parks found to be beyond the carrying capacity level may be perceived as being managed in an unsustainable manner.

Though this model is essentially conceptual, it was applied using the following data between 1993 and 1997: the length of time since the park was created, the physical size of the park, visitation counts over time (see Table 8.1), type of impacts (stresses/threats) facing parks and the ability of managers to address them (see Table 8.2) on the basis of the State of the Parks profiles over the time period. It may be argued that this range of information can provide, at best, crude indicators of the physical and environmental carrying capacities of parks, which in turn enable one to determine the general position of parks along the curve.

Given that these indicators provide at best a general impression of individual parks, each park's position is shown not as a specific point but as falling within a certain range (see Figure 8.2). For logistic purposes regarding visualising the findings and to avoid concealing regional differences, parks are presented on a regional basis with one curve being used to show parks in the Ontario and Quebec region of the overall parks system. Space does not permit a detailed explanation of where individual parks were placed on the curve, and so a number of case examples are drawn from Figure 8.2 as way of explanation for positioning.

For the Atlantic Region, all parks are plotted as falling between the 'development' and 'consolidation' stage, a fact not surprising given the range of park ages (Kejimkujik was established in 1969, compared to Cape Breton Highland in 1936). Further, a pattern of decline in visitation, increased threats and the lack of attention to external pressures on some parks may imply that the positions along the curve may be closer to 'consolidation' than to 'development'. A similar pattern is evident, albeit with some exceptions when parks in Ontario and Quebec are considered. For instance, Point Pelee is a park with an ecologically sensitive environment, a long history (established in 1929), small in size (16 km^2), but one that has had to cope with development (cottaging) and seasonal variation in visitation (dramatic increase during the bird-watching season). With increased stress placed on the natural environment from overuse and pressure from outside interests, it could be argued that this park is between 'consolidation' and 'stagnation'. However, management actions and strategies within this park (including the establishment of boardwalks and the absence of motorised transport) may help to ensure that 'stagnation' is not reached. The Prairie and Northern Region may be

Table 8.1 Number of person-visits to Canadian national parks (1993–97)

Province	*Park*	*1993–94*	*1994–95*	*1995–96*	*1996–97*
Newfoundland & Labrador	Gros Morne	126,019	124,729	129,083	120,943
	Terra Nova	233,783	237,978	241,567	232,616
Prince Edward Island	Prince Edward Island	690,645	808,899	836,344	749,212
Nova Scotia	Cape Breton Highlands	594,384	598,474	379,894	379,894
	Kejimkujik	55,469	58,552	58,308	56,592
New Brunswick	Fundy	223,357	241,087	233,486	220,725
	Kouchibouguac	210,684	230,089	226,631	229,562
Quebec	Forillon	169,412	181,953	180,816	173,914
	La Mauricie	247,104	232,765	239,774	215,888
	Mingan Arch.	25,350	27,125	28,596	19,860
	Saguenay			421,452	377,382
Ontario	Bruce Peninsula	144,650	163,255	210,980	207,444
	Fathom Five	390,562	335,412	411,867	399,054
	Georgian Bay Is	86,589	86,720	72,954	69,252
	Point Pelee	448,655	500,282	439,196	384,682
	Pukaskwa	13,298	13,252	19,180	7940
	St Lawrence Is.	43,980	58,365	73,021	63,278

Table 8.1 (*Continued*)

Province	*Park*	*1993–94*	*1994–95*	*1995–96*	*1996–97*
Manitoba	Riding Mtn	286,574	360,165	368,886	353,134
Saskatchewan	Grasslands	2528	2796	5082	3451
	Prince Albert	178,523	184,346	171,669	172,194
Alberta	Banff	4,395,400	4,892,551	4,858,161	4,453,021
	Elk Island	302,023	264,214	217,395	152,852
	Jasper	1,511,853	1,587,402	1,605,941	2,100,089
	Waterton Lakes	349,393	351,990	456,507	330,939
British Columbia	Glacier	173,321	194,751	143,085	101,924
	Gwaii Haanas	1902	2768	2775	2077
	Kootenay	1,263,412	1,323,913	1,288,495	1,113,795
	Mt Revelstoke	203,751	205,916	163,687	163,687
	Pacific Rim	1,102,559	1,121,145	920,795	836,120
	Yoho	747,292	848,321	761,871	678,189
Yukon	Ivvavik	429	129	244	152
	Kluane	78,996	72,511	66,489	69,924

Table 8.1 (*Continued*)

Province	*Park*	*1993–94*	*1994–95*	*1995–96*	*1996–97*
Northwest Territories	Aulavik		151	20	20
	Auyuittuq	379	349	507	470
	Ellesmere Is.	451	454	462	462
	Nahanni	3793	3095	4551	4605
	Wood Buffalo	6251	6231	6444	6040
Total		14,312,771	15,322,135	15,246,215	14,451,383

Table 8.2 Internal and external threats facing Canadian national parks

Region	*Park*	*Internal threats*							*External threats*					
		A	*B*	*C*	*D*	*E*	*F*	*G*	*H*	*I*	*J*	*K*	*L*	*M*
Atlantic	Cape Breton Highlands			X	X					X				
	Prince Edward Island	X	X			X		X	X	X				
	Fundy	X	X							X	X	X		
	Terra Nova		X		XX		XX			X		X		
	Kejimkujik	X	X		XX	X	X			X	X			
	Kouchibouguac	X	X			X	X		X	X		X		
	Gros Morne		XX	X	X	X				X				
Quebec	Forillon				X	X				XX		X		
	La Mauricie	X			X					X	X	X		
	Mingan Archipelago				XX		X			X		X		
Ontario	St Lawrence Islands	X			XX		X			X		XX		
	Point Pelee	XXX			XX				X	XX		XX		
	Georgian Bay Islands			X	X		X			X	X	XX		
	Pukaskwa			X						X	X			
	Bruce Peninsula													

Table 8.2 (*Continued*)

Region	*Park*	*Internal threats*							*External threats*					
		A	*B*	*C*	*D*	*E*	*F*	*G*	*H*	*I*	*J*	*K*	*L*	*M*
Prairie/Northern	Wood Buffalo	X				XX				XX		X	X	
	Prince Albert	X	X						X	X				
	Riding Mountain		X	X			X		X	X		X	X	
	Kluane			X					XX	X				
	Nahanni		X					X			X			
	Auyuittuq			X				X						
	Grasslands	X				X			X					
	Northern Yukon						X			X				
	Ellesmere Island			X			X			X	X			
Western	Banff	X	X		X		X			XX		X		XX
	Waterton Lakes	XX	X							XX				
	Jasper	XX		X			XX			X				
	Yoho	X		XX	XX		XX		XX	XX		X		X
	Glacier			XX	XX		X		X	XX				
	Elk Island	XXX										XX	X	X

Table 8.2 (*Continued*)

Region	*Park*	*Internal threats*							*External threats*					
		A	*B*	*C*	*D*	*E*	*F*	*G*	*H*	*I*	*J*	*K*	*L*	*M*
	Mount Revelstoke								X	XX				XX
	Kootenay	XX		X	X		XX			X				X
	Pacific Rim		X		XX					X				X
	Gwaii Haanas	XX			X							XX		

X, limited; XX, major; XXX, extensive

Internal threats: A, natural threats; B, tourism and recreation related; C, waste management and services; D, heavy use/overuse of area; E, traditional activities/commercial activities; F, conflict between wildlife and users; G, modification of the physical environment of parks

External threats: H, removal of buffers around parks, foreign species; I, nonconforming uses outside park boundaries; J, climatic influences (e.g. acid rain); K, pollution; L, community development; M, accessing parks from areas outside parks

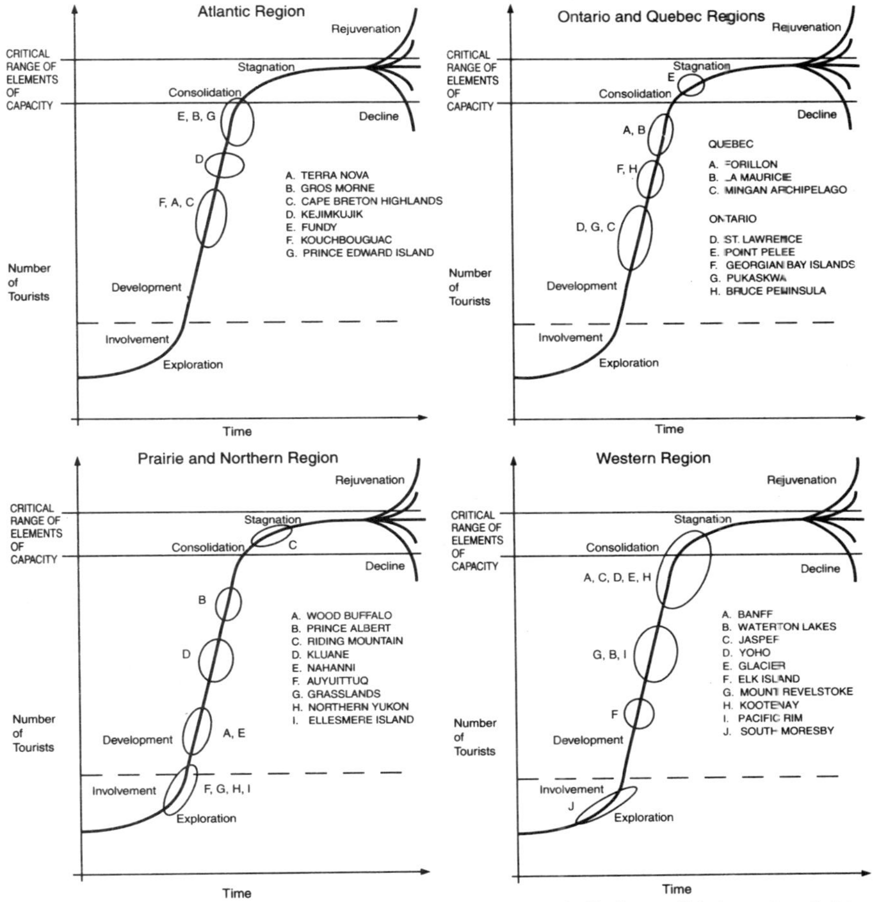

Note: the detailed labels for the modified model (diagram B, Figure 4.3) are left off to leave sufficient room to apply the model to the Canadian national park system. Given the data, it is impossible to accurately position each park on the curve. Therefore, the region of the curve considered most applicable to each park is shown instead.

Figure 8.2 Application of the modified tourist area cycle of evolution model to Canada's national parks

categorised into a number of divisions. First, Prince Albert and Riding Mountain National Parks, which have had a long history of recreation and tourism, with large visitor counts and severe external pressures, are plotted as approaching 'consolidation' and 'stagnation', respectively. Second, parks established in the North (Auyuittuq, 1974; Nahanni, 1976; Kluane, 1976; Northern Yukon, 1984; Ellesmere Island, 1988), where visitor counts are low, growth moderate and impacts minimal, are plotted between the 'involvement' and 'exploration' stage, with some approaching the level of 'development'. Wood Buffalo National Park is one park that resembles the pattern identified for the latter category, but with a number of differences, namely a longer history (established in 1911), being developed as an animal sanctuary, with the greatest impact coming not from outside the park from nonconforming land-uses but from the within the park in the form of an outbreak of disease amongst the bison herd and from indigenous uses.

The Western Region reflects parks that may be categorised as ranging between 'development' and 'consolidation', with the exception of South Moresby/Gwaii Haanas that has not advanced much beyond the 'involvement' stage given that it was only established in 1992 and is relatively inaccessible because of its location. Parks such as Banff, Jasper, Yoho, Glacier and Kootenay are seen as having reached or being close to 'consolidation'. With the exception of Glacier, these parks have continued to attract large numbers of visitors over time, but with the development of specific management strategies to address internal problems and the cooperative arrangements existing with neighbouring jurisdictions for many external issues, it may be argued that these parks have not yet reached the point of 'stagnation'. The large numbers of visitors and the conflicts between wildlife and visitors would suggest, however, that capacity limits have been reached and exceeded for some sections within these parks (e.g. Lake O'Hara in Yoho and the montane valley section in Banff). The Banff–Bow Valley study released in 1996 would support the latter argument. However, the history of tourism in specific parks (e.g. Banff), the attraction of recreation with a Rocky Mountain setting and the presence of a large urban market in the Calgary–Edmonton corridor, make it very likely that these parks will continue to receive large numbers of visitors.

Both axes in Figure 8.2 are produced as constants, but it may be argued that given the diversity of parks that comprise the system, the shape of individual curves would reflect a range of factors. These could include park history with respect to tourism, recreation and general visitor use, size, type of environment present, park location and management ability to redress internal and external problems. As such, it is possible to argue that the shape of individual park curves would fall between both scenarios presented in Figure 8.3, where scenario A depicts a park that is well established, popular, but increasingly facing stresses both external and internal, whereas Scenario B is reflective of parks that have been recently established, located within extremely sensitive isolated environments, where levels of visitation remain low. Regardless of whether graphs are plotted on axes that vary or are held as constants, the overall utility of applying the TALC model to Canada's national parks remains. Its application may reveal the extent of

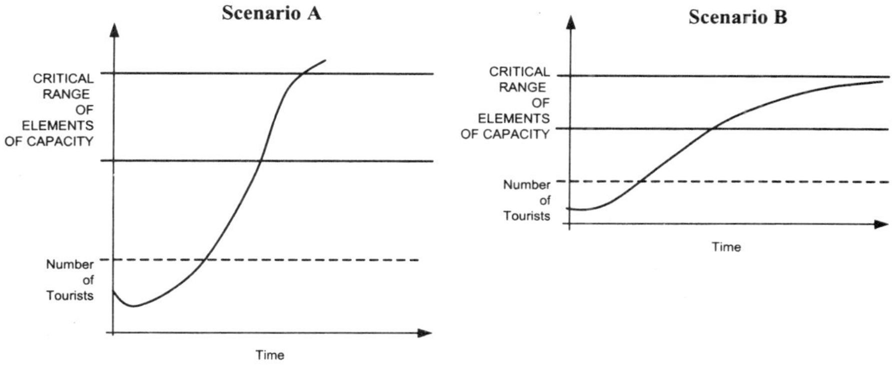

Figure 8.3 Alternative scenarios of park development

'development' that each park has reached, which in turn may be useful in indicating their potential to be sustainable landscapes.

Discussion

The focus in this chapter has been to illustrate the application of the TALC in a national park context. Attention now shifts to discussing how park management can redress the situation where parks have moved into the latter stages of the model, and what specific strategies can be employed to ensure that the 'critical range of elements of capacity' is not overstepped. Discussion is directed at specific policy developments that can shape individual park management plans as well as offering some comment on the extent to which partnership development, alluded to earlier in this chapter, is providing a new means of park management. In both cases, Banff National Park is highlighted as it remains the most visited and yet atypical park within the Canadian system, and if strategies can be employed here and be successful, then they have potentially wide utility across parks within the system as a whole.

National park policy, stemming from the 1930 Parks Act to the current policy released in 1994, can be compared to the analogy of a pendulum, swinging between development (use) and protection and ensuring ecological integrity (Boyd, 2000). At present, current Acts and institutional arrangements, previously discussed in this chapter, imply that the pendulum has clearly moved towards ecological integrity. The guiding principles outlined in the Parks Policy of 1994 (Parks Canada, 1994) place ecological and commemorative integrity as taking precedence with respect to acquisition, management and the administration of heritage places and programmes. The policy goes on to state that management decisions must be made on the basis of ecosystem-based management practices and sound cultural resource management, respectively. Other guiding principles and strategies include leadership and stewardship, new protected heritage areas, education and presentation, human–environment relationship, research and science, appropriate visitor activities, public involvement, collaboration and cooperation and accountability. These broad guiding principles, when translated into specific management plans at the level of individual parks, are applied by management which stresses ecosystem-based protection. In the case of Banff National Park, the current management plan was released in 1997 and provides a blueprint for action between 1997 and 2012. Sheila Copps, then Deputy Prime Minister and Minister of Canadian Heritage, in the foreword to the Banff National Park Management Plan (Parks Canada, 1997), states clearly that first and foremost, Banff is a place for nature in which ecological integrity is the cornerstone of the park as well as its key to the future, but that it is also a place for people, a place for heritage tourism, a place for community and a place for environmental stewardship. The plan is strategic, offering a clear and core vision shaped around a range of themes such as an integrated approach to decision-making, and that the parks tourism strategy shaped around heritage will serve as a model of integrated management. Specific strategic goals have been established for each section of the plan.

Much has been written about specific management strategies within the tourism heritage literature (see Hall & McArthur, 1998; Timothy & Boyd, 2003) and managing visitor impacts in general (see Garrod, 2003) and no attempt is made here to repeat familiar ground, other than to make the point that national park environments have often been the setting against which management strategies have been assessed. A strategy such as zoning regions based on their suitability for activity, for example, has a long history where national parks are concerned. The point to be made here is that a plethora of management strategies and procedures now exist at the discretion of park managers, and the history of park management would suggest that overall, they have been well used.

A recent strategy that has been commented on earlier in this chapter is that of building partnerships, and although the term is a relatively old concept, it is a relatively new one where tourism thinking is concerned (see Bramwell & Lane, 2000). In the case of Banff National Park, partnerships have emerged as one of the key components of the park's vision, namely 'people who live and work in the park will be a "community of communication", welcoming visitors and enhancing their understanding of the nature, culture and history of the park' (Parks Canada, 1997: 10). This thinking emerged as one outcome of the Banff–Bow Valley Study of 1996, which helped develop a heritage tourism strategy for the park (Parks Canada, 1997). The heritage tourism strategy has the following four goals:

(1) Create visitor awareness of being in a national park through fostering visitor appreciation and understanding of nature, culture and history of the park itself.
(2) Encourage and develop opportunities, products and services that are consistent with heritage values.
(3) Encourage environmental stewardship initiatives upon which sustainable heritage tourism could be based.
(4) Set up a heritage orientation programme with the express purpose of giving residents the knowledge base on which they could share their understanding of heritage of the park, both natural and human, with visitors.

It is the latter goal that attempts to foster a 'community of communication' by selling heritage through an orientation programme. Boyd (2003) commented that this education programme provides a new marketing approach, creating opportunity where heritage tourism is concerned, and that as a model has utility for 'educating' visitors as to the purpose, heritage or otherwise, of national parks and historic sites across Canada, and, indeed, more widely.

While this discussion has been limited, the point to be made is that the direction that national policy and specific management plans have taken and the initiatives behind building partnerships, for example, imply that national park management has the tools to avoid parks moving towards stagnation, indicated by their environments having overreached their capacity.

Conclusion

This chapter has presented an alternative application of the TALC model. National parks remain popular venues for leisure, recreation and tourism, and in many cases represent the majority of World Heritage Sites that were inscribed on the basis of natural criteria. It is therefore fitting and relevant to consider the merits of this popular tourism model in this context. As many of the chapters in this book will attest, the TALC model has moved well beyond the initial thinking around which Butler wrote of in 1980. Butler himself has noted that the model has utility beyond the level of destinations to that of tourism within regions and to specific types of tourism in general. Within the context of national parks, it is postulated here that the TALC model is applicable in broad terms as a descriptor of how entire park systems have developed, as well as offering utility in the placement of individual parks along the curve. The chapter provides yet another example of the difficulty of determining where individual cases may be best represented within the model. Despite this weakness, the modifications of the original TALC model provide the opportunity to think beyond the boundaries and justify the model's application to landscapes such as those found within national parks in a protected situation. A final point is that the importance of the TALC model and its application to national parks lies not in pinpointing the position of where parks lie along the curve, but rather in highlighting the need for good management of parks to avoid them reaching the latter stages of the model's cycle of development. National parks have a long history of management strategies and the ongoing application of these will be vital if national parks are to become and remain representative examples of sustainable landscapes.

Chapter 9

A Re-foundation of the TALC for Heritage Cities

ANTONIO PAOLO RUSSO

Introduction

Drawing on the example of Venice and similar congested destinations, this chapter looks at the way in which destinations have become overdeveloped or overused. It examines tourism development in the context of limited accommodation capacity and discusses the implications of the strategic responses from the market players, as well as alternative options which such destinations might adopt to bring their evolution to sustainable tracks. Cultural tourism is an important resource for cities and regions. It provides solid opportunities for growth that are not limited to direct employment and revenue generation. A visitor-friendly environment enhances the quality of life of a place – and consequently its capacity to attract new and strategic functions, contributing to general goals of urban development in the global economy (Russo & van den Berg, 2002). In fact, a culture-rich environment is not only attractive to visitors, but also to new citizens and firms. Apart from their ethical value, historical buildings, monuments and sights enhance the atmosphere of a city, providing prestige to the urban environment. Cultural attractions score high in the preferences of agents in the new service class (Dziembowska-Kowalska & Funck, 2000), and influence the development plans of companies and multinationals. This feeds a process in which tourism is the engine of economic regeneration.

For those reasons, an increasing number of cities invest in promoting their historical and cultural resources and making them accessible to residents and visitors. In doing so, however, they risk an unbalanced and short-lived development. The experience with tourism in many European cities suggests that the results of such efforts are often unsatisfactory (Russo *et al*., 2001; van der Borg & Gotti, 1995). Tourism pressure grows unbridled in heritage and cultural destinations, with negative consequences in terms of costs and lost opportunities for cities as living and working locations. As a strategy for urban growth, is has been proved largely nonviable in the long term.

This is especially a problem for a city whose mass is small with respect to the flow of visitors that it attracts – such as the small and medium 'stars' of European urban tourism, Bruges, Salzburg, Toledo and Venice. Not only the socioeconomic profile of entire communities, for which tourism is far too often the only source of wealth, is at stake in this process. Perhaps even worse is the risk that as a result of the loss of competitiveness of tourism, the very opportunities for the protection of the cultural heritage are eroded. To the extent that this patrimony represents an element of the foundation of the civil society and the collective memory of the past, its loss would be disrupting.

The challenge for such cities is to develop as thriving and attractive places without missing the opportunities offered by tourism. Hence the need for an integral policy that prevents the worse effects of tourism development, allowing the urban economy to grow harmoniously, and preserves in the process the valuable assets on which such growth is based, according to the general principles of sustainability. Yet, few sound explanations have been given of possible undesirable outcomes. Urban tourism remains in a sort of 'scientific vacuum', which Cazes and Potier (1996) attribute to the difficulty of establishing disciplinary boundaries in the study of the phenomena. It is somewhat surprising to find that in the top journals in the field, for instance *Annals of Tourism Research and Tourism Management*, only a small number of articles have been devoted to urban heritage tourism in the last decade. However, any mayor of a historical city in Western Europe is likely to put visitor management high on the political agenda, together with closely associated issues such as economic regeneration, traffic and environmental control, and infrastructure development. Policy practice calls for more scientific elaboration, but science hardly responds.

This chapter addresses these issues, starting with a discussion of the shortcomings of the most current Tourism Area Life Cycle (TALC) conceptualisations and applications in explaining the unsustainable outcome of tourism development in heritage cities. It is argued that a specific approach to tourist cycles based on spatial issues should be considered in such contexts. A 'vicious circle' model of tourism development is then presented, which puts the interrelations between the spatial development of tourism and market strategies at centre stage. The long-term developments of this model and the necessary policy responses are also discussed. The fourth section illustrates the working of the model and its implications in the case of a world-famous heritage destination, Venice. Finally, the conclusions draw useful insights for a more effective comprehensibility and use of the TALC framework as an instrument for planning.

TALC as a Policy Tool for Heritage Destinations: Problems and Extensions

Cities and urban regions are complex systems; any change in their component parts is likely to have repercussions in other domains, influencing the welfare and quality of life of various groups of citizens, or the power and legitimacy of organisations. While the expectation is that tourism development makes a city as a whole better off, this is not always the case. In some cases, development processes take place outside the city. The costs generated by development would eventually outweigh the benefits, in a zero-sum game in which there are 'winners' and 'losers'. Whereas benefits may be gauged by simple multiplier analysis, the disenfranchised spatial and temporal nature of development costs makes their evaluation particularly hard; sophisticated, complex tools are required for this analysis.

One such instrument is the TALC model, which provides a framework to analyse tourism in an evolutionary context. The destination-cycle scheme is complementary to multiplier analysis as it provides a 'reduced form' of the dynamic relations that are implied in tourism development. It gives an idea of 'what to expect' from a certain structure of the tourist economy and its relations with the local context, be it economic, environmental or social.

Despite its widespread influence in tourism studies, the destination cycle has attracted criticism. Part of the literature argues that the 'deterministic' nature of the model does not leave room for a diversity of outcomes in the development process (Prideaux, 2000), or points the finger to the unclear consideration of demand–supply interaction (Haywood, 1986). Another problem is that most studies focus on applications regarding beach resorts and other 'new' tourist products (for instance, Debbage, 1990; Holder, 1991; Knowles & Curtis, 1999). Little attention has been given to urban tourism, and to heritage cities in particular (Garrod & Fyall, 2000). One reason may be that the late development of this form of tourism (compared to other forms of recreational and '3S' travel) does not offer many examples of complete cycles to be observed and analysed. However, heritage destinations do have peculiar characteristics that make the straightforward application of the TALC framework not as credible as in other contexts. Whereas we can rely on arguments derived from aggregate consumption theory (as in Towse, 1991) to explain the rise in popularity of heritage destinations, it is difficult to grasp how in practice a 'decline' in tourism could occur. The cultural assets inherited from the past are irreproducible and highly specific to the local historical and cultural context, hence the 'substitutability' between destinations is limited. The decline stage of the destination cycle, hardly observed in the real world, would not even be an expected outcome of tourism development. Though authors such as Butler (1980), Haywood (1986), Ioannides (1992) and Plog (1973) offer arguments that could be adapted to the problems in question, none of these is thoroughly convincing in the case of heritage cities and anyway their approaches have not been applied to these destinations. However, socioeconomic impacts from tourism on heritage cities are perceptible (van den Berg & Gotti, 1995). Cities like Venice and Bruges have tripled their visitor/resident ratios in the last few years and tourism is perceived today as a 'danger'.

Following on, the least attractive aspect of the destination cycle is its poor use as a tool for policy (Haywood, 1998). The simple description of the trend does not capture the nature of the linkages that make the cycle self-propelling. One major consequence is that while TALC theorists prescribe that policy should act proactively to smooth the fluctuations of the cycle and prevent decline, it is not clear how these objectives should be achieved, nor which variables should be the object of regulation at each stage. According to authors such as Martin and Uysal (1990) and Canestrelli and Costa (1991), the challenge for tourism managers is to keep flows under the threshold of carrying capacity. This is generally defined as 'the number of visitors that an area can accommodate before negative impacts occur' (Martin & Uysal, 1990: 329). Yet few authors manage to define precisely the link between carrying capacity violations and the life cycle. Is carrying capacity the point beyond which, if repeatedly violated, the visitors' flows start to decline? Or rather does it cause tourist receipts to perform a cyclic path, affecting the performance of the urban economy? That is completely unclear, and contradicted by empirical observation. In cities such as Bruges or Venice, visitor flows – both in the resident tourist segment and in the excursionist segment – are still increasing, even at sustained rates, but carrying capacity is violated for many days in a year (Costa & van der Borg, 1988). Martin and Uysal (1990) suggest that each stage in the cycle will reveal different capacity thresholds, and requires distinct policy responses. Hence, we are not in a position to give clear indications for a long-term strategic policy to tourist planners, based on the notion of carrying capacity alone.

We adhere to the remark made by Haywood (1992: 353): decision-makers need to know what strategic moves are appropriate in each specific situation, and the destination cycle has no immediate prescriptive implication unless it explicitly takes into consideration the characteristics of places and resources. A promising step forward in this sense is provided by authors who focus on the changes in the spatial organisation of the tourist system (Debbage, 1990; Gormsen, 1981; Miossec, 1976; van der Borg, 1991) and on the repercussions on the performance of the destination. The original TALC model can be extended by a qualitative element, that is, the kind of visitor that is attracted (van der Borg, 1991). A close scrutiny of the characteristic of the visitor flows in cities at different stages of their life cycle suggests that not only the absolute number of visitors is changing, but also their mix, with major consequences in terms of associated costs and benefits in the space. This interpretation seems appropriate to describe the situation of historical urban destinations, as it hints at a specialisation of the space in and around the city, induced by the peculiar structure of the destination area. In the upper part of Figure 9.1, this 'revisited' version of the tourist life-cycle scheme is presented. Each stage of the cycle can be associated with a specific distribution of the costs and benefits arising from the tourist activities (lower part of the figure). At the first stage, the area benefiting from tourism is different from the newly discovered destination. As development proceeds (e.g. with the building of hotels), the two regions almost coincide. Municipalities are able to cover the costs

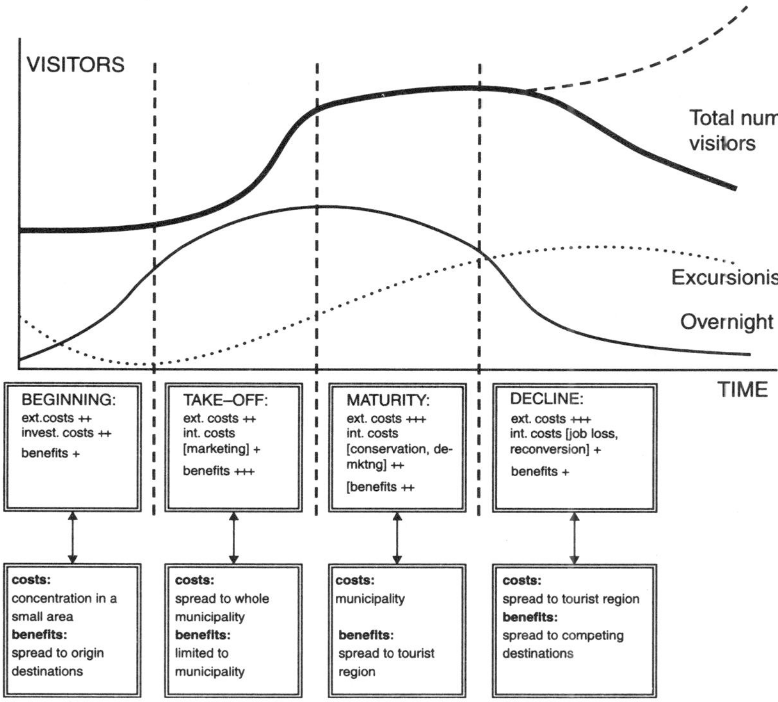

Figure 9.1 The destination life cycle reinterpreted: Visitor mix and spatial allocation of costs and benefits from tourism development in a site Adapted from van der Borg (1991).

generated by tourism with the receipts from tourism that at this stage are concentrated in the locality. At a later stage, the tourist revenues are diffused to the rest of the region as a result of the emergence of a tourist region, while costs remain concentrated.

According to this view, the negative effects of development are associated with the enlargement of the tourism region, pushed by the emergence of a class of 'false excursionists': would-be tourists that, faced with the high prices and the limited capacity of central facilities, choose a peripheral site for their visit to the main destination. A conflict arises between the centre – bearing the costs of tourism activity and retaining a decreasing share of the benefits – and the neighbouring communities. The latter enjoy as *free-riders* the advantages of proximity to the main destination; the core, instead, is pushed to impose higher taxes, and the budgets for heritage maintenance, cleaning of the city and marketing become overstretched. In the end, the possibility to preserve and market the cultural supply depends on the availability of external sources of income, like special laws or governmental transfers, increasing the rigidity of the context in which tourism policies operate. At the same time, tourism imposes a new valorisation dynamic, with devastating effects on the less competitive sectors of the urban economy (Sasson, 1995). The destination is transformed into a tourism monoculture and lacks any other economic activity that might balance a possible decline of the local industry. This 'spatial-economic' approach to destination cycles paves the way to a thorough analysis of the inter-relations between spatial development and changes in the competitiveness and performance of the tourist city. This insight may give arguments to policy-makers to calibrate their policy. What factors may lead to a decline of tourism in heritage cities? How can this process be redressed towards a sustainable path? The next section proposes an analytic framework to describe why tourism development in heritage destinations is likely to be unsustainable.

Space and Market: The Tourist Region as a 'Strategic Space'

The 'vicious circle' model consists of a series of logical *steps*, leading from the enlargement of a destination's Functional Tourist Region (FTR) under the pressure of persisting demand increases, to changes in the market structure and in the behaviour of visitors, and feeding back to the competitiveness of the destination. The main assumption is that visitors are attracted to heritage cities because they hope to enjoy a 'heritage experience', which materially takes place through the aggregate consumption of a set of goods and services, among which are the cultural assets. Such assets are virtually irreproducible and remarkably concentrated in historical centres (HCs). The quality of the experience depends not only on the quality of the primary heritage assets, but also on the quality of the environment in which the act of consumption takes place.

Tourism may grow 'undisturbed' in a city until some critical level of tourist development is reached. Beyond that point, problems begin. This critical threshold is easy to detect. The first visible sign of excessive tourism growth is the saturation of the central accommodation supply, which implies the expansion of supply facilities in the FTR around destinations.

In historical cities, the socioeconomic carrying capacity is likely to be violated at lower levels than the physical. However, even before getting to the point of physical or 'economic' saturation, the complementary industry will start to grow more dispersed, particularly those activities for which centrality becomes increasingly costly, such as new hotels, recreation areas and transport facilities. Therefore, the first step of the 'vicious circle' springs from the incapacity of the heritage city to limit the growth of tourism in accordance with its physical resources. The complementary product is much more mobile than the primary assets, and the administrative boundaries of the city are to a large extent insensitive to these dynamics. The region involved in tourist production tends to become larger, overstepping the boundaries of the municipality, as in the classic scheme of Miossec (1976). However, if the city is a very attractive one – as is the case of principal European cultural destinations like Venice, Bruges or Salzburg – it might well exceed regional or even national boundaries. As a consequence, the share of day-trippers among the overall number of visitors increases (Figure 9.2A). Among these, the

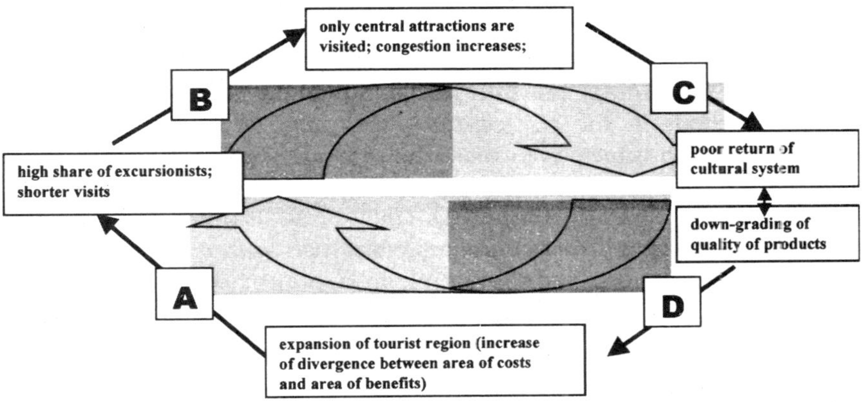

Figure 9.2 The 'vicious circle' of tourism development in heritage destinations

number of would-be tourists who turn into *false excursionists* because they cannot find a place in the city centre or because it is too expensive for their limited budgets, becomes higher and higher. (Van den Berg (1991) defines *real* excursionists as all those day-trippers who come to the visited city during the day from their normal place of residence and go back there in the evening: *indirect* excursionists are all those who visit the city during the day coming from and going back to another place that is the main destination of their journey; *false* excursionists are all those day visitors that spend the night in a different place from the city itself which remains the main destination of their excursion.)

This mode of visiting the city is remarkably less flexible than overnight-staying visits. On the one hand, day trips are typically more sensitive to weather conditions and 'special occasions', so that their seasonal pattern is more pronounced. On the other, visitors who commute have less time for retrieving 'tacit' information about the cultural and the complementary products. Consequently they tend to be (i) less aware of the qualitative content of the tourist goods and (ii) less reachable by traditional information tools. Therefore, they tend to concentrate in space, as the centrally located attractions are reached (and experienced) with a minimum level of information. This point is made by Towse (1991: 3–4). She assumes that visitors meet 'search costs' to gather information about the exact location, content and access of the cultural-tourist supply. In tourist gatherings around 'superstar' attractions, such costs are minimised. A further step in the vicious circle can thus be identified (Figure 9.2B). Day trips produce more congestion (and associated costs) than overnight stays, and their share of the total number of visits increases in the light of persistent demand pressure.

However, the imposition of costs on residents is not central to the present analysis. More relevant to this study is the impact of such an inefficient organisation of the visits on the quality of the tourist experience. Visitors now come from a wide (and widening) area and are therefore on average less informed about quality. Hence the suppliers of tourist goods in the city centre will be able to curtail the quality content of their products to increase their market share. This may happen with increased likeliness as the share of uninformed visitors increases. Pursuing this strategy, suppliers may lose some 'sophisticated' customers, but appeal to visitors less concerned with quality and much more sensitive to prices. In the end, in a typical process of adverse selection, only low-quality suppliers are left in the market. Whereas in the initial stages of growth the economic strength of tourism causes the displacement of other economic activities, at this later stage tourism tends to crowd itself out, replacing high-quality products with cheap standardised ones. At that point, the tourism space undergoes what is often referred to as 'McDonaldisation'. Not only is the capacity of products to match the demand of a certain segment of tourism compromised, but the whole aesthetic quality of the landscape and the system of cultural values embodied in the city is in jeopardy (Figure 9.2C).

The consequence of this decline in quality is a strong feedback to the very origin of such mechanisms. In the fourth and last step of the vicious circle, the regional dispersion of tourist activities has far-reaching implications on the sustainability of the development process. Visitors would set the cost of distance against prices and the quality of the complementary facilities, and find it more convenient to consume non-central facilities. The budget of visitors is reallocated between the goods in the tourist package in such a way that as many goods as possible are purchased outside the city, to save money and escape possible 'quality traps'. Indeed, more and more of those who still wish to visit the city will choose peripheral accommodation, thus feeding the dynamics of the vicious circle. The circle is now complete (Figure 9.2D). The expansion of the tourist region beyond the boundaries of the city centre, due first and foremost to the growth in demand, in the end causes that very expansion to continue.

Caserta and Russo (2002) analyse the process of quality downscaling in heritage destinations through a formal model. Utilising the reputation model toolbox developed by Tirole (1997) and applied to the tourist market by Keane (1997), they find that in order to continue to offer high quality, tourist suppliers charge a mark-up on prices. This depends on parameters such as the share of 'informed' visitors, which is most likely to be the resident tourists rather than the excursionists, whose learning capacity is eroded by time lost in commuting and compromised by lack of opportunities to compare or fewer contacts with informers. On this account, the widening of the tourist region is linked with the market behaviour of suppliers. As tourist regions become larger (due to persistent pressure from the world market), the conditions that are compatible with high quality are not sustained. Destinations are 'forced' to reorient themselves towards low-quality and low-budget visitors, those that are less likely to be struck by declines in quality. Caserta and Russo (2002) also discuss the full implications of this market change for the sustainability of tourism development in heritage destinations. To this aim they look at the effect on the performance and viability of the 'heritage industry' that is in charge of preserving the heritage and making it accessible to visitors and citizens. The combined effect of congestion and lack of information is that some cultural resources are underutilised while some others are overutilised. On the whole, far fewer visitors enjoy the cultural heritage than the city could afford. As a result, heritage attractions are less able to generate value. A larger share of the visitor budget comes to be spent on pricey tourist goods or simply leaks out of the destination to peripheral and unattractive places where better conditions are offered. To the extent that 'less sophisticated visitors' replace quality-sensitive tourists disaffected with the destination, the budgets spent on culture shrink.

In the end, this process affects the very competitive capacity of heritage cities. In fact, the resources needed for the maintenance of the heritage, for innovations in products, and for implementing information and marketing strategies cease, to a large extent, to be any longer in the control of the local institutions. That is particularly true in an era of decreasing transfers from central governments. Even if monuments and historical sites were subsidised, the conservation standards would be low and excessively rigid. In a 'user pays' approach, tourism should produce extra revenue to be channelled into heritage protection. If the tourist region around heritage centres is small, and/or it falls under the jurisdiction of an authority that can reallocate the tourist revenue generated in the periphery to the enhancement of the cultural assets in the core, then these mechanisms may operate. Yet, this may well not be the case, for two reasons.

i. Despite any redistribution, the pressure for the enlargement of the tourist region will persist, leading to higher prices/lower quality than in competing destinations.
ii. Frequently, tourist regions extend over regional or even national boundaries (as in the case of famous cultural cities such as Venice, Salzburg or Bruges), and then heritage preservation through fiscal mechanisms may be hard or impossible to enforce. Peripheral localities would *free-ride* on their proximity to the heritage centre until this loses its attraction capacity due to the changes experienced.

The 'vicious circle' provides a rationale for the decline of heritage destinations that one expects from a straightforward application of the TALC model. It emphasises that the maintenance of the 'place qualities' that make a destination attractive involve both direct maintenance and management costs and opportunity costs (like the 'information rents' captured by tourist suppliers). If tourism development does not generate in the process the resources that are needed to cover these costs, or leaks them out to a wider region, then this is not a sustainable process. The myopic, fragmented and preindustrial nature of the local tourist cluster (as analysed by authors such as Tremblay (1998) and Keane (1997)) ensures that such agents would not anticipate a foreseeable decline internalising the heritage conservation costs through responsible behaviour. A noteworthy element of this framework is the role of tourist regions, which present themselves as 'strategic spaces'. Tourist suppliers can relocate out of the city centre to escape physical and economic constraints, and in this way they produce spatial imbalance in the costs

make tourism a real engine of sustainable urban development. Demand regulation has often been directed at the wrong objectives – for instance, failing to discriminate between tourists and excursionists in visitor management policies – and has achieved poor results. As a consequence, today the pressure of tourism on urban centres and heritage assets is more critical than ever. A recent study on the 'sustainable use' of European heritage (van den Berg *et al.*, 2000) points out that the areas of 'crisis' for a sustainable use of the heritage are scattered throughout Europe. Among these, the heritage star attraction *par excellence* is the city of Venice.

A Case Study of the Vicious Circle Mechanism: Venice

The observation of tourist development trends in the city of Venice – possibly the most famous heritage destination in the world – may be a way to test the validity of the assumptions of the 'vicious circle'. Moreover, the sustainability of tourism development in Venice may be evaluated in the light of the prescriptions following from the use of that model.

Context

Venice is a well known international attraction. Yet, its HC in the heart of the lagoon is a 'problem area', whereas the mainland section of the city is well integrated in a booming regional economy. With young households pushed out by inaccessible housing prices and lack of specialised jobs, the population in the HC of Venice declined from 170,000 to 70,000 over the past half a century, and is still decreasing at a yearly rate of ca. 0.5%. The poor accessibility of the HC is one reason for workers to move outside to pursue jobs. The reoccurring floods generate economic instability. As a consequence, tourism is one of the few economic sectors experiencing full development left in the city. At the same time, it is seen by many as the main culprit of the irresistible decline faced by the city, because it produces all sorts of management and opportunity costs.

Visitors crowd the main attractions of the city – a sample of the best architecture spanning 13 centuries, inestimable collections and top cultural events. However, most visitors come for the city in itself rather than for any individual attraction. Its millenary history, its urban fabric, its atmosphere, the delicate interweaving of its water and built environment, suggest that the city as a whole should be considered a piece of art and a world heritage site, and it is deemed as such by international organisations such as UNESCO.

The visitors-to-residents ratio reached a peak of 50 to 1 in 2000 in Venice HC (175 to 1 if excursionists are considered as well, on the assumption that each tourist wants to visit the HC at least once during their vacation). Faced with this tourist pressure, which has increased further after the recent geopolitical changes in Europe and the rest of the world, Venice started a wide-ranging reflection on possible viable options for its development and on the role that tourism could play. One imperative was the necessity to quantify the tolerance of the city with regard to tourism, as it seemed clear that the costs of tourism could become unsustainable and compromise the endurance of the city's functionality and economic soundness. Canestrelli and Costa (1991) estimated the optimal level and composition of the visitor flow that is compatible with the full functionality of the different subsystems used by citizens and tourists alike (including transport, waste collection and access to cultural assets): i.e. the socioeconomic carrying capacity. This exercise indicated that Venice could absorb a total number of about 22,500 visitors, but only a maximum of 10,700 of these should be excursionists. This limit was surpassed in 1987 for 156 days in the year; the number of yearly violations has been increasing since then, despite any attempt to smooth the peaks through regulation and planning.

Analysis

Apart from its validity as a management prescription, this exercise made it clear once and for all that Venice attracts a flow comprised of very different types of visitors. Excursions represent by far the most popular way to visit the city, and have distinct profiles regarding their impact and management requirements. Moreover, even within the excursionist category, different types can be identified. Consequently, the territory involved in the delivery of the tourist product 'Venice' is much larger than the city itself. The FTR (the region where a substantial share of the visitors of the city is hosted overnight) has surpassed the provincial scale, extending to foreign countries like Austria and Slovenia, and has become specialised. Part of the territory surrounding Venice, whatever its (sometimes nil) intrinsic cultural richness, attracts a flow of visitors just because of its proximity to the city. In addition, another portion of the region, which is specialised in seaside tourism, generates a substantial share of 'indirect' excursions to the city that adds to the 'normal' tourist flow.

Though upgraded information is badly missing, it is today accepted that more than 80% of the daily arrivals in the HC are excursionists. On average, daily visitors spend less in the city than overnight-staying visitors (as a substantial part of their budget – an estimated 60% – is spent in hotel accommodations elsewhere) and have a distinct logistic behaviour that supports the assumption of the 'vicious circle' mechanism. Excursionists do not only spend less money in the city, producing a spatial mismatch between costs and benefits generated by tourism, but they also have less time and information, attributes that are needed to spend their budgets 'efficiently', as suggested by the model presented earlier.

A visitor survey of 1997 allowed reconstruction of the main directions of visitor behaviour in the city. A random sample of 1500 visitors over a one-year period was surveyed (the main results are summarised in ICARE, 1997). Sixty to seventy per cent of the daily flow of people (and vehicles) is concentrated in a couple of hours in the morning and another couple of hours in the afternoon. The average duration of a day trip to Venice is about eight hours, three-fifths of the visits being shorter. Moreover, the bulk of this flow approaches Venice through its only road/rail connection with the mainland, provoking congestion on the main routes connecting that terminal to the central areas.

The choice of the attractions to visit and the itinerary are consequently affected, supporting Towse's (1991) hypothesis about crowding to 'superstar' attractions as a result of trying to minimise search costs and time in situations of limited information. The resulting maps of visitor itineraries with different time budgets (Figure 9.3a–d) illustrates that for the biggest share of visitors, who stay in the city for less than 12 h, the number of attractions accessed is severely limited. Visitors are on the whole more likely to 'discover' attractions that they did not explicitly wish to visit before their arrival in Venice, the closer the locations of such attractions are to the main tourist routes. Location – and not intrinsic cultural motives – guides the visiting patterns, and that trend is reinforced as time is shorter and information scarcer. The impact on the cultural system is a serious mismatch between potential capacity and actual visiting on a territorial basis.

As a result of the combined effect of congestion and lack of information, some cultural resources – the most central ones – are overcrowded whereas others, slightly out of the main tourist corridors, are utilised below their capacity. On the whole, far fewer visitors are able to enjoy the cultural heritage than the city could afford. Data relative to the main attractions show that on average one out of 4.4 visitors buys a ticket to one museum and just one out of 55.7 enters a church when they have to pay for it. In aggregate, visitation rates decrease in time. Figure 9.4 describes the extent of the mismatch between visits to the city (grey bars) and visits to its main cultural institutions, such as the centrally located Doges' Palace, the Guggenheim collection and the Academia Art Gallery, possibly one of the greatest collections of Italian renaissance arts.

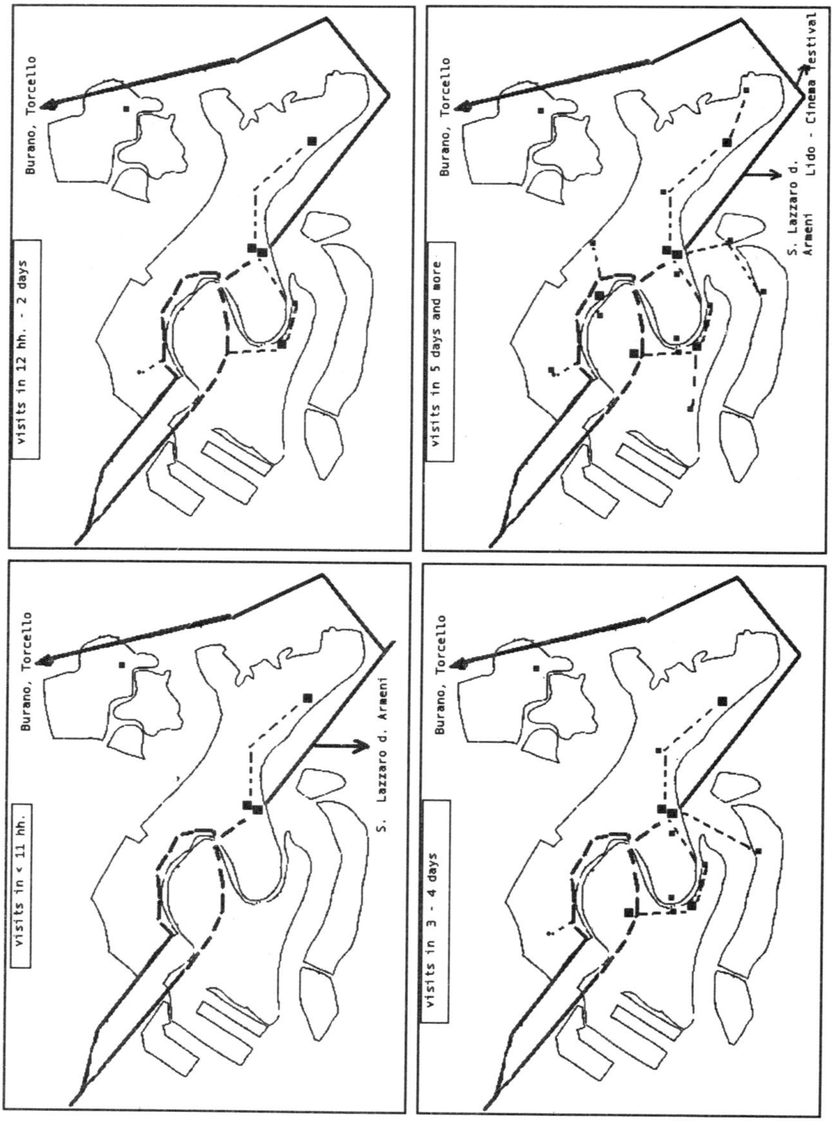

Figure 9.3a–d Time–budget analysis of cultural visits in Venice

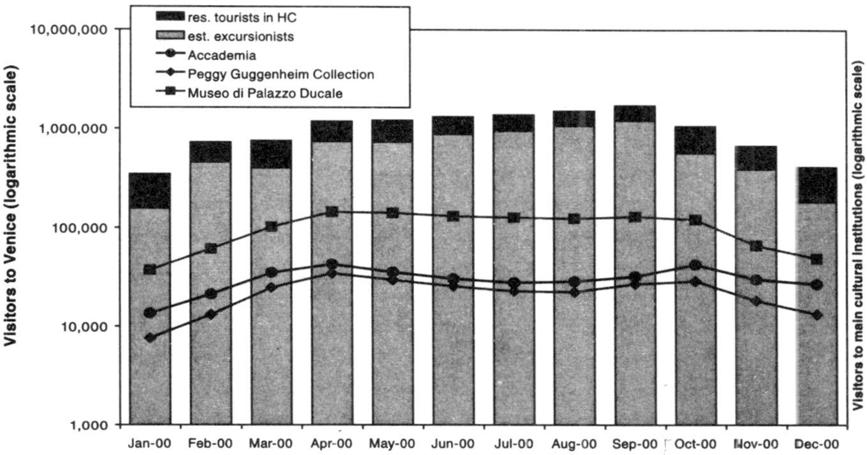

Figure 9.4 Visits to the city and visits to the main cultural institutions, Year 2000. Logarithmic scale.

However, as was argued earlier, primary cultural products are not the only elements to be affected in the vicious circle mechanism; more importantly, the very market structure for secondary or complementary tourist goods changes, provoking unsustainable effects in terms of consumption decisions of visitors. Unfortunately, it is rather hard to monitor the quality of the tourist goods on offer. The only sector for which reliable and comparable information is available is hospitality.

In Figure 9.5 the mapping of price-to-quality ratios (calculated as the average price of one star in a hotel room) shows that the priciest rooms are clustered around the main tourist gathering point of St. Mark's Square, where the first hotels were erected at the beginning of the 20th century. These hotels clearly count on a 'reputation rent' in fixing prices. Aside from them, one can see newer expensive hotels along the main corridors from the central station to St. Mark and in the proximity of the station itself. In these locations they exploit 'accessibility rents'. The same trends would be observed in relation to other tourist subsectors. For the sake of simplicity, the local tourist industry has been further divided isolating those activities called 'ancillary' by Jansen-Verbeke (1986), which in the light of the vicious circle models are more likely to seek the 'window effect', charging highest prices on account of imperfect consumer information. Among these are souvenir shops, street vendors and entertainment facilities. The concentration of these outlets in the most central areas (Figure 9.6) is again revelatory of an ongoing change in the tourist market. The location patterns of such subsectors reveal that whereas the traditional form of tourist crowding-out results in the substitution of a resident activity with a tourist activity, a new

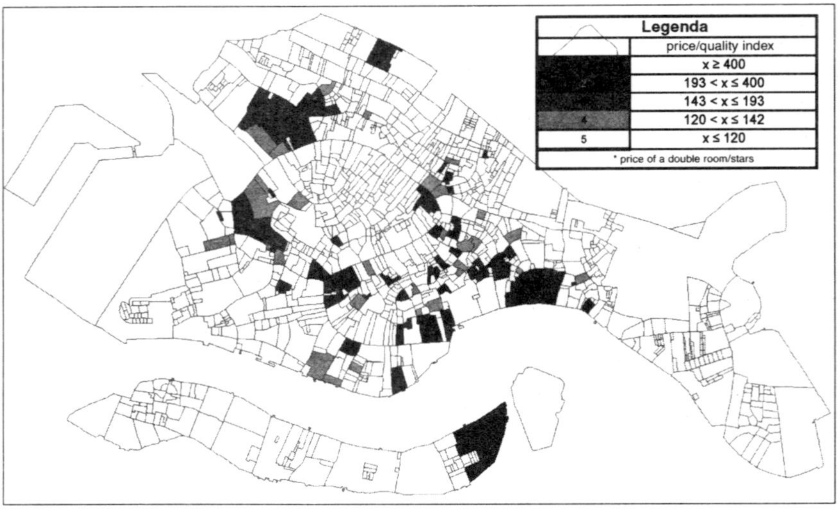

Figure 9.5 Price-to-quality ratios (av. price of stars) in Venice HC, Year 2001, census zones

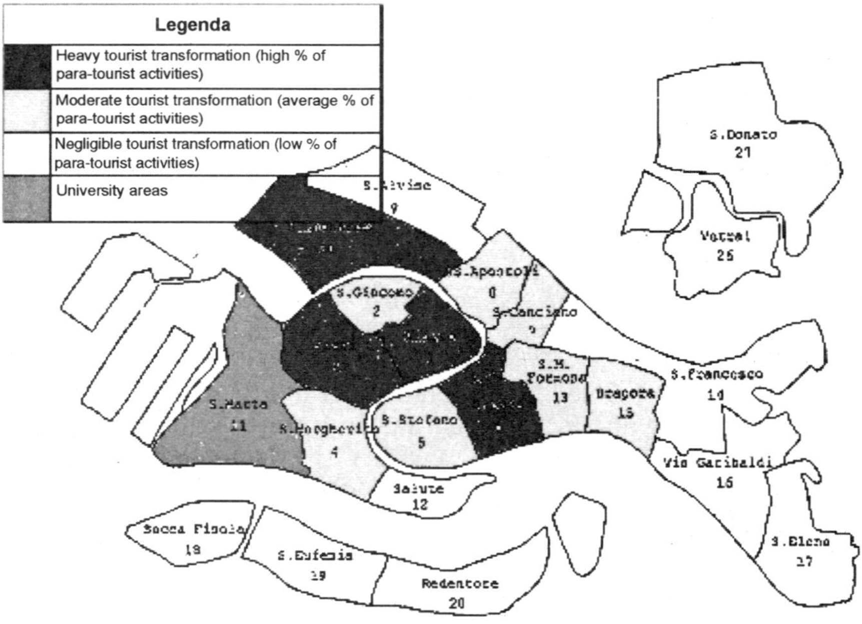

Figure 9.6 Tourist transformation in different areas within Venice HC

dimension is emerging today: the substitution within the tourist industry of high-quality with low-quality suppliers.

There are signs that in Venice the process of quality downscaling has in fact started to affect the consumption decisions of visitors, as foreseen in the fourth step of the vicious circle. Even on peak days, the hotel rooms in the upper categories are not fully occupied, and this occurs with increasing frequency.

The number of 'repeat visitors' is decreasing. Despite different interpretations in the literature (Darnell & Johnson, 2001), a decrease in interest from the 'traditional', high-paying segments and a simultaneous expansion of new origin markets does not suggest an improvement, as the new market segments have a lesser capacity to pay and a less sustainable logistic behaviour.

The share of 'group visits' in total tourism is increasing with respect to individual tourists. The most recent information estimates group visits at 32% of the total.

Tour operators are selling packages including daily visits to Venice that include overnight stays at increasingly distant locations. A number of interviews with local travel agents clarified that there is a relationship between the type of clientele and the location that is offered, especially to groups and other price-sensitive visitor types. This information should be read in conjunction with the analysis of Costa and Manente (1995: 67), who indicate that 'repeat' visitors are the most likely to spend the night in the hinterland of Venice: those who have already visited the city, on their return are likely to come as 'false excursionists'.

These 'clues' indicate that the prevalence of day trips as a means to visit Venice is less and less linked to the saturation of central accommodation, and more the result of a decision taking into consideration some of the perceived 'costs' of sleeping in Venice. As the concept of the vicious circle suggests, the elements of distortion in the tourist use of the city become self-feeding, creating further distortions.

Policy

Where is Venice going? Is tourism development in Venice proceeding relentlessly, as the main indicators would suggest, or might we expect a 'decline' in its life cycle? And what can the city do about it? The immediate suggestion from the data illustrated is that despite the richness and variety of the cultural system of Venice, both the heritage and the events, the capacity of this system to generate value is rather low. Moreover, the tourist market is not supporting a 'sustainable use' of that heritage. The price–quality spiral threatens to affect the reputation of Venice as a destination in the long term, to the benefit of its competitors. The very structure of the tourist region, where many of the benefits accrue to distant second-order destinations, is producing a 'fiscal crisis' for the maintenance of the heritage. The necessary funds, which depend on national transfers and international donors, are increasingly at stake. What is worse, this system is not inducing responsible behaviour on the supply side, which is oriented to rent extraction more than ever.

In other words, the developments conceptualised in the vicious circle model are largely present and the model seems to be developing to the full, requiring an integral policy response that addresses each of the steps of that mechanism. Hence, local policymakers should act to smooth the visitor pressure through effective tourism planning and management tools, but they also have to consider the market variables, reducing information asymmetries and controlling quality. They also have to bring forward an enhancement of the system of value generation from the cultural supply, in at least two directions: (a) intercepting a larger share of visitor expenditure and (b) becoming more diverse and spatially articulated.

The poor return from a policy approach totally focusing on demand regulation – perhaps hiding the lack of any approach whatsoever – started to be acknowledged by decision-makers and public opinion in the last few years. However, it would never have reached the top of the political agenda were it not for a series of unfortunate circumstances. First of all, there was a boom in day visits from former socialist countries in the late 1980s. These new flows spend practically nothing, have pushed congestion to the extreme, and produced a lot of waste, for which Venetians have come to pay the highest collection tax rate in Italy. The public resentment, misunderstood at that time as 'tourist racism', made it clear and very apparent that not all tourism is good, and that tourism may change for the worse if unguided. This argument was reinforced by two dramatic incidents. The first was the concert of Pink Floyd off St. Mark Square in 1989 – the event attracted a crowd of more than 200,000 without adequate facilities being set up for resting, sleeping or restoring, paralysing the city for days. The second was the fire that destroyed the city's prestigious theatre, La Fenice, in 1995. Another proposed mass event, the International Expo 2000, was finally turned down after the mobilisation of public opinion, supported by national and international organisations. It was then finally accepted that the management of tourism had to change, that the cultural heritage was a precious resource demanding preservation, and that tourism had to be a lever and not an impediment to other activities.

A number of new projects may finally trigger an appropriate process, as they are likely to improve the spatial and industrial configuration of various elements in the Venetian tourist system. On the marketing side, the promotion and commercialisation of most cultural assets as an integrated system (involving common ticketing, coordination of events, websites and the creation of a marketing agency) has been accepted, overcoming a long-lasting fragmentation in the management and ownership structure of cultural goods. Zago (1996) counts at least 10 institutions, public or private, directly responsible for the museums of Venice. Proactive cultural marketing is a new thing for a city that used to consider its international fame sufficient to attract a steadily growing flow of visitors. Moreover, an effort is being made to link the existing resources through advanced communication technologies, with the provision of online archival services and information facilities. Internal accessibility will be enhanced with the rationalisation of water transport, the diversification of access points to the HC and the creation of alternative itineraries and water routes. In the absence of such facilities as signposts or kiosks, this would result in a simple shift of crowds from one part to the other. However, the city is now convinced that the spatial management of the tourist flows must be pursued through an integral approach that also considers the accessibility and strategic location of the cultural supply.

Two management tools worth mentioning have been introduced recently:

(1) One is the ALATA partnership, a consortium of municipalities and provinces around Venice that got together to manage more effectively the incoming flows on the occasion of the Holy Year, 2000. A complex information system and a series of information points were set up to this aim. The rationale for this partnership is that the excess visitor flow expected in that year (approximately 6 million) would saturate Venice's capacity but would be attractive for peripheral destinations which are generally overlooked by tourists, starting a process of 'dispersion' of the flows in the tourist region of Venice.

(2) The second is the Venice Card, a pass (utilising 'contact-less' technology) to access a variety of facilities and functions. The Card is purchased by tourists when they send in the booking for their accommodation, and physically collected upon arrival at one of the city's terminals. The number of Cards issued is to be equal to the tolerance threshold, to be periodically determined. In that way, motivated cultural tourists get a better deal because they can more easily discover what is on offer, and then arrange their itineraries, expediently benefiting from free parking, access to limited-number events, reduced time in queues and reductions of transport fares. At the same time, the city is better off because it attracts relatively high-spending and well organised tourists.

Overall, these projects are fully consistent with the integral, complex and spatially inclusive policy approach dictated by the vicious circle.

It should be noted however that none of them was completely successful. ALATA collapsed when the 'business model' provided by the Holy Year extra-movement (and funding) was over. After the event, the peripheral sites in the tourist region of Venice found it again more convenient to play against Venice as free-riders. The Venice Card has finally been issued; however it is not the 'smart card' version originally planned, but a normal ticket, which is fine as a marketing tool but hardly achieves any of the logistic/management objectives. It is thus insufficiently flexible to manage different kinds of visitors in an interactive environment. That was due to the difficulty in getting all the stakeholders to participate in the system right from the start, and to the related delay in establishing the necessary infrastructure. The Venice Card's managing company has opted, therefore, for a 'low-profile' introduction, hoping to build up a consensus for the 'smart' version of the card. These partial failures are illustrative of the implementation difficulties faced by many heritage-city managers. Policy changes of this magnitude require a high 'organising capacity' through strategic networking and capacity building, as suggested by van den Berg and Braun (1999).

Conclusions and Implications for Life-cycle Models

This chapter has presented an original interpretation of the relations between space and market which supports the assumption of a cyclical development pattern in urban heritage destinations, for which relatively little evidence has been produced in the literature. The application of this model, however, can be extended to a variety of contexts, and in particular to those in which the local capacity is negligible with respect to the global dimension of tourism.

The vicious circle model should not be confused with the destination cycle; rather, it should be seen as an 'appendix' to it, providing a spatial–economic explanation for the decline stage of the TALC. It is argued that the reasons for decline have to be looked for in the inability of tourism to generate the resources that are needed to 'keep up' the quality of the destination, both for what is the market for tourist goods, and the heritage itself. We are not concerned in this study with the start-up process. In fact, it is assumed that tourism is a viable industry in the beginning, and attention is focused on the mature stage of the tourist industry, in order to better understand the determinants and the consequences of change within a region. Another point of distinction is that the time horizon of destination cycles is medium to long, whereas the four steps of the vicious circle model, while logically sequential, may in fact occur simultaneously from the moment of saturation of the accommodation capacity in the city centre.

One of the main difficulties with the operational use of the TALC has been in its 'tautological' nature (see, for instance, Martin & Uysal, 1990): the cyclical trend is likely to be perceived as a problem when the problem is already there. This springs from the difficulty of using it as a forecasting model. The underlying economic variables are not clearly identified, and neither is the dynamic mechanism; moreover the critical thresholds tend to be different in each context or type of destination. The TALC methodology may gain from the vicious circle conceptualisation, because this framework can easily be benchmarked through indicators that are valid in all circumstances and may anticipate the likely emergence of decline (see chapters by Berry and Manente and Pechlaner in other volume, editor). Policymakers may set up an apparatus to signal when any step of the vicious circle is critical, and act to smooth it. The 'economic nature' of these indicators makes it possible to calibrate policy tools accordingly. As long as the pressure from visitor demand persists, the circle will continue to operate, and when it is endogenously reduced as a consequence of the model's mechanism, the sustainable development of the destination is at stake. Hence policy should be integral in character, preventing the model from operating, and at the same time reducing the pressure factors at the relevant territorial level.

There is however another strong message emerging from the use of this model, one vital matter that has been largely left out of the destination-cycle literature: the fact that unsustainable tourism development may come not only from abuse of the heritage, but also from its insufficient use (van der Borg *et al*., 2000). This idea underscores the fact that even though physical impacts must remain a focus of the management of sustainable tourism, there should be more attention paid to the question of how to link heritage preservation to an integrated and balanced tourism development. As Gartner (2002: 11) puts it,

> Whether one believes in product life-cycle to explain the rise and fall of consumer acceptance, or not, it is clear that demand for culturally-based tourism products, which is reported to have increased substantially in recent times, is still lower than the supply of products. In this situation, other factors such as service, value added, niche marketing take on greater importance.

Tourism management often seems to miss the point, treating tourism as a sector to be 'isolated' from other functions performed by a city, rather than as an engine of harmonious, synergetic regional development. The peculiar nature of the resources on which heritage tourism is based, and the extreme complexity of the environment with which tourism strategies have to cope, contribute to the incapacity of traditional policy approaches to fully grasp and govern the process.

Chapter 10
The TALC and Heritage Sites

JANE MALCOLM-DAVIES

Introduction

The democratisation of culture has permitted the British bourgeoisie to participate in ways previously reserved for the elite before the two world wars. Long before that, Napoleon sneered at the English as a nation of shopkeepers. Now, it seems, even the symbols of power – royal palaces, stately homes, ancient cathedrals – are in the hands of middle-class marketeers, desperate to attract visitors. Heritage sites are being redefined as products and this new perspective suggests that they are subject to the vagaries of the product life-cycle. It is the purpose of this paper to investigate whether this revolution is actually taking place and, if so, whether it threatens what it promises to preserve.

Heritage attractions, whatever their original functions, found themselves thrust into a highly competitive marketplace during the 1980s. There are myriad activities that offer alternative leisure experiences. There has been a growth in book sales and an expansion of networked entertainment services in the home in addition to walking for pleasure and sports or leisure centre activities (Davies, 1994: 23). The attractions sector itself has boomed. In the UK, the number of tourist attractions increased dramatically at the end of the 20th century – 47% of all existing attractions have appeared since 1980 (Middleton, 2001: 196). There is much evidence of a growth in heritage attractions in particular (Hall & McArthur, 1996; Hooper-Greenhill, 1994; Yale, 1998). It is difficult to think in terms of competition for attractions such as Notre Dame Cathedral, the Pyramids and Buckingham Palace because they are all unique (Swarbrooke, 1995: 49). But it is nevertheless true that Notre Dame is just one of many great cathedrals, the Pyramids one of many ancient burial complexes and Buckingham Palace one of many royal residences.

The competition phenomenon has not been confined to those places where the economics of the marketplace held sway: 'The number of museums in both western and eastern European countries increased substantially during the 1970s and 1980s ... Museum growth was also encouraged by Communist regimes in eastern Europe during the 1980s, although arguably with different motives from their western counterparts' (Richards, 1996: 10–11). With the collapse of the Soviet Union and the reunification of Germany, the last bastion of market-protected heritage bit the dust.

The test for success for cultural institutions can no longer be a purely aesthetic one. They must justify themselves in quantitative terms, such as the number of visitors or income generated. These performance indicators are equally important for institutions which operate in a wholly commercial environment and for publicly funded organisations which have to demonstrate the effectiveness of subsidy (Richards, 1996: 13). Improved access or display is now essential for a successful Heritage Lottery Fund grant in the UK (Heritage Lottery Fund, 1997). Much that has been written about these trends focuses on museums, which stand as representatives of what is happening in other heritage sectors (Davies, 1994: 24; Light, 1995: 118). Peter Longman of the Museums and Galleries Commission remarked in 1994: 'All museums now exist in a mixed economy. Very few can rely solely on the public purse... This means that they are subject to fluctuations in the economy, and prey to demographic and social trends in much the same way as any other industry' (Davies, 1994: 4).

The move to the marketplace has brought about fundamental changes in the management of heritage attractions. There has been a discernible shift from historical monument to heritage product since 1850 (Figure 10.1). Three successive management approaches are identifiable – preservation, conservation and heritage (Ashworth, 1994: 15). The 'heritage' phase is the one in which the resource is transformed into a product for consumption in the marketplace. In this transformation many managers and commentators ignore any distinction between the management of a historic site and a theme park, applying mass-market concepts to heritage attractions without a second thought (Swarbrooke, 1995; Walsh-Heron & Stevens, 1990). This belittles the real challenges facing fragile sites under increasing visitor pressure. Some authors are more sensitive to historic sites' particular concerns, noting that heritage attractions are, for the most part, concerned with the management of vulnerable resources (Richards, 1996).

Nevertheless, the stress now is on inviting people in, not tolerating them if they arrive. 'The balance of power in museums is shifting from those who care for objects to include, and often prioritise those who care for people' (Hooper-Greenhill, 1994: 1). These changed priorities are due in part to political forces. The withdrawal of state funding from the arts in general has forced heritage attractions to face up to the challenge of making money. Government-created quangos in the UK have been charged with making ruins (English Heritage) and redundant official residences (Historic Royal Palaces) accessible to wider audiences both physically and intellectually (HRPA, 1995). While public responsibilities have been shifted to the private sector, entrepreneurs

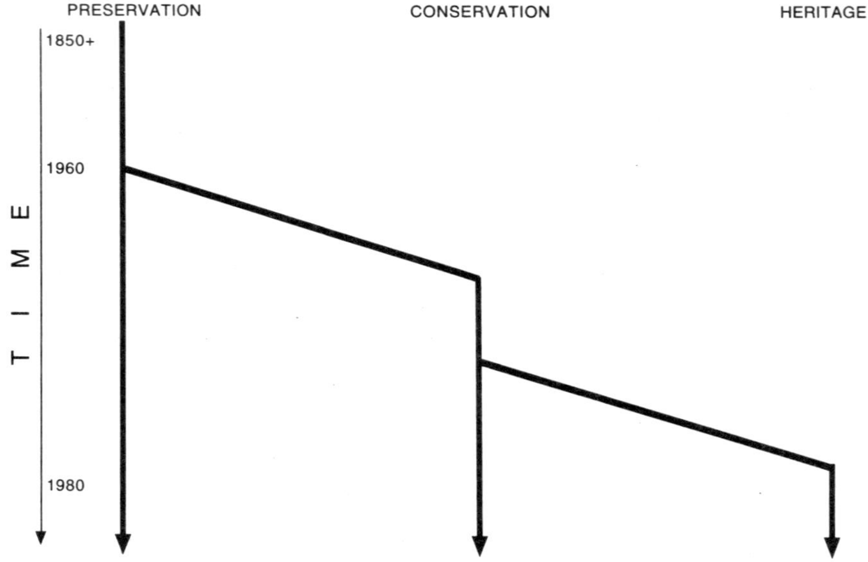

Figure 10.1 Phases in the evolutionary process: Historical monument to heritage product (Ashworth, 1994: 15)

have moved in on the same market: 'One striking feature of these recent developments has been the increased privatisation of the heritage/museum industry, with 56% of recently opened museums being in the private sector' (Urry, 1990: 107).

The theory of the product life-cycle, which is frequently discussed in relation to destinations (Cooper, 1992), is applicable to heritage attractions, although few authors note it. A detailed study of visitor figures to 16 ecomuseums such as Skansen in Stockholm, Old Sturbridge Village in Massachusetts, and the Museum of Welsh Life in Cardiff, demonstrated the classic product life-cycle despite geographical and economic differences (Figure 10.2). Having recognised the downturn in their visitorship, several of the ecomuseums set about rejuvenating their product. At Sovereign Hill in Victoria (Australia), a *son-et-lumière* experience was developed to rekindle interest in the site; while at the Museum of Welsh Life a competitively priced season ticket contributed to a recovery (de Haan, 1997: 26–27).

Rejuvenation

A Confederation of British Industry survey showed that 'mature attractions which recognised/anticipated changing market trends, had successfully developed to meet those needs, and experienced sustained

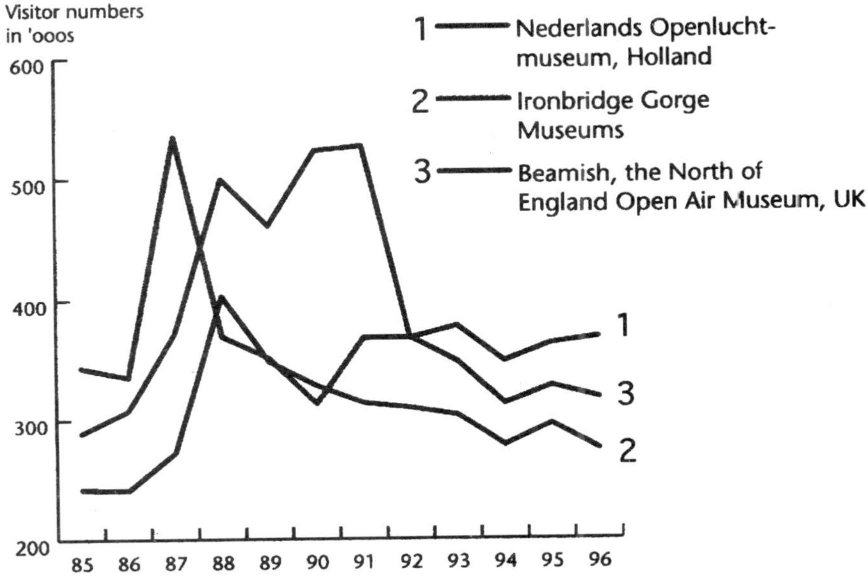

Promotional activities and local events generate noticeable peaks in visits, but are rarely sustained

Figure 10.2 The product life cycle theory applied to ecomuseums (de Haan, 1997: 26)

growth as a result' (CBI, 1998: 20). The need for rejuvenation of resources as visitor numbers fall over time is recognised in the management of theme parks and addressed by the development of new and yet more thrilling rides, often costing as much as £1 million each (Gilling, 1995: 41). Heritage sites may introduce new methods of presentation or improved support services such as dining facilities in order to boost falling admissions, although usually at considerably less cost (Swarbrooke, 1995: 48).

In 1996, the Jorvik Viking Centre in York (UK) updated its static displays, added an opportunity for visitor participation and introduced costumed interpreters (Yale, 1998: 131). The introduction or retraining of front-of-house staff is a way of introducing novelty (Holloway, 1994: 144) and enhancing the visitor experience (Richards, 1992: 39), and thereafter, regular changes to their activities and presentations are cheaper than replacing technological systems of display (Binks *et al.*, 1988: 39). But even these relatively inexpensive ways of rejuvenating an experience are not without difficulties for the heritage sector. People are a bothersome business and few heritage organisations have the time or expertise to recruit, train, motivate and retrain staff in what can become a boring and repetitive job (Risk, 1994: 326).

Heritage sector rejuvenations are cheap, expedient solutions compared to those dreamed up by private attractions such as Camelot, Alton Towers and Blackpool Pleasure Beach where £3–5 million is spent on rejuvenation every few years (Davis, 2001: 26). Wigan Pier's *The way we were* heritage centre undertook a major overhaul of what it was offering in 1999/2000 when a Single Regeneration Budget grant permitted an investment of £2.2 million in Robert Opie's Museum of Memories. In its first year, the Opie collection attracted 260,000 visitors but in 2000/01 visitation fell back to 160,000 again. How often may a heritage attraction tap into such funds? One historic house owner reported that having received a government grant in 1969, he had been refused every application ever since (Williams & Bradlaw, 2001: 286).

If rejuvenation at heritage sites is not possible through major new projects, the facilities at heritage sites may be tailored to match the benefits sought by specific visitors in order to exploit a target market successfully (Swarbrooke, 1995) but it is not often that this happens. Manchester's Museum of Science and Industry published a marketing plan in 1992, which presented information on the current visitor profile and the potential for development in the main segments of that market with strategies to increase the existing customer base and attract new audiences (Hooper-Greenhill, 1994: 175). By the mid-1990s, *The way we were* recognised that most of its 160,000 visitors were schoolchildren. The management did something rare in the 'We're here for everyone' world of heritage attractions – it chose a target market and worked to produce specially tailored packages. It focused firmly on the educational market: 'Schools are our lifeblood', maintains the council's group marketing officer (Davis, 2001: 24–27).

Marketing Heritage Sites

The postmodern era has been marked by the emergence of new interest groups and specialised markets (Richards, 1996: 10–11). A heritage market segment may be identified by grouping all potential visitors with similar motivations and propensities towards particular types of heritage or visitor experiences (Hall & MacArthur, 1996). Social psychologists, market researchers and business forecasters have identified attitudes and lifestyles as important alternatives to the traditional classification of people by demographics and socioeconomic groups (Middleton, 1990: 29–31). Middleton argues that museums should target an 'inner directed' group which has been growing in significance (from 25% to over 40% of the population) over the past 20 years. This group is made up of 'people of all social groups and income levels, mostly educated beyond school leaving age and typically aged over 40, who have achieved the self confidence, maturity of personality and tolerance to be able to live easily with themselves and social contacts' (Middleton, 1990: 30). This is a significant alternative to more traditional segmentation approaches (Davies, 1994: 58). Another alternative is the 'values and lifestyles' framework, which identifies nine different types of consumer (Gunther, 1999: 119). This has been used to target adults most likely to visit museums (Mitchell, 1984: 8).

A further attempt to segment the London (UK) tourist attraction market in a different way (Figure 10.3) is based on a psychographic analysis of motivation (Plog, 1991). It puts the Tower of London on the itinerary of the psychocentric visitor and the Hayward Gallery on that of the allocentric (Richards, 1992: 7). The Canadian Museum of Civilization in Hull has segmented its market according to patterns of behaviour and designed exhibits to suit: visitors can be characterised as 'streakers', 'strollers' or 'students' (MacDonald & Alsford, 1989: 74). Both these approaches go some way to differentiating the visitors in terms of personality but their usefulness is questionable in a sector lacking the management skills to innovate and take risks (Graham & Lennon, 2002: 216).

Nevertheless, the application of mass marketing ideas to heritage sites has had the advantage of freeing some from old-fashioned notions of exclusivity. The shift from the traditional collection, care and conservation-centred approach to a concern for the visitors' welfare is analogous to the switch from a product-orientated approach to a

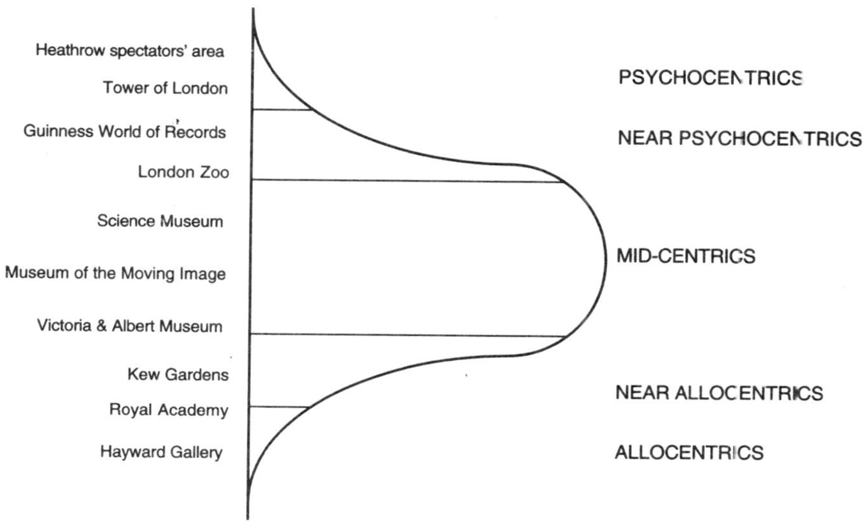

Figure 10.3 Psychographic positions of London paid admission visitor attractions (Richards, 1992: 7)

customer-orientated culture (Kotler, 1984: 23). A marketing manager's attention usually focuses on the four elements of the marketing mix (price, product, place and promotion) and how they may be manipulated to increase market share and revenue generation (Hall & McArthur, 1996: 26). Each may be used to stimulate visitation at a time when the life-cycle curve suggests the market is ready for a boost.

The price

One predictable manifestation of heritage sites being treated as products would be a new emphasis on price as a strategic component of the marketing mix. Some museums and other heritage attractions have attempted to cover their costs with increased admission charges or introduced them for the first time. Kirby (1988) provides an excellent résumé of the resulting controversy in the UK – attendances at the National Maritime Museum in London fell by 37% in the year charges were imposed. However, other museums reported initial problems followed by a gradual rise in numbers or an increase in visitation, such as that experienced by the Imperial War Museum in London (UK), when admission fees coincided with a major redevelopment programme (Lilley, 1990: 12). More recently, the sudden absence of admission charges at national (i.e. government-funded) museums in December 2001 resulted in the doubling of numbers at many (DCMS, 7 January 2002), stealing visitors from their competitors who have not benefited from the government's largesse. In this context, the decision to charge, and what to charge, has not been in line with sharp-nosed business practices. This is a marketplace where producers are not free to set competitive prices because the government is subsidising major players (HCCMSC, 2002: 88).

There is also some prejudice against charging premium prices at heritage sites because their mission is frequently seen as primarily educational and that therefore they should be accessible to all. For example, under the government legislation of 1983 that created English Heritage in the United Kingdom, it has a statutory duty to provide educational facilities, advice and information to the public (Prentice & Prentice, 1989: 155). One of its aims is the promotion of wider knowledge and enjoyment of England's heritage of ancient monuments and historic buildings (English Heritage Education Service, 1986). Meanwhile, Cadw (the government body responsible for Welsh historic monuments in the UK) 'seeks to broaden the awareness of all Welsh people wherever they may be, and the visitors to Wales, to help them learn, to understand, to enjoy the 6,000 years of history visible in the landscape' (Prentice & Prentice, 1989: 155–156). Many recently established heritage attractions incorporate educational aims in their mission statements (in the UK, the Ironbridge Gorge Museum, the York Archaeological Trust and Wigan Pier Heritage Centre are to a greater or lesser extent established as charitable educational organisations), although this does not stop them from charging higher prices than their publicly managed competitors.

In a study of factors affecting visitation in 1999, just 4% of historical, garden and museum attraction managers suggested that changes in admission charges were responsible for falling numbers, whereas 32% of them identified the weather as the cause (Hanna, 1994: A61). A study of pricing decisions at attractions in England concluded that the sector is cautious and conservative in its pricing decisions, with respondents stating that their admission fees were primarily linked to 'what the market will bear' (65%), costs (51%) or competitors' prices (23%) (Rogers, 1995). Rarely is price used to differentiate sites in the marketplace and the range of admission charges in the UK is very narrow – just 14% charge up to £1, while only 9% charge more than £5. The average price is £2.97 (Hanna, 1998: 29). Tourist attractions in general are thought to be overpriced by UK residents (MAI, 2000: 42). However, there is evidence that this is not true of heritage sites. A study of visitors at Warkworth Castle in 1994 suggested that they were (on average) prepared to pay 91 pence (29%) more than the adult admission price of £1.80 (Powe & Willis, 1996: 266). Studies of price elasticity in relation to increases at heritage sites have shown that it is generally low, particularly in the long term (Bouvaird *et al*., 1984; Jones, 1984; Snaith, 1975).

There are few instances of cut-price admission fees offered in the last few days of an exhibition or lower prices for admission in the off-season. Still fewer heritage sites willingly banish charging altogether despite the clear relationship between free access and increased admission. When the National Museum and Galleries in Merseyside became free in December 2001, the number of visitors for the month rose by 56% on the previous December; and at the National Railway Museum in York there was an increase of 66% (DCMS, 7 January 2002). However, a MORI poll in September 2002 revealed that 41% of visitors to museums were not influenced by the abolition of entry fees and a further 40% were not aware that fees had been abolished (HCCMSC, 2002: 89).

Pricing policies may also be employed to preserve cultural assets intact both in terms of the visitor experience and the longevity of the resource. A £5 admission charge at Westminster Abbey was intended to reduce the impact on the building of nearly three million visitors a year and restore its atmosphere as a place of prayer (Fyall & Garrod, 1998: 226).

The UK lacks a tradition of philanthropy towards heritage resources in stark contrast to North America, where many museums and historic sites have enjoyed long associations with successive generations of a generous family (Alberge & Rumbelow, 2003: 3). In Europe too there are examples of art collections housed and presented at the expense of individual patrons such as the Museo Thyssen-Bornemisza in Madrid (Shnayerson, 2002: 74–83). Admission charges are therefore a fact of life for many heritage sites in the UK and yet there is little evidence that price is manipulated as a strategic component of their marketing mix.

The promotion

Heritage sites do not spend a great deal of money on promotion, whether it be through public relations or advertising campaigns. Alton Towers Pleasure Park spent £2.6 million on advertising in 1998 compared to Beaulieu's (a stately home with a Motor Museum) £175,000 and Historic Scotland's £153,000 (for 300 properties, 70 of which charge admission) in 1997 (Griffiths, 1998: 45). Hampton Court Palace struck a deal with media production company Bazal to develop a 'behind the scenes' television series to promote it around the world (Sturgis: 1998). Both Chatsworth and Woburn Abbey have offered similar televised peeps behind their green baize doors in the hope of boosting visitor numbers. However, promotional activity for most heritage sites is confined to a special events programme. These are often managed in-house, exploit local volunteer labour and use craftsworkers who sell their wares, amateur re-enactment societies or may rely on enthusiasts with visually impressive hobbies such as ballooning or vintage car restoration. Historically themed events are often designed to maximise attendance by taking a cavalier approach to the known history of the site. In order that special events are possible at Plimoth Plantation in Massachusetts (USA), 'historical events have to be glamourised a bit or historical dates shifted a little' (Snow, 1993: 88). A wedding of 1627 is knowingly recreated each year more lavishly than is 'probably proper' for the time and place. At other times of year, simple weddings are staged as a counterbalance to this festive special event (Snow, 1993: 88–89).

It is difficult to reconcile the promotional needs of a site with the reality of the place recorded in historical documents. Colonial Williamsburg in Virginia (USA) has wrestled with the evidence of 'unpleasant subjects, unappetising smells, and ugly sights' in 1770s Virginia, while offering 'itself as a holiday destination, a place for relaxing, entertaining, even romantic, vacation' (Leon & Piatt, 1989: 75). Themes are often reduced to simple dichotomies which are easy to transmit in advertising material and on-site information. Lévi-Strauss and other structuralists argued that humans establish oppositional sets in their minds (high/low, wet/dry, black/white) in order to process and store information (MacDonald & Alsford, 1989: 62). This tendency frequently reduces complex cultural phenomena to simplistic scenarios. The medieval tournament with its chivalric pomp and careful ceremony is often presented as the black knight (bad) losing to the white knight (good). A comprehensive survey of special events associated with historic houses in the USA found that a great many focus on 'mundane activities' such as household chores, often on seasonal themes, because 'they are fairly simple to stage' (Janiskee, 1996: 410). The special events are, for the most part, superficial representations of the history of the houses at which they are held (Janiskee, 1996: 407–409).

The chief executive of English Heritage has argued that special events are a 'taster', and that they invite people to investigate further these aspects of English history. Critics do not agree:

> These events are nothing but mere titillation, meaningless amateur dramatics promoting the postmodern simulacrum, a hazy image of a manipulated and trivialised past. The most ridiculous was the American Civil War garrison at Fort Brockhurst, Hampshire... History is decontextualised and mixed with non-history in a promotion of a pastiche. English Heritage has argued that because these so-called recreations are popular, that makes them acceptable. (Walsh, 1991: 102–103)

Promotion is not implemented with the rigour of commercial operations at most heritage sites. Low cost special events tend to be the mainstay of their promotional efforts and there is some evidence that their transience permits a lowering of curatorial standards (Sansom, 1996: 120).

The place

This element of the marketing mix has a radically different application to tourist attractions in that the customer travels to the product, rather than vice versa, and prepurchase is rare. It is theme parks which tend to use intermediaries to widen their point-of-sale via ticketing agencies as their prices offer a viable level of income as commission (Swarbrooke, 1995: 210–211). However, there are examples of heritage sites using intermediaries to sell advance tickets: for example, Buckingham Palace which also exploits the internet as a point-of-sale, levying a £1 booking fee on each transaction. Few tourist attraction websites allow online ticketing in this way, although they clearly fulfil a promotional role in offering up-to-date, comprehensive information about a site, its location and the visitor experience (Fenn, 2001: 53). There have been some questionable marriages between the commercial world and historic houses in attempts to widen the point-of-sale. In 2001, Historic Royal Palaces offered Sainsbury supermarket customers discounted admission tickets. However, heritage sites' use of this element of the marketing mix does not seem to have brought about a ruthless change in the way heritage sites sell themselves to potential visitors.

The product

Most commercial operations recognise the need to update and redesign their products for specific target markets. Critics (for example, Newby, 1994) suggest the consequence of this is that the presentation of heritage resources is primarily a marketing activity rather than marketing acting as a servant of the resource (Figure 10.4):

> This is a process involving both resource selection and packaging. It is not a marginal enhancement of a product but is, from the producer's viewpoint, the means by which the diverse elements are integrated... [it] involves a conscious series of choices about which history-derived products are to be produced, and conversely which are not. (Ashworth, 1994: 17)

It is arguable, however, that this selectivity has always been the case at museums, historic houses and other cultural resources. Usually owned and managed by the state or wealthy individuals, these places have rarely been hotbeds of subversive or radical re-presentations of the past. This view also suggests that visitors are passive receivers of heritage experiences, which is not borne out by studies into their methods of constructing meaning for themselves (Goulding, 2000: 849).

There are some aspects of heritage management activity that suggest that the visitor experience is being redesigned in subtle if not radical ways. Many subsidised historic sites are in the care of state or other public authorities and even here 'recent years have seen an increased

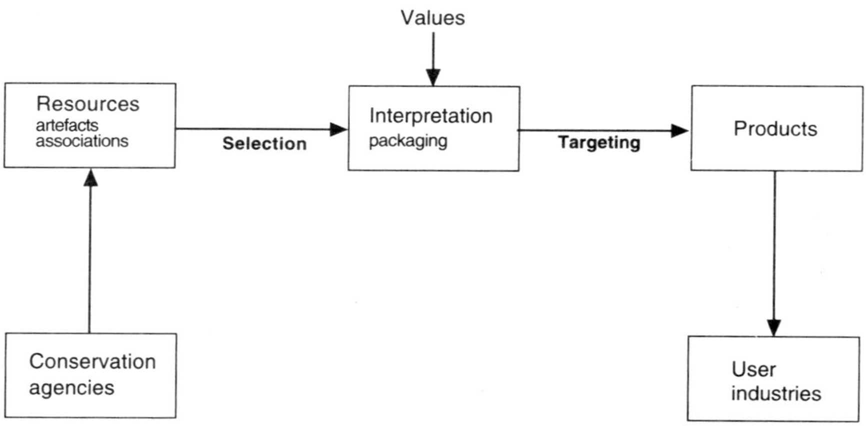

Figure 10.4 Components of the heritage industry (Ashworth, 1994: 17)

emphasis on customer care, corporate planning, greater management flexibility and performance measurement' (Davies, 1994: 25). The heritage sector of old tended to see the visitor as a disruptive force – an attitude long-held in service industries but undergoing a fundamental change (Bowen & Schneider, 1985: 132). Guidelines published by the then Museums and Galleries Commission urged museums to adopt ideas based on the 'National code of practice for visitor attractions' developed by the English Tourist Board (Hooper-Greenhill, 1994: 182).

If the theory of 'the augmented product' (Kotler, 1984: 463) was successfully applied to a package holiday (Callaghan *et al.*, 1994) and a theme park (Swarbrooke, 1995), why not a heritage site? For a product to be successful, all its constituent parts must be shaped to complement each other – from the core benefits, through its tangible features to the augmented elements (Figures 10.5 and 10.6). Catering, gift shops and membership schemes have been introduced or improved to make heritage sites more attractive to the visiting public (Crighton, 1992; Herbert, 1989; Palmer, 1994).

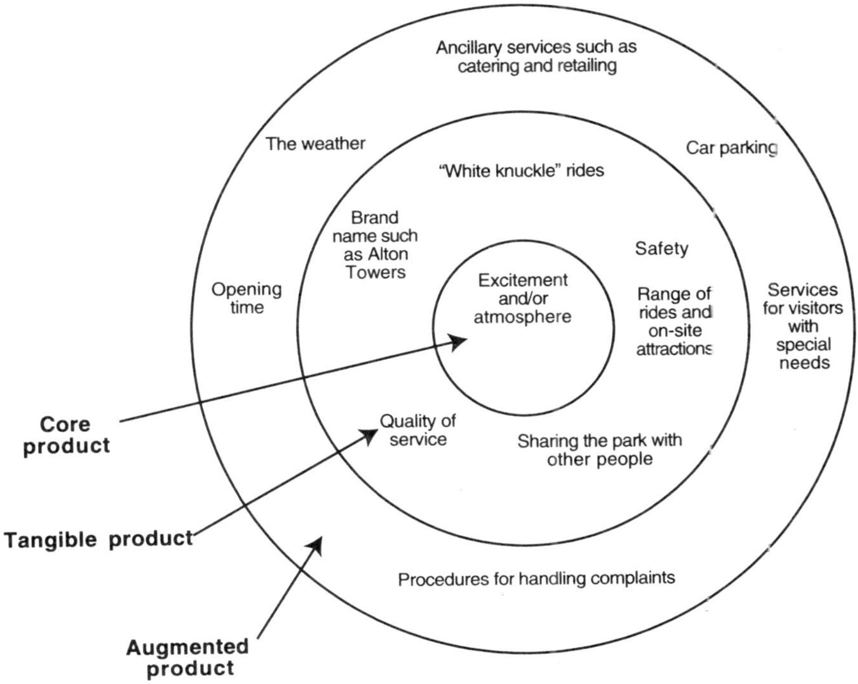

Figure 10.5 The three levels of product, the example of a theme park: After Kotler, 1994 (Swarbrooke, 1995: 40)

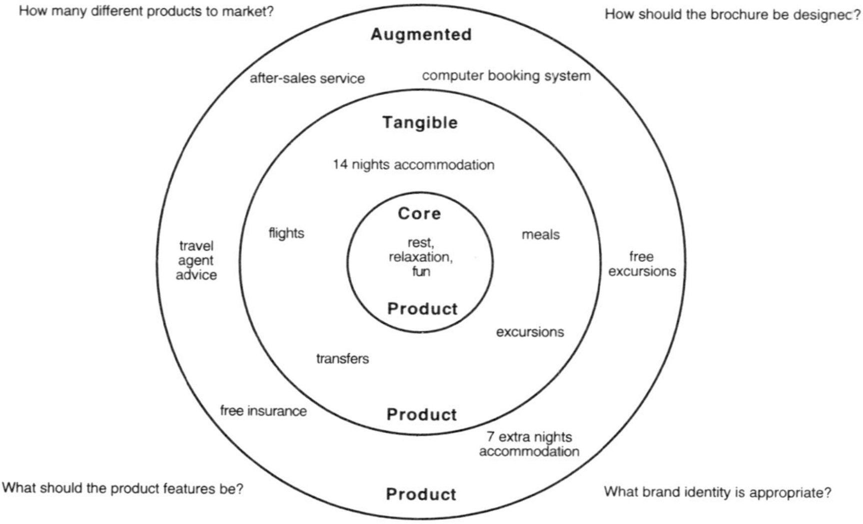

Figure 10.6 The elements of the travel and tourism products (Callaghan & Bottomley Renshaw, 1994: 213)

A great deal of effort has gone into the tangible and augmented levels of the heritage site product (mainly because these raise extra revenue) yet it seems unlikely that the visitor comes to a heritage attraction with expectations which may be marked off on a checklist: 'Tourists do not arrive in a destination simply in order to sleep, eat, drink, buy petrol and park their cars, and yet these amenities are said to produce the benefits of tourism' (Bull, 1985: 19). There is something beyond these facilities on offer, something beyond the physical properties of the place which satisfy other needs for the visitor. A product (or a heritage attraction) possesses two major characteristics: what it is and what it does (sometimes referred to as its extrinsic and intrinsic qualities). Its extrinsic features are what are usually described in brochures and in industry classifications. The intrinsic value of an attraction is the need it satisfies; its utility – what it does rather than what it looks like or how it is described (Bull, 1985: 24). While there is evidence that heritage site 'products' have been tinkered with at the edges, there is little to suggest that the core benefits have been challenged. Indeed, a typical example of an attempt to assess the quality of service at historic houses uses a checklist of 24 items. The items identify needs, such as the restaurant and directional signs (Frochot & Hughes, 2000: 161). None of them addresses the intangibles, the historic house's 'utility' for the visitor. If evaluations concentrate on the peripherals in this way, there is little likelihood that the heritage resource is seriously threatened by the results they provide.

Research has suggested that there are three main components to a heritage site's core product: atmosphere, learning and personal experience.

Atmosphere

Visitor surveys conducted by the United States National Trust for Historic Preservation and Colonial Williamsburg in Virginia have shown that people visiting historic sites were primarily attracted by the 'atmosphere' and ambience associated with them (Colonial Williamsburg, 1985; Mawson, 1984). 'A shock of confrontation with "the Other" is essential to a memorable museum experience' (Lowenthal, 1992: 26). Heritage tourism offers an encounter with nature or an opportunity to feel part of the history of the place (Hall & Zeppel, 1990: 87). 'Travel is no longer to see for the first time. It is to experience' (Collins, 1983: 59). It is the experiential nature of a visit to a heritage site which sets it apart from tangible products and other services too (Prentice, 1993: 202; Prentice *et al*., 1993).

Heritage attractions put people in contact with the tangible remains of the past and this relationship is 'something we want to appreciate and experience to the fullest extent' (Masser *et al*., 1994: 31). It is important, then, that each site offers visitors a unique and impressive atmospheric experience. Visitors to New Lanark in Scotland suggested that the lack of exhibits which offered immersion in the past (such as an underground mine trip or costumed demonstrators re-enacting what life would have been like) was a weakness in its provision compared to similar attractions (Beeho & Prentice, 1997: 84).

This emphasis on the visitors' opportunities for immersion rather than an attraction's physical features or facilities sits well with the 'gestalt' theory of museum experience (Falk & Dierking, 1992: 81). Gestalt is 'a structure or configuration of... phenomena, so integrated as to constitute a functional unit with properties not derivable from its parts in summation' (Webster's, 1983; Johns & Tyas, 1997: 475). All the parts must be considered within the context of the whole visitor experience (Johns, 1999: 127). That an experience cannot easily be broken down into its elements for analysis explains why well meaning research, which concentrates on facilities, reveals little about successful heritage site management.

Visitors have identified 'a sense of the past' as being an important component of the visitor experience (Malcolm-Davies, 2002: 577). This sense of the past may be connected with issues of perceived authenticity, which has been identified as 'the best predictor of visitor satisfaction' (see Figure 10.7) (Pearce, 1988: 77). Visitors may want an empirically 'real' experience of the past (an objective authenticity), their own idea of a 'real' experience (a constructivist authenticity), a 'real' fake experience

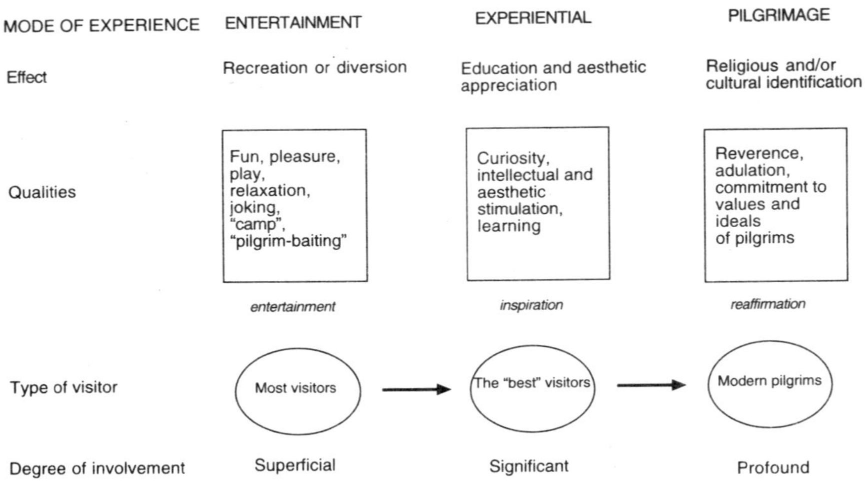

Figure 10.7 Three modes of tourist experience (Cohen, 1988) at Plimoth Plantation, Massachusetts, USA (Snow, 1993)

(a postmodern authenticity), a 'real' personal experience (existential authenticity) or a mix of these 'realities' (Wang, 1999).

Learning

Research into historic site visitors' priorities in four countries revealed that learning something is more important than atmosphere, although together they top the list of what people want from their visits (Malcolm-Davies, 2002: 469). Education was what most visitors to Burgos Cathedral (Spain), Nottingham Castle (UK) and Paleis Het Loo (Netherlands) identified as their motivation for visiting in a 1995 survey (Richards, 1996: 25). Visits to New Lanark in Scotland were perceived to have increased visitors' knowledge through a beneficial learning experience (Beeho & Prentice, 1997: 84). Another research project in Scotland suggests that a quest for active learning takes second place to enjoying oneself. A study of visitors to the ship Discovery in Dundee (UK) showed that 82% went to learn, compared with 63% who went to be entertained. However, these were secondary motivations indicated after 99.5% of visitors had already noted more pragmatic reasons for going, such as being on holiday and having a day out (Prentice *et al.*, 1998: 9). While 48% of visitors to an Australian ecomuseum said their principal reason for visiting was an interest in history or a desire to learn (Moscardo & Pearce, 1986: 473), only 2% of visitors identified 'self-education' as a reason for their last museum visit in another study (Merriman, 1991: 55).

Surveys of visitors to historic sites in Wales in the 1980s showed 62% of respondents wanting to be informed or educated (Light, 1995: 125).

A study at Cadw sites in Wales suggested that a small minority seek to be taught about a site in a formal sense but that a large group is interested in acquiring some knowledge (Herbert, 1989b: 198). The Commission on Museums for a New Century acknowledged this difference by committing itself to the concept of lifelong learning rather than formal education (CMNC, 1984: 59). The many and varied definitions of museums have adapted to these new expectations; the well founded 'functions' of a museum as defined by the American Association of Museums (collection, conservation, exhibition) are giving way to a more progressive idea of the 'purposes' of a museum (study, education, enjoyment) as defined by the International Council of Museums (MacDonald & Alsford, 1989: 37; Weil, 1986: 26–27).

Personal experience

The essential magic of a heritage attraction is that it provides a touchstone for the perceived benefits of the past. It is not necessary to feel dissatisfied with the modern world to appreciate these benefits, as critics of 'the heritage industry' have asserted (Hewison, 1987; Lowenthal, 1985; Samuel, 1994; Wright, 1985). A change of scene, an encounter with something other than the regular routine, was a feature of leisure activity long before it extended to the many rather than being limited to the few. Consumers are increasingly sophisticated and self-centred – because most people in industrialised societies are relatively comfortable, they seek experiences that offer more than sustenance, warmth and shelter (Maslow, 1954: 80–106). A new postmaterialist set of values has emerged, defined as needs for 'self-realisation, self-esteem, affection, a better quality of life and improved social relationships' (Walsh, 1991: 62).

Economic, social and technological changes have produced 'the thoughtful consumer', who puts more emphasis on the quality of life than material affluence (Martin & Mason, 1993: 37). Visitors seek quality of experience with opportunities for greater personal participation, whether they define quality by recreational values, intellectual stimulation or cultural meaningfulness (MacDonald & Alsford, 1989: 41). 'The emphasis is likely to be more on visiting with a purpose, going to an attraction because it offers something of particular interest or relevance to the visitor, rather than just because the destination exists and there is time to be occupied' (Martin & Mason, 1993: 39). Sociopsychological studies of leisure have revealed that such activities are goal driven and linked to the expected benefits or rewards gained. An individual will undertake those activities that produce a sense of competence, satisfaction and fulfilment (Light, 1995: 126). Facilities that help a visitor to develop a critical insight and appreciation of historic buildings provide a boost to self esteem (Herbert, 1989b: 197).

Arguably, visitors in the 21st century are more conscious of the way in which the world around them is constructed than visitors were in the 20th century. Gone, or going, is the classic realist text with its authoritative linear narrative and empirical truths (MacCabe, 1974: 8). *Tristram Shandy* (Sterne, 1760–1767), *Ulysses* (Joyce, 1914), *To the Lighthouse* (Woolf, 1927) and *The garden of forking paths* (Borges, 1941) paved the way in literature for fragmented narrative in film (for example, in *Natural Born Killers*, Oliver Stone, 1994) and (in the USA) television (for example, in Courthouse, Deborah Joy LeVine, 1995). All of these demonstrate the variety of ways a story can be told (Gibson, 1996). 'Most visitors today are oriented toward a multichannelled, cool-media approach to experience. They expect to be able to switch back and forth among channels easily, to experience a rapid transformation of frames' (Snow, 1993: 192).

The 'thoughtful' visitor is looking for something more nebulous – a 'real' experience (Martin & Mason, 1993: 39). They may enjoy it with their tongues firmly in their cheeks or see it as an opportunity to learn, depending on the authority with which it is delivered and the respect they accord it. The integrity and genuineness of what is offered will, in part, determine the lasting quality of the experience (Martin & Mason, 1993: 40). Whether the visitors actually learn anything is irrelevant; what is more important is that they think they have learnt something and learning can therefore be identified as a perceived benefit of their visit (Light, 1995: 134; Prentice, 1993).

Conclusions

If marketing theory were applied with rigour, product development techniques would be used to devise, pilot and refine visitor experiences at historic sites to provide learning, atmosphere and personal experience. Any assessment of a heritage attraction's strengths and weaknesses should attempt to gauge how effective it is in 'raising curiosity, appealing to fantasy, and in providing a challenge' (Schouten, 1995: 260).

One commentator notes 'the introduction of marketing as a concept has not always been easy in museums... None the less, suitable approaches have begun to emerge and there is now a growing body both of literature and good practice' (Hooper-Greenhill, 1994: 24). However, there is a paucity of radical examples of marketing theory applied to heritage sites. This may serve to demonstrate that lip-service only has been paid to the notion of market-led management. Promotion has been and remains heritage managers' priority to the exclusion of more developed marketing applications. Expansion has been based largely on opportunism, rather than on market research. Critics assert that many attractions have been product-led, promoting an otherwise redundant resource to a new market (Prentice, 1993: 223). Too many heritage sites continue to serve up the same old things or simply tart them up with quick fixes, which are assumed to bring the crowds. Costumed guides, for example, are often introduced in the belief that they act as a primary motivator when research has shown that this is true only for a minority of visitors (Malcolm-Davies, 2002: 477).

A truly market-led approach to heritage management would note the need for regular, expensive rejuvenation of the resource (such as the arrival of annual blockbuster exhibitions at national museums), widen the range of admission charges from bargain basement attractions to premium-priced exclusive visits (such as Dennis Severs' £12 visits to his tiny house in Spitalfields and evening tours at Buckingham Palace at £25), enhance the quality of the experience in line with what the traditional visitor segments like (as at Waddesdon Manor in Buckinghamshire), and pay attention to visitors' priorities as revealed by research. The introduction of the 'audience advocate', who researches the needs of visitors to aid exhibition design indicates museums may be leading the way in the proper application of marketing principles: 'Where in the past collections were researched, now audiences are also being researched' (Hooper-Greenhill, 1994: 1, 9). Croydon Clock Tower's museum galleries in Surrey were devised after an extensive public consultation process, which included questionnaires, interviews and focus groups (Susie Fisher Group, 1990). Academic research into visitors' responses to heritage sites has offered ideas for imaginative product development which have been translated into action at Blists Hill, Ironbridge (Goulding, 2000), the Black Country Museum in the West Midlands (Beeho & Prentice, 1996) and Castlefield in Manchester (Schofield, 2001).

It is not surprising, therefore, to discover that heritage attractions that are owned or operated by industrial production outlets or retailing groups (for example, Cadbury World in Birmingham) offer the clearest examples of marketing principles put into practice (Swarbrooke, 1995: 319, 322). Tetley Brewery Wharf was planned with a life cycle of three years while the brewery obtained planning permission for residential development of its site. Similarly, the Granada Studios Tour in Manchester closed after it had worked through a life cycle of eight years which began with 659,000 visitors per year, peaking at 750,000 and declining to 500,000 (Hanna, 1991, 1992, 1993, 1994, 1995, 1996, 1997, 1998). These, of course, are exceptions because they are not listed buildings, registered collections or symbolic ruins and battlefields. They are free to operate as commercial ventures. The difficulty for many historic properties competing in the marketplace is that they do not have the capacity to respond to the warning signs offered by the product life-cycle. Few can raise capital with ease and many lack the freedom to alter the layout of the building or dispose and collect in creative ways because of laudable legislation that preserves the remnants of the past from wilful destruction. Heritage attraction managers are fighting for market share with both hands tied behind their backs.

While curators cry over a revolution that has brought 'people who don't have a clue about heritage into the heritage sector' (Alberge, 2003: 3), the real tragedy is that proper application of marketing theories, including the product life-cycle, is long overdue in a sector that is fighting for its very existence. The traditional market for cultural resources is well heeled, well educated and in search of meaning in their lives – why aren't their millions subsidising the assets of the nation for those who have nothing?

Part 4
The TALC and Local Involvement

RICHARD W. BUTLER

One of the aspects of tourism destination growth that was not explicitly dealt with in the original article was the politics of development. It has become clear over the years that much more attention needs to be paid to the relationships between politics and development, both with respect to the impacts of politics at all levels on the nature and scale of development, and the impacts of such development on the political situation in destinations. The process of development discussed in the original model suggested that the stages of development would be affected by different levels of political (and economic) involvement. Keller (1987) argued that changes in the level of control and investment could be matched by periods of instability and turbulence (or chaos) in destination systems, but the general suggestion was that involvement would move consistently from local to regional to national and to international levels.

The first to challenge this view was Weaver (1990) and the first chapter in this section summarises and expands his arguments with respect to the different pattern of early development followed by destinations which had experienced a plantation type of initial economic development. He notes the different early patterns of development in such economies and the implications for the later stages. The chapter raises some interesting issues not explored fully here, relating to who might be termed a 'local' and who an outsider, and at what stage the latter may become the former. It also hints at some of the issues involved when the interests of various groups are not the same and thus the potential for conflict over the rate, scale and nature of development.

Johnston's discussion of the development process of Kona, on the Big Island, Hawaii, demonstrates the interplay between local residents and tourists. One of the themes which emerges is the growing power of local groups over tourism, as well the increasing role which they can play in shaping the direction of growth. The fairly long history of tourism on the Big Island reveals a variety of roles for local participants and the potential and actual conflicts that can emerge from increased visitation and development. Johnston's detailed review of this tropical island destination's relationship with tourism is marked by a more detailed identification of stages and phases of development, with marked changes in local involvement in development and limitations on development.

While Johnston's examination of development is more qualitative and descriptive, the chapter by Johnson and Snepenger takes a much more quantitative approach. Their study is the first detailed review of resident attitudes to tourism and tourism development in the early stages of the TALC. The location in which their study was undertaken is typical of many locations that in recent years have seen tourism replace other, more traditional resource-related activities when these resources have become uneconomic to continue to extract, or have been exhausted. They use four models to see if it is possible to predict residents' attitudes towards the overall impact of tourism in the early stages of the TALC in a specific community. They conclude that the stages of development are critical to understanding the perceived impacts of tourism in a community and that dispersing economic benefits across a community and encouraging positive interaction can aid the acceptance of tourism. Such longitudinal studies are clearly essential if a full understanding of the relationship between involvement and development through the TALC process are to be understood.

That theme is supported by Martin in her chapter, which examines the local politics in another North American location, Hilton Head in North Carolina. In her study she examines in detail local political attitudes and actions in a destination which has progressed a considerable way through its TALC. Confusion over the role tourism should play and the way that role could be controlled and directed had direct and unfortunate political results. There have been very few studies that have examined the transformation of attitudes of residents in a tourist destination into political action and the effect that these resulting political actions can have on subsequent tourism development and the direction of the TALC. The study makes it clear that there is often considerable apprehension about the process of the TALC and the nature of development in destinations, particularly those with a considerable proportion of the resident population not keen to see continued major change in the destination and not wanting to lose elements of local control over development.

The final chapter in this section by Marois and Hinch shifts location to South East Asia, and describes and analyses the process of tourism development in a Thai hill village. The community examined has proceeded through the TALC, with accompanying changes in emphasis on services provided and visitors received and local response and involvement have changed with the various stages of development. The level of control by locals has shifted and the roles they now undertake in tourism have changed considerably from the first period of contact with tourists. Efforts to ensure that the tourism industry on which the community has become partly dependent remains sustainable have not been entirely successful but the problems have been acknowledged. Even at the relatively small scale at which tourism occurs in this community, the problems of loss of control over development and subsequent changes in the tourist product which may threaten the viability and authenticity of the tourism experience are clear to the local population.

Chapter 11

The 'Plantation' Variant of the TALC in the Small-island Caribbean

D.B. WEAVER

Introduction

Harrison (1995) contends that the Butler sequence, as the most prominent TALC model, is most effectively regarded and utilised as an 'ideal type', or undistorted model of tourism development against which real life situations can be measured and compared. Once this has been achieved for a given destination, then the factors that account for the deviation (or the 'why') can be identified, with the aim of attaining a greater understanding of destination life cycle dynamics and diversity. Weaver and Oppermann (2000: 331), accordingly, argue that TALC researchers should focus on constructing around the ideal type a 'constellation of modified resort cycle models that take these real life circumstances into account'. Earlier research by Weaver (1988, 1990, 1993) has identified distinctive TALC processes in the British Caribbean islands that could contribute to the development of this constellation. Specifically, a 'plantation' model of tourism evolution is evident in Antigua (Weaver, 1988), while Grand Cayman Island displays significant deviations from the Butler sequence, especially in regard to the issue of empowerment (Weaver, 1990). An urban variant of the plantation model has also been proposed (Weaver, 1993). Each of these case studies, it is important to note, displays not just deviations but also a substantial level of conformity to Butler's ideal type. This chapter incorporates the above research into a broader investigation of small-island Caribbean TALC dynamics, toward the enunciation of one or more variant TALC ideal types. Modifications as well as conformities to the Butler model are accommodated in these models. The first section outlines the theoretical context that has influenced the study of the evolution of Caribbean tourism, with an emphasis on dependency theory. Subsequent sections examine this evolution in the sequence of stages and in reference to the characteristics provided by Butler (1980) in his original paper. Preliminary consideration is given in this context to the role of contemporary activities such as ecotourism and offshore finance.

Dependency Theory

Dependency theory, in its classical form, describes a group of neo-Marxist hypotheses which assert that low levels of development in the so-called 'third world' are primarily the consequence of the latter's chronic dependence (both economic and cultural) on the more advanced regions of the world, rather than of any innate shortcomings (Amin, 1976; Beckford, 1972; Frank, 1967; Rodney, 1972). This relationship is often described as a 'core–periphery' dichotomy in which the surplus produced in the periphery is commandeered by the core initially through the apparatus of formal colonialism (e.g. the British empire), and then (i.e. in the postcolonial era) through informal channels of transnational capitalism. The unequal and interdependent nature of this relationship is captured by Buchanan (1968: 83), who states that 'capitalist development simultaneously generated development and underdevelopment, not as separate processes but as related facets of one single process'. Accordingly, only by extricating itself from such a system can a country or society hope to achieve true development.

Modifications and reassessment

The harsh dichotomy of dependency theory has since been challenged by Wallerstein (1974, 1980, 1989), whose less ideologically charged world-system theory proposes the formation since 1492 of one global capitalist system with a single core, a single periphery and a transitional semi-periphery, the memberships of which are in a constant state of flux. Contemporary dynamics of globalisation, coupled with the collapse of the Soviet bloc (i.e. potentially the socialist alternative desired by the dependency theorists) and the rise of the East Asian economic bloc, appear to further elevate world-system theory at the expense of dependency theory. However, Surin (1998) argues that the fundamental elements (the phenomenon and persistence of uneven development that derive from the asymmetries of political and economic forces inherent to capitalism) of the latter remain valid. He consequently calls for a 'reanimation' of dependency theory based mainly on contentions that inter-regional (and internal) disparities have for the most part dramatically increased since the 1980s due to the very dynamics of globalisation, including the erosion of state control over economic policy and the substitution of highly mobile financial capital for productive capital. Yet, because these dynamics are significantly different from those that animated debate during the era of dependency theory, Surin admits that the called-for reanimation needs to be set in very different terms from the classic dependency theory prototype.

Relevance to the Caribbean and tourism

More than perhaps any other major world region, the Caribbean experience lends support to the basics of dependency theory. Five hundred years of interaction with the global core have witnessed the wholesale erasure of the indigenous Caribbean presence and its replacement by a 'plantation' system of production designed to create maximum wealth for the core with minimal consideration for the wellbeing of the periphery. The peripheralisation of the region within the global capitalist system was based initially on the production of agricultural goods, of which sugar was the mainstay and primary symbol (Mintz, 1971). For lack of viable alternatives, plantation-based agriculture dominated the Caribbean economy well into the 20th century despite chronic price instability, competition from European beet sugar and mainland producers (in the case of sugar), natural hazards, soil erosion and other problems. Tourism has existed in the Caribbean since the earliest days of the peripheralisation process, but it was not until after World War II that demand and supply factors combined to position tourism as a serious alternative (see below). Tourism eventually became dominant over agriculture in most Caribbean economies. However, this transformation from one sector to another was not accompanied by any systemic change in the essential core–periphery relationship. Tourism was introduced and evolved within a rigid and pervasive plantation system that maintained racially based social hierarchies (e.g. white hotel owners instead of white plantation owners), the diversion of profits to the core and other characteristics well familiar to the era of the sugar plantation (Beckford, 1972; Harrigan, 1974). It is because of this close association between tourism and the plantation system that Weaver (1988) refers to Antigua as an example of a 3S (sea, sand, sun)-based 'plantation' tourism landscape that fits well within Turner and Ash's (1975) concept of a global 'pleasure periphery'. The extent to which this has distorted Butler's TALC ideal type is discussed below. This discussion, moreover, also takes into account more recent tourism-related developments that appear to move beyond the 3S plantation model, such as the widespread adoption of ecotourism.

Exploration and Involvement

An interesting but rarely considered characteristic of the TALC is the absence of a commencement point. This appears to allow that some form of tourism, however negligible, may have occurred in any given area long before the arrival of individuals whose identity as tourists, at least in the contemporary sense, is indisputable. In the Caribbean, the existence of Carib, Arawak and other intraregional Amerindian 'tourists' prior to European settlement is an intriguing possibility that, accordingly, cannot be discounted. However, it also cannot be denied that the initial settlement process after 1492 dramatically altered the tourism situation by facilitating the arrival of visitors other than explorers, soldiers, missionaries and migrants. Hence, the plantation model per se begins with an *incorporation* phase during the exploration stage in which the indigenous population is subdued or at least held in check, formal claim is made over the land, and a rudimentary infrastructure of ports, fortresses and settlements is established to accommodate explorer-type tourism activity. In dependency theory terminology, incorporation is coexistent with the early *peripheralisation* process. In the case of Antigua and most eastern Caribbean islands, this occurred approximately from the 1620s to the 1640s.

Tourist motivations and markets

As per Butler, the tourists who visited the Caribbean from the mid-17th century to the mid-20th century were small in numbers, nonseasonal and motivated by a variety of factors related to the uniqueness of the area. These patterns are evident in the written accounts that were provided by these visitors, which include incidental descriptions of other visitors. Four primary motivations are evident in these written accounts. First, many tourists arrived in the West Indies for personal adventure, in keeping with the essence of the allocentric tourist who is purported to be prevalent during the early stages of the TALC. Examples include Brassey (1886), Paton (1887), Franck (1920) and Aspinall (1928). The travels described by these and other authors mostly consist of a multiple itinerary encompassing a sequence of islands, in keeping with the modern backpacker type of 'explorer' tourist. These adventurers, with their idiosyncratic and personal ruminations, are distinct in motivation from the tour guides, who intended their writings to provide factual guidance for other visitors. Examples of this typically more recent genre include Stark (1902), Ober (1908), Roberts (1948) and Clark (1952). A third motivation is health. This is cited as a personal factor by only a few of these authors (e.g. Baird, 1850), but is described by many others as a common motivation for visiting the Caribbean (e.g. Olley, 1937; Phillippo, 1843).

Significantly from a plantation model perspective, the fourth main motivation involves visitors, primarily members of Christian churches, who were interested in investigating the effects of Emancipation upon the black underclass (e.g. Bigelow, 1851; Gurney, 1840; Sturge & Harvey, 1838; Truman *et al*., 1844). Like the other types of visitor, these 'social tourists' came mainly from the mother country of the UK, although some were also Americans monitoring the Caribbean experience as evidence for their opposition or support for slavery in the USA. This concentration of the market in just one or two source regions is contrary to Butler's proposal that such market concentration typically does not occur until the development stage, but it is entirely consistent with the nature of the plantation system wherein peripheralised islands are almost completely tied to their respective cores (e.g. Barbados and Antigua to Great Britain, Martinique and Guadeloupe to France, etc.), making visits from other core regions extremely difficult.

Accommodation

The pattern of accommodation revealed in the Caribbean during the exploration and involvement stages provides further support for a distinctive plantation variant of the TALC. A critical element here is the extent to which many visitors were literally accommodated within the plantation structure. For example, Baird (1850) stayed in the 'country homes' (i.e. plantations) of his Antiguan acquaintances, while Paton (1887) spent most of his time on that island residing with an 'estate owner'. Bigelow (1851) advises that visitors to Jamaica must look to the homes of planters for overnight accommodations when visiting any rural districts outside of Kingston. It is interesting to note that this use of active plantations for accommodation purposes persisted well into the 20th century. Cundall (1928: 127), writing about Jamaica in the 1920s, states for example that 'on enquiry may be found a few planters, pen keepers and others who are willing to take paying guests on suitable introduction'. This need for an advance 'introduction' is mentioned by other writers, and indicates that visitors so accommodated were members of the higher classes in the core region, that is, persons who had benefited directly or indirectly from the peripheralisation of their intended destination region.

Plantation owners who accommodated visitors were no doubt partly motivated by the desire for revenue as well as by a culture of hospitality projected toward individuals of similar class standing. However, there is ample evidence that planter openness to guests was more deeply motivated at least in some cases by the desire to attract white settlers, which would help to perpetuate the plantation system by reducing, however modestly, the huge disparity in population between whites and blacks. Phillippo (1843) explicitly states that planters were trying to attract visitors in the hope that they would settle permanently in Jamaica, where whites constituted just 3 or 4% of the population. More recently, Cundall's (1928) *Handbook of Jamaica* was targeted toward 'intending residents' as well as visitors, while the Tourist Trade Development Board (Olley 1937) was also mandated to provide advice for prospective settlers. Referring to one of the earliest hotels in Tobago, the Robinson Crusoe Hotel, Alford (1962: 27) describes its lounge in the following terms:

> this lounge is largely used as a meeting-place and sort of informal club by the local residents, so giving visitors a chance to meet the local planters, officials and British and American settlers and to enjoy their hospitality, of great assistance to those people who also might be thinking of settling in this beautiful island.

Taylor (1988: 214), moreover, suggests that the government-supported effort to develop good hotels in Jamaica during the 1890s 'would encourage visitors to come to Jamaica who, seeing at first hand the economic potential of the island, might decide to invest or even settle there'. The concept of 'involvement' in the plantation model, therefore, appears to extend well beyond the conventional and more superficial motivation of attracting temporary paying visitors, and thus is not of just 'relatively little significance' to the social life of the planters. Furthermore, this motivation is evident as early as the 1800s (and probably earlier), suggesting the onset at an earlier stage than anticipated in Butler's model. There is, however, little indication of the extent to which visitors were significantly motivated by the prospect of settlement or actually became settlers as a result of their tourism experience in the Caribbean. Certainly, this is not a motivation that is encountered in any of the travel accounts cited above.

Not all tourists were accommodated in plantation homes. Tobago, as well as most other British-controlled islands, also provided 'resthouses' in remote villages, which, while intended mainly for government officials while on duty, were also made available to tourists (Trinidad and Tobago 1912). More significantly, the plantation homes were paralleled on all islands by a network of guesthouses and similar accommodations located within prime urban areas such as Kingston (Jamaica), Saint Johns (Antigua), Bridgetown (Barbados), Basseterre (St. Kitts) and Port-of-Spain (Trinidad). Descriptions, locations and price structures of these facilities suggest that they catered to a middle class clientele, those with business in the urban area, and anyone newly arrived and unable to obtain immediate accommodation in a rural plantation. These guesthouses and small hotels are more indicative of the conventional involvement stage in that they catered specifically to tourists and other visitors.

More intriguing, however, is the ownership structure of these facilities as well as the plantations. Expatriates and the local elite controlled the plantations in roughly equal terms, with the boundary between the two being very fuzzy in many cases (e.g. a plantation owner who lives six months each year in England and six months in Antigua). This high level of non-local involvement contradicts a fundamental ascription of the early-stage TALC model regarding local ownership. Moreover, the resident planter class itself requires an important qualification because of its elitist character and very close ties to the mother country – characteristics that are not usually associated with the 'local community' described by Butler. But again, this anomalous profile of accommodation owners is entirely consistent with tourism's assimilation within a plantation system of production and social exchange. The above-mentioned guesthouses appear on perusal to be another matter entirely. Truman, Jackson and Longstreth (1844) stayed at urban guesthouses in Basseterre, Bridgetown and Port-of-Spain owned by 'coloured' women. Bigelow (1851) mentions that 'coloured people' kept all the boarding houses of Kingston, while Taylor (1988) cites a writer from the 1870s who bemoans the control held by 'lazy and independent negroes' over the small hotel sector in Jamaica. A more recent and detailed list of all such Kingston-based facilities provided by Olley (1937) confirms this remarkable pattern of female, non-white dominance, which is more in keeping with Butler's description of involvement-stage dynamics. Yet even this apparent anomaly can be explained in terms of the plantation system. Such owners are members of a small and mainly urban emergent class of free blacks, mainly mulatto, who occupy entrepreneurial and artisan positions that cannot be filled by the small white population and are considered inappropriate for slaves.

Development and Beyond

In most British Caribbean islands, the development stage (measured in terms of increases in visitation) commenced in the 1960s. The emergence of tourism as a viable alternative to agriculture during this time, as mentioned above, provided an incentive for suitably located plantation owners to pursue this sector more formally and vigorously. Often, this involved the physical conversion of their plantation homes and properties into resorts, expatriate housing estates and golf courses. Such conversions, an illustration of tourism-related functional adaptation in response to the demand for 3S tourism, were already evident during the involvement stage. The above-mentioned Robinson Crusoe Hotel in Tobago, for example, was originally a plantation home, as were two other coastally sited hotels established respectively in the 1930s and 1950s – the Bacolet and the Arnos Vale (both of which, interestingly, used the original estate name). In Antigua, the Antigua Beach Hotel opened in 1940 as a restored estate home (Weaver, 1988). The conversion process, however, accelerated during the development stage, which in Jamaica began in the 1950s. Chapman (1961) cites at least five plantation homes – Flamstead, Shaw Park, San San, Good Hope and the Manor House – that were converted into hotels during that time, although other Jamaican examples occurred as early as the 1920s (Taylor, 1973). In many of the smaller islands, similar transformations occurred in the 1960s. Even more common was the transformation of abandoned plantation properties into space-extensive tourism facilities such as golf courses. But as Harrigan (1974) reminds us, the occupational hierarchy of these hotels mirrored the plantation, with a typical structure of white and largely expatriate ownership, mulatto or 'coloured' middle management and Afro-Caribbean labourers.

Because the peripheralisation process encompasses small islands almost completely (excepting remote mountainous areas in some cases), the plantation TALC variant incorporates the indirect effect of tourism on noncoastal landscapes not directly impacted by this new sector. Weaver (1988) refers to this as 'tertiary' space that contrasts with 'primary' hotel strips along the beach and 'secondary' tourist housing estates adjacent to these hotels. Tertiary space, best exemplified by Antigua, consists of abandoned plantation lands whose condition is partly attributable to the transfer of investment to coastal tourism. This interior landscape also houses the Afro-Caribbean labourers who work in the coastal tourism industry. In conjunction with Butler's characterisation of the development stage, links between the remaining agricultural activity in this area and tourism are minimal, due to the maintenance of links with wholesale suppliers based in the core.

Other elements of the original TALC model are retained in the plantation variant, including the entry of new foreign hotel interests, increases in average hotel size, the use of imported labour and the dominance of a mid-centric tourist market. However, the pattern of locally owned urban guesthouses and small hotels persists (Weaver, 1993), perhaps reflecting a continuing lack of interest on the part of the core to become involved in this less lucrative aspect of the sector. With regard to market origins, the dependence on visitors from the mother country is replaced, contrary to Butler, by a pattern of greater market diversity, so that destinations such as Antigua and Barbados now count UK residents as a minority among a diverse clientele that also includes Americans, Canadians, mainland Europeans, other Caribbean islanders and South Americans. The 'monoculture' of 3S tourism also precludes the establishment of 'man-made imported facilities' such as theme parks and other contrivances. The peculiar, monocultural nature of the plantation system, furthermore, results in the pre-eminence of tourism within the island economy well before the consolidation stage (which is when Butler suggests that this pre-eminence will occur). Agriculture in Antigua still accounted for two-thirds of the island's GNP by 1950, but just 20 years later it was tourism that contributed a similar share (Weaver, 1988). This rapid transformation owes to the process through which opportunistic plantation owners took advantage of the 3S tourism market to abandon an agricultural sector that, as seen above, was plagued by chronic shortcomings.

Carrying capacity threshold range

Arguably the most significant characteristic of the original TALC model is the provision of the carrying capacity threshold range, the breeching of which eventuates in the decline of the tourism industry if no countermanding measures are adopted. This threshold implies a potential transition from a sustainable, functional state to one that is unsustainable and dysfunctional. The nature of the peripheralisation process, however, necessitates a rethinking of this concept. Beginning with the incorporation phase, indigenous societies in the Caribbean islands were brutally eradicated and supplanted by an imported population of African slaves. Emancipation in the 1830s did little to elevate the social or economic empowerment of this Afro-Caribbean underclass whose numbers were augmented on some islands by indentured labourers of Asian descent. Concurrently, natural environments were devastated as native habitat was converted into plantation land, which was in turn exhausted as a consequence of predatory farming practices. Again, Antigua provides the extreme example of this devastation. The implication for the TALC is that the environmental and social carrying capacities of these destinations were already exceeded during the exploration stage. However, because the breeching was the consequence of the overall early peripheralisation process rather than tourism itself, it is useful to refer to this breeching in terms of a *contextual carrying capacity*. Not surprisingly, the tourism that subsequently evolved in this unsustainable and dysfunctional setting was itself unsustainable and dysfunctional, relying for its existence on the apparatus of suppression instituted by the core and its local agents (e.g. local planters and police). Hence, early travellers refer to nervous planter-hosts keeping a close eye on their workers, and to blacks seen as sullen and silently hostile, or overly deferential. Of course, the writers in turn invariably perceive the black underclass in patronising or contemptible terms. Such dysfunctional relationships are evident in Trollope's visit to Jamaica during the 1860s, in which the author's constant frustration with the apparent impudence of the Afro-Caribbean hotel staff is interpreted by Taylor (1988: 212) as part of the latter's 'subtle struggle for dignity' and a 'manifestation(s) of passive resistance by the native hotel staff' (p. 213).

As the islands have progressed through the development stage, it is still relevant in the plantation model to retain the concept of the *tourism carrying capacity*, as by this time it is the growth of tourism per se that potentially induces a new round of environmental and social dysfunction. It would be greatly misleading to characterise this new round as an assault on a stable social and environmental setting, but new tourism-related problems are possible. For example, a devastated terrestrial environment (i.e. caused by three centuries of plantation agriculture) could now be accompanied by the destruction of coral reefs and offshore pollution. Similarly, an already dysfunctional social structure could be further skewed by the activities of 'beach boys' (i.e. male sex workers targeting mainly female tourists), the commodification of local culture and the need to compete with tourists for water and other vital services. Such tourism-related problems may indeed result in the predicted onset of 'consolidation', 'stagnation' and 'decline' dynamics, as demonstrated by the experience of New Providence Island (Bahamas) and parts of the US Virgin Islands. However, this is not inevitable. If the pre-existing conditions were already appalling, then local residents may perceive tourism, for all its faults and adherence to the plantation system, as a positive development. That is, employment as a low-paid bellhop in an air-conditioned Antiguan resort may be regarded as preferable to unemployment or backbreaking work as a labourer in the sugar cane fields. If such sentiments are widespread (and the critique of Harrigan (1974) and other dependency theorists is therefore just an elitist academic conceit), then the outbreak of widespread antagonism (as per Doxey's irridex) is unlikely. Indeed, tourism has not yet produced such an outcome on Antigua, Barbados or any of the other islands where the plantation model is evident. The plantation model, therefore, should be accompanied by the caveat that these tourism capacity thresholds may not have quite the import on plantation system islands as they do in other kinds of destinations.

Ecotourism and tax havens

A factor that complicates the discussion of the plantation model of tourism development is the recent emergence in the Caribbean of alternative 'postmodern' activities such as ecotourism and offshore finance that deviate from the 3S monoculture. Virtually every Caribbean island, including unlikely prospects such as Antigua and Barbados, now offers ecotourism as a component of their destination product mix. On first appearance, this sector offers an 'escape' from the plantation syndrome in so far as it purports to entail nature-based tourism experiences that are educational and contribute to the environmental, sociocultural and economic sustainability of the destination (Blamey, 1997). Ecotourism, however, can meet these criteria and still reinforce the plantation system by functioning as an auxiliary activity that diversifies and enhances the core beach-based 3S experience (Weaver, 2001). Ecotourism can also serve to incorporate remnant natural areas of the interior – that is, areas unsuitable for plantation agriculture or 3S tourism – into the economic orbit of the core, thereby extending the peripheralisation process. In this context, it is fitting that ecotourism, despite its alleged adherence to the principle of local community empowerment, is essentially an elitist Eurocentric concept with its own idealised perceptions of a (fictitious) pristine natural environment juxtaposed with traditional (primitive?) local communities. Ecotourism represents, by this logic, the most recent or 'post-modern' means by which the core imposes its demands on the small-island Caribbean periphery.

Some Caribbean destinations, the most notable example being the Cayman Islands, have opted to position themselves as offshore financial centres. In concert with the plantation model, early tourism initiatives on Grand Cayman Island were associated with expatriate interests (Weaver, 1990). However, the plantation system as such was never established in the Cayman Islands as an integral component of its peripheralisation, due to its low capacity for agriculture. This lack of a plantation system may have encouraged innovative responses to the lack of economic opportunity, including legislation in the 1960s establishing the colony as a tax haven. The subsequent accumulation of wealth enabled the resident population to invest in the rapidly growing tourism sector, thereby inverting the conventional TALC model wherein local ownership is superseded by non-local control. The Caymans example might be dismissed as a regional anomaly, except that many other Caribbean destinations (e.g. Dominica, St. Kitts, Antigua, Turks & Caicos Islands, Bahamas, Anguilla, Montserrat, Grenada, St. Lucia, St. Vincent) have since attempted to emulate its success as a centre for offshore finance. However, upon closer examination, it is clear that Grand Cayman Island is indeed an anomaly. The pursuit of offshore financial opportunities in virtually all other Caribbean destinations, while bound to be negatively affected by oversaturation, has been tainted by accusations of chronic impropriety, shady dealings and by the pursuit of related questionable (and desperate?) practices such as the sale of 'convenience' citizenships and the establishment of offshore medical schools and online gambling operations (Weaver, 2003). All of these other destinations, to a greater or lesser extent, are characterised by plantation systems, and therefore the question must be raised as to whether the unhappy story of these 'innovations' is yet another (nontourism) extension of the plantation model, wherein the prospect of increased local ownership of the tourism industry, unlike Grand Cayman Island, is remote. Certainly, this is compatible with Surin's (1998) contention (see above) that highly mobile financial capital has replaced productive capital as the main impetus underlying postmodern core–periphery relationships.

Conclusions

The following points reiterate and summarise the salient characteristics of the plantation variant of the TALC.

- The plantation model formally commences with an *incorporation* phase, which entails the beginnings of the peripheralisation process that opens the door to core-based tourists.
- Incorporation and its aftermath coincides with the breeching of the destination's contextual carrying capacity, that is, with the eradication of indigenous people and natural environments to accommodate, subsequently, a plantation system of agriculture.
- Early visitation patterns adhere strongly to the prevalent core–periphery relationship, so that the 'mother country' accounts for the overwhelmingly share of visitors.
- Early visitor motivations are focused on adventure, providing a guidebook for future visitors, health and 'social' considerations surrounding Emancipation. The latter is closely linked with the plantation system.
- Overnight accommodations outside of urban areas are mainly in plantation homes, indicating the degree to which early tourism is integrated into the plantation system.
- Host planters have, as at least one motive for their 'involvement', the desire to attract white settlers in order to help perpetuate the plantation system. Tourism is therefore of considerable significance to the white elite despite low levels of visitation.
- Expatriate interests rather than members of the local community own many if not most plantations.
- Local 'coloured' females control most urban guesthouses. This apparent conformity to Butler's statement about local ownership is actually consistent with the plantation model, as it indicates the existence of an intermediate class that occupies a niche unacceptable to whites and unattainable for the black underclass.
- Underclass Afro-Caribbean employees of the early hotels display passive forms of resistance toward tourism that are similar in essence to those adopted toward plantation owners.
- Tourism tends to supplant agriculture during the development stage, thereby indicating the opportunistic conversion of investment from a monoculture of the primary sector to a monoculture of the tertiary sector.
- The functional adaptation of some plantation homes into hotels is an important and widespread manifestation of this conversion.

- The development of the coast into a 3S tourism landscape is paralleled by the marginalisation of the interior, which serves mainly as a labour reservoir.
- Markets become more diverse as the strict core-to-periphery pattern of the past gives way to greater accessibility.
- Built attractions are conspicuous by their absence because of the monocultural nature of the 3S tourism product.
- This monocultural dimension also means that tourism becomes dominant within the destination economy long before the advent of the consolidation stage.
- The breeching of the *tourist carrying capacity* does not necessarily signal the demise of the destination, due to the distortions created when the contextual carrying capacity was breeched (see above). For example, passive resistance by Afro-Caribbean hotel employees toward tourists may actually diminish as markets diversify and working conditions improve.
- The introduction of ecotourism does not necessarily threaten, and may actually reinforce, the plantation system.

The above summary constitutes a preliminary profile of the plantation variant of the TALC, as a potential contribution to the constellation of variants proposed by Weaver and Oppermann (2000). Each characteristic, on its own, could be the topic of a full research project. Further study is also required to determine whether the model is a product of historically specific circumstances – that is, the peripheralisation process of the past 400 years, or whether more generic and timeless processes are at work. With regard to geographical coverage, it is likely that the plantation model in its essence captures the experience of many Pacific Ocean (e.g. Fiji, New Caledonia, Cook Islands) and Indian Ocean (e.g. Seychelles, Mauritius) island destinations, but may require revision in the case of island destinations that opt for a deliberately alternative tourism strategy focused on small-scale ecotourism, such as Dominica, St. Vincent, Montserrat and Samoa. In any case, this study has hopefully demonstrated the great utility of the original TALC model of Butler as an ideal type around which a more comprehensive understanding of destination dynamics can coalesce.

Chapter 12

Shoring the Foundations of the TALC in Tropical Island Destinations: Kona, Hawai'i

CHARLES S. JOHNSTON

This chapter is a case study of the TALC in Kona, Hawai'i Island (hereafter 'the Big Island', the name used throughout Hawai'i). The chapter attempts to integrate and apply the ontological and epistemological concepts that are discussed atomistically in the other volume. The purpose is to allow the research to function as a model for examining the TALC within the broader framework of 'place as process' (Pred, 1984).

The chapter is structured around two analyses, of unequal length. An initial boundary analysis focuses on establishing the spatial extent of the Kona destination region – the 'entity' being examined. The second, longer section of the paper is a 'sequence analysis' of the stages Kona has gone through as a tourist destination. This structure is similar to previous case studies in that a chronological discussion of stages is provided. It goes beyond the typical treatment through the use of two analyses that are embedded within the discussion of each stage. First, an identification of mechanisms introduces events that can be interpreted as defining changes in the stage or phase (substage) sequence. The importance of specifying mechanisms is to improve temporal bounding of stages by eliminating the arbitrary selection of cut-off dates. Mechanisms may be 'critical events' or 'blurry transitions'. The former affect the development of the institution of tourism in a profound way. Critical events may be different from 'critical junctures'. The latter focus on periods of crisis and/or issues of controversy but their resolution may not result in a stage or phase change. 'Blurry transitions' are more subtle; they are defined as the occurrence of a series of events subliminal to the scale of analysis. All events, critical or not, may be considered abstractly as 'additions', 'alterations', or 'cessations'.

Second, for each stage, after mechanisms have been identified, a 'pathway analysis' will look at epistemological features such as the 'internal characteristics' of the institution of tourism (including change in the resource attraction base and in resort morphology), the 'macrostructural' conditions (broad external factors), as well as the 'users' (tourists themselves). A pathway analysis focuses on the full development of the institution of tourism at the destination. Discussion in such a manner permits projection (though not prediction) of development patterns into the future.

For Kona, these analyses reveal that the destination has passed through a 'classical' stage sequence and is now in the stability phase of the maturity stage. The very success of the tourism industry, however, has led Kona into a broader urban era in its sequent occupance (Whittlesey, 1929). Tourism in the early 21st century is still important and still likely far away from the conclusion of its *longue durée* (Giddens, 1984), but it is no longer the driving institutional force in Kona.

Bounding the Destination Region

The word 'Kona' is typically translated as meaning 'leeward' in Hawaiian (Fornander, 1980; Pukui *et al.*, 1974). Figure 12.1 shows Kona to be roughly in the middle of the leeward (western) side of the Big Island, bounded by Kohala to the north and Ka'u to the south. The region is located on the steep slopes of two of the Big Island's five volcanoes, Mauna Loa and Hualalai. The recency of the island's creation means most of the Kona coastline is rugged lava bench, not white sand, a fact that has disturbed beach-seeking tourists for decades.

Kona's climate is somewhat atypical for Hawai'i. The great heights of Mauna Loa, Hualalai, and also Mauna Kea to the north prevent the trade winds from reaching the region. A localized diurnal land–sea breeze regime prevails instead (Juvik *et al.*, 1978). Precipitation is thus low *makai* (along the coast) but increases quickly *mauka* (upland) (Giambelluca *et al.*, 1986). Since Hawaiians first began to inhabit the region, most residents have lived in the wetter areas between Kailua and Kealakekua Bay. The different climatic conditions, hot and dry coastlines but cool mountain heights, have appealed to different visitors in different time periods. Charmian London (1917: 204), for example, noted that her husband, writer Jack, thought mauka Kona had a 'matchless equable climate'. This opinion has probably not been shared by most tourists since the 1950s, who have come for the makai sun and heat.

For purposes of analysis, the epistemological need to properly bound the area under study requires the selection of a destination that is appropriate in size and complexity of institutional tourist development. The Kona region, rather than the entire Big Island or the western half, was chosen as the most appropriate scale for analysis. The latter – 'West Hawai'i' – became quite important for planning by the State government beginning in the late 1960s. The town of Kailua (sometimes known as 'Kailua-Kona') was the site where tourism first became institutionalized. Since then, resort development has occurred in two

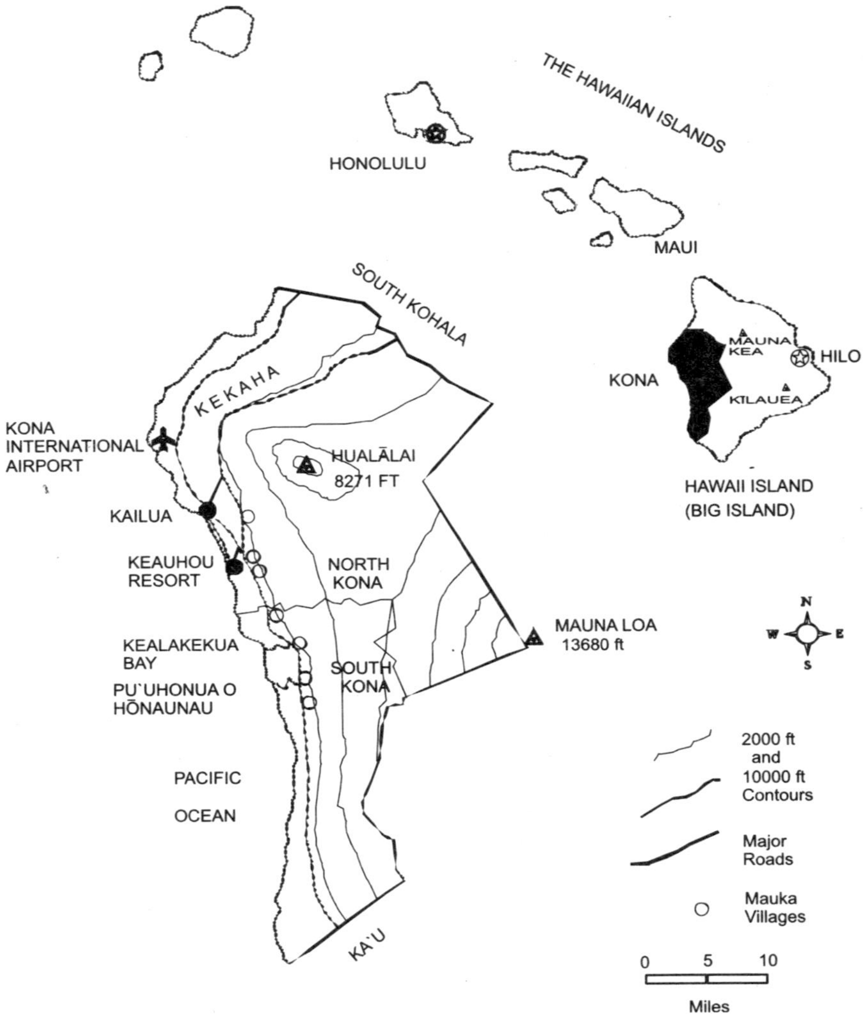

Figure 12.1 The Kona districts within the Hawaiian islands

other contiguous areas (Keauhou and Ali'i Drive) along the coastline, creating a 'linked' morphology, but the Kona district itself retains a distinctive identity that is meaningfully differentiated from the Kohala resort area to the north and Ka'u to the south. Kona was therefore chosen for study on the basis that it was of a spatial scale that destination life cycle theory could handle in its present state of development. Problems from multiple-site development were minimized, though not entirely eliminated.

Sequence Analysis of Life-cycle Stages

Table 12.1 shows the stages and phases of tourism development through which Kona has passed; it also shows the eras in the regional sequent occupance. To date, the Kona region's sequent occupance has consisted of four eras. Kona is also interpreted to have gone through a 'classical' set of stages. The Hawaiian royal capital and exploration stages (pretourism – see Young, 1983) have been followed by initiation, which led to a development-stage building boom that was in turn followed by maturity as growth slowed. All but the first of the stages are interpreted to have had two phases, as well. A variety of mechanisms – critical events and blurry transitions – have been listed in Table 12.1 to account for the changes.

Hawaiian Royal Capital stage

The first stage in the sequence has been named 'Hawaiian Royal Capital' on the basis that Kailua town was occupied by royalty – King Kamehameha and Governor Kuakini – much of the time between 1779 and 1844. During these 60+ years the presence and actions of royal rulers created a history for the region that was later used by tourists as an experiential (cultural) resource (see Table 12.2). The fact that Kona was the original seat of the Hawaiian kingdom established the region as the premier place for later visitors to see 'old Hawai'i'. This nostalgic longing for heritage experiences has been an institutional feature of tourist demand going well back into the 19th century.

Few people visited Kona during this time who could be called tourists. The arrival of the Wilkes (1970) expedition in 1840 was perhaps most typical: Kona was visited more by true explorers than explorer tourists. The years of the stage completed the 'Hawaiian' era of the sequent occupance, which had lasted several centuries (see Kirch, 1983). The stage and the era are interpreted to have ended on the basis of a cessation – Governor Kuakini's death in 1844.

Exploration stage

The second stage, exploration, is considered to be pretourism on the basis that although some tourists did come, there was little development of a tourism industry. The institution was thus incomplete. During these years ranching and coffee came to dominate the landscape and economic activity of residents (and thus the era in the sequent occupance has been termed 'agricultural hinterland'). Two phases of the exploration stage have occurred. The early phase is defined by the absence of Hawaiian royalty in Kona; the district became very isolated with the capital located in Honolulu. The late phase is interpreted to have begun in 1910, when

Table 12.1 Stages and phases of tourism development in Kona

Era in sequent occupance	*Stage and phase in tourism life cycle*	*Date*	*Mechanism of change initiating stage/phase; critical event or blurry transition (addition, alteration, cessation), plus critical junctures*
Hawaiian, prehistory to 1844	Hawaiian Royal Capital	1779–1844	Critical-addition: Cook reaches, and is killed at, Kealakekua Bay Critical-addition: Kamehameha sets up throne at Kailua, after establishing power over Hawai'i Nei Critical-cessation: Kuakini dies 1844
Agricultural hinterland 1844 to 1953	Exploration	1845–1928	
	Early	1845–1910	Blurry-cessation: (above)
	Late	1910–27	Critical-addition: Circle-island auto road completed
	Involvement	1928–63	
	Pioneer hotel	1928–48	Critical-addition: Kona Inn opened Critical-addition: Old Kona Airport opened, facilitates local-scale recreational business district in Kailua
	Local morphology	1949–63	• Juncture: large accommodation projects inhibited • Juncture: regional development plans inhibited

Table 12.1 (*Continued*)

Era in sequent occupance	*Stage and phase in tourism life cycle*	*Date*	*Mechanism of change initiating stage/phase; critical event or blurry transition (addition, alteration, cessation), plus critical junctures*
Tourism	Development	1964–88	
1954 to	Domestic morphology	1964–75	Blurry-addition: Accommodation unit numbers break out above 400; rise continuously for a decade; multi-story hotels constructed ● Juncture: Natural and cultural resource development projects inhibited ● Juncture: Kailua pedestrian mall and high rises inhibited ● Juncture: Keauhou Resort built nearby Critical-addition: Kailua Village Special District Commission created
1988	Linked morphology	1976–88	Blurry-addition: Heliotrophic development links Kailua and Keauhou; condominiums co-dominate with hotels
Urban	Maturity	1989–present	
1989	Consolidation	1989–93	Blurry-cessation: Accommodation unit growth peaks ● Juncture: Kekaha subregion resort enclave projects inhibited
to present	Stability	1994–present	Critical-addition: Runway extension completed, renamed Kona International Airport; infilling of Kailua recreational business district facilitated

Table 12.2 Chronology of major historical events occurring in Kona during the Royal Hawaiian Capital stage

Year	*Historical event*
1779	Cook reaches Kealakekua Bay, Jan. 16, in the *Resolution* and *Endeavor*. He is worshipped as the god Lono the next day then is killed by Hawaiians on Feb. 14.
1792–93	Vancouver's expedition visits Kona.
1812	Having conquered the island-chain, by force or negotiation, Kamehameha returns to Kona to set up the seat of his kingdom from fortress 'Kamakahonu' on the north side of Kailua Bay. Several exploration expeditions (Arago 1971, Freycinet 1978, Von Chamisso 1986, von Kotzebue 1967) visit, spreading the fame of Kamehameha and Kona throughout the known world.
1819	May: Kamehameha dies; October: Liholiho (Kamehameha II) publicly eats with women, thus officially renouncing the *kapu* system, effectively overthrowing the traditional religion and the basis for priestly authority.
1820	January: Lihohiho wins the Battle of Kuamo'o at Keauhou Bay; advocates of *kapu* restoration are defeated. April: Missionaries arrive from North America. Step ashore onto 'Plymouth Rock' in Kailua. Liholiho moves royal court from Kailua to Honolulu. Kona is politically peripheralized.
1825	Kuakini, Governor of the Big Island, builds the first Christian church, Mokuaikaua, in Kailua. Made of wood, it burns in 1837.
1837	Kuakini builds Hulihe'i Palace as the governor's mansion, across from the church.
1838	Kuakini rebuilds Mokuaikaua Church, this time of stone.
1844	Kuakini dies.

a circle-island road for automobiles was completed. This addition enabled tourists to purchase circle-island trips in touring cars based in Hilo; they stayed at mauka hotels in Kona and took day trips to see important historical sites makai.

Early phase

In the early phase there were no major historical events to describe. A distinctive type of local did come into existence – the *paniolo* – a Hawaiian cowboy, who was to be a common sight on the Kona landscape well into the 20th century. The number of visitors was small. Travel, nearly always by ship, was difficult. Initially, interisland boat passage was on Hawaiian-owned 'poi clippers' (Day, 1955), referred to as 'the haole's [foreigner's] horror, the Hawaiians' pleasure' (Thomas, 1983: 31). By the 1870s, steamers built especially for Hawaii's rough interisland channels began to ply the waters regularly.

The major attraction of the Big Island was Kilauea Volcano. It was nearly continuously active during this time and the boiling cauldrons of the lava lake in central Halema'uma'u Crater drew tourists from around the world. Package tours from Honolulu were developed as early as the 1880s to facilitate access (Thrum, 1886). For these visitors, Kona was but a stopover on the return to Honolulu. From the decks tourists watched Hawaiians 'come galloping in' (Whitney, 1890: 29) from mauka villages, excited by 'steamer day' (Stevenson, 1973). Ships would stop at Kealakekua Bay, tourists would then go ashore to stand at the spot where Cook had been slain and re-live the scene. In the 1860s, after he recovered from seasickness traveling on a poi clipper, Twain (1966) visited the site and lampooned this behavior.

Along the coast, there was not much to do. In 1858, King Kamehameha IV visited the Hulihe'e Palace; his secretary later recorded him remarking that 'the place itself is so desolate that ennui was the order of the day' (Neilson, cited in Daughters of Hawai'i, 1979: 2). This opinion slowly began to alter in the 1890s, when tourists on steamers began to consider these sleepy coastal villages as 'romantic' (Burnett, 1892: 202).

Those tourists who did get off the boat in Kona generally went mauka, where they enjoyed themselves by riding through the forests (Chaney, 1879) to the summit of Hualalai. The truly adventurous, such as Isabella Bird (1966), went hunting for wild cattle with the Hawaiians. Robert Louis Stevenson (1973) was more sedate, limiting himself to a week's homestay with a Hawaiian judge who augmented his income through providing lodging and board to tourists.

Late phase

Change was slow to come to Kona, but around 1910 the district began to catch up with civilization as completion of the circle-island road, the Mamalahoa Highway, made auto travel possible. The circle-island tour was an attraction itself: it was conducted in large touring cars driven by Hawaiians, who made the long, dusty trip less arduous by entertaining the tourists with picnics and by singing and playing the ukulele (Morrill, 1919). Once in Kona, most visitors continued to stay mauka in small hotels, two of which are still popular with 'alternative tourists' today (Sodetani, 1985).

The historical features dating from the Hawaiian era, which had been slowly deteriorating in the sunny coastal landscape, were now legitimately old and represented the major attraction resources. Mokuaikaua Church and Hulihe'e Palace in Kailua, the twin landmarks left from Kuakini's rule, were particularly important. Several other historically and culturally important sites were improved, though not specifically for the purpose of attracting visitors. What MacCannell (1976) has referred to as 'sight sacralization' was beginning to occur. Kona's 'past glory' (*Paradise of the Pacific*, 1924) was more imaginable to the tourist. These makai sites were now visited during day trips by car. The long slow horse rides through the forest were ending. Cook's death site receded somewhat in importance for it was much less accessible (and remains so) by car than by steamer; reaching it required a long walk down and up the steep, hot and dusty Kealakekua fault line.

Other events occurred to increase the value of Kona as a destination. The first was an addition: the discovery around 1920 that billfish were abundant just offshore in the calm but deep leeward waters. Kona quickly attained a reputation as a 'rendezvous for game fishermen' (Sabin, 1921: 37) intent on catching marlin, swordfish and tuna. Second, an unusual cessation occurred that represented a change in the macrostructural tourist conditions. In 1924, the lava lake within Kilauea crater hardened over, and the living volcano became dormant. People came to Kilauea in ever-increasing numbers (Hawai'i Volcanoes National Park officials, October 1991, personal interview), but now the circle-island trip to see Hawaiian history had more appeal.

Kona was also one of the few places where it was still easy to meet and interact with 'native' Hawaiian people. Honolulu had become a modern city (a macrostructural alteration); the old ways of life were going fast. Photos taken well into the 1930s (e.g. *Paradise of the Pacific*, 1939) show Hawaiians smiling for the tourist cameras, or wearing only loincloths, frolicking with tourist ladies on the pocket beaches. Paniolos still walked the dusty streets of Kailua and the mauka villages.

By the mid-1920s, Kona had an identity as a tourist destination. The regional appeal was based on a diverse set of resources – environmental, cultural, and social. What Miossec (1977) has called the *perception globale* – tourists' ability to differentiate the destination as an attraction area from the neutral space surrounding it – had occurred. The only element missing from the picture was the true presence of the tourist industry itself.

Involvement stage, 1928–63

Butler (1980) defined an 'involvement' stage as when residents begin to provide facilities exclusively for tourists. The literature has described variations in how this happens; Din (1992) and Douglas (1997), in particular, have questioned whether 'residents' are not in fact immigrants. A variation along these lines also occurred in Kona, on the basis that outsiders from Honolulu were responsible for the event that initiated the stage. Two phases are interpreted to have occurred. A pioneer hotel phase first institutionalized Kailua as the nucleus for tourism. Later, the opening of the region's first airport helped bring in a local phase, when a local-scale resort morphology developed in the village.

Pioneer hotel phase 1928–48

The critical event that institutionalized tourism in Kona, and to the outside world, was the addition of a hotel in Kailua town, thus anchoring tourism on the coast rather than the uplands. The event occurred in 1928 when the Inter-Island Steamship Navigation Company (1930) opened the Kona Inn. The company had been actively trying to expand travel throughout the islands so that more tourists (especially residents of Honolulu – Hawai'i's 'domestic tourists') would book passage on its ships. The Kona Inn was a good example of a 'pioneer hotel'; it was built at higher-than-local standards and became an attraction in its own right. The hotel was an instant success and became 'the spot in all Hawai'i where you can utterly, completely relax in surroundings of modern comfort' (Thrum, 1940–41: 267).

Beyond the opening of the Kona Inn there were no other additions of significance in the tourism industry during this phase. Rather, the old Hawai'i ambience, which Kona contained in abundance, continued to age like good wine. A phrase – the 'Kona Way of Life' – made its way into the vocabulary to describe it. Tourists during the late 1920s and the 1930s went to Kona to steep themselves in the Kona Way of Life – a feeling that had faded in much of the rest of the Territory, particularly in Honolulu. The ambience took on an almost spiritual flavor; De Vis-Norton's (1925) comment that 'Kona is one of the most soul-satisfying districts on earth' is typical.

This phase carried on through World War II, when civilian interisland travel was completely halted. The war did not function as a macro-structural constraint; it seems to have been more of a hiatus to a region already known for slowness.

After the war, life for a few years returned to what it had been before. Locals were still living the Kona Way of Life; the Kona Inn was again open for business. At the mid-century point, Coll (1950: 17) would write that tourists were 'flocking' to Kona, on the basis that it was 'a place to get a quiet rest amid soothing tropic surroundings but if you feel a bit lively one can find plenty to do'. Yet even as he wrote, change had begun to occur. Progress was about to catch up to the sleepy little village, and it would come in the form of a developing tourism industry.

Local phase, 1949–63

The local phase began just before mid-century. The mechanism of change was an infrastructural addition, the opening of what is now called the 'Old Kona' airport on July 10, 1949 (HNCM, 1949). This was a critical event for within a year a local-scale resort morphology began to appear in Kailua village. Growth was not happening only in tourism, however. Agriculture still dominated the region as an economic activity and the ranching industry, in particular, also had infrastructural needs. The most important of these was for an up-to-date facility from which to transfer cattle onto boats going to Honolulu. For a century, cattle had been herded to the shore in Kailua Bay, and then paniolos on horseback swam with them out to the boat where they were lassoed and hoisted on board. This colorful procedure had been a tourist attraction of sorts for a long time but was not easy to accomplish. To improve the situation, a pier was built on the shore in the early 1950s. A resource conflict issue arose: whether to use the Bay for tourism or agriculture; but ultimately, tourist interests won, the shed was removed, and cattle were trucked to a different port. This conflict represents a critical juncture in the sequent occupance. Agricultural interests dominated less and less after this and Kona became perceived more as a tourist region than an agricultural one. The tourism era is interpreted to have begun at this time.

The construction of the Old Kona Airport in 1949 was brought about by the locals' need to be less isolated. Even before opening, it was considered responsible for inducing new business to Kailua (HNCM, 1949). Within a year, new hotels had opened, and houses were being converted into shops. A local-scale recreational business district had come into existence – 'the sleepy port of Kailua has become a bustling community' (HNCM, 1951). This growth was deemed good for the entire Territory, and the status quo understanding was that Kona was the rightful heir to becoming the no. 2 tourist destination in Hawai'i, after Waikiki (*Honolulu Advertiser* 1954, 1956, 1956b). Though people knew early on that this growth would affect the Kona Way of Life (Doyle, 1957; Stermer, 1954), the small scale of additions built throughout the phase did not impact it severely.

Two notable additions to the resource base occurred: the Pu'uhunua o Honaunau ('City of Refuge') was given US National Historical Site status in 1961 (Clark, 1985) and the annual Hawai'i International Billfish Tournament began in 1959 (Peter Fithian, tournament organizer, December 1991, personal communication). The latter event helped institutionalize Kona as a world-class destination for big game fishing. However, the 1950s penchant for the sun-sand-sea vacation was altering the use of the resource base in Kona. History and culture slowly ceased to be as important to visitors.

There were two developmental junctures in Kona during this phase, which are important to consider – even though they did not eventuate. They had a virtual quality that was real to residents at the time, even though tourists who passed through were probably unaware of the storms around them. The first juncture concerned accommodation. Throughout this phase only one domestic-scale facility was built, the

King Kamehameha Hotel, which opened in 1960 with 94 rooms. Several others, however, were announced in the newspapers. The aluminum magnate, Henry Kaiser, proposed constructing a megaresort consisting of four hotels with 800 rooms, a new beach, three yacht harbors, and hundreds of apartments and private homes on the site of the existing airport (*Honolulu Advertiser*, 1955). Bureaucratic inhibition constrained progress, and by 1957 Kaiser was to note that Kona 'wasn't ready for another big hotel' (*Honolulu Star Bulletin*, 1957). Nothing was ever built. Plans for at least three other domestic-scale hotel projects met the same fate during this substage, though none of them were as big as Kaiser's (*Honolulu Advertiser*, 1955b; *Honolulu Star Bulletin*, 1956).

The second juncture concerned planning. Territorial government development plans began to specify guidelines during this period. Height limits on buildings were set at two stories in central Kailua (Scott, 1957). Regional master plans were also done. The most ambitious, by the Territorial Planning Commission, was presented to the public in 1958 (Harland Bartholomew and Associates, 1960). This promoted tourism development but maintained the ambience of the region by specifying a set of seven 'resort centers' up and down the coastline. Residents' reaction to the plan was positive: 'They all like it, with few exceptions' (*Honolulu Star Bulletin*, 1958b). But, as with Kaiser's private sector project, nothing from the plan ever appeared on the landscape. Funding was dropped from the State budget in 1960, and jealousy from Hilo, the county capital, seems to have played a role in inhibiting any action to implement the plan (HNCM, 1960).

Throughout the 1950s and into the early 1960s, then, Kona's pathway was typified by a state of tension between what was perceived as the region's rightful position – the no. 2 destination in Hawai'i – and the slower pace of development that actually occurred. Facilitational forces made some small additions, but inhibitional forces had constrained all the 'big' projects that would have quickly shifted Kona into the development stage. Residents and members of the business community were left waiting, wondering when true development would come.

Development stage, 1964–88

One way to identify a 'development' stage is to look for a building boom, characterized by additions to the tourist landscape and particularly to the accommodation sector. Before 1960, statistics for numbers of accommodation units in Kona were nonexistent or approximate. After this, data on accommodation units outside of Waikiki began to be published for some resort areas, including Kona. It is possible to use these data as a means of interpreting stage and phase changes. On the basis of Figure 12.2, it can be interpreted that a 'breakout' occurred

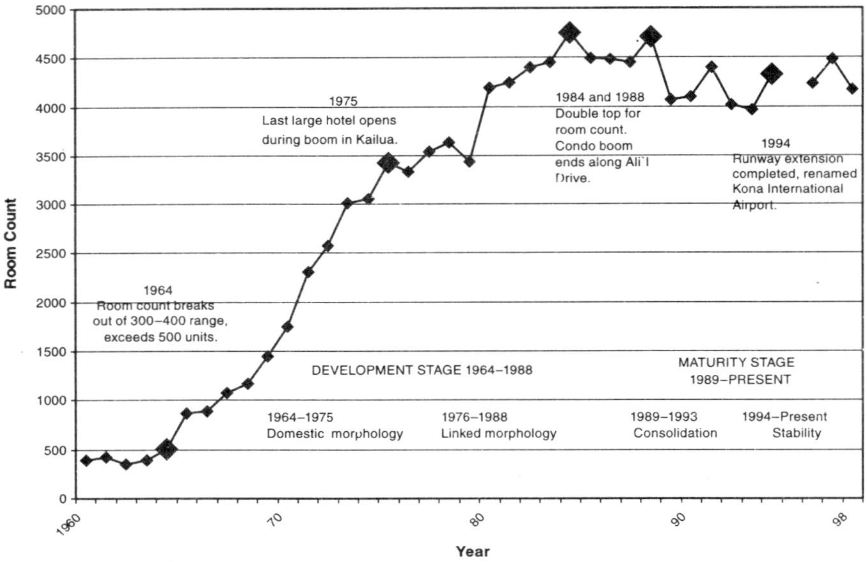

Figure 12.2 Accommodation totals for Kona
*1995: No survey was done by HVB
Source: Hawai'i Visitors' Bureau *Annual Research Reports* for years shown and Thrum's *Annual* 1960–63

during 1964; the number of accommodation units rose above the 300–400 unit range and exceeded 500 units for the first time. A change of this nature constitutes a blurry transition because no major event occurred. Annual increases in accommodation would be the norm for the next two decades. The development stage has been defined on the basis of this graphical pattern.

Within the stage, two phases – domestic and linked – are interpreted to have occurred, based on changes in the resort accommodation morphology. Between 1964 and 1975, new hotels built in Kailua Village were mainly of a domestic scale and attained several stories in height. About five miles to the south, Keauhou resort was developed by a large land-owning estate, and three enclave-scale hotel resorts were constructed within it by 1974. The final large hotel project built during the phase – the King Kamehameha – was completed in Kailua in December, 1975. The domestic phase is interpreted to have ended with the opening of this hotel and the corresponding cessation of construction in Kailua. Room numbers had increased over seven-fold during this decade.

During the next phase, 1976–1988, increases in accommodation facilities would mainly take the form of condominiums. The two separate resort areas – Kailua and Keauhou – would become morphologically and functionally 'linked' by condos built along the connecting coastline road – Ali'i Drive. Room totals were to reach a maximum of 4748 units in 1984 but would nearly reach this again in 1988. This 'double top' represents the end of the development stage. There has been a notable cessation of accommodation construction since, though one large enclave resort did open in the Kekaha subregion north of Kailua in the mid-1990s.

Domestic phase, 1964–75

The domestic phase of development for Kona was just over a decade long. Much was built, but much was prevented from being built. The conflict over the direction of growth was intense. It was notable that all contestants were seemingly protourism. It was particular visions of growth and Kailua's place-identity that were contested. Facilitational aspects will be discussed first, followed by inhibitional conflicts.

Hotel size in Kailua grew more or less organically. During the 1950s, the hotels that had been built in Kailua were nearly all small, averaging about 20 rooms. After 1964, however, facilities of three-to-four stories (height limits had been raised) with more than 100 rooms were the norm, over-topping the earlier generation. Just south of the existing village, on the south side of 'One'o Bay (Figure 12.3), Hilton opened a hotel in 1968, with over 300 rooms (Hawai'i *Tribune Herald*, 1968). This was Kona's first international-scale facility. Several other domestic-scale hotels were built nearby, either along the coast or just inland. These created a new southern anchor to the village, with empty land directly behind 'One'o Bay.

At about the same time, the Bishop Estate, Hawai'i's largest land owner, began work on a megaresort at Keauhou (West, 1967), about five miles south of Kailua, connected to the village by Ali'i Drive. Plans called for nine hotels, along with hundreds of condominium units, residential housing, shopping areas, coastal walkways, a golf course, and other recreational features. Keauhou was in fact to be a new city, larger than Kailua. Had development gone as planned, Kona might have ended up with two distinct destinations. However, private sector hotel developers did not come forward with the anticipated eagerness. Only three hotels had opened by 1974. These were international-scale enclave resorts, each containing several hundred rooms.

In addition to hotels, Kailua's recreational business district developed considerably. The shops of the 1950s were in turn replaced by small tourist-oriented malls in the 1960s and 1970s. By the late 1970s, when the trend had ceased, a travel writer was to note, 'The resort town of Kailua features . . . more shopping malls per square mile than I have ever seen' (Riegert, 1979: 115). Together, the addition of these hotels and shops constituted the 'boom' typical of a development stage. Kailua had been

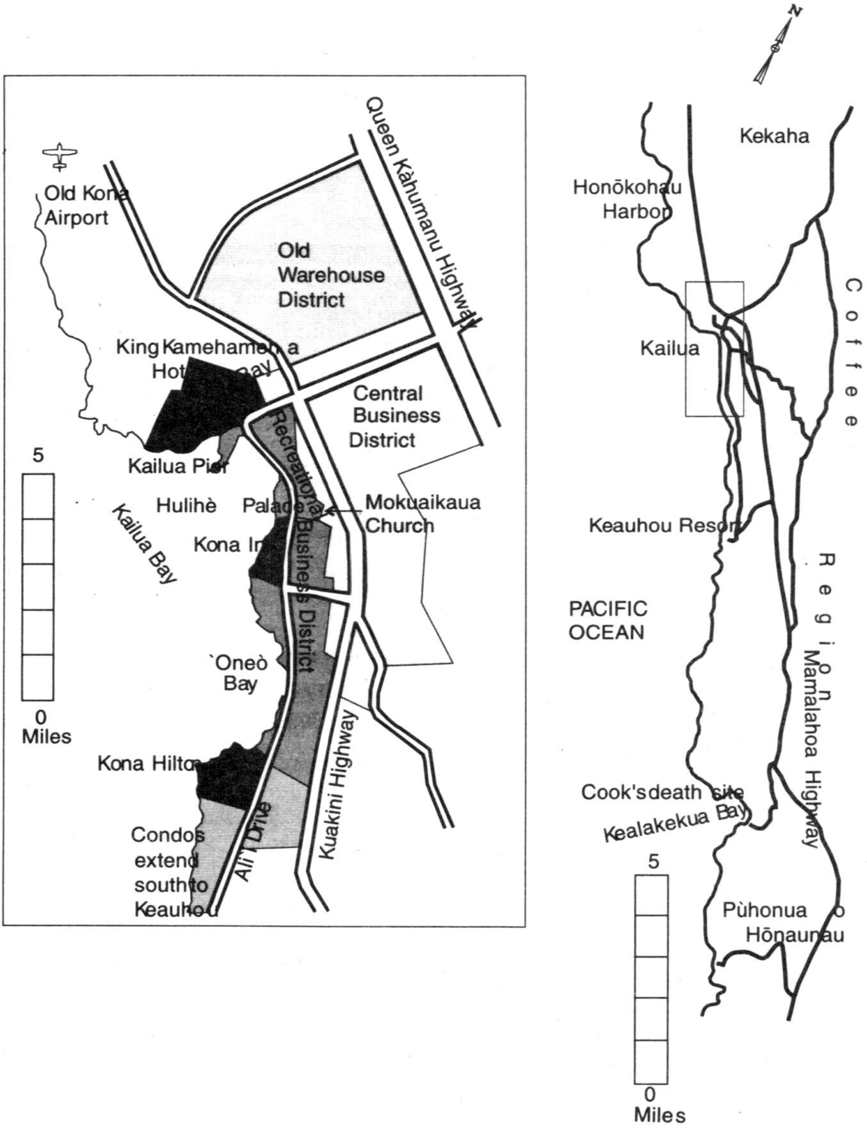

Figure 12.3 Major features of Kona's tourist landscape

attractive because of its ambience, its 'way of life'; this resource was severely degraded during the domestic phase. A series of newspaper articles complained about how noisy the village had become (Benham, 1970b; Hawai'i *Tribune Herald*, 1969, 1970). What were described as 'signs of growing pains' (Bryan, 1965) became more harshly phrased as a situation of 'Nightmare Not Over For Kailua' (Shapiro, 1974: A12). Shapiro went on to note that 'the tourist boom of the 1960s brought uncontrolled growth and tackiness, erasing much of Kailua's old charm.'

Another aspect of the building boom involved improving the regional infrastructure. In the late 1960s, Governor Burns had a dream of creating a 'Gold Coast' in West Hawai'i, running from the Kohala district north of Kona to the Pu'uhunua 'o Honauanu in South Kona (Hawai'i *Tribune Herald*, 1968b; *Honolulu Advertiser*, 1968). As governor, he directed millions of dollars into three particular projects so that private industry would find conditions feasible for investment in resorts. These projects were a new airport, a coastal highway connecting Kona with Kohala, and a new harbor blasted from the Kekaha lava shoreline. These three projects were of considerable importance in providing Kona with an adequate infrastructure. None, however, had the mechanistic impact of the original airport's opening. Rather, they fit in with other developments going on in the tourism industry itself during those years. Put abstractly, they could be considered to be 'tolerance' pathway factors; their construction in the 1970s would enable developers in the 1980s to propose large-scale resort projects.

Turning to inhibitional issues, several projects were highly contested, and discussion of these perhaps best brings out aspects of Kona's pathway. Two of these projects focused on developing natural and cultural attraction resources; they were proposed at almost the same time. The summit of Hualalai volcano had been a day-trip destination of 19th century tourists on horseback. Nearby, Hawai'i Volcanoes National Park included the summit of Mauna Loa. In the 1960s the National Park Service realized the landscape of the summit area of Hualalai was not of inferior quality and proposed expanding the park to include it (Hawai'i *Tribune Herald*, 1967b; Ketchum, 1969, 1969b). Road access from Kona would have made the national park much more accessible. Opposition developed from locals, however, who saw the expansion as a land grab by the federal government. The proposal collapsed, and the summit of Hualalai today remains off-limits to tourists.

The second project involved State plans for developing the land area around Kealakekua Bay. Nineteen seventy-nine was the bicentennial year of Cook's 'discovery' of Hawai'i and a decade earlier a plan had been made for upgrading the area (Creighton & Walters, 1969). The plan specified construction of educationally oriented facilities, focusing not only on Cook's death, but also on the archaeological ruins from nearby Hawaiian settlements. Again, conflict with residents inhibited the project. Probably the most offensive element in the plan was to turn the site of a small village on the south side of the Bay into a parking lot, displacing the residents (Benham, 1971; Hawai'i *Tribune Herald*, 1972).

The project did not receive approval, and the land surrounding Kealakekua Bay area remains 'unelevated' (after MacCannell, 1976) as a resource. The Bay area today is marketed more towards day-trip snorkelers than towards people curious about one of the major events in the history of Pacific exploration – the death of Cook.

These resource-related issues were of considerable importance, but inhibitional junctures within prodevelopment groups were even more so. Two burning issues arose during the phase – whether to turn Ali'i Drive into a pedestrian mall, and whether to allow high-rise buildings in the Kailua village center. In 1965, the owners of the Kona Inn had become concerned about the excessive traffic on Ali'i Drive and proposed turning the road into a pedestrian mall. They also proposed constructing a new road behind the growing recreational business district to eliminate this negative impact on the village ambience. An article written during that time stated bluntly that bus tours to the Kona Inn were responsible for most of the traffic 'chaos' (Hawai'i *Tribune Herald*, 1967). The business community reacted with extreme hostility towards the proposal, on the bases of prohibitive cost and that supplies could not be delivered to their small shops and hotels (Southward, 1966). Numerous plans regarding the mall were advanced (Southward, 1968), but all failed to satisfy the business community. The issue of the mall would wax and wane for a full decade. Some changes were made (e.g. Ali'i Drive was made into a one-way street), but there was no comprehensive solution.

The second issue was over high-rise buildings within Kailua Village. This erupted in 1968 when a developer proposed constructing a seven-story condominium adjacent to Mokuaikaua Church. The past few years had seen building heights gradually increase. For example, the King Kamehameha Hotel, built to four stories originally, had added two more. The Hilton, almost completed, was about to reach seven stories. There had been no major public opposition to the height of these structures. But such height next to one of the town's major landmarks was considered sacrilege by many, and the protest against the development was just as vehement as it had been against the pedestrian mall. At a 'Citizen's Conference' held in May 1968, residents debated the future identity of the village. There was a strong feeling that permitting high-rises would 'ruin' (Harada, 1968) Kailua by making it a 'poor cousin' (Southward, 1968b) of Waikiki. The twin landmarks of Hulihe'e Palace and Mokuaikaua Church, now 130 years old, also perpetuated Kailua's 'old Hawai'i' ambience, in spite of the construction chaos. The argument that the project would destroy the ambience of the 'picturesque little village' (*Honolulu Advertiser*, 1969: B2) had some credibility (see Martin, this volume for a similar development, editor's note). The project was completely legal and within zoning allowances, but public opposition delayed groundbreaking ceremonies until 1972. By that time, the developer had conceded to community concerns. The site of the building was moved further away from the church and its height was limited to four stories (Tao, 1972).

The community impasse over these two issues did not mean there was a lack of vision about Kailua's future. There was nearly constant talk of creating a 'special and historic district' (*Honolulu Advertiser*, 1973). Yet by the early 1970s there was little left that was truly historic other than Kuakini's buildings. At one point a state legislator proposed the State buy the entire village (*Honolulu Advertiser*, 1970). The fighting finally ended in 1974, when money was released for a new urban plan (*Honolulu Star Bulletin*, 1974); by the end of the summer the central village area was given 'special district' status (Hawai'i *Tribune Herald*, 1974, 1974b, 1974c). The theme of the plan was that the appearance of central Kailua should be perpetuated as a small village. To oversee the implementation of the plan, the Kailua Village Special District Commission was created. From this time on the village has had an official body to mediate disputes. There have been no major variations permitted to builders for the past quarter-century. The 'tentacles of blight' (Southward, 1967) from the development boom were no longer present. Contemporary tourists strolling along Ali'i Drive continue to experience a pleasant ambience, though not one representing the 'Kona Way of Life'.

In December 1975, the second incarnation of the King Kamehameha Hotel opened to the public. With this event, the domestic phase came to a close for Kona. No major hotels have been constructed in Kailua since. Overall, the impact of inhibitional forces had dealt a severe blow to the organic development of tourism. Future development would be kept rigidly along community-approved lines. An international phase, identified by high-rise hotels, had been completely prevented. Kona thus did not fully complete the 'classical' development stage, as did Waikiki.

Linked phase, 1976–88

Figure 12.2 shows a continued rise in the number of accommodation units between 1975 and 1988. The linked phase has been interpreted on the basis of this pattern. Virtually all accommodation constructed was in the form of condominiums. The increase in numbers is significant; the 1984 peak (4748 rooms) is nearly 40% higher than the total for 1975 (3423 rooms). The initial condominium boom resulted from a spillover of demand for properties on Maui (Tune, 1980). Prices in Kona were considerably lower. The condos were mostly built during the good economic years; the second oil crisis in 1979 brought development to a halt for a while (*Sunday Star Bulletin and Advertiser*, 1984).

At the end of 1975, tourism development in Kona was still mainly centered in Kailua Village, with the Bishop Estate having partly developed Keauhou resort five miles away. Keauhou represented newness, high-quality facilities, and planning; Kailua was old and messy. One writer (Krauss, 1974b) noted that only 5–10% of visitors staying in Keauhou went into Kailua. Had the Bishop Estate's plans come to fruition, Kona would have become a binodal tourist destination. What resulted instead was that the Village and resort became spatially and functionally 'linked' through condominium construction along the coastal road, Ali'i Drive, which ran between them. For the next decade, development of condominiums gradually merged the two resort subregions. The district, as a destination, remained 'Kona' in identity.

Compared to the previous substage, the linked phase occurred in a straightforward manner. No major issues came to the fore. In terms of ambience, Kailua Village re-established something of its 'old Hawai'i' identity in the late 1970s, after the Planning Committee took control. The major event of the phase was the closing of the Kona Inn. The hotel was purchased by a local group, who closed it in 1978 and built a large shopping mall on the lawn (William Kimi, CEO, December 1991, personal communication). The change from a hotel to a shopping mall represented a major alteration for the Village. It was not a critical event in the life cycle, however, because a sufficient supply of room stock now existed elsewhere to meet demand.

One notable addition occurred during this phase, an annual special event. In the late 1970s, the original 'Ironman' triathlon had begun in Honolulu. The race was moved to Kona in the early 1980s (Hawai'i *Tribune Herald*, 1989). It has grown in popularity and, along with the Hawai'i International Billfish Tournament, has become what Getz (1991) referred to as an 'image-maker'. The Kona Way of Life was gone, but a new theme – sports – would begin to define the region.

Maturity stage, 1989–present

If the envisioning idea of development is growth, then maturity brings to mind the image of completed growth. Since 1989, the amount of accommodation available in Kona has remained fairly steady at just over 4000 units – defining the maturity stage. Not many events have occurred that produced visible changes on the resort landscape. The years between 1989 and 1993 have been interpreted as the consolidation phase on the basis of this lack of activity. In 1994, the runway at Ke'ahole Airport was extended, and it was renamed 'Kona International'. Long-distance jumbo jets could now land and take off. This alteration is considered to have initiated the present stability phase, on the basis that Kona is now directly connected to the rest of the world.

Consolidation phase, 1989–93

The consolidation phase will likely be remembered most for what did not happen – a failed third phase of development. To examine the situation properly it is necessary to return to the 1960s. In the middle years of the 1960s decade, two resorts opened north of Kailua Village. One was the Mauna Kea Beach Hotel complex, in South Kohala. The other was the Kona Village in Kekaha. Both catered to a luxury clientele and were quite successful. Governor Burns had understood the potential for luxury tourism when pushing through the infrastructure projects in the early 1970s. Had the private sector done its part, Kona and Kohala may have merged in identity as a tourist destination, as the Gold Coast. Two hotels did open in South Kohala in the early 1980s, both catering to a luxury segment. The fabulous Gold Coast, however, never really came into existence.

The land ownership pattern in Kekaha dated back to the 1850s. Extremely large ranches covered the lava desert. This pattern was suitable for megaresorts costing hundreds of millions of dollars. The necessary infrastructure (airport, highway, harbor) was in place. In the mid- to late 1980s, six projects were proposed. There was little difference in the plans; each specified large hotels, condominiums, and one or more golf courses set inland from one of the Kekaha's pocket beaches (County of Hawai'i, 1987). If completed as proposed, they would have added approximately 5000 hotel units and 6000 condo units (not all in the vacation rental market), more than doubling Kona's accommodation stock. Access to beaches by the public at this time was severely restricted. The public needed to cross private land to reach the beaches, but many were able to do so, and thus these were popular recreation sites, particularly on weekends.

The furor of the community over these projects was just as intense as it had been with previous issues. Unlike earlier fights in Kailua, the battles in the 1980s were between protourism developers (mainly outsiders) and anti-development residents. Two projects were proposed near a large pond that was a protected bird sanctuary. After initial permits were granted by the County, the State of Hawai'i itself came out in opposition to these (*Honolulu Star Bulletin*, 1988). Project-by-project, fights went on in public planning meetings throughout the late 1980s and into the early 1990s. One corporation did manage to get enough permits to begin construction (Hawai'i *Tribune Herald*, 1989) and eventually opened a large, luxurious resort enclave next to the Kona Village. By 2000, the remaining projects were still listed in the 'planned development' accommodation statistics collected on by the State of Hawai'i. Nothing about them has been mentioned for years however (Annie Earl, County of Hawai'i Planning Department, March 1999, personal communication).

One addition of note occurred during this phase, the elevation of coffee as a tourist resource. Kona had been a noted coffee district since at least the 1860s, when Twain (1966) made favorable comments about its quality. Tourists had often noted the presence of coffee growing in the mauka village areas, and aspects of its production had been an attractive feature for decades (Harlow, 1928; Musick, 1898). The development of tourism in the 1950s and 1960s had, however, hurt production; better paying jobs meant the crop was sometimes not picked (Smyser, 1972). The subdivisions that had followed tourism had also caused the price for land to explode during the 1980s. There was concern that the land would be rezoned for residences, though this did not eventuate (Harada-Stone, 1989). By the early 1990s, however, the coffee lifestyle of cities had diffused to the source region, and entrepreneurs in Kona were exploiting this resource by opening shops at which freshly roasted coffee could be consumed and purchased. The annual Kona Coffee Festival has also become elevated in importance and now represents a third 'image-maker' for the destination.

Stability phase, 1994–present

A stability phase suggests that little new is happening, but that existing businesses are doing well. This situation has existed in Kona for the past few years. Accommodation numbers have never reached the peaks of the 1980s but have remained at the levels of the early 1990s (Figure 12.2). The opening of the longer airport runway reduced dependence on Honolulu. Since then, more malls and restaurants have filled in the vacant lots inland from 'One'o Bay. This is now the new 'center' of nightlife. Kailua's recreational business district now is completely developed along the shores of Kailua and 'One'o Bays, but because planning guidelines remain effective, the recreational business district still looks and feels like a village (field inspection, April, 2000).

Though this took years to achieve, Kona presents itself as a contemporary tourist destination that has been able to reach a balance between facilitational and inhibitional forces. The growing pains of the development stage have ended. Attraction resources have changed and continue to do so. The Kona Way of Life ambience is gone but the region effuses an idyllic quality that is pleasant to experience. There is something of a new image that is distinctive in the State and not yet completely defined, based around sports-health and coffee. Kilauea Volcano, on the windward side of the Big Island, remains a day trip. The challenge for the community in the years to come will be to prevent the decline in quality of these attraction resources.

The Future of Kona's Tourist Life Cycle

Research on a destination life cycle that incorporates the concepts of mechanisms and pathways permits a limited projection into the future, on the basis that the past provides a certain understanding of what cannot likely happen again. Of course, there is no crystal ball, and so *ceteris paribus* is assumed. It is unlikely that Kona will undergo a further boom period, akin to what occurred during the development stage. There are three factors that suggest this. First, the entire length of coastline has by now either been developed for tourism or has had projects proposed then inhibited by community pressure. Further development faces tight planning guidelines, and the Kohala districts to the north are in the midst of their own destination life cycle and compete for tourists.

Second, by the early 1990s, the condominiums constructed during the development stage were being increasingly inhabited by their owners, not listed as available vacation rentals (field inspection, 1991–1992). Part-time residents do not behave exactly like tourists, hence the nature of the institution of tourism is slowly changing. Were tourist numbers to drop considerably and stay down for a period of time, Kona could likely be interpreted as being in the residential stage.

Third, Kona's success as a tourism destination has enabled it to grow into a multifunctional urban area. Prior to the 1950s, most inhabitants in Kona lived in mauka villages. Kailua's recreational business district then developed makai. However, there was no corresponding central business district; this was constructed behind the recreational business district along Kuakini Highway, beginning in the 1970s (Figure 12.3). Subdivisions for local residents were built back from the coast as well. In 1989, the Hawai'i County Planning Department released a *General Plan* that projected land use zonation into the future. The plan shows that most new development would be zoned residential, industrial, or urban, but not tourist or resort. When the planning maps are analyzed in relation to the nontourist types of additions that have already been constructed, it is feasible to interpret that Kona ended its tourism era in the sequent occupance around 1989, at the same time the maturity stage began. The plan thus represents a mechanism – the agency of County government – which had decided to concentrate on other forms of urban development. Though still a mainstay of the local economy, after a reign of roughly 35 years tourism gave way to urbanization at large, which is now in its own development stage. As an institution, tourism may remain stable for a long time; the life cycle cannot be expected to end soon. But a greatly expanded Kailua is fast becoming an important city in the State of Hawai'i, and tourism in the future can be projected to be just one of many institutionalized activities occurring there.

On the other hand, if *ceterius paribus* assumptions were removed, it is possible to conceive that Kona might yet have another developmental phase. It has been repeatedly noted that the base resources for tourists keep changing. Were tourists' tastes to return to those of a century or more ago, features of Kona that have been 'de-elevated' could again become resources for the industry. For example, if global warming worsens, appreciation of the cooler upland climates could cause a new 'boom' in the mauka areas to occur. Also, the continued appreciation of 'old Hawai'i', today redefined as heritage tourism, could result in the restoration of literally hundreds of important archaeological sites that have been left to weather in the tropical sun. The identifiable presence of additional, though currently undeveloped, attraction resources indicates that the future pathway of Kona as a tourist destination has not been completely predetermined by past events and accommodation trends and thus cannot be predicted.

Conclusion

This paper has presented a case study of the Kona region of the Big Island, Hawai'i. The structure and content have utilized an ontologically and epistemologically underpinned version of Butler's (1980) destination life cycle model. As a way of delimiting the scale of analysis Kona has, first of all, been spatially bounded. As a destination, Kona was shown to have had tourism development occur in three contiguous subregions, Kailua, Ali'i Drive, and Keauhou. Attempts to develop a fourth area, Kekaha, have mostly failed to date. Features of development in each of the three subregions were quite distinctive; yet the region as a whole retained an intact identity as a single destination. On this basis, Kona can be interpreted to be at the large end of the spatial scale appropriate for study in terms of presently developed theory.

Second, the paper analyzed the chronological stage sequence of development that has occurred, in terms of the mechanisms that have been interpreted to have caused stage and phase changes, and in terms of the pathway features that were most pertinent during each. This sequence analysis has shown that Kona has gone through a classical set of stages – none has been skipped or reached in an unusual order. All stages attained can be divided into phases, based on the occurrence of events functioning as mechanisms of change. In particular, analysis of change in accommodation units was useful in interpreting stage and phase change, particularly when the graph of room totals was discussed in terms of morphology – what types were built, where, and when.

Kona's pathway as a destination, however, has been much more complicated than a study of the mechanisms alone would indicate. Facilitational and inhibitional forces (with a bit of 'tolerance') collided for much of the second half of the 20th century. Developmental victories have produced the existing tourist landscape. Developmental failures, sometimes representing victories for anti-growth forces, meant a Waikiki-type environment (international-scale morphology) did not come into existence, and kept the Kekaha lava desert mostly free of large resort enclaves. The broader growth of Kona as an urban region, however, was not contained. Success at tourism has led to Kona becoming a sprawling urban area. Whether the region can maintain the idyllic quality for tourists, or whether it becomes a nice place to live, but not to visit, remains to be seen. The process of tourism development appears to be nearly completed, but the process of place-development at-large appears by no means finished.

Chapter 13

Residents' Perceptions of Tourism Development Over the Early Stages of the TALC

JERRY D. JOHNSON and DAVID J. SNEPENGER

Introduction

The Tourism Area Life Cycle (TALC) model is conceptually longitudinal; however, most studies applying the model are cross-sectional. There are many reasons why the literature is dominated by cross-sectional studies. First, it is pragmatically easier to acquire information at one point in time and then analyze the data across a sample of residents of the area. Secondly, the need for expedient publication motivates most researchers to publish cross-sectional studies. Third, there are few resources available to tourism researchers by way of grants or contracts to support impact studies over a decade or more.

Three notable longitudinal studies employing the life cycle model illustrate the research design complexity and the rich information available from these types of studies. The first study is 'Lifecycle models for Pacific Island destinations' (Choy, 1992). He employed visitation volumes over time for several popular and emergent island destinations in the Pacific. The most extensive set of data was for Hawaii and incorporated data from 1946 to 1988. Other island destinations utilized a smaller time frame for examining aggregate visitation patterns. Choy concluded that a general destination lifecycle model does not apply to most Pacific island destinations. A large variation in growth patterns was observed across the 13 destinations.

Another study by Johnson and Snepenger (1992) examined tourism development in Yellowstone National Park over two decades. 'Application of the tourism life cycle concept in the Greater Yellowstone Region' applied several elements to the TALC – the traditional tourism impact dimension, visitation trends, economic indicators, and biological indicators for the ecosystem. They concluded that tourism in the Greater Yellowstone is an intricate system where multifaceted parts can be in different stages of the TALC and that public land managers, private entrepreneurs and local government decision makers should coordinate development and maintenance of tourism assets.

The third paper, 'Tourism planning and destination life cycle', investigated Niagara Falls over the entire tourism destination life cycle (Getz, 1992). This comprehensive examination traces the chronological changes to Niagara Falls (New York, USA and Ontario, Canada) from the early inception of the attraction in the 1820s through to its consolidation in the 1990s and anticipated rejuvenation. Getz utilizes historical qualitative data, visitation and business data, and survey data from industry and municipal groups to conclude that stages within the TALC can be delineated and that it can be a useful construct if attention is also paid to monitoring and forecasting the complex market and product of the tourism attraction.

Measuring Tourism Impacts

Although others (Ap & Compton, 1998; Lankford & Howard, 1994) have designed alternative impact scales, conventional tourism impact studies use a generally accepted battery of 16 questions that investigate the economic, social, and environmental positive and negative consequences of hosting tourists (Lui & Var, 1986). The study of impacts from tourism on local communities takes in a range of literature that includes both the positive and negative effects of hosting tourists to a community.

Andereck and Vogt (2000) point out that residents of a tourist community differ with respect to the impacts resulting from tourism development. However, researchers agree that a necessary condition of successful tourism development strategy is the inclusion of residents of the entire community if tourism investment is to yield substantial returns (Allen *et al.*, 1988, 1993; Jurowski & Uysal, 1997; Long *et al.*, 1990; Snepenger & Johnson, 1991).

The existing tourism impact literature has for the most part relied on cross-sectional data (Allen *et al.*, 1993; Andereck & Vogt, 2000; Ap, 1990; Jurowski & Uysal, 1997; Long *et al.*, 1990; Snepenger & Johnson, 1991; Var & Kim, 1989). However, the TALC implicitly demands that any study of tourism dynamics view changes over time (Ap, 1990; Butler, 1980) and that the economic, social, and cultural impacts evident in any community are best viewed within a longitudinal context. One of the attractive features of repeated or longitudinal measures is that they allow for general statements of change over long periods of time. Knowledge of trends can lead to a better understanding of the community tourism system and may provide useful managerial information to community and tourism planners (Mueller *et al.*, 1970; Snepenger & Ditton, 1985). Longitudinal analysis as utilized in this study is useful to indicate which, if any, demographic and tourism iteration variables explain how the community opinion toward tourism development changes over time. These trends may be important because as stated by many researchers, cohesive community feelings toward tourism aid in the development of sustainable tourism policy (Ap, 1992; Jones, 1993; Madrigal, 1994; Martin & Uysal, 1990; Teye *et al*., 2002). In other words, unwilling hosts are not conducive to an effective tourism industry.

Longitudinal Investigation of Silver Valley, Idaho (USA)

The purpose of this chapter is to examine the early stages of the TALC in a regional economy previously based on natural resource extraction. The region is experiencing a transition from mining and timber production to one increasingly diversified to incorporate tourism attractions and services. The investigation utilized a longitudinal research design incorporating survey data from four different points in time.

The research setting for the study is Shoshone County, in the northern panhandle of Idaho, USA. The area is known as the Silver Valley, a narrow mountain river valley. Mineral deposits of silver, gold, zinc, and lead discovered in 1883 led to the development of underground mines throughout the 14-mile long valley. The Valley at one time produced over one-third of the world's supply of silver.

The valley is surrounded by National Forest lands that produce many of the local amenities residents find desirable and act as attractants for tourist visitors. Mountain biking, hiking, big game hunting, cross country and alpine skiing as well as water-based recreation opportunities such as fishing, river floating, and waterfowl hunting are available throughout the year. The small communities of the Silver Valley are developing into bedroom communities for nearby Coeur D'Alene, Idaho – a community of 35,000 people that is itself a popular tourist destination for year-round recreation only 56 km (35 miles) to the west via interstate highway. Lower housing prices in the Valley provide an incentive for people to drive the relatively short distance to employment in the larger urban center.

The local mining industry in the Valley collapsed in the early 1980s due to a multiplicity of issues and local residents were encouraged by community leaders to collectively rethink the basis of the local economy (Johnson *et al*., 1994). The idea eventually presented to locals was to transform a 20-year-old local ski area into a four-season destination resort. The ensuing vision was a radically different way of thinking about the local economic base and centered on building a gondola to move skiers from a central location in the town of Kellogg, Idaho to the ski area over 5 km (3 miles) away and several thousand vertical meters above the community. Public meetings were held to educate residents and local business owners, politicians and community leaders to advance the idea of promoting tourism.

In 1986 political leaders initiated a market study to investigate the feasibility of a major year-round destination resort development for the Valley. The resort would be focused around a $20 million dollar project that at 3.1 miles in length would be the world's longest passenger-carrying gondola. It would serve the alpine ski area and eventually a year-round destination resort complex. Several setbacks occurred over the course of the development but by Fall 1990 the initial stages of the project, including the gondola, were completed and the new Silver Mountain Ski and Summer Resort, owned and operated by the City of Kellogg, Idaho began operations. The public ownership made the resort one of the few public sector owned ski resorts in the country.

However, confusing the economic and quality of life circumstances is the designation of the Valley as an Environmental Protection Agency (EPA) Superfund site. The designation constrains local business investment and pervades the local politics of the area. During the course of the ski area development, as part of the Superfund activity, all remnants of the mining operations that polluted the area were removed and the land mitigated. The Superfund designation has infused significant amounts of Federal spending into the Valley but uncertain liability concerns makes future business investment an unsure proposition (Fernandez, 1999). As a result, contrary to hopes and government efforts, very little non-mining and non-recreation investment has taken hold in the region.

The literature provides a few studies addressing the nature of transitional economies from resource dependency to one based on tourism, retirees, and attendant professional and consumer services. Historically, the economic base in most rural communities in the Rocky Mountain West was found in agriculture and natural resource extraction. Today, the contemporary economies of the West are more easily described as progressively more diversified. Timber harvest, mining, and agricultural production are still in evidence in much of the rural west but at diminished levels, but those employment opportunities are giving way to service-related employment including tourism, non-labor income, small business startups, light manufacturing, retail, and construction jobs. These nontraditional employment sectors dominate regional urban centers and adjacent rural communities (Beyers & Nelson, 2000).

An important component of the economic restructuring is tourism (Fly, 1986; Getz, 1986; Gunn, 1988; Liu & Var, 1986; Long *et al*., 1990; Loyacono, 1991; Luloff & Steahr, 1985; Rafool & Loyacono, 1997). In the Rocky Mountains (USA) the travel industry provides over 381,300 jobs and accounts for approximately 6.5% of total state employment and in Idaho, the setting for this study, tourism generates almost 22,000 jobs or 4.8% of total employment in the state (Rafool & Loyacono, 1997). Future tourism-related job growth will continue to be an important component of the rural economies of the western USA (English *et al*., 2000).

For natural resource dependent communities, tourism may be a last attempt at economic survival as the market for natural resources is increasingly global, regulated, or displaced with technological substitutes. Many rural locations, especially in the Western USA, enjoy close proximity to existing tourism resources such as national parks or scenic/ historical resources (i.e. Yellowstone, Lewis and Clark route locations) and can take advantage of readily available nearby recreation on public lands (i.e. skiing, river recreation, mountain biking).

The issue of community acceptance of tourism or other form of economic diversification is important for communities where the economic shift away from commodity production is taking place. Power (1995) advises that there may be a considerable lag between recognition of economic myth about how the community formerly made a living and the acceptance of the new reality and eventual acceptance of the new set of economic conditions. This may be particularly acute in the case of tourism – an industry generally perceived to result in low quality jobs, part-time, or seasonal work, and low pay. Accordingly, Jurowyski and Uysal (1997) and Teye *et al*. (2002) suggest that given a lack of understanding or approval for an ongoing economic transition, tourism development efforts will suffer from a lack of local community support.

Three major communities comprise the Silver Valley: Pinehurst (pop. 1800), Kellogg (pop. 2591) – the location of the ski area base operation, and Wallace (pop. 1100). Total population for the region at the inception of the study was 5491 (US Census 2000). A random geographic cluster sampling design was utilized to acquire data from residents. A grid system was developed which partitioned each of the communities into several neighborhoods. Within each neighborhood a random sample of 30–35 households were surveyed. This was initiated by selecting a random starting point in each neighborhood and then randomly selecting dwellings within the neighborhood to contact. The self-administered questionnaires were given to one adult in each household and later retrieved at a predetermined time. Response rates and sample sizes for the four survey periods varied but were within acceptable limits for similar community surveys (Babbie, 2002: 256) and appear in Table 13.1.

Four household surveys monitored area residents' expectations of tourism development conducted in 1991, 1994, 1997, and 1999. The first survey was initiated at the end of the first season of operation. Because residents did not have enough experience with ski area resort destination tourism, the questions were reworded to query area residents' expectations and thereby their level of optimism, of tourism impacts as a result of development in the Silver Valley. These items asked respondents in 1991 to assess expected impacts and were reworded to assign values five years into the future. For example, where the original question was

Table 13.1 Response rates for survey periods 1991, 1994, 1997 in Silver Valley, Idaho

Year	*Sample size*	*Response rate (%)*
1991	385	349 (91)
1993	400	367 (91)
1997	300	221 (74)
1999	400	307 (76)

stated as 'One of the most important aspects of tourism is that it provides more jobs in the Silver Valley', the question was rephrased to read: 'One of the most important aspects of tourism is that it will provide more jobs in the next five years in the Silver Valley'. The questions for all surveys were developed using previously tested questions developed by Lui and Var (1986), Lui *et al*., (1987), and Snepenger and Johnson (1991). The surveys were repeated during the same time of year in spring at the end of the winter ski season. These four data collection periods captured information during the exploration, involvement and early development stages of the TALC. Specifically two research questions were examined. The first was whether demographic variables, residents' contact with tourists, perceived economic consequences, and congestion scales predict residents' attitude about the overall impact of tourism across the early stages in the TALC.

This question examined the variables driving the residents' view of tourism development at each point in time. Furthermore, it analyzes the direction and magnitude of the demographic, contact, and impact variables on the dependent variable.

The second question compares results across the four models to assess the consistency or dissimilarity with respect to predictors and overall explanatory power across the early stages of the TALC. In other words, this question examines the stability of variables to predict and the level of prediction for tourism development across the early stages of the TALC.

In 1990 the resort was in the exploration stage of the TALC. As part of the economic redevelopment process the City of Kellogg adopted a mountain theme and sought to refurbish storefronts with alpine architecture. The nearby City of Wallace adopted an early mining theme. But most skier visits to the area were within a 100–150 mile radius – the locally defined skier market. Little additional tourism investment was taking place and the resort was not a major employer in the area.

By 1993 the town was experiencing some growth in the local business mix aimed at the tourism market and can be said to be in the involvement stage. A 61-room hotel was constructed at the ski area base and several eating establishments were built. In 1997, citing financial and management limitations, city officials sold the area to a tourism specialty firm based in Oregon. After some initial fear that the gondola complex would be moved to a ski area development in Oregon, the investors were able to assure residents that the ski area would remain in operation as they continued to invest in and expand the operation. At full operational levels the resort employed over 100 full- and part-time employees.

As early as 1999 the area can be said to be well within the development stage of the TALC. In 2000 the US Forest Service completed the conversion of a scenic section of abandoned rail-bed from the Milwaukee Road that has transformed the unused rail bed into a world-class bike and walking path. This adventurous 13-mile trail takes mountain bikers (and hikers) through nine tunnels and over seven high wooden rail trestles. The *Route of the Hiawatha* is already a regional attraction and expected to expand the visitor base to the region considerably. Also slated for completion in 2002 is a regional 75-mile long 'rails to trails' development, much of which will traverse the Valley. These developments will expand the tourist visitor base to include more seasons. In 2002 the present owners handed management of ski area services to a ski area specialty firm and planned for 2002–2003 is a new ski lift and condominium development at a second base location. The ski area has received some favorable national press coverage and continually expands skier visitor days.

The first set of questions asked respondents for demographic information including marital status, age, years of residency, political self-identification, education level, and household income. Two additional questions that inquired about respondent contact with tourists probed their frequency of contact with tourists and the sociability of contact. Quality of interaction was operationalized using the following question: 'When you talk with tourists around town, which one of the following best describes your contact with tourists?' The response format was five point scale ranging from: 'very negative' to 'very positive'. The frequency item was stated as follows: 'During an average week, how often do you talk with tourists around town?' The response format was: 'daily', 'almost every day', 'a couple times a week', 'once a week', and 'seldom or never'. 'Daily' was scored a five and 'seldom or never' was scored one.

The instrument contained five items for each of the three impact areas – economic, social, and environmental. These items were measured on a five-point Likert scale where 1 = strongly disagree and 5 = strongly agree. Two scales of three items each were developed to measure respondents' attitude about the economic aspects of tourism development and congestion resulting from tourism. The first scale was designed to quantify the potential consequences of tourism development on the local economy. The economic development scale consisted of the following three questions:

- Tourism provides more jobs in the Silver Valley.
- Tourism attracts more investment in the Silver Valley.
- Our standard of living has increased because of tourism.

In contrast, the other scale was developed to ascertain the perceived level of congestion resulting from the presence of tourists in the small communities. The congestion scale included the following items all reverse coded:

- Local residents suffer from living in a tourist destination area.
- Tourism results in overcrowded lakes, hiking trails, parks, and other outdoor places for locals.
- Tourists add greatly to traffic congestion, noise.

Presented in Table 13.2 is the reliability analysis for each of the two scales for each year of the study. The economic development scale and the congestion scale manifested acceptable internal consistency across all four time periods (Berman, 2002: 96). The higher the Cronbach alpha, the greater the internal consistency of the items in the scale. Scales with high internal consistency provide relevant measures of theoretical constructs (Babbie, 2001).

The dependent variable for the study was a single item statement that elicited information on the overall perceived benefits and costs that might be anticipated from tourism development: 'Overall, the benefits are greater than the costs of tourism to the people of the Silver Valley.' The item was scored 5 = strongly agree and 1 = strongly disagree.

Significant predictors of perceived overall tourism development were identified using stepwise multiple regression. Separate models were developed for demographics, the contact variables, the impact scales, and an overall model that utilized all predicators. Standardized betas are reported for each of the significant independent variables. Standardized betas allow direct comparisons for the importance of significant predictors which are measured on different units or scales. The larger the standardized beta, the greater the change in the dependent variable

Table 13.2 Reliability analysis of economic development and congestion scales using Cronbach's alpha

Scale	*1991*	*1993*	*1997*	*1999*
Economic development	0.7633	0.6628	0.7428	0.6836
Congestion	0.8561	0.7866	0.7992	0.8115

given a one unit change in the independent variable. An alpha level of 0.05 was utilized to trim the stepwise regression models.

Findings

In order to investigate whether demographic variables, residents' contact with tourists, perceived economic consequences, and congestion scales predict residents' attitudes about the overall impact of tourism across the early stages in the TALC, stepwise multiple regression analyses were performed for the three sets of independent variables.

Table 13.3 delineates the four separate models that were constructed at each point in time. The first model examined demographics, the second the influence of contact between residents and tourists, the third the significance of the impact scales, and the fourth was an overall model predicting the overall costs and benefits of tourism development. The demographic model in the exploration stage did not predict overall attitudes towards tourism development. The R^2 was 0.032 and the two significant predictors were political self-identity and years in residence.

The contact model, in contrast, did predict overall attitude towards tourism development. The quality and frequency of interactions with tourists were used as predictors. However, in 1991 only quality of interaction was significant and it explained almost 82% of the variance. The higher the quality of the interaction residents had with tourists, the more positive they were toward this form of economic development.

The third model employed the two impact scales: economic development and congestion. Only the economic development scale was significant with an R^2 of 0.867. The more positive residents viewed the economic impacts, the more favorable they were towards tourism development. Lastly, the overall model using all of the predictors identified the economic development scale and quality of interaction as significant predictors. The most important of these was economic development. The overall model had an R^2 of 0.879.

The next series of models explored predictors for the involvement stage. The early involvement stage used survey data from 1993, while the later involvement models used data collected in 1997. Several demographic variables were significant in 1993. Marital status was the most important followed by level of education, political self-identity, age, and lastly by income. For the contact model in 1993, only quality of interaction was significant with a beta of 0.940 and R^2 of 0.883. The impact scales model revealed that both scales were significant. The standardized beta for congestion was 0.320 and for economic development 0.655. The model had an R^2 of 0.924. Finally, the overall model for 1993 shows two significant variables as predictors – the economic

Table 13.3 Stepwise regression analysis for attitude towards overall benefits and costs of tourism to Silver Valley, Idaho using demographics, contact, and tourism impact scale variables as predictor variables*

Predictor variables	***Stage in TALC***			
	Exploration	***Involvement***		***Development***
	1991	***1993***	***1997***	***1999***
	$n = 294$	$n = 272$	$n = 173$	$n = 261$
Demographic model				
Age		0.168	0.304	0.205
Years in residence	0.116			
Income		0.132	0.208	
Marriage status		0.248		0.217
Education		0.235	0.342	0.317
Political self-identity	– 0.147	0.200	0.156	0.254
R^2	0.032	0.862	0.924	0.903
Contact model				
Quality of interaction with tourists	0.905	0.940	0.867	0.889
Frequency of interaction with tourists			0.103	0.087
R^2	0.819	0.883	0.915	0.927
Impact Scales Model				
Congestion		0.320	0.279	0.376
Economic development	0.931	0.655	0.704	0.610
R^2	0.867	0.924	0.939	0.946
Overall model				
Economic development	0.641	0.678	0.440	0.424
Quality	0.320		0.220	0.319
Education			0.134	
Age			0.133	
Congestion		0.300		0.247

Table 13.3 (*Continued*)

Predictor variables	*Stage in TALC*			
	Exploration	*Involvement*		*Development*
	1991	*1993*	*1997*	*1999*
Frequency			0.079	
R^2	0.879	0.928	0.948	0.951

*Standardized betas reported, alpha = 0.05

development scale and the congestion scale. The overall model had an R^2 of 0.928.

The later involvement stage in 1997 was more complex. For the demographic model four variables – education, age, income, and political self-identity – were significant. Both interaction variables were significant as were both impact scales. In the overall model five variables were found to be significant with an overall R^2 of 0.948.

The final year of survey data describes the early development stage of the TALC in 1999. The demographic model explained 90% of the variance in the dependent variable and four variables were significant predictors: education, political self-identity, marital status, and years of residency. Both contact variables were significant and had an R^2 of 0.927. The impact scale items were also significant: R^2 was 0.946. The overall model contained three variables that were found to be significant: economic development, quality of contact with tourists, and the congestion scale item. Overall R^2 in 1999 was 0.951.

The ability of the models to demonstrate consistency or dissimilarity with respect to predictors and overall explanatory power across the early stages of the TALC was the next area of inquiry.

The level of prediction for tourism development across the early stages of the TALC improved over time. At the exploration stage respondents had a difficult time assessing tourism impacts. As the community tourism economy transitioned through the involvement and development stages, residents had a better sense of the benefits and costs of tourism development and the results for the statistical modeling became more convincing. Concurrently, those favoring and not favoring tourism development became easier to identify using demographic measures, contact, and impact variables. Over time, as evidenced by the increasing R^2 values, each of the four general models explained more of the variance in the independent variable.

Modeling perceived overall benefits and costs of tourism revealed that some variables were stable predictors over time. Across all four time periods the overall model demonstrated that economic development is the major driver in how residents view tourism. Those residents who believe tourism enhances the local economy tend to also have a positive overall view of tourism on their lives and the community while those who do not view tourism positively tend to believe that tourism will have negative effects.

The second most important variable across the stages of the TALC was the quality of interaction locals have with tourists. Those who enjoy favorable interaction tend to view tourism development positively. For those whose interaction with tourists is negative, their view of tourism is also negative.

The third variable that shows a systematic relationship over time is the congestion impact scale. Those who favor tourism tended to believe that congestion was not a problem with respect to overcrowded parks and other recreational facilities in the region. Those who perceive a crowding or congestion problem tend to hold a negative view of tourism development.

Finally, three demographic variables emerged as stable predictors in three of the four years. Education produced relatively high standardized betas and was the most important demographic predictor. The higher the educational attainment, the more predisposed toward tourism development they tended to be. Political self-identity was a weaker but consistent predictor. In the first year conservatives tended to favor tourism but the relationship shifted to reveal that the more liberal political stance favored tourism and a conservative political position held negative views toward tourism development. The last demographic variable that showed stability as a predictor over time was age; the relationship with the dependent variable was that older respondents supported tourism development while younger respondents were less supportive.

Discussion

Stages in the TALC are critical to understanding perceived overall impacts of tourism development (Johnson & Snepenger, 1992). In this study, different relationships between overall impacts, demographic measures, contact between locals and tourists, and tourism impacts emerged along the exploration, involvement, and development continuum. These changing relationships can be effectively modeled as noted by the increasingly high regression coefficients in the four models. A set of robust predictors were identified in this study as measures of economic development, quality of interaction, and congestion.

The economic development impacts of tourism are perhaps the most important to any community undergoing a planned economic transition. The economic development scale assesses (1) enhanced employment opportunity, (2) investments resulting from increased tourism activity, and (3) the possibility of enhanced standard of living for locals. Clearly, these were consistently the most important predictors of support for tourism. Local governments and tourism developers will find greater community support for tourism development if these economic criteria are explicitly addressed. For example, owners and promoters of emergent tourism enterprises can hire local labor and pay a living wage. Community economic development efforts can work to attract secondary businesses to a region that complements an attraction but can also help diversify the tourism economy by attracting other business not directly associated with tourism (Snepenger *et al*., 1995). Local option tourist taxes can be utilized to make community and social investments to the region so that all residents share in the benefits of tourism development. Some tourist communities provide heavily subsidized public transportation or provide locals with inexpensive season ski passes. The fundamental lesson for tourism developers is that if residents believe that economic attributes for them are enhanced as a result of tourism development, they will tend to support it.

Related to increasingly positive economic activity is the quality of contact between tourists and locals. As long as that interaction is enjoyable and positive in nature, residents will tend to support tourism development. Public and private managers can encourage positive interactions by planning for community events that appeal to both locals and tourists – winter and summer festivals, farmers markets, and community free ski days are just a few examples. Locals can be encouraged to open their homes as B&Bs and can do so with planning and capital startup loans from various sources.

As previously noted, the TALC is both a cross-sectional and longitudinal construct, however there are very few longitudinal studies in the literature and further research is needed to explore the shifting long-term relationships between residents and tourism development. The tourism impact literature begs for additional longitudinal studies in other settings with other characteristics such as different economic transitions, ethnicity, level of tourism development, urbanization, and cultural settings, which could all provide valuable insight into the changing nature of tourism impacts and destination maturation processes.

In the Silver Valley, future research could include utilizing the scales discussed here as well as others by Ap and Crompton (1998), Lankford and Howard (1994), and Snepenger *et al*. (2001) to investigate both summer and winter tourism. The region will expand the visitor base and seasonality of visitation as mountain biking, bike touring, and water-based recreation continue to develop in future years. As the region moves through the TALC it will be critical to continue to monitor the impacts of the growing tourism segment of the economy – this is especially true as second home development grows in importance to the region (Johnson *et al*., 2002; Snepenger *et al*., 1995) and the traditional mining and timber economy recover from past decline.

Conclusion

Very few longitudinal empirical studies exist that help operationalize the TALC model. This study examines the early stages of the TALC from exploration through early development for a regional economy previously based on natural resource extraction and now increasingly diversified toward tourism and tourism services. The study examines the results of four surveys of residents in the region that monitor the perceived economic, social, and environmental tourism impacts over the 1990s.

The first research question examined which variables best explained residents' view of tourism development for each of the four time periods. The analysis included the direction and magnitude of demographic measures, residents' contact with tourists, and tourism impact variables. The results show that an economic development scale constructed from three of five standardized economic impact questions from the tourism literature was the most robust predictor of feelings toward tourism development for all four time periods.

The second research question compared results across time and TALC stages. This question examined the stability of variables to predict and the level of prediction for tourism development. The results again showed that the economic development scale was the most powerful predictor across the TALC continuum.

The findings present some opportunities for supporters of tourism development and it was suggested that policies that spread out the economic benefits of tourism development to include locals and at the same time enhance tourist/resident interactions can help ensure the community will be a willing host to tourists as visitation expands.

Continued monitoring of the expanding tourism base is suggested as a management tool to help foster a sustainable tourism economy in the region. This monitoring can prove useful to help foster lasting and expanding support for tourism development as the Silver Valley rebuilds its local economy and social infrastructure that were lost with the decline of the mining industry after 100 years of prosperity.

Finally, similar longitudinal studies may prove valuable across all stages in the TALC and could help manage existing tourism activity as it inevitably adjusts to emergent and shifting markets. As it does so, the impacts on residents of tourism-dependent communities will certainly change and it is possible that a different demographic, economic, and political cohort may be attracted (or repelled) to the community. These new residents may desire something different for their quality of life and their opinions may significantly impact the tourism economy. For example, as retirees who are uncoupled from the local economy are attracted to an area rich in recreational opportunities, they may wish for lower levels of tourism development in order to avoid perceived overcrowding (see Martin, this volume, editor's comment). In mature or declining tourism markets, residents may desire to radically retool the local economy as experienced in the Silver Valley. Other scenarios can be imagined. Local government decision makers and tourism entrepreneurs would be well advised to consider investing in continued and long-term monitoring of those who act as hosts for community tourism.

Chapter 14

The TALC Model and Politics

B. MARTIN

Introduction

'If you are leaving Hilton Head ... please take our mayor.' That bumper sticker seen on cars in Hilton Head, South Carolina in the mid-1990s signaled an increasing dissatisfaction with the mayor who had been elected a year and a half earlier. Hilton Head was in a political uproar, with the tourism industry at the center of the controversy. The mayor, a planner by profession, had been elected with strong support from the retirees on the island on what he construed as a 'no-more-tourism' platform. When he was elected, many had assumed that the incumbent would be re-elected and had complacently failed to vote. During his term, the mayor had created a furor because of his interpretation of his mandate. In interviews on national television and state papers he indicated that Hilton Head wanted less tourism. Many of the town's residents were quite disappointed with what they considered to be his irresponsible behavior (Hammond, 1993; Lofton, 1993). Even those who had voted for him believed that he had misinterpreted a controlled growth mandate as a 'no-more-tourism' mandate. For many, the bumper sticker quite clearly expressed their feelings.

The tourism industry on Hilton Head at that time enjoyed a visitation rate of 1.6 million people who spent $577 million on their visits (Lofton, 1993). There was no question that tourism was important to the economy of the town. Unlike many destinations, tourism in Hilton Head had been planned. According to the original major developer, Charles Fraser, Hilton Head had been planned to be both a resort and a retirement community. It had been highly successful in attracting both retirees and tourists, and therein lay the problem. Many residents, and especially retirees, were concerned that the number of tourists was growing and becoming a problem. A carrying capacity study conducted a few years previously had shown that transportation was the limiting factor for the island (Bell, 1994). Residents did not have to be convinced of that. There was only one major road through the island and only one bridge to be used for evacuation in the event of a hurricane. Traffic congestion was a serious problem and many on the island feared that Hilton Head was headed for other serious problems. This group was called the 'burn the bridgers', referring to their perceived desire to protect the community by burning the only bridge that gives access to Hilton Head. These were ostensibly the residents who had voted for the controversial mayor.

Both development and the control of development are based on political decision making. Governments are made up of politicians who are elected on specific platforms, supported by the public vote. It is quite common for that platform to be economic growth and development, which makes the situation in Hilton Head even more interesting, as the mayor's platform had appeared to be anti-growth. In addition, government agencies decide the rules of development through formulation of laws and regulations. Recognizing this is important to the study of the tourism life cycle. Government leaders, elected by interested citizens, who provide the framework for the development and growth of tourism. But are these government leaders always following the desires of their constituencies? Or are there other pressures put upon them that benefit a few but may not be in the best interest of the community. And what backlash can be expected when the public is discontented with government involvement?

Butler (1980) refers to some of these political pressures when discussing the involvement stage of the tourism life cycle. He states that in this early stage of tourism, development pressure will be put upon government and public agencies to provide or improve transportation and other facilities for visitors. Who is exerting this pressure and why? Is it simply those in the tourism industry that apply the pressure or might there be others within the community interested in growth from tourism? Although there has been some previous recognition of the involvement of government in the tourism development process (Elliot, 1997: 8; Getz, 1991: 134), not enough attention has been paid to the politics of tourism (Hall, 1994: 1; Hall & Jenkins, 1995: 97). This study of resident attitudes toward tourism in Hilton Head provides a unique view of some of the political ramifications of tourism development. Election of an anti-tourism mayor and his eventual political demise provide an interesting backdrop for enhancing understanding of the political aspects of the tourism life cycle. This chapter is a snapshot of Hilton Head in the mid-1990s that provides insight into the relationship between political processes and the tourism life cycle, from the perspective of the town's residents.

Historical Perspective of the Development of Hilton Head

Development of Hilton Head Island commenced in the late 1950s with the building of the James F. Byrnes Bridge to the mainland. In 1956 the Frasers acquired a totally uninhabited 5200-acre tract, which encompassed the entire southern end of the island, comprising approximately 20% of the total land area of the island. Charles Fraser proceeded to develop Sea Pines Plantation into a resort community designed to serve both retirees and vacationers. Fraser's development was based on a master plan that included the establishment of, and adherence to, three fundamental commitments: strict control of land use, the development of recreation land, and the preservation of two square miles of wildlife refuge. Fraser's goal was to maintain the natural beauty of the area by developing it in such a way that the island's natural attributes would be enhanced rather than destroyed. Careful planning and rigid standards were seen as the method for accomplishing this (Fraser, 1995). The early development of Sea Pines Plantation by Fraser implemented those standards. Homes blended in with the natural environment and wildlife roamed free. Fraser also had a great influence on other aspects of the island's development. Even today, Hilton Head is noted for its strict regulation of signage throughout the town.

Since the original development of Sea Pines, much development has occurred, not all of which adheres to the original goals. Charles Fraser never owned the entire island but the areas that he did own were well planned and protected. However, other developers during the 1980s were more interested in turning a profit than protecting the island. While a great deal of the island is comprised of gated communities in which care has been taken to provide only the best in amenities for the wealthy residents, several resort developments provide rental accommodations that barely meet city standards (Shields, 1987).

Most of the remaining undeveloped land in Hilton Head is owned by the African-American indigenous population. The town planner, as well as an African-American city councilman who is a native of the island, reported that some of these native islanders felt that their right to develop their land was being threatened by both current and proposed land use restrictions. According to one real estate agent (Kenney, 1994), some business people also felt that the island was not 'built out' and that there was room for continued growth. On the other hand, the election of the mayor gave evidence that many of the residents felt that restrictions on growth were very important.

Some residents believed the town administrators were attempting to control growth in what some considered a backdoor method; implementing regulations on new developments that would be restrictive enough to halt most development. For example, traffic impact statements were required for new developments. Developers had to show that their new facilities provided acceptable access to the only major road on the island and pay impact fees according to potential impact.

During this unsettled period in Hilton Head's history, the incumbent mayor was running for re-election. Ironically, his opponent was a local building contractor. Would the mayor be re-elected to continue his anti-tourism campaign? This was a vital question for the future of Hilton

Head. The mayor's political viewpoints had the potential to send Hilton Head into the decline stage of the tourism life cycle (Butler, 1980). A study that determined resident attitudes toward various aspects of tourism development could provide the answer to important questions. Were the residents of Hilton Head anti-tourism, anti-growth or neither? Were there differences in the opinions among residents about the future of Hilton Head, according to whether or not they were retirees, business leaders, or government administrators? Where did resident attitudes indicate that Hilton Head was on the life cycle continuum and what did residents want for their future? And what role did politics play in determining Hilton Head's progression through the tourism life cycle? Resident attitudes are an important determinant in assessing whether social carrying capacity is being exceeded in a manner that will affect the tourism life cycle stage of the community (Martin & Uysal, 1990)

A study of tourism in Hilton Head was conducted with the intent of discovering whether or not various groups of residents had consistent views of the future of tourism and whether there was indeed an indication of a political growth machine in Hilton Head that might be inclined to pressure the government into decisions that could result in the eventual demise of the tourism industry. Resident attitudes were the basis for this determination. The study was conducted using the Tourism Impact Attitude Scale to determine resident attitudes toward tourism and its continued growth on Hilton Head. Some of the results of that study have been reported previously (Martin, 1999; Martin *et al*., 1998) and will be reviewed here. Not previously reported were the many long discussions held with the residents after they had completed the standardized questionnaire. The qualitative aspects of the research yielded valuable information for assessing the dynamics between politics and tourism growth that might propel a destination through the life cycle. Those conversations provide much of the basis for this chapter.

Growth Machine Theory and the Tourism Life Cycle

There are several theories of political influence on the development of communities (Harrigan, 1989). A year of background research on the situation in Hilton Head revealed that growth machine theory would be most useful in describing resident attitudes and the political atmosphere in Hilton Head (Canan & Hennessy, 1989; Danielson, 1995; Martin, 1998). Growth machine theory (Molotch, 1976) is based on the concept that community growth is frequently used as a platform for political gain, driven by influential members of the community, the 'elites'. Molotch contended that land-holding community leaders, and those in whose best interest community growth lies, dominate community policymaking. That faction makes up the growth machine. The main goal of the growth machine is to promote growth in order to maximize the economic return to land holders, as well as others in the community who benefit from growth. The growth machine is made up of landowners, financial institutions, lawyers, and local newspaper owners who are in a position to benefit from growth. This faction of the community dominates local government and seeks to influence local political leaders in order to bring them into the progrowth machine. Generally, city government plays a dichotomous role in dealing with the growth machine. First, it must support the growth machine's promotion of economic (i.e. tourism in the case of Hilton Head) growth on the grounds that growth increases job opportunities for residents and makes land more valuable. On the other hand, because it represents people in local neighborhoods, city government frequently finds itself playing an intermediary role in conflicts that arise when residents oppose particular development projects (Harrigan, 1989). According to Logan and Molotch (1987: 51), those who make up the progrowth machine 'use their growth consensus to eliminate any alternative vision of the purpose of local government or the meaning of community.'

Growth machine theory has important implications for discussions and assessments using the tourism life cycle model. The life cycle model is based on the concept that tourism destinations change over time (Butler, 1980). Those changes in the stage of tourism development generally are occurring based on various aspects of growth within the destination. Growth in tourist numbers and tourist facilities generates both potential benefits and costs to the community. These costs and benefits vary as the destination changes over time, *due to growth*. Resident attitudes may also change over time due to growth in the number of outsiders with whom they must share resources and space. Attitudes on the part of community residents are recognized as playing a vital role in the success of tourism for the community. Negative attitudes of residents are commonly acknowledged to result in reduced popularity of the destination for visitors (Doxey, 1975; Martin & Uysal, 1990). Resident attitudes toward tourism can also be manifested through the political processes that elect officials according to their plans for the community. Therefore, it would seem that more attention needs to be paid to the role of politics in the tourism life cycle process.

While it is often difficult to assess just how much growth is spurred by tourism and how much by other types of business in the community, in the case of Hilton Head it is far easier to see the effect of tourism. Tourism is the main economic engine on the island, with real estate running second in importance. However, real estate sales and tourism development are intricately connected to each other. As in many attractive resort areas, new residents are frequently prior tourists. Sometimes they purchase second homes during their working lives and then retire to live there permanently, and sometimes they move there for the first time when they retire. In either case, often their first attraction to the island is as a tourist. There is no doubt that Hilton Head has changed over time, with more and more residents living in more and more gated communities, as well as an increase in service industries to support the growing number of hotels and restaurants built for tourists. All of these changes could be expected to affect resident attitudes toward tourism. Did this growth result in negative attitudes of the residents toward current or future tourism development? What impact did resident attitudes have on the political processes that affect the tourism life cycle of resort communities?

Hilton Head Study

A survey of Hilton Head residents' attitudes was conducted during the summer of 1995. The data for this study were collected using a questionnaire based on the Tourism Impact Attitude Scale (TIAS) developed by Lankford (1994). The TIAS is a 29-item scale used to assess resident attitudes toward tourism development. It is a five-point Likert-type attitudinal scale, with possible responses ranging from strongly agree to strongly disagree. The questionnaire was slightly modified for relevance in Hilton Head. At the end of the questionnaire respondents were asked if there was anything else they wanted to discuss or clarify.

The sampling frame for the study was rather complex. A market research firm located in Hilton Head provided the list of businesses, as well as a list of permanent home owners. Business leaders were identified as owners or managers of all businesses on Hilton Head. Government administrators were identified by the Town Manager, using the criteria that those town employees who were in administrative positions which allow them to have input in the decision-making process would be surveyed. The six members of city council and the Mayor were also included in the sample of government administrators. Retirees were identified using a screening question for home owners. Those residents who were not retirees, business leaders or government administrators were identified as 'general residents'.

All respondents except government administrators were interviewed by telephone using the Dillman Total Design Method (1978) for telephone interviews. The Town Manager asked that government employees self-administer the questionnaire rather than participate in the telephone interviewing. A total of 287 respondents participated in the study, representing an 86% response rate. The breakdown of respondents by areas of interest showed that there were: 120 business leaders, 100 retirees, 28 government administrators, and 39 general residents.

Results

A sociodemographic profile of the respondents showed that 53.5% of the respondents were male and 46.5% female, 44.6% were over 55 years of age, and nearly 45% had incomes over $60,000. The vast majority of respondents reported that they were non-natives of Hilton Head. Although 81% reported being non-natives, this number was actually higher, as many who reported being natives also reported only living on Hilton Head for a fairly short period of time. The question was 'do you consider yourself to be a native of Hilton Head?' Perhaps due to the wording of the question, personal views of 'belonging' may have complicated the results.

An analysis of resident attitudes toward tourism revealed interesting results. Respondents were asked to rate their opinion of the statements on a scale from 1 to 5, with 1 being strongly disagree and 5 being strongly agree. Three statements stand out as having the highest means. One was that 'tourism is responsible for the traffic congestion in Hilton Head.' Another was 'long-term planning by city government can control the negative impacts of tourism on the environment.' The statement with the highest mean was 'the tourism industry will continue to play a major economic role in Hilton Head.'

A factor analysis was performed to examine underlying dimensions that would provide information for measuring attitudes toward the issue of growth from tourism development. A four-factor solution with high alpha reliabilities for each of the factors emerged. The four factors were: increased development, positive impacts, tourism support, and negative impacts.

The increased development factor contained items related to resident attitudes toward more development. These items included attitudes concerning more intensive development of facilities, becoming more of a tourist destination, attracting more visitors, development of more tourism facilities, and further tourism growth.

The second factor, positive impacts, included attitudes toward tourism's impact on recreational opportunities, the quality of public services, the standard of living, economic wellbeing, the job market, shopping opportunities, as well as generic benefits of tourism and the type of jobs provided by tourism.

The third factor was termed tourism support because all the items related to resident support for tourism in the community. The items in this factor included attitudes about government control of impacts, the value of tourists, government role in promoting tourism, support of tourism as vital to the community, support for tourism as the main industry, promotion of tourism, and support for tourism as a continuing economic force in the community.

The fourth factor, negative impacts, ascertained resident attitudes toward litter, crime, environmental impacts, and traffic congestion.

In order to test for differences among the four groups on the four factors, an analysis of variance (ANOVA) was performed. There was a statistically significant difference among the groups on each of the four factors at the 0.05 or better level. The first factor, Increased Development, was directly related to the issue of whether or not residents were interested in continued or increased growth as a result of tourism development. This factor explained 35.6% of the variance while all the other factors together explained 17.1%. According to Kachigan (1986), it is important to note the importance of the first factor when it explains an overwhelming percentage of the variance in comparison to other factors. As it was considered most important to assess attitudes toward growth, the Increased Development factor was considered an important indicator of those attitudes. Business leaders showed the strongest support for increased development, with general residents and government administrators showing more modest support and retirees being the mostly strongly opposed to further tourism development.

On the Positive Impacts factor, retirees and government administrators viewed tourism as having less positive impacts than did the general residents and business leaders. Business leaders were most aware of the positive impacts.

On the Tourism Support factor, retirees and government administrators showed significant differences from business leaders and general residents. There was more support for tourism from business leaders than from the retirees and government administrators.

On the Negative Impacts factor the only significant difference was shown between business leaders and all the other groups. Business leaders felt that there was less negative impact on the community from tourism development than did all the other groups.

Although significant differences were shown, it is important to understand that the differences were only in the *strength* of opinion or feelings on the issues. Differences did not indicate that different groups were pro or con on the issues. All residents' attitudes were on the same side of the spectrum. It was only the strength of their attitudes that was different. For example, all groups showed low support for the items in the factor Increased Development, ranging from 2.04 for retirees to 2.89 for business leaders. Although they were technically significantly different, it was not because any of the groups agreed with statements such as: 'Hilton Head should encourage more intensive development of tourist facilities'; 'Hilton Head should become more of a tourist destination'; and 'Overall, you are in favor of further growth from tourism development in Hilton Head'. The same was true of respondents for all of the factors. There were differences in the intensity of their agreement or disagreement with the statements but they were never polar opposites in their views.

Conversations with respondents

At the end of the questionnaire, respondents were asked if there was anything they would like to add to their responses on the questionnaire. Most residents were very willing to discuss issues not specifically addressed in the questionnaire or to explain their responses. Government leaders did not participate in this portion of the research because their questionnaires were not completed by phone. However, they did have a section at the end of the questionnaire for writing in comments.

Respondents were most anxious to express their dismay about the mayor's behavior. As for their attitudes toward the mayor and their intentions politically, respondents were overwhelmingly negative toward his bid for re-election. Retirees and business leaders alike felt that a new mayor was necessary. It was quite clear that the mayor was highly unlikely to be re-elected. Even those who had voted for him previously were against his re-election. They were pleased to be able to explain why they had voted for him originally and their comments gave a much richer understanding of the dynamics of politics, tourism, and growth on Hilton Head. Several respondents mentioned that the conversations were therapeutic, reflecting their emotions about the subject. Through these discussions, it became clear that these residents were indeed concerned about where the town was headed if growth of the tourism industry continued unabated. They were disappointed that the man elected to help solve the problems had created such negative, erroneous perceptions of the Hilton Head tourism industry.

There were several other consistent themes running through the comments of the residents. Many residents reported that they felt that Hilton Head had 'reached saturation point'. They believed that Hilton Head was a thriving resort and retirement community but that it was essential that 'future growth be managed'. The term 'managed growth' was used many times in conversations with the residents in the study. They did not see themselves as anti-growth or anti-tourism. They believed that the best protection for Hilton Head would be in controlled and managed growth. Whether the respondents were business owners or retirees, their desires for controlling growth of the community were consistent.

Residents were quite fearful that Hilton Head would 'become another Myrtle Beach'. Myrtle Beach is also a coastal community in South Carolina, located approximately three hours north of Hilton Head. Myrtle Beach is highly developed, with many reasonably priced motels, restaurants, and a variety of amusement parks and country music entertainment. It is predominantly marketed to the middle class and has a very different image from that of Hilton Head. Myrtle Beach had gone through a rejuvenation stage during the late 1980s and early 1990s but was still not the type of high-class resort that Hilton Head had always been.

Many of the residents of Hilton Head were concerned about the ability of Hilton Head to maintain its upper-class image. They were hesitant in explaining their thoughts on this issue but nevertheless, many expressed concern that overbuilding and continued growth that was not consistent with this high-class image would result in the attraction of a type of tourist that would change the character of their community. The life cycle model predicts that the type of tourist will change over time and residents of Hilton Head were aware that they were in peril of watching this phenomenon become reality. There was a time in the 1980s when new construction in the upper end of the island was shoddy, resulting in what locals call 'stack a shacks'. These were poorly constructed condominiums that were much more affordable to the less affluent than the upper-class hotels such as the Westin and Hyatt. In addition, many new fast-food restaurants and low-cost motels had opened in the previous decade. Residents were concerned that this would lead to the end of the 'classiness' of their town. Business leaders and residents alike were concerned about the potential for negative change in the *type* of tourism Hilton Head had always enjoyed, as Butler predicts will happen without stringent controls.

Discussion

The consistency with which the residents were concerned about continued growth due to tourism was unexpected based on observation of the political dynamics of the town. It was expected that the residents would be divided along the lines suggested by growth machine theory; that business leaders would be much more supportive of growth of tourism than retirees and other residents. It seemed logical that business owners and managers would differ significantly from retirees and government officials in their opinions of the benefits and costs of tourism, as predicted by growth machine theory and by the mayor's election. Such was not the case. Despite the reported statistical differences, the residents were surprisingly on the same side in their views of the future of Hilton Head. Perhaps the fact that Hilton Head attracts so many highly educated, successful retirees who have themselves previously run large businesses, means that residents have more understanding of the importance of 'not killing the goose that lays the golden egg'. The business owners were quite savvy in understanding that principle and the retirees were quite aware of the importance of protecting the economy. After all, it is an economy that provides everyone with a number of amenities. Although many residents felt that a lot of the shopping opportunities are geared toward the tourists and frequently shop in upper-class shops in Savannah, the residents generally take advantage of the many other amenities such as the excellent restaurants and golf courses. Several of the retirees who were interviewed not only played on the golf courses but worked there part-time in what some might consider menial jobs but which they considered to be fun and interesting ways to keep busy.

What impact did the desire of Hilton Head residents to protect the image of the community have on the determination of life cycle stage? The fact that residents were concerned about the image of the town indicates that a change in image might have been occurring. The building of low-income tourist accommodations and fast-food restaurants certainly indicates that Hilton Head may be on the verge of a downturn in the ability to attract the high-income tourist. This would be one more indication that Hilton Head is moving towards a later stage of the life cycle and that it may need to take stringent measures to protect the resort from a potential decline stage. It is unlikely that Hilton Head will ever deteriorate to the point that tourists will not actually visit. However, there are several indications that the town is becoming less exclusive and becoming more attractive to the average-income tourist.

A confounding issue for keeping the image of Hilton Head intact is the inability of those who work in the tourism industry to actually live on Hilton Head. Most of the service workers are bused as much as an hour and half to work in tourism positions. Low-income housing is simply not available and therefore, the image of Hilton Head is, in an interesting manner, more easily protected. Molotch (1976) calls those who promote growth the 'elites'. Is the lack of affordable housing a case of the 'elites' of the growth machine protecting the image of the town in order to keep land values at a premium?

One important aspect of growth machine theory is the potential for an anti-growth coalition. Hilton Head did indeed appear to have a type of anti-growth coalition; one that wanted strictly controlled and managed growth. However, this is not to be mistaken for an anti-tourism coalition. Although it is difficult to distinguish between anti-growth and anti-tourism when it is generally tourism that is spurring the growth, residents made it clear that they were not anti-tourism. In the end, it seems that the residents were being proactive in demanding managed growth, rather than negative in being strongly anti-growth. Residents want the town to have the ability to maintain a viable and profitable tourism industry while residents enjoy a high quality of life. For them, being in favor of managed growth is the best possible method of protecting their quality of life and allowing for continued economic prosperity. Several residents commented that they believed that the physical limitation of the island would in itself be the final limitation to growth. As there are strict limitations on the height of buildings, which make it impossible for the town to grow *up*, there is some credibility to that idea.

Not taking any chances in protecting their island, the residents exercised their right to elect a true representative of their views in the Fall of 1995. A native of the local area who was an award-winning building contractor was elected as the new mayor. He then became the first mayor in the history of Hilton Head ever to be re-elected to a second term and recently won a third election. What makes this contractor-turned-politician so popular when a planner was so unpopular? His answers to questions posed by local media before his third election help explain (*Carolina Morning News*, 2001). He was asked what he saw as the top two issues facing the town and how he would address them. The first issue he stated was 'mainland growth', alluding to the impact that growth occurring just outside the town from a large retirement community is having on the town of Hilton Head. He stated that he would address the issue by working with the county 'to implement growth management techniques and ordinances that will allow growth to be implemented in a more orderly and less intense fashion'. The second issue was 'enhancing our sense of community'. When asked what experiences or qualities he had that would make him a good mayor for the next four years his answer was 'I am a consensus builder'. A consensus builder who understands the need for growth management and protection of their sense of community was exactly what the people of Hilton Head were seeking. His commitment to listening to the desires of the community in their vision of the future of the town has not only kept him in office but bodes well for keeping Hilton Head as a viable tourism destination.

Conclusion

The tourism life cycle as proposed by Butler (1980) has for many years provided a mechanism for studying the future of tourism destinations. However, little has been noted of the political aspect of the growth that occurs as tourism progresses through the different stages of the life cycle. The events in Hilton Head of the mid 1990s provide an interesting laboratory for assessing the relevance of the political aspects inherent in promoting growth. Growth machine theory postulates that avaricious residents will inordinately influence local politics in a manner that leads to excessive growth and the rise of an anti-growth coalition. On the surface, this did indeed appear to be the case in Hilton Head. However, the study of resident attitudes that specifically compared views of business leaders, government officials, and retirees did not find that in fact to be true. No group was found to want the growth of Hilton Head to occur at any cost. Instead, even retirees who would not monetarily benefit from allowing tourism to thrive were in favor of maintaining the current level of tourism. Business leaders with more to gain monetarily from tourism growth were prudent in acknowledging that too much growth could eventually destroy their profitable businesses. Government leaders were trying to provide the mechanism through regulation that would control growth.

Overall, all groups of residents made it clear that maintaining the quality of life and sense of community were what concerned them most. Business leaders were just as interested in maintaining a high quality of tourism business. It was evident that residents would take control of the political process in order to do so. The election of a mayor who became very unpopular was quite possibly the best thing ever to happen to Hilton Head. Although he did not turn out to be the right man for the job, never again could it be assumed that concerned citizens would not be heard on their views of the future of their community. The election that year and in subsequent years of a building contractor who understands the issues of growth was a direct result of the disastrous prior administration. It would seem that the best method of controlling an anti-tourism coalition that could result in descent into a decline stage is to elect a leader who cares about resident attitudes and takes action on their behalf.

As for the tourism life cycle, resident attitudes toward tourism provide evidence to support determination of the stage of the life cycle in which Hilton Head appeared to be at that particular time. Butler's consolidation stage seems to best represent Hilton Head's position on the life cycle. A major part of the island's economy is tied to tourism, major franchises and chains are well established, and efforts have certainly succeeded in extending the tourist season. Perhaps most importantly, the large numbers of visitors and facilities for tourists have aroused just enough opposition and discontent among residents to make them vigilant in protecting their quality of life.

From the first introductory stages of development in the late 1950s through the maturing of the town in the mid 1990s, Hilton Head has progressed from an inaccessible island to one of the world's greatest resorts. With savvy and concerned residents who are willing to use the political process to proactively protect the island's future, Hilton Head may never arrive at the decline stage of the life cycle.

Chapter 15

Seeking Sustainable Tourism in Northern Thailand: The Dynamics of the TALC

J. MAROIS and T. HINCH

Introduction

The concept of tourism area life cycles (TALC) is germane to this book. For the purposes of this chapter, however, it is also important to understand the concept of sustainable tourism development, as well as the general environment of TALC in Thailand. Sustainable tourism development is defined as:

> tourism which is developed and maintained in an area (community, environment) in such a manner and at such a scale that it remains viable over an indefinite period of time and does not degrade or alter the environment (human and physical) in which it exists to such a degree that it prohibits the successful development and well-being of other activities and processes. (Butler, 1993: 29)

Ideally, tourism developments should respect, and even improve, the viability of the natural environment and the social community.

Butler's (1980) conceptualisation of TALCs suggests that tourist destinations will not be sustainable indefinitely, at least in terms of tourism activity. The more pertinent question is, therefore, how to extend a constructive form of tourism in the destination rather than how to ensure the destination equivalent of immortality.

The essence of the tourist attraction in Ban Raummit, Thailand is the tribal culture of the Karen people. Tourists, particularly Westerners, travel to the hills of Northern Thailand in search of primitive 'others'. The distinct culture of the Karen has proven to be a powerful draw. Any discussion of the sustainability of tourism development in this village must, therefore, consider culture as a defining element of the community, as well as its manifestation in various tourism products. Although the TALC has already been used to examine sustainable tourism development in Northern Thailand (Cohen, 1979; Dearden, 1991; Dearden & Harron, 1994; Maneeorasert *et al*., 1975), the dynamic inter-relationships between product and destination life cycles have not been emphasised. The purpose of this chapter is to consider the sustainability of hill tribe tourism in the Karen village of Ban Raummit, Thailand by examining these inter-relationships.

Previous studies indicate that commercial trekking began in this area around 1970 as small-scale operations in which a limited number of people, mostly scientists, travelled to learn about the hill tribes (Cohen, 1996). Guides were tribal people who knew how to access the villages. Dramatic growth over the next two and a half decades is reflected in the currently more than 200 trekking operators in Chiang Mai, the major starting point for treks into northern hill tribe villages by the mid-1990s (Cohen, 1996; Dearden, 1991). As the number of trekkers increased, Chiang Rai and Mae Hong Son have also grown as major departure points.

Two different types of tours emerged. The first was a *jungle trek* consisting of a guided trek into the forest to visit more remote and traditional hill tribe villages with few tourist facilities. These treks operate with an average of 10–12 participants and last three to ten days. The second type was a *tribal village or sightseeing tour* in which most of the transportation is by van, bus or boat. These tours travel through Northern Thailand, stopping at various villages for short 'picture opportunities'. Typically, sightseeing tours consist of relatively large groups of 20–40 people and last from one to three days. For both types of tours, the tour operator is responsible for the operational details including transportation, accommodation, food and luggage handling, thereby making these tours accessible to a wide range of visitors.

Dearden and Harron (1994) estimate that more than 100,000 people participated in jungle treks each year during the early 1990s. Given the high growth rates of this type of tourism and the rapid modernisation of hill tribe cultures, Dearden (1991) suggests that areas promoting jungle treks and sightseeing tours tend to move through their tourism life cycles relatively quickly. Other factors contributing to this rapid progression include increased accessibility to hill tribe villages by walking trail, road and waterways. The cycle formally begins for a village on the jungle trek when the trek operators make initial contact. These operators will continue to visit a village with their tours until their clients perceive it to be too developed or modern. As the number of visitors increase, the interactions between the visitors and the villagers become less intimate and more institutionalised. Villages originally featured as part of a jungle trek may be rejuvenated as destinations on the tribal village sightseeing tours as they become more accessible by land or waterway, but even these sightseeing stops may eventually be abandoned when visitors feel that they have become too modern.

Dearden and Harron (1994) argue that currently this cycle is not sustainable. Some operators have responded by adding more components to the treks such as commercial elephant and raft rides basing the tours more on adventure than culture. Although these changes make the industry more viable for the tourism operators, they tend to remove visitors from the villages, reducing opportunities for economic development. Nevertheless, Dearden (1991: 412) suggested 'trekking, appropriately managed and with input from the hill tribes, could become a key component in sustaining these communities in the future.' A greater understanding of the life cycles of these tourism products will provide a tool with which to better manage development within the villages.

The Tourism Area Life Cycle Revisited

Johnston (2001, other volume) suggests that, after 20 years, Butler's original TALC model needs some modification. In addition to the traditional graphic representation of TALC's general stages, he suggests three types of analysis are required. The first is a 'boundary analysis' in which the destination is defined to facilitate comparisons between like destinations. This analysis addresses two key questions. What is the region and what type of region is it?

The second type of analysis focuses on 'pathways'. It examines the internal characteristics, the users and the macrostructural conditions of the destination. A discussion of the scale of development and the ambience of a destination is required. Users are discussed in terms of quantity and type. This analysis also highlights macrostructural conditions including external elements that either constrain or enable the development of the destination. Once organised chronologically, these descriptions are used to identify the corresponding stages of the TALC.

Finally, an 'analysis of mechanisms' identifies the turning points that shift a destination from one stage to another. Three types of mechanisms are discussed: critical juncture, critical event and blurry transition.

Methods

An interpretive paradigm was used in this study. This approach 'seeks to describe and analyse the culture and behaviour of humans and their groups from the point of view of those being studied' (Bryman, 1988: 46). Because the reality experienced by the tribal group in Ban Raummit was different from that of other stakeholders, and because their culture was the tourist attraction, it was important to understand the tourism life cycles from their perspective.

Like many peripheral communities, a formal education system had only recently been introduced in Ban Raummit and the literacy rate among community members over the age of 20 was low. In addition, until recently few community members saw a need to record information about the number or type of visitor arrivals. Like many indigenous cultures, information had traditionally been communicated verbally rather than in written form. Detailed data related to visitor arrivals or visitor nights were, therefore, not available for TALC analysis. Instead, oral history as told by various community members served as the basis for the following analysis. The dates and numbers provided in this chapter are therefore approximations, but these oral histories have provided a rich description of development from the villager perspective.

The cross-cultural situation within which the research was conducted required the flexibility inherent in the emergent design of the case study approach. Data collection consisted of informal semi-structured interviews and participant observation conducted between September and December of 1997. Interviews were more structured than originally planned due to the challenges of working through an interpreter, but each new interview built on information gathered in the previous ones.

A combination of Butler's (1980) TALC, Dearden's (1991) study of hill tribe trekking and Johnston's (2001) reassessment of TALC is used as a framework for the analysis of the sustainability of cultural tourism in Ban Raummit. The balance of this chapter consists of a boundary analysis in which the village of Ban Raummit is described in terms of its tourism products and destination status. This description is followed by a chronological analysis based on Johnston's pathway analysis. Finally, analyses of three distinct tourism life cycles and the mechanisms of change within these cycles are provided. A tabular presentation of the mechanisms and stages is also presented in this section. This table draws from the chronological analysis to highlight the mechanisms of stage change. In doing so, it demonstrates the independent progression of the three inter-related life cycles of the trekking product, the tribal village or sightseeing product, and the destination in general.

Boundary analysis

The Karen is one of nine major ethnic tribal groups in this region of Northern Thailand. These ethnic groups have become known as the 'chao khao' or hill tribes. Less than one-third of all tribal people have Thai citizenship, and even fewer own land, reflecting their relatively low political status in Thailand. In 1959 the National Committee for Hill Tribes was created by the government of Thailand, and this group began to address what was known as the 'hill tribe problem' (TRI, 1995).

Hill tribes were initially considered a threat to national security as possible agents for the spread of Communism. The government also believed, and continues to believe, that the hill tribes have had a detrimental effect on the natural environment. Deforestation is seen as a major problem in Thailand with an estimated loss of about 75% of its natural forest cover between 1961 and 1994. Although the government has blamed hill tribe agricultural practices for much of this loss, others have suggested that non-hill tribe logging schemes are largely responsible (McCaskill, 1997). Another concern of the Thai government has been hill tribe involvement with the production of illegal narcotics. Reducing the amount of opium cultivation and use by tribal people in Thailand is a major objective of the government.

One development strategy that the Karen in Ban Raummit have pursued within this political and economic climate is to develop the regional tourism industry. The Karen culture is at the heart of this area's attraction. Tourists coming to this village hope to gain experiences with people significantly different than themselves. For example, one particularly popular manifestation of the Karen culture in Ban Raummit is the domestication of elephants. Traditionally, the Karen used elephants to work in the forests and as a means of transportation. Their self-identity is tied to this practice as suggested by an elephant controller's observation that 'after WWII, the government told the Karen people to take food to Japan with their elephants ... because only Karen people can control elephants' (elephant controller).

The spatial scale of this destination is that of a village with a population of approximately 600 residents. Ban Raummit is located along the Mae Kok River in Chiang Rai province in Northern Thailand. Access to Ban Raummit is dominated by boat and motor vehicle. The road to Chiang Rai is partially paved and a one-way trip takes 40 minutes.

A tourist district has developed within the community along the river where most tourists arrive and is extended along a few main roads in town. While most tourists remain in this area, tourism activity is dispersed beyond this service district into the surrounding bamboo forests where visitors hike or ride elephants. A small number of the more intrepid visitors also venture into the nearby rice fields to watch and photograph farming activities.

Chronological analysis

Ban Raummit provides a unique opportunity to follow the evolution of a village from the time of its conception to the present due to its relatively recent creation. Tourism product life cycles (trekking and sightseeing), as well as the overall destination life cycle clearly emerged over this period.

1962–1974

This village was created about 35 years ago [~ 1962]. Mr. Oo gave the name to this village. He was the first man to build here. The groups

> of people that lived here came from Mae Tro in Chiang Mai province. It was near Doi Inthanon. There were four families that left this place [Mae Tro] because of opium. They did not want to smoke it so they left. (Karen elder)

While the village was originally named for the first man who lived in the area, the name was recently changed to Ban Raummit. 'Raummit' is a Thai word meaning a mixture, and 'ban' means town. The name change occurred to reflect the changing nature of the village given the multiple ethnic groups now living in the community.

This particular site was chosen because 'this land is good to make agriculture. Have good farm. It is near the river' (Karen resident). Its location made it a favoured spot because of the accessible water source and plentiful fish supply. In addition, the forests were rich and the land was fertile. These traits were well suited to the subsistence lifestyle of the Karen.

About 10 years after the creation of the village (~ 1972), the area was placed under the control of Thailand's Royal Forestry Department (RFD) as a forest conservation area. Village boundaries were defined and the RFD implemented strict land use controls including the restrictive distribution of land titles (Sumrauy Nhusaeng, personal communication, November 15, 1997). Technically, people were not allowed to purchase the land in the conservation forest, but the Karen feel that exceptions have been made in the case of well financed buyers.

> The villagers want to have the documents for the land, but when they ask the RFD they cannot. They will not sign because this is a conservation forest. But, if the person has money, they will get the documents. (Karen resident)

For the first 15 years, the village grew at a moderate rate. People who moved to this village were mostly relatives of the first families. The headman gave each family a parcel of land to farm. An older villager described the process by stating that:

> . . .after one year he said that he want everyone in this place to go and choose the land where they want to live and farm. The headman will share it with the others so they will have one rai [land area measurement] for each family. (Karen elder)

1975–1979

Tourism began in this village during this period. It was introduced by a missionary who had spent some time in Japan where he learned about trekking. Upon his return to Thailand, he came to Ban Raummit and suggested that they begin to offer elephant treks. At that time, the village had three elephants that they used to work in the forest.

> In the past, the elephants were used for labour in the forest. They had only three elephants to start with. There were no roads, so they used the elephants for transportation to the fields. The fields were far from home. . . . After that, villagers used them for trekking. They took the trekkers to the Lahu and Yao villages. When they did this there were only 5-6 people at a time (not Thai people just foreigners). They used to spend the night. (elephant controller)

The total number of visitors to Ban Raummit averaged about 20 people per month. During this early stage, there were no specific tourist facilities or infrastructure. Most trekkers stayed and ate in the villagers' homes, particularly the home of the headman. Their visits were irregular so none of the elephants were solely dedicated to transporting tourists. Because the trekking groups were small and these groups stayed in the homes of the tribal people, interactions between these visitors and the Karen were fairly intimate.

> Before we only had older tourist about 40–50 years old. They liked to experience the culture. Some were even 60–70 years old and very fat. They could only put one on each elephant. When they stayed over night the Karen did show performances at night. Tourists could talk to the Karen and eat their food. (village headman)

During this period, the tourists were as interesting and different to the Karen as the Karen were to the tourists. The Karen people considered these visitors to be their distant brothers and sisters, therefore making this stage of tourism development quite enjoyable for them. They appreciated the opportunity to demonstrate parts of their culture to others. Tourism was also a relatively minor activity in the community. Only 'seven to eight of the villagers were involved with the trekkers' (elephant controller), so the impacts of trekking were not widespread.

Basic services were also introduced around 1975 with the construction of the first school in the community. Volunteers from Julalongkan University in Bangkok came to teach in the village. Today, this school is run by the national government and it services the surrounding villages as well. Another structure included 'the first church built 1 kilometre from here. The Karen would walk to that church. Then it changed to be built in this village about 20 years ago (1977). It was built by missionaries from the United States' (Karen resident). These missionaries still come to this village on a regular basis to distribute shirts, blankets, mosquito nets and similar goods.

1980–1991

A significant amount of tourist development occurred during this period. One operator noted, 'I was one of the first tour companies here – more than 12 years. When I first came, there was no guesthouse, there were no toilets... Well there were toilets, but not up to European standards' (Thai tourism operator). This early tourist development was led by Thai people who moved to the village rather than by the original Karen residents. For example, a Thai-owned tourist restaurant opened along the river. The next tourist operation, a Thai-owned souvenir shop, opened shortly afterwards. Two more Thai-owned restaurants were in operation by 1988.

A permanent tourist police station was built in 1983. The police presence was needed partly in response to some problems with robberies and shootings of trekkers near the Burmese border. Trekking guides and their tourists were required to register here prior to entering more remote areas.

1992–1995

> The big companies came about five years ago [1992]. Big groups are sightseeing not trekking. They started to come because Chiang Mai, these places not have many elephants and big groups needed lots of elephants. (Karen resident)

Several developments occurred between 1992 and 1997 led by an increase in the number of elephants used in the tourism industry. By 1994, there were over 40 elephants in the village that were actively used for tourism. Because of the limited disposable income of most Karen persons, one elephant was often owned by a group of local investors who pooled their resources to purchase the animal. 'Elephants cost about 150,000 Baht. This is very expensive here. That means that many people put their money together to buy the elephants. Ten people may save to buy one elephant' (elephant controller). Each elephant has its own 'mahout' or elephant controller. The construction of an elephant loading area was also completed during this period to make elephant rides accessible to a broader range of clients including less mobile village tour participants.

By 1993, ten tourist shops and three local shops were operating in the village. At this point, only one of the shops was Karen operated. For many years, the village authorities had not allowed other tribal groups to open tourist shops, but the Karen were apparently not interested in, or possibly not able to, pursue these opportunities themselves. Thai people led this type of development. As visitation continued to grow, the pressure for further development increased. Finally, however, the village authorities agreed to let other tribal groups open shops. By 1996 there were over 40 shops in Ban Raummit operated by a broad range of ethnic groups.

Most tourist shops sold crafts, souvenirs and postcards. Few of these crafts were made in this village, or by the tribal person selling them. One Karen vendor noted, 'My crafts come from Mae Sai or Lamphun. I do not go there because I have no transportation. People [wholesalers] come here to sell the stuff. Sometimes they may come two–three times each month, other times only once' (Karen villager). There were a few exceptions to this practice of importing goods. The Karen weavers who worked by the river making belts, bracelets and bags sometimes sold their wares in the local shops. Most shops were located along the roads frequented by tourists including the main one connecting Ban Raummit to Chiang Rai, and the two smaller connector roadways leading to the boat docks.

Allowing other tribal groups to own and operate shops has influenced immigration to the community. Karen villagers differentiate people moving into Ban Raummit in terms of their ethnicity and livelihoods.

> People that move here have two styles. From Mae Tro, they come because they have family here and they give them the land to come here. Another group that want to sell. They are not Karen. They buy the land to do the shops for sell from the Karen people, but not buy the land to do the farm. (elephant controller)

As the number of other tribal people moving to Ban Raummit has increased, conflicts have begun to emerge.

> First time have one or two families. I never mind cause there was little. They have shop so nothing. Now there are many, many. The Lisu and Hmong, they cut the trees everywhere. When I tell them 'don't do,' they don't listen. Some people who buy land to stay here are good. But, those who rent the land are not so good. (Karen elder)

Most of these people do not plan to stay in the village indefinitely. They follow the tourists, and as a result, their investment in village development was lower than the Karen's. The newcomers appear to be gaining significant benefits from the visitors while the Karen people are forced to deal with many of the costs.

Vehicle access was greatly improved around 1993, when a portion of the road from Chiang Rai to Ban Raummit was paved. Although the pavement did not reach all the way to the village, even the unpaved section was widened to improve access. A portion of these road improvements was financed by revenues earned through elephant treks. Prior to these improvements, the trail to Chiang Rai was only passable by foot or motorcycle. With the completion of the roadwork, a one-way trip by car between Chiang Rai and Ban Raummit was only 40 minutes.

1996–1997

Electricity was introduced to the village after a visit from Thailand's royal family in 1996. This development seemed to change the attitude of the Karen people towards their involvement in tourism. Prior to this point, they perceived little need for additional cash income and were content with a subsistence lifestyle based on agriculture. However, the introduction of electrical power created new demands for rice cookers, refrigerators, stereos and an assortment of other appliances. Karen involvement in tourism increased as one way to earn the disposable income necessary to make these purchases.

By this point, the villagers had reduced the number of elephants that they owned and managed to 32. In addition, Karen shop ownership had increased to 14 of the 51 shops in operation (Table 15.1).

Because there were no controls over entrance to this village, the exact number of visitors was impossible to determine, but information from the records of the Tourist Police and the elephant operators provide an indication of the magnitude of the tourism in the community. During November 1997, an estimated 2500 people visited Ban Raummit. Of this total, about 1800 people rode the elephants. November was considered an average month for tourism visitation as a villager explained that, 'July and August are the busiest. March, April, May and September are the slowest.'

Although Ban Raummit was no longer considered one of the better villages in which to observe traditional Karen culture, trekking tours continued to visit. The village's location made it a convenient staging point for their journey into the hills to visit more remote and primitive villages. Many trekking groups hired the elephants in Ban Raummit for the next portion of their journey. These trekkers often bought food and drink in the village to prepare for their expeditions, but they purchased few souvenirs. Local villagers made a clear distinction between trekkers and sightseers.

> If the people have backpacks they are trekkers. But if they have only a camera and a small purse they are sightseers. There are more of these tourist. They don't want to take the elephant rides. (elephant controller)

Table 15.1 Shop ownership and target markets

Target market	*Operator ethnicity*							*Total*
	Karen	*Thai*	*Hmong*	*Akha*	*Lisu*	*Yao*	*Swiss*	
Tourist	11	4	17	10	2	1	1	46
Local	3	2	0	0	0	0	0	5

Relatively easy access by road or waterway, good linkages to other destinations, along with improved tourist services and infrastructure, made Ban Raummit an increasingly popular stop on tribal village sightseeing tours. A typical itinerary for a sightseeing tour was described as:

> [After leaving Chiang Mai and travelling to Thaton], they go on to Chiang Rai by boat. Along the river they see the hill tribes; about 20 in total. May stop at four to five villages along the way. After Chiang Rai, they go on to the Golden Triangle and Mae Sai. Stop at interesting villages – not the small ones. They may have four to five families. Hill tribes stay by the water so it is easy to see them. (International sightseeing operator)

The sightseers accounted for the majority of the visitors to Ban Raummit during this period. Most of these visitors arrived in groups of 20–30 people while other visitors came in groups as small as two to four people.

Those sightseers with limited interest in the Karen culture typically stayed in one of the restaurants by the river enjoying the scenery and a soda. Others ventured into the village to shop or take pictures of the various tribal shopkeepers or Karen villagers. Still others rode the elephants. These rides tended to be shorter village tours of 20–30 minutes rather than the longer forest treks. Some sightseeing tour groups with their own guides took time to find a Karen person with whom they could talk. One Karen elder in particular enjoyed the opportunities to share his stories with these visitors. 'Tourists have tour guide to talk with me. Tour guide knows me and bring tourists to tell stories. I enjoy it very much to tell them my stories' (Karen elder).

As the number and type of tourists have changed, villagers directly involved in the provision of tourism services increasingly received formal training in customer service. Sightseers tend to have higher service expectations than trekkers. At the same time, villagers have developed a deeper appreciation of the important role that tourism plays in generating income for the village. The villagers therefore decided to address these expectations as 'everybody wants to have tourists because they can make money' (elephant controller). Formal customer service training seminars were offered to the mahouts, shop keepers and boat drivers by the Tourism Authority of Thailand (TAT) at the Mae Kok Farm across the river from this village.

While the growth in tourism was significant, it was still not the most prominent industry in the village. Agriculture had continued to dominate. Few of the Karen villagers who generated income through participation in the tourism industry considered it their main source for survival as reflected in the following statements.

- Mostly I make rice on the farm.
- Now only this, but before corn too. I make corn at the same time as rice, but corn is finished. I grow it to eat and sell: rice and corn... Farm about the same with or without tourism.
- I built the store with my husband. Now he still works in the field as a farmer. (Karen villagers)

Even the mahouts, who have invested significant amounts of time into tourism, acknowledged that tourism would not be the main source of income throughout their lifetimes.

> Old people cannot control elephants. If they control one day, they are sore with back aches the next few. Usually they stop controlling around 36 years old... Then he will go work on the farm. All the controllers have farm land. (elephant controller)

Plans emerged in 1997 to create a formal 'cultural village' attraction. The village authorities anticipated that this addition would serve multiple purposes. It was seen as an enjoyable activity and source of information for sightseers, thereby encouraging increased spending in the village. To the trekkers heading to more primitive villages, it would provide vital information to prepare them for more intimate interactions. Finally, and potentially more importantly, it would be an instrument through which elements of tribal cultures could be maintained, taught and enjoyed.

> We are working on a project now to build a place in this village to show people about the Karen lifestyle. They will be able to go to the farm and show about agriculture. This will be not only for Karen though. They want to show all tribes. The more they conserve, the more tourists. (village headman)

Mechanisms and Stages

The preceding chronological analysis has outlined the history of Ban Raummit in relation to tourism development. Table 15.2 draws from this analysis to highlight the existence of three separate tourism life cycles and the turning points within each of these. These turning points are labelled as critical junctures, critical events or blurry transitions. A critical juncture is an issue that once resolved moves the destination to a new stage. Critical events are particular actions that trigger the progression from one stage to the next. Finally, blurry transitions are turning points that occur as the result of a number of smaller events that combine to bring about a shift to the next stage. Typically any of these mechanisms can manifest itself as an addition, alteration or cessation in terms of the product or destination life cycles.

A critical event began the life cycle of the trekking product in 1975 with the introduction of elephant treks (Table 15.2). Initial interactions between the Karen villagers and trekkers were based on mutual interest. The blurry transition to the development stage occurred around 1980 when outside influences such as the introduction of the Thai police and entrepreneurs institutionalised the trekking product. Another blurry transition led to the consolidation stage around 1992. More tourist infrastructure was added and the village modernised. Other tribal groups opened shops along the main streets creating a tourist space that limited interactions between the Karen hosts and the trekkers. Much of the primitive nature of the village disappeared, however, many trekking groups continued to use the village as a staging point to get supplies and purchase elephant rides to more remote villages. In 1996 a critical event, the introduction of electricity, spurred an increase in Karen involvement, and began trekking's reorientation stage. This event increased the Karen's demand for consumer items, and tourism was identified as a viable cash income generator. The Karen recognised that the village was no longer as attractive to those trekkers seeking contact with primitive others but was well positioned to serve as a staging point. Village authorities determined that the addition of a cultural village could fulfil an educational function to prepare these trekking groups for more intimate interactions in remote villages.

The exploration stage for the sightseeing product began around 1980. Simple tourist services had been added to the village and a few Thai operators brought small groups of sightseeing tourists. A number of additions led to the blurry transition initiating the development stage around 1992. Larger groups started to arrive, precipitating the purchase of more elephants. In addition, the type of visitors arriving required additional services such as a loading dock for elephant rides and more shops. To facilitate this growth, the village authorities allowed other tribal groups to open shops. Development continued into the late 1990s as Karen interest in tourism increased, leading to more Karen shop ownership. In addition, the village committee decided to build a cultural village to showcase tribal cultures and gain additional income from the sightseers.

The third life cycle concerns the village of Ban Raummit as a tourist destination. It is shaped by the life cycles of each individual product along with an assortment of other trends. Like the trekking product, the arrival of the first trekkers initiated the exploration stage, and the process of commercialising the Karen culture for visitors. A blurry transition moved the destination to the development stage. This transition resulted from the institutionalisation of tourism and the beginning of outside involvement. The Thai police station was built to minimise danger to international tourists because of incursions around the Burmese border.

Table 15.2 Mechanisms of change for three tourism-related life cycles in Ban Raummit

Chronological era	*Trekking product*		*Sightseeing product*		*Destination*	
	Mechanism	*Stage*	*Mechanism*	*Stage*	*Mechanism*	*Stage*
1962–1974	N/A	Pretourism	N/A	Pretourism	N/A	Pretourism
1975–1979	Critical event additions • Missionary recommends offering elephant treks • First trekkers arrive • Natural interactions between hosts and guests begin	Exploration	N/A	Pretourism product	Critical event additions • First trekkers arrive • Initial stage of the commercialisation of culture	Exploration
1980–1991	Blurry transition Addition • Tourist police station is built Alterations • 3 Thai-owned restaurants open	Development	Blurry transition Additions • 3 Thai-owned restaurants open • 1 Thai-owned shop opens	Exploration	Blurry transition Additions • State involvement in village tourism begins • Involvement of international	Exploration

Table 15.2 (*Continued*)

Chronological era	*Trekking product*		*Sightseeing product*		*Destination*	
	Mechanism	*Stage*	*Mechanism*	*Stage*	*Mechanism*	*Stage*
	• 1 Thai-owned shop opens • More trekkers stay in village		• 1 Thai-owned shop opens • Sightseeing operators begin to visit with small groups		tour companies and Thai entrepreneurs begins • Trekkers outnumber sightseers • Initial tourist services and infrastructure develop	
1992–1995	Blurry transition Alteration • Other tribal shops open (~40) Cessations • Interactions between hosts and guests are institutionalised	Consolidation	Blurry transition Additions • More elephants are bought • Elephant loading dock is built • Road access improves • Large sightseeing groups arrive	Development	Critical juncture Additions • Policy change occurs • Other tribal groups become active in tourism • Front stage develops	Development

Table 15.2 (*Continued*)

Chronological era	*Trekking product*		*Sightseeing product*		*Destination*	
	Mechanism	*Stage*	*Mechanism*	*Stage*	*Mechanism*	*Stage*
	• Fewer overnight stays occur • Karen identity of village decreases Additions • Becomes a staging point for treks rather than a stop on route		• Customer service training begins Alterations • Policy change facilitates arrival of other tribal vendors • Commodification of culture increases		Alterations • Tourist infrastructure increases • Road access improves • Population increases • Village modernises • Sightseers outnumber trekkers Cessation • Fewer natural interactions between hosts and guests occur	

Table 15.2 (*Continued*)

Chronological era	*Trekking product*		*Sightseeing product*		*Destination*	
	Mechanism	*Stage*	*Mechanism*	*Stage*	*Mechanism*	*Stage*
1996–1997	Critical event Additions • Electricity is introduced • Village authority proposes plans for cultural village Cessation • Loss of primitive image in village	Reorientation	No stage change Addition • Village authority proposes plans for cultural village Alterations • Infrastructure upgrades continue • Increases in Karen involvement in shop ownership continues	Late development	No stage change Addition • Electricity is introduced Alterations • Village infrastructure improves: roads, sewage • Increases in Karen interest and involvement in directing future growth • Conflict between Karen and other tribal groups emerges	Mid-development

Thai entrepreneurs opened businesses to earn tourism income. The number of visitors continued to increase, encouraging the further development of tourist services. A policy change allowing other tribal vendors led to a critical juncture in the early 1990s. The arrival of these vendors altered the appearance of the village through the development of a front stage that further formalised host–guest interactions. As this process continued into the late 1990s, conflict between the Karen and other tribal vendors emerged. Although 1997 marked a stage change for the two product life cycles, it was not a turning point for the overall destination. The cumulative effects of the changes were becoming evident, but neither the villagers nor their village committee had begun to address them in a dramatic way.

By examining the three life cycles separately and identifying the stages and mechanisms in each, Table 15.2 clarifies some seemingly contradictory occurrences. Turning points classified as additions to one product represent cessations for other products. This is not surprising considering the base of Ban Raummit's attraction is culture, and culture is dynamic. Tourism products cannot remain static while their base moves forward. The relatively rapid progression of the trekking product through its life cycle stages is indicative of the rapid pace of change faced by tribal cultures here and elsewhere (Butler & Hinch, 1996).

Conclusion

Ban Raummit has been a dynamic tourism destination over its relatively short existence. The hill tribe trekking product has progressed rapidly through its life cycle with a shift from the village being a featured stop on the early trekking tours to it being an important staging point for treks to more isolated villages. As the village was losing its appeal as a 'primitive' stop for trekking tours, it was gaining popularity as a major stop on sightseeing tours. Indicators suggest this sightseeing product is currently in a mid to advanced development stage. Visitor demands are being met through increased tourism services and infrastructure. Yet, these vestiges of modernity have reduced its 'charm' as a relatively traditional village. Manifestations of modern life are undercutting Ban Raummit's appeal as a stop on sightseeing tours and accelerating its trajectory through the TALC. The proposal to commodify the Karen culture through the development of a 'cultural village' represents a new type of cultural product, which by its institutionalised nature may provide greater control over this life cycle. Finally, the destination itself has undergone a cycle of development that is a complex amalgam of individual tourism product cycles and a multitude of external cycles and trends. The fact that the economy of Ban Raummit remains based in agriculture serves as a buffer to the volatility of tourism. It is clear, however, that tourism has become an important contributor to economic development in the community. Tourism has enabled the Karen to continue residing in a rural area by integrating them into the global cash economy. In the process, they have retained more control over their culture than have other hill tribe peoples that have been forced to move to large urban areas in order to survive. It is clear, however, that Ban Raummit's residents must actively manage tourism if it is to serve them well in the future.

Beyond the direct insights that this chapter has provided about tourism in Ban Raummit, it has also provided insight into the TALC. Two of the most important contributions concern the confirmation of multiple life cycles and the merit of using qualitative data to examine tourism-related life cycles. In the first instance, it has been demonstrated that there are multiple life cycles that have a direct bearing on tourism destinations. Even in the case of destinations that are based on sensitive cultural attractions, a variety of tourism products may emerge and interact with each other and the life cycle of the community as a whole. Researchers need to appreciate this complexity if these analyses are to be beneficial. Secondly, tourism destinations populated by indigenous people living traditional lifestyles are not likely to be characterised by data bases neatly organised into time series formats that can accurately quantify the number of visitors for TALC analysis. Qualitative data can, however, be used to provide a useful approximation of TALC patterns in terms of boundaries, chronological progression and the mechanisms of change. In fact, qualitative data can be used to interpret quantitative data, thereby providing a much richer understanding of tourism area cycles.

Finally, the relationship between cultural attractions, the TALC and sustainability bears additional consideration. This chapter has demonstrated that cultural tourism products like hill tribe treks are dynamic. Tourism is one of many agents for change in these communities and ultimately serves as a factor in changing the culture of the hosts or the 'others' in this case. This change in culture is one of the factors that moves tourism products through their life cycles. Yet in the case of tourism in Ban Raummit, the culturally based tourism product of hill tribe trekking appears to be being replaced by other forms of cultural tourism like sightseeing tours. The proposed cultural village represents yet another generation of cultural tourism products in this village. Ban Raummit has retained its vibrancy throughout these various product life cycles. The perplexing question of when life starts or finishes must be asked in the case of TALCs just as it is asked in the case of human life cycles. The TALC offers a useful tool to track development, make decisions about the pace and nature of change in the present and to predict change in the future. It does not, however, allow for definitive statements on sustainability.

Part 5
The TALC and Rejuvenation

RICHARD W. BUTLER

The conclusion of the TALC model in its original form was that without appropriate intervention a destination would eventually enter into decline. Two possibilities were proposed as being capable of altering this result. One was suggested to be a continuation of operation at a level that remained within the capacities of the destination, so that its attractivity remained at a sufficiently high level to continue to attract investment and visitation to remain viable, in other words, to achieve sustainability (although the term had not been used then in its now current context). The other was for the destination to be rejuvenated in a variety of ways, including changing to a new focus, finding an additional focus and repositioning the destination with respect to markets. It is this stage of the TALC that is examined in the three chapters in this last section, which provide specific examples of the way destinations have redeveloped themselves. A more conceptual discussion of the rejuvenation and exit processes is dealt with in the other volume by Agarwal, Cooper and Baum.

In her chapter, Corak discusses the case of the Opatija Riviera on the Adriatic Coast of Croatia, a destination that has experienced a wide range of circumstances and influences. She argues that there have really been four cycles which this destination has gone through and is experiencing. The intervention of three wars has served to move the destination back, if not to the beginning of a new cycle, at least some way in reverse, and forced it to reposition itself several times. The changes in accessibility, in markets, in political and other exogenous forces have meant that the destination has suffered from instability and enforced change, and thus had to attempt to rejuvenate itself three times at least. She posits a somewhat different development curve in this case because of the unique forces to which this area has been exposed.

The example of Atlantic City described by Stansfield represents what is, perhaps, the most classic of all attempts at rejuvenation by a mature tourist destination. Atlantic City, like the 19th century resorts of Northern Europe, had had a full cycle of development through to decline by the last quarter of the 20th century. Without rejuvenation it was dying a slow but inevitable death as far as tourism was concerned. The identification of legalised gambling as a tool of rejuvenation was the first step in a relatively rapid process that has seen Atlantic City experience massive reinvestment and redevelopment on a scale not anticipated initially. How long the new cycle will last is unknown. The explosion of legalised gambling across the USA and Canada has undoubtedly deprived Atlantic City, earlier than it would have wished, of its unique comparative advantage on the East coast of the USA, similar to that held by Nevada in the West. It still remains, however, probably the best example anywhere of successful large-scale rejuvenation of a resort that had almost completed its TALC.

The Gold Coast of Queensland, Australia, has had a much more rapid process of development and potential decline than the New Jersey shore, but gambling and private investment on a large scale have also been witnessed there. Faulkner and Tideswell describe and interpret in considerable detail the process of rejuvenating this area. Sadly, this chapter marks one of the last pieces of research and writing undertaken by Bill Faulkner before his tragically early death in 2002. He completed the first draft less than two months before his death. The chapter reveals the full and complex process that he and colleagues had organised to identify, evaluate and decide on specific directions for the future development of the region. One of the great successes of the CRC programme in Sustainable Tourism has been achieved by involving the private sector with the academic sector in identifying best practice and development options. The model developed and discussed in this chapter represents a successful approach to the complicated and often undesired process of repositioning a mature destination. The initial reluctance of the private sector to accept the idea of a 'revisioning' exercise and the final acceptance of a 'visioning' exercise (because the latter did not imply the change of direction and hence implication of earlier mistakes or a current need for a change in direction) is indicative of the reluctance of those in destinations to admit that all may not be well in tourism and that rejuvenation is needed.

Chapter 16

The Modification of the Tourism Area Life Cycle Model for (Re)inventing a Destination: The Case of the Opatija Riviera, Croatia

SANDA CORAK

Introduction

In the rich tourism literature on TALC, many studies have demonstrated the general validity of observing tourism development within an evolutionary framework. In this study, the life cycle model is used to determine the stages and to analyse the market position of the Opatija Riviera, a destination that has been developing tourism for more than 150 years. The TALC is applied to identify four distinct stages and it is argued that those stages could also be analysed as separate life cycles. The chapter also discusses how the strategic options proposed by the original model could help destination managers and planners to 'reinvent' this heritage resort on the Adriatic coast.

Croatia is a Mediterranean tourism destination and a country with a long tourism tradition. Although the most intensive tourism development in Croatia started after World War II, its tourism history began at the end of the last century when Opatija, located on the Northern Adriatic coast, emerged as the first tourism destination in this country. The long and rich tourism history of the Opatija Riviera is the focus of this chapter.

Tourism in the Opatija Riviera (stretch of 15 km, Figure 16.1) is traced back to 1844, when Higinio Scarpa, a wealthy wheat and timber merchant from the nearby industrial and port town of Rijeka, built his villa 'Angiolina', where he hosted guests such as Josip Jelacic, Croatian governor of the time, Maria Anna, the Queen of Austria, Romanian King Karol and the likes. In particular, a visit of the Empress of the Austrian–Hungarian Empire sparked much interest for this completely unknown place. A further impetus for the popularity of Opatija came when a group of eminent professors from the Vienna University opened a health retreat there (at the time a so-called 'sanatorium'), taking advantage of the

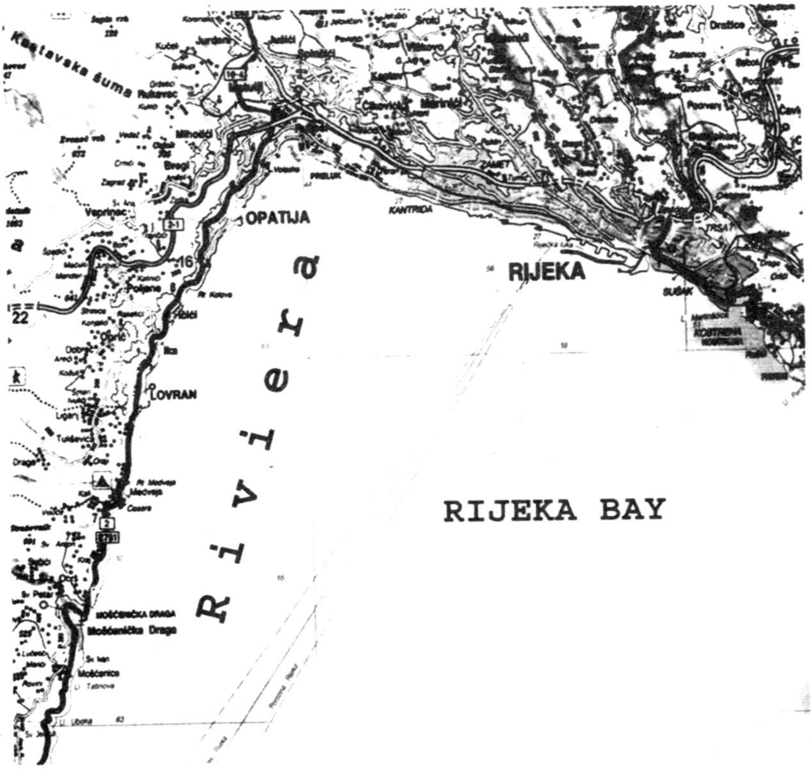

Figure 16.1 The Opatija Riviera

healing properties of the Riviera's mild climate and Adriatic Sea. Subsequently, in 1889, Opatija was given official *'kurort'* or health retreat status. The accelerated development of health retreat facilities and hotels was accompanied by diversification of additional services and facilities. A public library and tennis courts were opened, while there were music events staged in the central park as well as regular morning and evening music concerts. The flow of visitors was increasing steadily and their numbers were statistically recorded from 1883.

From that time until today the Riviera has travelled a long and often rough road of tourism development. Three key phases can be identified. It was initially a health retreat and winter tourism destination for wealthy aristocracy. In the second phase of its development the Opatija Riviera became a summer holiday destination for mass tourism. Currently, attempts are being made to rejuvenate Opatija's tourism through the introduction of new products that would make Opatija one of the most important conference centres in Croatia. Proximity to major urban centres together with increasing road accessibility make it viable for day-trippers and short-break tourists drawn to the Opatija Riviera by a variety of revived traditional events and festivals. Such a long and rich history of tourism lends itself to analysis based on the tourism area life cycle (TALC) model. Through such analysis it is possible to identify the turning points in the Opatija Riviera's history and also to discuss the current tourism development policy of what is still one of the most developed destinations in Croatia.

Many well known tourism destinations started to develop touristically only after World War II and their tourism products are currently in the growth or maturity phase. Application of the TALC model, in general, faces certain difficulties. Wall (1982) and Haywood (1986) discussed difficulties of gathering sufficiently suitable data to test models, and the operational problems involved in defining and distinguishing the individual phases. The problems most frequently encountered are those of comparability of spatial units and of interpreting transition points on the curve where the end of one phase and the beginning of another must be identified. The utility and applicability of the TALC model to destinations with a centennial tourism history has been tested in several cases (e.g. Cooper & Jackson, 1989; Getz, 1992; Russell & Faulkner, 1999). From the existing literature it can be concluded that such analysis enables a more holistic approach to the planning of a destination's future development options. Given that Opatija's tourism industry is currently undergoing restructuring (especially of its accommodation sector) accompanied by the reconstruction of many attractions, a decision was made that a strategic marketing plan ought also to be developed. For the purpose of that plan, the TALC model was used to evaluate tourism development to date and to assess the strategic steps that need to be taken to (re)invent Opatija's attractive, but at the moment neglected and insufficiently utilised, resources. These resources, due to the long and interesting history of the area, make it not only an attractive seaside destination, but, providing the heritage buildings are restored to their original glory, it could also become one of the leading heritage tourism destinations in the Adriatic region.

In this chapter, the analysis is conducted using Butler's model (1980) combined with a historical analysis approach in order to investigate the trends in tourism development on the Opatija Riviera and provide insights into issues affecting the rejuvenation of this area as a tourism destination. Stages in the life cycle of the Riviera are identified, graphically presented and described. It is argued that, because the area's tourism development was halted four times due to the wars that have affected this region, each of the four periods should also be examined as a separate life cycle.

The Life Cycle Model and the Opatija Riviera

For the purpose of this research, historical records were collected from official statistical data, historical monographs, brochures, tourist guides, articles in newspapers and magazines. Most time studies have suffered problems in the operationalisation of the concept (Foster & Murphy, 1991), in the search for appropriate indicators of development and concrete historic data to define the various phases. However, in contrast, as already noted, statistical data on tourist numbers were officially collected in Opatija from 1883.

Data for the Opatija Riviera indicate that the area has, through its centennial history, witnessed all phases of the life cycle (Figure 16.2). Throughout, the same area is analysed – the coastal region, hinterland and several microlocations as illustrated in Figure 16.1. Detailed analysis of the data for the number of arrivals in this area indicates that the entire life cycle could be divided not only into separate phases of development, but also some phases could be analysed in terms of separate life cycles. The sharp declines in visitor numbers were not caused by strategic development measures, but by the same exogenous factor – the wars that routinely halt tourism activity in affected areas. These were World War I, World War II and the most recent War of Independence from 1991

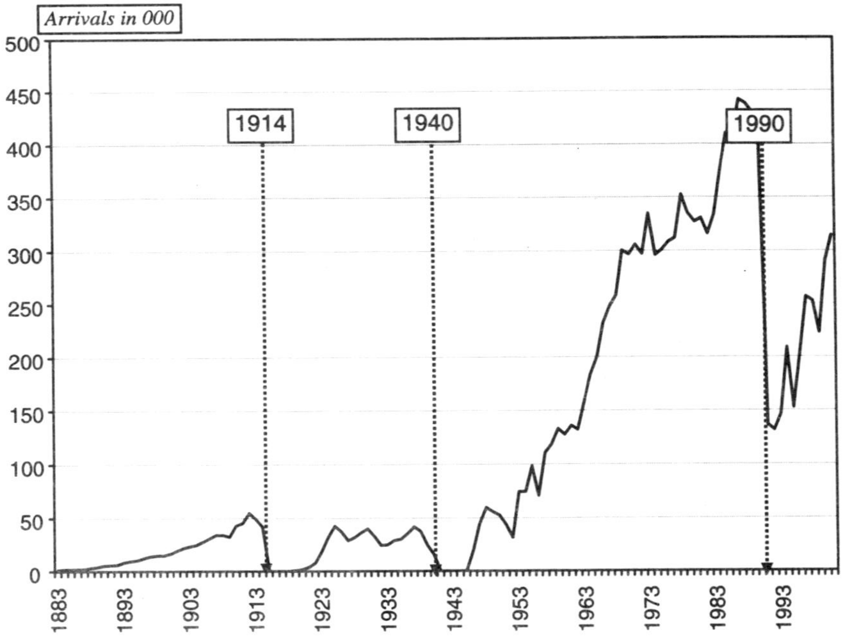

Figure 16.2 TALC for the Opatija Riviera (1883–2001)

to 1995. Thus, in this area tourism has developed from almost zero activity four times and, not surprisingly, each phase is characterised by a different nature of tourism development. The turning points of particular significance are: (a) the transition from an exclusive, winter resort to the summer holiday destination which occurred between 1915 and 1940; (b) development of a mass holiday destination after World War II and, finally, (c) the attempt to manage the maturity and differentiate the destination through the introduction of new products. The tourism history of the Opatija Riviera provides also an impetus and a source of inspiration for crafting its future tourism development. At the same time its history acts as a constraint, given that the history does not necessarily provide all the solutions to the dilemmas faced when planning future tourism development.

Tourism development and growth (1883–1914)

The first phase of tourism development on the Opatija Riviera was marked by a slow but steady growth of visitor arrivals. Construction of the road connecting the main port town in Croatia (Rijeka) with the seaside resort (Lovran) facilitated better communication between these two localities, influencing Mr. Scarpa's decision to build his villa 'Angiolina', named after his wife. The attractiveness of the villa was further enriched by the lush landscape dotted with exotic plants that thrived in the mild climate of Opatija, the centre of the Riviera. As mentioned earlier, Opatija became the favourite excursion spot for the wealthy citizens of Rijeka, while Scarpa himself hosted an array of friends, among whom were some of the leading figures of the public life of the time. The arrival of the Empress, Maria Anna, the wife of the Austrian Emperor, Ferdinand I, in this area in the 1860s marked another turning point when Opatija started to be considered a health retreat. The Empress stayed there on the recommendation of her doctors and this 'royal confirmation' generated much interest for visiting this place within the boundaries of her monarchy. This was followed by the construction of the first sanatorium and the important transport connection of the railway line between Vienna and Rijeka, built by the South Railway Company.

Tourism development of Opatija accelerated when the area was officially declared a health winter resort (on the basis of climate and spa) and the first hotel, a pavilion with a warm seawater pool, a beach pavilion and a coastal walking path were constructed in 1883. From the very beginning of Opatija's development great attention was given to the construction of buildings, their design and the equipment of the sanatoria. Newly built hotels offered additional services and accommodation, in particular massage and warm sea baths. Finally, when hotels were electrified in 1896 and running water installed, conditions for even more accelerated growth were provided. The growth in popularity of the resort was further fuelled by the official meeting there between the Emperor, Franjo Josip I, and the German Emperor, Vilim I. This event ensured Opatija the status of a first-class elite health retreat and fashionable gathering spot. The fact that Opatija was the first resort to host an international conference on thalassotherapy in 1908 testified to its reputation as a health resort. After the meeting of the emperors, Opatija was visited by the heads of many European monarchies and the Austria-Hungarian aristocracy, to industrial elite and many writers of repute. In the records of the time it could be found that the Romanian royal couple donated a significant sum of money for construction of walkways, a forest path and a viewing platform, which still carry the king's name – Karol I – today.

At that time the health tourism product dominated. The main season had different characteristics from the main summer season, as we know it today in Opatija. The largest number of guests was in the wintertime, as visitors were drawn to the mild climate in their desire to avoid the severity of the winters in the North. Historical records indicate that, at the beginning of the 20th century, Opatija Riviera had 10 large hotels, 44 pensions, 83 villas and five baths. Given the steady increase in popularity and accommodation capacity, the number of tourists grew continuously (Figure 16.3).

The best results were recorded in 1912 when there were almost 55,000 overnight guests. The jobs generated by such demand could not be met by the local population, therefore many Austrians with experience in hospitality and trade were attracted to Opatija to take advantage of the growing opportunities that tourism development offered. At that time a

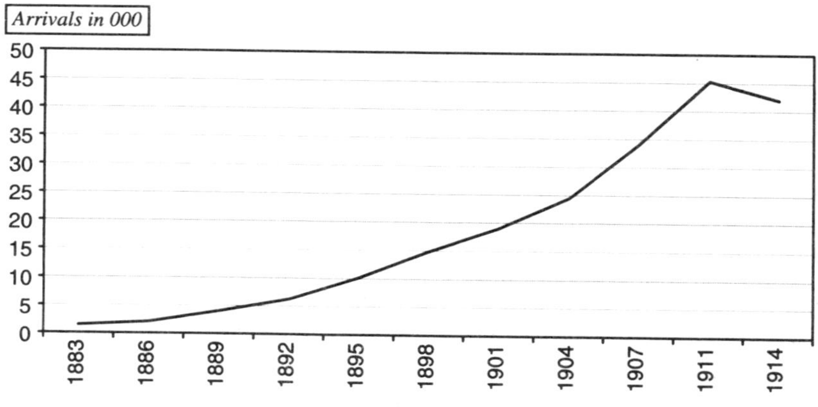

Figure 16.3 Arrivals to the Opatija Riviera (1883–1914)

regional tourism association with its headquarters in Opatija was established, while a weekly tourist newspaper was published to update visitors on events and attractions. Transport connections were also improved by regular bus line between Trieste and Opatija, while an electric tram operated along the Riviera.

Opatija in that era was a lively and vibrant destination with continuous special events. Apart from the beautiful villas built mostly in secession style, the Austrian Tourist Club 'Abbazia' started construction of the 12-km long coastal walkway, called *lungomare*, which is still one of the Riviera landmarks today. Its numerous meticulously maintained parks further enhanced the exclusive atmosphere of the place. Historical documents include some information on the construction of the park around the villa 'Angiolina' between 1845 and 1860, where exotic plants from Japan, China, South America, Australia and other parts of the world were planted. Among them is the *Camellia japonica* that has also become the flower symbol of Opatija. In this period the vision of a few enthusiastic individuals that pictured Opatija as an exclusive health resort was fully achieved. It could be assumed that tourism would continue to grow, but it was halted abruptly with World War I in 1914, an event that stopped all tourists flows for several years.

The changing tourist product (1919–1940)

The next phase in the tourism development of the Opatija Riviera was characterised by the weakening of the quality of the entire tourism product. The absence of a tourism development vision had an adverse effect on tourism activity in the period between the two world wars and as a consequence, great fluctuations in tourism demand were recorded. In this period the area was under Italian rule and with the introduction of the Italian government the number of visitors declined significantly. While the former Austria-Hungarian rulers had stimulated development of tourism in the Opatija Riviera, seeing it as part of their own territory, the newly established Italian government did not have the same attitude. For them the region was simply an occupied territory to be exploited (Miskulin, 1994). With such an attitude, they perceived Opatija as a strong competitor to their own resorts and therefore introduced measures degrading Opatija from an official health resort to firstly, a health and bathing place (*stazione climatica e balneare*), and then further degrading it in 1933 to simply a tourism destination (*luogo di soggiorno*).

By losing the status of health centre, converting sanatoria into hotels, letting the existing hotels go into decay and not investing in new facilities, the Opatija Riviera quickly lost its noted reputation. Consequently, this led to changes in market demand turning to less demanding clientele. From being initially a winter destination, Opatija became a summer holiday resort. The tourist season was shortened and hotels

Figure 16.4 Arrivals to the Opatija Riviera (1919–1939)

operated for only three summer months. The largest number of arrivals during the period of Italian rule, of about 43,000, was recorded in 1925, but soon the economic depression that hit Europe between 1929 and 1933 adversely affected tourism flows again (Figure 16.4).

The change in tourism orientation that was most noticeable in the change of the main tourist product and the nature of visitors attracted to this area led to the decrease in the visitor numbers, so that the peak performance from 1912, when almost 55,000 arrivals were recorded, was never repeated between the two world wars. A particularly vivid illustration of the drop in tourism numbers could be found in the daily papers of the time and various chronicles. There, for example, one could read an article from 1930 which noted that Opatija had only 45 taxis and four horse carriages, in comparison to hundreds of these that were cruising the town at the beginning of the century (Blazevic, 1994). In this phase, political decisions adversely affected tourism development, leading to a lowering of the product quality and an unsuccessful reorientation to a different tourist product. Thus, in the period between the two world wars tourism development in Opatija stagnated. This phase, just like the earlier one, finished with the beginning of another world war.

Transition to mass tourism (1946–1990)

For the third time, the Opatija Riviera was back on the tourist map and with the available resources attempted to create an interesting tourism product. Tourism started to grow more intensely after 1948 when numbers of 50,000 bed-nights were reached again. The 1950s continued to witness a sharp increase in visitations levels, when the travel agency 'Kvarner Express' opened and particularly in the late 1950s with the opening of the Institute for Thalasso-Therapy, specialising in curing respiratory and heart diseases. At the same time the College for Tourism Studies was established, and was later upgraded to University level.

This was the era of mass tourism with the 'sun and sea' product prevailing internationally. This product was developed largely unplanned and lacked development controls along the entire Croatian Adriatic coast (Weber, 1998), and the Opatija Riviera was not spared. Tourism development in Croatia was affected by two factors: the demand of the citizens of Western and Northern Europe for a holiday in the sun and a warm, clean sea, and the country's proximity to the main generating markets. The practically continuous growth in tourism demand over a period of 30 years (1957–1987) illustrates the attractiveness of the Opatija Riviera as a summer holiday destination (Figure 16.5).

Its tourism product has occupied a relatively stable market position, mainly relying on exploitation of the natural and ecological components of supply that consumers of that era preferred. Following growth that only occasionally fluctuated during the 1980s (1982), there were no noticeable trends of the stagnation that characterised tourism demand in other Adriatic destinations.

Throughout the 1960s and 1970s several large up-market hotels with congress facilities were constructed in an attempt to introduce new products and diversify demand. However, these were only sporadic efforts, which did not demonstrate expected financial returns although the number of visitors and bed-nights were still on the increase. In that period the quality of the entire tourism industry of the area was well below the quality of the destination itself. A more detailed examination into the tourism supply indicated a decline in quality of service and a loss of identity of accommodation facilities, as architecturally the new

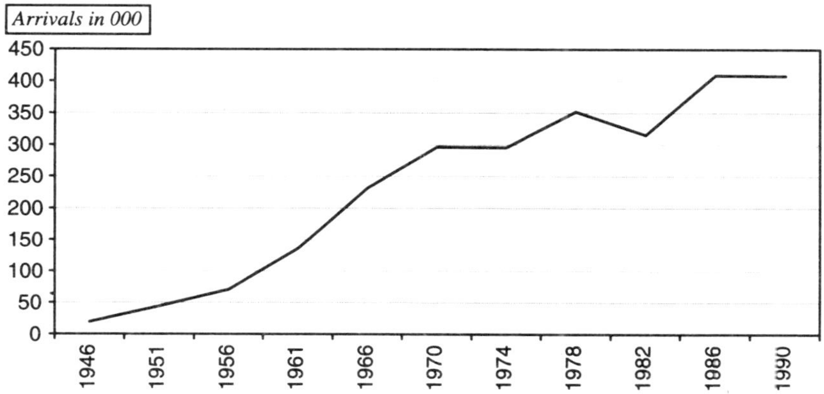

Figure 16.5 Arrivals to the Opatija Riviera (1946–1990)

hotels were not in harmony with their surroundings. There was also a lack of inventiveness in creating the various activities and services. This 'mediocracy' of supply and standardisation of individual elements of supply lead, for example, to identical forms of entertainment and menus in restaurants. This resulted in a decline in tourism numbers, an increased discrepancy between declared and achieved average prices, large price reductions outside the main season and loss of any real relationship between price and quality of supply. Destination marketing did not exist as a business philosophy. Suppliers relied mainly on infrequent and uncoordinated promotional efforts and there was a complete lack of a consistent and innovative product policy.

This was the period when Croatia was part of the former socialist Republic of Yugoslavia when the entire tourism development was characterised by unplanned activities, and when the success of the tourism sector was measured only superficially in terms of tourist flows and not the income generated from tourism. Nevertheless, there were attempts over that period to diversify the product and extend the summer season from three months. Thus, in addition to the classical 'sun and sea' product, congress tourism was stimulated (10% of all overnights). Likewise, the hotels introduced new health services in an attempt to revive Opatija's century-old reputation as a health retreat destination. The entire product was enriched by the construction of a marina, which is still one of the best in Croatia. However, the quality of product offered was still well below the product that was offered in the previous eras. For the third time the growth phase was abruptly interrupted by external factors.

Differentiating the tourist product (1991–...)

Although the War of Independence did not directly affect the area, it did nevertheless result in a drastic reduction of tourism activity for several years (see Figure 16.6). Tourism in the area has been rejuvenated again, although affected by both positive and negative consequences of the rich tourism history. Although the Riviera has an indisputably valuable architectural and urban heritage, long tourism tradition, favourable geographical location and good accessibility, it has to face numerous problems associated with a mature tourism product. Although this area is already recognisable as the 'Riviera' product, the old-fashioned concept of accommodation facilities and entire tourism infrastructure necessitated relatively unfavourable market positioning, despite the fact that growth of visitors was still recorded (Figure 16.6). While the Opatija Riviera can match competitors in Italy and France in terms of physical attractiveness, it falls behind in many other aspects, such as restaurants, shopping, entertainment and recreation and even

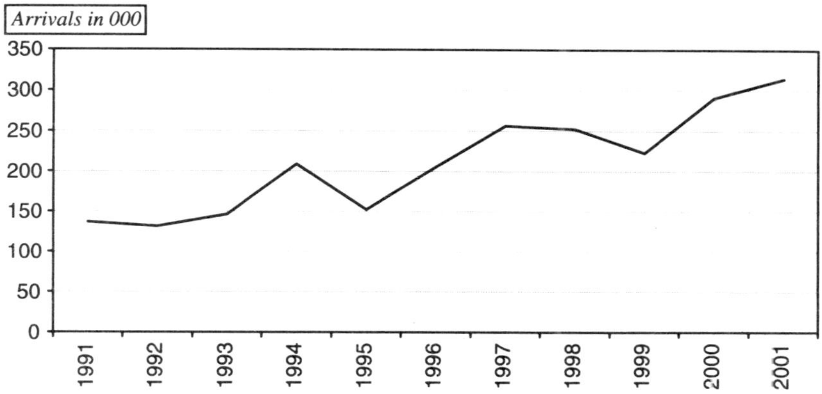

Figure 16.6 Arrivals to the Opatija Riviera (1991–2001)

hotels. To a large extent these are problems inherited from the past as over the long period there was little investment in maintaining and upgrading existing hotels, and these were further degraded when refugees were housed in them for four years of war. The last 10 years have witnessed also significant residential development that, coupled with the poor standard of the wastewater treatment, has resulted in marine pollution. A permanent problem also has been the lack of parking spaces in the town centre, while beaches and public spaces have not been maintained at the appropriate standard.

In this period the Riviera, in addition to maintaining the classic summer tourism, has continually strived to develop congress tourism. Attempts have also been made to upgrade and innovate the traditional health product to modern standards. To this end a few hotels are developing 'wellness' centres with a variety of services – fitness, massage, baths, beauty treatments and a variety of specialised health products, ranging from thalassotherapy to aromatherapy. It is still customary that most hotels sell half and full-board packages instead of offering the variety of services and experiences necessary to suit current demand. The Opatija Riviera is currently positioning itself as a non-stop event destination, packed with festivals and carnivals that are slowly becoming a symbol of Opatija. These events also provide an impetus for maintaining and reviving historical traditions and are, as such, important for the local community. There are also two casinos in the area and attempts are currently being made to improve the range of entertainment opportunities.

Overall, the marketing efforts of the Opatija Riviera could be assessed as insufficient and poorly targeted. However, in the current circumstances intensive tourism development and improvement in accommodation facilities are obstructed by the lack of development capital and a slow privatisation of hotels. It is encouraging though that the development plan for the Riviera, which defines development vision, market positioning and mix strategies is near to completion. The future of tourism development now depends mostly on the extent to which the main stakeholders of the area – the tourism industry, local government and the local community – will endorse this plan.

Applicability and Modification of the TALC Model

The aim of this chapter is to evaluate the manner in which the TALC model could be used in the case of the life cycle of the Opatija Riviera – an area with specific features of tourism development. The long tourism life of this destination was abruptly halted three times by wars so that the destination has not followed the classic development curve of the original TALC model. The main departure from the original model has been that in each era several life-cycle stages could be identified, as illustrated by Table 16.1.

Period I: 'Exploration and involvement'

Applying Butler's life-cycle stages, it is clear that the first period of tourism development on the Riviera could be identified as going through the exploration and involvement stages if the entire period is analysed as part of the development cycle. In this first era the destination partly

Table 16.1 Phases of destination development: The experience of the Opatija Riviera

Phase	*Period I (1883–1914)*	*Period II (1919–1940)*	*Period III (1946–1990)*	*Period IV (1991–)*
Exploration	Completely	Partly	Partly	Partly
Involvement	Completely	Partly	Partly	Partly
Development	Partly	Skipped	Almost completely	Completely
Consolidation	Skipped	Skipped	Partly	Partly
Stagnation	Skipped	No	No	Partly
Decline	Complete	Several times	Completely	No (can be expected)
Rejuvenation	No	No	No	No (can be expected)

experienced a development phase, although it is, because of the time and data available, difficult to assess with a degree of certainty. Consolidation and stagnation were not experienced as tourism development was halted under the influence of external factors. This first period of the tourism history was also marked by a clear vision of its development driven by several actors who, sensing the area's attractiveness and its potential including its favourable geographical location, developed the infrastructure and built capacity necessary for tourism development. As health tourism dominated in this period it could be said that the destination product was homogeneous and thus it is relatively easy to apply the TALC model. Recommended strategies for this stage of tourism development were selling new products/services to new markets (Ansoff, 1965) and building market share (Heath & Wall, 1992). According to the data available it could be safely concluded that the area successfully applied the latter strategy. Key development directions of this period were quality of services, hotel accommodation, care for the environment, and product exclusivity that enabled it to attract tourists with a high spending power and to develop unique product features.

Period II: 'Involvement and decline'

The second period was characterised by the development of new products and thus health tourism ceased to dominate. The development features lead to a conclusion that the destination was at this time in the involvement phase with some characteristics of the decline stage. The destination product was no longer homogeneous; the destination used the risky strategy of new product development, including orientation to new markets and new market segments. However, this reorientation was mostly driven politically, rather than by the stakeholders involved in tourism development. The consequence of such repositioning was a fluctuation in tourist numbers while the product itself suffered degradation in quality. The growth of demand in certain years could be attributed mostly to the area's inherent attractiveness and uniqueness.

Period III: 'Development'

Following several years of war, when all tourism activity ceased, the Opatija Riviera again experienced initial stages of tourism development – exploration and involvement, but this time it relatively quickly entered the development phase. However, that time was marked by the nonexistence of a tourism development plan. The principles of the market economy were applied only partially and, therefore, tourism development was not a subject of strategic decisions. There was some evidence that the overall cost leadership strategy was applied rather intuitively. Such a strategy, in general, can return a profit even from consumers at the lower end of the market who are those mostly attracted to a destination. That was not achieved at the Opatija Riviera for several reasons, primarily because of insufficient marketing, unsophisticated promotional efforts and at best a confused development vision. In this phase, congress tourism was developed as a new product and slowly introduced to the market. However, this product was still not accompanied by the necessary investments in infrastructure, research, customer service and marketing. In this period an opportunity to better utilise the area's attractiveness and to build on the experiences gained from past successes was lost.

Period IV: 'Development and consolidation'

In this period, after the War of Independence, the area was again on the tourist market but this time really carrying the burden of the inherited problems. It went through initial and development phases. It can be argued that the Opatija Riviera also entered a phase of consolidation and partly stagnation according to some parameters such as slowing growth rate, low occupancy rate, heavy reliance on repeat trade and reaching the limits of carrying capacity. Along with the dominant holiday tourism product, congress and health tourism were in a growth phase. Although tourism continued to grow, because of several problems with infrastructure and an aging product, the decline stage began to emerge slowly. Thus if the area fails to increase investments and does not apply appropriate strategic measures that would enable it to enter the rejuvenation phase, decline is inevitable. Some commentators, such as Gilbert (1990), suggest that one of the recommended strategies in this case would be to move from a position of 'commodity area' to a position of 'status area' by differentiating its products from competitors. Extending existing products/services for sale to new markets as suggested by Ansoff (1965) would also help the Opatija Riviera to enhance its attractiveness and competitiveness.

Conclusions

Assuming that the Opatija Riviera opts for a successful expanded tourism future, development should not be left to uncontrolled, sporadic activities, as has been the case in the past. A planned approach to tourism, which identifies and evaluates the optimal development options, should be applied.

The most important benefits derived from the application of the TALC model are:

- Identification of the phases in the life cycle of a destination indicate different characteristics of tourism development, of which the most important in this case is the reorientation from a winter health tourism to a mass summer holiday destination. That, in turn, led to an overall decrease in destination attractiveness and associated unsatisfactory financial returns.

- Tourism development was successful in the periods when a clear vision existed (mostly in the first phase), when the product responded to market demand and when the entire destination's development was in harmony with the specific products that were dominant at the time.
- Identification of the positive and negative effects of tourism, as it is worth remembering that the 'exclusivity and quality' achieved in the first phase positioned the Riviera on the tourist map of Europe, while this reputation was quickly lost in the period between the two world wars due to the absence of a planned approach.
- Although most of the turning points to date depended on the external factors and not on destination planning and management, further growth of tourism, in the face of strong market competition, will depend on the ability of the Opatija Riviera to reposition itself and reinvent its products. This could be achieved only if development is planned and the appropriate destination management tools applied. The planning options are partly determined by the specificities of the development to date (i.e. several introduction phases, simultaneous existence of two phases), where the measures characteristic of the rejuvenation phase should be applied, such as combined efforts from government and private bodies or the construction of artificial attractions such as theme parks.

The case study of tourism development on the Opatija Riviera illustrates how extrinsic factors can influence the evolution of a destination and make it unique. It can be concluded that several phases existed simultaneously and this was a result of tourism activities being halted several times due to the armed conflicts, creating a necessity to start tourism development from scratch each time. The TALC model is fully applicable in the situation where a single tourism product dominates a destination. In the case of the Opatija Riviera, where the latest phase of development is characterised by several products, the model should be applied to each product separately. Development of a tourism destination database and continuous market research into tourist motives will make it possible to test the applicability of the TALC model at this destination in the future.

Although in the tourism literature there are many case studies demonstrating the conformity/validity of Butler's model (e.g. Cooper & Jackson, 1989; Hovinen, 1982; Meyer-Arendt, 1985; Strapp, 1988), there are also cases demonstrating deviation from the model (Agarwal, 1997;

Choy, 1992; Getz, 1992). Regardless of the outcome, all derive conclusions and evaluate past and expected developments of a destination under study. The applicability of the TALC model in the case of the Opatija Riviera lies in its ability to identify development phases according to the stipulated characteristics and recommended strategies and not solely in their succession according to the classical model. A relatively simple model such as the TALC also assists a combination with other methods such as market share analysis, portfolio management model and various planning indices to determine what could be a direction for future research.

Chapter 17

The Rejuvenation of Atlantic City: The Resort Cycle Recycles

CHARLES STANSFIELD

Introduction

Geographers and other scholars long have been intrigued that it might be possible to better comprehend the apparent waxing and waning of a region's economic or political fortunes as evidence of a predictable sequence or cycle. Economists study, interpret and try to predict a variety of business activity cycles. Climatologists seek to understand possible climate cycles. Noted political geographer Samuel Van Valkenburg compared the state's 'life cycle' to a human life cycle, noting that the organism of the state could repeat, or recycle, this sequence.

Stansfield appears to have been the first to use and exemplify the term 'resort cycle' in a publication in 1978 (Stansfield, 1978). Butler was the first to define, structure, and generalize the specific stages of this cycle (Butler, 1980). Can the resort cycle 'recycle' or repeat, as in the manner of Van Valkenburg's age cycle of states? Atlantic City's 'rebirth' as a world-class, successful resort seems to be evidence that it can.

Why Atlantic City?

An important question about Atlantic City's spectacular renaissance through the agency of legalized gambling is, why Atlantic City? Why was Atlantic City the first jurisdiction in the USA to break Nevada's long monopoly on legalized gambling? The answer lies in the resort cycle as exemplified by Atlantic City's history, its sad decline, and in political solutions to economic problems. Politics – lots of politics – are involved.

The old Atlantic City, 'B.C.' (Before Casinos) suffered from a combination of economic and social problems. Chief among them were seasonality, obsolescence of tourism infrastructure and changing life-styles and vacation habits. To be sure, this list applies to all aging resorts; in Atlantic City's case, though, it was the scale and intensity of those problems that contributed to a bold move to use legalized gambling as a tool of urban renewal.

Gambling on Renewal: Background to the Legalization of Gambling

By the 1970s, Atlantic City was in deepening trouble. Approximately 120 years after Atlantic City was founded on a then desolate offshore sandbar, the city's economy, social health and reputation all were in desperate condition. The once glamorous, fabled 'Queen of the Jersey Shore' had sagged into a frayed and peeling version of its glory days. Atlantic City's appeal, its crowd-attracting formula combining natural and created attractions, no longer encapsulated the extravagant and fantastic illusion on which great resorts flourished. In his landmark study of Atlantic City, Charles Funnell concluded

> ultimately, changing modes of transportation practically destroyed the resort's ability to attract patronage across class lines, threatened the physical appearance of the city, and sapped the illusion – creating potential the town once so vigorously exploited. Atlantic City did not 'fall' – it was abandoned. It persevered in formulas which had been highly successful, but though a large part of its patronage continued to respond eagerly to what it offered, an important minority left it behind, to return no more. (Funnell, 1975: 154)

Atlantic City's plight by the 1970s explains much of its determination to seek revitalization through legalized gambling. Some of Atlantic City's problems can be viewed as yet another instance of the urban cancer affecting virtually all aging cities in America. Other aspects of the resort's decline are related to causes unique to resorts. Atlantic City's sad decay is illustrated by data from the 1970 census. The city's census tract (neighborhood) with the lowest mean income had less than half the county mean, while only two tracts of 21 in Atlantic City exceeded the county mean. The percentage of families below the official poverty level, slightly under 10% for the entire county, varied within Atlantic City from 3.5% to 46% in the north end urban renewal area. Some neighborhoods reported as much as 80% of the population over 65, and old age and lower incomes often go together. Two-thirds of the housing occupied year-round had been built before 1940, and looked it. This was a city that had 40 pawnshops, but not a single supermarket or movie theater (if we don't count porno).

Basically, the people of New Jersey felt sorry for Atlantic City and its citizens. It had been such a great place in memory; now it needed help. If Atlantic City couldn't help itself – and evidently it couldn't – how could the state help the old resort to once again rise to success? What to do?

The road to renewal first needed an answer to the question, what went wrong? For one thing, owners and operators of hotels, restaurants, and entertainment businesses had failed to keep up with changing tastes. Aging buildings weren't kept fresh and up-to-date, typical of the decline stage in the resort cycle. New facilities just were not being built. The places that attracted, accommodated, and entertained visitors had become shabby and old-fashioned. Profits were being drained away without making necessary reinvestments in modernization or replacement.

Early success: The period of rapid expansion

Obviously, all the facilities in Atlantic City's early days were new, and new commonly equals desirable for American tourists. The early success of Atlantic City is illustrated by the size and plush nature of its hotels. For example, the United States Hotel, which occupied an entire city block, was described in a contemporary account as having rooms for 600 guests which were

> large, airy, comfortable, carpeted and furnished in walnut, with gas in every room and in every respect will compare with a first class city hotel. There are also attractive billiard rooms, ten pin alleys and shooting galleries and daily morning, afternoon and evening open air concerts are given by a celebrated orchestra. (Rose, 1878: 42)

Host to President Grant in 1874, the hotel was one of the most successful ventures of the railroad company which had literally created the resort. By 1894 it had been torn down, an example of the energetic drive to 'keep up to date'. New resorts as summarized and generalized in Butler's landmark study on resort cycles (Butler, 1980) are characterized by intensive real estate speculation, and rapid construction of new, plush accommodations, restaurants, and transport facilities of the latest design. The reputation of the resort, carefully nourished by enthusiastic public relations efforts, is at its height. It is an 'in' place with a magnetic appeal to the trend-followers.

As leisure time and disposable income were democratized, successively lower income groups arrived to sample Atlantic City's well publicized delights. This trend toward a broadening of the social strata patronizing the resort is closely related to the progressive lowering of the time and money cost of travel to the resort.

At the apex: Triumph and decline

By World War I, Atlantic City had reached a plateau. It appeared that all was well, that the tried and true formulas still worked, but by that time, most of the resplendent and extravagant seafront hotels had been built; few more on the truly grandiose scale would be added. The railroad was still fulfilling its dominant role although motorists were beginning to clog the highways in summer. The costs of reaching Atlantic City were decreasing. The railroad, whose speed made day-trips feasible, was carrying progressively lower income groups to Atlantic City. The entertainment complex increasingly reflected their tastes and disposable incomes. This shift in emphasis towards working class tastes was both a cause of and a consequence of the upper middle class's declining allegiance to Atlantic City. As observed of Coney Island at the same period, 'The working classes, those most effected by the increasing pace and increasing mechanization of life, accepted mechanized Coney most readily... they did not see close contact with nature as a "spiritual necessity"... mechanized, time structured leisure may simply reflect mechanized, time structured lives.' (Snow & Wright, 1976: 960–975).

The mechanical amusements, cheap vaudeville theaters and garish entertainments which so thrilled the working classes helped to drive away the upper middle class from the ornate hotels and high-class restaurants. The 'takeover' of a resort by a lower-income group than had originally dominated it may be partially explained, however, by the upper-income group's desire for new recreation environments. Tourism is an industry in which fashion and the search for the new and different play important roles.

The physical complex of hotels, restaurants, and the more expensive, higher-class entertainments was allowed to slowly deteriorate. No new investment was attracted due to diminishing patronage, at least of the higher-priced facilities. Unfortunately, the fact that Atlantic City's fortunes were tied to trains was both good and bad news. Trains had created, and built, Atlantic City. The last excursion trains were phased out after World War II, leaving Atlantic City with only minimal, commuter-oriented train service. The two replacements for trains in vacation travel, limited-access, high-speed highways and jet airplanes, both favored other resorts over Atlantic City. Atlantic City was the loser under these new rules. Although Atlantic City's Bader Field, the first municipal airport in the nation, is convenient to downtown and nearby Atlantic City, Pomona can accommodate large jets, the air age has not greatly benefited Atlantic City. Other than convention trade, few visitors arrived by air until after the casinos were built. The time in the air from most of the neighboring cities of the northeast Megalopolis to other resorts such as those of southern Florida is not all that much greater than that to Atlantic City. Also, economical operation of fast jets on a regularly scheduled basis requires termini in busy markets. A short-haul service to Atlantic City from Philadelphia has continued, and a longer-distance jet service has a bright future.

Obsolescence of infrastructure

The individual mobility of automobile vacations led to a quite different style of vacation from that of the old railroad resorts. The railroad had provided only point-to-point mobility for its users. Whether for a day or a month, the Victorian vacationer was tied to that one city, perhaps even to the vicinity of a particular hotel. The vacationer's dollars were spent mostly within the confines of that resort. Private automobiles had two major impacts upon recreation patterns, neither of which really benefited Atlantic City. Vacationers arriving in cars wanted to be able to park their cars conveniently and, preferably, free of charge. Crowded, densely built-up Atlantic City was friendly to pedestrians but not to cars. By the auto age, most of the city's buildable land was occupied by multi-story structures packed tightly together. The narrow streets of an earlier era could not accommodate both heavier traffic and curb parking on both sides. Relatively few new, large motels were constructed in a city where many hotel rooms were empty even in peak season. Cost-conscious vacationers could stay at cut-price motels constructed along the highways and drive daily to the beaches, crowding Atlantic City's beaches and streets, but leaving little money behind. The much sought-after middle class 'family trade' increasingly preferred the smaller, less crowded, less expensive, less noisy towns along the coast. The new highways that brought vacationers to Atlantic City also facilitated their going to other resorts, or their commuting into Atlantic City from less expensive locations. Highway improvements ever increased the distance that day-trippers could travel from home to resort to home in one day.

Proof of Atlantic City's decline and obsolescence was the loss of about 3500 hotel rooms (to demolition, mostly) between 1964 and 1969, accompanied by a loss of 2500 'guest house' rooms. While motels did add approximately 1000 rooms during this period, the net decrease in transient rooms available was nearly 20% of the total in just five years. In this last stage of the resort cycle, the natural amenities that led to the founding of the resort were of deteriorated quality, with environmental pollution a serious and intensifying problem. Commonly, declining resorts attempt to modify and rejuvenate their appeal to vacationers. Due in some measure to uncontrollable or unforeseeable changes in leisure patterns, transport technology, and fashion, and through environmental pollution and plant obsolescence, the resort can no longer rely on its original set of attractions. The resort may choose to emphasize its historical and cultural uniqueness rather than its deteriorated, less-attractive physical site amenities. In other words, superior climates, lower costs, relatively comparable degrees of accessibility resulting from changing transport technology, more modern and glamorous facilities, less crowded beaches – all of these assets may characterize other and newer resorts. Some unique quality of the artificial or human-created environment can, conceivably, be emphasized to lure tourists, for example, the huge stock of accommodations and entertainment facilities which are available at lower rates in attracting conventions.

A notable example of capitalizing upon the historic cultural landscape is nearby Cape May's largely successful preservation of its Victorian townscape. Cape May's stock of 1850s through 1890s architecture helps draw visitors to an otherwise out of the way site with relatively narrow beaches. By the 1970s, Atlantic City's architecture, while flamboyant and varied in the remaining great hotels of the turn-of-the-century through 1920s period, was not quite old enough to yet draw the full interest of the preservationists and nostalgia buffs who had made a pet of Cape May. At that time, great gaps in Atlantic City's oceanfront skyline, the product of demolition of antiquated hotels, resembled broken or missing teeth in a smile – a reminder of old age and neglect. While small town Victoriana at Cape May is charming, Atlantic City's seafront, what there was left of it, seemed more isolated in a sea of slums and consequently dreary. Atlantic City simply could not become another, larger Cape May.

Atlantic City was beginning to show its age. No major new hotels had been built for decades. The all-too-short 'season' left many locals on the unemployment rolls for about eight months a year. For the first time, local business and political leaders publicly discussed the possibility of legalized gambling as an economic stimulus. Major hotel owners were split on the controversial proposal. The owners of the Chalfonte-Haddon Hall Hotel, for example, who were Quakers, strongly opposed legalizing casinos. The year? 1956. Twenty years later, a referendum question approving casinos in Atlantic City was successful. The first casino to open, in 1978, was Resorts International, the new owner of the Chalfonte-Haddon Hall property.

The Beginning of a New Beginning: Recycling the Resort Cycle

The problems of Atlantic City spurred a variety of governmental efforts to revitalize the city by the 1960s. A new high-speed toll highway, the Atlantic City Expressway, was built to the aging resort. A new state college was built on the mainland nearby. There was talk of extending a suburban high-speed commuter railway from Philadelphia all the way to Atlantic City. The most intriguing (and, initially, controversial) suggestion was to legalize gambling. Legalization was at first opposed on the grounds that it might attract organized crime. A referendum on gambling casinos, which appeared on the November 1974 ballot, was resoundingly defeated, three to two. The defeat was achieved by well organized opposition ('no dice on casino gambling'), particularly from church groups. The 1974 proposal, however, while supposedly designed to help Atlantic City, would have made casinos a matter of local option anywhere in the state. Clearly, the possibility of a casino in everyone's hometown was unpopular. The 1976 ballot proposal was restricted to legalized casinos in Atlantic City only. This time, state revenues from casinos were to be devoted to property tax and utility bill relief for the elderly poor – a maneuver which attracted many votes. The sugar coating of charitable impulse helped ease the pill of legalization of casino gambling down the throats of the voters. Popular ambivalence toward casino gambling has characterized Americans long before the 1976 referendum, and it continues. The campaign of the 'Committee to Rebuild Atlantic City' succeeded.

But, would casinos thrive by the sea? Would the new industry bring prosperity to the old resort? New Jersey's governor helped open the first casino, Resorts International, on the Memorial Day weekend of 1978. It was a winner – an instant hit. Local legend has it that this pioneer casino took in so much money in those first days that the 'counting room' couldn't handle the volume of cash. It is said that supermarket bags full of bills accumulated on the floor until the accounting staff caught up. Resorts' seven-month-long first year of operations earned a gross income of $156 million, representing a 200% return on equity (Hawkins, 1982: 120–128).

Here is a snapshot of the casino industry 19 years after Resorts International first opened its doors to the crowds lined up on the boardwalk. This is Atlantic City about midway from the first legalized gambling to the present:

> On an average day in Atlantic City, nineteen years into the casino era, 110,000 visitors and non-resident workers joined the city's 37,000 residents. Over 82,000 people visited the city's twelve casinos and gross winnings in casinos amounted to about 6.5 million dollars. At the same time, 1,452 charter buses arrived in town. Gamblers dropped over 46 million quarters in slot machines. (Russell, 1987: np)

By the dawn of the new century, Atlantic City had become America's most popular resort destination, with over 37 million visitor-days per year. In comparison, Walt Disney World hosts about 18 million visitor-days per year. Hotel/casino industry wages topped $700 million a year, employing over 46,000 people directly in an industry that did not exist until 1978. Between 1976, the year in which the casino referendum was approved by New Jersey voters, and 1984, per capita income in the US doubled. In the same period, New Jersey's per capita income increased faster, 109%, while Atlantic City's grew by 134%. In 1976, Atlantic City had one-tenth as many visitors as it had by 1987. The state's 8% tax on gross revenues of casinos already had transferred over $1 billion to the state treasury. Indirect taxes – sales taxes and the city's luxury tax paid by casino patrons – generated another $20 million per year.

Early impacts of casinos

The visible impacts of the casino industry on Atlantic City can be compared to a growing snowball, or maybe it was more like an avalanche filmed in slow motion. At first, little seemed to be happening, at least for the better. In her book about Resorts International, owners of the first casino to open in Atlantic City in May 1978, author Gigi Mahon described the scene in the summer of 1977 – a year after the voter approval of legalized gaming in Atlantic City, but a year before opening day.

> Up at the Chalfonte-Haddon Hall, a handful of construction men labored through the heat, a renovation under way. But for that, the facades of the old hotels remained as they had for years, sagging, gray, like the faces of the people who sat on the Boardwalk day after day. It was the same Atlantic City, long ago duchess of resorts, now an arthritic and dowdy dowager trying desperately to cling to her past. A bag of worn-out bricks on splintered pilings. (Mahon, 1980: prologue)

Did legalization of gambling work?

In a word, yes. Look at the skyline of Atlantic City, then consider this: $60 billion dollars. That is the total brought to the State of New Jersey's treasury by casino revenues from 1978 to the present. That is enough money that the state could have written a check for over $7200 to every one of the state's estimated 8,359,000 citizens and it is 60 billion dollars worth of state services that New Jersey taxpayers didn't have to pay for directly.

The legalization of casinos in Atlantic City has created almost 50,000 jobs directly in the casino industry, and an estimated additional 50,000 jobs in industries within New Jersey that supply and service the casinos. This creation of approximately 100,000 jobs in the state did not cost the state, or any of its municipalities, anything directly.

In contrast, other states and local governments have not hesitated to spend millions in efforts to attract new jobs into their economies. Pennsylvania spent a quarter of a billion dollars to secure a Volkswagen assembly plant near New Stanton, PA. Tennessee paid for $15 million worth of site improvements and issued $450 million in bonds to build a facility in order to lure a Nissan assembly plant; Nissan also was given a substantial tax exemption, all to add 6000 jobs to the state's economy (Sternlieb & Hughes, 1983: 3).

Gambling on the future, gambling in the future

Atlantic City's present and future depends on Americans' attitudes toward gambling. The industry itself prefers the term 'gaming' – it sounds classier and less controversial than 'gambling.' Americans have changed their attitudes several times about permitting, encouraging, or criminalizing gambling, er, gaming. Colonial America openly tolerated lotteries. Such upright citizens as Benjamin Franklin printed lottery tickets, which were sold to support good causes, much as 'chances' today are sold on new cars to raise money for volunteer fire departments. Many a colonial college and church were built with lottery proceeds. Then, in the mid-19th century, Americans evidently decided that gambling was undesirable and should be officially frowned upon. By the 1890s, though, state lotteries again were common and gaming was widely tolerated. The notoriously crooked Louisiana State Lottery, however, caused a national scandal and by the early 20th century, public opinion had once again swung in favor of criminalizing gambling.

Using legalized gaming as a tool for urban renewal in Atlantic City was not the first time that gambling was used to revitalize a depressed economy. In the Great Depression of the 1930s, Nevada was particularly hard hit. Mining and ranching jobs were declining. With the important exception of the Sierras along the California border (such as at Lake Tahoe), Nevada had no natural landscapes of special appeal to tourists. Plenty of people crossed Nevada, to or from San Francisco and the rest of the country, but few planned to stay. Nevadans decided to legalize all forms of gambling anywhere in the state, and the modern gaming industry was born. Until 1978, when New Jersey's first casino opened, Nevada enjoyed a national monopoly on legal gaming.

If gaming could rescue a whole state's economy, maybe it could also rescue Atlantic City.

Gambling industry expert Jerome Skolnik (1978: 8) has observed,

> Vice is a fascinating social phenomenon. Leading dictionaries define it as immoral or evil conduct. But the dictionary definition is incomplete. The term vice suggests pleasure – and popularity – as well as immorality. Murder, robbery, and theft are generally regarded as immoral, but not much fun. In contrast, gambling, illicit sex and drug use are vices because they combine pleasure with 'evil.' The whole point about the phenomenon of vice is its duality: it is conduct that can be enjoyed and deplored at the same time, sometimes by the same people.

It is this duality that, combined with the charitable destination of a portion of the revenues, helps explain the geographic pattern of casino gambling in the USA.

Easy money: Gambling as voluntary taxation

By 1984, 17 states and the District of Columbia had legal, government-run lotteries; these lotteries had total sales approaching $7 billion. Typically, states keep about 30–40% of ticket sales, after paying out prize money and administrative costs. As with legalized casinos in Atlantic City, some portion of revenues is allocated to projects that appeal to social consciousness – to a conservation trust fund in Colorado, aid to the elderly in Pennsylvania, and funds for the arts in Massachusetts. State lotteries tend to spread geographically as the government and citizens of a state without a lottery, but adjacent to one with one, see their own residents buying lottery tickets from their neighbor. Now 48 states have some form of state-sponsored gaming – lotteries, off-track betting, casinos, or a combination of these. Utah and Hawaii are the only exceptions to this relatively recent trend.

Lotteries, and now casinos, are seen as a painless form of voluntary taxation. Legalized casino gambling is most attractive to states when most of the gamblers are from out-of-state. In this way, most of the gambling losses are 'exported.' After all, revenues from gambling are based entirely on net losses by gamblers. This 'export' of gambling losses is the factor that makes Nevada's legalized gambling so lucrative to that state. State lotteries, while serving as tax collectors from volunteer taxpayers, are non-basic economic activities; they do not expand the state's economic base to any significant degree. As long as legal casinos serve largely out-of-state gamblers, they contribute to basic economic growth within that state.

Nevada's nationwide monopoly on legalized gaming ruled until Atlantic City became a competitor. Still, at least the Western half of the country was closer to Nevada than Atlantic City. But, Atlantic City had not only become a competitor to Nevada. Its success served as a role model for depressed regions elsewhere. Gambling came to many reservations as Native Americans (the poorest of the Census-tabulated minorities) sought economic growth. Riverboat gaming came to many of the Midwest's depressed old industrial cities, and to Mississippi, America's poorest state.

Expansion of the casino industry

Expectations for legalized gaming in Atlantic City ran from strongly negative to equally strongly positive. Just exactly why did the 1974 public question on the ballot (legalizing casinos anywhere in the state) lose but the 1976 question, legalizing casinos only in Atlantic City, win? Richard Lehne pointed out that public opinion polls showed little change in attitude from 1974 to 1976 (Lehne, 1986) (see Table 17.1).

Table 17.1 Opinion poll results

Month, Year	*Yes on casinos (%)*	*No on casinos (%)*	*No opinions (%)*
1, 74	59	34	7
9, 74	56	38	6
9, 76	59	36	5

Source: Lehne, 1986

Voter turnout in 1974 was less than 2 million. But in 1976, a presidential year, voter turnout was over 2.7 million. It seems that the legalization of casinos was a 'hot button issue', highly motivating those opposed, but when more voters showed up, the 'yes' votes prevailed. An analysis of who voted how summarized the yes vote as favored by males, inner city residents, and Catholics. Those opposing tended to be females, Protestants, and suburban residents.

Expansion of the casino industry in Atlantic City has not been one of continuous growth at a steady pace. Instead, as shown in Table 17.2, the early success of Resorts International produced a boom between 1978 and 1981, in which the number of casinos jumped from one to nine. In those first three years, casino square footage multiplied almost eight times, casino employees increased from 3226 to almost 28,000, and hotel rooms in casino hotels went from 724 to 4781. The legalization authorizing casinos in Atlantic City stipulated that casino hotels must have a minimum of 500 rooms. To guarantee more construction jobs, each hotel room had to be of sufficient square footage that old hotels, with their characteristically smaller rooms, would have to be substantially renovated. The annual increase in casino gross revenue or 'winnings' remained in the double digits until 1985. Between 1981 and 2002, only three more (net) casinos opened, and growth rates slowed noticeably. The increase rate of the gross 'win' stayed below 10% per year after 1984. During the 1990s decade, the number of casino employees fluctuated between about 44,000 and 49,000.

However, both casino floor areas and number of hotel rooms were higher by 2001 than they had been in 1991. Casino floor area, which since 1993 has included simulcast horseracing rooms, has gone from 773,000 square feet in 1991 to 1,230,000 square feet by 2001, a percentage increase of just under 60%. What is even more impressive is the growth in casino hotel rooms, from 9419 in 1991 to 11,466 by 2001, a somewhat surprising and healthy 22%.

The increase in the number of hotel rooms is significant because it points to a new trend that few had predicted. Atlantic City clearly is moving from a largely 'daytrip' resort towards a destination resort, in

Table 17.2 Expansion of casino gaming in Atlantic City

Year	*No. of casinos*	*Casino floor sq. footage (000s)*	*Casino employees*	*Gross revenues (000s)*	*% Increase in win*	*No. of hotel rooms*
1978*	1	52	3226	134,073	–	724
1979	3	160	11,301	325,480	42.7	1572
1980	6	281	21,351	642,693	97.4	3257
1981	9	412	27,842	1,099,799	71.1	4781
1982	9	425	28,093	1,493,164	35.7	4770
1983	9	422	30,958	1,770,941	18.6	4779
1984	10	510	35,356	1,951,766	10.2	5503
1985	11	577	38,686	2,138,651	9.5	6342
1986	11	593	37,251	2,281,206	6.6	6351
1987	12	664	39,336	2,495,728	9.4	6835
1988	12	696	41,205	2,734,775	9.5	7314
1989	12**	648	39,603	2,806,990	2.6	7584
1990	12**	770	43,399	2,952,582	5.1	8828
1991	12	773	41,473	2,991,562	1.3	9419
1992	12	777	44,240	3,215,968	7.5	8961
1993	12	854***	44,111	3,301,366	2.6	8946

Table 17.2 *(Continued)*

Year	*No. of casinos*	*Casino floor sq. footage (000s)*	*Casino employees*	*Gross revenues (000s)*	*% Increase in win*	*No. of hotel rooms*
1994	12	928	43,900	3,422,614	3.7	9227
1995	12	959	46,513	3,748,158	9.5	9404
1996	12	1081	48,956	3,813,598	1.7	10,533
1997	12	1173	49,123	3,879,651	1.7	11,891
1998	12	1211	48,542	3,991,612	2.8	11,880
1999	12	1170	47,366	4,119,507	3.2	11,361
2000	12	1198	47,426	4,275,783	3.8	11,361
2001	12	1230	45,592	4,279,034	0.07	11,466

Source: Compiled from the annual reports of the New Jersey Casino Control Commission, 1978–2001

*220 days

**Eleven casinos from 22 May 1989 to 4 April 1990

***From 1993 forward, figure includes simulcast-racing room

which vacationers stay longer and to which they travel increasing distances. In 1979, Economic Research Associates made the following predictions, based on an analysis of trends in the overall economy, legalized gaming in general, and Atlantic City's casino industry in particular. By 1990 there would be: 26 casinos (compared to 1979's three); a permanent population of 75,000 (there were 41,322 in 1979); 24 million visitors a year (7,500,000 in 1979), and 55,000 hotel rooms by 1990 (as against 1572 in 1979).

So much for scientific predictions, especially those made during a period of rapid expansion with the assumption that expansion will continue at a frantic pace. However, the 22% increase in hotel rooms, 1991 to 2001, is a respectable achievement, and one trend that will continue. 'By the summer of 2004, Atlantic City should have an additional 3,200 hotel rooms – an increase of approximately 33 percent over what currently exists.' (Casino Control Commission, 2001: 4).

Since the 2001 figure of 11,466 rooms was reported, Harrah's has built another 452-room addition; Resorts is adding another 459-room tower; Tropicana is adding 502 rooms; and Showboat is adding 544 rooms. The Borgata, opening in 2003, will contribute another 2010 rooms. The Sheraton Atlantic, a new, non-casino hotel next to the $268 million Convention Center, has 502 rooms. A Boardwalk non-casino hotel, Atlantic Palace, has 302 units, many of them two-bedroom suites.

Atlantic City seems poised for another period of fast growth despite the miniscule increase in win reported for 2001 – a year of deepening recession, falling stock markets, and, of course, the tragedy of September 11, which considerably slowed the entire tourism and travel industry. Indeed, the disasters of September 11, which had a strongly negative impact on air travel, may have actually helped Atlantic City in the long run by increasing tourism at resorts that can be reached by road and rail rather than by air. Atlantic City's casino industry enjoyed a remarkable fourth quarter, with gross operating profits up almost 25% over the October–December period of 2000 (Casino Control Commission, 2001: 4).

The casinos

Before the first casino opened in Atlantic City, the size of the legalized gambling market was unknown. The 'convincer' that a huge, formerly unserved market existed in the Northeast was the success of Atlantic City's first casino, Resorts International. Resort's seven-month long first year generated a gross income of $156 million, which was a 200% return on equity. In its first full month of operation, Resorts' 'win' was $16 million.

> When Resorts had the only game in town during the summer of 1978, the only 'marketing' problem was one of security and crowd control.

> Lines of people four or five abreast waited on the Boardwalk for hours before being admitted, and once a patron got inside his most lucky break of the day might be finding a spot of play! But as each new casino opened, patrons began to choose their casino, and the market was shared even though it continued to grow. (Smith, 1982: 116)

'Casino fever,' a belief that there would be no end to the boom, prevailed among otherwise sane people.

As more and more casinos opened, they began to develop marketing strategies to differentiate themselves and establish unique identities. James Smith (1982) pointed out that Nevada's casinos generally fell into one of two categories: 'premium' or 'grind joints'. Premium casinos strove for an upscale image. Lavishly decorated, they emphasized table games with fairly high minimum wagers. Premium casinos rely heavily on 'high rollers' who may stay several days and gamble large sums. For their select clientele, premium casinos are happy to 'comp' them with complimentary luxury suites, preferred seating at shows featuring big-name entertainment, and any other services that will keep the high rollers coming back. These wealthy players routinely risk many thousands of dollars. Typically, they stay for days, not hours, and expect elegant and impeccable service. They play table games in which experience and familiarity with the rules count in their favor, they hope. Premium houses' showrooms feature top name entertainment (it is said that the late Frank Sinatra was the champion 'draw' for high-rollers) (Smith, 1982).

In contrast, 'grind' houses (also known as 'sawdust joints' in contrast to 'carpet' or premium casinos) prospered on a high volume of gamblers who bet less individually, a lot less, than the high rollers. Grind houses typically featured many slot machines, with relatively fewer table games. Grind houses thus rely on large numbers of low-rollers who, individually, wager modestly but who as a group, are highly profitable. Senior citizens arriving by chartered bus, prepared to lose little more than the $10 roll of quarters that is part of their daytrip package, are the main patrons of the grind houses. Food is often buffet-style, most patrons do not stay overnight, and the showrooms feature revues rather than renowned stars. While premium houses offer tickets to boxing matches and other special events to their high-rolling clientele, grind houses offer meal coupons, chances to win cars and discounted revue tickets to their clients. Many patrons of grind houses have too little experience to confidently play table games where skill counts; instead they prefer the no-skill slot machines.

Historically, Nevada's casinos were mostly grind houses. Ben 'Bugsy' Siegel's ground breaking 'Flamingo', opened at Las Vegas in 1946, not only pioneered the Vegas Strip (as opposed to downtown's Fremont Street) but was a true premium house. High rollers arrived by chartered planes; dealers wore tuxedoes.

Smith (1982) illustrated the premium–grind contrast by comparing the MGM Grand in Las Vegas with Atlantic City's Resorts International. The MGM Grand was the largest hotel in the state when it opened (1973) and boasted the largest casino. In addition to 2100 rooms, it featured a shopping arcade, two large showrooms and a jai alai fronton. Resorts, Atlantic City's first casino, and its largest in 1981, had little more than a third of MGM's hotel rooms, and a very different mix of games.

MGM versus Resorts offered a strong and obvious contrast (see Table 17.3). However, contrasts among Atlantic City's casinos in 2001 are much less obvious or consistent. Table 17.4 lists number of slot machines, number of (all) table games, the ratio of gaming tables to slots, and the percentage of slot machines that are nickel slots. Premium houses would be expected to have lower ratios of slots to tables, and lower proportions of nickel slots. The table also shows that Showboat, at 56 slots per gaming table, has a much higher ratio of slots to tables than Tropicana, with a 1 to 24 ratio, or Trump Taj Mahal (1 to 23). Harrah's, another high slots to gaming tables operation, suggesting a possible 'grind' classification along with Showboat, has less emphasis on nickel slots (which are surely an indicator of 'grind' appeal) than five other casinos, including the more prestigious Hilton and Bally's. All of Atlantic City's casinos seem to be aiming at as broad a market segment as possible. Economic survival requires satisfying all varieties of gamblers. Atlantic City operations may emphasize their appeals to premium or grind clienteles, but they are determined to discourage no one.

Atlantic City seems to have pioneered a hybrid premium–grind operation. These premium–grind operations seek distinctive identities

Table 17.3 Contrasts between casino characteristics

	MGM (1973 data)	*Resorts (1981 data)*
Hotel rooms	2100	723
Slots	930	1698
Blackjack tables	61	82
Crap tables	10	20
Roulette wheels	6	14
Big 6 wheels	3	4
Baccarat tables	3	3

Table 17.4 'Premium–grind' characteristics of Atlantic City casinos

	No. slots	*No. table games*	*Ratio of table/slots*	*Nickel slots as % slots*
Atlantic City Hilton	2024	84	1/24	24
Bally's Park Place*	4316	155	1/28	24
Caesar's	3856	123	1/31	19
Claridge	1777	63	1/28	20
Harrah's	3171	69	1/49	20
Resorts	2583	74	1/35	18
Sands	2060	79	1/26	19
Showboat	3390	61	1/56	22
Tropicana	4114	171	1/24	21
Trump Marina	2528	78	1/32	22
Trump Taj Mahal	4825	207	1/23	17
Industry	37,483	1247	1/30	20

*Includes Bally's Wild, Wild West
All data calculated from New Jersey Casino Control Commission Annual Report, 2001

through 'themes', which are shaped and expressed by architecture, interior decoration, costumes of dealers, bartenders, waitresses, etc., and even names of lounges, showrooms, and restaurants. The most obvious example of theme operations include Showboat's 'New Orleans Mardi Gras,' Taj Mahal's Oriental–Arabian nights fantasy and Caesar's Imperial Roman orgy.

Atlantic City's 13th casino, the Borgata, at the time of writing is under construction in the Marina District. The $1-billion, 480-foot high casino will open in the summer of 2003. The Borgata will add 135,000 square feet to Atlantic City's casino floor space, will house 11 restaurants, and will employ 4700. Plans are firming for a $1.5 billion MGM Mirage to be located next to the Borgata on what was, until recently, the city dump. A recent expansion of Harrah's Atlantic City will (temporarily) make it the state's largest hotel at 1626 rooms. Gaming industry insiders predict that Atlantic City will be home to 17 casinos within five years. Atlantic City will continue to reign as the Queen of the Jersey Shore as it moves to more closely resemble its original model, Las Vegas.

The revitalized resort draws more visitors than any other single locale in the USA, more than 37 million visitor-days per year. About 7 million were overnight guests. At 94% occupancy year-round, Atlantic City has a much higher occupancy rate for hotels than the US average. The casinos are a big draw, but not the only attraction.

Atlantic City's casinos pay 70% of all property taxes collected by the city. There are now over 1 million square feet of casino 'floors' (including simulcast rooms), over 10,000 rooms in casino hotels, and nearly 50,000 casino employees (compared to Atlantic City's resident population of some 38,000).

Conclusions: The Coming Megaresorts

The casino industry has big plans for Atlantic City. Huge new 'megaresorts' are planned for vacant land on the bayside. These future mammoth hotels will out-glitz the city's existing casinos – no small challenge there. They will feature 'total resort environments', more family-oriented, with amusement rides, video games, shopping areas, lavish showrooms, continuous entertainment and, of course, a slot machine or two. Sound familiar? As in the 'New' Las Vegas? Atlantic City has consciously imitated Las Vegas since New Jerseyans authorized casinos at the beach in 1976. Las Vegas' fantastic success made it Atlantic City's role model.

The success formula for Las Vegas' incredible expansion (the city grew by 86%, 1990–2000) has been Bigger! Better! More extravagant! More fantastic buildings! Set new standards of size, design, and flamboyance and blow away the competition! And when the competition begins to catch up, raise the stakes again.

Las Vegas, which has featured gambling joints since the 1930s, has witnessed several escalations in investment and the scale and lavishness of casinos. When gangster Bugsy Siegel built the 'Flamingo' in 1946, its glitz set new standards. When Caesar's Palace opened in 1966, its fabulous blend of fantasy theme park and casino was hugely popular; there was a new game in town, again. Then came the first mega resort, the $630-million Mirage in 1989. Again, the challenge to the competition was clear: match it or fold.

Atlantic City certainly will soon enter the era of megaresorts. Increasing competition from riverboats and Amerindian reservation gambling leaves little choice. Besides, when did Atlantic City shrink from a little more glitz and hype? Clearly, the resort cycle is well into its second sequence; the cycle recycles.

Note

Some of this material has been adapted from Charles A. Stansfield, Jr., 'Atlantic City and the Resort Cycle', published in *Annals of Tourism Research* 5 (1978), 238–251. Reprinted by permission, Pergamon Press. Discussion of more recent developments in Atlantic City is adapted from Charles A. Stansfield, Jr. (1998) 'From East Coast Monopoly to Destination Resort: The Geographic Content of Atlantic City's Transformation' in K. Meyer-Arendt and R. Hartmann (eds) *Casino Gambling in America: Origins, Trends, and Impacts*. Elmsford, NY: Cognizant Communications. Reprinted by permission.

Chapter 18

Rejuvenating a Maturing Tourist Destination: The Case of the Gold Coast, Australia

BILL FAULKNER and CARMEN TIDESWELL

Introduction

In an increasingly competitive global environment, strategic planning has become a fundamental element of business survival. The lead times involved in effectively responding to market trends mean that an on-going environmental scanning and strategic assessment process is necessary. This is no less so in the tourism industry than in any other area of economic activity. As Ritchie and Crouch (2000) have observed, while tourism has been growing over the last 50 years, it has been relatively easy for most tourist destinations to maintain a healthy rate of growth despite declining market shares. They add, however, that this is changing as growth in the total market size is slowing down and more destinations are emerging to compete within this market. Competitiveness in this setting requires the establishment of a more strategic focus at both the individual enterprise level and for the destination as a whole. Indeed, planning at these two levels needs to be an integrated process. The tourism product in any setting is a composite of services and goods, and the quality of the visitor's experience depends, to some degree, upon the extent to which the range of providers involved coordinate their efforts and have a common sense of purpose. A 'whole of destination' approach is therefore required in the development of the strategic focus and it has been the recognition of this imperative that has underpinned the creation of tourist destination marketing organisations.

In assessing the competitive position of a tourist destination and extrapolating this assessment to the consideration of future directions of development and the strategic measures necessary to ensure competitiveness within the emerging environment, consideration needs to be given to how the destination has evolved. An understanding of the sequence of events or phases that have marked the history of the destination can assist in bringing its inherent potential and the impediments to achieving this into sharper focus. Also, it enables comparisons with general patterns of destination development as an aid to understanding the dynamics of destination development and predicting what might happen in the future. In this latter regard, in particular, Butler's (1980) Tourist Area Life Cycle (TALC) has proven to be a useful organising framework for interpreting the stage of development of a destination and canvassing scenarios regarding its potential future.

This paper looks at the specific case of Australia's Gold Coast as an example of a maturing and potentially stagnating destination to illustrate the methods being developed in that context to avert stagnation. These methods are discussed in the context of the Gold Coast Visioning (GCV) project, the overall aim of which was to construct a vision for the future of Gold Coast tourism. More specifically, the objectives of this project were:

- To provide a systematic and comprehensive overview of the current status of Gold Coast tourism, covering such considerations as market position, competitiveness and a variety of tourism impacts.
- To develop scenarios for future global, national and local socio-economic, technological and environmental conditions and assess the implications of these trends at the Gold Coast destination level.
- To combine insights from the above with the principles of sustainable tourism development to produce a shared vision for the Gold Coast's tourism future.
- To utilise the shared vision as a framework for generating a set of issues, core values and principles for evaluating future development options.
- To arrive at a consensus on preferred tourism development options consistent with the vision and the actions/approaches necessary for this to become a reality.

Given that the GCV project was essentially concerned with establishing directions for tourism development in the longer term, the principles of sustainable tourism development were adopted as a fundamental philosophical foundation for the planning process. That is, only those options for the Gold Coast's tourism future that satisfy the needs of residents and visitors alike, preserve the cultural and natural assets of the region, and are economically viable were considered (Bramwell & Lane, 1993; Twining-Ward, 1999). There are two basic implications of this caveat, which are reflected in the approach described below. Firstly, the achievement of sustainable tourism objectives hinged on the adoption of a participatory model (Murphy, 1985), involving the meaningful engagement of the community, along with industry stakeholders and relevant government agencies. Secondly, the 'whole of destination' approach referred to earlier was necessary, encompassing the integration of tourism with other sectors of the economy along with an understanding of the inter-relationships and synergies between sociocultural and environmental dimensions. A shift from a 'destination marketing' to a 'destination management' approach was therefore advocated (see Cooper, other volume, editor's comment).

The paper begins with an overview of the status of the Gold Coast as a tourist destination, with particular reference to the indicators of impending stagnation. Background on the methodological foundations of the GCV project is then provided, with specific attention being given. Finally, the translation of these principles into the approach to rejuvenating the Gold Coast is described.

The Gold Coast at a Turning Point

The Gold Coast has long been acknowledged as one of Australia's premier tourist destinations (Gold Coast City Council, 2000). In 1999 it was the third most popular tourism region visited by Australia's international visitors, behind the key arrival ports of Sydney and Melbourne (Bureau of Tourism Research, 2000). This position has been established because of a fortunate combination of natural assets and a sequence of visionary entrepreneurs whose initiatives ensured that this destination was always at the cutting edge of many innovations in Australian tourism development (Russell & Faulkner, 1999). This history is reflected in the destination's international market performance in particular, as indicated in Figure 18.1, which reveals strong growth in the number of international visitors to the Gold Coast from the mid-1980s, when Australia's appeal as an international destination first began to gain momentum (Faulkner, 1990), through to the late 1990s. The profile also reveals a strong resemblance to Butler's scenario, to the extent that the rate of growth is declining in later years and, indeed, suggests that the Gold Coast had already entered the stagnation stage. The dramatic

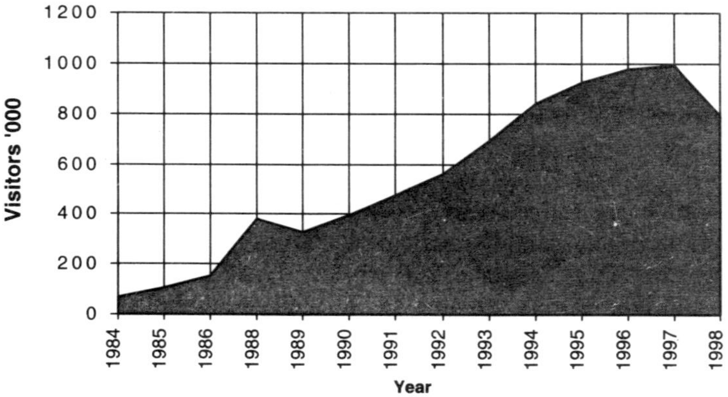

Source: Bureau of Tourism Research (2000a)

Figure 18.1 Trends in international visitor numbers to the Gold Coast

decline in international visitors in the late 1990s, however, is a reflection of the impact of the Asian financial shock, rather than a long-term trend that might suggest the destination is already in decline. While this market has recovered more recently, the dramatic impact of this event highlights the destination's vulnerability arising from its heavy dependence on a narrow band of the market. As illustrated in Figure 18.2, the Gold Coast's performance in the domestic market had been somewhat erratic and less conclusive in terms of any interpretations regarding the Butler model.

While trends in visitor numbers have been the most commonly used indicator of the stage reached in a destination's evolution, a number of authors have identified a more comprehensive range of indicators of stagnation (Butler, 1980; Cooper, 1990; Haywood, 1986; Morgan, 1991). These are outlined in Table 18.1. Preliminary analysis of the Gold Coast's position with respect to some of the indicators contained in Table 18.1 is useful for the purposes of highlighting the rationale underpinning the objectives of the GCV Project.

An examination of data from the Australian International Visitors' Survey (IVS) and the Domestic Tourism Monitor (DTM) reveals a consistent downward trend in the duration of stay of both international and domestic visitors to the Gold Coast over the last decade – from 7 to 4.5 days in the former and from 5.5 to 4.5 in the latter (Bureau of Tourism Research, 2000a,b). The IVS also reveals an increased emphasis on 'organised mass tourism' within the international market, with the proportion of visitors on package, all-inclusive tours increasing from 48 to 75% over the last decade. The plateauing of the international visitor

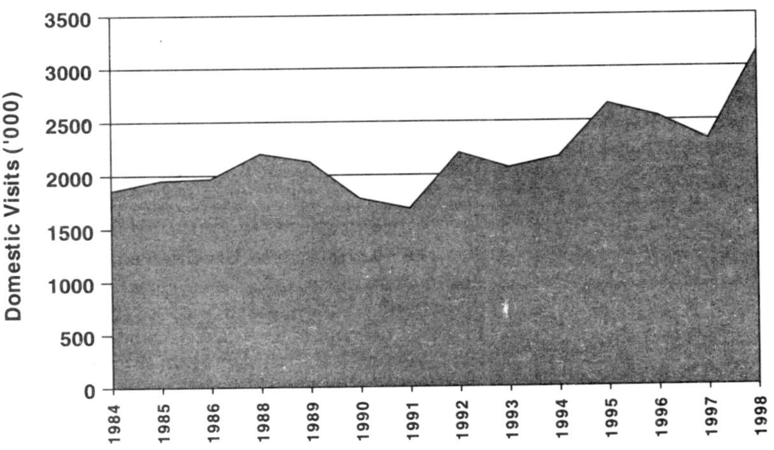

Figure 18.2 Trends in domestic visitor numbers to the Gold Coast. *Source*: Bureau of Tourism Research (2000b)

Table 18.1 Indicators of stagnation and their potential relevance to the Gold Coast

Area of destination performance	*Indicators*
1. Changing markets	• Growth in low-status, low-spend visitors and day visitors. • Overdependence on long-haul market, and lack of penetration of short-stay market. • **Emphasis on high-volume, low-yield inclusive tour market.** • **A decline in visitors length of stay.** • **Type of tourists increasingly organised mass tourists.** • A declining proportion of first-time visitors, as opposed to repeat visitors. • **Limited or declining appeal to overseas visitors.** • Highly seasonal.
2. Emerging newer destinations	• Competition from emerging newer destinations. • The destination is well known, but no longer fashionable.
3. Infrastructure	• Outdated, poorly maintained accommodation and amenities. • Older properties are changing hands and newer properties, if they are being built are on the periphery of the original tourist areas. • **Market perceptions of the destination becoming overcommercialised, crowded and 'tacky'.** • **Tourism industry over capacity.** • **Diversification into conventions and conferences to maintain numbers.** • **Large number of man-made attractions, which start to outnumber the more natural attractions that made the place popular in the first place.**
4. Business performance	• **Declining profits of major tourism businesses.** • Lack of confidence in the tourism business community. • A decline in the elasticity of advertising (lower return in terms of increased visitors per advertising dollar investment) and an increase in process elasticity. • Lack of professional, experienced staff.

Table 18.1 (*Continued*)	
Area of destination performance	***Indicators***
5. Social and environmental carrying capacities	• Visitor levels approaching or exceeding social and environmental carrying capacities. • Local opposition to tourism as the resort's residential role increases;
6. Institutional environment	• Local government reorganisation (amalgamation) diluting the political power of resorts in larger authorities. • Demands for increased operational efficiency and entrepreneurial activity in local government. • Short-term planning horizons in local government owing to financial restrictions and a low priority given to strategic thinking. • Shortage of research data.

Indicators in bold apply to the Gold Coast on the basis of existing data (based on Butler, 1980; Cooper, 1990; Haywood, 1986; Morgan, 1991; Russell & Faulkner, 1999)

numbers shown in Figure 18.1 suggests that the destination was losing some of its appeal in the international market, while the shift-share analysis contained in the Vision Project's Market Analysis Report (Faulkner & Tideswell, 2002) indicated that newer destinations, such as Tropical North Queensland, had eroded the Gold Coast's market share in both the international and domestic markets. It appeared possible that the destination had become 'well known, but no longer fashionable'. Furthermore, even though there had been no marked or consistent decline in hotel occupancy rates, it is arguable that this is only so because of aggressive price cutting in room rates, which has produced a persistent profitless volume problem. The high volume/low yield syndrome is also a reflection of the heavy reliance on the inclusive tour market and the tight margins associated with this market. Finally, while it cannot be claimed that the Gold Coast's tourism infrastructure is aging and in need of refurbishment generally, the Visioning Project's Infrastructure Audit study indicated there were pockets of decay that presented a real prospect of an 'infrastructure time-bomb' (Moore, 2002). The symptoms of stagnation that appear to apply to the Gold Coast have been highlighted in bold in Table 18.1.

The destination's heavy reliance on built attractions (theme parks) and the increasing emphasis on the convention sector that will follow the completion of the convention centre which was under construction in 2002/03 could be cited as symptoms of stagnation according to the literature. However, it might be equally argued that such developments are manifestations of rejuvenation strategies.

On the basis of this overview of the current status of the destination, it is reasonable to conclude at least that the Gold Coast is a mature destination showing some early signs of stagnation. Given this, it is clear that a fundamental shift in the approach to destination planning and management is necessary if the region is to rejuvenate and remain competitive in the longer term. In short, a reorientation from destination marketing to a more encompassing destination management approach was necessary. One of the Gold Coast's major competitors (at least, in the Japanese market) had recognised this and adjusted its approach to tourism development and marketing accordingly, as the following excerpt from an Hawaii Tourism Authority (1999: 9) report reveals.

> Destination tourism management is increasingly becoming more sophisticated worldwide. The success of many tourism destinations has been driven by an integrated tourism management structure, including effective integration of tourism policy, long-term planning, product development and marketing. This successful tourism management approach has also led to strong and mutually supportive private/public sector partnerships that have been driven by a common tourism strategy and policy.

Apart from the tourism development and marketing considerations emphasised above, it is also arguable that the challenge confronting the region was heightened by the need to reconcile the demands of tourism with those of urban growth currently being experienced and likely to continue in the future. With a population of over 400,000 residents, the Gold Coast has been one of the fastest growing urban areas in Australia over the last 10 years. The same assets of the area that make it as a pleasant place to visit also make it an attractive lifestyle choice for new residents and the quality of life of these residents in the future will depend to a large extent on how effectively the potentially competing demands of tourism and urban growth are managed.

Steps Towards a Rejuvenation Strategy: Methodological Issues

Any meaningful strategic assessment of a destination's tourism development future must involve at least the basic ingredients of the traditional strategic planning approach recognised in the literature (Getz, 1986; Gunn, 1988; Heath & Wall, 1992; Inskeep, 1991). It is envisaged that refinements of the strategic planning model are applicable to maturing destinations in general. Each of the key refinements considered in the

GCV Program are now discussed in turn and elaborated on in relation to the TALC Model.

The sustainable tourism development framework

Since sustainable tourism development principles were formally recognised as a goal for modern tourism development, initially in the Manila Declaration (WTO, 1980) and later in the Hague Declaration (WTO, 1989), this set of guidelines has become, in principle at least, the universally accepted basis for destination management and planning.

The emerging sustainable tourism development philosophy of the 1990s can be viewed as an extension of a broader realisation that a preoccupation with economic growth without due regard to its social and environmental consequences is self-defeating in the longer term. Within this perspective, tourism can be construed as essentially a resource-based industry, where the integrity and continuity of the tourism product in a region is inextricably linked with the preservation of its natural, social and cultural assets (Murphy, 1985).

The impediments to the implementation of sustainable tourism development principles go beyond simply a question of awareness levels and intentions among decision makers at the destination level. Noting the tendency for socioculturally and environmentally pristine locations to be degraded once they become too popular as mature tourist destinations, Twining-Ward (1999: 187) asks 'why is it that despite knowledge of the risks, as well as increased understanding of conservation issues, destinations continue to make the same mistakes?' She offered three basic reasons:

- Ecologically and culturally sensitive areas that are most vulnerable to deterioration are also the most attractive to tourists.
- Many of the resources that are so important for the tourism product are 'common pool' resources which the private sector taps free of charge and over which no single company or authority has responsibility for management. They therefore suffer from the 'tragedy of the commons' syndrome, with over-use and a lack of investment in management ultimately degrading the resource (Healy, 1994).
- A reluctance on the part of government to regulate economic activity and thus control levels of activity within sustainable limits.

Earlier interpretations of sustainable tourism development have been criticised on the basis of their focus on ecological sustainability, at the expense of sociocultural and economic, and for the fixation of alternative tourism as the route to sustainability (Farrell, 1999; Twining-Ward, 1999). Farrell (1999) has noted how the sustainable development agenda was captured by the environmental movement and how this has distorted policy and planning practice in a manner that tends to overlook the social and economic dimensions of the 'three dimensional sustainability trinity'. He referred to this trend as a form of 'environmental fundamentalism', which produced a tendency for those responsible for this agenda to resist change of all kinds irrespective of the bigger picture issues re longer-term sustainability. This agenda also encouraged a belief that only alternative forms of tourism (Krippendorf, 1987) (i.e. alternatives to organised mass tourism) were consistent with sustainable tourism objectives. This assumption has since been challenged by many authors, who have pointed out that alternative forms of tourism can have an equally devastating effect, especially where this involves the dispersion of tourists to environmentally or culturally fragile areas (Butler, 1990, 1992; Cater, 1993; Javiluoma, 1992; Wheeller, 1993; Zurick, 1992). Alternatively, if managed properly, mass tourism can be instrumental in controlling tourist movements more effectively, thus enabling them to be contained within 'site hardened' areas where their impacts can be managed.

Farrell (1999: 91) advocated an interdisciplinary and more encompassing approach to sustainable tourism development, involving 'a commitment to provide healthy long-term tourism thoroughly integrated with other elements of the economy, and with the environment and society in such a manner that a policy change in one does not unduly interfere with the optimal functioning of any of the others.' Drawing on this and other insights referred to above for the purposes of the Gold Coast strategy, the objectives of sustainable tourism development are summarised in Table 18.2.

There are several general implications raised by Ritchie (1999) that had a particular bearing on the proposed approach to the GCV Program. Firstly, the need for 'long term planning horizons' and an 'integrated

Table 18.2 Sustainable tourism objectives for the Gold Coast

- To enhance visitor satisfaction and the competitiveness of the destination within the tourist market;
- To improved profitability and the return on investment of the industry;
- To maximise economic benefits to the region;
- To protect and enhance natural environmental assets;
- To provide a foundation for enhancing the host community's quality of life and life opportunities;
- To ensure that development is consistent with the local community's sociocultural values.

Source: Faulkner, 2002

cumulative perspective' highlight the need for a shift from the destination marketing orientation. Secondly, Ritchie (1999) refers to the need for the meaningful involvement of the community, with industry stakeholders, in the development of a consensus on the directions of future development and the actions necessary for the preferred outcomes to be realised. This consensus might be expressed through 'the sharing of a common destination vision'.

Shifting from a destination marketing to a destination management perspective

As emphasised by Ritchie's (1999) initial two points, one of the more obvious implications of the sustainable tourism development agenda is the need for a more comprehensive, integrated and holistic approach that goes beyond the traditional focus on destination marketing to take into account a broader range of environmental, social and economic issues. The fact that the necessity of such an approach is beginning to be recognised by major tourism destinations has been referred to earlier in the reference to the Hawaii Tourism Authority's (1999) latest tourism plan.

The failure of more traditional tourism development plans, with their 'top-down', market-oriented approach, has been observed in several settings (e.g. Alipour, 1996; Choy, 1991; King *et al.*, 2000). Choy (1991: 329) has suggested that, given that 'tourism plans have little probability of influencing market forces to achieve economic success, government planning efforts might be better spent on resolving issues involving. . .market failure, leaving the private sector to assume the planning and financial risk of tourism projects.' Areas of market failure he referred to include: public interest in products and services which are consumed collectively (parks, beaches, historic sites); external effects (positive and negative) that affect people not directly involved in tourism activity (e.g. construction of a resort may restrict locals' access to the beach); and costs and benefits not reflected in market prices (value of open space, costs of social impacts, benefits from environmental preservation). However, while there are obvious differences in the focus of public and private sector interest, the demarcation of their involvement in this way loses sight of the inter-relationships and synergies that need to be developed. A demarcated, as opposed to a truly integrated, approach will produce the sort of 'dysfunctionality' in tourism plans observed by Butler (1991). Thus, for instance, it might produce a conflict between policy mechanisms aimed at limiting environmental impacts by minimising tourist numbers, at one level, and elements of policy at a higher level that encourage increases in visitor numbers in order to improve economic benefits.

An approach that gives due consideration to the various dimensions of the sustainability agenda, while at the same time avoiding the dysfunctionality trap, hinges on a process involving participation by a broad range of stakeholders within a framework that fosters the development of a consensus on preferred directions of future development and the building of collaborative relationships. The key issue related to the desire to rejuvenate a destination following maturity is that continuing growth should not be attempted by merely chasing larger numbers of tourists through increased marketing initiatives, but rather it should be pursued through better management of the industry as a whole.

Community participation and the building of collaborative relationships

One of the seminal works on community participation in tourism development planning is Murphy's (1985) book, *Tourism: A Community Approach*. Murphy proposed an ecological/systems-based model for community involvement in tourism planning and in the process anticipated many of the elements of sustainable tourism development principles described above. In particular, he argued that:

> Residents must put up with the physical development, but have little say so in the decision-making process that will inevitably affect their community and way of life. Development and planning in isolation from the community at large cannot continue if the industry is to develop in harmony with the capacity and aspirations of destination areas. To become self renewable resource industry and agent of hospitality will require more citizen participation in the development, or non-development, of a destination. (Murphy, 1985: 163)

The above rationale for community involvement is largely based on ethical considerations, in the sense that it emphasises the resident's stake in the process in terms of the potential impacts of tourism on their way of life. Emphasis is therefore placed on the need to ensure that changes associated with tourism are both within the bounds of their adaptive capabilities and consistent with the retention or enhancement of their quality of life. There is, however, another perspective, which has a more pragmatic orientation. Kotler and Armstrong's (1984) societal marketing concept has been invoked to highlight that members of the host population are simultaneously consumers of product and beneficiaries or victims of the effects of production (King *et al.*, 2000; Mill, 1996). Thus, if the industry can be construed as using the community itself as part of the product it sells to the market, then a planning and management regime that becomes insensitive to community interests will undermine the quality of the product, to the extent that this will precipitate a community backlash. From the perspective of the TALC model, a destination which has reached maturity and may be experiencing some of the traditional tensions between local residents and supporters of further tourism development cannot hope to resolve these issues and move forward towards rejuvenation without the support and involvement of community members.

While the rationale for a community-based approach to tourism planning is compelling, how extensively and effectively this approach has been adopted is another question. As Joppe (1996) has observed, despite the rhetoric about community participation in tourism planning, most instances of this are driven by government (and business) agendas, rather than community interests. Part of the problem arises from the difficulty of defining the community and assumptions made about the homogeneity of interests within it. While to some the notion of community implies a coherent entity with a shared identity and common sense of purpose, in reality communities generally consist of an agglomeration of special interest groups who are often antagonistic towards each other and competing for scarce resources or power (Manning, 1999). Thus, for example, it is not uncommon for residents to favour options that will benefit them personally in some manner (e.g. product based on parks, outdoor recreation, restaurants) regardless of market conditions or the potential of the area (Andereck & Vogt, 2000). In such circumstances, the task of building a consensus or shared vision on the future of tourism in the destination is a major challenge that is compounded by the need to reconcile a diversity of views and interests.

The need for such an approach is illustrated by Backman *et al.*'s (2001) reference to how planning in the ecotourism context involves overlapping agendas of various stakeholders. The distinction between public and private sector involvement has therefore become blurred and, as observed by Backman *et al*. (2001: 454), this provides the opportunity for previously unrecognised synergies to be developed:

> Whether the motivation is economic or stewardship, organisational missions and strategies are beginning to coalesce around the idea of ecotourism, capitalising on public interest in the environment. Therefore the need for collaboration, cooperation and synergy among this multitude is as obvious as it will be challenging. In the past, economics have often run counter to protection and preservation interests. But ecotourism, perhaps for the first time, provides a feasible mechanism to align economic incentives with stewardship of the environment.

The specifics of the above argument apply to the Gold Coast situation to the extent that the natural environment is an integral part of this destination's tourism product. There are a range of potential synergies between the tourism sector and various avenues of economic development recognised in the Gold Coast's economic development strategy. Significantly, many of these synergies hinge on the potential of tourism development to enhance the lifestyle of residents.

Building a shared vision

The articulation of a shared vision among stakeholders was envisaged as being the initial and most critical step in the consultative process that would lead to the development of the Gold Coast's tourism strategy. In its simplest terms, a vision can be construed as a shared view on a preferred future. Alternatively, as described by Senge *et al.* (1994: 302), a vision can be construed as '...sense of shared purpose and destiny...', '...a picture of the future we want to create...that gives shape and direction to the organisation's future'.

The visioning exercise was critical in two respects. Firstly, a well designed visioning exercise had the potential to provide a 'circuit-breaker' and a 'call to action', to the extent that it was instrumental in galvanizing opinion on the need for a fundamentally different approach from that which had prevailed in the past to allow rejuvenation to occur.

Secondly, a well articulated vision that has been constructed in a manner that ensures it represents a consensus among primary stakeholders provides a focus for the strategic planning process and a vehicle for mobilising cooperative action. Here, the word 'cooperative' is used very deliberately as an alternative to 'coordinated' action. The former implies a group of equal stakeholders working together towards the same end, while the latter implies one party exerting control over others to ensure that all their activities contribute to a mutually agreed outcome. The distinction is subtle and, in reality, one cannot be achieved without the other. However, the emphasis on the equality of stakeholders in the achievement of mutually agreed outcome and the reciprocity implied by the word 'cooperation' makes this a more meaningful concept in this context. The nexus between the visioning process and action is fundamental, as implied in the following popular quote from Joel Barker (1992).

> A vision without action is merely dream. Action without vision just passes the time. Vision with action can change the world.

A vision provides a framework for choosing appropriate responses and for cooperative action. External events (including changes in government policy agendas at all levels, international developments and random disasters) have the potential to profoundly affect the competitiveness of the Gold Coast as a tourism destination, and thus the direction of tourism development. While we have little control over these events, a long-term shared perspective (a vision) is necessary for not only determining how we respond, but also for ensuring that we respond in a coordinated and effective way. Without a vision, we will become locked into the past. That is, an incremental approach, where the focus is on responding to immediate contingencies in a piecemeal fashion, leads us to a position where the options available for us to cope with longer-term eventualities are progressively reduced.

Like most elements of strategic analysis and planning, it might be said that the route taken in constructing a vision is as important as the destination. The meaningful engagement of the community, with industry stakeholders and relevant public sector agencies, in the development of a consensus on the directions of future development and the actions necessary for the preferred outcomes to be realised is an essential ingredient in the visioning process. Such engagement of stakeholders is essential if the vision that eventuates is to provide an accurate reflection of a truly shared position of all concerned and if it is to provide a relatively stable reference point for future action. The importance of this has been emphasised by Senge *et al.* (1994: 313):

> A vision is not really shared unless it has staying power and evolving life force that lasts for years, propelling people through a continuous cycle of action, learning and reflection.

The following comment by Mintzberg (2000: 209–210) provides a useful summary of the main point regarding the role of a vision and, in particular, it alludes to linkages with the learning organisation concept, which is explored further below:

> The visionary approach is a more flexible way to deal with an uncertain world. Vision sets the broad outlines of a strategy, while leaving the specific details to be worked out. In other words, the broad perspective may be deliberate but the specific position can emerge. So when the unexpected happens, assuming the vision is sufficiently robust, the organization can adapt – it learns. Certain change is thus easily accommodated. Of course, when even vision cannot cope, then the organization may have to revert to a pure learning approach – to experiment in the hope of capturing some basic message and converging behaviors on them.

Learning organisations and organisational change

The notion of learning organisations has been developed as a tool for assisting commercial organisations to adjust to change primarily in the North American context (Senge *et al.*, 1994). In one sense, a tourist destination represents a more complex situation, at least to the degree that it involves an amalgam of separate public and private sector organisations, along with a loose array of community-based interests and alliances, all pursuing separate agendas that both overlap and conflict with each other to varying degrees. However, as Senge *et al.* observe, these characteristics are not uncommon within large corporations and the art of developing a learning organisation approach involves reconciling the tensions, finding common ground for collective action and channelling rivalries into creative energy that benefits the organisation as a whole. It follows that elements of the learning organisation philosophy may be applicable to the development of a strategic approach to destination management.

As defined by Senge *et al.* (1994: 4), a learning organisation is one that is '...able to deal with the problems and opportunities of today, and invest in its capacity to embrace tomorrow, because its members are continually focused on enhancing and expanding their collective awareness and capabilities.' It would become integral to the planning and management process, rather than, as is too often the case, a marginal activity restricted to a few specialist researchers.

The introduction of the learning organisation approach to the Gold Coast setting required a fundamental shift in mindsets and organisational approaches in that setting. The Gold Coast had grown and flourished in a relatively benign regulatory regime, which had fostered a combative private enterprise mentality driven by market forces and a fiercely competitive business culture. Public sector engagement in aspects of tourism development had been minimal and regarded with suspicion by the business community. One of the consequences of this had been a policy and planning void, whereby the lack of a tourism agenda within the state and local government bureaucratic structures had meant that the tourism implications of various policy and infrastructure initiatives have not been adequately addressed. Despite this, the laissez-faire environment provided a fertile setting for a range of flamboyant entrepreneurs to introduce innovations that have rejuvenated the destination at various points in its history (Russell & Faulkner, 1999). However, the scale and complexity of tourism development in the region had reached a point where it was increasingly difficult for the actions of individual entrepreneurs to initiate major shifts in the fortunes of the destination as a whole. A more collaborative and cooperative approach, involving the private, public sector agencies and other stakeholder groups within the community, was necessary if the challenges of the future were to be effectively addressed. This implies that the Gold Coast's problem was essentially one of organisational change.

Like organisations in general, the Gold Coast can be envisaged as having evolved towards a point where internal rigidities associated with hierarchical structures, specialisations and demarcations have impeded internal communication, and the inertia of established values and approaches threaten to constrain responsiveness to changing conditions (Hurst, 1995). This makes the destination both less adaptive and more prone to disaster. In an observation that perhaps encapsulates the 'catch-22' predicament of many maturing destinations, Hurst (1995: 139) suggested that many organisations were caught by the 'renewal process paradox', whereby 'the change process cannot begin until the failure of the old order is manifest, but the process is likely to be more successful if it gets underway before too much damage is done.' Given the symptoms of stagnation evident in the Gold Coast case, as demonstrated in the analysis in earlier sections of this paper, it could be argued that 'the failure of the older order' was clearly manifest. While it may be overstating the case to suggest that too much damage has already been done to make the situation retrievable, it was certainly evident that any delay in the reassessment of future directions and approaches, such as that proposed in the GCV process, would make the eventual demise of the destination inevitable.

Scenarios and the art of strategic conversion

Visions can be construed as 'complexity reducers', which provide a common frame of reference for organising information. They provide the signpost for signals for navigating against a noisy background. Scenarios, on the other hand, are 'shared and agreed upon mental models of the external world...created as internally consistent and challenging descriptions of possible futures...' (van der Heijden, 1997: 5). They complement the visioning process through their value as a basis for exploring possible futures and the opportunity they provide for stakeholders to see the world through different lenses. Scenario-generating exercises help participants to see things they may not have otherwise been disposed to look for, thus dislodging them from established mindsets.

Scenario planning is distinct from the more traditional approaches to strategic planning by virtue of its more specific focus on ambiguity and uncertainty in the strategic issues being examined. The affinities of this approach to the learning organisation perspective are explicit in the following observation:

> The most fundamental aspect of introducing uncertainty into the strategic equation is that it turns planning for the future from a once-off episodic activity into an ongoing learning proposition. In a situation of uncertainty planning becomes learning and never stops. (van der Heijden, 1997: 7)

Recognising that we operate within a turbulent environment which makes our efforts to predict the future with any degree of certainty a futile endeavour, scenario planning instead aims to identify and consider multiple, equally plausible futures. Scenarios are helpful in assisting organisations to cope with future events in three ways. Firstly, they help organisations to understand the environment, and allow many decisions to be put into perspective through them being seen not so much as isolated events, but as part of a process of 'swings and roundabouts'. Secondly, they highlight the inherent uncertainty of the environment and, in the process, foster an appreciation of exposure to 'accidents' and undue risk. Finally, they help organisations 'to become more adaptable by expanding their mental models and thereby enhancing the perceptual capabilities needed to recognize unexpected events' (van der Heijden, 1997: 86).

To add one final clarification of the nature of scenarios, it is useful to consider the distinctions between scenarios and forecasting. Forecasting assumes that the future can be accurately predicted and is usually carried out be 'experts' who are detached from decision makers, whereas scenario planning is process oriented and accepts that uncertainties invariably restrict the extent to which the future can be predicted. But by involving decision-makers in the process, rather than the latter abdicating responsibility to detached experts, the planning process is more attuned to the risks and variety of possibilities involved. In short, scenario planning is more consistent with the type of informed decision-making identified with learning organisations.

The use of scenarios was incorporated into the GCV project to provide a set of 'what if' situations for stakeholder groups to consider in relation to their potential impact on the future movement of the region along the destination life cycle mode.

The Gold Coast Visioning (GCV) Project Approach

In order to ensure that the stagnation stage of the TALC did not become engrained in the Gold Coast region, the approach adopted in the GCV project involved a combination of the methods employed in traditional strategic planning with refinements involving the concepts of visioning, organisational learning and scenario-based strategic conversion. The approach adopted included the following components.

An 'audit' process involving an integrated series of research projects aimed at overviewing the current status of Gold Coast tourism in terms of social, economic (including tourism marketing) and environmental considerations has been carried out as 'front-end' inputs to the process.

- A survey of tourism industry stakeholders (Tourism Industry Barometer) was conducted to provide an indication of industry perceptions on the status of tourism development on the Gold Coast, individual visions of the future and preferred options for tourism development.
- A one-day futures workshop, involving representatives of key stakeholder groups, was planned with the aim of producing a consensus on likely future scenarios affecting the Gold Coast.
- A two-day workshop aimed at constructing the vision and strategy for the Gold Coast's tourism future was to be convened.

The above activities were carried out in five stages as identified in Figure 18.3. As the figure suggests, the approach involved a systematic examination of the Gold Coast situation at the time (Destination Audit); an analysis of the implications of this audit and the future prospects for tourism on the Gold Coast (Destination Barometer and Megatrends Analysis) and, finally, it culminated in the development of a shared vision for the future via the 'Visioning Workshop'. The last four of these steps are described in more detail in Table 18.3.

Outcomes

The Visioning Program produced a number of significant outcomes, known as the 'Visioning Statement' that linked the past, present and future position of the Gold Coast tourism industry. The generic outcomes of the process are highlighted in Table 18.4. Beginning with a historical overview of what had occurred within the region's tourism environment to date, the process was concluded with the formulation of an ultimate 'vision' of how the industry should progress in the future in order to ensure not only that rejuvenation of the destination continues, but also that the needs of both residents and tourists alike are managed in an optimal manner.

In terms of specific outcomes of the GCV Project, a series of reports were produced and disseminated to key stakeholders involved in the industry for consideration. A summary of the key issues raised in these documents is contained in Table 18.5.

Related Initiatives

The outcomes of two other initiatives that had a bearing on the examination of strategic directions for the Gold Coast tourism industry were also taken into account in the approach outlined above. These initiatives included the 1999 Edward de Bono Workshop organised by the Property Council of Australia's Gold Coast Chapter (PCAGC) and

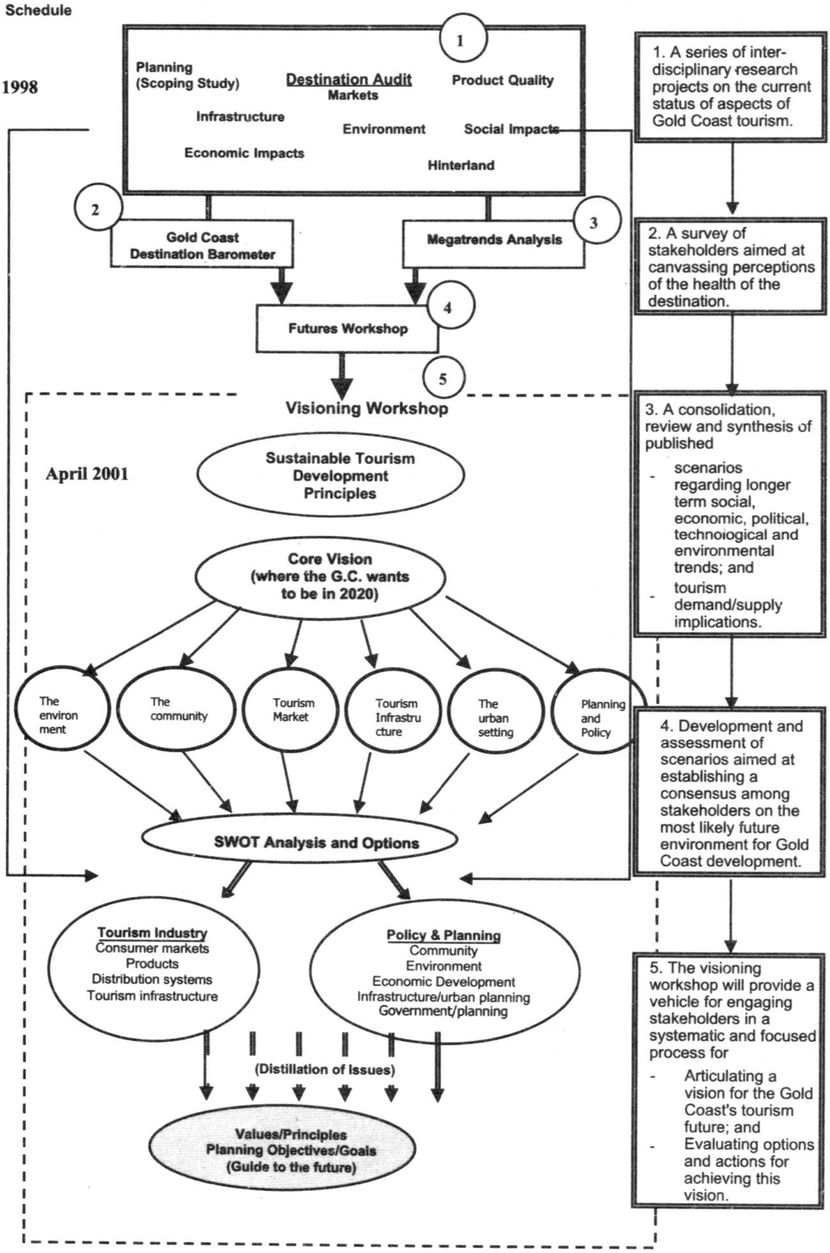

Figure 18.3 The Gold Coast Visioning approach
Source: Faulkner, 2002

Table 18.3 Method of the GCV Process

Phase	*Method*	*Objectives/desired outcomes*
1. Gold Coast Destination Barometer	Survey of key stakeholders aimed at gauging perceptions of the health of the destination in terms of: • Image and positioning. • Competitiveness. • Market trends. • Yields and profitability. • Aging and condition of infrastructure. • Community reactions.	• To encourage participants to reflect on the health of the destination and begin focusing on the issues that were eventually addressed in the workshops. • To highlight indicators of the Gold Coast's stagnation and thus reinforce the need for challenges confronting the destination to be addressed.
2. Mega-trends Analysis	Consolidation, review and synthesis of: • Scenarios regarding longer-term social, economic, political, technological and environmental trends; and • tourism demand and supply-side implications of these trends.	• To ensure that the development of scenarios and consideration of their tourism implications in the futures workshop were informed by analyses carried out elsewhere.
3. Futures Workshop	A one- or two-day workshop involving panel discussions on long-term trends in each dimension followed by break out groups aimed at constructing most likely scenarios and considering their tourism demand and supply side implications. Key issues covered include: a. Panel discussion on socioeconomic and political/policy (global and domestic) scenarios. b. Panel discussion on technological,	• Long-term scenarios regarding social, economic, political, technological and environmental trends at the macro level; • The general tourism implications of these trends. • A consensus on the most likely general, global and domestic scenarios on socioeconomic, technological, environmental and political/policy trends in 2020 and their tourism implications.

Table 18.3 (*Continued*)

Phase	***Method***	***Objectives/desired outcomes***
	environmental and urban/regional planning scenarios, followed by break-out groups and plenary session.	
4. Visioning Workshop	A two-day workshop aimed at construction of a vision for Gold Coast tourism in 2020. Key components of the workshop included: • A reiteration of the need for, and objectives of, the visioning process, with reference to the linkages between this and the previous workshop. • A guide to sustainable tourism development principles in the future; • Where do we want to be in 2020? • Future Scenarios Revisited. A briefing on the outcomes of the Futures Workshop. • Issues and actions. Key planning, policy and management issues emerging were addressed.	• A shared view among stakeholders on a preferred future for Gold coast tourism. • An appreciation of the importance of the project and an understanding of the approach among participants. • A draft core vision comprising a brief statement encapsulating the essential ingredients of the desired tourism future of the region. • To refocus participants' minds on the likely emerging environment in which the preferred future identified in the vision statement was to be achieved. • A synthesis of threats, challenges and opportunities affecting the achievement of the vision was produced. • A consensus view on key planning, policy and management issues associated with the vision and the actions required to achieve the vision.

Source: Faulkner, 2002

Table 18.4 Indicative format of the GCV Statement

Component	*Description*
Executive summary	A one-page outline indicating the purpose of the visioning process and summarising key outcomes produced by the process.
Introduction	A concise statement addressing the following points: • The history of the Gold Coast as a growing urban conurbation and tourist destination. • The current status of the Gold Coast as a tourist destination and place to live. • The challenges confronting the destination in terms of the achievement of sustainable tourism development objectives. • Why a vision is necessary. • The nature of, and approach to, constructing a vision. • A 'mud map' indicating the format and contents of the document.
The core vision and elements of the vision	A brief statement encapsulating the essential ingredients of the desired future of the region. This was supplemented by a series of more detailed statements, articulating principles and benchmarks for preferred outcomes in specific dimensions of tourism development: • The environment (ecological impacts). • The community (social impacts). • Tourism markets and visitor experiences (tourism demand). • The tourism sector (supply side development). • The urban environment (infrastructure and urban planning). • Governance and urban planning/policy frameworks.
Future scenarios and their implications for the Gold Coast	A summary of outcomes of the futures and SWOT analysis, structured in terms of the dimensions identified above: • Future scenarios. • SWOT analysis. • Core issues vis-à-vis the dimensions of the vision.

Table 18.4 (*Continued*)

Component	*Description*
Conclusion	The visioning exercise, and the documents that record its outcomes, aims to provide a framework for developing a tourism strategy for the region, rather than being a strategic plan in its own right. This document will therefore fall short of providing explicit guidelines for implementation. Within the conclusion, however, recommendations will be provided on how the visioning process might be carried forward to the development of the strategy.

Source: Faulkner, 2002

the Gold Coast City Council's (GCCC) Draft Economic Development Strategy (2000).

The de Bono Workshop

A workshop organised by the PCAGC in October 1999 engaged Edward de Bono to assist business leaders and other stakeholders to focus on issues associated with setting some strategic directions for the refurbishment and rejuvenation of the Gold Coast. Initially concerned primarily with the Surfers Paradise precinct of the Gold Coast, it was recognised that issues affecting the rejuvenation of Surfers Paradise could not be examined in isolation from the rest of the Gold Coast. A 'whole of Gold Coast' approach was therefore advocated, and it was also realised that this implied that a diverse range of stakeholders needed to be engaged in the process (The Property Council of Australia Gold Coast Chapter, 2000).

What was of particular interest to the process of averting the onset of the stagnation stage of the TALC model was the realisation of the need to counteract negative perceptions of the Surfers Paradise precinct through cooperation and education. Here it was recognised that the business community could play a lead role in this by 'adopting a broader all-encompassing view' and not allowing personal agendas to distract them from an approach that leads to benefits for the whole community. The remainder of the recommendations focused on the measures necessary to reinvigorate Surfers Paradise specifically and these generally amounted to the presentation of a case for additional local government support to strengthen the role of the public sector subsidised Surfers Paradise central management association.

Table 18.5 Core issues generated by GCV research projects

Research project	***Issues***
Issues, policy and Planning Audit (Scoping Study)	• A tourism policy and planning void exists on the Gold Coast (GC): the actions of the various (state and local) government and quasi-government (GC Tourism Bureau) agencies who have a role to play in tourism development are not well coordinated, and the tourism implications of their policy and planning agendas are not taken into account. • The ad hoc, incremental approach to tourism development of the past will not work in the future: the scale and complexity of tourism development in the region means that a more holistic, strategic approach is necessary in the future. • The region suffers from a major image and positioning problem in the domestic market in particular: this problem is compounded by the dominance of Surfers Paradise as a visual icon, and the perception of this precinct as 'glitzy' and deteriorating. • The lack of tourism industry involvement in environmental planning needs to be remedied: the natural assets of the region, encompassing the beaches, waterways and hinterland areas, remain as fundamental ingredients of the area's attractiveness. • A purpose-built convention centre is essential if the GC is to build on it natural advantages as a MICE destination and retain its pre-eminent position.
Market Audit	• While the GC has consistently exceeded national average growth rates in inbound tourist numbers over the last 15–20 years, its performance in the domestic market has been patchy: there have been periods where GC domestic tourism growth has both exceeded and lagged behind national levels. • The strength of the GC in the inbound market has been particularly attributable to its performance in Asian markets: with two-thirds of all international visitors coming from Asian countries, however, the vulnerability of the Gold Coast to potentially crippling impacts of external shocks was highlighted during the Asian financial crisis. • Far North Queensland (FNQ) and Sydney are the main competitors in the inbound market, while Victoria, FNQ and, to a lesser extent, the ACT, have been the main competitors in the domestic market.

Table 18.5 (*Continued*)

Research project	***Issues***
	• The core attractions of the GC revolve around four elements: beaches/relaxation; theme parks/ excitement; nightlife/action; and nature and wildlife. The main market segments associated with these attractions are families, midlife and older couples and younger singles/couples. • The GC has consistently performed well in the young families and younger solos markets, but its younger and older couples markets have stagnated.
Infrastructure Audit	• There is an 'infrastructure time-bomb' on the GC, with there being a number of potential black spots arising from concentrations of high-rise accommodation of similar age: refurbishment or replacement of buildings in these areas will be inhibited by mixed ownership and associated unrealistic expectations regarding capital appreciation. • There is a substantial high-volume, low-yield ('profit-less volume') problem in GC accommodation infrastructure: this has emerged as a consequence of the over-reliance upon inclusive tour markets and the erosion of margins associated with this. • An unresolved question concerns the extent to which a large holiday flat/unit rental sector exacerbates or ameliorates this problem.
Product Quality Audit	• Satisfaction levels among visitors regarding the quality of services and experiences associated with the GC's accommodation, theme parks, restaurants and beaches are generally high. • The main negative perception among visitors concerns value for money from theme parks. • The major danger for the GC regarding service quality is the prospect of high satisfaction levels encouraging complacency: regular monitoring of satisfaction levels is essential so that lapses in the quality of services can be promptly detected and remedied, while the competitiveness of the environment necessitates a more systematic approach to the continuous improvement of services in all areas.

Table 18.5 (*Continued*)

Research project	***Issues***
Social Impacts Audit (preliminary)	• GC residents are generally positively disposed towards tourism and its impact on the community: tourism is seen to have a positive effect on the economy, job opportunities lifestyle and aspects of amenity, although costs associated with noise and congestion are also recognised. • At the aggregate level, perceptions about the impacts of tourism do not appear to vary among major demographic groups: older residents appear to be no more or less vulnerable to negative impacts of tourism and, indeed, appear to benefit from the same features of the GC that make it an appealing destination for visitors. • Supplementary work needs to be carried out to canvas resident reactions to alternative approaches to tourism development in the future and the impacts of tourism in specific situations, such as in areas where permanent resident and visitor accommodation are integrated.

Source: Faulkner, 2002

Draft Gold Coast 2010: Economic Development Strategy

This document also reinforced the theme that the Gold Coast was at 'the cross-roads', with the vulnerability of the region associated with its dependence on the narrow economic base provided by tourism and construction being emphasised (Gold Coast City Council, 2000).

The strategy document acknowledged the inescapable – that is, whether we like it or not, tourism would have a continuing and significant role in the economy. However, the report appeared to imply this was a liability, rather than a potential strength. That is, the dominance of tourism (and the associated sunbelt migration phenomenon) may provide some resistance to the diversification agenda to the extent, for instance, that this produces employment and demographic patterns that are not consistent with the development of 'clever', 'new-age' industries. Reference was made to the Gold Coast as a city of 'experiences', but it did not give sufficient emphasis to this theme. It is a distinctive feature of the Gold Coast that separates it from a myriad of other regions that are probably putting together similar arguments for the development of a knowledge-based focus for regional development at this time, and would, therefore, serve as a useful platform from which to launch the destination into the rejuvenation phase of the TALC model.

Table 18.6 Tourism synergies associated with key industry strategies identified in the draft economic strategy

Key industry strategy	*Tourism synergies*
Communication and information	• Lifestyle implications of tourism's enhancement of leisure opportunities have the potential to play a role in locational decisions of IT firms/ entrepreneurs.
Education and training	• Educational tourism: educational services attract international students who, with visiting family members, also become tourists. • Lifestyle factors in student choice: the attractiveness of the Gold Coast as a tourist destination also makes this region an attractive place to live while studying. • Alumni networks: former international students become ambassadors for Gold Coast tourism and the Gold Coast generally upon their return home. • Tourism management and planning research capabilities of the CRC and Griffith University are elements of the 'knowledge industry' development
Environmental	• Adoption of 'Green Globe' as a framework for benchmarking tourism-related environmental management on the Gold Coast, along with the identification of this concept with the CRC for Sustainable Tourism, provides an opportunity for the Gold Coast to promote both its environmental management technical capabilities abroad and its environmental tourism destination assets. • A stringent environmental management regime is essential for protecting environmental assets that are central to the region's sustainability as a tourist destination.
Film and interactive media	• Film and interactive media applications to entertainment technology underpin the continual renewal of theme parks such as Movieworld. • Reinforcement of the leisure theme, which is central to the Gold coast's image as a tourist destination.
Food, beverage and aquaculture	• Restaurants and fine food are essential elements of the range of services that make the Gold Coast an attractive destination. • There are potential synergies between the marketing of the Gold Coast as a tourist destination and the marketing of its food products.

Table 18.6 (*Continued*)

Key industry strategy	*Tourism synergies*
Health and medical	• There are tourism sector spin-offs from the provision of medical services to international markets (families accompanying patients and patients themselves during recuperation may engage in tourist activities). • For the reasons alluded to in the previous point the Gold Coast's attractiveness as a tourist destination can give its medical providers a competitive edge in international markets.
Marine	• The marine environment constitutes a major tourism asset in the area and potential synergies exist between the marketing of pleasure craft manufactured in the area and the recreational boating opportunities available to tourists. • The proposed cruise shipping terminal would provide access to an additional tourism market.
Urban development	• Urban development capabilities will support the enhancement of existing tourism infrastructure and the construction of new quality infrastructure, such as resorts, marinas, etc.

Source: Faulkner, 2002

There are many synergies between tourism and the key industry strategies identified in the report. Some examples are provided in Table 18.6, which are also useful in analysing the prospect of rejuvenation and growth of the tourism industry in the region.

Conclusion

As with any industry, a tourism destination must keep pace with the growing pressures of increasing competition for the tourists' attention and, as a result, must continually reassess its position and ensure that sufficient change and improvement takes place to maintain its attraction to key markets. It must also maintain a quality of life for its local resident population which is not hindered by further tourism growth. The ultimate challenge, faced by a mature destination such as the Gold Coast, is to avoid becoming too locked into strategies used in the past to develop tourism within the region. Change and new directions are often required to ensure that stagnation does not occur and that the area follows the rejuvenation path of the TALC model.

In the Gold Coast setting, the need for a more focused strategic approach to destination management and planning is accentuated by a history that has been distinctively ad hoc and piecemeal. At the outset of the GCV Program, many of the key indicators suggested the destination may have already entered the stagnation phase. This chapter has provided an example, based on the GCV Program, of how an agreement on a shared vision among stakeholders represents the first step towards developing a strategy for rejuvenating the destination. In this context, the relevant stakeholders were broadly defined to include tourism and other businesses, industry organisations, public sector agencies at the local and state government levels, and representatives of the resident community. Such a broad spectrum of involvement reflects the necessity of a holistic approach, which recognises that social and environmental considerations warrant equal consideration with the economic dimension in the mapping of a course toward a sustainable tourism future.

The difficulties apparent in rejuvenating a mature tourist destination such as the Gold Coast were highlighted through the GCV Project. Growth and continual change to ensure the destination meets the ever-changing needs of both visitors and residents cannot be achieved merely by adding new attractions or increasing marketing exposure for the destination. The GCV Project was founded on the acknowledgement that a shared vision had to be achieved by industry stakeholders including tourism developers, industry managers, government departments involved in the region and local residents of the region. The process of developing the vision was instrumental in developing an informed and considered dialogue among stakeholders, to such an extent that the destination will represent not only a consensus among this group, but also it will reflect a thorough and rigorous analysis of the issues. Such

Table 18.7 Why a vision and a plan are so necessary for Gold Coast tourism

- By creating a more structured, strategically focused and shared framework for individual enterprises and organisations to operate within, we can ensure that decision makers at all levels take longer-term considerations into account in their day-by-day decisions.
- A modest up-front investment in planning avoids the need to think through every crisis situation from scratch. It creates a readiness for the unexpected.
- Appropriate planning facilitates the transition from individual insights to collective/institutional action.
- Well developed planning systems create an institutional learning and memory system.
- Reduce the prospects of repeating past mistakes and/or reinventing the wheel.

Based on van der Heijden, 1997

support and involvement of a wide range of stakeholders is essential to ensuring the path taken to rejuvenation of the destination is not only agreed upon, but is the ultimate vision towards which those involved in the community will work towards achieving.

The Visioning exercise itself was used as a catalyst for bringing about the permanent changes in the structure of the destination planning and management process that were necessary for the Gold Coast to become a 'learning organisation' at the destination level. That is, the visioning project was instrumental in establishing a systematic planning regime that was supported by a strong research base and a rigorous evaluation system. Such a regime will underpin the institutional learning process and memory that is so essential for creative adaptation to the challenges of the future and reducing the prospect of repeating past mistakes or reinventing the wheel (van der Heijden, 1997).

Strategies for rejuvenation of tourism in the Gold Coast region were developed in a strategic and comprehensive manner through the GCV Project. The integration of sustainable tourism principles into the shared vision for the future direction of the industry was the lynchpin to the future success of the region's tourism potential. Rejuvenation of the destination life cycle was the ultimate goal, and, as summarised in Table 18.7, the creation of a suitable industry 'vision' was the key to developing a platform from which this objective can be pursued.

Part 6
Conclusion

RICHARD W. BUTLER

One of the common problems with edited books is that there is often no final chapter that provides a conclusion to the often widely differing contributions from the set of authors. It had been my intention to write such a chapter for this volume to avoid that problem. It is not an easy task, as, having written the links to the sections, it would have been redundant to make similar summarising comments in the conclusions. Given that the focus of this volume is on the application and modification of the TALC as demonstrated in the previous chapters, it would not have been appropriate either to write a general conclusion to the TALC and therein discuss some of its relevance for the future in terms of conceptual development. That is dealt with in the final chapter to the other volume that deals with theories and concepts relating to the TALC, particularly with respect to the nature of future development in tourism and its implications for destinations.

The preceding chapters have provided some excellent examples of the settings in which the TALC has been applied, and some of the ways in which it has been modified to better fit specific destinations and their unique situations. Clearly no destination is exactly the same as another, despite the best efforts of many tour companies, their marketing agencies and developers. Each one represents a unique mix of geography, politics, economics and ethnography at least, along with elements such as individual behaviour and chance. To model the infinite variety of pathways that development can take is unrealistic except at a general level, and that is what the TALC attempted to do. It would be amazing, indeed impossible, to produce a 'one size fits all' practical model, but it may be possible to produce such a conceptual model. Whether the TALC really fits each and every destination to a reasonable and acceptable degree is yet to be determined, and probably never will be. It does remain intuitively appropriate and after the large number of applications discussed earlier in this book in the specific chapters, it still appears to be generally accurate. Refinements which make the fit better in one location may make it worse in another, and whenever trying to fit a line to data, compromise has to be made to obtain the best overall fit. It is clear that more than one cycle may be in operation at any one time in many destinations, as most locations cater to more than one market segment. The TALC is an attempt to model the overall pattern and process of development for destinations and the existence of multiple cycles does not invalidate that. In the future, further application and subsequent modification of the TALC may result in a more accurate and more widely applicable curve, a more precisely defined set of stages and a better explained process of development for destinations. At the end however, they are still products and will have a pattern of development and ultimately decline. The most we can do is intervene and manage appropriately in order to maximise the successful period of operation for residents and visitors.

In looking for a chapter, therefore, to close this volume, the solution emerged fortuitously. Those who have read his works, and particularly those who have heard Brian Wheeller present his views on tourism development and on rock and roll in person, will realise that it is next to impossible to follow him at a podium or in a volume (and to follow Elvis Presley is something which no-one has dared try to do since 1954). In his chapter Wheeller takes the unlikely pairing of Elvis Presley and sustainable tourism and manages to make sense of their seemingly impossible relationship in the context of the TALC. He argues effectively that what may seem like deterioration and reduced appeal to one 'market' is not always that to all markets. Perhaps more importantly, he links spatial location and stage of development in the context of ecolodges that are likened to the King of Rock and Roll. He also focuses, unlike most of the other authors, on the analogy of the TALC to the population life cycle of wildlife, again, with comparisons to Presley. Apart from containing many images that are poignant and relevant to those of us who grew up with real rock and roll, it is both a perceptive and thought-provoking chapter with which to end this volume.

Chapter 19

The King is Dead. Long Live the Product: Elvis, Authenticity, Sustainability and the Product Life Cycle

BRIAN WHEELLER

Introduction

In the welter of references to, and articles on, Butler's Tourist Area Life Cycle model (TALC) there has, to my knowledge at least, been no mention of Elvis Presley. So far.

Clearly, there are a number of ways Elvis, and the Elvis phenomenon, can be seen as a part of tourism and the tourist industry – manifesting, most obviously, as a generator of tourism trips. Evidenced in the pilgrimages to Graceland, to locations featured in his dubious backlog of films, even to Prestwick Airport in West Scotland, site of Elvis's only – recent sightings apart – visit to the UK, there can be no doubt that Elvis is big tourism business. Appearing regularly in the travel pages of contemporary newspapers and magazines, he remains a huge attraction – Graceland is second only to the White House for tourist visits to US Historic Places (Davis, 1997).

But there are other, somewhat more tenuous, links between Elvis and tourism. It is these that are, perhaps ambitiously, suggested and explored in this chapter. Just how he fits in with the TALC model might at first sight seem tangential – and with ecolodges, obtuse. And yet 'sustainable' tourism developments in the Amazon jungle seem to me an admittedly quirky, yet appropriate, environment in which to locate Elvis. The parallels drawn in this chapter then, call for considerable flexibility and (vivid?) imagination on the part of the reader. What is more, although traditionally set in a linear/temporal, evolutionary framework, the intention here is to tentatively explore a spatial dimension to the life cycle concept. It is recognised that adopting a two-tier analytical framework on which to hang unconventional empiricism, further complicates the picture. Hopefully, however, it is considered neither irreverent nor irrelevant, but simply seen as an attempt at an unorthodox take on the TALC.

Of the two fundamental supports underpinning Butler's model, the concept of the life cycle of animal species in the wild appears to be relatively unexplored (although discussed earlier in this volume, and by Coles, and Ravenscroft & Hjihambi, other volume; editor's comment). Relative that is, to the considerable attention afforded the other pillar – namely the concept of the life cycle of the product. If the sheer volume of subsequent written material on the subject reflects the relative importance of the two founding concepts, one is left with the suggestion of somewhat uneven foundations and (possibly) an unbalanced structure. However, I suspect, it could simply be the result of unbalanced critique rather than lop-sided edifice.

Going some way to addressing this imbalance, initial attention is focused here on the animal/nature perspective – though clearly the notion of 'the product' remains crucial to any discussion or, indeed, analysis. Elvis, it could be argued, bridges these two concepts. He was the wild animal that became the managed, domesticated, cultivated product. He metamorphosed from a feral, wild cat – a hip, hep, hell cat – to the big, flabby, neutered pet pussy cat of his later years. His rise, decline – from erotic to neurotic, demise and then subsequent rejuvenation (resurrection might be more apposite here) mirrors, and serves as metaphor for, the well researched phases of the resort life cycle.

Ecolodges and The Jungle Cycle

Given some poetic licence, Butler's reference to 'the life cycle of animal species in the wild' (Butler, 2000: 288) could be interpreted loosely and widely (though not necessarily wisely) to embrace all species including man in the wild. Now, it would seem, modern man trapped in the 'urban jungle' yearns, ostensibly at least, to escape from civilisation by going back to nature and experiencing the wild.

Where better to engage with nature at its most sublime, and encounter wild animals, than the jungle? And where more evocative than the mythical Amazon jungle? Fabled for its golden roofed opera house, Manaus, the city in the jungle, is the tourist gateway into the Amazon. Once there, tourists partake to varying degrees in the jungle experience. In the mid 1990s I was afforded the wonderful opportunity and experience of several field study visits to the Amazon to explore the developing eco-lodge phenomenon. Somewhat surprisingly it was there, during those forays into the jungle, that the relationships and parallels between Elvis, ecotourism, sustainability and the life cycle first struck me – as did the relevance of incorporating a linked spatial/temporal perspective to the analysis.

To establish a sequential profile of change, the tendency is to view the resort development through a linear time frame. To actually achieve this we mentally, and instantaneously, leap back – usually to the time when the resort was created/born – and begin our analysis there and then. Tracing, as we do, the resort's progress from its inception, we move to the present day and on to predictions of future options. When we 'read' the resultant graph, our eyes glide from left to right, taking in and absorbing chronologically the life cycle from birth – youth – maturity – old age; from A → B → C etc. Although how we leave the present and arrive mentally at the birth of the resort is ignored and may be of more significance than we think, once there at the origin, the process, and our analysis, appears to flow naturally and chronologically.

While travelling, against the current, back in time up the Amazon (more precisely, the tributary River Negro), I experienced this process in reverse. The 40-hour boat trip (in effect the often overlooked, neglected and, for me up until then, instantaneous, 'leap back' stage of the TALC) furnished me with time for literal – and littoral – reflection. Time to reflect on the passing of time, of, for example, the realisation of distant childhood dreams of the jungle. But only now venturing there (both childhood and jungle) from the vantage – or disadvantage – of middle age. And time to realise that the subjectivity inherent in where one is in terms of one's own personal life cycle must surely have some relevance to any analysis one attempts.

It was this journey up the river from Manaus that made me aware of going back in time. This spatial/temporal dimension was later reinforced when reading Winchester's *The River at the Centre of the World. A Journey up the Yangtze, and Back in Chinese Time.* 'The Yangtze flows for 4,000 miles from the pristine glaciers of the pre-industrial Tibetan plateau to the polluted, extended mouth in Shanghai. As it flows it traces China's history' (Winchester, 1997: 17). A graphic account of journeying up the Yangtze (a slow boat in China?), as the title suggests travelling upstream from Shanghai was to Winchester, searching for China's heart and soul, like retreating from civilisation – like going back in time. Similarly in the Amazon, the further the distance up river by boat from Manaus then, generally speaking, the wilder, the more primeval the environment/ambience. This, in turn, is reflected in the 'nature' of the ecolodge situated on the banks. The further up river they are then, as a rough indicator, the more 'primitive' the ecolodge, and concomitantly the more natural, the more supposedly authentic the visitor experience. Conversely, those lodges in close proximity to Manaus offer the tourist a safer, sanitised environmental bubble. Generally speaking then, the distance from the tourist gateway influences/determines at what stage each ecolodge is at in terms of the overall life cycle of the generic Eco-Lodge.

To me, each successive individual ecolodge I encountered on my journey up river epitomised a different stage in the life cycle of the still growing and evolving generic Eco-Lodge. Logistically the picture unfurled in reverse. The isolation of the ecolodges in the Amazon makes it possible to establish their respective characteristics in a cross-sectional analysis and to locate their comparative position in the overall life cycle of the Eco-Lodge – as opposed to a conventional time-series analysis of an individual resort. Different stages of the product life cycle can, in these circumstances, be determined therefore not by tracing the life cycle of one single 'resort'/product over time but rather by identifying at what stage of the generic life cycle model the particular lodge is at. Here space/distance represent time. Consequently we can view each individual ecolodge as a manifestation of a different life cycle phase, in this case chronicling the process in reverse sequence from the luxurious to the primitive.

For this purpose, the Ariau Tower, situated approximately three hours by boat from Manaus, serves as an example of the lodge where ecotourists are pampered, in a protected environment offering the relative luxuries of air-conditioning, swimming pool and, perhaps the ultimate convenience, flush toilets. At the other end of the spectrum, for those prepared to penetrate further in their quest for the authentic, is the small Xixuau Nature Reserve. This basic ecolodge, bereft of creature comforts, is some 40 hours by boat from Manaus. Put rather simplistically, the sizeable Ariau Tower was catering for the mass ecotourist, the Xixuau for the would-be intrepid traveller.

The Life Cycle from Memphis to Las Vegas

Now superimpose on this profile Elvis's earthly life cycle, from youth to premature death at 42. The Xixuau reserve then equates to the raw teen idol Elvis circa 1956 and the Ariau tower to the commodified, bloated, idle Elvis of later years.

Distanced from civilisation, the wildness of the Xixuau lodge – its primitive, unpretentious, no frills, natural authenticity – represents the unconstructed Elvis from his early days. Aptly monikered 'King of the Cats', he was then both the Lion and Loin King. Roar/raw sex. Via the racially slurred, nastily labelled 'jungle music' of rock'n'roll (itself jazz terminology for sex) he brought black music to a white audience – the dark, the dangerous and the forbidden. Effortlessly mimicking the 'primitive', King not by birthright but by revolution, he brought rebellion. And he was sex, animal sex. The impact was cataclysmic. 'Elvis was electric, when he sang "Turn me Loose" that was the feeling. And he spat out his songs and shook and murmured with the bottled up emotion we felt. When he moved we knew it was sex. Rock'n'roll was a euphemism for sex, but not the girl next door. We wanted to fuck the world' (Gosling, 1980: 39) This Elvis was not for the fainthearted.

But already there were problems. How to maintain, and sustain, the momentum of success? 'By 1958, Elvis had ruled for two years solid ... He had racked up twenty world-wide million sellers. Still, he had some long term problems. He was already twenty three, he could not go on being a teen idol for ever. The difficulty was how to turn him from an adolescent rebel into a respectable established figure ...' (Cohn, 1973: 26).

His manager, the enigmatic impresario, Colonel Parker, had the answer 'The King of the Cats' was to be emasculated, tamed and domesticated: turned from beast to cuddly toy. Initially, Elvis seemingly acquiesced in this transition. 'Put a chain around my neck and lead me anywhere' (Mann & Lowe, 1956) proved painfully prophetic. 'I don't want to be your tiger, cos tigers play too rough. I don't want to be your lion, cos lions aren't the sort your lovin' of – I just want to be your teddy bear.' (Mann & Lowe, 1956). The lyrics say it all.

Already the wheels had been set in motion. Elvis had moved from Sun Records to RCA, from specialist to mainstream; from small to mass market, from local to national to international. Moulded to take full advantage of market opportunities, Elvis was stage managed.

Some might see Elvis's commodification and concomitant democratisation as a positive, not negative evolution/development – simultaneously becoming more acceptable and accessible to a far wider audience. To others though, the taming of the wild, dangerous Elvis, his sanitisation and commodification marked the beginning of the end. Are there specific pivotal moments to which decline can be attributed? Or, being evolutionary, is the process slow and defining moment indecipherable? For John Lennon it was Elvis joining the army, and the haircut; for Gambacini it was the contrived television appearance where Elvis, in tuxedo, sang 'Hound Dog' to a lugubrious Basset hound (Gambacini, 2002). To them the 'true', 'authentic' Elvis has been irretrievably lost. This is assuming that there was such a thing in the first place. But what was the 'real' Elvis, and the 'authentic' Elvis experience? At his wildest while performing, apparently off stage he was just a Bible reading country boy from the backwoods who loved his mother. Frontstage–backstage authenticity epitomised? (A perfect paradigm for a cross-sectional analysis.) So was the 'real' Elvis the one performing on stage or was it the shy, polite Elvis backstage?

To find out, Dunk (2002: 63), in his newspaper article 'Discovering the real Elvis in folksy Tupelo' suggests distancing yourself from the gaudy Graceland and commercialisation of the big city, and going (backwards?) to the backwoods to discover the home-spun country boy – his private persona.

Even on stage though, things were not necessarily all they seemed. Decoding early Elvis appearances, Cohn believes '... it was sex in a vacuum. He looked dangerous but ultimately he was safe and clean. That is what young girls have always wanted from their idols, an illusion of danger, and Elvis brought a new thrill of semi-reality to the game' (Cohn, 1973: 26). The girls in the audience were uninhibited, shouting, screaming, fainting, whatever, while Elvis was performing on stage because that precisely was where he was – on stage. There was always a safety belt because he was unreachable, unreal and nothing could actually happen.

From Natural to Comfortable

The audience desires excitement and danger, but only from afar. Like viewing caged creatures in the zoo, or perhaps a tamed circus act. Or, from the safely strapped sanctuary of a Land Rover, the 'wild', exotic animals at a safari park. While fostering our delusion of wanting the authentic, in reality we much prefer a sanitised, safe and commodified version of nature – the staging of the wild.

So too with tourism. According to Dunn (1998: 38), 'MacCannell (1976) draws on Goffman's (1959) recognition of the division between public and private to suggest that tourists seek out the authentic in the private back regions in places which they visit' (Shades of the 'real' jungle adventure of the Xixuau compared with the staged Ariau Tower experience). He continues 'Much of MacCannell's *The Tourist* is concerned with deliberate staging of authenticity and whether tourists are in a position to differentiate between staged and actual' (Dunn, 1998: 38).

With the ecolodge, the jungle adventure is experienced from the safety of the environmental bubble. Even at the edge, as tourist/travellers in the most 'authentic' ecolodge we, of course, don't experience the 'true' experience of the wild. We are protected, cocooned. We have the safety (and mosquito) net of Mosiguard and malaria tablets, our purified water tablets. We have our tampons and suntan lotion. And our indefatigable illusion/delusion of being at one with nature.

Further down river, in close proximity to the tourist gateway, we have the 'staged authenticity', the sham experience of the Ariau tower, the commodified ecolodge 'hotel', representing the kitsch, Graceland Elvis of the mid 1970s. Pseudo-ecotourists cosseted in the comfort zone of the Ariau tower lounge; Elvis, corseted, lounge lizarding in the jungle room at Graceland.

Certainly, the décor of this jungle room is more pseudo experience than real. Graceland is, in effect, the mummification of 1970s garish Elvis (should that be mummyfication? He did, after all, originally purchase Graceland partly for his adored, and adoring mother, Gladys). Equally, it could be argued, by that time Elvis had himself become a pseudo-experience. A far cry from his own younger self, he was reliant on artificial stimulants and drugs to generate the energy and vitality that in his youth had come naturally to him – a contrived effort to maintain his younger unspoiled, uncultivated persona, to prolong his success and avert decline. When exactly did Elvis become the first Elvis impersonator? And which of them was 'real'?

Not easy. As Harry Chapin says, 'Reality is only just a word' (Chapin, 1976). Adopting a time series rather than cross-sectional perspective, should we be looking at a youthful Elvis or the Elvis approaching middle age? Both were 'real' and both had their own frontstage/backstage personas. Latter day impersonators of Elvis usually opt for mimicking his rhinestoned, jump suited days/daze. Yet the purists unequivocally see the early Elvis, before he was corrupted by commodification, as being the 'real', 'authentic' Elvis. Ironically though, it was this early Elvis that was seen by many as a, if not the, corrupting influence – more the devil incarnate than in disguise. In much the same way, to aficionados of travel, the traveller and the travel experience are held in high esteem, above reproach, whereas the tourist and mass tourism are worthy of only ridicule and scorn. But isn't the very same traveller the vanguard of the tourist, the harbinger of change/decline? Isn't there a familiar inevitable process – that inextricably links conspicuous consumption (Veblen, 1970), successive class intrusion (Pearce, 1982) and the pleasure periphery (Turner & Ash, 1975)? And, at the macrolevel, isn't tourism surely beyond coordinated management (Wheeller, 1991)?

However, it would appear that (at the microlevel?) Butler is more positive – if only in the sense that he believes management can avert the otherwise inevitable decline. To Butler, the process of development, unless managed appropriately, is invariably linked with decline. In order to stave off deterioration he calls for 'responsibility and control over development' (Butler, 2000: 294) and consequently views management as the means of sustaining the product and ensuring its long-term survival. This seems optimistic. To me, too optimistic. It calls, on the part of management, for the replacement of short-term profit maximisation blinkers by unimpeded vision, imagination, integrity and compassion. (However, one might argue that the Rolling Stones have survived four decades as the greatest rock and roll group in the world through 'sustainable change' and still sound as good on stage as in the 1960s, so perhaps I am not being too optimistic, editor's comment).

Certainly with Elvis, the role of management seemed somewhat dubious, less altruistic. Parker had control, but whether he matched this with responsibility is another matter. Lacking in integrity, his prime agenda appears to have been procurement of maximum cash flow. Short-term this managerial approach had paid dividends. Mid-term, fuelled by industrial quantities of drugs, gluttony and indolence, Elvis's decline was exacerbated further by those perhaps initially responsible. First by rapacious management,

> If he had held control of his own life, he might have chosen to lock himself away in Graceland and never come out again. That wasn't an option. Tom Parker was a compulsive gambler and needed Elvis to keep working. So the King was dispatched to Vegas again, and then on tour, zig-zag-ing across America, with ever decreasing breaks, until he finally imploded. (Cohn, 2002: 23)

And then secondly by leeching friends. Desperate to sustain their milch cow, his immediate 'friends' – whose sobriquet the 'Memphis Mafia' seems so apposite – fed him a potent cocktail of drugs. Rejuvenation/regeneration at all costs. Rather than taking care of Elvis, their motto 'Taking care of Business', attested to their priorities and true loyalties.

This potent cocktail progressively took its toll. Elvis the Pelvis became Elvis the Product. The cost? Elvis the Person. Local boy made god, his fall from grace was one of tragic proportions. 'It is a sad and salutary tale: the beautiful prince, kissed by Fate, who turned into a toad' (Melly, 2002: 15). But as in all true tragedies it was one of overwhelming irony. Because of course, long term for the Elvis phenomenon death proved the ultimate career move. Elvis the idle idol becomes Elvis the icon.

Conclusion

Does it matter if the product 'deteriorates' and is 'ruined' in the process? If the prince turns into a toad? If the proverbial goose is cooked? As sustenance to the masses, maybe it is easier to digest that way. The venerated golden goose may, after all, be a dispensable luxury. While the product undergoes physical decline and decay, the assumption that the utility derived simultaneously declines seems a little doubtful. Individual utility might, or might not, decline. But given the increased accessibility to, and acceptance of, the product by a wider (less discerning?) market, then even though the product deteriorates, the aggregate pleasure/utility may very well increase.

Simple common sense – surely? But maybe, in a sense, simply because it is 'common' it is conveniently ignored, indeed eschewed, by the 'sophisticated'. We need only look at the huge tourist numbers to Las Vegas, Niagara or the Blackpools of the world to realise this. Comparing these figures with visitor numbers to the niche, ecodestinations of say, Costa Rica and Belize, confirms the fact that despite its prominence in tourism academic research, and gushing rhetoric from politicians and the tourism industry, eco/sustainable tourism is still only a small, very minor segment of the overall tourism market. Like it or not, mass tourism demand reigns supreme. When it suits, the 'informed', the 'educated', the 'sophisticated' again choose to ignore this too.

And so with Elvis. Because of, rather than despite, commodification and 'inauthenticity', the number seeing the King – live or on film – in the

1960s and 1970s far exceeded the rock'n'roll aficionados of his mid-1950s, early 'authentic' years. What to some constituted Elvis's decline to others was, perversely, the very reason for his continued success. His transition from rebel outsider to mainstream good guy and the subsequent pathos of the ultimately sad, suffering tragic hero ensured his enduring popularity – albeit with an (arguably) less discerning market. Beauty is in the eye of the beholder – what to some is ugly and degenerate to others appeals. Content with kitsch, for many this is beauty.

Pilgrims to Graceland:

> are not the cool or the hip. Like Elvis himself, they come from the great amorphous white millions, who scuffle to get by, who blunder through lives filled with mess and waste and odd moments of joy, untouched by changing fashion. Small wonder Elvis is their once and future king. They love him, not in spite of his excesses and his grotesque end, but in large part because of them. He suffered so much. He is their martyr. (Cohn, 2002: 23)

And this is the conundrum possibly at the heart of the life cycle/ sustainability model – Is (perceived) deterioration in quality necessarily synonymous with decline?

To some – often the pretentious and condescending – be they academic experts, pseudo-travellers or music connoisseurs, the answer invariable is 'yes'. But the majority – the mass market – maybe see things from a different, less privileged, more prosaic angle. To them, the supposed decline may appear merely as a shift in focus, a change that brings the product within their economic and cultural compass. Happily wrapped in their safety blanket, it is suggested here that many don't feel the need or even want to see beneath the surface, beyond the immediate – particularly if that necessitates any potential discomfort or danger. They prefer the staged to the actual, the superficial to the real.

Similarly, with the ecolodges. While changes to facilities may make the product more attractive to the wider market, do they enhance the jungle experience? The introduction of air-conditioning dilutes the experience of the wild but simultaneously makes it more bearable and, therefore, acceptable to more tourists – who without the decadence of incongruous luxury would not be prepared to experience the jungle at all. And, of course, because it maintains cash flow, the modification is, in a sense, 'sustainable' (Wheeller, 1994). So changes determined by market forces/ entrepreneurial intervention do not necessarily enhance the soul of the product – indeed they may remove the essence, the very heart. But does it really matter as long as it keeps the customer satisfied? The supposedly progressively less discerning customer, that is.

The King is Dead. Long Live the Product.

References

Abernatthy, W. and Utterback, J. (1978) Patterns of industrial innovation. *Technology Review* 80, 41–47.

Agarwal, S. (1994) The resort cycle revisited: Implications for resorts. In C.P. Cooper and A. Lockwood (eds) *Progress in Tourism, Recreation and Hospitality Management* (Vol.5, pp. 194–208). Chichester: Wiley.

Agarwal, S. (1997) The resort cycle and seaside tourism: An assessment of its applicability and validity. *Tourism Management* 18 (3), 65–73.

Agarwal, S. (1998) Reply – What is new with the resort cycle? *Tourism Management* 19 (2), 181–182.

Agarwal, S. (1999) Restructuring and local economic development: Implications for seaside resort regeneration in South West Britain. *Tourism Management* 20 (5), 511–522.

Agarwal, S. (2002) Restructuring seaside tourism. The resort life-cycle. *Annals of Tourism Research* 29 (1), 25–55.

Aglietta, M. (1979) *A Theory of Capitalist Regulation*. London: New Left Books.

Aiken, K.G. (1994) Not long ago a smoking chimney was a sign of prosperity: Corporate and community response to pollution at the Bunker Hill Smelter in Kellogg, Idaho. *Environmental Values* Summer, 67–86.

Alford, C. (1962) *The Island of Tobago* (Vol. 7). London: The Ranelagh Press.

Alipour, H. (1996) Tourism development within planning paradigms: The case of Turkey. *Tourism Management* 17 (5), 367–377.

Allen, L., Long, P.T., Perdue, R.R. and Kieselbach, S. (1988) The impact of tourism development on residents' perceptions of community life. *Journal of Travel Research* Summer, 16–21.

Allen, L.R., Hafer, H.R., Long, P.T. and Perdue, R.R. (1993) Rural residents' attitudes toward recreation and tourism development. *Journal of Travel Research* Spring, 27–33.

AMBIO (1877) The Mediterranean, Special issue. Stockholm: Royal Swedish Academy of Science.

AMBIO (1981) The Caribbean, Special Issue. Stockholm: Royal Swedish Academy of Science.

Amin, A. and Thrift, N. (1994) *Globalisation, Institutions and Regional Development in Europe*. Oxford: Oxford University Press.

Amir, S. (1976) *Unequal Development: An Essay on the Social Formations of Peripheral Capitalism*. New York: Monthly Review Press.

Andereck, K.L. and Vogt, C.A. (2000) The relationship between residents' attitudes towards tourism and tourism development options. *Journal of Travel Research* 39 (1), 27–36.

Anonymous (no date) *Renewal Scheme for Traditional Seaside Resorts*. On WWW at http://www.mayo-ireland.ie/Mayo/CoDev/RenSeaRs.htm. Accessed 23.2.2001.

Ansoff, H. (1965) *Corporate Strategy*. Harmondsworth: Penguin.

Ap, J. (1990) Residents' perceptions: Research on the social impacts of tourism. *Annals of Tourism Research* 17 (4), 610–615.

Ap, J. and Crompton, J. (1998) Developing a tourism impact scale. *Journal of Travel Research* 37 (2), 120.
Apo, P. (2000) Waikiki: At heart a Hawaiian destination. *Waikiki News* July. On WWW at http://www.waikikinews.com/0700/0700apo.html. Accessed 22.3.2001.
A.R. (1883) The preservation of Mt. Desert. *The Nation* August 9, 116–117.
Arthur, B. (1994) *Increasing Returns and Path Dependence in the Economy.* Ann Arbor: The University of Michigan Press.
Arthur, W.B. (1990) Positive feedbacks in the economy. *Scientific American* 262 (2), 92–99.
Aspinall, A. (1928) *A Wayfarer in the West Indies.* London: Methuen.
L'Association des Vingerons du Quebec (1995) Prenez le chemin des vignobles du Quebec. Pamphlet et communications orales.
Ateljevic, I. and Doorne, S. (2000) Staying within the fence: Lifestyle entrepreneurship in tourism. *Journal of Sustainable Tourism* 8 (5), 378–392.
Atkinson, J. (1984) Manpower strategies for flexible organisations. *Personnel Management* 16 (8), 28–31.
Atkinson, J. (1986) *Changing Work Patterns: How Companies Achieve Flexibility to Meet New Needs*. London: National Economic Development Office.
Aunger, R. (2001) Review of technological innovation as an evolutionary process (Zimon, J., ed). *Journal of Artificial Societies and Social Simulation* 4 (4). On WWW at http://jasss.soc.surrey.ac.uk/4/4/reviews/ziman.html.
Australian Bureau of Statistics (1999) *Consumer Price Index: Table 1B. All Groups Index Numbers – Quarterly (Base Year 1989–90 = 100)*. Product number 6401.0. Canberra: Australian Government.
Avlonitis, G.J. (1990) Project dropstart: Product elimination and the product life cycle concept. *European Journal of Marketing* 24 (9), 55–67.
Babbie, E. (2000) *Practicing Social Research*. Belmont, CA: Wadsworth Publishing.
Backman, S., Patrick, J. and Wright, B.A. (2001) Management tools and techniques: An integrated approach to planning. In D.B. Weaver (ed.) *The Encyclopedia of Ecotourism* (pp. 451–462). Wallingford, UK: CABI Publishing.
Bacon, W. (1998) Economic systems and their impact on tourist resort development: The case of the spa in Europe. *Tourism Economics* 4 (1), 21–32.
Bagguley, P. (1987) *Flexibility, Restructuring and Gender: Changing Employment in Britain's Hotels.* Lancaster Regionalism Working Group Working Paper No. 24, University of Lancaster, Lancaster Regionalism Group.
Bagguley, P., Mark-Lawson, J., Shapiro, D., Urry, J., Walby, S. and Warde, A. (1990) *Restructuring Place, Class and Gender.* London: Sage.
Bagus Oka, I. (1992) Traditional tourist resorts; problems and solutions: The case of Bali. International Forum on Tourism to the Year 2000: Prospects and Challenges, Acapulco, Mexico.
Baird, R. (1850) *Impressions and Experiences of the West Indies and North America in 1849*. Philadelphia, PA: Lea & Blanchard.
Baker, M. (1991) One more time – what is marketing? In M. Baker (ed.) *The Marketing Book* (Vol.2, pp. 3–9). Oxford: Butterworth-Heinemann.
Bao, J. (1994) Big theme park distribution research. *Research of Georgraphy* 13 (3), 83–89.
Bao, J. (1998) Tourism planning and tourist area lifecycle model. *Architect* 12, 170–178.
Bao, J. and Peng, H. (1995) Tourist area expanding research: Case study of Danxia Mountain. *Science of Geography* 15 (1), 63–70.

Bao, J., Chu, Y. and Peng, H. (1993) *Tourism Geography* (p. 134). Beijing: Higher Education Press.

Bao, J. (1994) Tourism development of karst cave. *Geographic Sinica* 50 (4), 353–359.

Barker, J.A. (1992) *Discovering the Future: The Power of Vision*. Florida: Infinity Limited.

Barr, T. (1990) From quirky islanders to entrepreneurial magnates: The transition of the Whitsundays. *Journal of Tourism Studies* 1 (2), 26–32.

Barrett, J. (1958) The seaside resort towns of England and Wales. Unpublished PhD thesis. London: University of London.

Barrot, T-A. (1978) *Unless Haste is Made: A French Skeptic's Account of the Hawaiian Islands in 1836*. Kailua, HI: Press Pacifica.

Basalla, G. (1988) *The Evolution of Technology*. Cambridge: Cambridge University Press.

Baum, T. (1998a) Taking the exit route: Extending the tourism area life cycle model. *Current Issues in Tourism* 1 (2), 167–175.

Baum, T. (1998b) Tourism marketing and the small island environment. Cases from the periphery. In E. Laws *et al*. (eds) *Embracing and Managing Change in Tourism*. London: Routledge.

Baum, J.A. and Singh, J.V. (1994) *Evolutionary Dynamics of Organisations*. New York: Oxford University Press.

Beckford, G. (1972) *Persistent Poverty: Underdevelopment in Plantation Economies of the Third World*. New York: Oxford University Press.

Bell, M. (1994) Personal interview, Hilton Head Island Planning Office, Hilton Head, SC.

Benham, B. (1970) Kealakekua Bay remains 'unlisted'. Hawaii *Tribune Herald* 9 August, 2.

Bennett, R.C. and Cooper, R.G. (1984) The product life cycle trap. *Business Horizons* 27 (Sept–Oct), 7–16.

Benson, J. and Shaw, G. (eds) (1999) *The Retailing Industry. Volume I: Perspectives and the Early Modern Period*. London: I.B. Tauris.

Berman, E.M. (2002) *Essential Statistics for Public Managers and Policy Analysts*. Washington, DC: CQ Press.

Berry, E.N. (2001) An Application of Butler's (1980) Tourist Area Life Cycle Theory to the Cairns Region, Australia, 1876–1998. PhD Thesis, Tropical Environment and Geography, James Cook University, Cairns Campus. On WWW at www.geocities.com/tedberry_aus/tourismarealifecycle.html.

Beverland, M.B., Hoffman, D. and Rasmussen, M. (2001) The evolution of events in the Australasian wine sector. *Tourism Recreation Research* 26 (2), 35–44.

Beyers, W.B. and Nelson, P.B. (2000) Contemporary development forces in the nonmetropolitan West: New insights from rapidly growing communities. *Journal of Rural Studies* 16, 459–474.

Bianchi, R. (1994) Tourism development and resort dynamics: An alternative approach. In C. Cooper and A. Lockwood (eds) *Progress in Tourism, Recreation and Hospitality Management* (Vol.5, pp. 183–193). New York: John Wiley & Sons.

Bieger, T. (2000) *Management von Destinationen und Tourismusorganisationen*. München, Wien: Oldenbourg.

Bigelow, J. (1851) *Jamaica in 1850. Or, the Effects of Sixteen Years of Freedom on a Slave Colony*. New York: George P. Putnam.

Bird, I.L. (1966) *Six Months in the Sandwich Islands*. Honolulu: University of Hawaii Press.

Bird, J. (1963) *The Major Seaports of the United Kingdom*. Hutchinson of London.

Blamey, R. (1997) Ecotourism: The search for an operational definition. *Journal of Sustainable Tourism* 5, 109–130.
Blanchard, O.J. and Fischer, S. (1989) *Lectures on Macroeconomics*. Cambridge, MA: MIT Press.
Blazevic, I. (1994) Opatija Chronicle. In Proceedings, *150th Anniversary of Tourism in Opatija* (pp. 15–24). University of Rijeka, Faculty of Hotel Management, Opatija.
Boniface, B. and Cooper, C. (1987) *The Geography of Travel and Tourism*. Oxford: Butterworth Heinemann.
Booth, J.D. (1982) *Railways of Southern Quebec* (Vol.I, 1982; Vol.II, 1985). Toronto: Railfare Enterprises Ltd.
Bordieu, P. (1977) *Outline of a Theory of Practice*. Cambridge: Cambridge University Press.
Bordieu, P. (1984) *Distinction: A Social Critique of the Judgement of Taste*. Andover: Routledge and Kegan Paul.
Borenstein, S. (1992) The evolution of U.S. airline competition. *Journal of Economic Perspectives* 6 (2), 45–73.
Bosselman, F.P., Peterson, C.A. and McCarthy, C. (1999) *Managing Tourism Growth: Issues and Applications*. Washington, D.C.: Island Press.
Bouchikhi, H. (1993) A constructivist framework for understanding entrepreneurship performance. *Organization Studies* 14 (4), 549–570.
Bournemouth Borough Council (2002) *Tourism Facts.* Bournemouth: Bournemouth Borough Council.
Boyd, S.W. (1995) Sustainability and Canada's national parks: Suitability for policy, planning and management. Unpublished PhD thesis: Department of Geography, University of Western Ontario, London, Canada.
Boyd, S.W. (2000) Tourism, national parks and sustainability. In R.W. Butler and S.W. Boyd (eds) *Tourism and National Parks: Issues and Implications* (pp. 161–186). Chichester: Wiley.
Boyd, S.W. (2003) Marketing challenges and opportunities for heritage tourism. In A. Fyall, B. Garrod and A. Leask (eds) *Managing Visitor Attractions: New Directions* (pp. 189–202). Oxford: Butterworth-Heinemann.
Boyd, S.W. and Butler, R.W. (2000) Tourism and national parks: The origin of the concept. In R.W. Butler and S.W. Boyd (eds) *Tourism and National Parks: Issues and Implications* (pp. 13–27). Chichester: Wiley.
Boyer, R. (1986) *La Theorie de la Regulation: Une Analyse Critique*. Paris: Editions La Decouverte.
Bramwell, B. and Lane, B. (1993) Sustainable tourism: An evolving global approach. *Journal of Sustainable Tourism* 1 (1), 1–5.
Bramwell, B. and Lane, B. (2000) (eds) *Tourism Collaboration and Partnerships: Politics, Practice and Sustainability*. Clevedon: Channel View Publications.
Brassey, S. (1886) *In the Trades, the Tropics, & the Roaring Forties*. London: Longmans, Green, & Co.
Braunlich, C.G. (1996) Lessons From the Atlantic City casino experiment. *Journal of Travel Research* 34 (3), 46–62.
Briere, R. (1966) Le Tourisme au Quebec. Unpublished PhD dissertation, Geography Department, Universite de Montreal.
Briere, R. (1967) Les grands Traits de l' Evolution du Tourisme au Quebec, *Bulletin de l'Association des Geographes de l'Amerique Francaise* No. 11, Quebec.
Briggs, J. and Peat, F.D. (1999) *Seven Life Lessons of Chaos*. St. Leonards, NSW: Allen & Unwin.

Britton, S. (1991) Tourism, capital and place: Towards a critical geography. *Environment and Planning D: Society and Space* 9, 451–478.
Brookes, R. (1989) *Managing the Enabling Authority*. Harlow: Longman.
Brougham, J.E. and Butler, R.W. (1972) The applicability of the asymptotic curve to the forecasting of tourism development. Paper presented to the Research Workshop, Travel Research Association 4th Annual Conference, Quebec, July 1972.
Brown, B.J.H. (1985) Personal perception and community speculation: A British resort in the 19th century. *Annals of Tourism Research* 12 (3), 355–369.
Brown, S. (1987) Institutional change in retailing: A geographical interpretation. *Progress in Human Geography* 11 (2), 181–206.
Brown, S. (1988) The wheel of the Wheel of Retailing. *International Journal of Retailing* 3 (1), 16–37.
Brown, C. (1995) *Chaos and Catastrophe Theories*. Thousand Oaks, CA: Sage Publications.
Brown, K. (2002) Innovations for conservation and development. *The Geographical Journal* 168 (1), 6–17.
Bryan, J. (1965) 3 new Kona resort areas planned. Honolulu *Star Bulletin* 24 March, A2.
Bryman, A. (1988) *Quantity and Quality in Social Research*. London: Routledge.
Buhalis, D. (2000) Marketing the competitive destination of the future. *Tourism Management* 21 (1), 97–116.
Bullock, W.B. (1926) *Beautiful Waters Devoted to the Memphremagog Region*. Vermont: Memphremagog Press.
Bunge, W. (1966) *Theoretical Geography*. Lund: C.W.K. Gleerup Publishers.
Bureau of Tourism Research (2000a) *International Visitor Survey*. Canberra: BTR.
Bureau of Tourism Research (2000b) *Domestic Tourism Monitor*. Canberra: BTR.
Burnett, C.C. (1892) *The Land of the O-o*. Cleveland, OH: The Cleveland Printing and Publishing Co.
Burns, D. and Murphy, L. (1998) An analysis of the promotion of marine tourism in Queensland, Australia. In E. Laws, B. Faulkner and G. Moscardo (eds) *Embracing and Managing Change in Tourism: International Case Studies* (pp. 415–430). London: Routledge.
Busenitz, L.W., Gomez, C. and Spencer, J.W. (2000) Country institutional profiles: Unlocking entrepreneurial phenomena. *Academy of Management Journal* 43 (5), 994–1003.
Butler, R.W. (1973) The tourist industry in the Highlands and Islands. Unpublished PhD thesis, Glasgow: University of Glasgow.
Butler, R.W. (1980) The concept of a tourist area cycle of evolution: Implications for management of resources. *The Canadian Geographer* 24 (1), 5–12.
Butler, R.W. (1990a) The resort cycle revisited – a decade of discussion. Paper presented to Association of American Geographers Conference, Toronto, April 1990.
Butler, R.W. (1990b) Alternative tourism: Pious hope or trojan horse. *Journal of Travel Research* 28 (3), 40–44.
Butler, R.W. (1991) Tourism, environment and sustainable development. *Environmental Conservation* 18 (3), 201–209.
Butler, R. (1993) *Pre- and Post-Impact Assessment of Tourism Development. Tourism Research: Critiques and Challenges*. New York: Routledge.
Butler, R.W. (1997) The destination life cycle: Implications for heritage site management and attractivity. In W. Nuryanti (ed.) *Tourism and Heritage Management* (pp. 44–53). Yogyakarta: Gadjah Mada University Press.

Butler, R.W. (1998a) Still peddling along. The resort cycle two decades on. Paper to *Progress in Tourism and Hospitality Research*. CAUTHE Conference, Gold Coast.

Butler, R. (1998b) Sustainable tourism – looking backwards in order to progress? In C.M. Hall and A. Lew (eds) *Sustainable Tourism: A Geographical Perspective* (pp. 25–34). New York: Addison Wesley Longman.

Butler, R.W. (2000) The resort cycle two decades on. In B. Faulkner, G. Moscardo and E. Laws (eds) *Tourism in the 21st Century: Reflections on Experience* (pp. 284–299). London, New York: Continuum.

Butler, R.W. and Boyd, S.W. (2000) Tourism and parks – a long but uneasy relationship. In R.W. Butler and S.W. Boyd (eds) *Tourism and National Parks. Issues and Implications* (pp. 3–11). Chichester: Wiley.

Bywater, M. (1992) *The European Tour Operator Industry.* Special Report No. 2141. London: Economic Intelligence Unit.

C.P. (1883) The boarder and the cottager. *The Nation* August 2, (944) NP Cairns Post. 1976–1998.

Canan, P. and Hennessy, M. (1989) The growth machine, tourism, and the selling of culture. *Sociological Perspectives* 32, 227–243.

Canestrelli, E. and Costa, P. (1991) Tourist carrying capacity: A fuzzy approach. *Annals of Tourism Research* 18 (2), 295–311.

Capra, F. (1982) *The Turning Point*. London: Flamingo.

Casagrandi, R. and Rinaldi, S. (2002) A theoretical approach to tourism sustainability. *Conservation Ecology* 6 (1), 13–35.

Caserta, S. and Russo, A.P. (2002) More means worse. Asymmetric information, spatial displacement and sustainable heritage tourism. *Journal of Cultural Economics* 26 (4).

Casino Control Commission Annual Report (2001) p. 4.

Cater, E. (1993) Ecotourism in the third world: Problems for sustainable tourism development. *Tourism Management* 14 (2), 85–90.

Catry, B. and Chevalier, M. (1974) Market share strategy and the product life cycle. *Journal of Marketing* 38, 29–34.

Cauthorn, R. (1989) *Contributions to a Theory of Entrepreneurship*. New York: Garland Publishing Inc.

Cazes, G. and Potier, F. (1996) *Le Tourisme Urbain*. Paris: Presses Universitaires de France.

Centre for Tourism Policy Studies, School of Travel Industry Management, University of Hawaii (1998) *Repositioning Hawaii's Visitor Industry Products: Development Strategies for the New Tourism Environment*. On WWW at http://www.state.hi.us/tourism/reposit.pdf. Accessed 14.2.2001.

Centre for Travel and Tourism, New College, Durham in association with Business Education Publishers Limited.

Chaney, G.L. (1879) *Aho-ha! A Hawaiian Salutation*. Boston: Roberts Brothers.

Chapin, H. (1976) Corey's Coming. From *On the Road to Kingdom Come*. Electra Records.

Chapman, E. (1961) *Pleasure Island: The Book of Jamaica* (Vol. 5). Kingston: Arawak Press.

Chemin des Vignobles du Quebec (2001) Pamphlet. Associaton des Vignerons du Quebec.

Chen, J. (2001) Disscusion on "the lifecycle of the tourist products". *Journal of Guilin Technical College* 3, 18–20.

Cheshire, P. and Gordon, I. (1996) Territorial competition and the predictability of collective (in)action. *International Journal of Urban and Regional Research* 20 (3), 383–399.
Chorley, R. and Haggett, P. (eds) (1967) *Models in Geography*. London: Methuen.
Choy, D.J.L. (1991) Tourism planning: The case for market failure. *Tourism Management* 12 (4), 313–330.
Choy, D. (1992) Life cycle models for Pacific island destinations. *Journal of Travel Research* 30 (3), 6–31.
Christaller, W. (1933) *Die Zentrale Orte in Süddeutschland* [*The Central Places in South Germany*]. Jena: Gustav Fischer Verlag.
Christaller, W. (1955) Beiträge zu einer Geographie der Fremdenverkehr. Erdkunde, Band IX, Heft 1, February 1955, 1–19.
Christaller, W. (1963) Some considerations of tourism location in Europe: The peripheral regions – underdeveloped countries – recreation areas. *Regional Science Association Papers* XII, Lund Congress, 95–105.
Chunxiao (1997) Thoughts on "tourist products lifecycle". *Tourism Tribune* 12 (5), 44–47.
Circuit des Arts (2002) pamphlet.
Clark, J.R.K. (1985) *Beaches of the Big Island*. Honolulu: University of Hawaii Press.
Clark, S. (1952) *All the Best in the Caribbean*. New York: Dodd, Mead & Co.
Clawson, M. and Knetch, J.L. (1963) *Economics of Outdoor Recreation, Resources of the Future Inc*. Baltimore: Johns Hopkins University Press.
Clegg, A. and Essex, S. (2000) Restructuring in tourism: The accommodation sector in a major British coastal resort. *International Journal of Tourism Research* 2 (2), 77–96.
CLICOR (1971) Canada Land Inventory Land Capability for (Outdoor) Recreation, Montreal H31 map sheet. Ottawa: Department of Energy, Mines and Resources.
Cloke, P., Philo, C. and Sadler, D. (1991) *Approaching Human Geography. An Introduction to Contemporary Theoretical Debates*. London: PCP.
COAST (1993) *COAST*. Brussels: European Commission.
Cohen, E. (1972) Toward a sociology of international tourism. *Social Research* 39 (1), 164–182.
Cohen, E. (1979a) Rethinking the sociology of tourism. *Annals of Tourism Research* 6 (1), 18–35.
Cohen, E. (1979b) The impact of tourism on the hill tribes of Northern Thailand. *International Asienforum* 10 (1/2), 5–38.
Cohen, E. (1996a) A phenomenology of tourist experiences. In Y. Apostolopoulos, S. Leivadi and A. Yiannakis (eds) *The Sociology of Tourism: Theoretical and Empirical Investigations* (pp. 90–114). London: Routledge.
Cohen, E. (1996b) *Thai Tourism, Hilltribes, Islands and Open-Ended Prostitution*. Bangkok: White Lotus and Co., Ltd.
Cohn, N. (1973) *AWopBop aLooBop ALopBamBoom*. St Alban: Paladin.
Cohn, N. (2002) The king is dead. *Observer Magazine* 11 September, 17–23.
Coles, T.E. (1999a) Competition, contested retail space and the rise of the German department store, c.1870–1914. *International Review of Retail Distribution and Consumer Research* 9 (3), 275–290.
Coles, T.E. (1999b) Department stores as innovations in retail marketing in Germany: Some observations on marketing practice and perception in the Wilhelmine Period. *Journal of Macromarketing* 19 (1), 34–47.

Coles, T.E. (2004) Tourism, shopping and retailing: An axiomatic relationship? In C.M. Hall, A. Lew and A.M. Williams (eds) *A Companion to Tourism* (pp. 360–373). Oxford: Blackwell.

Coll Jr., R. (1950) Visitors flocking to Kona. Honolulu *Advertiser* 17 January, 17.

Connely, W. (1955) *Beau Nash Monarch of Bath and Tunbridge Wells*. London: Werner Laurie Ltd.

Constant, E. (2000) Recursive practice and the evolution of technical knowledge. In J. Zimon (ed.) *Technological Innovation as an Evolutionary Process* (pp. 219–233). Cambridge: Cambridge University Press.

Convention Concerning the Protection of the World Cultural and Natural Heritage (16 November 1972) On WWW at www.unesco.org/whc. Accessed 12.2002.

Convention on Wetlands of International Importance (2 February 1971) On WWW at www.ramsar.org/. Accessed 12.2002.

Cooke, P. (1987) The changing urban and regional systems in the UK. *Regional Studies* 20 (3), 243–251.

Cooke, P. (1989) *Localities*. London: Unwin Hyman.

Cooper, C. (1990a) Resorts in decline – the management response. *Tourism Management* 11 (1), 63–67.

Cooper, C. (1990b) The life cycle concept and tourism. Unpublished Conference Paper, *Tourism Research into the 1990s*. University of Durham (cited in Shaw & Williams, 2002).

Cooper, C.P. (1992) The life cycle concept and strategic planning for coastal resorts. *Built Environment* 18 (1), 57–66.

Cooper, C.P. (1994) The destination life cycle: An update. In A.V. Seaton, C.L. Jenkins, R.C. Wood, Dieke, P.U.C., M.M. Bennett, L.R. MacLellan and R. Smith (eds) *Tourism: The State of the Art* (pp. 340–346). Brisbane: Wiley.

Cooper, C.P. (1995) Strategic planning for sustainable tourism: The case of the offshore islands in the UK. *Journal of Sustainable Tourism* 3 (4), 191–209.

Cooper, C.P. (1997a) *Inaugural Lecture*. University of Bournemouth.

Cooper, C.P. (1997b) The environmental consequences of declining destinations. *Progress in Tourism and Hospitality Research* 2 (3), 337–345.

Cooper, C.P. (1997c) Parameters and indicators of the decline of the British seaside resort. In G. Shaw and A. Williams (eds) *The Rise and Fall of British Coastal Resorts* (pp. 79–101). London: Cassell.

Cooper, C. and Jackson, S. (1989) Destination life cycle: The Isle of Man case study. *Annals of Tourism Research* 16 (3), 377–398.

Cooper, C.P. and Lockwood, A. (1993) *Progress in Tourism, Recreation and Hospitality Management* (Vol.5, pp. 181–193). Chichester: Wiley.

Cooper, R.G. and Kleinschmidt, E.J. (1993) Screening new products for potential winners. *Long Range Planning* 6 (6), 74–81.

Cooper, C., Fletcher, J., Noble, A. and Westlake, J. (1996) Changing tourism demand in Central Europe: The case of Romanian tourist spas. *Journal of Tourism Studies* 6 (2), 30–44.

Cooper, C., Fletcher, J., Gilbert, D. and Wanhill, S. (1998) In R. Shepherd (ed.) *Tourism: Principles and Practice* (2nd edn). Harlow: Longman.

CORD (Canadian Outdoor Recreation Demand) Surveys (1969–72) Ottawa: Parks Canada.

Coriat, B. (1979) *L'Atelier et al Chronometer*. Paris: Bourgois.

Costa, P. and Manente, M. (1995) Venice and its visitors: A survey and a model of qualitative choice. *Journal of Travel and Tourism Marketing* 4 (3), 45–69.

Costa, P. and van der Borg, J. (1988) Un modello lineare per la programmazione del turismo. *COSES Informazioni* 32/33, 21–26.

County of Hawaii: Office of the Mayor (1987) *A Summary of Planned Developments in West Hawaii, County of Hawaii*. Hawaii: Hilo.

Crawford, C.M. (1984) Business took the wrong cycle from biology. *Journal of Consumer Marketing* 1 (Summer), 5–11.

Creighton, T.H. and Walters, G.S. (1969) *The South Kona Coast Historic and Recreation Area, Island of Hawaii*. Honolulu: Hawaii Department of Land and Natural Resources.

Cundall, F. (1928) *Jamaica in 1928: A Handbook of Information for Visitors and Intending Residents with some Account of the Colony's History*. London: The Institute of Jamaica.

Curtis, S. (1997) Seaside resort: Spanish progress and British malaise. In *Insights* (C9–18). London: British Tourist Authority/English Tourist Board.

Cypriot Tourism Organisation (2002) Strategic tourism plan, 2010. Nicosia: Government of Cyprus.

da Conceiçáo Gonçalves, V.F. and Roque Águas, P.M. (1997) The concept of the life cycle: An application to the tourist product. *Journal of Travel Research* 36 (2), 12–22.

Danielson, M. (1995) *Profits and Politics in Paradise: The Development of Hilton Head Island*. Columbia, SC: The University of South Carolina Press.

Darling, F.F. (1936) *A Herd of Red Deer.* Oxford: Oxford University Press.

Darling, F.F. (1941) *Island Years*. London: G. Bell and Sons Ltd.

Darling, F.F. (1943) *Island Farm.* London: G. Bell and Sons Ltd.

Darnell, A.C. and Johnson, P.S. (2001) Repeat visits to attractions: A preliminary economic analysis. *Tourism Management* 22, 119–126.

Daru, R., Vreedenburgh, E. and Scha, R. (2000) Architectural innovation as an evolutionary process. Abstract of paper presented at the Generative Art Conference, Politecnico di Milano, Italy, 14–16 Dec 2000. On WWW at www.generativeart.com/abst2000/abst77.htm.

Darwin, C. (1859) *The Origin of the Species*. New York: P.F. Collier & Son.

Daughters of Hawaii (1979) *Treasures...Hulihee*. Honolulu.

Davidson, W.R., Bates, A.D. and Bass, S.J. (1976) The retail life cycle. *Harvard Business Review* 54 (November–December), 89–96.

Davies, P. (1992) Wish you here? *Landscape Design* (December), 21–24.

Davis, C. (1997) Bloated victim of a fallen world. *Sunday Times* 13 July.

Dawkins, R. (1986) *The Blind Watchmaker*. London: Penguin Books.

Day, A.G. (1955) *Hawaii and Its People*. New York: Dull, Sloan and Pearce.

Day, G.S. (1981) The product life cycle: Analysis and applications issues. *Journal of Marketing* 45 (Fall), 60–67.

de Albuquerque, K. and McElroy, J.L. (1992) Caribbean small-island tourism styles and sustainable strategies. *Environmental Management* 16 (5), 619–632.

Dean, J. (1950) Pricing policies for new products. *Harvard Business Review* November–December, 45–53.

Dearden, P. (1991) Tourism and sustainable development in Northern Thailand. *Geographic Review* 81, 400–413.

Dearden, P. and Harron, S. (1994) Alternative tourism and adaptive change. *Annals of Tourism Research* 21, 81–102.

Debbage, K. (1990) Oligopoly and the resort cycle in the Bahamas. *Annals of Tourism Research* 17, 513–527.

Debbage, K. (1992) Tourism oligopoly is at work. *Annals of Tourism Research* 19 (2), 355–359.

Decker, R.W., Wright, T.L. and Stauffer, P.H. (eds) *Volcanism in Hawaii* (pp. 149–189). US Geological Survey Professional Paper.

de Kadt, E. (1979) *Tourism: Passport to Development*. Oxford: Oxford University Press.

Del Viscio, J. (no date) Atlantic City: A Renaissance Resort. On WWW at http://www.travelbase.com/auto/localview-new.cgi?article = 142. Accessed 30.3.2001.

Department for Culture, Media and Sport (2000a) Seaside 2000 Consultation. London, DCMS.

Department for Culture, Media and Sport (2000b) Government Report to the Tourism Summit: Tomorrow's Tourism.

Department of Culture, Arts and Leisure (2001) *Guidance to District Councils on the Development of Local Cultural Strategies*. London: Department of Culture, Arts and Leisure. On WWW at http://www.culture.gov.uk/tourism/govt_report.html. Accessed 16.2.2001.

De Vis-Norton, L. (1925) The island of Hawaii, a paradise for tourists. *Paradise of the Pacific* 38, 13–15.

Dewailly, J-M. (1999) Sustainable tourist space: From reality to virtual reality? *Tourism Geographies* 1 (1), 41–55.

Dhalla, N.K. and Yuspeh, S. (1976) Forget the product life cycle concept. *Harvard Business Review* 54 (January/February), 102–112.

Diamond, N.P. (1988) A Strategy for Cold Water Resorts into the Year 2000. Unpublished MSc Thesis, University of Surrey, UK.

di Benedetto, A.C. and Bojanic, D. (1993) Tourism area life-cycles. *Annals of Tourism Research* 20 (3), 557–570.

Dicken, P. (1998) *Global Shift: The Internationalisation of Economic Activity* (3rd edn). London: Chapman.

Digance, J. (1997) Life cycle model. *Annals of Tourism Research* 24 (2), 452–455.

Dillman, D.A. (1978) *Mail and Telephone Surveys*. New York: John Wiley & Sons.

Din, K.H. (1992) The "involvement stage" in the evolution of a tourist destination. *Tourism Recreation Research* 17 (1), 10–20.

Din, J. and Bao, J. (2000) A study on the life cycle of special karst cave with a case of Jinashui Swallow Cave in Yunnan Provice. *Carsologica Sinica* 19 (3), 284–289.

Douglas, N. (1997) Applying the life cycle model to Melanesia. *Annals of Tourism Research* 24 (1), 1–22.

Doxey, G.V. (1975) A causation theory of visitor–resident irritants: Methodology and research inferences. *Proceedings of the Travel Research Association 6th Annual Conference* (pp. 195–198). San Diego: Travel Research Association.

Doyle, G. (1957) The magic of Kona coast. *Paradise of the Pacific* 69 (11), 22–41.

Drucker, P.F. (1973) *Management*. New York: Harper and Row.

Drucker, P.F. (1985) *Innovation and Entrepreneurship: Practices and Principles.* New York: Harper & Row.

Duncan, S. and Savage, M. (1989) Space, scale and locality. *Antipode* 21 (3), 179–206.

Duncan, S. and Savage, M. (1991) New perspectives on the locality debate. *Environment and Planning A* 23 (2), 155–164.

Dunk, M. (2000) All shook up by the King's birthplace. *Daily Express* 6 May.

Dunn, D. (1998) Home Truths from Abroad. PhD Thesis, University of Birmingham.

Dziembowska-Kowalska, J. and Funck, R.H. (2000) Cultural activities as a location factor in European competition between regions: Concepts and some evidence. *Annals of Regional Science* 34, 1–12.

Eadington, W. (1982) The Gambling Papers: Proceedings of the Fifth National Conference on Gambling and Risk Taking. Vols 8&9: Issues in Casino Gambling: Nevada and Atlantic City. Reno, NV: University of Nevada.

Eastern Townships regional Tourist Guidebooks (2000) Association Touristique des Cantons de l'Est, Tourisme Quebec.

Eidsvik, H.K. (1983) Parks Canada, conservation and tourism: A review of the seventies – a preview of the eighties. In P.E. Murphy (ed.) *Tourism in Canada: Selected Issues and Options.* Western Geographical Series, 21 (pp. 241–269). Victoria: University of Victoria.

English, D.B., Marcouiller, D.W. and Cordell, K.H. (2000) Tourism dependence in rural America: Estimates and effects. *Society and Natural Resources* 13, 185–202.

English Tourist Board (1991) *The Future of England's Smaller Seaside Resorts.* London: English Tourist Board.

EUROPARC and IUCN (2000) *Guidelines for Protected Area Management Categories.* Grafenau: EUROPARC and WCPA.

Evans, R. and Harding, A. (1997) Regionalisation, regional institutions and economic development. *Policy and Politics* 25, 19–30.

Evans, K., Barnes, J. and Schlacter, J. (1993) A general systems approach to retail evolution: An existing institutional perspective. *International Review of Retail, Distribution and Consumer Research* 3 (1), 79–100.

Farrell, B. (1992) Tourism as an element in sustainable development: Hana Maui. In V.L. Smith and W.R. Eadington (eds) *Tourism Alternatives* (pp. 115–132). Philadelphia: University of Pennsylvania Press.

Farrell, B.H. (1999) Conventional or sustainable tourism? No room for choice. *Tourism Management* 20 (2), 189–191.

Faulkner, B. (1999) Qualitative Research Methods (unpublished chapter).

Faulkner, B. (2002) *Our Gold Coast: The Preferred Future*. Gold Coast: Cooperative Research Centre for Sustainable Tourism.

Faulkner, B. (2003) Rejuvenating a maturing tourist destination: The case of the Gold Coast. In E. Fredline, L. Jago and C. Cooper (eds) *Progressing Tourism Research*. Clevedon: Channel View Publications.

Faulkner, H.W. (1990) Swings and roundabouts in Australian tourism. *Tourism Management* 11 (1), 29–37.

Faulkner, B. and Russell, R. (1997) Chaos and complexity in tourism: In search of a new perspective. *Pacific Tourism Review* 1 (2), 93–102.

Faulkner, B. and Russell, R. (2001) Turbulence, chaos and complexity in tourism systems: A research direction for the new millennium. In B. Faulkner, G. Moscardo and E. Laws (eds) *Tourism in the 21st Century*. London: Continuum.

Fayos Sola, E. (1992) A strategic outlook for regional tourism policy: The white paper on Valencian tourism. *Tourism Management* 13 (1), 45–49.

Fernandez (1999) *Shoshone News Press.* (personal communication).

Finch, J. and Groves, D. (1983) *Labour of Love: Women, Work and Caring*. London: Routledge and Kegan Paul.

Fly, J.M. (1986) Tourism and nature: The basis for growth in Northern Lower Michigan. Unpublished paper.

Foglesong, R. (1999) Walt Disney World and Orlando: Deregulation as a strategy for tourism. In D. Judd and S. Fainstein (eds) *The Tourist City* (pp. 89–106). Newhaven: Yale University Press.

Formica, S. and Uysal, M. (1996) The revitalisation of Italy as a tourist destination. *Tourism Management* 17 (5), 323–331.

Fornander, A. (1980) *An Account of the Polynesian Race: Its Origins and Migrations*. Rutland, VT: Chas. E. Tuttle Company.

Foster, D.M. and Murphy, P. (1991) Resort cycle revisited – The retirement connection. *Annals of Tourism Research* 18, 553–567.

Foster, C. (2000) A new look for Waikiki. *Travel Agent* May 1. On WWW at http://www.findarticles.com/cf_0/m0VOU/18_299/63298501/print.jhtml. Accessed 5.3.2001.

France, L. (1991) An application of the tourism destination area life cycle to Barbados. *Revue de Tourisme* 46 (3), 25–30.

France, L. and Barke, M. (1991) The development of Torremolinos as an international resort: Past, present and future. Occasional paper produced for the Centre for Travel and Toruism, New College, Durham, in association with Business Education Publishers Limited.

Franck, H. (1920) *Roaming through the West Indies*. New York: Blue Ribbon Books.

Frank, A. (1967) *Capitalism and Underdevelopment in Latin America*. New York: Monthly Review Press.

Franklin, A. and Crang, M. (2001) The trouble with tourism and travel theory? *Tourist Studies* 1 (1), 5–22.

Freidmann, J. and Alonso, W. (eds) (1974) *Regional Development and Planning: A Reader*. Cambridge, MA: MIT Press.

Fritz-Nemeth, P. and Lundgren, J.O. (1996) Tourist attractions – from natural to industrial. *TEOROS* 15 (2), 23–30, Montreal: UQAM.

Funnell, C. (1975) *By the Beautiful Sea: The Rise and High Times of That Great American Resort, Atlantic City* (p. 154). New York: Alfred A. Knopf.

Gambicini, P. (2002) *Elvis*. BBC Radio 2.

Gardner, D.M. (1987) The product life cycle: A critical look at the literature. *Review of Marketing* 162–194.

Garmise, S. and Rees, G. (1997) The role of institutional networks in local economic development. A new model of governance? *Local Economy* 12 (2), 104–118.

Garrod, B. (2003) Managing visitor impacts. In A. Fyall, B. Garrod and A. Leask (eds) *Managing Visitor Attractions: New Directions* (pp. 124–139). Oxford: Butterworth-Heinemann.

Garrod, B. and Fyall, A. (2000) Managing heritage tourism. *Annals of Tourism Research* 27 (3), 682–706.

Gartner, W.C. (2002) Cultural tourism trends and implications for tourism development. Paper Presented at the International Conference on: The Tourist-Historic City: Sharing Culture for the future, 17–20 March 2002, Bruges.

Gershuny, J. and Miles, I. (1983) *The New Services Economy: The Transformation of Employment in Industrial Societies*. London: Frances Pinter.

Getz, D. (1983) Capacity to absorb tourism concepts and implications for strategic planning. *Annals of Tourism Research* 10 (1), 245–257.

Getz, D. (1986) Models of tourism planning. Towards integration of theory and practice. *Tourism Management* 7 (1), 21–32.

Getz, D. (1991) *Festivals, Special Events, and Tourism*. New York: Van Nostrand Reinhold.

Getz, D. (1992) Tourism planning and destination lifecycle. *Annals of Tourism Research* 19 (4), 752–770.
Getz, D. (2000) Festivals and special events: Life cycle and saturation issues. In W.C. Gartner and D.W. Lime (eds) *Trends in Outdoor Recreation, Leisure and Saturation Issues* (pp. 175–185). Wallingford: CABI.
Giambelluca, T.W., Nullet, M.A. and Schroeder, T.A. (1986) *Rainfall Atlas of Hawaii*. Honolulu: State of Hawaii. DLNR.
Giddens, A. (1984) *The Constitution of Society*. Berkeley: University of California Press.
Gilbert, D. (1990) Strategic marketing planning for national tourism. *Tourist Review* 45 (1), 18–27.
Gilbert, E.W. (1939) The growth of inland and seaside health resorts in England. *Scottish Geographical Magazine* 55, 16–35.
Gilbert, E.W. (1954) *Brighton – Old Ocean's Bauble*. London: Methuen.
Gist, R.R. (1968) *Retailing. Concepts and Decisions*. New York: Wiley and Sons.
Glaser, B. (1978) *Theoretical Sensitivity*. Mill Valley, CA: The Sociology Press.
Glaser, B. and Strauss, A. (1967) *The Discovery of Grounded Theory: Strategies for Qualitative Research*. New York: Aldine De Gruyter.
Gleick, J. (1987) *Chaos: Making a New Science*. London: Heinemann.
Goad, P. and Crispin, S.W. (1999) Tourism: Wish you were here. *Far Eastern Economic Review*. On WWW at http://www.feer.com/9909_30/p60tourism.html. Accessed 21.2.2001.
Godkin, E.L. (1883) Evolution of the summer resort. *The Nation* July 19, 47–48.
Goffman, E. (1959) *Presentation of Self in Everyday Life*. New York: Doubleday.
Gold Coast City Council (2000) Draft Gold Coast 2010: Economic Development Strategy. GCCC.
Gordon, I. and Goodall, B. (1992) Resort cycles and development processes. *Built Environment* 18 (4), 41–56.
Gordon, I. and Goodall, B. (2000) Localities and tourism. *Tourism Geographies* 2 (3), 290–311.
Gormsen, E. (1981) The spatio-temporal development of international tourism, attempt at a centre–periphery model. In *La Consommation d'Espace par le Tourisme et sa Preservation*. Aix-en-Provence: Centre d'etudes touristiques.
Gosling, R. (1980) *Personal Copy. A Memoir of the Sixties*. London: Faber and Faber.
Gössling, S. (2000) Tourism development in Sri Lanka: The case of Ethukala and Unawatuna. *Tourism Recreation Research* 25 (3), 103–114.
Gould, S.J. (1980) *The Panda's Thumb*. New York: W.W. Norton & Co.
Graham, B. (1998) Liberalization, regional economic development and the geography of demand for air transport in the European Union. *Journal of Transport Geography* 6 (2), 87–104.
Green Globe News (2000) Country Focus: Spain. On WWW at http://www.greenglobe21.com/pdf_files/june2000.pdf. Accessed 13.2.2001.
Gregory, D.J. (1994) 'Logical positivism', 'model', 'structurialism' entries. In R.J. Johnston, D. Gregory and D.M. Smith (eds) *The Dictionary of Human Geography* (3rd edn, pp. 350–351, 385–386, 599–600). Oxford: Blackwell.
Gunn, C.A. (1988) *Tourism Planning*. New York: Taylor and Francis.
Gunn, C.A. (1993) *Tourism Planning: Basics, Concepts, Cases* (3rd edn). Washington, D.C.: Taylor & Francis.
Gurney, J. (1840) *A Winter in the West Indies, Described in Familiar Letters to Henry Clay, of Kentucky*. London: John Murray.
Hall, C.M. (1996) Personal communication on the relevance of lines in sand pits to resort life cycles. April, London, Ontario.

Hall, C.M. (2000) *Tourism Planning – Policies, Processes and Relationships*. Harlow: Prentice Hall.
Hall, C.M. and McArthur, S. (1998) *Integrated Heritage Management*. London: The Stationery Office.
Hall, C.M. and Page, S.J. (1999) *The Geography of Tourism and Recreation: Environment, Place and Space*. London: Routledge.
Hall, C.M. and Page, S.J. (2005) *The Geography of Tourism and Recreation: Environment, Place and Space* (3rd edn). London: Routledge.
Hall, C.M., Williams, A.M. and Lew, A. (2004) Tourism: Conceptualisations, institutions and issues. In A. Lew, C.M. Hall and A. Williams (eds) *Companion to Tourism* (pp. 3–21). Oxford: Blackwells.
Hammond, J.T. (1993) Hilton Head Island's growing pains centered on mayor-elect. *The News* 29 November.
Handy, C. (1994) *The Age of Paradox*. Boston: Harvard Business School Press.
Harada, W. (1968) Kona group seeks 3-story limitation. Honolulu *Advertiser* 29 May [Hawaii Newspaper Clippings Morgue, Hamilton Library, University of Hawaii-file Kona Building Heights]
Harada-Stone, D. (1989) Kealakekua ranch's plans worry neighbours. Hawaii *Tribune Herald* 10 January, 1.
Harland Bartholomew and Associates (1960) *A Plan for Kona*. Honolulu: Prepared for the Hawaii State Planning Office.
Harlow, G.S. (1928) *Hawaii: By a Tourist*. Los Angeles, CA: West Coast Publishing.
Harmon, M. (1999) Long Beach, Successful Meetings, June. http://global.umi.com/pqdweb?ts = 98. . .&Sid = 7&Idx = 10&Deli = 1&RQT = 309&Dtp = 1. Accessed 9.3.2001.
Harnischfeger, U. (2000) Preussag focuses on leisure. *Financial Times* 5th October.
Harrigan, J.J. (1989) *Political Change in the Metropolis*. Illinois: Scott, Foresman and Company.
Harrigan, N. (1974) The legacy of Caribbean history and tourism. *Annals of Tourism Research* 2 (1), 13–25.
Harris, C. (1954) The market as a factor in the localization of industry in the United States. *Annals of the Association of American Geographers* 64, 315–348.
Harrison, D. (1995) Development of tourism in Swaziland. *Annals of Tourism Research* 22 (1), 135–156.
Hart, C. (1999) The retail accordion and assortment strategies: An exploratory study. *International Review of Retail, Distribution and Consumer Research* 8 (2), 165–182.
Hart, C.W., Casserley, G. and Lawless, M.J. (1984) The product life cycle: How useful? *The Cornell Quarterly* 25, 54–63.
Hartwell, M. and Lane, J. (1991) *Champions of Enterprise*. Double Bay, NSW: Focus Books Pty Ltd.
Harvey, D. (1969) *Explanation in Geography*. London: Edward Arnold.
Harvey, D. (1989) *The Condition of Post-Modernity*. Oxford: Blackwell.
Hawaii County Planning Department (HCPD) (1999) On WWW at http://www.hawaii-county.com/text.version/annual96_97/r&d01.htm. Accessed 21.1.2000.
Hawaii Newspaper Clippings Morgue (HNCM), Hamilton Library, University of Hawaii [original newspaper unknown, subject heading shown in brackets below]
_____ (1949) Kona airport induces new business. 9 Sept. [Kona Airport 1929/1953]
_____ (1951) Kona's airport: An asset for Hawaii. [Kona Airport 1929/1953]

_____ (1953) 'Cow pen' battle continues at Kona. 30 Apr. [Kona Cattle Pen Controversy at Kailua Wharf]

_____ (1957) 'Natural' look to prevail by Kona landscaping project. 5 June [Kona Sea Wall]

_____ (1959) Kona water supply called adequate for now. 17 Nov. [Kona Water 1957/1958]

_____ (1960) Sen. Lymanm Moves to drop $1.7M Kona area projects [Kona Master Plan]

Hawaii Tourism Authority (HTA) (1999) *Competitive strategic assessment of Hawaii tourism* (Executive Summary). Hawaiian Tourism Authority.

Hawaii Tribune Herald (HTH) (1967a) Planners recommend Kona maps. 21 February, 1.

Hawaii Tribune Herald (1967b) New golf course proposed by County for South Kona. 25 October, 8.

Hawaii Tribune Herald (1968a) Kona Hilton opening brings room level to over 2,100. 25 February, 3.

Hawaii Tribune Herald (1968b) Editorial. Emphasis on 'Gold Coast'. 5 February, 4.

Hawaii Tribune Herald (1969) Nearly 3,500 new rooms planned for Kona. 26 January, 3.

Hawaii Tribune Herald (1970) Girders, construction worker's pounding reshape Kailua and ... New Kona of modern buildings rises along isle's 'sun coast'. 26 July, 2–3.

Hawaii Tribune Herald (1972) Proposed development, scenic route are termed 'monstrosity'. 18 January, 1.

Hawaii Tribune Herald (1974a) Kailua Village development bill gets county support. 31 July, 1.

Hawaii Tribune Herald (1974b) Council oks bill for Kailua-Kona. 22 August, 10.

Hawaii Tribune Herald (1974c) Kona chamber applauds district approval. 18 September, 16.

Hawaii Tribune Herald (1989) Ground blessing held or Ka'upulehu Four Seasons. 2 May, 1.

Hawken, P., Lovins, A. and Lovins, L.H. (1999) *Natural Capitalism: Creating the Next Industrial Revolution*. Boston, MA: Little, Brown and Company.

Hawkins, M. (1982) The Atlantic City Experience: Casino Gambling as an Economic Recovery Program.

Haywood, K.M. (1986) Can the tourist area life-cycle be made operational? *Tourism Management* 7 (3), 154–167.

Haywood, K.M. (1988) Responsible and responsive tourism planning in the community. *Tourism Management* June.

Haywood, K.M. (1992) Revisiting resort cycle. *Annals of Tourism Research* 19 (2), 351–354.

Haywood, K.M. (1998) Economic business cycles and the tourism life-cycle concept. In D. Ioniddes and K. Debbage (eds) *The Economic Geography of the Tourist Industry* (pp. 273–284). London: Routledge.

Heath, E. and Wall, G. (1992) *Marketing Tourism Destination: A Strategic Planning Approach*. New York: Wiley.

Hiss, T. (1990) *The Experience of Place*. New York: Alfred A. Knopf.

Hobbs, C. (1913) The ruin or the redemption of Lake Quinsigamond. *The Worcester Magazine* February, 35–38.

Hodgson, G.M. (2002) Darwinism in economics: From analogy to ontology. *Journal of Evolutionary Economics* 12 (3), 259–281.

Hofer, C.W. (1975) Toward a contingency theory of business strategy. *Academy of Management Journal* 18 (December), 784–809.

Holder, J.S. (1991) Pattern and impact of tourism on the environment of the Caribbeans. In S. Medlik (ed.) *Managing Tourism*. Oxford: Butterworth-Heinemann.

Hollander, S.C. (1960) The wheel of retailing. *Journal of Marketing* 25 (July), 37–42.

Hollander, S.C. (1980) Oddities, nostalgia, wheels and other patterns in retail evolution. In R.W. Stampfl and E.C. Hirschmann (eds) *Competitive Structure in Retail Markets: The Department Store Perspective* (pp. 84–94). Chicago: American Marketing Association.

Holloway, J.C. (1994) *The Business of Tourism* (Vol. 4). London: Pitman.

Holloway, J.C. (1998) *The Business of Tourism* (Vol. 5). Harlow: Longman.

Honolulu Advertiser (HA) (1954) Long range thinking urged in Kona area. 13 January, 1.

Honolulu Advertiser (1955a) Chamber unit ok's Kaiser Kona tourist project. 11 January, A1.

Honolulu Advertiser (1955b) Local corporation plans $1 million Kona resort. 5 August, A3.

Honolulu Advertiser (1956a) Time grows short. 3 August, A3.

Honolulu Advertiser (1956b) Kona backs four-point development. 17 September, B1.

Honolulu Advertiser (1968) Kimurao opposes Kona high-rises. 18 May, A10.

Honolulu Advertiser (1969) Editorial. Saving Kona's assets. 5 February, B2.

Honolulu Advertiser (1970) Bill proposes State buy Kailua-Kona village. 7 March, A6.

Honolulu Advertiser (1973) Historic district proposed for Kona resort area. 7 February, B6.

Honolulu Star Bulletin (HSB) (1956) Plans for Two $1 Million Hotels in Kona Announced. 10 July, 1B.

Honolulu Star Bulletin (1957) Kaiser pegs plans to tourist growth. 14 February, 1B.

Honolulu Star Bulletin (1958a) Navy barge reaches Kona with 9-to-10 day water supply. [HNCM Kona Drought]

Honolulu Star Bulletin (1958b) Big Isle reaction to Kona plan stresses water, airport need. 2 Dec. [HNCM Kona Master Plan]

Honolulu Star Bulletin (1970) Kona's time to plan. 1 July, A14.

Honolulu Star Bulletin (1974) On the Big Island. 31 Mar. [HNCM Kailua-Kona 1962/1975]

Honolulu Star Bulletin (1988) State opposes resort near wildlife area. 13 July, A4.

Hough, M. (1990) *Out of Place: Restoring Identity to the Regional Landscape*. New Haven, CT: Yale University Press.

Hourglass Foundation (2001) *Where Are We Headed?* Lancaster, PA: Hourglass Foundation.

House, J. (1954) Geographical aspects of coastal holiday resorts. Unpublished PhD thesis, Durham: Kings College.

Hovinen, G.R. (1981) A tourist cycle in Lancaster County, Pennsylvania. *The Canadian Geographer* 25 (3), 283–286.

Hovinen, G.R. (1982) Visitor cycles: Outlook for tourism in Lancaster County. *Annals of Tourism Research* 9, 565–583.

Hovinen, G.R. (1995) Heritage issues in urban tourism: An assessment of new trends in Lancaster County. *Tourism Management* 16 (5), 381–388.

Hovinen, G. (1997) Lancaster County, Pennsylvania's heritage tourism initiative: A preliminary assessment. *Small Town* 27, 4–11.

Hovinen, G.R. (2002) Revisiting the destination lifecycle model. *Annals of Tourism Research* 29 (1), 209–230.

Hudson, R. (1992) Industrial restructuring and spatial change: Myths and realities in the changing geography of production in the 1980s. *Scottish Geographical Magazine* 108 (2), 74–81.

Hunziker, W. (1942) *The Tourist Doctrine*. Switzerland: St. Gallen.

Hurst, D.K. (1995) *Crisis and Renewal: Meeting the Challenge of Organizational Change*. Boston, MA: Harvard Business School Press.

ICARE – International Center for Art Economics (1997) *Applicazione della Telematica alla Gestione dei Flussi di Visitatori*. Research Center Telecom Italia S. Salvador, mimeo.

Idzes, I. (1988) *Corporate Lifecycles: How and Why Corporations Grow and Die and What To Do About It*. Englewood Cliffs, NJ: Prentice Hall.

Inskeep, E. (1991) *Tourism Planning: An Integrated and Sustainable Development Approach.* New York: Van Nostrand Reinhold.

Inskeep, E. (1994) *National and Regional Tourism Planning: Methodologies and Case Studies*, edited by the World Tourism Organization. UK: Routledge.

Inter-Island Steam Navigation Company, Ltd. (1917–44) *President's Report for the Year.* Honolulu: Advertiser Publishing Co.

Ioannides, D. (1992) Tourism development agents: The Cypriot resort cycle. *Annals of Tourism Research* 19 (4), 711–731.

Ioannides, D. and Debbage, K. (1998) *The Economic Geography of the Tourist Industry: A Supply-side Analysis.* London: Routledge.

Irish Tourist Board (2001) On WWW at
http://www.ireland.travel.ie/aboutus/tourismfacts.asp;
http://www.irlgov.ie/finance/budget/budget01/budmeasu.htm#PARTIII;
http://www.irlgov.ie/finance/budget/budget01/speech01.htm.
Accessed 6.3.2001.

Ishii, K. and Stevels, A. (2000) *Environmental Value Chain Analysis: A Tool for Product Definition in Eco Design*. San Francisco, CA: IEEE ISEE.

Isle of Man Department of Tourism and Leisure (1996) *Marketing Plan 1996*. Douglas: Government of the Isle of Man.

IUCN (1994) *Richtlinien für Management-Kategorien von Schutzgebieten*. Gland, Cambridge, Grafenau: IUCN, WCMC and FÖNAD.

IUCN (1998) *1997 United Nations List of Protected Areas.* Gland and Cambridge: WCMC and WCPA.

IUCN, UNEP and WWF (1980) World Conservation Strategy. Living Resource Conservation for Sustainable Development. Gland: IUCN.

Jablonka, E. (2000) Lamarckian inheritance systems in biology: A source of metaphors and models in technological evolution. In J. Zimon (ed.) *Technological Innovation as an Evolutionary Process* (pp. 27–40). Cambridge: Cambridge University Press.

Jain, S.C. (1985) *Market Planning and Strategy.* Cincinnati, OH: South Western.

Jansen-Verbeke, M. (1986) Inner-city tourism: Resources, tourists and promoters. *Annals of Tourism Research* 13 (1), 79–100.

Javiluoma, J. (1992) Alternative tourism and the evolution of tourist areas, *Tourism Management*, 13 (1), 118–120.

Jawahar, I.M. and McLaughlin, G.L. (2001) Toward a descriptive stakeholder theory: An organisational life cycle approach. *Academy of Management Review* 26 (3), 397–414.

Job, H. and Weizenegger, S. (1999) Anspruch und Realität einer integrierten Naturschutz- und Entwicklungspolitik in den Großschutzgebieten Schwarzafrikas. In G. Meyer and A. Thimm (eds) *Naturräume in der Dritten Welt. Ausbeutung, nachhaltige Nutzung oder Schutz?* (pp. 37–64). Mainz: Interdisziplinärer Arbeitskreis Dritte Welt, Veröffentlichungen 12.

Johnson, J.D. and Rasker, R. (1995) The role of economic and quality of life values in rural business location. *Journal of Rural Studies* 11 (4), 323–332.

Johnson, J. and Snepenger, D. (1993) Application of the tourism life cycle concept in the Greater Yellowstone Region. *Society and Natural Resources* 6, 127–148.

Johnson, J.D. and Snepenger, D.J. (in progress) Community solidarity regarding tourism development in a transitional rural economy.

Johnson, J.D., Snepenger, D.J. and Akis, S. (1994) Host resident perceptions of tourism in a transitional rural economy. *Annals of Tourism Research* 21 (3).

Johnson, J.D., Maxwell, B.M. and Aspinall, R. (2003) Moving nearer to heaven: Growth and change in the Greater Yellowstone Region. In R. Buckley, C. Pickering and D. Weaver (eds) *Nature Tourism and Environment*. Wallingford: CAB International.

Johnston, C. (1995) Enduring idylls? A geographical study of tourism in Kona, Hawaii Island. University of Hawaii: Unpublished PhD dissertation.

Johnston, C.S. (2001) Shoring the foundations of the destination life cycle model. Part 1: Ontological and epistemological considerations. *Tourism Geographies* 3 (1), 2–28.

Johnston, R.J. (1991) *Geography and Geographers. Anglo-American Human Geography since 1945* (Vol. 4). London: Arnold.

Johnston, R.J., Gregory, D. and Smith, D. (1986) *The Dictionary of Human Geography* (2nd edn). Oxford: Blackwell.

Jones, P. and Pizam, A. (1993) *The International Hospitality Industry – Organizational and Operational Issues*. London: Pitman.

Joppe, M. (1996) Sustainable community tourism development revisited. *Tourism Management* 17 (7), 475–479.

Jordon, P. (2000) Restructuring Croatia's coastal resorts: Change, sustainable development and the incorporation of rural hinterlands. *Journal of Sustainable Tourism* 8 (6), 525–539.

Juelg, F. (1993) Tourism product life cycles in the Central Eastern Alps: A case study of Heiligenblut on the Grossglockner. *Tourism Recreation Research* 18 (1), 20–26.

Jurowski, C., Uysal, M. and Williams, D.R. (1997) A theoretical analysis of host community resident reactions to tourism. *Journal of Travel Research* 36 (2), 3–9.

Juvik, J.O., Singleton, D.C. and Clarke, G.G. (1978) Climate and Water Balance on the Island of Hawaii. *Mauna Loa Observatory, a 20th Anniversary Report* (pp. 129–139). National Oceanic and Atmospheric Administration.

Kachigan, S.K. (1986) *Statistical Analysis*. New York: Radius Press.

Kaplan, R.S. and Norton, D.P. (1990) *The Balanced Scorecard: Translating Strategy into Action*. Boston, MA: Harvard Business School Press.

Kaplan, R.S. and Norton, D.P. (2001) *The Strategy Focused Organisation: How Balanced Scorecard Companies Thrive in the New Business Environment*. Boston, MA: Harvard Business School Press.

Katsanis, L.P. and Pitta, D.A. (1995) Punctuated equilibrium and the evolution of the product manager. *Journal of Product and Brand Management* 4 (3), 49–60.

Keane, M.J. (1997) Quality and pricing in tourism destinations. *Annals of Tourism Research* 24 (1), 117–130.